Arik

Arik

The Life of Ariel Sharon

DAVID LANDAU

ALFRED A. KNOPF · NEW YORK · 2013

THIS IS A BORZOI BOOK
PUBLISHED BY ALFRED A. KNOPF

www.aaknopf.com

Library of Congress Cataloging-in-Publication Data
Landau, David.
Arik : the life of Ariel Sharon / by David Landau.—First edition.
pages cm
"This is a Borzoi book"—Title page verso.
Includes bibliographical references and index.
ISBN 978-1-4000-4241-8
1. Sharon, Ariel. 2. Prime ministers—Israel—Biography. 3. Generals—
Israel—Biography. 4. Israel—Politics and government—20th
century. 5. Israel—History, Military—20th century. 6. Arab-Israeli
conflict. 7. Israel—Biography. I. Title.
DS126.6.S42L36 2013
956.94054092—dc23
[B]   2012049631

Front-of-jacket photograph: 1969 Portrait of Israeli General Ariel Sharon
© Gamma-Keystone/Getty Images
Jacket design by Carol Devine Carson
Maps © Soffer Mapping

Manufactured in the United States of America

FIRST EDITION

For Jerrold

The righteous, in death, are called living.—Talmud

CONTENTS

My grandfather was a Hebrew teacher in Rehovot at the beginning of the last century." Ariel Sharon, corpulent, white-haired, looked up over his reading glasses at the half-full Knesset, the Israeli parliament. Members were listening politely or quietly reading. "I have a deep love for the Hebrew language," he read on in his incongruously high-pitched voice. "For the miracle of its revival, for the historical wellsprings from which it draws its words and phrases."

There was no tension in the chamber that afternoon in January 2005. No catcalls, no heckling. A parliamentary moment without politics. Sharon could have asked one of his two deputy prime ministers to represent the government at the largely ceremonial debate marking Hebrew Language Day. But he wanted to speak himself. He had a point to make.

Mordechai Scheinerman, Sharon's grandfather, came to Palestine in 1910 and settled with his wife and children in the still-tiny Jewish village of Rehovot, southeast of the barely existent Jewish town of Tel Aviv. That made him sort of aristocracy. Not quite a *Mayflower* man of the First Aliya (1882–1902), but still an early Zionist pioneer of pre–World War I days. Palestine was a derelict corner of the crumbling Ottoman Empire then. The dream of the Zionist visionary Theodor Herzl (d. 1904), that it would one day become a Jewish state, seemed just that: a dream.

In his native town, Brest Litovsk in White Russia, Mordechai was an early convert to Zionism. He became a Hebrew teacher. That was a career choice reflecting real commitment. Hebrew, the ancient language of the Bible and the rabbis, was struggling to reincarnate itself as a modern vernacular. The Zionists promoted it as the language of the new-old Jewish nationalism. But the Zionists themselves were a struggling minority within the Jewish people. Millions of Jews, fleeing czarist oppression, set sail for the New World rather than for sandy, sweaty Palestine.

Mordechai Scheinerman endured the heat and mosquitoes of Rehovot for two years, then packed up, as did so many of the early pioneers, and headed back to Brest Litovsk. When war broke out, the family fled east, ending up in Tbilisi, Georgia. His faith in Zionism never wavered, though, and he instilled it in his son Samuil. Samuil Scheinerman taught Hebrew too, but, chastened by his father's experience, he studied agronomy at the local university as a practical preparation for his own eventual aliya.*

This came more quickly than planned. Walking toward the Tbilisi Zionist club, where he held his Hebrew classes, one night in 1921, he found the area swarming with security police of the newly formed communist government. He veered away, hastened to the home of his girlfriend, Vera Schneeroff, and offered her two peremptory proposals: marriage and aliya. She was a fourth-year medical student, the daughter of a well-to-do Jewish family, also from Belarus, and, by her own admission, not much of a Zionist. But she accepted Samuil's plan. They were married forthwith and fled to the Black Sea port of Baku, from where, some months later, they embarked for Palestine.

Samuil had completed his studies in Tbilisi; Vera nursed the hope that she would graduate someday too, perhaps at the University of Beirut since there were no universities or medical schools in Palestine. On a bleak February day in 1922 they arrived in Jaffa. Vera, to her consternation, was lifted bodily from boat to shore by a gigantic Arab stevedore. The experience confirmed her general impression of Palestine as a backward and uncouth place.

By then, the Zionist dream had advanced a little closer to reality, at least on paper. The wartime British government issued its Balfour Declaration in November 1917, favoring "the establishment in Palestine of a national home for the Jewish people." In 1920, the San Remo Conference of principal Allied powers granted a mandate over Palestine to Great Britain, specifically enjoining it to "put into effect" the Balfour Declaration.† But beyond emotional rhetoric, the response among Diaspora Jewish communities was disappointing from the Zionist standpoint. The Zionist movement campaigned hard to per-

---

* Literally, "ascent"; the Hebrew term for immigration to Eretz Yisrael, the Land of Israel.
† The San Remo resolution, like the Balfour Declaration itself, contained the following caveat: "It being clearly understood that nothing shall be done which may prejudice the civil and religious rights of existing non-Jewish communities in Palestine, or the rights and political status enjoyed by Jews in any other country."

suade young Jewish people to make aliya. It achieved only modest success.

His son's aliya, and his own subsequent return to Eretz Yisrael—Mordechai Scheinerman lived out his last years in Tel Aviv—restored the old Hebrew teacher's right to a place of honor in the annals of the Zionist enterprise. A century later, his grandson pointedly read the family narrative into the record of the Zionist state's parliament. His Zionist credentials, Sharon was signaling, were unimpeachable.

The point was not superfluous. The momentary calm in the Knesset was deceptive. Parliament and the country were seething with disaffection. It was spearheaded by the Jewish settlers in the occupied* Palestinian territories of the West Bank and Gaza, who defined themselves as today's true Zionists. It was directed against Sharon, who for long years had been their champion but whom they now portrayed as a traitor. To many, the atmosphere was reminiscent of 1995, when Prime Minister Yitzhak Rabin was decried by the national-religious Right as a traitor and eventually felled by an assassin's bullets.

Rabin died for signing a peace accord with Yasser Arafat's Palestine Liberation Organization (PLO). That agreement held out the prospect of a Palestinian state eventually arising alongside Israel, thus bringing the century-old conflict over Palestine to an equitable end. But Arafat, once Rabin had gone, proved incapable of leading his people to peace. A decade later, the two-state solution was foundering in a welter of bloodshed and failed diplomacy.

Ariel Sharon, the hard-line ex-general who had been elected prime minister in 2001 to crush the Palestinians' intifada, now proposed to dismantle Jewish settlements and withdraw Israeli troops from parts of the occupied territories. To the settlers and their supporters—his erstwhile political constituency—that was heresy, a denial both of Judaism and of Zionism. To the peace camp at home and to governments and public opinion around the world, Sharon's dramatic turnabout was a hugely hopeful change. It meant the beginning, at last, of a repartition of Palestine between the two nations vying for it. Sharon found himself suddenly praised where he had previously been loathed and feared.

He looked back to his text. "Eliezer Ben-Yehuda, the man who revived the Hebrew language, said: 'There are two things without which the Jews will not be a nation—their land and their language.' " The subtext was clear. He, the old warrior turned statesman, the

---

* Occupied, that is, since the 1967 Six-Day War, when the Israeli army took over the West Bank, previously held by Jordan.

true-blue Zionist, could be depended on to protect and defend both of those pillars of Jewish nationhood. The imminent withdrawal from parts of Palestine would strengthen, not weaken, the future of the Jewish state.

Half a year later, in August 2005, the withdrawal took place. Israel evacuated its settlers and its army from the Gaza Strip and from a small area of the northern West Bank. Sharon called it "disengagement." The settlers called it "uprooting" and "expulsion," terms taken from the most macabre chapters in Jewish history.

But the settlers' threats of violent resistance, of massive civil strife, and of rebellion in the army melted away in the face of Sharon's iron will. He deployed forty thousand soldiers and policemen around the doomed settlements and won the day without a battle. Not a shot was fired. Resistance was almost all passive. In one settlement a few young militants hurled paint balls from a rooftop. It was all over in hardly more than a week, and the country resumed its interrupted summer vacation.

The anticlimactic absence of trauma raised Sharon's stock even higher both at home and abroad. Israel's misguided colonization of the Palestinian territories, which Sharon himself had done more than any man to put in place, was neither immutable nor irrevocable, as many had feared. Sharon had shown it could be undone with relative ease, if only there was the political will to undo it. The Palestinians could still have their state. Israel could still save itself from the morally and politically crippling sickness of occupation. It could recover its identity and its cohesion as a Jewish and democratic state.

That destiny had been receding over the long years of occupation and settlement building. Yet the majority of people in both nations still supported the two-state solution, as poll after poll attested. The majority of Israelis supported Sharon's disengagement from Gaza and believed it would lead to disengagement from the West Bank, too.

That bright moment of hope that Ariel Sharon created in the summer of 2005 still shines, though the powerful forces in both nations who oppose the two-state solution have conspired to obscure it. Sharon's collapse in January 2006 into a stroke-induced coma has forced Israeli history into the subjunctive mode: Had he survived in power, would he have been able to complete the decolonization process that he boldly began?

What he began, during the dramatic years of his prime ministership (2001–2006), contradicting a lifetime of military extremism and political obduracy, entitles him, like his grandfather, to a place of honor in Israel's annals.

What might have been—what could still be, despite the intervening years of setbacks and disappointment—makes him the worthy subject of this effort to understand his life and times. When he was elected prime minister, many proud and patriotic Israelis talked seriously of leaving the country. His accession to power was the stuff of nightmares. The future seemed to hold only war and bloodshed. When he collapsed, less than five years later, we wept. Not just for him; for ourselves.

In the Knesset that January, he read on monotonously, now deploring the pervasive infiltration of foreign words and phrases into Eliezer Ben-Yehuda's pristine Hebrew. "I don't understand, for instance, how that anomalous alloy '*Yallah,* bye' has supplanted our own beautiful '*Shalom*' for saying farewell."

His secretary, Marit Danon, who served five previous prime ministers, recalled years later her double surprise when, days after he took over in 2001, he sent out for a falafel for his lunch from a popular Jerusalem street stand. She duly served up the plebeian fare and was leaving the room when Sharon invited her to share the meal. "Marit," he asked, "does not your soul yearn for the falafel?" On another occasion, hungry as always but never willing to admit it, he lifted the phone to tell her, "Uri [his aide] is assailed by famine."[1]

For "famine," Sharon used the word *kafan,* a rare term unknown to many Hebrew speakers. Danon would have a two-volume Hebrew dictionary always at hand on her trolley when she took dictation from the prime minister.[2] "Almost daily I was on the phone to the Hebrew Language Academy," she recalled, "asking for the correct pointing of a particular word in a speech, because of his obsession to get every word perfectly right."* The language, like the land, was his responsibility.

---

* In Hebrew, vowels are shown by a system of dots and dashes placed under, over, or inside the letters. These can change with the construction or declension of words. Most texts dispense with them; the letters appear unpointed, leaving the reader to envision the vowels. Not all readers know all the rules, and this frequently leads to minor mispronunciations.

Arik

CHAPTER 1 · POOR LITTLE FAT BOY

Ariel Sharon probably had a much nicer childhood than he admitted to. In family photographs from the 1930s he looks happy enough. A plump, clear-eyed little boy, neatly, almost fussily turned out, staring boldly at the camera, comfortable with his parents, his sister, his various uncles and aunts.

The backdrop is usually poor looking. The walls of the family homestead, both inside and out, expose bare boards and rough-hewn doors. The farmyard is unkempt, but it is clearly a busy and active place.

In later years, as a politician and eventually as leader of the rightist Likud Party, Sharon often spoke of the tensions between his parents and the other farming families in their moshav, or cooperative village, of Kfar Malal, nine miles northeast of Tel Aviv. He never tired of telling how he, at age five, fell off a donkey and cut his chin and how his mother carried him bleeding through the fields to a private doctor in the township of Kfar Saba, nearly two miles away, rather than have him treated at the clinic in Kfar Malal. The clinic was run by Kupat Holim, part of the Histadrut trade union organization. Samuil and Vera Scheinerman, Sharon's parents, refused to belong to Kupat Holim.

Some of the village old-timers, though, pooh-poohed his account. It was hyped, they hinted: the auto-hagiography of a rightist arriviste who grew up, in fact, a Labor boy in a thoroughly Labor village. Vera, too, the lonely heroine of her son's reminiscences, failed to confirm the ideological motives to which Arik ascribed her and Samuil's running feuds with the village committee. "Revisionists?* We weren't Revi-

---

* The Revisionist Zionist movement, founded in 1925 by Ze'ev (Vladimir) Jabotinsky, became the main opposition to the Labor-led World Zionist Organization and the Jewish Agency for Palestine, the Jewish state in the making. The Revisionists evolved over the years into the Likud.

sionists," she told an interviewer at the age of eighty-five, still running the farm at Kfar Malal. "Who even knew what that meant around here? It was simply that anyone who tried to demand a bit of order was immediately dubbed a Revisionist."[1]

But Arik's depiction of his parents as loners, tough and obstinate individualists in a society that preferred conformism, was basically right. Samuil and Vera were among the earliest settlers at Kfar Malal. New immigrants from Russia, they joined in 1922. First they lived in a tent. Then Samuil built the rickety cabin that, with additions, was to house the family till the mid-1940s, when they could finally afford a house of bricks and mortar. Yehudit, always called Dita, was born in 1926, and Ariel, called Arik, arrived two years later. There were quarrels over land. Kfar Malal was required to donate some of its fields to nearby settlements founded later. On one occasion—this, too, made famous by Arik's incessant, proud narration of it—Vera resolved on the unilateral disengagement of the Scheinermans' little vineyard from the annexationist designs of neighboring Ramot Hashavim. Husband away, children asleep, she crept out at midnight with rifle in one hand and wire cutters in the other and dismantled the new demarcation. The village suspected Bedouin marauders, but she put them right—and threatened to do it again unless the fence was restored to the far side of her vineyard.

As an individualist and as a trained agronomist with novel ideas, Samuil Scheinerman tried to introduce crops new to Palestine on his little farm. He planted peanuts and sweet potatoes. They were family staples for years. "So what? Arik doesn't look small or stunted on them," Vera observed years later.[2] But neither of these niche foods swept the market, and making a living remained a problem. Vera swallowed her pride and wrote to her brother, Joseph, who had settled in Istanbul, asking if he could find work for Samuil.

For two years Samuil worked in Turkey. He came back full of plans for growing cotton, but no one in the Jewish Agency Settlement Department wanted to listen. In time, he planted avocados, another exotic novelty in those days, mangoes, and clementine oranges. Slowly his finances improved, but Dita and Arik's high-school fees were still a heavy drag on the family budget.

High school for village kids was by no means the norm, and Vera and Samuil's insistence on it exacerbated the charges of snobbishness and hauteur constantly muttered by their neighbors. Most of the other Kfar Malal children made do with eight years at the local elementary school, graduating at fourteen to become full-time farmhands. Arik did his share of farmwork before dawn. Then, in a blue shirt with red lacing and khaki shorts,[3] the de rigueur dress code for kibbutz and moshav youngsters, he bused in to Tel Aviv.

The Geula High School, a private institution catering mainly to the sons and daughters of the Yishuv's* bourgeois gentlefolk, stood by the seashore. Arik strode the half hour from the bus terminal, saving his fare money for a falafel and soda after classes. By late afternoon he was back home again, working in the fields until nightfall. Then—homework.

In later life, Sharon praised his parents for inculcating in him both the stomach and the stamina for sustained, hard work. "As a child," he wrote in *Warrior*, the autobiography he published, in English, in the 1980s, "I listened to my father talk about the nobility of physical labor. By the time I was old enough to have my own thoughts on the subject, the work itself was in my bones . . . By the age of eight or nine I was doing the heavier work on my own. In the spring I would take the horse and wagon out to the vineyard and hitch up the plow."

In Tel Aviv, after school, Sharon would sometimes spend his afternoons with his paternal grandmother, Miriam, Mordechai's widow. She regaled him in Russian with "stories of her life in Petrograd, where she had studied to be a midwife; in Brest Litovsk, where she had practiced her profession; and in Baku, where the family had fled during the war." Russian forebears and a good smattering of the language were to stand the politician Sharon in good stead decades later, when more than a million Jewish immigrants from the former Soviet Union poured into Israel. So was the snippet of Scheinerman family lore, of uncertain provenance, that the midwife Miriam had actually brought the Likud leader and prime minister Menachem Begin into the world. Begin was certainly born in Brest Litovsk, and his father and Mordechai were certainly friends and fellow activists in the local Zionist cell.

The adult Sharon always praised his parents, too, for dinning into him a love of culture. "Be a *ben kfar*, a man of the soil," the agronomist Samuil urged his son. "But be a *ben tarbut*, a man of culture, too."[4] Samuil was an enthusiastic amateur musician, and despite his prickly personality he found a few like-minded souls to make music with. He painted too. Vera read constantly. She made sure her children imbibed the Russian classics. From the tight domestic budget they bought little Arik a quarter-size violin and the lessons to go with it. They took him to musical soirees in neighboring Ramot Hashavim, at the home of Dr. Steinitz, an accomplished pianist and lecturer on music.†

---

* Yishuv: the pre-state Jewish community in Palestine.
† Like many of the people in Ramot Hashavim, the Steinitzes—both he and she

While his young farmer's fingers showed little aptitude for the fiddle, Arik took away with him a lifelong devotion to classical music from his incongruous childhood conservatory at Kfar Malal and Ramat Hashavim. Political rivals who suffered the sharp side of his tongue during the day knew they would find him all smiles and good cheer at night, in his regular seat at the Tel Aviv concert hall, for a performance of the Israel Philharmonic.*

At school, a classmate recalled, Arik was a good student and generally liked by the teachers. But where he really shone was in the martial arts class. Here he served as the instructor's aide, helping to teach the boys and girls how to wield a cudgel to maximal effect. His budding military prowess was in evidence, too, on a class outing in tenth grade when the teacher lost his way and Arik led the hot and worried city kids back to safety.

Samuil kept quarreling and bickering with other families till the end. He died young, in 1956. At the burial in the village cemetery Arik himself eulogized his father. Standing at attention in his red paratrooper boots and red paratrooper beret, Colonel Ariel Sharon, a national hero by then, though already a controversial one, pulled out a folded paper from his tunic pocket and read appropriately uncontroversial words of love and longing for the dogged, hard-bitten idealist.

ARMS AND THE MAN

There was one item on Kfar Malal's agenda that provoked no discord at all between the regimented village families and the cantankerous Scheinermans: defense against the Palestinian Arabs who lived all around. Vera never forgot the sense of near terror one night during the

---

were medical doctors—had fled Hitler's Germany and were now reinventing themselves as farmers in the Jewish homeland. Their Bechstein grand made the bucolic life a little more palatable for them. "Now your grandfather," Prime Minister Sharon used to needle the young Likud hard-liner Yuval Steinitz nearly seventy years later, "*there* was a sensible man." Yuval, a left-wing professor of philosophy turned right-wing politician, was chairman of the Knesset Foreign Affairs and Defense Committee. Sharon alternated irony and charm in an unremitting effort to winkle him away from the camp of his archenemy, Benjamin Netanyahu, into the dovish camp that supported his disengagement from Gaza. In charming mode, he would recall at Steinitz's committee how, as a youngster driving his oxen into the fields, he would stop and listen to the music wafting from the open windows of Grandfather Steinitz's house.

* This stopped, for security reasons, when he became prime minister.

countrywide violent riots of 1929, when rumors reached the village that thousands of Arabs were massing in Kalkilya, a nearby town, to overrun Kfar Malal. With the other mothers she cowered with Dita and baby Arik in a concrete cowshed while the men made ready to fight for their lives. The attack never came. For his bar mitzvah, Samuil gave Arik a richly decorated Caucasian dagger he had brought with him from Baku. It was a symbolic gift but one whose import both giver and receiver recognized.

Guarding and patrolling the village at night was always part of the farmers' lives. After his bar mitzvah, Arik was on the roster. At fourteen, like other likely lads, he took his oath of allegiance to the Haganah, the underground army of the Jewish state in the making. The rite duly took place at dead of night, replete with Bible and revolver and flickering candle. The Haganah was supposedly secret, but everyone knew it existed, and most people encouraged the boys and young men to volunteer. Training at Kfar Malal took place on Saturdays and one weekday evening.

No sooner had Arik taken up arms as an eager young teenager than he found himself involved in the first of the historical disputes that were to dog his military career and later darken his political life. For Arik, they were historical in two senses: they became key episodes in the history of Zionism; and his own specific role in them was debated, often bitterly, for long years and even decades after the episodes themselves had become history.

The *saison*, or hunting season, was the cynical sobriquet attached to the period from December 1944 to April 1945 during which the Haganah actively pursued members of the Etzel,* the rival underground army of the Revisionists, and the Lehi,† an even more radical underground group. Some of these "dissidents" apprehended by the Haganah were handed over to the British, who deported them to detention camps in East Africa. Others were held in secret kibbutz lockups or merely roughed up and released.

Most of the serious pursuing, apprehending, and roughing up was done by the Palmach, the Haganah's two-thousand-strong full-time guerrilla force. But the part-time soldiers sometimes played a role, too. Did young Arik Scheinerman, a dab hand with a cudgel, swing his

---

* An acronym for Irgun Zvai Leumi, or National Military Organization, commanded by Menachem Begin.
† Lohamei Herut Yisrael, or Fighters for Israel's Freedom, known by the British as the Stern Gang. One of its leaders was another future prime minister—Yitzhak Shamir.

stick and his fists in the *saison* of 1945? That was hardly something the future leader of the Likud would want to be remembered for. The evidence is sketchy. Sharon himself denied any such thing. "I hated [the *saison*]," he wrote in *Warrior.* "Even arresting and punishing the militants seemed reasonable enough. But turning them over to the British? How could Jews turn over other Jews? It seemed criminal, a shameful thing to be associated with."

Two years later, with the Palestine issue before the newly formed United Nations, the Zionist leadership again clamped down on the Revisionist underground. This time, Arik Scheinerman seems to have joined in with gusto. By now he was an unofficial NCO in the unofficial army of the state-to-be. After graduating from high school in the summer of 1945, he had been picked to take part in a Haganah platoon commander's course in the remote southern kibbutz of Ruhama. Here again he distinguished himself in hand-to-hand combat training and field craft, though he graduated, to his chagrin, only a probationary corporal, not a full corporal.

He wanted to enlist in the Palmach. His parents wanted him to register for studies in agricultural science. Instead, he did neither but enrolled in the Jewish Settlement Police. This was a legitimate branch of the Mandatory security forces, designated to protect the Jewish settlements and patrol the roads between them. But it was also a convenient cover under which military-minded youngsters like Arik could continue their own weapons training, and train other Jewish youth, without harassment from the authorities.

It also allowed him plenty of spare time to work on the family farm. "One day," he writes, "as we were working together in the orange groves . . . [Samuil] said, 'Arik, I want to tell you, anything you decide to do with your life is all right with me. But you have to promise me one thing. Never, never take part in turning Jews over to non-Jews. You must promise me that you will never do that.' "[5]

In fact, though, the second *saison,* in 1947, did not entail collaboration with the British forces. These, still vigorously enforcing their blockade of Palestine's shores against Jewish refugee-immigrants from post-Holocaust Europe, were by this time seen as outright enemies by David Ben-Gurion, leader of the Yishuv, and the mainstream Zionist leadership. The Haganah made do with beatings and incarceration of Etzel activists. In the area around Kfar Malal, known Etzel recruiters were warned away, and when the warnings went unheeded, one of them had his arms thrust in an irrigation pipe and deliberately broken. Another was locked in a refrigeration plant for twenty-four hours. Arik, attached now to the Haganah's fledgling intelligence branch, is said to have gathered the information that led to these brutal assaults. In another incident, Arik tracked five Etzel men carrying tommy guns and engineered their ambush by a Haganah unit. But they opened fire and escaped, leaving a Haganah man shot through the buttocks.

Periodically over the years, people would come forward with vivid recollections of these activities that the adult Arik would have preferred to forget. "He was very, very active in everything we did against the Etzel," said Dedi Zalmanson, one of Arik's Haganah comrades, in 1983.[6] "He chased after me with a pickax handle," said Yosef Menkes, an old-time Etzelnik, in 1990.[7] "He smashed up my coffee shop," said Ben-Ami Zamir, another ex-Etzel man, in 1995.[8] Arik, he recalled, arrived by truck at the head of a Haganah posse. "He asked me for a soda, pointing to a crate on the floor. As I bent over to fetch it, he whacked me over the head with the wooden club he was carrying. I was covered in blood. Unluckily for him, my brother, who was in the Palmach, happened to be around, and he fought back. My sister, who'd been boiling up water for coffee, poured it all over them." Arik, prime minister by this time, issued a categorical denial. "I never took part in the first *saison* nor in the second *saison,* and I never hit a Jew with a pickax handle."[9]

In *Warrior,* Sharon wrote that he was attracted to the militants, jealous of "their actions and their heroism. But I was also in the Haganah, and I believe that people did not have the right to go off and do whatever they wanted, no matter how courageous they might be."[10] It was a delicate balancing act by a general whose own subsequent military career was stained by acts of excessive and wanton retribution and who now, as a politician, aspired to lead the party that still adulated the Etzel. Sharon often claimed that his military career was in fact stymied—he was held back for years and was never appointed chief of staff—because he wasn't "one of us," in other words, a reliably anti-Revisionist Laborite. "What do you mean 'not one of them'?" one lifelong Revisionist, Mordechai Zippori, snorted contemptuously. " 'Not one of them'?! He took part in the *saison* and beat up Etzel men."[11]

L ife was not all cudgels and plowshares. Arik was in love. "She was not exactly my first love," he wrote years later. "But what I felt now seemed completely different from anything I had felt before." Margalit Zimmerman, whom everyone called Gali, was just sixteen, a student at the boarding school for immigrant children next door to his parents' farm. He had furtively watched her weeding and was smitten. Happily, his Haganah duties required him to impart military rudiments to the boys in Gali's class, and through them he communicated his first request for a date. "I cut a hole in the wire fence that surrounded the yard so she could sneak through . . . In the evenings we would go out and sit next to the old village well in the middle of the groves, holding hands and talking in the dark."[12]

On November 29, 1947, endorsing the recommendations of a special commission of inquiry, the United Nations General Assembly voted by 33 to 13 with 10 abstentions to partition Palestine into a Jewish and an Arab state. Jerusalem was to remain under international control. Throughout the country, Jews took to the streets dancing, singing, and weeping with joy. Ben-Gurion watched the celebrations with a heavy heart. "I knew that we faced war," he wrote in his diary, "and that in it we would lose the finest of our youth."

The youth were now called up in their thousands for full-time service as the Haganah steadily morphed into a regular army, ready to be proclaimed as such as soon as the British flag was hauled down and the Jewish state declared, the following May. The intervening months quickly deteriorated into countrywide civil war. The Palestinian political leadership flatly rejected partition. Palestinian fighters, backed by Arab volunteers from Iraq, Syria, and Egypt, attacked Jewish settlements and transportation. The Haganah, spread too thin to defend the entire Yishuv, attacked city suburbs and villages seen as strongholds of the Palestinian forces. The British for their part, having announced their departure date, effectively washed their hands of their security responsibilities. Their troops protected only their own evacuation routes. Ben-Gurion sent emissaries abroad on a desperate quest for arms; he anticipated with dire certainty that the Arab states would pitch their regular armies into the battle once the Jewish state came into being.

Arik was mobilized on December 12. He did his initial fighting in the general area of Kfar Malal, in the center of the country. "Operating around the old coastal highway, we raided Arab bases and set ambushes . . . Typically we would leave our camp in the middle of the night, picking our way through the orchards . . . [W]e would be at our ambush site before first light, waiting for the early-morning traffic between the Arab villages and bases . . . As one action followed the next, I became aware that the others in our platoon had developed confidence in my ability to lead them into these actions."

The guerrilla war was "vicious, cruel and littered with atrocities."[13] On the last day of 1947, armed Arabs killed 39 Jewish workers at the Haifa oil refineries. The Haganah hit back, killing 60 Arabs in the village of Balad el-Sheikh. In February, two terrorist bombs in Jerusalem killed a dozen Arabs and 60 Jews. In March another 17 Jews died and many more were injured in a truck bombing at the Jewish Agency headquarters in Jerusalem. On April 9, 110 Palestinian civilians were killed by the Etzel in an attack on the village of Deir Yassin, just outside Jerusalem. Four days later, in a revenge attack, 77 Jewish medical staff died in an ambush on a convoy traveling to a beleaguered Jewish hospital on Mount Scopus, in east Jerusalem.

Arik was part of the Alexandroni Brigade, a loose collection of local Haganah units gradually taking shape into a regular military formation. After a large-scale night attack on Iraqi irregulars in the village of Bir Addas, he was formally appointed a platoon commander. "A good many of the soldiers I was now leading were from Kfar Malal, boys I had studied with and played with, but whose families had been at odds with mine for ages. But now our relationships had become something else entirely."[14]

Some of these boyhood friends were lost during the months of guerrilla warfare that preceded the "real" war against the invading Arab armies after the State of Israel was declared on May 14, 1948. At the time, there seemed little difference between before and after.

> What set that day [May 14] apart was the short pass I had. I would be seeing Gali for the first time in almost two months. That night I was scheduled to lead a raid on the bridge to Kalkilya . . . [T]here was just enough time to get home, give Gali a kiss, and say goodbye. As I walked toward the children's school where she still lived, I heard a radio . . . Ben-Gurion's voice . . . announcing the establishment of the State of Israel. "In the Land of Israel the Jewish People came into being. In this land their character was shaped." These were beautiful words, sonorous words. But they did not excite me . . . It seemed to me that we already had our independence for the past six months. We had been neck-deep in it and fighting for it since November. The coming night at the bridge to Kalkilya would be no different from all the other nights.

The Haganah, hard-pressed in the early months after the Partition Resolution, scored some successes in the weeks before independence. In April, Haganah forces broke the Arab blockade on the road up through the hills from the coastal plain to Jerusalem. Convoys of supply trucks brought food, fuel, and ammunition to the city. Mixed cities designated part of the proposed Jewish state were overrun: Tiberias on April 18, Haifa on April 22–23, Safed on May 13–14. Many of their

Arab inhabitants fled. Jaffa and Acre, which were both to have been within the proposed Arab state, were also taken. So was much of the western Galilee. On the other hand, a Jewish bloc of settlements south of Jerusalem, Gush Etzion, fell to the Arab Legion and local Palestinian fighters. Hundreds of settlers and soldiers were killed or taken into captivity in Jordan.

The fate of Jerusalem hung in the balance. The city had been designated a *corpus separatum* in the UN resolution, but once it became clear that the fate of Palestine would be decided by war and not diplomacy, Jerusalem became the most sought-after prize—both for Ben-Gurion and for the Transjordanian leader, the emir Abdullah.* The two wily neighbors had hoped not to fight. Ben-Gurion sent Golda Meir to negotiate with the emir, with a view to Transjordan peaceably annexing part of Palestine to his kingdom. But the talks failed. Jordan's small but well-trained Arab Legion acquitted itself by far the best of all the invading Arab armies.

It was against units of the Legion, well dug in around a British-built fortress at Latrun, commanding the road to Jerusalem, that young Arik Scheinerman now found himself deployed. This was to be not another derring-do night raid against ill-trained irregulars but a pitched battle against disciplined soldiers, equipped with artillery and heavy machine guns. The Israeli side, moreover, was dishearteningly ill-prepared.

On May 26, 2005, at a memorial event for the dead of his regiment, the Thirty-Second Regiment of the Alexandroni Brigade, Prime Minister Sharon reflected on that fateful night, fifty-seven years before:

> An olive grove near ancient Hulda. My platoon and I lie sprawled in the afternoon heat under the shade of the trees. Thoughts before the battle. We blend into the scrubby soil, as though we were an integral part of it. Feelings of rootedness, of homeland, of belonging, of ownership.
>
> Suddenly a line of trucks pulls up nearby. New recruits, foreign looking, pale, in sleeveless pullovers, gray trousers, striped shirts. A mélange of languages. Names like Herschel and Jazek are bandied about, Yanem, Jonzi, Peter. They so don't blend with the olive trees,

---

* Shimon Peres, then a junior aide to Ben-Gurion, makes the point in *Ben-Gurion*: "[Priority] Number one for Ben-Gurion was Jerusalem. That was his argument with Yigael Yadin [the deputy chief of staff], who wanted to fight in Ashkelon because the Egyptians had reached Ashkelon. And Ben-Gurion said no; Jerusalem first. It was the same on the Jordanian front: John Glubb [the Transjordanian commander] said we'll cross from Beisan to Haifa and bisect the Jewish state, and Emir Abdullah said no; first Jerusalem. Interesting, that parallel."

the rocks, the yellow earth. They came to us from the death camps of
Europe . . .

They stripped off, white-skinned bodies, tried to find uniforms
that fit, struggled with buckles and belts helped by young commanders they have only just met. All are quiet. Acquiescent. Not one of
them shouts, Give us a chance at least to breathe a little air after the
terrible years we have been through. As though they know this is
another battle, the last battle, for Jewish survival.

The new recruits didn't yet know, Sharon continued, of the draft
dodgers in the Yishuv who failed to enlist or of "moneyed aristocracy who sent their sons abroad lest they be harmed in the war. No
one sang of these new recruits, the 'overseas draftees,' as they were
called . . . Numbers on their arms. The lone remnants of their families,
of their entire communities, cinders salvaged from the flames . . . No
one told stories around the bonfire about their exploits. They had no
one waiting for them at home, with whom to share their experiences.
They had no homes. Men from another world, young like us but a
thousand years older."

It was a subtly political speech, but for his peroration Sharon cast
aside subtlety:

My comrades and my commanders are assembled here. With you I
started on my life's path. From you I learned. After the war, I thought
I'd go back home to work and to study. But our need to stand firm in
the battle lines did not end then, and it still has not ended. Looking
back, I feel as though I've been at the front for sixty years. Now I have
decided on a great effort designed to bring about different days, days
of peace and quiet. It is a difficult and painful effort, and I am on
the front line in a hard battle, perhaps the hardest I have ever fought.
But I will persevere because I know it is both right and vital for our
nation. And for that, too, I need your comradeship.

He carried the memory of that day with him all his life. It taught
him tactical truths that he was later to employ in much larger engagements. It taught him lessons of leadership, basics of battlefield morale.
Arguably, it taught him, too, some basic truths about Israel's place
in Palestine and in the wider region. He needed a whole lifetime,
though, to learn them. But in the end—before the end—they sank in.

He nearly died there that day, of thirst, of blood loss from a bullet
that struck him in the thigh and exited through his stomach. His son
Omri attested that whenever his father passed that place, for the next

fifty years and more, he was assailed by an overwhelming thirst.[15] His own platoon, much better kitted out than the newcomers, had nevertheless somehow not been provided with water canteens. The platoon was supposed to lead the attack on the hilltop Jordanian emplacements and the fortress and monastery below. Arik planned to cross the Jerusalem highway and come upon the defenders under cover of darkness. The rest of the force would follow.

But logistical delays—a critical unit of mortars failed to arrive; the buses ferrying the troops to the battlefield lost their way[16]—meant that the attack didn't get going till nearly dawn. The rising sun caught the platoon in open country, still on the wrong side of the road, and drew down on them a relentless hail of mortar bombs and machine-gun bullets from the hilltop. Casualties quickly mounted; the radio set was hit. The soldiers tried to flatten themselves into a shallow gully, waiting with gradually flagging confidence for reinforcements.

The Jordanians and the Palestinian irregulars, meanwhile, sensing that Arik was effectively abandoned, advanced on foot toward the beleaguered Israeli platoon.

[They] came again and again . . . moving in, shouting "*Etbach al Yahud*," "Kill the Jews," firing. Each time we drove them back, choking as the stench of cordite mixed with the smoke billowing over us from the fires in the wheat field . . . Between the fighting, the sun, and the hot wind coming across the plain, we were dying of thirst.

Around noon, the Jordanians on the hill intensified their fire, the usual forerunner of another assault. Raising myself to see what was happening, I felt something thud into my belly, knocking me back. I heard my mouth say "*ima*"—mother, and the instant it was out I glanced around to see if anybody had heard. Already blood was seeping through my shirt and from my shorts, where another wound in my thigh had appeared as if by magic. I lay down, still lucid, but feeling my strength ebbing away.

By this time, almost half of the thirty-six-man platoon were dead and most of the others wounded. The Israeli field guns suddenly fell silent, and Arik, looking around gingerly, saw Arab soldiers on a hill to the rear where another Israeli unit had previously been deployed.

Now and then they stooped down over black shapes that were just barely distinguishable . . . Instantly I realized what the scene meant. Our people there were gone—dead or withdrawn. The black shapes on the hillside were their casualties; the Arabs stooping over them were looting and mutilating the bodies. Then I understood the silence. We were alone on the field. The other units had been ordered back. That was what the artillery fire had been for, to cover the retreat . . . They had not known that we were still here, and still alive . . . I gave the order and pointed out the direction—straight back through the smoke and over the terraces.

[T]he Arabs on the hillside were moving slowly, going from body to body, oblivious that we were down here . . . Simcha Pinchasi, a wonderful boy from Kfar Saba, had been hit badly in both legs and could not move. With a look and a quick nod he indicated that he would cover the withdrawal . . . "But Arik," he said, "before you go, give me a grenade." I gave it to him, knowing there was no hope whatsoever, not for him and most likely not for the rest of us either. There was no one whom I could ask to carry him, just as there was no one who could carry me.[17]

Arik crawled painfully on all fours toward the terraces that rose up out of the burning field. He knew he lacked the strength to climb along them. A young soldier from his platoon half dragged him along. "He was a new boy, just sixteen years old. He had joined us only two days earlier, and somehow I could not remember his name. I stared at him in horror. The bottom of his jaw had been shot up, leaving a mass of gore . . . He was unable to talk. I was too tired."

"He kept saying, 'Get away. Save yourself; run for it,' " the young savior recalled years later. "But I insisted. I wouldn't obey him."[18] "Together we crawled over one rocky terrace, then another," Sharon continued his account. Eventually, they were picked up by a jeep, driven, coincidentally, by Rifka and Shmuel Bogin, a brother and sister from Kfar Malal. "Then the name of the boy who saved my life came to me. It was Yaakov Bogin, a cousin of theirs. A moment later . . . I passed out."

Half conscious on the long and much-interrupted ride to the hospital, he thought he overheard people remark that he had been hit "right in the genitals . . . [At Ekron] some of the village women came in carrying cans of milk and filling glasses for us. I was so thirsty; but looking down at my abdomen, they wouldn't give me any. I couldn't keep my eyes open . . . But when I was awake I couldn't keep my mind off my wound."[19] At a field hospital in Rehovot, "my stretcher was placed on the ground, and a charming volunteer nurse asked me to urinate. I couldn't. She asked for a catheter to be brought, and I said, 'Wait, I'll try again.' This time I succeeded. She kissed me on the mouth, and then I realized that my wound was not where I had feared."[20]

Lying in the hospital in Tel Aviv for several weeks, he reviewed the battle in his mind over and over. Fifteen of his soldiers had been killed and eleven others wounded. He had known most of them well; they were from Kfar Malal and the surrounding settlements. He knew many of their families, whose lives would never be the same again. Some of the parents came to visit him in the hospital. He didn't know what to say to them. He felt he could not claim with conviction that their loved ones' deaths had been unavoidable.

He never, then or later, questioned the strategic decision by Ben-Gurion to hurl regiment after regiment, some barely trained to shoot a rifle, against the Latrun defenses, in three successive and failed assaults. In the event, the army found an alternative route up to Jerusalem, dubbed the Burma road, which it was able to roughly pave and use to send in supplies to the city. Military historians argued subsequently over whether the dogged and costly harassment of the Arab Legion forces at Latrun served at least to reduce their numbers and their effectiveness in the fight for Jerusalem itself (which ended with both sides exhausted and the city divided by concrete walls, barbed wire, and pillboxes for the next nineteen years). Arik's criticisms were on the tactical level, and they were bitter and devastating. He faulted the more senior commanders for failing to plan the operation in greater detail, failing to ensure that it was launched on time, and above all failing to command the forces in person and from the front—so that they could change plans and improvise as the battle ebbed and flowed. "There wasn't a single senior officer on the ground, and that was what was lacking at the critical moment," Sharon told his longtime friend and amanuensis, Uri Dan, years later.[21]

Arik was troubled, too, by the almost blithe stoicism with which both officers and other ranks in the fledgling Israel Defense Forces (IDF) seemed resigned to leaving the injured as well as the dead on the battlefield. He found himself wondering what the proper code of conduct ought to be, especially given that he had seen with his own eyes acts of cold-blooded barbarism perpetrated on abandoned soldiers, both living and dead.

"The decision to withdraw and to leave wounded men in the field was mine, and I had to live with it," said Brigadier General (res.) Asher Levy, Arik's company commander at Latrun. "If I hadn't taken that decision, they'd have all been killed. As it was, some were killed, and some were taken into captivity by the Jordanians. Of course the battle was a deep trauma both for Arik and for me. The realization that you've left your comrades wounded or dead on the battlefield, justifiedly or not, is a most terrible experience."

Sharon was later to claim that as a result of his experience at Latrun he instituted in the forces he commanded—and this later percolated throughout the army—a strict, almost hallowed code that forbade leaving anyone, alive or dead, on the field of battle. In fact, Asher Levy explained, that principle was rehearsed, and was supposed to apply, in the pre-state Haganah and in the IDF from its very first day. The question was how determinedly the principle was put into practice.[22]

D espite the repeated defeats at Latrun, the IDF held its ground else-where until a truce brokered by the UN mediator Count Folke Bernadotte went into effect on June 11. It was to last for just one month, but Ben-Gurion made good use of every moment of it, dra-matically bolstering the firepower of his army with weapons that his emissaries had purchased around the world and that were now flowing freely into the country. The size of Israel's armed forces also increased significantly as the inflow of immigrants swelled the available pool of manpower. In early June, 40,000 men (and women: about 10 percent of those mobilized were women) were under arms; by mid-July, the figure had risen to 63,500. By the end of the year, it stood at more than 100,000. The invading Arab states—Syria, Iraq, Lebanon, Egypt, Transjordan, and Saudi Arabia—were vastly larger than Israel, but they failed to bring to bear their manpower potential on the Palestine front.

Ben-Gurion used the brief respite, too, to organize and consolidate the IDF. He insisted that the Etzel, and the Palmach, too, merge into the general army and not retain a separate command structure or sep-arate units. The standoff with the Etzel climaxed with the arrival of an arms ship, the *Altalena,* which Ben-Gurion ordered shelled rather than allow its cargo to be distributed in large part to Etzel units, as the Etzel leader, Menachem Begin, was demanding. Historians give credit to Begin for avoiding a civil war in the midst of the War of Indepen-dence by ordering his men not to fight back.

On July 9 the fighting resumed. The IDF quickly conquered the Arab towns of Ramle and Lydda in the center of the country. They were both to have been included in the Arab state under the Partition Resolution of the previous year. Their fifty thousand inhabitants fled east, actively impelled to do so by the victorious Israeli forces. Arik had recovered sufficiently to rejoin his battalion by this time, and he took part in operations in the Lydda area. In his memoirs he wrote of a Transjordanian counterattack, "overrunning a unit, then massacring the wounded. Twenty-eight bodies had been found, many with their ears missing, some with their genitals cut off and stuffed into their mouths. For days we scoured the area looking for missing pieces, and scattered around the hills we found them: fingers, ears, penises caked into the dusty earth . . . I caught myself thinking about having been left behind on the field."[23]

After ten days of intense fighting a second truce was called. Arik spent this one, too, in the hospital. Driving his jeep with his company commander alongside him, "somehow I managed to roll it over on us, breaking some ribs and injuring my spine in the process."[24] In mid-October, the fighting resumed for a third and last time. Israel strove mightily to drive the Egyptians out of the Negev, the south of the country, and the Syrians, the Iraqis, and the Lebanese out of the Galilee, the north. It was largely but not entirely successful. The main Negev town of Beersheba was taken on October 21, and IDF units swept across the northern border into Lebanon later that month. But an Egyptian brigade of some four thousand men was dug in around the area of Faluja in the northern Negev and refused to give ground.

Arik, on his feet again and now serving as reconnaissance officer of his battalion, tasted bloody defeat once again. "This Taha Bey [the Egyptian brigadier] was a true hero. Without any real hope of breaking out or being rescued, his brigade was . . . repelling every attack . . . Finally a major effort was planned for the night of December 27. Our battalion would keep the village of Faluja busy while a second battalion would carry out the main assault on Iraq Manshiyeh [a British-built fortress held by the Egyptians]. It was a disaster. By the time we were able to disengage we had lost ninety-eight men out of a total of six hundred."

The war ended with armistice agreements, signed during the first half of 1949, with Egypt, Lebanon, Transjordan, and Syria (Iraq refused to sign). Israel had expanded from the 55 percent of Palestine allocated to it under the UN Partition Resolution to 78 percent. Most Palestinian inhabitants of this expanded Jewish state had gone or been expelled. Of the remaining land, the West Bank was annexed by Transjordan (henceforth known as the Hashemite Kingdom of Jordan), and the Gaza Strip was taken over by Egypt.

Despite the very steep price in blood—5,682 dead, almost 1 percent of the population—the IDF had emerged victorious.

With demobilization, the IDF lost not only its wartime bulk but also many of its best young officers. The Palmach, which had been the Haganah's only professional fighting force before the state, did not take kindly to being disbanded and merged without trace into the regular army at Ben-Gurion's insistence. Many of its men preferred to return to their kibbutzim rather than pursue military careers.

Arik was appointed commander of the reconnaissance company of the Golani Brigade. "The end of the war had left many frontier areas disputed or unclear, and skirmishes with the Egyptians, Jordanians, and Lebanese were a regular fact of life. It was a time for establishing borders and training new recruits in patrolling, intelligence gathering, and night fighting. The job was just down my alley." His commanding officer, Colonel Avraham Yoffe, promoted him to captain in 1950 and recommended him for a battalion commander's course.

It was run by Yitzhak Rabin, a former top Palmach commander who had distinguished himself in the war and had decided to swallow the forcible disbandment of the Palmach and make his career in the IDF. On completing the course, Arik was appointed intelligence officer of Central Command, an unexpectedly steep step up on the ladder of promotion and an opportunity to make his mark on the top brass. His first contact with Moshe Dayan, then commanding officer (CO) of Southern Command, came in a large-scale training exercise. Arik was intrigued to find that the already-famous general scored his successes by not playing by the rules. Dayan launched his attack on Central Command before the war game had officially begun, gaining a strategic advantage but eventually running out of fuel. Arik led a counterattack that salvaged some at least of Central's honor. Later he was carpeted on the grounds that intelligence officers do not lead field operations—and resolved there and then to quit the intelligence corps.

His activities during this year were repeatedly stymied by bouts of malaria, for which the antidote was increasingly large doses of quinine. In the end the army doctors recommended a complete break and change of climate as a way of ridding his system of the bug, and he set out to see the world. But first, "My father and I went to a clothing store in Tel Aviv, where I bought my first sport jacket and a pair of what were then known in Israel as 'half shoes,' to distinguish them from the high-top boots that everyone always wore on the farm. When I arrived at Orly airport in Paris, my uncle took one look at my outfit and blanched."[25] Duly kitted out by his uncle Joseph's bespoke tailor, Arik spent a fortnight taking in the culture and living the high life in Paris. Then it was on to London, where he had three friends from the war: Yitzhak Modai and Dov Sion, both young Israeli officers, and Cyril Kern, an English Jew who had volunteered for the IDF in 1948 and was now back in the U.K. making money in the rag trade.

From London, Arik flew to New York, where his host was his aunt

Sana. She helped him get a driver's license, explaining to the examiner that he was an Israeli army officer and hence his rudimentary English. She flew down to Florida, and he took her car on a leisurely swing through Tennessee, Louisiana, and Texas, joining her in Palm Beach for New Year's 1952. "By the time I returned to Israel I felt like a man of the world. More important, the malaria seemed to have disappeared."

Back in uniform, he found himself assigned to Northern Command, where once again his path crossed that of Dayan and once again Arik signaled to the famous general that they were two of a kind: single-minded, devious, and resourceful. Two Israeli soldiers had crossed the border with Jordan and been captured. Dayan, now CO Northern Command, asked his intelligence officer whether he thought it might be possible to pick up a couple of Jordanian soldiers to help expedite the Israelis' repatriation. Arik, careful to sound equally blasé, merely offered a noncommittal "I'll look into it." But as soon as Dayan left his room, he phoned one of his officers, Shlomo Hefer, and arranged for the two of them to drive to a remote spot on the border.

They pretended they were looking for a lost cow and got into a shouted conversation with a Jordanian sergeant and three soldiers, inviting them across to drink coffee under a tree. Arik, in reasonable Arabic, asked the sergeant to send one of his men back to ask about the cow. He sent two. No sooner were they out of sight than Arik and Hefer drew their weapons and bundled the remaining two into their vehicle. The next morning, Dayan found a note on his desk: two Jordanians were in the cells below his office, waiting to be interviewed. Dayan, in a cover note to the chief of staff attached to Arik's report of the capture, wrote, "In my opinion, this operation, which was carried out with sense and with daring, is worthy of special mention."[26]

"It was the beginning of a complicated lifelong relationship between us," Sharon wrote later, "that was to be marked by deep feelings of respect, but by suspicion too . . . He positively relished the idea that someone would do this kind of thing . . . Typically he would convey his intentions in an ambiguous way, leaving plenty of room for initiative and interpretation . . . If the result was success, fine. But if it was a failure, well then, the responsibility was not his but yours."[27]

BORDERLINE

Dayan's tenure at Northern Command lasted only half a year; he was promoted to deputy chief of staff and moved to the High Command in Tel Aviv. Arik was all the more susceptible to a sustained barrage of nagging from his parents, especially his mother, to continue his education. The army, reluctant to lose a promising officer, suggested a leave of absence for the purposes of study at the Hebrew University of Jerusalem. During this period he would be commander of a reserve battalion in the Jerusalem Brigade. Perfecting the picture from Arik's viewpoint, Gali was moving to Jerusalem too. Having completed her studies as a psychiatric nurse, she was to work in a small psychiatric hospital in the suburbs of the capital. The couple married without much ado at the office of a military chaplain whom Arik knew. They found a basement apartment for rent, and Arik began diligently taking classes in Middle Eastern history. "It was a wonderful time," he writes.[28]

But it didn't last. The situation on the borders was steadily worsening. Ever since the war ended (and indeed, even before), Palestinian refugees had been infiltrating back across the unmarked frontiers of the West Bank and the Gaza Strip. Some sought to return to their former homes: if one member of a family could establish residency, there was a chance for the others to come back under a family reunification scheme. Others simply tried to harvest the crops, the fruits, or the olives growing on their former lands. Often the land was now worked by Jews: the government deliberately located new settlements close to the armistice lines in order to stake the state's claim to every inch of the territory that remained in its hands after the war. New immigrants were channeled to these border settlements and encouraged to farm the land. Government instructors gave rudimentary guidance to those who had never been farmers before.

The infiltration soon gave rise to violent and sometimes fatal confrontations. Some refugee-infiltrators did not confine themselves to their own former farms or villages but scoured the wider area for produce, tools, irrigation pipes, livestock, anything worth taking. Some settlements formed vigilante groups to protect their property, since the border was wide open and the army was plainly unable to patrol its entire winding length.

The government for its part ordered the army to maintain a ruthless shoot-to-kill policy along the armistice lines.[29] The purpose was twofold: to keep the refugee-infiltrators out for fear of a mass return that could quickly undermine the new state's conveniently manageable 80/20 Jewish/Arab demographic; and to reaffirm, each day anew, the inviolability of the armistice lines, even in the absence of full peace treaties. Subsequent orders issued by the IDF High Command forbade shooting at women and children. Male infiltrators, too, were not to be shot at without due warning, unless they opened fire first. In practice, even after these limitations were imposed, shoot to kill continued to be the order of the day in some IDF units. In others, nonviolent infiltrators were rounded up and sent back or handed over to the UN observers.

The harsh deterrent policy against the refugee-infiltrators was the focus of political argument then and thereafter. Also still in dispute is whether the Israeli policy caused or at least catalyzed the next spiral of escalation. Increasingly, the Palestinian infiltrators came in armed bands, out to kill and maim indiscriminately. Israel's response was to launch reprisal raids across the borders, against the villages or refugee camps from which the marauders were believed to have set out.

It was the dissonance that developed between that vaunted policy and its execution on the ground that sucked Arik back into the army and catapulted him to military prominence and national fame. Time and again, reprisal actions over the borders ended in frustrating failure. The postwar army seemed to have lost its fighting edge. IDF units were driven off with ease by poorly armed Jordanian militiamen. Often, the raiding party failed to make contact altogether, losing its way in the dark.

Arik had an opportunity to show how it should be done in July 1953. Mishael Shaham, commander of the Jerusalem Brigade, won approval from the High Command to go after a particularly lethal Palestinian marauder who lived in the village of Nebi Samuel, overlooking Jerusalem from the north. But Shaham could not get a regular IDF infantry unit to take on the assignment. So he called in Arik, one of his reserve battalion commanders, and asked him to undertake the mission with whatever men he could pull together. By nightfall, seven crack fighters were strapping on their webbing and checking their tommy guns. They were a motley collection: not men from his battalion at all, but comrades from war days and a couple of present-day soldiers discreetly wooed out of their units. The fact that Shaham, a regular army colonel, countenanced this semi-guerrilla setup reflected his desperation at the almost daily toll of Israeli lives and property that the infiltrators were exacting in the area under his command.

In the event, the reprisal raid was a flop. The man was not at home, and anyway the dynamite charge that Arik's men laid failed to blow off the door of his house. It did, however, rouse other villagers who began firing vigorously at the raiders, who in turn chucked a few grenades and beat a retreat. Yet when they returned to base at dawn and told their story, Shaham was well pleased. At least they had reached the target and engaged it. That was a lot more than most such operations achieved.

Shaham wrote to Ben-Gurion, prime minister and minister of defense, urging that the army set up a special force to conduct reprisal raids. Asked to recommend a commanding officer, he said he had the very man. Arik, sorely tempted, shrank back at the thought of Gali's likely reaction, let alone Vera's. He had an important test in history the next day, he muttered to Shaham. "Why study history when you can *make* history?" the colonel replied.[30] A fortnight later Arik was called before the chief of staff, Mordechai Makleff, and formally offered the task of creating and commanding the proposed special force.

"I'm dying of hunger. Where's that porcupine we hunted yesterday?" "Coming right up! He's on the grill with onions as big as a bull's balls."

This gastronomical exchange between Major Arik, big-bellied, silver-haired, but baby-faced commander of Unit 101, and his deputy, Shlomo Baum, is one of the salient memories of one young officer, Moshe Yenuka, who had come for an interview at the elite unit's base in the Jerusalem hills. The commander, Yenuka recalled, wore sandals on his bare feet and a large pistol strapped to his belt.

Arik cherry-picked his men from all over the army, often to the chagrin of rival commanders. While he encouraged an atmosphere of informality between officers and men that harked back to the egalitarian traditions of the Palmach, he was demanding and unforgiving in the strenuous training programs that he put in place in Unit 101. And while discipline was lax on base, it was harsh and inflexible on operations. Unit 101's esprit de corps rested on a new, much higher benchmark of what constituted "mission accomplished." The officers exhorted the men, and the men exhorted each other, to persevere despite casualties, to drive home their attacks, and always to bring their dead and wounded back with them, never leaving them to the enemy's mercies.

Arik began pressing Shaham and the High Command for assignments. Among the first was a mission to drive a clan of Bedouin encamped in the Negev back across the border into Sinai. Jeep-borne soldiers of Unit 101 stormed through the encampment firing their weapons at will. A few of the Bedouin were wounded; the rest fled in panic. The Israelis burned their tents and confiscated abandoned weapons. They chased the fleeing Bedouin to the border, where, in a demilitarized zone between Israeli and Egyptian territory, Unit 101's jeeps ran into a larger Egyptian force. "Get out, or we'll do to you what we did to you in '48," Arik barked at the Egyptian troops. "We're leaving now. If you shoot, we will immediately turn back and attack you."

It worked and gave the guys a lot to laugh about when they got back to base. But some in the unit were uncomfortable with the action against the Bedouin. Meir Har-Zion, a Unit 101 man whom Moshe Dayan was later to praise as the finest soldier Israel ever had, recorded years later in his memoirs a "sense of imperfection" that pervaded him at the time. "Is this the enemy? Is it all justified?"[31] Arik tried to persuade them that Israel needed to assert its sovereignty and shore up its borders and this was the only way to do it. Dayan himself, in his memoirs, writes that these Bedouin, members of the Azazme tribe, "served Egyptian intelligence by passing on information and by planting mines and carrying out acts of violence inside Israel."[32]

Shortly after, Unit 101 was ordered into action against the al-Burej refugee camp in the Gaza Strip, and again a dispute arose over the likely fates of innocent civilians. Shmuel Falah, one of the soldiers, refused to take part in the attack. Arik allowed him to switch to a second platoon whose task was to blow up the home of an Egyptian military commander. In the debriefing, defending the deaths of women and children, Arik railed that the women were "prostitutes serving the armed infiltrators who kill our innocent civilians." The chief of staff, Mordechai Makleff, phoned Shaham to demand an explanation of how fifteen civilians had died in the operation. Shaham called in Arik. Arik explained that a guard had given the alarm; the Unit 101 men found themselves in a tight spot; they had had to shoot their way out of the refugee camp.

Perhaps it was his cavalier attitude to Arab lives that had persuaded the Jerusalem Brigade commander, Shaham, to recommend Arik for Unit 101 in the first place. Shaham himself once recounted how he had been assigned two new battalion commanders, Arik and Shlomo Lahat, nicknamed Chich, who was also studying at the Hebrew University.* "Chich arrived, took command of a battalion, and the first thing he asked was, 'Where do we train?' Arik came and received a battalion too, and his first question was, 'Where can we fight Arabs,

---

* Lahat went on to become a major general in the army and, later, mayor of Tel Aviv.

where can we kill Arabs around here?' That was the difference between him and others."[33]

But Major Arik Scheinerman, aged twenty-five, did not make the policy. He merely executed it more effectively than it had been executed before Unit 101 came into being. His military leadership, first at Unit 101 and afterward as commander of the paratroopers, meant that the reprisal operations achieved greater success than in the past. It also meant that the conflict with the surrounding states escalated; the operations achieved *too* great success, as Ben-Gurion himself later observed.

Like Shaham, though, like Moshe Dayan and other top officers, Arik wholeheartedly identified with the reprisals policy. Indeed, time and again at Unit 101's camp at Sataf, in the Jerusalem hills, the unit commander's voice was to be heard blasting and cursing the powers that be for not being even tougher in the border warfare and specifically for not approving more cross-border operations for Unit 101.

On October 12, 1953, Palestinian infiltrators gruesomely murdered a mother and her two children in the Israeli village of Yahud, east of Tel Aviv. General Glubb, the British commander of the Arab Legion, promised to hunt down the killers. He invited Israel to send tracker dogs over the border to help in the search, but they lost the scent. Glubb condemned the murders at Yahud.

Nevertheless, Mordechai Makleff, the chief of staff, and his deputy, Moshe Dayan, met the next morning with the acting defense minister, Pinhas Lavon, and with Ben-Gurion, who was vacationing and thus formally not involved in the decision making. They decided on a reprisal operation against Kibbiya, a nearby Palestinian village on the West Bank. Fifty of Kibbiya's 280 homes were to be blown up. Arik was called to Central Command headquarters at Ramle. Unit 101 was to give diversionary support to the paratroop battalion that would conduct the large-scale operation. The paratroop commander was hesitant, explaining that his men were neither trained nor prepared for the action. Arik stepped in immediately. Unit 101 was trained and prepared, he said. He could take command of the whole force and lead the operation the following night.

Arik himself led the combined force of a hundred paratroopers and twenty-five men from Unit 101. Returning at dawn, he reported that a dozen Jordanian National Guardsmen and two legionnaires had been killed in exchanges of fire early in the operation.

"In a few more minutes we were in the village proper," Sharon recorded in his memoirs.

As we walked through the streets an eerie silence hung over the place, broken only by the strains of Arab music coming from a radio that had been left playing in an empty café. A report came in from one of the roadblocks that hundreds of villagers were streaming by them . . . At midnight we began to demolish the village's big stone buildings . . . Soldiers were sent to look through each house to make sure no one was inside; then the charges were placed and set off.[34]

But there were people inside. Sharon writes that he went home to Jerusalem to sleep and learned only later in the day, from Jordanian radio, that "sixty-nine people had been killed, mostly civilians and many of them women and children. I couldn't believe my ears."

Israel claimed the victims must have been cowering unnoticed in cellars or basements and were killed by mistake in the explosions. The Arab Legion claimed many of the bodies had bullet wounds.[35] Ben-Gurion made matters worse by going on the radio several days later to claim that the attack on Kibbiya had been carried out not by the IDF but by a vigilante group of local Jewish villagers enraged by the incessant raids on the border settlements and finally by the triple murder in Yahud. This was not the first time that Israel had denied the IDF's role in reprisals and resorted to the vigilante canard.[36] It fooled no one, especially since some thirteen hundred pounds of explosives had been expertly laid to blow up forty-six buildings in Kibbiya—hardly the work of an enraged posse. Great Britain, Jordan's patron, voiced "distress and horror" at the outrage. Washington said that "those responsible should be brought to account." Israel was condemned and excoriated around the world.

Behind the self-righteous facade there was both shock and worry in Jerusalem. Ben-Gurion asked to see the officer in charge of the Kibbiya operation. "It was an exciting moment for me," Sharon recorded later, in unwonted understatement. He was fairly bursting with pride. The "Old Man" quizzed him about the operation and about the men of Unit 101. Perhaps he suspected they were ex-Etzel fighters, prone to massacring and to disobedience. Arik told him they were mostly moshav and kibbutz youth. "They were the finest boys we had, I said, and there was no chance they would ever act except under orders. Then Ben-Gurion said, 'It doesn't make any real difference what will be said about Kibbiya around the world. The important thing is how it will be looked at here in this region. This is going to give us the possibility of living here.' "[37]

Sharon may have been embellishing, but his grasp of the prime minister's remarks was accurate. Alongside the concern over international fallout from Kibbiya there was a grim gratification in Ben-Gurion's circle that at last the army could be relied on to deliver a bloody but unmistakable message to the other side. "There were tragic consequences that were nobody's fault," Dayan wrote. "But from a purely military perspective, this was a first-class operation . . . The lesson for the whole army was that the government's instructions were no longer mere wishful thinking but rather minimal expectations. Instead of army units returning from operations and explaining why they had failed to carry out the assignment, the paratroopers were explaining why they had done more than expected."

Still, the worldwide castigation was a sober reminder of Israel's vulnerability. "The lesson," Dayan wrote, "was that we must direct our reprisals against military targets. What was 'permitted' to the Arabs, and indeed to other nations, was forbidden for Jews and Israelis and would not be forgiven them. Not only foreigners but citizens of Israel themselves and Jews overseas expect from us a 'purity of arms' far more exacting than that demanded of any other army."[38]

The reprisals policy was drastically revised. No longer were Arab civilians and Arab villages and refugee camps to be considered legitimate targets. The IDF's border war now shifted to focus on the armies of the states flanking Israel. Their regular armies, especially the Egyptian troops in the Gaza Strip, were actively supporting, arming, and encouraging the bands of armed Palestinian infiltrators, known as *fedayun*. The states, therefore, were responsible. Repeated military discomfiture could bring them, it was held or hoped, to rein in the marauders.

The exploits of Unit 101, although not public knowledge at the time, were the stuff of word-of-mouth legend throughout the army. So were its off-duty feats, which of course contributed to its dazzling panache in the eyes of less privileged soldiers. Unit 101's camaraderie was elitist, brash, and brutal. One Friday evening in December 1953, a 101 man driving one of the unit's jeeps was stopped by military police in Tiberias. He failed to address them with due deference, and they took him to their base, where three of them knocked him about a bit. He reported to his own base. Within hours, a posse of comrades had been rounded up, made its way to Tiberias, stormed the MP base, located the three assailants, and set about them with clubs. All three required hospitalization.

An inquiry was duly launched; Shaham was carpeted; Shaham called in Arik. Arik penned a fulsome apology to the IDF chief of operations, expressing "the most profound regret in my own name and in the name of every one of my men, for the grave incident that took place . . . I am confident such an incident will never recur. I do hope this incident will not cast a shadow on the excellent relations between my unit and the Military Police."[39] Back at Sataf, the posse members were sent home on a two-week furlough; when they returned, Arik informed them that they had been confined to base for a fortnight.

Five months after Kibbiya, Unit 101 ceased to exist as an independent military formation. It was merged with the paratroop battalion. Presumably, both lessons of Kibbiya were at play here: on the one hand, Dayan (who was appointed chief of staff in December 1953) wanted a larger fighting force imbued with the spirit of Arik's commandos; on the other hand, he wanted that spirit embraced, contained, and rendered more disciplined and less antiestablishment—less prone, in other words, to embarrass Israel by intemperate action.

The merger was seen as a hostile takeover by the men themselves, and there were murmurs of defiance. Some of the best fighters in the unit had joined it in order to escape the spit and polish of the regular army. There would be no more beating up of MPs when they were part of a proper battalion. Arik invited Dayan to Sataf to woo and win them over. "You have established new standards of combat, new benchmarks for completing missions," Dayan said, stroking their individual and collective egos. "Now it's time to instill those standards into the entire army."

There was not much enthusiasm for the merger on either side. Lieutenant Colonel Yehuda Harari, the commander of the paratroopers, a former British army officer, fully expected to command the enlarged battalion. Dayan disabused him. The paratroopers themselves looked askance at the scruffy crew who sidled reluctantly into their spick-and-span base at Beit Lid, north of Tel Aviv.

The handover ceremony said it all. Harari, ramrod straight, starched, and buckled, precision marched to his spot on the parade ground, facing the flagpole. He read out a terse parting speech and ordered officers who had asked to leave with him to fall out and line up beside him. Many did.

Arik quickly distributed the few dozen Unit 101 men among the different companies of the four-hundred-strong battalion. And he sent all the companies off on prolonged training exercises in different parts of the country, so as to dissipate any lingering umbrage. "Within weeks," a young officer wrote decades later, "it became clear that 101 had not merged into 890 the paratroop battalion but rather 890 had merged into 101."

The 101 commandos-now-890-paratroopers ceased their excesses against the military police and, much more important, against Palestinian civilians. But with the new pattern of attacking military targets, and attacking on a much larger scale than previously, the risks inherent in the reprisal operations became even greater, certainly in the eyes of the foreign minister, Moshe Sharett, and the doves in government. Escalation was inevitable, given that the clashes were now between armies. The numbers of soldiers killed, wounded, and captured—Egyptian soldiers, Jordanian soldiers, and also Syrian soldiers—were embarrassingly high for their respective governments. Yet the *fedayun* infiltrations persisted. The atmosphere in the region steadily, dangerously deteriorated.

Again, it was Sharon's military prowess, tactical skills, and leadership gifts that contributed significantly to the success of the military operations conducted within the revised reprisals policy. Again, though, he did not make the policy. However enthusiastic an executor he was of it, he was only that—the executor, not the architect. He did not conceive it, nor was he ultimately responsible for it. Retrospective discussions of this period that blame Sharon for triggering the chain of events that led to the 1956 Sinai War give him too much credit (or discredit). Granted, his own incessant pushiness, his expansive, extroverted personality, his unbridled, loudmouthed criticism of the moderates, all contributed to his ostensible importance in the scheme of things (and all enhanced the strictures of his critics). Granted, too, he was much coddled by Ben-Gurion. And he for his part took every available advantage of his access to the premier and defense minister. But he was never in the inner coterie, not one of the bright young men like Dayan and Shimon Peres and Teddy Kollek whom the Old Man nurtured and whose company he patently preferred to that of his own old party comrades. They were policy makers, inasmuch as they were present at the conception and formulation of policy. Sharon never was.

It was Ben-Gurion who required Arik, as he did other officers and diplomats, to Hebraize his diasporic-sounding name. The Sharon is the name of the geographic district around Kfar Malal, and it vaguely emulates the sound of Scheinerman. Vera and Samuil (who had long used his Hebrew first name, Shmuel) readily concurred, although they themselves kept the old family name.

There is no record of what Gali thought. There are hints, however, of broader dissatisfaction on the part of Arik's young bride over the dramatic change of course their life had taken. When he went back into the army and started coming home late, or not at all, from raids or training exercises, Gali's frayed nerves showed through. "She used to give him a hard time," an army comrade, Gideon Altschuler, recalled more than fifty years later. "My wife and I lived near them in Jerusalem, and we were good friends. The two of them didn't always live harmoniously. She didn't understand that when your man comes back from an operation across the border, that's not the time to pick a quarrel with him."[40] When Arik took over the paratroop battalion, the young and still-childless marriage was strained even more. "He hardly ever came home," according to one account, "and when he did, it was only for a few hours—during which time he subjected her to long-winded army stories. She asked him many times to be around more often, but Sharon was engrossed in his military life."[41]

One of the revamped paratroop battalion's earliest operations, in March 1954, followed the murder of eleven bus passengers on a winding road in the Negev called Ma'aleh Akrabim, or Scorpions Hill. The assailants were *fedayun* from across the Jordan border. The target chosen for reprisal was the West Bank village of Nahalin, where the paratroopers were to blow up houses again. The new policy of attacking only military targets had not yet fully gelled. Arik handed out flashlights to the troops with which they were to scour the homes before demolishing them. In the event, Arab Legion units tried to block their access, and a pitched battle developed between the two forces. The end result was seven legionnaires killed in the operation and three civilians, including the *mukhtar,* or headman, of Nahalin.

Three months later, following the murder of a farmer near Kfar Saba, the target was an Arab Legion camp at Azoun, on the West Bank. The dovish Sharett was now prime minister, Ben-Gurion having retired, at least temporarily, and gone to live on a remote Negev kibbutz, Sde Boker. Sharett approved the army's reprisal plan. Arik handpicked seven of his men to carry out this mission. The commander was Aharon Davidi, Arik's deputy. Leading the squad through nine miles of West Bank territory on the dark, moonless night was Meir Har-Zion, commander of the battalion's reconnaissance company and a man with uncanny navigational skills. Two of the others were also ex–Unit 101 men, Yitzhak Gibli and Yoram Nahari. Sharon sat with the seven as they pored over aerial photographs and maps and saw them off at the border at nightfall. They were kitted out in civilian clothes and armed with non-army-issue tommy guns. Even though the IDF was now beginning to direct its reprisals at the neighboring armies, it apparently still sought to cling to the ostensible deniability of the "vigilante" fiction.

At the camp, they split into two groups. Each stormed a large tent, spraying automatic fire and hurling grenades. As they withdrew, Gibli was hit in the leg. They lifted him and kept running, but he was hit again, this time in the neck. They bandaged him quickly. The surviving legionnaires were firing wildly in all directions. Soon they would come after them. Gibli begged to be left. "Just give me a grenade," he told Davidi. "When they reach me, I'll blow myself up with them." Davidi consulted with Har-Zion. It was against their battle ethic to leave a wounded man in the field. But they decided there was no choice; if they stayed, they would all suffer the wounded man's fate (which they fully assumed would be death or suicide). But Gibli was not killed and instead was taken prisoner. On his cell wall, he recalled four decades later, he scratched the first letters of Arik's and Davidi's names, "to remind myself who I am and where I come from."[42]

Arik for his part, surprised and delighted to learn that Gibli was alive, now embarked on a determined effort to get him back in the way he knew best: kidnapping Jordanian soldiers wherever he could pounce on them. In one instance, he had a jeep painted in white with UN markings and dressed up two of his men as Palestinian peasants and Har-Zion as an Israeli policeman. They were to drive to the border to "return" the two straying peasants. When a Jordanian patrol came to "receive" them, they would grab the officer and head back with him to Israel. The officer in question saw through the fresh paint or the peasant dress and backed away in time. On another occasion, Arik sent two women soldiers across the border to entice legionnaires, also without success.

He was like a man possessed, endlessly repeating the mantras that the paratroopers don't leave a man in the field (which they had) and that the IDF does everything possible to bring its men home. He was a lieutenant colonel by now, having been promoted after being wounded leading an attack in July 1954 on a fortified Egyptian army position near Khan Yunis, in the Gaza Strip. "I was hit in the thigh," he recounted in a nostalgic lecture, as prime minister, forty-nine years later.

The same searing physical pain. But whereas at Latrun I was a young platoon commander abandoned on the field of battle after a bitter fight and a crushing defeat, this time, despite the pain, I had a feeling of confidence. I'd been wounded again, but in a battle that we'd won. And I was among comrades in a unit suffused with self-confidence and fighting spirit. Above all, I myself was confident in the certain knowledge that I would never be abandoned on the field. That knowledge, that our comradeship would sustain every test, was what gave us all the determination and the strength to carry out every mission assigned to us throughout that period and in the wars that followed.[43]

Sharon's mantras reflected the spirit he inculcated in the paratroopers, and these did in time pervade the whole army as ideals to be aspired to.

Under Arik, a commander's decision to leave a wounded man would be justified only in the direst straits, as Gibli's case proved. For Arik, what also changed was the lengths to which he believed the IDF should go to get its POWs back. His unremitting attempts to seize Jordanians led to serious strains with Dayan and his head of operations, Colonel Meir Amit. Dayan wrote in his diary:

> I called in Arik on August 25 and told him he had no approval to cross the border and grab a hostage to exchange for Gibli . . . To resolve this business of unapproved operations [I said], there was one single condition: that we worked in cooperation. If he wasn't satisfied with the approval given for a particular operation, he could always come and present alternatives. I would not be angry or surprised if a particular operation with a particular purpose changed under the circumstances and produced different results. But I would not tolerate the defined purpose of an operation being altered before the operation had begun. Arik said he understood, agreed and promised.[44]

The "business of unapproved operations" was never really resolved between the two men. This conversation was a harbinger of many conversations to come over the next two years and further in the future, when Sharon was to lead much larger formations under Dayan's overall command.

In his memoirs, Dayan wrote of Ben-Gurion's "special affection" for three IDF officers: Haim Laskov,* Assaf Simchoni, and Sharon. The founding father saw in all three of them "the antithesis of the *galuti,* or diasporic Jew. The New Jew was a fighter, bold, self-confident, expert in the art of war, in weaponry, in field craft, in the region, and in the Arabs. Ben-Gurion could not bear casuistry and beating around the bush. He didn't like the Talmud; his heart rebelled against two thousand years of exile. He yearned for the Israelites of the Bible, living on their land, farming and fighting, independent and proud and building

---

* Chief of staff from 1958 to 1961.

their national culture. Haim, Assaf, and Arik were like those ancient Israelites in his eyes."[45] Ben-Gurion's biographer Michael Bar-Zohar writes that the Old Man told him he admired two soldiers above all for their bravery and resourcefulness: Dayan and Sharon.

Sharon himself failed to understand that his easy and frequent access to Ben-Gurion rankled with other, more senior officers. "With the room full of generals and staff officers, he would call me to be next to him . . . It was a situation that cried out for tact on my part, but at the age of twenty-six I didn't recognize the need."[46]

Regardless of the tension between Sharon and himself, Dayan was consistent and unequivocal in recognizing the reprisal operations as a key factor in strengthening the IDF. "Dayan saw the reprisals as a means of educating and training the army," writes his then aide-de-camp, Mordechai Bar-On. "The long series of combat failures during the years before his appointment as chief of staff, and especially during 1953, worried him deeply, and he saw his main task as chief of staff to restore the IDF to fighting efficacy . . . The reprisal actions were the chief instrument."[47]

Dayan insisted that the army's regular infantry brigades improve their combat effectiveness and that more units develop the commando skills which the paratroopers expended so much effort acquiring. With time, Dayan records in his memoirs, other units began to take part in the reprisal operations. "The paratroopers ceased to be solely an army formation and became a concept and a symbol—the symbol of courageous combat."

The paratroop battalion "has set high standards of combat," Dayan told the General Staff in February 1956. "It has proved that we can achieve those high standards, and has thereby had an influence throughout the army. It has demonstrated what the level of commitment of the individual fighter can be and ought to be in battle. If one man had succeeded in moving the entire army forward in this regard, it is Arik."[48]

But there were moments of weakness, too, even of cowardice. And there were serious lapses of ethical standards, despite the lessons ostensibly learned from the Kibbiya operation. In February 1955, Meir Har-Zion and three other paratroopers crossed the border and killed five Bedouin in cold-blooded revenge for the murder of Har-Zion's sister. The sister, Shoshana, and a friend had gone hiking on the Jordanian side of the border, heading for the Dead Sea. They never returned. Har-Zion formally quit the army, enlisted three paratrooper friends, and went after the killers. They picked up six Bedouin, murdered five, and left the sixth alive to tell the tale. Har-Zion maintained that these were the killers, but there was no clear proof of that.[49] "The entire episode was a throwback to tribal days," Sharon writes in *Warrior*.

Tribal or not, Sharon provided Har-Zion with a tracked vehicle, a driver to take him right up to the border ("the best I had"—Yitzhak Gibli, now back from Jordanian captivity), and weapons with which to conduct his vendetta. And what's more, Dayan knew in real time that he had done so. "Dayan called to ask what had happened . . . 'I tried to persuade him [Har-Zion],' I said. 'But he wouldn't listen. So I gave him some help.' 'Can we still stop him?' Dayan asked. 'No,' I answered. 'It's too late for that.' "[50] When the four returned, they were feasted and feted by the paratroopers.

Prime Minister Sharett demanded that the four men stand trial "or else we will lose the right to demand that neighboring states try and punish murderers [of Jews]." Ben-Gurion, who had now returned from his desert retreat and was serving as minister of defense, agreed. Har-Zion and his friends were arrested. Sharon hired an able young lawyer, Shmuel Tamir, to plead their case. But Tamir was a vocal and eloquent member of Menachem Begin's Herut Party and a thorn in the government's flesh. Ben-Gurion was furious, more over the political deviation in hiring Tamir, apparently, than over the killings that Sharon had abetted. Ben-Gurion gave Sharon a stark choice: sever your ties with Tamir at once, without telling him why, or leave the army at once. Sharon chose the former, explaining to Tamir only years later why he had been forced to do so.[51]

In a fawning and disingenuous letter to Dayan—disingenuous, it would seem, on both their parts—Sharon vigorously denied any taint of disloyalty. "There is no unit in the army more admiring of and loyal to the chief of staff than the paratroop battalion." He admitted to "mistakes" in the Har-Zion affair but insisted that he "genuinely and sincerely believed at the time I was doing the right thing . . . I never intended, Heaven forbid, to embarrass the IDF in any show trial, and I certainly had no political intent regarding the lawyer."[52]

Ben-Gurion, in his diary, faulted Sharett for publishing the names of Har-Zion's three accomplices and justified Har-Zion's refusal to cooperate with the police investigators. The upshot was an internal IDF investigation. There was no trial and no punishment. Har-Zion was back in uniform within months. "The final outcome of the affair," writes the historian Benny Morris, "reflected Ben-Gurion's position in general. He never really wanted to prosecute four of his most favorite soldiers, especially since a trial might have thrown light on other ethically dubious actions of Unit 101 and the paratroopers."[53]

A much more ominous drama was meanwhile building up between Israel and Egypt. On February 17, 1955, an Israeli farmer was murdered near Rehovot. Clearly the killers had infiltrated from the Gaza Strip. Sharon submitted a plan to attack in reprisal a small Egyptian army unit encamped south of Gaza City. Ben-Gurion and Dayan together persuaded Sharett to agree. The order to the paratroopers, they explained, would strictly forbid them to kill enemy soldiers "except if that proves vital for the fulfillment of the mission," which was defined as blowing up buildings in the camp and in the nearby railway station.

To ward off suspicious snooping by UN observers, the paratroopers left their forward camp at the kibbutz of Kfar Azza together with girl soldiers, all singing and laughing as if they were off on a hike. As they approached the border, they split off into separate attacking forces. One headed for the Egyptian army camp, another for the station; a third set up an ambush on the main road from the south, to intercept reinforcements.

Bad navigating led to mistakes, and the first and second forces found themselves in a vicious firefight with Egyptian soldiers. Eight paratroopers died, and a dozen more were injured. The Egyptians lost fourteen men. A number of buildings were destroyed, and the attacking units withdrew under fire, carrying their dead and wounded with them. The third force, meanwhile, wiped out a column of Egyptian reinforcements, killing twenty-two men without loss. Waiting on the border, Dayan listened to Sharon's grim report impassively. "The living are alive and the dead are dead," he said, wheeled around, and left the scene.

Ben-Gurion published a paean of praise for the paratroopers. "The cabinet has unanimously asked me to convey to the paratroop battalion our feelings of appreciation and admiration for the spirit of Jewish heroism demonstrated in this battle . . . I am sure that these feelings are shared by the entire country. The paratroop battalion, which enjoys the love of the whole nation, has proven once again for all the world to see the triumph of Jewish heroism and has added a glowing page to the annals of the Israel Defense Forces.

"We do not lust for battle," the defense minister continued, "and we regret all loss of life, Jewish and non-Jewish alike. But it is as well that all should know that we are strong and that our blood is not to be spilled with impunity . . . Your glorious, all-volunteer battalion, comprising native-born Israelis and immigrants, members of oriental communities and of western communities, young men from all the lands of Asia, Africa, Europe, and America—your battalion is the living embodiment of the unity of the Jewish people." Ben-Gurion signed, "With love and admiration."

A PASS TOO FAR

From the immediate political perspective the Gaza operation was profitless: Israel was condemned by the UN Security Council. From a historical perspective, the operation stands out as a catalyst of escalation in the tension between the two armies, in the arms race between the two governments, and, ultimately, in the process by which the Arab-Israeli conflict grew into a vicarious battle between the superpowers.[54]

Egypt fueled the tension by ratcheting up its support for the Palestinian infiltrators. The *fedayun* groups operating out of the Gaza Strip became effectively an agency of the Egyptian military, armed and paid by army intelligence. They raided deep into Israel, occasioning ever larger reprisal attacks, usually by the paratroopers, against Egyptian military units. In one four-day period in August 1955, *fedayun* units ranged through southern and central Israel killing 11 civilians, injuring 9, and causing extensive damage to property. The paratroopers, in their first mechanized attack, captured and destroyed an Egyptian police station at Khan Yunis in the Gaza Strip, killing 72 Egyptians and wounding 58 for the loss of 1 dead and 11 wounded on their own side.[55]

A month later, after repeated Syrian shelling of Israeli fishermen, the paratroopers swept up the northeastern (Syrian) shore of the Sea of Galilee (Lake Kinneret), overrunning Syrian gun posts and killing more than 50 Syrian soldiers, wounding at least that number, and taking dozens more prisoner. Sharon's men suffered 6 dead and 10 wounded. The operation was "too successful," Ben-Gurion (now back in the dual role of prime minister and defense minister) complained when Dayan, with Sharon in tow, came to Tel Aviv to explain what had happened.

The border escalation was doubly disturbing because by this time Israel was facing the threat of a hugely more powerful Egypt, backed by the Soviets' military arsenal. The stunning shock was delivered by Gamal Abdel Nasser, the charismatic new leader of the country, in a speech in September 1955. Egypt, he announced, had signed a major arms deal with Czechoslovakia and would soon be receiving the first deliveries of state-of-the-art Soviet weaponry. The Americans knew something of this imminent Egyptian turnabout. Through intelligence contacts they tried to head off Cairo's shift into the Soviet sphere, but without success. For Israel, it was a bolt from the blue. The three Western powers, the United States, Britain, and France, had agreed in a 1950 concordat to severely restrict their arms sales to all Middle Eastern countries. Would they now ease those restrictions in the face of the challenge from Moscow?

In August 1956, an ambush laid by the paratroopers on the Gaza border against infiltrators again developed into a full-pitched battle with Egyptian forces. A dozen Egyptians were killed, among them a medical team. Israel's consternation was all the greater because by this time secret negotiations were under way with France on possible military collusion against Egypt. The last thing Ben-Gurion and Dayan needed at that point was a border skirmish triggering an unplanned and premature conflagration. "Dayan's anger at the paratroop commander became more open and more pronounced," wrote an Israeli military historian. "[Sharon] was conducting 'his own independent policy,' in Dayan's words."[56]

The tension between Dayan and Sharon flared again in October, around a reprisal action against a Jordanian police station at Kalkilya, on the West Bank, which turned into a battle between the two armies and left 18 Israeli dead and 68 injured. These were far higher casualty figures than the public and the prime minister were prepared to stomach for any reprisal operation that was less than all-out war. The fact that almost a hundred Jordanian soldiers, militiamen, and police were killed in the Kalkilya raid did not mitigate the losses. The fact that it came just a fortnight after another costly reprisal action, at Hussan, near Bethlehem, where ten paratroopers died, made it even harder to take.

A week later, on October 17, Dayan called in the officers who took part in the Kalkilya operation for a debriefing. He explained the constraints under which the government operated: the need to avoid civilian casualties and to avoid triggering intervention by British air force units stationed in Cyprus. He urged the officers to speak out freely, but when Sharon and others criticized his policy and his behavior, he lashed back. He accused Sharon of indifference to Israeli casualties. Sharon needlessly risked soldiers' lives, he charged, in order to kill greater numbers of Arab soldiers and score "fuller" victories. Whatever the rights and wrongs of the battlefield tactics at Kalkilya, everyone realized that the reprisals strategy had become counterproductive, escalating the tit-for-tat violence to unacceptable levels. "I think," Dayan confided, "that there will be a pause in operations while we carefully reconsider our policy."[57]

Alone in that room, Dayan knew that a large-scale war between Israel and Egypt, and also between France and Egypt, was likely to break out within weeks. He knew that Britain, too, might take part alongside France. Together with Shimon Peres, the director general of the Defense Ministry, and a handful of aides, Dayan was deeply involved in secret negotiations with the French over this fateful scenario. In five days, with dark glasses shielding his telltale eye patch, he would accompany Ben-Gurion—the Old Man's disguise was a trilby hat pulled down over his famous, flowing demi-tonsure—and Peres on a French air force plane via North Africa to a top-level summit conference at Sèvres, near Paris, where the details of this military collusion finally would be worked out. Guy Mollet, France's Socialist prime minister, Christian Pineau, the foreign minister, and Maurice Bourgès-Maunoury, the minister of defense, promised Ben-Gurion to protect Israel's skies from Egyptian bombers while the IDF struck at Egyptian forces in Sinai. In a separate understanding negotiated by Peres, the French leaders agreed to provide Israel with the technical assistance and the uranium required to create its own nuclear weapons program.[58]

For France and Britain, the Sèvres Protocol was a last-ditch attempt to dislodge Nasser and prevent a total Egyptian takeover of the Suez Canal. Britain had reluctantly agreed in 1954 to withdraw its forces from the Canal Zone over a two-year period, thereby ending the seventy-seven-year British military presence protecting the waterway.* The agreement provided that Britain could keep up some of its

---

* Israel tried to head off this Anglo-Egyptian agreement by ordering a network of Egyptian-Jewish agents to carry out provocative attacks against American cultural centers and other institutions in Egypt. The idea, breathtaking in its naïveté and irresponsibility, was that such attacks would poison Egypt's relations with the West and prompt Britain to keep its troops on the canal. The amateurish attacks all failed hopelessly; two of the Jews were executed; an Israeli agent committed suicide in prison; six other Egyptian-Jewish members of the group received long prison terms. What was poisoned as a result, terminally in the view of many historians, was the cohesive solidarity within the ruling Mapai Party. Ben-Gurion, who was on his Negev kibbutz and out of power during "the unfortunate mishap," as it was called for years in the censored Israeli press, insisted on a judicial process to determine if his stand-in as defense minister, Pinhas Lavon, had ordered the operation. Lavon put the blame on the head of Military Intelligence, Binyamin Gibli (no relation to Yitzhak). Luckily for Chief of Staff Dayan, he was out of the country when the order was given. Ben-Gurion's veteran Mapai colleagues, led by his close lieutenant and eventual successor, Levi Eshkol, wanted to make do with a ministerial committee that had delivered an inconclusive verdict on who gave the order. After years of simmering conflict, Ben-Gurion eventually resigned from office and seceded from Mapai in 1963, taking Dayan and Peres with him. The labor movement as a whole was seriously weakened by this infighting. In time, this decline helped pave the way for the Likud's accession to power in 1977, after three decades of Labor rule.

bases in the Canal Zone, under civilian maintenance, for use by its troops in wartime. In July 1956, a month after the last British military units left, Nasser announced that Egypt was nationalizing the Suez Canal Company, largely owned by the British government and French shareholders. He said the company's future revenues would go toward the cost of the Aswan High Dam project in Upper Egypt, which the United States and Britain had recently pulled out of. (The dam was subsequently built with Soviet aid.) While the canal no longer served as an imperial lifeline from the mother country to British India, it was still a vital and lucrative route for international trade and especially for the constantly expanding traffic in oil tankers. Britain was both damaged and humiliated by Nasser's action. France, in addition, bitterly resented Egypt's support for the FLN rebels in Algeria.

For Israel, the war with Egypt was designed to achieve three goals:

- to maul the Egyptian army and smash as much of its newly supplied Soviet weaponry as possible;
- to break the blockade of the Straits of Tiran, at the tip of the Red Sea, and open up the southern port of Eilat to commercial shipping; and
- to end the Egyptian-run *fedayun* infiltration from the Gaza Strip. If that were stopped, it was held, Jordan would rein in its own *fedayun,* too.[59]

Sharon's paratroopers were to play a key role in the opening phase of the clandestinely coordinated hostilities. The Sèvres Protocol provided that Israeli forces were to launch "a large-scale attack on the Egyptian forces on the evening of October 29, with the aim of reaching the Canal Zone the following day." The only way that could realistically happen was by a parachute drop. "On being apprised of these events," the protocol continued, "the British and French Governments during the day of 30 October 1956 [will] respectively and simultaneously make two appeals to the Egyptian Government and the Israeli Government" to withdraw their forces ten miles from the canal. Egypt, in addition, would be required to "accept temporary occupation of key positions on the Canal by the Anglo-French forces to guarantee freedom of passage through the Canal by vessels of all nations until a final settlement."

Egypt, of course, was not expected to agree to any of this, in which case "the Anglo-French forces will launch military operations against the Egyptian forces in the early hours of the morning of 31 October." Israel, meanwhile, released from its own requirement to heed to Anglo-French demands, would "send forces to occupy the western shore of the Gulf of Aqaba and the group of islands Tirane and Sanafir to ensure freedom of navigation in the Gulf of Aqaba." Another paragraph provided that "the arrangements of the present protocol must remain strictly secret."

How secret did Ben-Gurion keep it, and for how long? Specifically, how much did Sharon know and understand of the larger picture before and during the fighting? The question is important in understanding Sharon's conduct, which resulted, according to his critics, in the needless deaths of nearly forty paratroopers and the injury of more than a hundred.

Sharon himself claimed he knew everything before everyone. "As we licked our wounds after Kalkilya," he wrote, "Ben-Gurion, Dayan, and Shimon Peres left for Paris to try to conclude negotiations with the French and British that would bring all three countries into a concerted action against Egypt. When they returned on October 25, I went to see Ben-Gurion. He told me briefly that a deal had been struck by which Israel, France, and Great Britain would each gain their objectives . . . Events that would shake our world were now only days away. As I stood there absorbing it, I could almost feel the wings of history brushing the air."

This is not quite as bizarre as it sounds: a young lieutenant colonel dropping in on the prime minister and defense minister to hear secret plans to which senior generals were not yet privy.[60] Sharon did frequently call on the Old Man. Indeed, on November 4, as the Sinai War was winding down, Sharon was at Ben-Gurion's home reporting in person on the operation he had led, and his wife, Margalit, also came in and was greeted warmly by the prime minister.[61]

On the afternoon of October 29, Sharon's lead battalion under Rafael Eitan, 395 men in all, took off as planned in a fleet of DC-3s and flew toward the Mitle Pass, 150 miles from the Israel-Sinai border. The original intention had been to drop on the western end of the pass, a bare dozen miles from the canal. But intelligence reports pointed to an Egyptian deployment in that area, and so the drop was moved to the eastern end of the pass. The change of plan proved fateful.

Sharon himself led the rest of the paratroop brigade, reinforced by an armored company of thirteen French AMX light tanks, on a dash across the desert to link up with Eitan's force. Three Egyptian fortified positions stood in their way. On the evening of the twenty-ninth they took Kuntilla, some twelve miles inside Egyptian territory, "moving the attacking units around to the rear," Sharon writes, "so they could come in out of the setting sun."

At dawn on the thirtieth, "we were in position in front of Themed, a Bedouin oasis that had been heavily fortified with minefields and perimeter fences and was held by two companies of Egyptian infantry." This time he attacked head-on, with the sun behind him. Tanks, half-tracks, and jeeps all surged forward. "Huge whirls of dust clouded the desert from the charging vehicles, illuminated from behind by the bright morning glare. Emerging from the cloud, at the last moment, we formed a single line and smashed into the middle of the Egyptian defenses. Themed, too, fell quickly."

The last obstacle was the little township of Nakhl, with an adjoining military camp, forty miles farther west. Sharon's forces took them by late afternoon in another swift frontal assault. "I had left a company behind to secure Themed, and now I left a battalion at Nakhl . . . In the back of my mind was the thought that the British and French might not act, and if they didn't I would have to have a protected line of withdrawal out of the desert." The rest of the brigade swept across the remaining seventy miles without opposition, and by ten that evening the first units entered Eitan's encampment.

Eitan, Sharon writes, had been strafed during the day by Egyptian warplanes and shelled by a motorized infantry unit advancing through the Mitle from the west. But Israeli planes had bombed and destroyed this force, and the pilots had reported "that the pass was now free of any discernible Egyptian presence." Sharon determined to press on through the pass to the western end. In his testimony after the war to General Haim Laskov, who was appointed by Dayan to investigate the fighting at the Mitle, Sharon said he had met with the CO of Southern Command, General Assaf Simchoni, at 3:00 a.m. on October 29, and the two of them had agreed that the paratroopers, once they had linked up, would push on through the Mitle Pass to the original drop site at the western end. They would then station one battalion at each end of the pass.[62]

At dawn on the thirty-first, however, an order came through from the High Command in Tel Aviv forbidding further movement westward. Egyptian jets swooped down to strafe the paratroopers, vulnerable targets in their shallow foxholes. The Egyptian planes were chased off by a squadron of Israeli fighters, and three of them were downed. But the Israeli pilots radioed to the paratroopers, Sharon writes, "that an Egyptian armored brigade was moving toward us" from the direction of Bir Gafgafa, a large military base to the northeast. Again Sharon proposed moving his force into the Mitle. His reasoning this time was that his twelve hundred lightly armed men—only three of the brand-new AMXs had made the journey to the end; the others had broken down, and there were no spare parts to fix them—would be sitting ducks for the oncoming Egyptian armor, spread-eagled as they were on the flat ground east of the pass. They needed to take up defensive positions on the slopes of the Mitle from where they could pick off the Egyptian tanks with bazookas and recoilless rifles as they made their way through the narrow defile. Again, though, the order came back from Tel Aviv: stay put. Southern Command sent its chief of operations, Rehavam Ze'evi, by Piper plane to survey the scene and to make sure the order was obeyed.

Sharon persuaded Ze'evi to approve sending a reconnaissance patrol into the pass, to confirm that it was free from Egyptian forces. " 'You can go as deep as possible,' " Sharon recalled Ze'evi saying, " 'just don't get involved in a battle . . .' Immediately I put together a unit to go into the pass. My idea was that this unit would move the twenty miles to the western end and hold the position there, preventing Egyptian forces from attacking from that direction. Then the rest of the brigade could move inside, deploying to defend themselves against the armored forces . . . For this job I put the three tanks together with two companies of infantry in half-tracks."

Ze'evi remembered things rather differently. "I told [Sharon] that a reconnaissance patrol was approved but nothing more than that," Ze'evi testified to Laskov. "We're sitting and talking, and I see that a whole column of vehicles is lining up, half-tracks, jeeps, AMX tanks. I say to Arik, 'What's all this?' He says, 'Those sons of bitches, when I tell them to prepare a reconnaissance patrol, everyone starts pumping it up out of all proportion. But don't worry, it's just a patrol.' I said to Arik, 'I'm warning you, this patrol is to bring back nothing but information.' "[63]

Sharon put one of his battalion commanders, Mordechai Gur, in command of this ill-defined force with its ill-defined mission. He gave him, he writes, "strict orders not to get involved in any fights . . . But within a mile of the entrance the first half-track was slammed by a volley of fire from hidden positions high on the defile walls. The driver was killed instantly and the half-track swerved sideways and stopped. The second half-track moved up and was also hit and stopped."[64]

Gur's force had driven into a well-laid trap. Egyptian troops, holed up in caves and dugouts high above the pass, virtually invisible from the air, rained down mortar and machine-gun cross fire on the Israeli vehicles. The paratroopers, those who were not hit in the first fusillade, tried to clamber out, to find what cover they could, and to return largely ineffective fire at their tormentors. Gur resolved to stand and fight rather than try to back away. He managed to send a runner back to Sharon to describe the inferno in which he found himself. He begged urgently for help.

Sharon sent in two units of reinforcements, under Eitan and Davidi, to join the battle. "It was a precarious situation. We were exposed on the flatland at the end of the pass. Many wounded were already being brought out of the battle. I felt I had to take immediate steps to create a defensive perimeter facing the approaching Egyptian armor and to have the wounded evacuated." He began redeploying the rest of the brigade on the slopes at the entrance to the pass and at the same time arguing with the air force, who were reluctant to land their DC-3s in the soft desert sand. In the end, they took the chance and began ferrying the casualties out of the battle zone.

Gur and his dwindling force were pinned down and fought desperately until sunset, when Yitzhak Hofi, the deputy brigade commander who had joined the original patrol and made it westward with two tanks and several half-tracks, charged back through the pass and provided fire cover, under which, with the help of the reinforcements, the paratroopers finally withdrew. After nightfall, Sharon sent two small units to creep along the sides of the pass and ferret out the Egyptian positions. "They attacked one Egyptian cave and firing hole after another in hand-to-hand fighting. For two hours the sounds of battle reverberated through the pass before finally giving way around eight o'clock to an ominous silence."[65]

The next morning, Sharon recalls, his troops were poised to give battle to the column of Egyptian tanks. But the only sound from the desert was the drone of two Israeli Piper Cubs, searching in vain for the Egyptian armor. With the Anglo-French intervention now (belatedly) imminent, the Egyptians had preferred to turn northwest and withdraw across the canal.

More than 250 Egyptians died in the caves overlooking the Mitle. But the paratroopers' losses—38 killed* and 120 wounded—were a grievous blow to the brigade. They would represent some 20 percent of all the IDF's losses in the hundred-hour Sinai War, which ended, for Israel at any rate, as a huge and resounding success. Three IDF columns, mainly comprising reservists, struck into Sinai in the wake of the paratroopers' jump. One headed south from Eilat, took Sharm el-Sheikh at the southern tip of Sinai, and spiked the guns that had blockaded the Straits of Tiran. The paratroopers had been designated to attack Sharm el-Sheikh, too. But by the time they regrouped after the battle of the Mitle and dashed down the western Sinai coast, it was

---

* Two more died in separate incidents.

too late. Another armored column attacked the heavily fortified Egyptian complex at Abu Agheila in northeastern Sinai. This was the heaviest fighting of the campaign, but eventually the Israeli force overran the defenders and pushed on toward Ismailia on the Suez Canal. The third, northernmost column skirted the Gaza Strip, taking Rafah at its southern end and then splitting. Half the force doubled back through the Strip, attacking the Egyptian units stationed there. The other half raced on along the Mediterranean coast, taking el-Arish and surging on toward Kantara, on the canal.

The final cost to Israel was 172 dead, 700 wounded, and 4 prisoners of war. Egypt suffered thousands of dead, great numbers of wounded, and 5,581 prisoners of war.

The British and French experience was far less favorable than Israel's: their combined land, sea, and air forces, operating—albeit not without copious snafus and delays—out of Cyprus and Malta and from half a dozen aircraft carriers, crushed Egyptian resistance. But Nasser had ordered all the cargo ships in the canal to be sunk, and so, while British troops were back in control of the waterway, Britain and France could not reopen it for maritime traffic. And Nasser, though his army was trounced, claimed a great victory. Far from being overthrown, he seemed more popular than ever.

The reaction from the two superpowers, the United States and the U.S.S.R., was wholly and vociferously negative. President Eisenhower, who had been reelected on November 6, threatened to induce a run on sterling unless Britain withdrew forthwith. Israel for its part was the target of some ominous nuclear saber rattling from the Soviet leader, Marshal Bulganin, and more civilized but no less stern admonishments from Eisenhower. Ben-Gurion, who had waxed lyrical over his expansive "Third Kingdom of Israel" with its biblically named outposts in the far south, quickly folded and agreed to pull out. The UN Security Council set up a peacekeeping force that it deployed along the Israel-Sinai border and at Sharm el-Sheikh. In March 1957, the blue berets moved into the Gaza Strip, too, and the last IDF units pulled back across the armistice lines.

The war left Sharon's standing and prestige in the army seriously weakened and his military career compromised. "Why are we, the best fighters, not in the fighting?" he had remonstrated with Southern Command by radio on October 31, in the course of his pleading to be allowed to move into the Mitle Pass. "When are we going to stop this guarding and start some fighting?" To the historian Motti Golani, this radio message shows that Sharon did not understand "the bigger picture" even when he was right in the thick of it.[66] There was no need to advance into the Mitle and risk a bloody battle now that the intended effect of the parachute drop was in train. The Anglo-French ultimatum had been delivered on the morning of the thirtieth, twelve hours after the Israeli parachute drop, as planned. It had been duly rejected by Egypt, and the two European powers launched their military operations that morning, the thirty-first, with bombing runs over the Canal Zone. There was no purpose, therefore, in Sharon's troops advancing west.

Mordechai Gur, who led the "patrol" into the pass, was scathing in his criticism of Sharon:

> He didn't direct the battle. No one directed it . . . Sharon was physically exhausted on the way down to the Mitle, after all the planning and conferring that preceded it. When Arik's there—he's there. Now he simply wasn't there. He slept the whole time or dealt with other things. When we saw he wasn't functioning, Davidi took the decisions instead of him. That's how we overran Kuntilla, Themed, and Nakhl. [At the Mitle] he wasn't functioning for hours on end. He was panicked, presumably because he'd acted against orders and because the casualty figures scared him. He collapsed under the stress . . . The brigade commander was totally out of it.[67]

That public indictment came thirty years after the Sinai War, when Sharon and Gur were rival politicians. But Gur leveled the same accusations against Sharon inside the army as soon as the fighting was over. And there was worse. "I never saw his back when we were charging the enemy," Gur said at a tense and bitter meeting of the paratroop officers that Sharon himself convened in March 1957. "Not at Gaza. Not at Khan Yunis. Nor at Hussan. Nor Kinneret. Nor Kalkilya. And most of all, not at the Mitle. Where was he from 1:30 in the afternoon till 8:30 at night? He wasn't there. He didn't take part in the fighting. He wasn't even on the radio."

By then, many of the officers were in open revolt against their commander. They wanted him out. He had urged them to speak freely; they accused him, in effect, of cowardice. He tried to defend his behavior at the Mitle. He needed to organize the rest of the brigade, he said, for the armored Egyptian assault that he expected imminently. He needed to organize a makeshift landing strip in the desert for urgent medevac flights. He had directed the battle from the entrance to the pass, feeding in reinforcements, planning how to outflank the Egyptians dug into the hillsides.

Was Sharon, Ben-Gurion's paragon of the courageous new Jew, in fact a coward? Some of his critics inside the paratroop brigade cast this ultimate aspersion openly. "He was not a brave man," said Brigadier General (res.) Dov Tamari, then a platoon commander who was wounded at the Mitle. "He was fearful for his own personal safety."[68]

Others confirmed that he did not often lead his men into battle but acknowledged that, at his rank, this was not necessarily the criterion by which to judge his bravery. Yitzhak Hofi, his deputy at the Mitle, said Sharon's behavior was entirely acceptable by the yardstick of any other fighting unit, where senior officers controlled the battle from behind the front line. "But by the standards of the paratroopers, which he himself had inculcated, there was something strange in his conduct."[69] Even Gur, his most stringent critic, conceded in a 1986 interview that Sharon did lead in several of the reprisal operations. "But at a certain point he began to think that he was too important [to lead from the front]. In the Gaza operation, for instance, he went along with us and then, suddenly, he moved aside." Gur praised Sharon's unequaled ability to "read the battlefield." "That's why I was so furious with him at the Mitle, for simply not being there. If he'd have been in contact with us, everything would have ended differently."[70]

In the welter of recriminations after the Mitle, another charge surfaced. This one stuck to Sharon for the rest of his life: he was an inveterate liar. This, too, wasn't new. Ben-Gurion himself had gently suggested to his young hero a number of times that he needed to rein in his penchant for not quite telling the truth. "He never called him outright a liar," said Yitzhak Navon, Ben-Gurion's longtime bureau chief and most discreet and intimate aide who was later to become president of the state (1978–1983). "On one occasion when I was present, he spoke to him almost in a fatherly way. 'Arik, you know people say about you that you aren't always accurate . . .' He was being euphemistic. He knew from his military aide, Nehemia Argov, that that was the word inside the army. Arik: 'No, no. I do try to be accurate.' BG: 'Well, it's not good not to be accurate. One must be accurate.' Arik: 'Okay, okay.' "[71]

Dayan's criticism of Sharon's mendacity was withering. "[M]y complaint against the paratroop command was not so much over the battle itself as over their subterfuge in terming the operation a 'patrol' in order to satisfy the General Staff. This made me sad, and I regretted that I had not succeeded in molding such relations of mutual trust that if they had wished to defy my orders, they would have done so directly and openly."[72]

Shimon Peres watched these swirling emotions from his own position of close proximity to the prime minister and to the military leadership, and with an abiding affection for Sharon. Half a century later, he looked back on those events and on Sharon's subsequent, turbulent career and offered a trenchant observation of his own. "For Arik, the report on the battle was part of the battle. You've got to fight not just the enemy; you've got to fight your superiors, too. They're men of little faith."[73]

Shmuel Scheinerman's death from cancer on December 31, 1956, added to the gloom that seemed to envelop Sharon at this time. "I felt I had not known him. In my childhood everyone had been too busy. Then came the War of Independence, then Unit 101 and the paratroopers. Since the age of seventeen I had hardly been at home. Perhaps it is normal for children not to fully appreciate their parents until later in life. For me, unfortunately, the first intimations of that truth came with the blow of my father's passing." Just recently, moreover, he and Gali had bought a home—from General Laskov, as it happened—in the Tel Aviv suburb of Zahala, brushing aside the sick Shmuel's imprecations that they build a house and settle on his land at Kfar Malal. In the hospital, close to the end, Sharon recalled, "[Shmuel] said softly, 'It's a pity I'm going to die. You still need my help in so many ways.' "

Arik had been able, at least, to gladden the dying man's heart with the news that he had a grandson. On December 27, Gali gave birth. The couple was overwhelmed with joy: "Both of us had wanted many children. But two years earlier we had been told we would be unable to conceive. The news had put a cloud over our lives."[74] The circumcision ceremony, on the eighth day in Jewish law, was bittersweet. Shmuel was dead; the newborn was named after him: Gur Shmuel.

CHAPTER 2 · PROBATIONER

Please give our very best wishes and greetings to the Old Man. I hope that in case of need *you won't forget me here.* I'm particularly asking you this because, regretfully, the relations that have developed between the new 'court' and myself might cause some people over there to forget me." Sharon's letter from London, dated July 28, 1958, was addressed to "Dear Yitzhak"—Ben-Gurion's secretary, Yitzhak Navon. "Of course you're too busy with much bigger and more important matters," the plaintive cri de coeur continued, "for me to trouble you with these little things . . . But please—don't forget I'm here, waiting for a summons in case of need. Warm wishes from Margalit, Arik."[1]

He was at the Royal Military Academy in Camberley, Surrey, for a yearlong course for middle-ranking officers from Britain itself and from around the world. Gali lived in a rented flat in London with their newborn son, Gur, and Arik would come home for "weekends of music and theater in London . . . On the whole, I was happy about it, but I was concerned too. I had left my command, the source of my strength."[2]

Sharon's sojourn in the U.K. was an elegant form of exile, contrived by Chief of Staff Dayan. Sharon had not exactly left his command, but in effect had been fired, at the insistence of the CO of Central Command, Zvi Tzur. The disaffection among the paratroop brigade officers, which reached a crescendo at that day of open recriminations in March 1957, never really let up. Ben-Gurion was aware of it. He wrote to Dayan urging him to "try to overcome these manifestations of small-mindedness that plague our little country."

Dayan's evident failure to overcome the small-mindedness that Ben-Gurion discerned around Sharon, and his recommendation that Sharon spend a year in the U.K. rather than defending the borders, signaled two uncomfortable truths for the acerbic, arrogant, but gifted twenty-nine-year-old who had known nothing but combat since his teens. The first was that Israel's policy makers looked forward now to a period of peace after the IDF's success in the Sinai War. The second, even more difficult for Sharon to appreciate, was that life in a peacetime army is not nearly so fast moving and studded with opportunity as it is in an army engaged in constant conflict. Different qualities are required of peacetime officers: less panache and improvisation; more diligence and patient application to training and discipline.

Camberley drove home the same disquieting lesson. The military life, he discovered from his British comrades, is a long and dogged haul, punctuated by the surges of action and rapid promotions that wars provide. Looking around him, Sharon saw "people who years ago had been brigadier generals in France or Italy or the Western Desert [and] were now climbing slowly up the peacetime ladder. And by and large they accepted it with a casual nonchalance."[3] Casual nonchalance was not his strong suit.

"Dear Shimon," he wrote in September 1958 to the director general of the Defense Ministry, Shimon Peres. "Following our conversation several weeks ago about the structure of the IDF, I am sending you my thoughts on the subject." He believed that Ben-Gurion was grooming him as a future chief of staff, and he seems to have presumed that Peres, the Old Man's close aide, was privy to this intent. In fact, though, Peres insisted half a century later, "Ben-Gurion would never have appointed Arik. There is no question at all in my mind. Despite his abiding love and admiration for him. No question at all."[4]

Sharon wrote that he and Gali were taking back with them a little car that his uncle had bought them as a gift. "We're doing this so that Gali can work at the hospital [in Jerusalem] without wasting hours each day traveling up and down [by public transport]," he explained to Peres, apparently feeling the need to justify this conspicuous consumption in the still-austere Israeli environment.

His anticipated frustration on his return home proved well-founded. There was no field command for Sharon. The best the army could come up with was a desk job in Tel Aviv, in the training branch, as head of infantry training. If he took it, he was told, he would get full colonel, the rank he ought to have got, by his own reckoning, years earlier when the paratroopers became a brigade. In November, Ben-Gurion called him in. "Have you weaned yourself of your off-putting proclivity for not telling the truth?" Sharon meekly assured the Old Man that he had. "He admitted that he had not told the truth on occasion in the past," Ben-Gurion wrote in his diary, "but he said he doesn't anymore."

Sharon, at any rate, came away from the meeting with the sense that the Old Man was watching over him and would not let his detractors crush his career.[5] But for the present he must keep his head down. He agreed to take the proffered staff posting.

A few months later, he lost it. The head of training, General Yosef Geva, fired him for failing to turn up at a meeting and then lying about why he hadn't come. Ben-Gurion stepped in to make sure he wasn't ousted from the army altogether. "He is brave, original, and resourceful," Ben-Gurion remonstrated with Geva. "Yes, but he's not disciplined, and he doesn't tell the truth," was Geva's reply.[6] The general agreed to give him another chance, as commander of the army's infantry school. Here Sharon was to spend the next three years in what he himself called "exile in the wilderness."

He took the job seriously, at least at first, planning and implementing strenuous but imaginative training programs for the young officers and NCOs undergoing courses at the school. They all knew his history and regarded him with distant awe. His colleagues in the training department of the General Staff found him creative and stimulating in their discussions on military theory and in their work on training manuals. The staff of the infantry school, on the other hand, suffered from Sharon's moodiness and short temper. He seemed to take out all his frustration on them. Meetings too often ended with him bawling someone out for no reasonable cause. Time after time, an instructor or administrator would be seen hauling his kit bag to the camp gate, fired by Sharon for a trivial infringement or for nothing at all save getting on the commander's nerves.

After a time, he began getting on his own nerves. He registered at the Tel Aviv branch of the Hebrew University Law School. He would have preferred to study agriculture, he wrote later, as his father had wanted. But that would have required full-time attendance.*

The end of the dour Haim Laskov's term as chief of staff brought no relief: the new chief was Zvi Tzur, and he stolidly withstood all of Ben-Gurion's urgings to bring Sharon back in from the cold. "I even went to see Dayan," Sharon writes. "[He] . . . was serving as minister of agriculture . . . 'Arik,' he said, 'there is no way for you to get out of it. You will have to wait for a crisis to come along. It's only then that they will let you out.' "

Sharon enrolled in the army's tank school, diligently learning his way through all the courses: driver, gunner, loader, radioman, and

---

* He received his law degree in 1966.

tank commander. He studied the mechanics of the tank and the tactics for deploying platoons, then battalions, and finally whole brigades of tanks. As a rookie tank officer, Sharon displayed tactical boldness and originality that impressed the top instructor at the school, Yitzhak Ben-Ari. In every war game, Ben-Ari reported, Sharon would come up with novel suggestions that defied traditional armored corps theory. His schemes involved deep thrusts through the enemy defenses in order to precipitate a collapse. But other officers faulted Sharon's ideas as too risky and too costly in lives.

In early 1962, he was thrown a crumb of comfort: Chief of Staff Tzur grudgingly assigned a reserve mechanized brigade to Sharon's command. At least if there was a war he would have a substantial role in the fighting. He declined. "I was holding out for an armored brigade. Tanks were emerging as a crucial element in [Israel's] strategic thinking." Eventually, he got one. But his ambitions still soared much higher than that. He asked for the job of IDF chief of operations. This drew from Tzur another predictable refusal.

"On May 2 all these problems turned suddenly meaningless," Sharon writes in *Warrior.*[7] Gali was killed in her little Austin car on the winding road to Jerusalem, near the village of Abu Ghosh. She swerved out of her lane and was hit by an oncoming truck. Arik was brought the news by his next-door neighbor, Motti Hod, a senior air force officer. He wept inconsolably, Hod recalled. At the funeral the next day, though, he kept a stiff military bearing. In a deadpan voice, he read out the eulogy he had written, recalling their teenage love and their years together.

The British car was a right-hand drive, and there was speculation that perhaps that was a factor in the accident. But among Gali's colleagues and friends there was an acrid undercurrent of suspicion that the cause of her death was to be sought in her growing anguish over Arik's relationship with her younger sister, Lily. There had been rumors of a romance between them.

Lily, four years younger than Gali, was strikingly good-looking with long black hair. When she enlisted, Arik pulled strings for her to serve in the paratroop brigade. She was around the Sharon home a good deal, often looking after Gur when Gali was out working. Now she moved in full-time to take care of the orphaned child, who was deeply attached to her. Arik, too, made a point of spending time with his son and came home from his base almost every night. A year after Gali's death, Arik and Lily were married.

"I didn't go to the wedding," a close family friend recalled.

There was a sort of dark cloud hanging over it. I liked Margalit a lot. She was a very serious person. Very professional and accomplished in her work. An impressive young woman. But there was always something sad about her . . . [My husband] went. He said he didn't want to judge anyone, especially not a good friend. Many in our group of friends stayed away. But as I came to know Lily better, I changed my attitude toward her, especially when I saw how she brought up Gur . . . Over the years we grew close. She never mentioned Margalit, though. Not to me at any rate. I never heard her talk about her.[8]

In a newspaper interview years later, Lily said she had married Arik "because it was good for Gur. Today, looking back, I can say that in fact I loved him very much then already. But it wasn't love that decided it. The situation was that we were two people with a shared, sacred goal—to look after a little boy who had lost his mother."[9] The police examiners who investigated the accident, meanwhile, found significant contributory negligence in Margalit's driving. A suit filed by Arik and Gur against the truck driver's insurance company was settled out of court. The driver did not admit to any guilt on his part.[10]

In August 1964, Gur, now eight, welcomed a little brother into his life. Arik and Lily's firstborn, Omri, joined the family, living now in a rented home in the northern village of Nahalal. Gur also got a pony of his own, a gift from his father to help him take to life in the country. They often rode out together through the flat expanses of the Valley of Jezreel and the hills of lower Galilee. It was a happy time all around. Arik was back on the fast track. He was deputy commanding officer at Northern Command, serving on the front line directly under a man he respected and liked, General Avraham Yoffe.

Ben-Gurion handed over both the prime ministership and the Ministry of Defense to Levi Eshkol, and with them a strong recommendation to name Yitzhak Rabin chief of staff after Tzur. Eshkol seemed willing to comply, and Ben-Gurion called in Rabin to tell him. In that same conversation, Rabin wrote later, "he opened his heart to me and said, 'You know I have a special regard for Arik Sharon. I see him as one of our best military men and one of the finest fighters the State of Israel has had. If he would only tell the truth, that would help him get ahead. I'm asking you, please don't treat him the way he's been treated until now.' "

Rabin writes of his "personal commitment to Ben-Gurion . . . [But] I decided to advance Arik not just to fulfill Ben-Gurion's wish. In my own previous position on the General Staff, I had been extraordinarily impressed by Arik's work as a reserves brigade commander: his organization of the brigade, his training schedule, his guidance and leadership of the officers. He created a formidable fighting force. This showed me what he was capable of."

Rabin took over on January 1, 1964.

In my first week as chief of staff, I called him in and said, "Everyone knows you're a superb military man. Your trouble is, though, that people tend to believe you're not a decent human being. I don't know you well enough to say. I want to promote you, but I've got to be sure that your accusers aren't right. I am going to appoint you for one year as deputy commanding officer at Northern Command. If at the end of the year your direct superior, the CO of Northern Command, says that you behaved like a decent human being, then I'll promote you to general."[11]

Sharon's seven lean years were over.

Yoffe was one general who didn't want to oust Sharon or block his advancement. He accepted the new chief of staff's challenge, welcoming Sharon to the north but cautioning him—and reassuring his apprehensive staff—that his advent must not entail a purge. He must prove himself by proving he could run Northern Command, and run it well, with the help of all the officers currently serving there.

No sooner had Rabin (and Sharon) assumed their new roles than a sharp downturn occurred in relations between Israel and the Arab world, and most especially between Israel and Syria. An Arab League summit convened in Cairo in January 1964 and resolved to thwart Israel's National Water Carrier, a major new project that had been under construction for several years and was now nearing completion. The carrier was designed to siphon off Jordan River waters entering the Sea of Galilee from the north and transport them, by canal and by underground pipe, to the center and arid south of the country, where annual rainfall was much sparser.

The Zionist dream of "making the desert bloom"—meaning particularly the parched Negev desert, which constituted the bulk of Israel's territory—depended in large part on the success of this enterprise. The Arab states adopted a "headwater diversion plan" designed to divert much of the Jordan waters before they reached the Sea of Galilee. For Israel this was unacceptable. Eshkol, the new prime minister and minister of defense, made it clear that Israel would act to thwart the Arab plan.

The same Arab summit of 1964 also saluted the birth of the Palestine Liberation Organization (PLO), injecting new vigor into the Palestinian cause. The summit created the PLA, or Palestine Liberation Army, and resolved that all the armies of all the frontline states would operate under a single unified command. Palestinian guerrilla groups, among them Fatah, led by Yasser Arafat, began mounting attacks on civilian targets inside Israel. Syria gave active encouragement to such attacks. Jordan and Lebanon provided passive support.[12]

In November, Syrian tractors and bulldozers went to work on their planned canal. The IDF responded with artillery fire directed at the earthworks. Syrian artillery, high on the Golan escarpment, retaliated by firing down onto the Israeli settlements below. The escalation continued with Syrian attacks on Israeli fishermen out in the Sea of Galilee and Israeli reprisals along the border. Israeli tanks were frequently in action, too, and on several occasions the air force took part, providing firepower that countered Syria's topographical advantage.

Compounding the overall tension was incessant skirmishing over three "demilitarized zones" along the Israel-Syria border. Israel insisted on its right under the 1949 Armistice Agreement to cultivate these areas and retaliated forcefully against Syrian firing on the Israeli farmers.

Rabin writes that many, including Dayan, believed there was no way to stop the Syrian diversion work short of all-out war. He himself, however, believed with Eshkol that a firm but restrained strategy could be effective, both in stopping the Syrian project and in containing the Palestinian incursions. In the event, the Syrians halted their project in the summer of 1965. The sporadic clashes continued, however. They climaxed in April 1967 when Israeli pilots shot down six Syrian MiGs in a dogfight over the Golan Heights.

Sharon reveled in being back in the thick of things. He seemed to be present at every border skirmish and often took part in the shooting himself. When there was no skirmishing, he would tour the front incessantly and kept the units busy with training and snap inspections. Ehud Barak, a future prime minister and political rival, at the time an officer in the supersecret Sayeret Matkal commando unit, remembered years later "what a pleasure it was to be debriefed by Sharon after a mission across the border, or to be inspected by him before a mission. It was all at his fingertips: how to learn a route, how to prepare weapons and equipment, what would really be needed over there. He knew it all."[13]

Once again, as with the reprisal operations in the 1950s, Sharon was an instrument of the policy, which was determined not by him but by others much his senior in rank and authority. Once again, he was a convenient, prominent, self-aggrandizing target for critics who opposed the policy as excessively aggressive.

Sharon completed his year's probation and received a favorable report from Yoffe. "He passed the test without a shadow of a doubt," Rabin wrote in his memoirs.[14] But Yoffe retired at the end of 1964, and when David Elazar took over at Northern Command, Sharon found himself embroiled again in internal rivalries and backstabbing. He asked for time off and flew to East Africa with Yoffe for a long trekking and safari holiday. When he returned, another deputy had been appointed alongside him. "From then until the fall of 1965 I stepped as lightly as I could through a minefield of bickering and intrigue."[15]

Not lightly enough, though. When he finally left Northern Command in October, he was kept cooling his heels at home for three months between jobs.

> At last Rabin invited me in for a talk—a very blunt talk, as it turned out, with no pulled punches. He let me know precisely how he felt about my performance—the things I had done wrong, my relationship with . . . Elazar, everything . . .
>
> So it was something of a surprise to hear him finish up the litany of my failings by saying that despite the criticisms I was now promoted to major general* and appointed as director of military training [and] commander of a reserve division.
>
> I was as happy as I was surprised. Lily prepared a small party . . . Not too long afterward we moved back to the house in Zahala so that I could be closer to my new headquarters. There, six months later, our third son, Gilad Yehuda, was born. Our dream of having a large family seemed on its way to being fulfilled.

"Never, in all its wars," writes Yitzhak Rabin, asking his readers' indulgence for this rare immodesty, "was the IDF readied for war more perfectly than it was before the Six-Day War." As head of training from early 1966, Sharon was certainly entitled to take a share in the credit for that amazing military victory, over and above his direct role in it as the commander of an armored division in Sinai. His basic training manual was the "spirit of the paratroopers." He

---

* "Dear and Exalted Arik," Ben-Gurion wrote to him, "I was glad to hear that you've become a general. To me, you were a general years ago. But what has changed is that certain failings which you had then, I believe, you don't have anymore . . . My trust has not been disappointed" (IDF Archives).

instituted a commando course for all officers in field units as a way of inculcating the paratroop techniques and traditions throughout the fighting army.

He also worked diligently to keep abreast of everything that was known in Western armies of Russian weaponry and battlefield tactics. The Russians were steadily deepening their involvement in the equipping and training of the Egyptian and Syrian armies. Israel for its part was beginning to see some initial, limited success from its own persistent efforts to break down the arms embargo that America had imposed on the Jewish state since its inception. The first U.S. tanks—not, yet, the latest models—began to arrive, bolstering the IDF's British (also not the top of the line) and French armory.

Sharon's ability as a military commander and a leader of men came into its own during the critical period from the middle of May until June 5, 1967, when the army found itself suddenly plunged into an eve-of-war deployment, as the politicians scrambled desperately to avoid war. "Arik issued new instructions," a military correspondent wrote, describing life in Sharon's division, dug in on the Negev-Sinai border. "The spontaneous, rather casual appearance of the troops was to disappear, to be replaced by established military routine . . . [S]mall tents were erected in which barbers cut soldiers' hair. Shaving was compulsory and walking around without weapon or helmet resulted in punishment. Prisons were built and MP platoons arrived from Beersheba. Training was to resume in all units . . . An army of reservists was to be transformed into a body of regulars, united, trained, patient."

The correspondent was Lieutenant (res.) Yael Dayan, daughter of the former chief of staff. Moshe was now, since Ben-Gurion's break with his own Mapai Party, an opposition backbench member of the Knesset in the Old Man's new, disappointingly small Rafi Party. Yael, a successful author, was mobilized as one of the army spokesman's pool of correspondents whose dispatches were distributed to local and foreign media. "I had suggested I join Arik's headquarters . . . I am suspicious of all men who have become legends in their own lives, including my father. I [wanted] to verify or disprove the qualities attributed to him."[16]

Those qualities were all on show in abundance—both the legendary ones and Sharon's subversive proclivity for running down his superiors, military and civilian, in the hearing of his subordinates. This incessant, deliberate display of behind-the-back insubordination, a carryover from the wild days of Unit 101, was intended apparently to bond his officers together and to enhance his prestige in their eyes.

Now, however, Sharon's raucous whining was in tune with the general mood, both in the army and in the eerily quiet city streets. There was a mounting impatience, and beneath it a serious ebbing of confidence that threatened to weaken the nation under arms. "Guys, there's just no one up there to rely on," Sharon harangued his staff officers each time he returned from meetings in Tel Aviv. "This government is just no government at all."[17]

The crisis with Egypt was instigated by the Kremlin. On May 13, the Speaker of the Egyptian parliament, Anwar Sadat, visiting Moscow, was informed by his Soviet hosts—falsely—that Israel was massing troops in the north for an attack on Syria. The same message was delivered to President Nasser by the Soviet ambassador in Cairo. Nasser ordered two divisions into Sinai. The troops marched through Cairo shouting, "We're off to Tel-Aviv."[18]

Israel strenuously denied any buildup in the north. Eshkol invited the Soviet ambassador to go up there and look for himself. Neither Syria nor Egypt had any evidence of it. Nevertheless, Nasser's initial move engendered a momentum of its own. On May 16 he ordered more troops into Sinai and demanded that the UN Emergency Force (UNEF), deployed in the peninsula since the 1956 Sinai War, now withdraw from the border with Israel.

On May 23, Nasser announced the closure of the Straits of Tiran to Israeli shipping. This had been the casus belli for Israel in 1956, as he well knew. The Egyptian buildup was now approaching 100,000 men—seven full divisions and additional units. Egypt's army fielded nearly 1,000 tanks and 900 artillery pieces. Its air force numbered more than 400 warplanes. Syria had some 60,000 men in its armed forces with 200 tanks and more than 100 planes, including dozens of ultramodern MiG-21s. Jordan, too, could deploy close to 60,000 men, 200 tanks, and 24 British-made planes. On May 30, President Nasser and King Hussein signed a joint defense pact putting Jordan's Arab Legion under Egyptian command in case of war with Israel. Iraq sent a division into Jordan to join the Arab effort, and several other states sent smaller forces.

The IDF mustered some 1,300 tanks, 750 guns, and 250 warplanes, the best of them French-supplied Mirage fighters. Most of the land army was concentrated on the Sinai border, deployed in three beefed-up divisions commanded respectively by Yisrael Tal, by Sharon's friend and former commander Avraham Yoffe, and by Sharon himself. The basic strategy they hoped to apply called for attack, for taking the war to the enemy on his territory rather than within Israel's slender confines. The Egyptians, they assumed, were poised to slice into the southern Negev, cutting through to Jordan and severing Eilat from the rest of the country.

On May 24, Rabin took sick, purportedly from nicotine poisoning brought on by too much smoking but more likely from frayed nerves in the face of the unremitting tension. His collapse was kept from the public, and in forty-eight hours he recovered. But a halting and hesitant radio broadcast from Eshkol on May 28 heightened public apprehension instead of dispelling it. This was unfortunate and unnecessary, the product of sloppy staff work—the prime minister's typed text was full of semi-legible handwritten corrections—rather than reflecting any weakness on Eshkol's part. Indeed, as the industrious and serious-minded minister of defense during the past four years, he, no less than Rabin, deserved a major share of the credit for preparing the army to fight. But Eshkol was determined to exhaust every diplomatic option before giving the army the green light for war.

With each passing day the nation's fighting spirit seemed to sag. Among the generals of the High Command there was much grumbling, muted for the most part by the proper constitutional constraints and kept firmly out of the press. On May 28, though, after a particularly caustic meeting between senior ministers and the General Staff, Sharon said something to Rabin about the hypothetical possibility of a military coup in Israel. "Not in the sense of seizing power out of a desire to rule," Sharon himself explained years later to a high-ranking ex-military researcher. "But in the sense of taking a decision, a fundamental decision. The army could take such a decision, I suggested, without the cabinet. And it would be well received [by the public]."[19]

On the streets of Tel Aviv, meanwhile, a clamor arose to bring back Ben-Gurion. But to no avail. The venom that had poisoned relations in recent years between Eshkol and his erstwhile comrade and mentor made that impossible.[20]

The public pressure now shifted to appointing Dayan defense minister. To this, Eshkol reluctantly agreed. On June 2, the morning Dayan's appointment was announced, the ministers and the generals met again. Rabin warned of "a serious threat to Israel's very existence . . . The longer we wait passively, the stronger the Arabs' confidence grows that Israel is not capable of confronting this challenge." He urged "a decisive aerial strike" that would destroy the Egyptian air force "in a single day."

Sharon, the most junior of the generals, was the most outspoken. "Our goal is no less than to destroy the Egyptian forces . . . But because of hesitation and foot-dragging we have lost the key element of surprise." He praised the morale of the people, appearing to contrast it with the faintheartedness of the government. General Matti Peled, head of the logistics branch, also spoke sharply, warning of the effects on the national economy of the prolonged mobilization. "Why do you let this disgrace go on?" he hurled at the ministers.

Dayan broadly agreed. He said the IDF could achieve its war aims in six days. In the discussion that followed, Eshkol upbraided Sharon and Peled. He accused them of "rearing up against the government." He explained once again why it was important to give international diplomacy every opportunity to play out. The meeting broke up, still without a decision.

Once again, Sharon—as he himself testified—stayed behind chatting furtively with Rabin. "I said that if we had got up at a certain point and said, 'Listen, you lot, your decisions are endangering the State of Israel. And since the situation is extremely serious, you are hereby requested to go into the adjoining room and stay there while the chief of staff goes to the national radio station and broadcasts an announcement. In my judgment, if we did that they would have accepted it with a sense of relief and liberation."

Sharon first recounted these dramatic moments to the *Haaretz* military commentator Ze'ev Schiff, soon after the war. Sharon shared with the reporter his hypothetical fantasy of locking the ministers in a room while the chief of staff went on the air. But he did not mention that he had shared the idea with Rabin, as he claimed in his testimony to the military historian more than thirty years later. Schiff suggested that the later embellishment may well have been apocryphal.[21]

A decision to go to war on June 5, barring unforeseen developments, was made secretly by Eshkol and a small group of top ministers soon after the larger meeting with the generals on June 2. It was approved by the full cabinet on June 4.

Sharon admits that "with Dayan present, it was like a fresh wind." He had been railing for days against the High Command's original plan for a phased attack in Sinai, "one division first, then the other two twelve hours later. I argued vehemently against that . . . It would be a waste not to attack simultaneously everywhere, to devastate the entire Egyptian army at once."[22] This was Dayan's thinking, too. Sharon, moreover, had shared with Dayan, then still a backbencher, his complex scheme for a divisional assault on the formidable Egyptian defenses at Abu Agheila—Umm Katef, the "gateway to Sinai." This was his own division's main assignment in the war. In 1956, it had taken the IDF, commanded by Dayan, three full days of stubborn fighting before Abu Agheila fell. This time, Sharon proposed to over-run it in one night.

With great prescience—but without, as it turned out, the determi-nation to impose his orders—Dayan ordered the army not to occupy the Gaza Strip and not to advance right up to the Suez Canal.[23] In the event, both of these Pyrrhic successes occurred in the hectic, historic week ahead.

MODEL MAJOR GENERAL

Even Sharon's more consistent and implacable critics make an excep-tion for his performance in the Six-Day War.[24] It was classic: a battle-field commander in his métier, unsullied by outbursts of argument or disobedience. The conquest of Abu Agheila was accomplished in near perfection on the night of June 5–6, 1967. Once Sharon's division had taken this strategic junction, Yoffe's troops poured through it to the west, while Sharon's own armor continued south to overrun another key Egyptian fortified complex at Nakhl.

At dawn on the fifth, Sharon drove in his staff car for a final meet-ing with his three armored brigade commanders. They talked through the next day's plans one last time, shook hands, and embraced. Sharon took a small rucksack and blankets from the Studebaker sedan and stowed them in his jeep, amid the communication sets already hissing and chattering. Each of the brigades, and the headquarters team of jeeps and half-tracks, now trundled toward its assigned jumping-off point on the border.

Soon, the signal came through. Sharon took his microphone and, listing each of his brigades in a steady voice, he gave the order: "Nua, nua [move]." He watched through his binoculars as the columns of tanks lurched forward, churning the dust. Very soon they were shoot-ing, engaging small Egyptian units deployed in forward defensive out-posts close to the border.

By midday, when Sharon drove through the first Egyptian outposts overrun by his tanks, he knew that the war was essentially won. The air force had delivered what Rabin and the air force commander Motti Hod had promised the anxious ministers: the near-total destruction of the Egyptian air force. The first wave of Israeli jets came in from the sea and attacked Egyptian planes on the ground at 7:45. Many of the Egyptian pilots had been out on early morning patrols and were back at base, having breakfast. Israel hurled virtually its entire complement of frontline jets* into this operation, and it proved decisive. Time after time throughout the morning, the Israeli planes returned to hit planes, hangars, radar installations, and runways all over Sinai and Lower Egypt. By 11:00, Hod was able to report that at least 180 Egyptian planes had been destroyed and that all the air bases had been rendered inoperative at least for the next few hours. The air force next turned its attention to Syria and to Jordan, too, after King Hussein rejected Eshkol's appeals through the UN and the United States to hold his fire and stay out of the war. "Within two hours," Rabin records, "the Jordanian and Syrian air forces had been destroyed, as had the Iraqi air base, H3, near the Iraq-Jordan border. Four hundred planes of various types were destroyed by the IAF [Israeli Air Force] on the first day of the war. These incredible results of the air force operation determined to a large extent the fate of the whole war."[25]

As Sharon and his headquarters team advanced toward Abu Agheila in the afternoon, they saw IAF French-made Fouga Magister training jets swooping down on Egyptian forces giving battle to one of Sharon's brigades farther to the north. The Fougas had been fitted with machine guns and underwing rocket pods. They were the best the air force could spare for ground support on that first day of the war. Later, with the Sinai skies almost totally clear of enemy planes, the full power of the IAF's Mirages and Mystères would be brought to bear on the Egyptian divisions.

The northern brigade, equipped with British-made Centurion tanks, had run into trouble earlier in the morning from Egyptian artillery and antitank fire. A battalion commander and two other officers were killed and several tanks disabled. The brigadier, Natke Nir, pulled back, regrouped, and attacked again in the afternoon, this time succeeding in overrunning the defensive position north of Abu Agheila itself. Still, the firefight showed how strongly dug in the Egyptians were around and inside the Abu Agheila–Umm Katef complex. Their artillery in particular, some eighty 130- and 122-millimeter Russian guns, would take a heavy toll on the Israeli attackers unless they could be silenced.

This task was assigned to a brigade of paratroopers under Danny Matt, ferried into position by relays of helicopters after nightfall. Their job was to storm the Egyptian guns from the rear, where they were least expected. The Centurions were to attack from the north, engaging the hundred-odd tanks deployed within the complex. Nir's

---

* Twelve planes were left behind, Rabin writes. Their job was to defend the whole country for the first few hours of the war.

brigade was also to cut off the desert road from the northwest and the southwest, thus blocking reinforcements that might be sent in from deeper in Sinai.

At the same time—timing was the critical factor in Sharon's intricate planning—an infantry brigade under Kuti Adam would storm the three rows of Egyptian trenches and concrete bunkers facing east, which were the main bulwark of the fortified position. The triple trenches were a textbook Soviet-style defensive deployment with the added advantage of difficult terrain at both ends: "high soft dunes in the north," Sharon writes, "and in the south jagged ridges and broken foothills." The infantry would go in from the north. Sharon knew the terrain from surveys he himself conducted after the Sinai War. He knew they could get through. Next, another brigade of tanks under Mordechai Zippori would charge forward parallel with the road, clearing a path through the minefields to confront the trenches in a narrow frontal assault.

As evening fell, the infantry arrived, carried to battle aboard a motley fleet of civilian buses that had been mobilized for war along with the reservists. They drove as far as they could on the old, rutted road, then let off their passengers. "Bus after bus was lined up as far back as I could see," Sharon writes. "I went down to the road to watch the procession up close. Zippori's Super Shermans moved up to take positions for their frontal assault. Then Kuti's infantry, two endless lines along the side of the road, marching into the gritty wind from the dunes. Soon they would leave the road in a wide hook from the north . . . They saw me in the middle of the road, and it was impossible to miss their expressions of confidence and determination."

The division's third tank brigade, equipped with light French-made AMXs, was deployed farther to the south, blocking the road from the Egyptian divisional headquarters at Kseima, twenty miles to the southeast. There were also units engaged in an elaborate feint that Sharon mounted during the day in the direction of Kseima, in the hope of confusing the enemy as to his intentions. "Abu Agheila was the more formidable position," he explains in *Warrior.* "The Ismailia road led right through the Abu Agheila defenses. Were I to take Kseima first, I would still have to deal with Abu Agheila. But if Abu Agheila fell, we would be in control of the roads behind Kseima, and the Egyptians would find the position untenable."

Before his infantry and armor moved on their target with almost choreographed precision, Sharon unleashed a massive softening-up bombardment from the six artillery battalions attached to his division. "Let everything tremble," Sharon ordered the chief artillery officer, Yaacov Vaknin, just after 10:30 p.m. "Tremble it shall," came the reply, shouted from the artillery command half-track standing along-side Sharon's own half-track. For the next twenty minutes, shells and mortar bombs rained down on the Egyptian complex until Kuti Adam called a halt to it and his men began to advance on the center trench.

The paratroopers reached their target close to midnight. "Three batteries of field-guns were silenced in a matter of minutes," Yael Dayan recorded. The paras next ambushed a convoy of reinforcement trucks and destroyed them. One, however, was loaded with artillery ammunition, and in the explosion three Israelis were killed and many more wounded.

The two tank brigades also surged forward, from their opposite vectors, at around midnight and began engaging the Egyptian armor in earnest. The whole night and into the morning, Sharon orchestrated the battle by radio.

While the battle still raged, he received an order from the CO of Southern Command, Shaike Gavish, to enable a brigade of Yoffe's armor to pass through the complex on their dash west. "There below us on the main road," Yael Dayan wrote, "as far as I could see, were a thousand headlights advancing rapidly towards us. Arik was stand-ing erect in his command half-track, raising his hand to the horizon as if blessing the sight." Sharon ordered his own tanks to stop firing, "and we were treated," he writes, "to the remarkable sight of a brigade of tanks moving unscathed right through the two forces locked in combat."

By mid-morning the fighting had died away. The whole complex was in Sharon's hands. The price: 40 Israeli dead and 140 wounded. A high price, but the reward was high, too. "Our mission had been to open the main axis to our forces in Sinai, and we had now done that," Sharon writes. He goes on to fault the High Command for procrasti-nating the whole day before deciding on his division's next assignment.

On Wednesday morning, June 7, at any rate, the orders came through: Sharon was to head south for Nakhl, which he had taken in his charge across Sinai at the head of the paratroop brigade eleven years before. The assignment was to cut off an Egyptian division that had been deployed at Kuntilla on the Negev border and was now head-ing back west. "If the Egyptians succeeded in getting to the Mitle Pass before we hit them," Sharon explains, "they could close off our advance to the canal." Outside Nakhl, which was defended by a full brigade, the lead vehicles hit a minefield, and Sharon decided to defer the attack to Thursday morning.

They celebrated that night with the rest of the nation over the news that the Western Wall had been taken, along with the whole Old City of Jerusalem, held since 1948 by Jordan.* Mordechai Gur, Sharon's subordinate who had turned against him after the Mitle in 1956, led the paratroopers who liberated this holiest site in Judaism after a bloody battle outside the city ramparts.

When the tanks surged into Nakhl at dawn, they found the fortified complex deserted. "Everything was in place," Sharon writes. "Tents were up, self-propelled guns were ready to move, artillery and mortars dug in and ready to fire. Everything was there except the people. We called it the 'ghost brigade.' "

The division from Kuntilla, however, was fast approaching, chased by an IDF armored brigade that had been deployed defensively in the Negev at the start of the war but now crossed into Sinai to join the battle. "With a brigade of tanks, a reinforced battalion of half-tracks, and the divisional reconnaissance unit, I set an ambush for the fleeing Egyptians," Sharon recorded. "The Egyptian Sixth Division entered a terrible killing field . . . For miles the desert was covered by ruined tanks and burned-out armored personnel carriers. Bodies littered the ground, and here and there across the scene groups of Egyptians were standing with their hands behind their heads . . . By [evening] the Sixth Division had ceased to exist."[26] This time, the Centurions and Shermans were supported by frontline jets that swooped down, pouring napalm and cannon fire onto the Egyptian column.

The desert was teeming with Egyptian soldiers desperate to get back, many of them without water in the blazing summer heat. The orders were to enable—later it became actively to assist and facilitate—the return across the canal of enlisted men, while officers were to be taken prisoner. These—almost five thousand of them—were eventually exchanged for a handful of Israeli POWs and various spies and agents imprisoned in Egypt.

General Tal's division had had similarly stunning success along the northern axis. Starting from south of Gaza City on the first day, it swept west along the coast to take el-Arish. On the second day, as its forward units raced ahead toward central Sinai and the canal, other units swung back to conquer Gaza City and the rest of the Gaza Strip. Some writers attribute Dayan's turnabout on Gaza to pressure from kibbutzim along the Gaza border that came under fire from inside

---

* The Wall was to have been accessible to Israelis under a provision of the 1949 Armistice Agreement, but Jordan refused to honor it.

the Strip. It is hard, though, to see how Gaza could have remained an unoccupied enclave once Israel was in occupation of the whole of Sinai (and of the entire West Bank). On the third and fourth days, Tal, too, fought major tank battles, on the Bir Gafgafa–Ismailia road. His units finally reached the canal at Ismailia and points north—again, contrary to Dayan's original wishes.

The last two days of the Six-Day War were fought mainly between Israel and Syria, on the Golan Heights. Here, yet again, Dayan found his original intentions overturned by the pressure of events. The breathtaking speed and relative ease with which the IDF had smashed through the Egyptian divisions gave added weight to the demands of the kibbutzim beneath the Syrian escarpment to put an end to their sporadic shelling from the Syrian positions above. During the first four days of war the bombardment was incessant. Eshkol wavered, but Dayan was set against extending the war to Syria for fear of direct Soviet intervention. On Thursday night, though, he changed his mind. He gave David Elazar, the CO of Northern Command, two days—Soviet pressure for a cease-fire was already mounting—to push the Syrian army back across the escarpment on the top of the Golan Heights. The air force was available now for devastating close support. Armored reinforcements from Central Command were rushed up north to help. The fighting up the steep slopes of the Golan was brutal. But by midday Saturday the IDF was swarming across the plateau and digging in on a line anchored at Kuneitra, the main town on the Golan.

On Saturday, June 10, Sharon was summoned to meet with Gavish, the CO of Southern Command, and a helicopter was sent to pick him up. It developed engine trouble. "As we began to lose altitude," he recalled, "small groups of [wandering Egyptian soldiers] began shooting at us, and we traded fire with them. Landing on the road, I wondered briefly what was going to happen to us. It was too ironic for words."

Yisrael Tal took up the story in an interview years later:

> I received an order to present myself immediately at Jebel Libni for a meeting of divisional commanders with the CO. A helicopter was sent to pick me up from Bir Gafgafa. During the flight I was glued to the window, staring out at the expanses of Sinai beneath us. I saw hundreds of Egyptian soldiers with their personal weapons fleeing west toward the canal. Among them, I saw a conspicuous figure, moving heavily along the dunes. I saw at once that it was Arik Sharon. I was rather concerned for his well-being. I told the pilot to land at once.

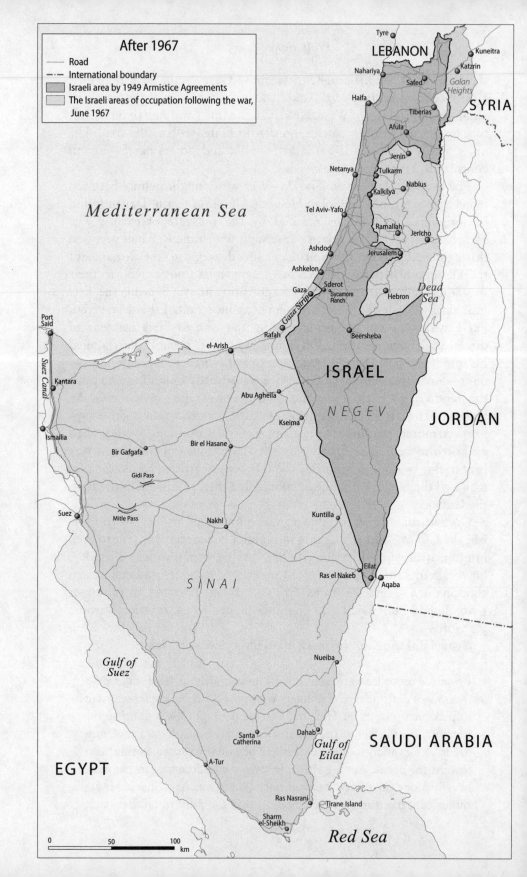

Tyre

LEBANON

Kuneitra

Nahariya

Katzrin

Safed

Golan
Heights

Haifa

SYRIA

Tiberias

Afula

Jenin

Netanya

Tulkarm

Nablus

Kalkilya

Tel Aviv-Yafo

Ramallah

Jericho

Ashdod

Jerusalem

Ashkelon

Sderot

Gaza

Sycamore
Ranch

Hebron

Dead
Sea

Mediterranean Sea

Gaza Strip

Rafah

Beersheba

Port
Said

el-Arish

ISRAEL

Suez Canal

Kantara

Abu Agheila

N E G E V

JORDAN

Kseima

Ismailia

Bir el Hasane

Bir Gafgafa

Gidi Pass

Suez

Mitle Pass

Nakhl

Kuntilla

S I N A I

Eilat

Ras el Nakeb

Aqaba

*Gulf of
Suez*

Nueiba

Santa
Catherina

Dahab

SAUDI ARABIA

*Gulf of
Eilat*

EGYPT

A-Tur

Ras Nasrani

Tirane Island

Sharm
el-Sheikh

Red Sea

0   50   100
km

I jumped out. Arik saw me and came running to the helicopter. He embraced me heartily and shouted above the din of the rotor, "Talik, we destroyed them." I shouted back, "Get into the helicopter right now, before these Egyptians kill you."[27]

At Jebel Libni there were more embraces with Gavish and Yoffe and posing for photographs. Then on to Tel Aviv to meet with Rabin. "Somehow Lily had learned that I was coming in and was waiting for me at the airport with Gur," Sharon writes. "It was a wonderful surprise despite the fact that we would not have any time together. She drove me to General Headquarters . . . Our meeting with Rabin was full of congratulations and warmth."

A week later, as the demobilization of the reserves wound down, Sharon flew home for his first real leave since the waiting period began a month before. It was, despite the mourning in some families and the suffering of the wounded, a triumphal return—for the army in general and for Sharon in particular. As he toured the Old City of Jerusalem with Lily and Gur, he was mobbed by well-wishers shouting his name, jostling to touch him and thank him. All the generals were instant heroes in those heady days, their photographs smiling out from magazine covers and victory albums. But he, somehow, seemed to attract special attention, to the chagrin of some of his colleagues. There was whispering that he and his friends had encouraged journalists, local and foreign, to cover his division to the exclusion of others. His trailer was depicted as something of a running buffet cum press conference. His name and voice seemed to appear all over, in print and on television, at home and abroad.

In the Diaspora, too, Jews basked in the glow of Israel's victory, which many saw as a salvation from the threat of another Holocaust. The Six-Day War marks the beginning of the renaissance, muted and hesitant at first, of Jewish identity among the three-million-odd Jews of the Soviet Union, where both Zionism and Judaism had been suppressed for decades. In the United States, home to more than six million Jews, the war—both the fear before and the relief and pride after—finally put to rest a certain ambivalence that many Jews there felt toward the Jewish state, as though its existence somehow threatened their Americanism.

Before the war, Sharon would later recall, he sometimes took young Gur to Mount Zion, on the borderline between the Israeli and the Jordanian sections of Jerusalem. From the buildings on the mount they could peer over into the Old City. "'Over there,' I would say, 'those places are not in our hands, but they are ours. They belong to us.'" Now he set out to show his oldest son the newly won territories. Many other Israeli families were doing the same that summer. "When they saw me, they would invariably gather around with congratulation, talk, and laughter. At these times I would look into Gur's eyes. Although he never said anything, a proud happiness lit his face . . . Watching him, I too felt an immense pride."

Sharon poured his love into the child, more especially since Gali's death. "He really was the most enchanting child," says Dalia Rabin, Yitzhak's daughter. She was Gur's group leader in the local scouts troop in Zahala. "He was the most beautiful boy in the group, and the most intelligent. I was at his funeral. I'll never forget it as long as I live."

Gur died in his father's arms, shot through the head by an antique gun he had taken down from the wall to play with together with a friend in the yard. " 'I'll be out in the front,' he told me, then turned around to leave. Just before he did, he gave me a playful salute, the gesture of a boy who had grown up around the army and who liked military things."

For the stricken, anguished father, the point was critical. Gur had been around guns all his life and knew how to handle them. Sharon never accepted the version of the other, older boy that Gur had shot himself by accident. Omri, then three and a half, and baby Gilad witnessed the accident. "He told the boy not to point," Sharon, in his account of the tragedy, recalls Omri saying. "Gur told the boy not to point it."[28]

It was the eve of Rosh Hashanah, the Jewish New Year. Lily had taken the car to go shopping. Sharon lifted the boy and ran out, screaming for help. A car stopped and sped with them to the local clinic and from there to the hospital. "I had seen so many wounds in my life; no one had to tell me that this one was hopeless . . . I sat in the back seat with Gur on my lap, my shirt soaked with his blood. Ages seemed to pass as we raced to the hospital. And as we did, he died in my arms.

"In keeping with Jewish law, the funeral would have to be held before sundown . . . They put him in a simple pine coffin, and I asked them to open it for a minute. I looked at him again, then watched as they closed the lid . . . Standing in front of the grave [alongside Gali's], I remembered five and a half years ago . . . that I had said, 'The only thing that I can promise you is that I will take care of Gur.' Now I could not shake the thought that I had not kept my promise . . . I didn't take care of him. I just didn't take care of him.

"For the first time in my life," Sharon wrote, "I felt I was facing something that I could not overcome, that I could not live through."

His friend Uri Dan remembers him saying at this time that life would
have no meaning anymore. He hired the attorney Shmuel Tamir to
demand that the police conduct a full inquiry. "I'm sure Gur didn't
shoot himself," he told the lawyer. "I don't want to sue anyone. I just
want all the facts to be investigated and the police to be convinced that
Gur didn't pull the trigger." The other boy's family claimed he had
held the gun first but that Gur had taken it and looked down the barrel, and then it fired. Tamir studied all the ballistic and other evidence,
"and in light of the facts I presented, the police investigators accepted
Arik's version."[29] Nevertheless, Sharon would sometimes hurl accusations at the other boy on the street. The boy was the son of an air
force pilot. His mother wrote to the chief of staff, Haim Bar-Lev, to
complain about this harassment, and Bar-Lev called in Sharon to try
to talk to him. Eventually, the boy and his family moved out of the
district.[30]

Sharon pulled through emotionally, thanks in large part to Lily.
"The hardest times were at night," he writes, "when sleep was impossible and the scene played and replayed itself in my head. Awake during the nights, Lily and I cried together. During the day there was
work, then at home if we did not talk about it we could hold the pain
inside. But once we would start to talk, it was impossible to put a barrier to the tears. Neither of us could find any comfort or relief from
the terrible grief."

Lily nevertheless often complained over the years to their friend—
who had been Gali's friend and now, with the two tragic deaths in the
family, grew ever closer to Lily—that Arik refused to talk about Gur,
that he kept his bereavement bottled up. In the trunk of his car he carried a rake, a hoe, and a watering can. When he passed the graveyard,
he would take them out, tend the double grave site, and shed a silent
tear.[31] He organized an annual horse race in memory of his boy, who
loved to ride; but he never spoke, even there, about Gur.[32]

Once, many years later, he let a rare shaft of light into this dark
place in his soul. It was during an interview as prime minister on Israel
TV Channel 2 in 2003. Looking at family snapshots, the interviewer,
Rafi Reshef, gingerly referred to Gur. "He looks like a lovely boy," he
ventured.

"Yes, he really was a lovely boy," the prime minister replied.

A boy with special leadership qualities. Very able. An excellent horse-
man. He took part in riding competitions. He was eleven years old
when he was killed. At first, the blow hits you a thousand times a
second. Later, it still keeps on hitting you all the time. If you ask

me—there isn't a day that I don't think about it. But if you're doing things—believe me, I don't know how a blow like this affects people who aren't busy doing things, and just live with their bereavement all the time—if you're doing things all the time, it helps you to cope . . . It's not that it doesn't hurt. You can see it hurts. But I have inside me an ability to overcome very, very difficult things.

WEST BANK, EAST BANK

Arik Sharon's efforts to colonize the captured territories, which were to preoccupy him for much of the remainder of his public life, began before the Six-Day War had even ended. "As soon as I heard that Samaria and Judea were liberated," he wrote in *Warrior,* "I had cabled instructions to the commander of the infantry school to move from the base in Netanya to a captured Jordanian army camp near Shechem. That was the first one I moved."

"Shechem," which Sharon deliberately used in his English text, is the biblical Hebrew name for the large West Bank town known in Arabic and English as Nablus. The religious and nationalistic yearnings to annex the West Bank were reinforced from the outset of this decades-long and still unresolved political struggle by the less biblical, more rational contention that the territories were crucial for Israel's defense. Given the enmity of the surrounding Arab states, it was argued, Israel was indefensible in its pre–Six-Day War borders. At one point, opposite Netanya on the Mediterranean coast, the country was less than ten miles wide.

Settlements, usually kibbutzim and moshavim, had been Zionism's way of staking out its claim to the land from its earliest days. After independence in 1948, the leadership continued to see settlements along the borders—inhabited first by soldier-farmers, then by immigrant-farmers—as the surest way to secure and solidify the 1948 armistice lines.

This settlement tradition, espoused mainly by the Labor Zionists who had dominated Jewish life and politics in Palestine both before and after independence, was now almost naturally espoused by all those who sought, for religious, nationalist, or security reasons—for many of them, it was an amalgam of all three—to perpetuate Israel's control over the West Bank (and the Gaza Strip, the Golan Heights, and strategic parts of Sinai).

Right from the start, though, such settlement ran into Arab and international opposition. The Arabs saw it, correctly, as a strategy ultimately designed to expand the borders of Israel at their expense. In November 1967 the UN Security Council passed Resolution 242 requiring Israel's "withdrawal . . . from territories occupied in the recent conflict" and at the same time acknowledging "the sovereignty, territorial integrity and political independence of every State in the area and their right to live in peace within secure and recognized boundaries." Israel argued that the resolution did not specify withdrawal from "all the territories" or even from "the territories"—just from "territories," meaning there was scope for adjustments. These needed to be negotiated between the parties, Israel maintained; that was the meaning of "secure and recognized boundaries."

Much of Israeli policy in the years and decades that followed the Six-Day War has been focused—though this was not often articulated—on how to avoid, allay, or weather international disapproval of Israeli settlement in the post-1967 territories while at the same time allowing the settlements to multiply and grow. "Allowing" covers a multitude of nuanced attitudes adopted over the years by various Israeli governments, of various ideological persuasions, to the diplomatic and legal problems posed by settlements and, in more recent years, to the domestic political power wielded by the growing settler constituency.

Sharon was brilliantly quick in grasping the dilemmas inherent in the Israeli yearning to settle the newly acquired territories—and in devising the first solution to get around them: army training camps. As the head of training, he was perfectly placed to implement his solution, which turned out to be no less than historic in affecting the course of the Israeli-Arab conflict for decades ahead. "Within a few months I was able to transfer quite a few [of the military training schools]: the infantry school, the engineering school, the military police school, part of the artillery school, the main basic training school for new recruits, the paratrooper recruit school, and others."

These military schools usually took over strategically positioned and now abandoned Arab Legion camps. But—and this was the long-term point—they naturally grew in size, and some became in time the nuclei of large civilian settlements in the populated Palestinian heartlands. At first, these civilian settlements were ostensibly mere adjuncts of the army bases, inhabited by people who provided various necessary services to the base. Gradually, though, they filled out, with families, with other settlers more loosely connected to the neighboring base, and finally with settlers not connected at all to the base, which by this time had itself become the adjunct of a swiftly expanding settlement.

If it had been up to Prime Minister Eshkol, there might well have been a deal with Jordan. King Hussein kept up discreet contacts with Israel despite the "Khartoum Noes."* But Dayan, the defense minister, was loath to cede the West Bank, theorizing instead about a "functional" sharing of sovereignty. Another key figure in the government, Deputy Prime Minister Yigal Allon, compiled a plan for the return of most of the West Bank to Jordan but with Israel keeping the Jordan valley, the area around Jerusalem, and a strip running along the narrow sections of the pre-1967 line.

The Allon Plan, as it became known, was always rejected by the king. But it became the effective blueprint for civilian settlement in the territories during the ten years of Labor rule that followed the war. Settlement was encouraged along the torrid and inhospitable Jordan valley, around Jerusalem, and at sites close to the former borderline. This was apart from large housing projects for Jews in East—that is, formerly Jordanian—Jerusalem. Israel formally annexed the eastern part of the city and sizable swaths of land around it immediately after the war, declaring the much-enlarged municipality its eternal and indivisible capital.

The "national camp," still a minority but growing, never acquiesced in the Labor governments' limitations on Jewish settlement. Partisan settlement efforts were sporadically attempted in areas beyond the Allon Plan, and, as we shall see, some took root during Yitzhak Rabin's first government (1974–1977). Sharon's training bases with their seeds of civilian adjuncts grew to become a means for the government and the army to circumvent their own Allon Plan restrictions.

Though severely mauled and deeply humiliated, Egypt was not giving up the long-term struggle against Israel. The occupation of Sinai and the paralysis of the Suez Canal—once again, as in 1956, Egypt deliberately sank ships in the waterway—made that struggle now all the more pressing. On June 22, 1967, barely two weeks after the defeat, Nasser told the Soviet president, "Because the Israelis are now in Sinai, we are building up our defences on the west bank of the Canal. If the Israelis refuse to leave peacefully, sooner or later we'll have to fight them to get them out."[33]

Even before the war was over, Nasser's Soviet patrons began pouring in new arms to replenish Egypt's stockpiles. New and better planes and tanks arrived in the following months, accompanied by more than a thousand Soviet advisers to help assimilate them. In September, the

---

* See below p. 73.

Arab League, meeting in Khartoum, vowed "No recognition, No negotiation, No peace" with Israel.

As if to demonstrate how vigorous and unbowed they still were, the Egyptians torpedoed and sank an Israeli destroyer off Port Said on October 21, 1967. Israel retaliated by shelling oil refineries and petrochemical plants at Suez. After this exchange, a tense quiet settled on the front for the following year. But President Nasser and his generals made it clear that once their army was fully refurbished, they intended to resume active hostilities and engage Israel in a sustained "war of attrition" on the canal front.

The first installment came unannounced on September 8, 1968. "The Egyptians launched a massive artillery attack on the sector from Kantara northward," writes Major General Avraham "Bren" Adan in his Yom Kippur War memoir, *On the Banks of the Suez*. "Our troops entered their defensive bunkers, but these had been prepared very amateurishly. Many were easily penetrated by the Egyptian artillery shells. So we suffered ten killed and eighteen wounded in one day, a heavy price by Israeli standards. This artillery barrage came as a surprise and jolted the IDF Headquarters . . . On October 26 there was another massive Egyptian artillery barrage, this time across the entire front line and over a period of nine hours. Fifteen of our men were killed and thirty-four wounded."[34]

Chief of Staff Bar-Lev now ordered General Adan, "at the head of an inter-service team, to bring to the General Staff a proposal for the creation of a defensive system in Sinai."[35] Chaim Herzog, a leading military historian and a future president of the state, treads ever so carefully as he recounts the beginnings of the "Bar-Lev Line," the defensive system in Sinai that was the focus of huge controversy four years later, at the outbreak of the Yom Kippur War.

The question was a classic one: Was the IDF to defend Sinai from the water's edge, which would mean building much stronger fortifications along the canal, or was it to rely on mobile defensive forces deployed farther back, beyond effective artillery range? Adan's team was to consult with the CO of Southern Command, Shaike Gavish. But, Herzog hints, Gavish's mind was already made up. "Gavish came to the conclusion that it would be advisable to hold positions on the waterfront, particularly at all points which were probable crossing areas for the Egyptians. Furthermore, since the Israeli concept invariably called for mounting a counter-offensive into the enemy's territory, it was important for [the Israelis] to sit in force along the Canal itself and not be in a position which would require fighting before they reached it."

Adan's final recommendation, which was adopted, was "a combination of the two systems of defense": position defense and mobile defense. He insists in his book that the strongpoints along the canal "were never planned to prevent a canal crossing or serve as a defensive line. They were only a warning line. The defensive role would fall to the armored forces in reserve."

Sharon presents a very different story. In his account, Adan's series of fortifications, or *ma'ozim*, fortresses, as they were called in Hebrew, were designed both to serve as forward observation posts *and* "to help stop the Egyptians on the water line, before they could establish any significant presence in the Sinai." He and Tal, alone among the generals, Sharon writes, consistently and unequivocally opposed this concept and argued in favor of a mobile defense.*

The crescendo came in April 1969. "During one of our regular Monday General Headquarters meetings . . . a particularly acrimonious exchange erupted . . . [F]or Bar-Lev it was apparently the last straw. That same evening he called a second meeting," Sharon recalls.

> When I walked [in] . . . I saw Moshe Dayan sitting there together with his deputy. Alongside them were Bar-Lev and every single one of my most vehement critics . . .
>
> Gavish . . . started things off with a wild attack that was personal as well as professional. While he was still speaking, I stood up and said, "I thought we were here to discuss the advantages and disadvantages of the Bar-Lev Line. That's the reason for this meeting and that's what I'm willing to participate in, so that I can tell you again what a dangerous and stupid idea it is . . ."
>
> Dayan cut in. "Arik, you've been invited to a General Headquarters meeting. It's not up to you to decide what's going to be discussed."
>
> "Maybe not," I said, "but if you proceed with this, it's going to be without me."
>
> When I sat down, everything was quiet for a moment; then Gavish took up right where he had left off. With that I got up again, announced that I wouldn't take part in it, then walked toward the door. Behind me I heard Dayan's, "Arik, you can't do that. You have to come back. *Come back!*" The door slamming behind me cut off his voice.

---

* "Specifically, I proposed that we should base our defense on the natural line of hills and dunes that runs parallel to the Canal five to eight miles to the east . . . A second line with our mobile reserves should be established fifteen to twenty miles from the Canal, where the mountains begin and the Mitla and Gidi passes cut toward the interior . . ." (*Warrior*, 220).

As I walked down the corridor, I knew with absolute certainty that I was right and they were wrong, that the Bar-Lev Line was bound to bring us disaster. But it was no pleasure when four years later it did exactly that.

A few days after the door-slamming episode, an officer from the adjutant general's office phoned to ask how Sharon wanted to receive his accumulated leave—as vacation or in cash. Bar-Lev, he learned, would not approve a further extension of his contract. He appealed to Dayan, only to be told, "Bar-Lev doesn't want you; I don't see how I can interfere." Golda Meir, the new prime minister (Eshkol had died suddenly in February 1969), also declined to step in on his behalf.

Sharon now conducted a brief but very public flirt with leaders of the parliamentary opposition. Was he just posturing in order to put pressure on Golda and the government to overrule Bar-Lev? Or was he seriously preparing to embark on a political career? Unsurprisingly, Sharon himself endorses the latter version. But even if he was being disingenuous, his account is entertaining:

At the age of forty-one I was not exactly ready for pipe and slippers.

As I thought about it, political life came to seem more and more attractive. I certainly had ideas . . . and 1969 was an election year. At that time I had two good friends in the political world with whom I occasionally talked about such things. One was Pinchas Sapir, the minister of finance and an important Labor party leader . . . He was from Kfar Saba, quite near my parents' farm, and I had known him from childhood.

The other was Josef Sapir (no relation to Pinchas), the head of the Liberal party. I had known him too since I was young. He had been born into a family of citrus growers in Petach Tikva . . . and when I was a child I occasionally went with my father to their farm to get graftings for our own trees.

Since 1965, Sapir's Liberals had been in alliance with Menachem Begin's Herut Party in an electoral bloc called Gahal,* a first attempt at creating a credible alternative to Labor. Sapir took Sharon to see Begin.

---

* Acronym for the Hebrew: Bloc (of) Herut, Liberals.

My meeting with Begin and Sapir took place in the King David Hotel, in a chilly air-conditioned room whose windows looked out on the walls of the Old City of Jerusalem. It was a cordial meeting. But as the talk went on, I began to feel a cold sweat forming on my back. In later years my relationship with Begin evolved considerably. But during this meeting I was more than a little uncomfortable. Although the discussion was friendly, there was something about the way Begin spoke, and especially the way he looked at me. The man had an extraordinarily powerful presence. And as he spoke, from minute to minute I had more of a feeling that I was getting involved in something I could not control . . .

He was talking about how I would be included with them in the election, and that if we were successful I would join them in the government, all the things that I had supposed I wanted to hear. But as he spoke, I became more and more aware of the man's strength and determination. Peering through his thick glasses, his eyes seemed to bore into me. I began to picture myself as Pinocchio when he got involved with the cat who wasn't blind and the fox who wasn't lame. But despite my growing if intangible misgivings, the discussion proceeded, and eventually we agreed to go ahead together. With that, Mr. Begin in his gallant way called room service and had a good brandy sent up. Then we drank to our understanding. But even as we raised our glasses, I felt that I was locked in and that I was locked in with someone about whom I had inexplicable feelings of apprehension.

The date was July 3, 1969. Election Day was October 28, and by law the parties' lists of candidates had to be submitted a hundred days ahead, by mid-July. As Sharon tells it, the understanding with Begin did not survive his drive back to Tel Aviv. He picked up a soldier-hitchhiker, who, "without paying the slightest deference to my rank or reputation . . . began telling me that I was making a terrible mistake, that I shouldn't do it, that I had to stay in the army . . . Lily was waiting for me, in bed already. I got in and covered myself up with the blanket. 'Lily,' I said, 'I feel as if I need to be protected.' I had already decided that I was not going to go through with it."

The next morning's headlines trumpeted the Begin-Sharon understanding. Sharon writes that he was in the act of composing embarrassing letters of withdrawal to Sapir and Begin when "fate intervened in my personal affairs . . . Pinchas Sapir was visiting the United States. When he heard about the newspaper headlines, he was livid. Calling Bar-Lev, Sapir asked the military's most prominent

Laborite* what he thought he was doing (as Sapir himself told me later) . . . Sapir told Bar-Lev to get busy and find some way of keeping me in the army and out of the hands of the 'enemy.' "

A way was duly, and quickly, found. He would be appointed to the hitherto nonexistent post of "lecturer for the IDF" and sent on an extended speaking tour to the United States, Mexico, Japan, Hong Kong, and South Korea. He would meet, too, with military and diplomatic officials in the various capitals. This eight-week foreign odyssey would end, by happy coincidence, the day before the election. He would thus be conveniently out of the country during the campaign, and everyone could forget his high-profile but now felicitously truncated tryst with the opposition.

He wrote a formal, pompous letter to Begin and Sapir explaining that after long and hard consideration he had decided that "in these difficult days, when the IDF is at war along the borders and its soldiers are shedding their blood in defense of Israel's freedom and independence," his place was "alongside them, and in the front line." To Josef Sapir he wrote a separate note, apologizing for the embarrassment and hinting at the unfavorable impact Begin had made on him. He was determined, he confided, not to enter political life "in a state of dependence on [Begin]."[36]

After the election, with Golda and Dayan and Sapir all safely back in their jobs, Bar-Lev obediently deposited the country's most fateful front, Southern Command, in the hands of the man he had wanted to fire. "In December," Sharon writes, "I received orders to take over Gavish's command."

Sharon seems to have persuaded Bar-Lev that whatever his past objections he would abide by the strategy that the High Command had decided upon, and to a large extent had already implemented, with the rapid fortification of the forward positions along the canal. Most of the fortification work had been finished before the War of Attrition began in earnest, in March 1969. Sharon did not abandon the fortress system and based the defense of Sinai on mobile forces, as Tal and he had advocated.† As CO of Southern Command, he tinkered

---

* A nasty sideswipe but not inaccurate: within ten weeks of his retirement as chief of staff in January 1972, Bar-Lev was in the Labor government as minister of trade and industry.
† After the War of Attrition ended, Tal pointed out that a very high proportion of Israel's casualties had been sustained inside the strongpoints or in the course of supplying them. The other school countered, reasonably enough, that without the strongpoints the casualty figures might have been higher.

with the Bar-Lev Line and ended up, in the words of Chaim Herzog, with "a form of compromise . . . which no military concept could accept." Far from abandoning the line of strongpoints, Sharon ordered many of them rebuilt and reinforced after the battering they took in the War of Attrition. In time, though, he persuaded Elazar, who succeeded Bar-Lev as IDF chief of staff on January 1, 1972, to let him "thin out" the line by closing some—by the end it was fourteen—of the thirty-two strongpoints.

In addition, he embarked on a massive building program of eleven underground fortifications in the hills some miles to the rear, where the massed armor and artillery were to be deployed that would ultimately defend Sinai in the face of an Egyptian crossing. He called these fortresses "*ta'ozim,* strongholds, to distinguish them from the *ma'ozim,* strongpoints," on the canal bank. "Here I put command and long-range surveillance posts, underground bunkers, firing positions, bases for forward reserve units, and emplacements for artillery."[37]

By mid-April 1970, the Israeli positions were being subjected not only to artillery barrages but also to attacks by Egyptian commando units crossing the canal in fast boats under cover of darkness. Israel responded with commando raids of its own, some deep inside Egypt. In one such raid, on July 28, paratroopers and naval commandos set down on the tiny, heavily defended Green Island, near the southern end of the canal in the Gulf of Suez, and destroyed key Egyptian radar and anti-aircraft installations housed there. This gave the air force freer rein to deploy above the Canal Zone as a sort of flying artillery, targeting Egyptian emplacements and armor.

In September, a force of Israeli infantry and armor was ferried across the Gulf of Suez to the port of Zafarana, from where it attacked and overran Egyptian positions along twenty miles of coastline in eight hours of sustained fighting before re-embarking. In December, just before Sharon took over, heli-borne commandos dismantled and transported back to the Israeli side a state-of-the-art Soviet radar system deployed at Ras Arab, also on the west bank of the gulf. And in January 1970, under the new CO a commando force overran Shadwan Island, 155 miles down the Gulf of Suez, killed or captured all of the hundred-man Egyptian garrison, and again made off with radar units and other military hardware.

Both sides now made moves that dangerously escalated the War of Attrition. Israel, worn down by the incessant toll of casualties on the canal, embarked on a policy of deep-penetration bombing raids against strategic targets throughout Egypt. President Nasser, acutely conscious of his vulnerability to Israeli airpower, demanded from his

Soviet patrons a drastic upgrading of Egypt's own air force and its anti-aircraft defenses, along with Soviet pilots and experts to help man the sophisticated new systems he wanted. In the first months of 1970, the Soviet presence in Egypt doubled and tripled, reaching more than twelve thousand men. Israeli pilots, some of them now flying American-supplied Skyhawk and Phantom warplanes, were ordered to back off from dogfights rather than risk downing Soviet airmen.

Israel's deep bombing campaign came to a peremptory end in April, when Phantom jets mistakenly bombed an elementary school, killing forty-seven children and injuring another fifty. The focus of the fighting returned to the Canal Zone, where the Egyptians, with Soviet help, were trying under the cover of almost constant artillery exchanges to deploy their Soviet SAM anti-aircraft missile batteries right up to the water's edge. On July 30, the undesired but inevitable dogfight took place and resulted in the downing of four Soviet-piloted MiGs and the deaths of the four pilots.

The escalation added urgency to U.S. diplomatic efforts to reach a peace agreement between Egypt and Israel, or, failing that, at least an end of the present round of fighting. The Nixon administration had been actively trying to broker a peace deal through Four Power (United States, U.S.S.R., Britain, and France) and Two Power (United States and U.S.S.R.) talks. These had failed to cut through Cold War rivalry, but in December 1969 Secretary of State William Rogers had announced a comprehensive American peace plan based on Israeli withdrawal from all Egyptian and Jordanian territory barring "minor adjustments" in the framework of a peace settlement. Golda Meir's government, still a unity coalition with Begin's Gahal in it, had rejected the proposal. Now, with the war at a global danger point, Rogers came back with a more modest plan, designed to achieve an immediate cease-fire in Sinai.

The American proposal had three parts: a ninety-day cease-fire and "standstill" in place for thirty miles on either side of the canal; a statement by Israel, Egypt, and Jordan that they accepted UN Security Council Resolution 242 and specifically its call for withdrawal from occupied territories; and an undertaking to resume peace talks through the UN peace envoy, Sweden's Gunnar Jarring, which had been conducted on and off since 1967 without registering any progress.

Golda Meir was under heavy international and domestic pressure to accept. Casualty figures mounted relentlessly. Since the end of the Six-Day War, 367 IDF soldiers had been killed on the canal front and 1,366 injured.[38] Almost daily, the black-bordered death notices appeared in the newspapers. The fact that Egyptian casualties were much higher was of no comfort and little strategic significance. As Nasser and his generals had rightly discerned at the outset, a war of attrition for a small, tightly knit society was much more damaging than for a country of tens of millions.

For the first time since the waiting period before the 1967 war, searching questions began to be aired not just on the leftist margin but in the political mainstream. In late July–early August, Israel, Egypt, and Jordan all announced their acceptance of the U.S. proposal. The cease-fire on the canal went into effect on August 7, 1970. Begin pulled his Gahal bloc out of the government, ending three years of unity rule.

Egypt, with Soviet connivance, immediately began advancing its SAM anti-aircraft batteries toward the canal bank, in brazen violation of the "standstill." The Egyptian push began on the very night of the cease-fire and continued in the days and weeks ahead. Israel strenuously protested to Washington, but the administration was reluctant to upend the cease-fire. Nixon preferred to step up the supply of advanced warplanes to Israel as a means of mollifying the anger and anxiety in Jerusalem.

Egypt's War of Attrition was supported by its Six-Day War allies, Syria and Jordan, through the activities from their soil of Palestinian guerrilla groups. Immediately after the war, the Palestinian nationalist group Fatah, under Yasser Arafat, tried to establish itself inside the occupied West Bank and lead resistance there. But it was eventually pushed out and forced to conduct its operations against Israel on a hit-and-run basis from over the border. Soon, Arafat was acting in defiance of Jordanian constraints. Increasingly, the armed Palestinian presence on the East Bank began to pose a threat to the stability of the Hashemite kingdom.

In September 1970, after two attempts on his life, King Hussein of Jordan lashed out at the armed PLO units that were running the border areas and the Palestinian refugee camps inside the kingdom as a veritable state within a state. The Arab Legion, comprising Bedouin tribesmen loyal to the royal house, crushed the PLO men and took a bloody toll of civilian camp dwellers, too. Hundreds of the armed Palestinians fled across the river, where IDF troops were ordered not to shoot them or send them back but to disarm and arrest them, "although," Sharon writes with evident disapproval, "these were the very terrorists who had carried out who knew how many murderous raids into Israel."

He voiced strident disapproval when Israel acceded to an urgent American request to mobilize its army in the face of a Syrian invasion of northern Jordan in support of the hard-pressed Palestinians. Israeli armor moved demonstratively into the Beisan valley, poised to cross into Jordan. The Syrians withdrew. "The resolution to this crisis was considered a success by the Americans and the Jordanians," Sharon writes. "Most Israelis were also pleased with the outcome. But I was not one of them." To most Israelis, guided by their government, the Hashemite house, formerly a British fiefdom and now an American client, was infinitely to be preferred as a neighbor to a Soviet-backed radical Palestinian state. But not to Sharon, as he argued vehemently but to no avail in the army High Command. Granted, he said, a Palestinian state in place of Jordan would probably remain hostile to Israel. "But the discussion will be about where the border should be. We will be arguing with them about territorial matters. We will no longer be dealing with the issue of Palestinian identity and about their right to a political expression of their identity."

This kind of bold, heterodox thinking about the Palestinian problem was the province in Israel at that time only of the Far Left. Prime Minister Meir blithely insisted that there was no Palestinian nation and therefore no need to grant it political expression. In the eyes of almost everyone in government and in the defense establishment, the disposition of the West Bank continued to be the business of its two neighbors: Israel and Jordan. Sharon's dissent from this article of faith would have reinforced his image in the eyes of the Labor old guard as a maverick, and a dangerously unpredictable one at that. Certainly it would not have improved his prospects, which he believed still existed, of ever being appointed chief of staff.

BRUTE FORCE

While the Suez front was the most significant area of Sharon's responsibility as CO of Southern Command, his tenure in that key post was overshadowed by two high-profile controversies that erupted far from the canal front line. The pattern was something of a throwback to the 1950s: Again he was carrying out government policy. Again he was doing so with excessive, wanton brutality. Again he was the convenient lightning rod to absorb and deflect criticism. And again his superiors—most especially Dayan—covered for him and protected him from serious fallout. Another episode in which his behavior was even crueler and more culpable never even became a controversy: it was hushed up at the time and has remained suppressed ever since.

With the canal front (deceptively) quiet after the August 1970 cease-fire, Sharon could spend much time during the next eighteen months focusing on Gaza. He had the territory mapped into small squares and deployed infantry teams in each square. "It is your job to know this square inside and out," he told them, "and it is your job to find and kill every terrorist in it." A shadowy unit, Rimon, commanded by a longtime Sharon acolyte, Meir Dagan,* drew veiled—and largely censored—criticism for shooting or hurling grenades first and asking questions later, or not at all. A particular source of criticism and controversy was the widespread use that Sharon's troops made of bulldozers, both in the fields and orchards and in the narrow alleys of the refugee camps. Trees and crops often fell before the bulldozers, as did many hundreds of modest homes, often hardly more than hovels, of many thousands of innocent people who found themselves in the path of Sharon's drive against the terrorists. The curfews clapped down on the camps, often for days on end as the soldiers went about their search-and-destroy missions, and the hours-long lineups imposed on the menfolk were also widely seen as forms of collective punishment.

In February 1972, Dayan publicly praised Sharon for the Gaza operation. But he went on to announce that the Strip would now come under the aegis of Central Command, effective immediately. Ze'ev Schiff wrote in *Haaretz* that "there may be reservations about Gen. Sharon's military methods, but the fact is that this commander has eliminated terror in Gaza . . . Sharon's determination, and perhaps, too, his lack of consideration of many things, have immeasurably improved the security situation there. Militarily, he leaves Gaza victorious."[39]

When ministers and Knesset members would come visiting Gaza, Sharon took them to the sand dunes overlooking the coast and urged the creation of blocs of Jewish settlements—"fingers," as he called them—between the major centers of Palestinian population. The concept evolved in government and military circles, moreover, that Israel needed to plant a permanent presence in the Rafah Salient, westward beyond the Gaza-Sinai border, in order to create a cordon sanitaire between Gaza and Egypt. Sharon claims that he was the progenitor of this strategic theory. It was vital for Israel, in his words, "to create a

---

* As prime minister, Sharon appointed Dagan, by then a reserves general, head of the Mossad. He held the post for eight years.

Jewish buffer between Gaza and the Sinai in order to cut off the flow of smuggled weapons and—looking forward to a future settlement with Egypt—to divide the two regions."

Progenitor or not, Sharon was the enthusiastic executor of the first stage of the scheme: ejecting the existing tenants. "It wouldn't be a bad thing if there were no Arabs here," Dayan mused to Sharon one day as they both flew over the Rafah Salient by helicopter. "Then we could fence the whole area and turn it into a security zone."[40]* That was enough for Sharon. Within days, some ten thousand Bedouin, most of them members of the Romeilah tribe and most of them not nomads but sedentary farmers long established in the area, were summarily ousted by soldiers of Southern Command.

The soldiers arrived unannounced at dawn on January 14, 1972, nine Bedouin sheikhs later recounted in their petition to the High Court of Justice.[†] They ordered the entire community to leave at once. They cited security grounds. That same day, according to the court depositions, the soldiers began physically demolishing the Bedouin's homes and outhouses. People were pushed around, and property was smashed and ruined. The eviction took several days. Once the Bedouin were all out, the army fenced off an area of some nineteen square miles to prevent them from getting back in.

The episode might have remained unknown, as Sharon (and Dayan?) apparently intended, had it not been for the protests of a few reservists, members of Mapam kibbutzim along the border who had witnessed the forcible evictions, and for the pointed inquiries of Red Cross officials. In mid-February, David Elazar, who succeeded Bar-Lev as chief of staff on January 1, set up an internal inquiry under General Aharon Yariv, the former head of Military Intelligence, to investigate the complaints.

Yariv focused on the decision to fence off areas of the Rafah Salient. Sharon admitted that he had given that order without explicit authorization from the chief of staff or the minister of defense. Yariv duly submitted his report. Elazar made do with a letter of reprimand to Sharon. A junior officer and a civilian were more severely punished: the officer was transferred; the civilian was dismissed. The military censorship kept a tight lid on the whole affair.

---

* In the Rafah Salient, too, as in the adjacent Gaza Strip, a couple of isolated settlements had come into being by this time. The Bedouin landholders were quietly compensated.
† The High Court of Justice in the Israeli system is the Supreme Court in its role as the court (of first instance) that hears petitions against the executive branch.

On the left, nevertheless, the controversy rumbled on for months, replete with demonstrations, counterdemonstrations, and angry articles in the press. The editor of the Labor Party's weekly, *Ot,* David Shaham, wrote an editorial demanding that the "very senior officer" be dismissed. What would happen in a normal country, Shaham asked, if an army commander went ahead and implemented a contingency plan without getting authorization from his civilian bosses? "Surely he would be appropriately punished."

This drew a rare and spirited defense of Sharon—still unnamed—by Moshe Dayan. The article was "wild and irresponsible incitement," he told the party central committee. The author did not know the facts and had not even heard the officer whose dismissal he was demanding. Neither the army's judge advocate general nor the attorney general had recommended legal or disciplinary action against Sharon.[41] Dayan demanded that Shaham, not the "very senior officer," be dismissed. Golda Meir rammed through a resolution requiring *Ot* to appoint an editorial board. Shaham was effectively neutered.

The government meanwhile announced that it would pay compensation to the Bedouin and help resettle them on nearby tracts of land, some inside the Gaza Strip. In the Knesset, the minister without portfolio Yisrael Galili, Golda's shadowy but powerful adviser, said that the government regarded the Gaza Strip and the adjoining Rafah Salient as territory that would remain under Israeli rule forever. Gaza thus now joined Jerusalem, the Golan Heights, the Jordan valley, and Sharm el-Sheikh in the list of places from which Israel proposed never to withdraw. This was a fairly momentous announcement and a remarkably backhanded way of making it. Within a few years, a string of Jewish agricultural settlements were up and thriving in the Rafah Salient area, along with a regional center, Yamit, which provided schools and services for the settlers.

Once again, Sharon was conveniently, indeed avidly available to "do the dirty work" of government policy and to take the heat from the humane Left. The eviction and the enclosure were decided above his pay grade. His methods of executing the decisions had been gratuitously excessive. But a thick blanket of censorship and political protection ensured that he emerged from the episode unscathed.

An infinitely thicker blanket, still unlifted to the present day, was required to shield Sharon from the consequences of *another,* much more heinous act of violence that he perpetrated at this same time against *other* tribes of Bedouin, deeper inside Sinai. Again it was a peremptory, forcible expulsion. Only this time it resulted in dozens of deaths, including of children and old people who died of exposure in the freezing desert night.

This time, there was no inquiry, no public outcry, no angry articles. There was a total, comprehensive cover-up, then and thereafter. The military censorship made sure that nothing was published. The chief of staff and at least one other general, Shlomo Gazit, the IDF's coordinator of operations in the territories, took no action against Sharon when they learned the shocking details of this episode. Presumably, Minister of Defense Dayan and probably Golda, too, knew of the outrage. Both of them visited the scene where it happened.

It took place on the night of January 12, 1972, with additional expulsions on the twentieth and the twenty-sixth, in the area of Sinai around Abu Agheila, about eighteen miles west of the Israeli border and twenty-eight miles south of the coast at el-Arish. This time the victims were some three thousand members of the Tarabin and Tiya'ha tribes, mainly nomads whose traditional camping grounds were in the area of Abu Agheila, north and south of Jebel Halal.

On January 12, a couple of jeep patrols from Southern Command cruised around the Bedouin encampments informing whomever they encountered that all the Bedouin were to be out of the area by the following morning. They left before sunset. When units of jeep-borne and camel-borne soldiers descended on the Bedouin after dark to enforce the order, some tried to argue. One sheikh said he would not move his tribe unless he received a formal, written order from the military governor of Sinai. The camel riders began tearing out tent poles and threatening to shoot. The same methods of persuasion were used in other encampments. The Bedouin began their trek the same night.

The temperature in Sinai that night, according to the Government Meteorological Office, was two degrees Celsius. On January 26, when other encampments in the area were expelled in this same way, it was zero. "Most of the Beduin did not possess sufficient animals to carry their families, their tents and their food," according to a detailed report submitted three months later to the chief of staff by an independent researcher. "As a result, they had to leave much of their property behind. As a result, too, old people were forced to walk. Many had to carry infants on their backs, or the infants had to trudge through the freezing sands. Many just slumped down and wept. When they reached their assigned destination [in one case some thirty-one miles to the south] many were unable to set up any kind of shelter for their families.

"As a result of their exertions and of exposure many became ill.

People of all ages died, by rough assessment more than forty. I myself counted 23 fresh graves at Jebel Jahem and five more at Wadi Seiseb. I heard from the Beduin that others were buried elsewhere."

The author of the report, a young American-born scholar of Bedouin life and lore named Dr. Clinton Bailey, attached a photograph of a line of tiny graves of infants who did not survive the transfer. He took his story first to General Gazit, "but nothing was done." He took it to a well-known journalist, but nothing was published. The journalist, though, telephoned the chief of staff in Tel Aviv. "I think there is something you ought to hear," he said.

Elazar read Bailey's five pages in his presence. He picked up the phone and asked for Sharon. "I understand the people displaced for the maneuvers haven't gone back yet . . . I want them back tomorrow! How do I know? There's a Dr. Bailey here. He's been there. He's written a report and submitted it to me."

A few days later, Bailey received a telephoned invitation to meet with the CO of Southern Command at his headquarters in Beersheba. Sharon positively radiated bonhomie. "We've got something in common," he said, beaming at Bailey, "because I really like the Bedouin." He regaled the scholar with stories of Bedouin trackers whom he'd fought alongside. He loved to spend time, he said, with the colorful sheikh Awda of the Azazme tribe, eating mutton and talking in his tent. "I don't know what happened here," he added breezily about Bailey's report. Anyway, the tribes were back on their land. If Dr. Bailey ever needed anything, any help with his research, he was to please feel free to ask.

No sooner had Bailey left than Sharon issued an order barring him from access to any IDF facility anywhere in Sinai. Bailey learned of it from a Bedouin officer-friend. He telephoned Elazar and reported this, too. "Soon they called me back and said, 'You can go wherever you want in Sinai . . .' Why didn't I press Sharon [about the deaths]? I was barely 30 years old. A kid doing research. He was a big war hero."

How was this appalling episode successfully hushed up? In part, presumably, it was because the tribes from deeper inside Sinai, unlike the Rafah Bedouin, had no neighborly relationship with the left-wing kibbutzim along the border. There was no one to encourage them to apply to the high court.

But more relevant, perhaps, was the top secret nature of the military maneuvers to which Chief of Staff Elazar referred in his phone call to Sharon and from which the Bedouin were so brutally distanced. On February 20–25, 1972, at the instance of Sharon and in the presence of Golda, Dayan, and the General Staff, the IDF exercised ferrying an entire armored division, under fire, across the Suez Canal. This remarkable war game was conducted at Abu Agheila, near the Bedouin's encampments.[42]

"Sharon had a great idea," writes General Bren Adan, then the Armored Corps commander and no admirer as a rule of Sharon. "Through relatively minor engineering work, he was able to enlarge the small Ruafa'a Dam, located in the middle of the desert in northern Sinai, which absorbs the flood waters that flow through the el-Arish wadi during the winter rains. Thus a small water obstacle was created that would enable us, despite the limitations of its location and its size, to conduct a 'wet' crossing operation combined with a live fire exercise."[43]

CASTLES IN THE SAND

The exercise at Abu Agheila, code-named Oz (Power), was not an unqualified success. It underscored the huge logistical problems involved in deploying bridging craft to get a large force of armor across the canal.

After the 1967 war, Adan writes, the IDF had purchased "floatable iron cubes—uni-floats—each of which measured 5 x 2.5 x 1.2 meters and weighed three tons." A large crane was required to unload them. Engineers then assembled them in the water in groups of nine, with hydraulically operated ramps on the front and back ends and outboard motors on the sides. These lumbering giant rafts could ferry tanks across. Assembling them took about an hour, Adan writes. Once there were several of them in operation, they could be linked together to form a bridge across the waterway.

After Oz, Adan writes, he worked with the deputy chief of staff, General Tal, to develop "a roller bridge." This monster "consisted of more than 100 iron rollers, two meters in diameter, which were attached together to make one rolling bridge 180 meters long. The main advantage of a roller bridge was that it could be pushed into the Canal." Among its many disadvantages, however, was that it took three days to build, it weighed four hundred tons,* it required an

---

* Sharon and his staff officers in the Yom Kippur War, who grappled with the rolling bridge and eventually laid it across the canal, claimed it weighed six hundred tons.

entire company of sixteen tanks to drag it along, and it could only travel in a straight line.

Given these drawbacks, the IDF wisely decided to invest, too, in a batch of fairly ancient amphibious bridging tugs, called Gilowas. These, Adan explains, were "very large vehicles with correspondingly large wheels that were capable of moving to the water, floating, and—by means of hydraulic power—opening up two treadways suitable for tank tracks . . . [T]hree such vehicles formed a raft unit capable of traveling across the water from bank to bank while carrying one tank. Six of them joined together would . . . carry two tanks." If there were enough of them, they could form a bridge. Their disadvantage was that they floated on inflatable rubber sleeves, easily perforated by enemy fire. "This problem could be overcome by filling the floats with a light foamy material."

Above all, Oz demonstrated that the army and the government were committed, should war come, to the basic strategy of crossing the canal and carrying the battle to the Egyptian side. This was the unanimous assumption and the unanimous intention. When war did come, and bitter fights erupted between Sharon, Adan, and other generals, the issue was never *whether* to cross but only when and how. The misconception in some popular quarters that Sharon initiated the canal crossing was just that—a misconception (eagerly propagated by Sharon). By the same token, Oz demonstrated that the Bar-Lev Line was never envisaged as a war winner in itself, even by its most ardent advocates. There was never any illusion of the attacking Egyptians dissipating their strength against a line of Israeli fortresses. Everyone on the Israeli side agreed that to win the war, the IDF would need to counterattack on the western bank of the canal.

President Nasser had died suddenly in September 1970 and was succeeded by the uncharismatic-looking Anwar Sadat, a more junior member of the original 1952 Free Officers' coup. Sadat announced publicly that he was prepared to make peace with Israel but got no commensurate response from Prime Minister Meir. Moshe Dayan had been promoting the idea of an interim agreement between the two countries. Israel, he suggested, would pull back from the Suez Canal to a distance of several miles, and Egypt would reopen the waterway and restore civilian life to the deserted towns on its banks. The Egyptian army would not be allowed back into Sinai, but civilian personnel, including police, would cross over in order to operate the waterway.

Once the canal was pulsing with commerce again, Dayan reasoned, Egypt would have much less incentive to resume hostilities.

In early 1971, Sadat put forward his own proposals for an interim agreement that in many respects overlapped with Dayan's. Sadat insisted, though, that the interim accord be integrally linked to a final accord, requiring complete Israeli withdrawal. Throughout 1971 indirect negotiations continued under the UN envoy Gunnar Jarring over ideas for an interim or partial settlement. The Americans, too, tried to build diplomatic momentum on the proximity of Sadat's and Dayan's thinking. They had to contend, though, with the sad reality that Dayan's thinking did not reflect Golda's and with the no less sad reality that he was not prepared to fight, politically, for his own view. The Israeli prime minister and key ministers around her—Galili, Allon, later Bar-Lev, too—were locked into the mind-set that there must be no withdrawal without full and final peace.

Sadat made an even more dramatic move in 1972, dismissing the fifteen-thousand-odd Soviet military advisers stationed in Egypt and arresting pro-Soviet figures among the Egyptian leadership. Clearly, he wanted to move Egypt back into the Western camp. Again, Israel read him wrong. The analysis in Jerusalem was that this move reduced the risk of war. In fact, Sadat felt he could not go to war so long as the overweening Russians were embedded in his army, presuming to constrain his actions and dictate his decisions. "Sadat's purpose was completely misunderstood [by Israel]," Herzog writes, "a fact that contributed in no small measure to the strengthening of the 'concept.' "[44]

The "concept," or in Hebrew *conceptziya,* was the term coined after the Yom Kippur War in 1973 to describe the blind arrogance that suffused the whole Israeli policy elite—the government and the army, but much of academia and the media, too—in the period leading up to the war. "We are all to blame," the president of the state, Ephraim Katzir, observed as the country grappled with its shock and mourning after the war ended. He was accused at the time of trying to deflect the main blame from the Labor government by dissipating it among the entire nation. But in a deep sense he was right. The hubris broadcast by the government reflected the corruption of the national ethos by delusions of grandeur in the wake of the 1967 conquests. The military intelligence assessment that Egypt and Syria would not go to war was rooted in a much broader national conviction that they would not dare to do it.

Sharon pretended in later years that he was not part of the hubristic overconfidence that deadened Israel's senses. "When Anwar Sadat announced in his 1972 Ramadan address that 'next year I will be blessing you from Sinai,' I for one had no doubts about his intentions. Unlike many Israelis, I had always considered the Arabs serious people . . . I had no doubt at all that at some point they would launch an attack."[45]

In fact, he was a pillar of the *conceptziya*. In July 1973 he assured the public in a newspaper interview that Israel's security situation was "wonderful." Israel had become "a middle-sized military power with enormous strength . . . As long as we stay on the present borders the Arabs have no chance of winning a war."

Two months later—and two weeks before the Yom Kippur War—he asserted with sweeping confidence, "Israel now stands before years of quiet in terms of defense. We need to use the time to deal with other issues that concern us. We are in the best possible situation in terms of defense."

By this time, the summer of 1973, he was speaking no longer as a soldier but as a prominent politician, the election campaign director of the Likud, a new amalgam of all the parties of the Right that in less than two months he had managed to weld together as the first-ever serious political challenge to Labor's hegemony. The election was set for October 31. Sharon seriously believed that the Likud could win, or could at least give Labor a much closer run than it had ever faced before. To that end, he had even embarked on a rigorous diet in order to make himself more attractive on the hustings.

His metamorphosis from grizzled warrior to political charmer came as a surprise to the public but not to him. David Elazar had made it clear soon after he took office as chief of staff the year before that he wanted him to retire from the army on completion of his term as CO of Southern Command. There was not much affection between the two of them.*

---

* With Bar-Lev, on the other hand, Sharon's relations had markedly improved. "You are an outstanding commander," the outgoing chief of staff told Sharon in their parting interview.

> You have strategic understanding and operational ability and the capacity to push things forward. As you know, I criticized aspects of your behavior in the past that were detrimental to the army's interests and detrimental to you, too. I am glad that in this latter period, as CO of Southern Command, these things have receded and over the past two years you have discharged your duties in a very professional way. I hope that as CO of Southern Command you have come to recognize the wisdom of the concept of holding strongpoints on the shore of the canal and that in the future, too, you will continue to deny the Egyptians any territorial gain. (Gai, *Bar-Lev,* 212)

But the new chief could argue that easing out Sharon was not personal: he planned a sweeping change of generation in the General Staff, with all those over forty-five making way for younger men. Sharon saw himself as by far the best-qualified candidate for chief of staff after Elazar. He appealed Elazar's decision to Dayan and then to Golda. But to no avail: both of them refused to intervene on his behalf.

Having decided to make his future in politics, Sharon proceeded to harness the ending of his old career to the launching of his new one. At a party in the garden of his home in Beersheba on the night of his formal retirement, July 15, he embarrassed the many serving officers present with a blistering attack on the chief of staff and the "top echelon of the defense establishment." He had to speak out, he said, because so many people had been urging him to stay on in uniform.[46] The subtext was clear: his military career had been stymied because he was not a supporter—but a critic—of the ruling Labor Party. There was a more important insinuation, too—and in a private conversation with Dayan, Sharon had spelled it out—that he did not consider his successor as CO of Southern Command, Shmuel Gonen, up to the job.[47]

Such washing of the army's dirty linen in public was unprecedented. Sharon added insult to insult by informing the chief of staff that he would not attend the traditional General Staff dinner given for every retiring general. They could send the engraved wristwatch in the mail, he wrote. He waived another "tradition"—the right to sum up his years of service at a press conference with military correspondents. He would speak with the press in his own way, he signaled, and in his own time. He did ask, though, to be invited one last time to the General Staff to take his leave of his colleagues there. Elazar agreed and Dayan attended, too, and heaped praise on the outgoing Sharon. This somewhat defused the tension and left no option for Sharon to be curmudgeonly in response. There was also a pleasant surprise for him: Dayan immediately concurred when he asked him for a reserves appointment as commander of an armored division on the southern front.

The next day, he met with the press, on his own terms. He hired a hall at the Tel Aviv press center and invited political, not military, correspondents to listen to him. But he was headline news and everyone came, including foreign correspondents. " 'Loyal opposition' is not good enough," he declared. "We need to create an alternative." This elusive goal he, a civilian of forty-eight hours' standing, proposed to achieve in time for the election in October. "Israel styles itself a democracy. But there is one area where our democracy is deficient: the realistic prospect of changing the government. It is totally wrong for one party to rule for decades on end, without facing any serious danger of being replaced."

He flatly denied reports that he had conducted secret contacts with Labor with a view to becoming a minister after the election.[48] Labor, realizing that he was headed to the other side, had nastily leaked the fact that he was a card-carrying member of the party. But Sharon at his press conference turned that to his advantage, demonstratively tearing up his party card.[49]

He proposed not a right-wing alliance but a centrist bloc. He would approach "Herut, the Liberals, the Free Center, the State List, and if possible the Independent Liberals too. These are the potential partners in an alignment of centrist parties that will stand against the Labor Alignment."[50]*

In the event, the intricate negotiations, which Sharon mediated with unflagging energy over the following weeks, boiled down to how to splice them all together equitably in a single list of candidates, and on September 13 the formal signing ceremony of the Likud took place at last. "You've shown the stubbornness of a mule," Yigael Hurwitz, the State List leader and a veteran farming man, said, showering compliments on Sharon. "And the belligerence of a bull," Sharon added, preferring his own farmyard metaphor.

Sharon spoke as a farmer, too. Not just as a son of Kfar Malal, where his mother, Vera, feisty as ever, was still running the family homestead, but as the proud new proprietor of a vast (by Israeli standards) ranch in the south of the country that he and Lily had named Sycamore Ranch.

They both wanted a farm, if only as an "insurance policy" given the fragility of a political career. But after twenty-five years in the military, he bridled at any thought of collective discipline, which is an inherent part of moshav farming in Israel. He would grow and raise

---

* The Free Center, with four members of the Knesset, was a breakaway from Herut, led by the lawyer Shmuel Tamir. Tamir had bridled at Menachem Begin's autocratic rule over his party and had been forced to secede. By listing the Free Center, Sharon was signaling that he, too, would not be cowed by Begin's authoritarian ways, which deterred middle-of-the-road voters. The State List, also with four members in the present Knesset, was the rump of Ben-Gurion's Rafi Party. Its hard core were salt-of-the-earth moshavniks. The Independent Liberals, also a Knesset faction of four, were out-and-out doves, a far cry from the old Irgun "fighting family" who were still the backbone of Begin's Herut. There was little chance they would join, and when it came to it, they didn't, but Sharon lost nothing by listing them. Another component of the new Likud was the Movement for Greater Israel, a group mainly of ex-Laborites headed by Sharon's old friend and commander, Avraham Yoffe.

what he wanted, how he wanted. Private farms in Israel are few and far between, but he alighted on one in the northern Negev near the little immigrant town of Sderot and immediately fell in love with it. It was a four-thousand-dunam holding,* most of it barren, with a farmhouse in fairly run-down condition and a few sycamore trees. Sharon liked the size, but also the remoteness. It had belonged in the 1950s to his old friend Rafi Eitan, who held a long-term lease from the state. Eitan later sold his rights to an Australian Zionist sheep rancher, but now it was on the market again.

"But how to buy it? I had received from my parents the greatest spiritual wealth a child could want, but not a penny of money—they had never had a penny free. My whole adult life I had spent in the army living on the subsistence salary of a career officer. So there were no savings to draw on. And now as I made the round of Israeli banks I found that a private person simply could not get a farm loan."[51]

He needed $600,000. He got it with the help of Avraham Krinitzi, the mayor of Ramat Gan, the town neighboring Tel Aviv that had "adopted" the paratroop brigade. Krinitzi had often heard his friend Meshulam Riklis, an ex-Israeli now living and flourishing in America, complaining that the IDF was forgoing bold, rightist generals like Ezer Weizman[†] and Arik Sharon. Now, Krinitzi suggested, Riklis could pitch in to help Sharon. Riklis agreed without hesitation. People like Sharon, he replied to Krinitzi, should not have to worry about money. They should worry about one thing: defending Israel.

Riklis met with Sharon, who was still in uniform, and offered him a standing loan of $200,000, interest-free, to help buy the ranch—but on one condition: that he did not make do with being a rancher but stayed involved in matters of defense and foreign policy. Riklis's views were of the Right, and he believed Sharon would champion them.

With the first $200,000 thus generously covered, Sharon was able to raise the rest of the money in the form of a loan from the Exchange National Bank of Chicago, which had recently opened a branch in Israel. Here, too, personal and political sympathies seem to have been interwoven with the lender's financial considerations: Samuel Sax, Exchange National's chairman, was a former U.S. Navy Reserve officer who knew Sharon and presumably supported his political ambitions. But his loan, linked to the dollar, was to be paid back at the rate of $50,000 a year, starting immediately.

---

* A dunam is one thousand square meters.
† Weizman, another avowed and outspoken right-winger, had left the army in 1969 and joined Herut, serving as a minister in the government of national unity.

CHAPTER 3 · DESERT STORM

Sharon arrived at the 143rd Division's forward base at Tasa, in western Sinai, in mid-afternoon on Sunday, October 7, 1973, to take command of the central sector. Avraham "Bren" Adan was deploying to his north with the 162nd Division, another reserve formation, while the peacetime commander of Sinai, Avraham "Albert" Mandler, took over the southern sector. Shmuel Gonen (still widely known by his original family name, Gorodish), Sharon's successor as CO of Southern Command, moved with his staff from Beersheba to the forward headquarters at Um Hashiba near the Gidi Pass, which was code-named Dvela.*

The Yom Kippur War was twenty-six hours old. Hundreds of Israeli soldiers were dead on the two fronts, the Egyptian and the Syrian. Hundreds of tanks had been destroyed or crippled. Five Egyptian infantry divisions had crossed the Suez Canal. The first waves of attackers had swarmed across in shoals of small boats. They then set about erecting ten bridges, swiftly and efficiently, down the entire length of the canal. Thousands of men and hundreds of vehicles were relentlessly streaming across. The Egyptian units were digging in on the eastern bank, fortifying bridgeheads two miles deep. Israeli warplanes sent to bomb the bridges and strafe the advancing columns were being picked off with alarming ease by the ground-to-air missile batteries on the western bank. Many of the Israeli canal-side strongpoints were surrounded and under attack. Others had simply been bypassed: they were six to seven miles apart, and the Egyptians poured through the gaps. The beleaguered men were begging for relief. But efforts to reach them had resulted only in more burned-out tanks and more dead crewmen.

"No, Arik didn't ask me why my tanks had not deployed according

---

* *Dvela* means "dried fig" in Hebrew. IDF code names are eclectic and arbitrary; they have no intrinsic significance.

to 'Dovecote.' " Colonel Amnon Reshef, whose Fourteenth Armored Brigade bore the brunt of the fighting in Sinai that first night and day of the war, was at Tasa to welcome Sharon. "Dovecote" was the defense plan centered on the Bar-Lev Line. At times of tension, regular army infantrymen were to man the strongpoints, and regular army tank units were to take up positions on ramps and high ground between them, ready to hold off an Egyptian attack until the reserve divisions arrived. On Yom Kippur, the strongpoints were manned by a battalion of 436 reservists from the Jerusalem Brigade, many of them noncombat soldiers. Reshef's tanks were assembled in the *ta'ozim*, the fortified rear staging areas miles back from the canal. The other two armored brigades in Sinai were camped even farther back.

"I was summoned to a briefing with Mandler on Saturday morning," Reshef recalled. "He was called to the phone. 'H hour is this evening at six,' he came back and told us. 'For what—they still don't know. It may be the end of the Egyptians' war games; it may be war.' We suggested moving the tanks forward to their firing positions, but Southern Command forbade it for fear of exacerbating the tension on the front line."

The war, confidently undetected by Israeli intelligence until almost too late, was now confidently predicted to begin at 6:00 p.m. precisely. The tanks were to take up their positions at 5:00, and in any event not before 4:00. But the Egyptian bombardment, and the Syrian assault in the north, started at 2:00. Some two thousand artillery pieces rained shells on the Israeli positions across the canal. At the same moment, 240 Egyptian warplanes roared overhead, en route to attack Israeli airfields, radar installations, anti-aircraft batteries, artillery emplacements, and rear bases throughout Sinai. "Over 3,000 tons of concentrated destruction were launched against a handful of Israeli fortifications in a barrage that turned the entire east bank of the Suez Canal into an inferno for fifty-three minutes."[1] Before the smoke cleared, the first Egyptian boats were in the water.

"The next afternoon, I reported to Arik what was happening," Reshef said drily. "I explained that opposite each company of mine an entire Egyptian division had crossed. By the time my tanks had reached their firing positions, Egyptian commandos were waiting for them with antitank weapons. Arik didn't cast blame, and he didn't complain. There wasn't time for that. The situation was catastrophic. He was focused, businesslike, constructive."

Reshef was businesslike, too, despite his night and day of relentless fighting. A soldier's soldier, six feet tall, ramrod straight with a handlebar mustache, he cut a very different figure from the bulky, silver-haired Sharon. His mauled and shrunken brigade was now ordered integrated into Sharon's division. "I didn't know Sharon at all. I'd met him briefly just once, years before."*

In April, the IDF had gone on alert in response to intelligence reports that Egypt and Syria might be planning an attack in May. For several weeks, units in Sinai and on the Golan were beefed up with reserves, trained, and held in a high state of readiness. Sharon, still the CO of Southern Command, made plans for a possible crossing at Kantara and farther south at Deversoir, at the top of the Great Bitter Lake. The huge Israeli-built ramparts were a problem there, but he solved it by hollowing out a section from the inside "so that its outward appearance would remain the same, though in actuality it would be thinner and less dense." He marked out the section with a line of red bricks. "We also built a large enclosed yard with a hardened floor almost a thousand yards in length and several hundred in breadth with roads going in one side and out the other to facilitate traffic."[2]

Dayan urged the General Staff to be prepared for war from the end of June. But nothing happened, and by August the state of alert had been reduced, and the languid, torpid sense of false security had crept over the canal front again. On September 13, a dogfight developed over southern Syria in which the IAF brought down thirteen Syrian MiGs for the loss of one of its own planes. This naturally raised tensions again, and on September 24, at the request of the CO of Northern Command, Yitzhak Hofi, a decision was made to reinforce the front line on the Golan with extra tanks. This was done, in part, by bringing up an armored brigade from Sinai.

The next day, Prime Minister Meir met secretly with King Hussein of Jordan and heard from him an explicit warning that war was imminent. But, reassured by Military Intelligence that the likelihood of war was low, she paid little heed to this neighborly tip-off. The Egyptians had been observed working feverishly behind their canal embankment,

---

* Eight years later, with Reshef now a full general and Sharon the minister of defense, Reshef resigned from the army rather than fight, he says, in Sharon's looming war in Lebanon. In civilian life, he became a prominent dove. But his assessment of Sharon the battlefield commander never changed. "He radiated presence, charisma, leadership. Men followed him willingly. They heard his voice on the radio, his assurance, his encouragement, his motivation. They saw him; he was with us. He was always there." Reshef shared his memories and assessments in a series of interviews in his home in Tel Aviv in 2006–2007.

moving heavy equipment and drilling troops. But this was confidently explained by Military Intelligence as a large-scale training exercise.

Only near noon on Friday, October 5, as the country prepared to close down for the fast of Yom Kippur, the holiest day in the Jewish year, did Military Intelligence's stolid "low probability of war" assessment finally begin to crack. Reports had come in overnight of urgent instructions from Moscow to the families of Soviet personnel in Syria and Egypt to leave at once, and planes were being sent in to collect them. The standing army went on high alert. Mobilization orders were issued to some air force reserve crews. But it was still a far cry from full war footing. The head of Military Intelligence, Eli Zeira, told cabinet ministers called to a hasty meeting in Tel Aviv that he still believed war was unlikely. Chief of Staff Elazar agreed. The *conceptziya,* even now, continued to hold sway.

It gave way only during the night, when the director of the Mossad, Zvi Zamir, telephoned from London to say war would break out the following day at sunset. His source was Ashraf Marwan, Gamal Abdel Nasser's son-in-law and a close aide to his successor as president of Egypt, Anwar Sadat. The Mossad had been running him since 1969. At a dawn consultation in Tel Aviv, Elazar demanded a preemptive strike by the air force. But Dayan balked, and Golda backed him, arguing that the critical factor now was U.S. support. In order to retain it, Israel must be seen not to have started the war. Elazar then demanded total, immediate mobilization of the reserves. But again Dayan opposed him. He suggested two divisions were enough for the moment. At 9:00 a.m., Golda approved the two divisions. Twenty minutes later she approved two more.

Arik Sharon, busy all week running the Likud election staff from an office in Tel Aviv barely half a mile from IDF headquarters, knew nothing of the secret deliberations in the government and the army. On Friday morning, he took a call from Southern Command suggesting that he come down to look at some intelligence data that had been coming in. "One look was enough," he writes in *Warrior.* "Near the canal the Egyptians had concentrated all their crossing equipment, a massive deployment that was quantitatively different from the exercises we had gotten used to watching." "There's no question," he told his divisional intelligence officer, Yehoshua Saguy. "This time it's war."[3]

The next morning at 7:30 they both received their mobilization calls and headed for the division's base camp outside Beersheba. "During the three months since my retirement I had visited the division regularly," Sharon writes, "and only a short while before, I had conducted a training exercise with them. Knowing how competent the headquarters staff was, it was no surprise to find everything in order when I arrived at the base and the mobilization proceeding calmly."

This was one of Sharon's taller war stories. A less tendentious depiction of the scene at the divisional base was "near chaos." There had indeed been an exercise a short while before, and much of the equipment had not been re-stored or, where needed, repaired. "[A young officer] shot the lock off a storeroom with his pistol, and the crew of the command vehicles and the divisional war room charged in and grabbed whatever equipment was lying around . . . Technicians repaired communications gear as best they could."[4]

The tank and armored personnel carrier (APC) crews climbed aboard "and set out on the long drive to Refidim*—on their tracks." There were no flatbed tank transporters at this base and no time to wait for any available ones to be sent. The crews also lacked "goggles, personal weapons, fireproof overalls, torches, blankets."[5] In other reserve bases around the country, the picture was no different. This was not an army primed and poised for war, but rather one that had grown lax and decadent, basking in its overconfidence. The state of the IDF's emergency stores on that fateful Yom Kippur was to be one of the grave episodes of negligence investigated by a commission of inquiry, under the chief justice of the Supreme Court, Shimon Agranat, once the war was over.

"The strongpoints were strongpoints as long as the east bank of the canal was in our hands," Moshe Dayan writes in his memoirs. "Now they became traps for the units caught inside them and surrounded by Egyptian forces." All the passionate struggles over the Bar-Lev Line for years before the war and during the first, terrible days of the fighting are encapsulated in the defense minister's morose observation. The strongholds were still in with a chance, Dayan continues, "if we could succeed within a very short time either in evacuating them or in pushing the Egyptians back out of the east bank. The chief of staff and the CO of Southern Command seemed to think we could. I, sadly, did not share their optimism."

This unshared optimism apparently prompted both Gonen and

---

* The large IDF base in central Sinai.

Mandler to decide against ordering any of the strongpoints to be evacuated during the first twenty-four hours. "The soldiers were begging to be brought out," Sharon wrote, "but the tanks could not do it."

> They had their orders—not to extricate them but only to support the strongpoints and relieve the pressure. Some of the tanks were able to take wounded out. Others simply roared into the Egyptian lines blazing away in a futile attempt to push the enemy back. Suffering terrible losses, the tank crews continued to assault as long as they could. And as second-echelon tanks arrived they too were fed into the carnage . . . In the first twenty-four hours we lost two hundred of our three hundred first-line tanks.
>
> . . . It was outrageous that those men had been left in the strongpoints in the first place. But sending the tanks to support them in that fashion was a clear sign of panic and of an inability to read the battlefield. Instead of gathering our forces for a hard, fast counterattack, we were wasting them in hopeless small-unit actions . . . I began to feel that Gonen's headquarters was not comprehending the situation on the ground.[6]

As soon as he arrived at the front, Sharon began pressing to reverse the no-evacuation order and get the beleaguered men out. This quickly became an early flash point of tension between the 143rd Division and Southern Command. Making matters worse—and unforgettably poignant for everyone who heard those radio exchanges and lived through the war—the men in the strongpoints began addressing their increasingly desperate appeals to Sharon personally. "We recognize your voice, '40' "—this was Sharon's designation on the divisional network—"we know who you are. We know you will get us out of here. Please come to us. Please send us help." One soldier in Purkan, the strongpoint opposite Ismailia, recalled "a moment of exultation when we heard Sharon had arrived. If we'd had champagne we'd have opened it. Just his voice on the radio was like salvation." Sharon for his part promised them, for all to hear, that he would help them get out.

"It took years," Sharon reminded the commission of inquiry in his testimony months later, "until the IDF established the norm that we don't leave the wounded on the battlefield and we don't leave men to fall into the enemy's hands. To me, this matter is of cardinal importance." He said that he had submitted a detailed rescue plan on the afternoon of October 7, "based on the experience of the night before. We would break through on a very narrow front, creating a virtual moving box of fire with tanks and artillery. When we approach the strongpoints, we send a small force in, they get the men out, and we disengage."[7]

"Not only would they [the Command] not approve any attempt at evacuation that afternoon," Sharon recalled bitterly after the war to another of the men trapped in Purkan. "They told me to come and talk about it in the evening, and then they didn't send a helicopter for me. I waited for hours on some sand dune at Tasa until they deigned to send one to take me to Um Hashiba. They deliberately delayed so that I should not be able to raise the subject of the strongpoints at the meeting. I had called the minister of defense and told him that in my view it was possible to rescue the men from the strongpoints."[8]

This delayed helicopter—the Command's explanation was technical problems—became the next point of friction in the already-worsening relationship between Sharon and his erstwhile-subordinate-now-superior, Shmuel Gonen. Sharon repeatedly urged the CO of Southern Command to come up to the front and see the situation for himself. But Gonen preferred to run things from Um Hashiba. Now, on the night of the seventh, with the reserve divisions more or less deployed, they were to have a first war council there in the underground war room and decide on how to parry the Egyptian thrust. Thus far, as Dayan records in his stark, unvarnished tone, "We had not only failed to prevent the Egyptians from crossing; we had hardly hurt them at all. Their casualties . . . were negligible. Hardly any of their equipment had been destroyed. We had barely disrupted their crossing operation."

By the time Sharon arrived, close to 10:00 p.m. for the meeting scheduled for 7:00, the key decisions had been made. Dayan, who did not attend, had been lugubrious all afternoon, trying to persuade the army and the cabinet to abandon the canal altogether and withdraw to a new defensive line based on the Mitle and Gidi passes.

On the Syrian front, where Israel's lines had been breached, too, the defense minister believed there must be no withdrawal.

> It will be hard—but possible. In the south, though, I propose that we stabilize a new line . . . thirty or more kilometers from the canal. I propose that tonight we give orders that those strongpoints which we have no chance of reaching should try to evacuate . . . Those that can't should leave the wounded and try to escape. If they decide to surrender—then so be it. We should say to them, "We cannot reach you. Try to break through or else surrender." Every attempt to reach these strongpoints means losing more tanks. We should withdraw from the canal line with the intention not to return . . . The war will

continue. The Mitle line has its advantages and disadvantages. The canal line, at any rate, is lost.[9]

Chief of Staff Elazar was far from such despondent thinking. He believed the IDF, despite its early and heavy losses, would be able to beat back the Egyptians and eventually take the battle to them across the canal. He did, however, agree with Dayan that the talk—from Gonen and also from Sharon—of Israel crossing the canal in an immediate, large-scale counterattack was premature, unrealistic, and dangerous. If the IDF were to commit the bulk of its depleted southern forces to a cross-canal operation and get bogged down there, there would be precious little preventing the Egyptian forces already in Sinai from marching on toward Tel Aviv.

It was this strategic thinking that lay beneath Elazar's plan for the next day's fighting on the canal front, which he envisaged as an initial, limited counterattack on the Sinai side. He unfurled it before Gonen and his generals (minus Sharon) in the command bunker at Um Hashiba. Bren's division was to attack the Egyptian Second Army along the east bank of the canal, pressing its assault from north to south, starting in the area of Kantara. Sharon's division, deployed around Tasa, would serve as a reserve, supporting Bren if needed. Assuming Bren's attack went well, Sharon's division would then swing into action, attacking the Egyptian Third Army, also from north to south, along the shore of the Great Bitter Lake. Mandler's division would continue blocking attempted breakouts in the south and would support Sharon's attack if needed. "Two feet on the ground," Elazar said repeatedly, "and the third up and attacking."[10]

According to his biographer, Elazar also sketched out his longer-term strategy for the Egyptian front. "I want to attack [across the canal]," he said, "but first we will need to defend when they attack us." He anticipated the Egyptians hurling their heavy armored divisions across the canal, which they were scheduled to do, under their Soviet offense doctrine, once their infantry divisions had fully deployed. "We'll break that attacking force," said Elazar, "and when it has been seriously weakened—then we'll attack."[11]

Sharon met Elazar leaving the command bunker, accompanied by Yitzhak Rabin, the 1967 chief of staff. He immediately began expounding his own basic belief: that it would need a mighty armored fist comprising two whole divisions attacking together to smash through the Second Army and then move down to the Third. One division with the others held in reserve would not be enough. But Elazar rehearsed his view that one division needed to be ready at any time to block an

Egyptian advance toward the heart of the country. Sharon countered that the Egyptians were not aiming for Tel Aviv, but rather to consolidate their gains in Sinai to a depth of five to seven miles. They would not want to step beyond their surface-to-air missile coverage deployed on the west bank.

But Elazar's mind was made up. "Rabin put his hand on my shoulder," Sharon writes. " 'Arik,' he said, 'we're counting on you to change the situation.' With that they shook hands with me and disappeared into the darkness."[12] Sharon went down into the bunker and argued his case for trying again during the night to relieve the strongpoints. Gonen, despite himself, seems to have been affected by Sharon's remonstrations. "He did not turn him down flat," Bren writes, disapprovingly, in his own book on the war. "He said only that at this stage we were not going to approach the strongpoints, though developments during the night might lead to a change in plan." This nuance was to grow to critical importance in understanding what went so terribly wrong the following day.

OCTOBER 8

Gonen was accused by his many critics of arbitrarily changing Elazar's plan when he issued his final orders to his divisions. In his first order, issued during the night, he approved plans submitted by the 143rd Division to rescue the strongpoint crews in its sector—Hizayon, Purkan, and Matzmed*—before Bren began his attack. At dawn, however, he reverted to the original order for the 143rd to stand in reserve while the 162nd attacked. But he left in place, in his orders to the 162nd, the goal of rescuing strongpoints and even attempting a limited crossing. This implied, as Elazar's biographer points out, approaching the canal bank, which Elazar had explicitly forbidden; it implied attacking from east to west, whereas Elazar explicitly and repeatedly ordered a north-to-south attack across a narrow front; and it implied trying to cross the canal, which Elazar had expressly discouraged and hedged with conditions.[13]

Bren's brigades began to move south at 8:00 a.m. But it was far from a divisional armored fist scything through the Egyptian deploy-

---

* Lakekan, on the shore of the Great Bitter Lake to the south of Matzmed, had been successfully evacuated by order of Reshef the previous afternoon (http://www.hativa14.org.il/).

ments. While one brigade did encounter enemy infantry and armor, and engaged them successfully, the two others drove along in uneventful silence. Chaim Herzog writes sourly:

> In the late morning, it suddenly became clear to Bren that his brigades were not moving in accordance with orders and were, in fact, moving too far to the east, along the Artillery Road, and away from the bulk of the enemy forces. Arieh's brigade was actually some 20 miles from the Canal at one stage of the operation.
>
> The result of this mistake was that instead of rolling down the north flank of the narrow Egyptian bridgehead, the massed forces of Bren's division were moving across the front of the Egyptian bridgehead. Accordingly, when the attack was finally launched, it developed from east to west right into the deployed Egyptian positions—instead of from north to south, where the Egyptians least expected it.

The result was a veritable rout. Sharon, deployed in reserve to the west of Tasa, writes that he saw the disaster shaping up:

> At about 9:45 I saw them [the 162nd Division]. But they were not moving along the front a couple of miles east of the canal as I had expected. Instead, the dust columns were rising in back of us, seven or eight miles from the front. I watched as Adan's tanks pressed southward, passed to our rear, and then turned westward toward the Egyptians . . . I was dismayed by what was happening. Only a relatively small number of tanks were involved, perhaps two battalions charging valiantly into the Egyptian artillery fire. It was not a divisional attack; it was not even a concentrated effort. There was no way it could succeed.

"But," Sharon continues, "I did not have much time to worry about it." In a decision that remains essentially inexplicable to the present day, Gonen now ordered Sharon's division to pull back eastward to Tasa and drive south down the Lateral Road for some fifty miles with a view to seizing Egyptian bridges opposite the city of Suez and crossing on them.

> This idea seemed to be that since Adan had now rolled up the Egyptian Second Army, I could smash through the unsuspecting Third Army. It was unreal. First of all Adan had not rolled up anything . . . Second, my division was occupying critical high ground that would cost us dearly to get back if we gave it up. And if we did not get it back

we could forget about any future assault on the canal in this sector. Third, the idea that we might fight our way through to the canal in the south and find intact Egyptian bridges there was based on the merest wishful thinking. And even if we did, we knew the Egyptian bridges were constructed for the lighter Soviet-made tanks and would not support ours . . .

When I got the order to move south, I called Gonen immediately. In the strongest terms I told him that what he was asking would be a disastrous mistake . . . The answer was shouted back. If I didn't obey the order I would be dismissed immediately. Immediately! "Then come down here and look yourself," I repeated. "No!" Gonen shouted. "You will be dismissed. I will dismiss you right now!"

I thought about it for a moment, then decided I had no choice except to obey. So I gave my own order for the division to pull back to Tasa and head south . . . If I had to strike in the south I was going to do it as fast and as hard as I could. But even as I did, I deviated slightly from Gonen's order. Instead of disengaging completely, I left my divisional reconnaissance unit holding two absolutely critical ridges, one code-named Hamadia, the other Kishuf. These positions were on either side of the Akavish Road, which led to the canal in the region of Deversoir. This was where I had prepared the crossing site five months earlier, with its walled "yard" and its thinned-out ramparts. I was simply not going to hand control of these ridges over to the Egyptians.[14*]

Three and a half hours later, and fifty uneventful miles farther south,

a helicopter overflew the column and landed near my APC. A liaison officer from Southern Command climbed out and told me briefly that Adan's attack had failed. There had been no Israeli crossing as had been mistakenly reported to Southern Command . . . We were ordered to get back as fast as possible to support Adan and recover as much of the ridgeline as we could.

My inner feelings at that point were simply not describable. If on

---

* This is another of Sharon's tall war stories. "It was *I* who disobeyed orders," said his deputy divisional commander, General Jackie Even, "*his* orders. And after the war he thanked me for it." In fact, it was two of Sharon's most senior subordinates, Jackie Even and Colonel Gideon Altschuler, who together ensured that a sufficient force remained on the key strategic hill of Hamadia to stave off the Egyptian assaults.

the surface I appeared normal, it was because I was numbed with rage. It was now October 8. Two days earlier the entire division had been called out of their homes and synagogues. In less than twenty-four hours they had fully mobilized and had driven two hundred miles to the battlefield . . . And now, on this absolutely crucial day of battle, they had spent their time driving around the desert like idiots.

As the 143rd Division made its frustrating way back during the afternoon, Bren Adan's battered division was able to regroup and strongly resist Egyptian advances eastward opposite Firdan, taking a significant toll of Egyptian armor and infantry in some of the bitterest fighting of the war. Farther to the south, however, Bren's forces failed to hold the key area of Hamutal, which commands a section of the Talisman road from Tasa to Ismailia. Here, a tragedy of "friendly fire" was only narrowly averted when Bren's retreating forces encountered a brigade from Sharon's division, under Haim Erez, also intent on recapturing Hamutal. Neither brigade was aware of the other. "The confusion on and around Hamutal was tremendous," Bren writes.

Bren was sharply critical of Sharon's behavior once the 143rd Division had returned to within striking distance of the battlefield. He accused Sharon of evading appeals from Gonen that he deploy his unblooded brigades to assist the hard-pressed sister division.

But Bren directed the full brunt of his resentment, recrimination, and disdain at Gonen, accusing him of transmitting overoptimistic, inaccurate, and sometimes wholly fictitious reports to the High Command in Tel Aviv. These were based not on the 162nd Division's reporting to Southern Command, Bren insisted, but on Gonen's strange misunderstanding of the true situation on the battlefield. "Gonen behaved as if we were conducting some kind of war game, an exercise involving no troops—neither ours nor the enemy's—and in which there was no battlefield reality. For him the battle ended the moment he had had his say. The moment he made a decision, he could move ahead to the next stage."[15]

Elazar's approval of Gonen's wildly optimistic plans came after he had himself presented a wildly optimistic picture of Bren's unfolding attack to the cabinet. This fantasy world in Tel Aviv was not to be shattered until late in the evening of October 8. "I want to know," Golda Meir asked her top ministers and generals that night, "has the situation on the canal got better or worse since the morning?" The first, faint reply came from General (res.) Zvi Zamir, head of the Mossad. "My impression is that it hasn't got better . . . Our tanks are being consumed." "And only in the morning they had to 'hold Arik back,' " the prime minister retorted sardonically. The bitter irony in her comment echoes down the decades.[16]

In Gonen's view, the blame for the misreporting up the chain of command lay wholly with Bren, who "never reported to Southern Command on the setbacks he encountered. While he was reporting that everything was all right, key areas of high ground were falling into the Egyptians' hands . . . There was confusion, too, within his division. At one point, a brigade commander Natke Nir told Adan that [a battalion commander Assaf] Yaguri might have crossed the canal, when in fact he had already been taken prisoner and his battalion smashed. My sending Sharon's division south came in the wake of Adan's optimistic reporting."

Gonen denied, moreover, that he had changed the original plan. The main assignment remained destroying the Egyptian forces in Sinai. Bren was ordered, as concomitant assignments, to rescue Hizayon and Purkan and to cross to the other side there. "But the final decision on these was left in his hands, depending on the battlefield conditions, and he acknowledged as much in his response. The failure of his division was not in the assignment but in the execution. He never actually mounted a divisional attack."[17]*

---

* Sharon, in *Warrior,* delivers a trenchant critique of the day's disaster, setting it in the wider context of the cursed *conceptziya* that blighted the post-1967 IDF. He does not expressly include himself among the targets of his grim retrospective. But nor does he entirely exculpate himself. He scarcely could, given the central role he had played in the army over those past six years.

October 8 was the black day of the Israeli Defense Forces, a day that traumatized the army. On the first two days of the war in Sinai, we had suffered defeats. But for those defeats it was easy enough to find scapegoats; poor intelligence, Defense Minister Dayan's miscalculations, the government's errors. October 8, however, belonged to the IDF alone.

The failure stemmed from a combination of major tactical errors and also from an attitude of overconfidence that since the Six Day War had hardened into arrogance. After the victories then, the idea had taken hold that the tank was the ultimate weapon . . . The IDF was overcome by a kind of tank mania. Other combat arms—infantry, armored infantry, and artillery—were neglected. Standard battle doctrines such as ratios of force and concentration of effort were taken less seriously. The commanding idea seemed to be that the business of the Israeli tanks was to charge and the business of the Arab infantry was to run away . . . But this psychological flaw was not Gonen's alone. Adan's Centurion and Patton tanks were hit at long distances by a hail of Sagger missiles and other anti-tank fire. Those that managed to close with the enemy found themselves surrounded by swarms of Egyptians firing Sagger and RPG bazookas. Natke Nir, who led the attack, left eighteen of

. . .

Churning beneath all the arguments and analysis of the events of October 8 was an ugly subtext, replete with political rivalries and personal animosities. It ran through the minds of all the major players at the time and continued to fuel passions and suspicions long after. "They're turning us away [from the canal] deliberately," Sharon said to the officers in his APC when the order came through to head off to the south.

"I know what he thought," the division's chief intelligence officer, Yehoshua Saguy, recalled decades later.

He thought—and in fact he *said*—that they want to head him off because they envisage a great and glorious victory for Bren's forces. And the plain fact is that they did head us off southward. There was no way we were going to reach our ostensible destination in the south before nine or ten o'clock at night. This is a whole division traveling . . . hundreds of tanks and APCs and trucks. To launch an attack there at night would have been suicide.

Don't forget, Arik's not just a general. He's a political figure. He's just set up the Likud . . . After the cease-fire, we were called "the Likud division," and they [the 162nd] were called "the Labor division." Those were the names people used, even on the radio network.* In addition, the tank men were a junta—Dado [Elazar], Gorodish [Gonen], Bren. They stuck together and supported each other automatically.[18]

General Abrasha Tamir, another of Sharon's staff officers, put it even less subtly:

Arik thought Bren was an idiot before the war. He thought Gorodish was crazy before the war. And they thought the same about him. But Bren and Gorodish basked in Dado's favor. He always gave them his backing . . . There's a picture of me standing with Arik on the top of a hill on the first day of the war when we reached the front, with him looking ahead through his binoculars and me with my head turned around looking back. I remember he said to me, "What are you look-

---

his twenty-two tanks burning on the field. It was only by incredible courage that he managed to penetrate to within eight hundred yards of the canal before ordering his few survivors to withdraw in reverse gear, firing as they retreated.

* Saguy himself later entered the Knesset as a Likud member. He served as mayor of Bat Yam, a town bordering Tel Aviv, from 1993 to 2003.

ing at? The enemy's over there" [pointing forward]. And I said, "No, sir. The enemy's not there. The enemy's back here, behind us."[19]

One high-ranking officer who rejected this political subtext, at least as regards the events of October 8, was Sharon's old commander from 1948, Asher Levy. Levy, by now a brigadier general, served as operations officer (the No. 3 man) in the 162nd Division during the first week of the war, after which he was transferred to a senior post at Southern Command headquarters. His appraisal of Bren's performance on the eighth was devastating. He insisted, though, that Elazar's decision to split the two divisions rather than launching a combined two-divisional attack was made "because he genuinely believed we needed to sweep up the Egyptians all the way down the canal. The purpose was not to prevent Arik from crossing on Egyptian bridges . . . The 'war of the generals' started later."[20]

In Tel Aviv the day's disaster gave new impetus to Moshe Dayan's suggestion that Israel abandon the canal and pull back to a new line of defense deep inside Sinai. Other ministers and advisers now seemed prepared to consider it. But Golda Meir was rocklike in her resistance. "I warn us all against planning new defense lines. They won't hold. If we move to some new line inside Sinai, it will not hold." If there was no choice, she said, then of course they would have to dig in farther back. But that was not the situation at the present time, and she would not hear of withdrawal.[21]

The news from the Syrian front was better—though still far from good—and a consensus evolved that Israel must press home its counterattacks on the Golan while containing the Egyptian bridgeheads without initiating further risky and costly operations against them at this stage. This meant the air force would continue to devote most of its efforts to support the forces in the north and to bomb strategic targets inside Syria. Deputy Prime Minister Yigal Allon said it was important to defeat the Syrians quickly so as to deter Jordan and Iraq from entering the fray.

OCTOBER 9–14

The next morning, back from visiting the headquarters in Sinai, Dayan was still grim. "In my best judgment," he reported, "there is no chance of crossing the Canal. In the immediate future we should not try to cross, nor even to approach the Canal and drive back the

Egyptians. We'd pour out our life's blood and it wouldn't make any difference . . . Even Arik agrees that crossing the Canal now will not radically change things."

Elazar, once again, refused to be drawn into despondency. The day before had been a failure, he admitted. Now the divisions in Sinai would be on the defensive. But he hoped the Egyptians would attack—and be broken. Eventually, he insisted, the IDF would cross the canal.

> GOLDA: But when Arik's on the other side, won't he be in a trap?
> ELAZAR: In certain circumstances—yes. Right now, it's not possible. But it might become possible by Wednesday night or Thursday . . . or Friday . . .
> GOLDA: Tell it to me in plastic terms. He crosses; they've got tanks, etc., there; what happens?
> ELAZAR: They'll attack him. He'll go in with two hundred tanks. They won't have aerial superiority . . .
> GENERAL AHARON YARIV: He will neutralize the missiles; he'll destroy a lot of them. The Egyptians will direct part of their force to confront him. If it works, it will be very good.
> GOLDA: What I'm afraid of is if it doesn't work. It'll be a catastrophe. He'll be stuck over there, in their hands.
> ELAZAR: Anyway, it's not doable in the present situation. Only if things improve.[22]

One area where Dayan and Elazar did see eye to eye was the creaking command structure in Sinai. "I don't think Gonen can handle it," the defense minister told the other ministers bluntly, "especially with Arik under him." At a predawn meeting with Elazar, he proposed that either Sharon or Bar-Lev be appointed to head Southern Command.

Elazar, unsurprisingly given their various past histories, plumped for Bar-Lev. The eventual decision was not to depose Gonen but to appoint Bar-Lev over him as "personal representative of the chief of staff"—in effect, commander of the front. For Sharon this was "the last thing I needed to hear . . . I felt I was in a hornets' nest."[23] But for Golda and the ministers, the slow-talking, unflappable Bar-Lev inspired confidence.

Bar-Lev took up his new posting in Sinai on the morning of the tenth. Uri Ben-Ari, Gonen's deputy, later described to army historians the sense of calm he felt almost palpably descending on Southern Command from the moment Bar-Lev took over. "It began at HQ and spread instantly over the radio. Before he came, staff meetings were one long shout from Gonen. Bar-Lev put in place proper work methods. No one questioned his authority. The country owes him a great deal."[24]

The immediate upshot of Bar-Lev's appointment was that Sharon grew even more offhand and insolent toward Gonen. The crisis came on Tuesday, the ninth. "After that there was a complete rupture," according to Yisrael Itkin, who served as the staff sergeant aboard Sharon's command APC. "Arik ordered me not to reply to Gonen's calls. For me this was a really weird feeling. I'm sitting over the radio, and the CO of Southern Command calls and says, 'I know you're there. Answer me!' And Arik signals me with his hand not to answer. On the other hand, he was respectful toward Rabin, Tal, and Dayan. He would talk to them every day. From them he was ready to take any criticism."[25]

The ninth was to be another dramatic day, fraught with suspicion and recrimination among the Israeli commanders that resonated long after the din of battle died down and the dead were buried. "In accordance with the orders I had received," Sharon writes, "in the early morning of October 9, I gave instructions to my three brigade commanders—Amnon Reshef, Haim Erez, and Tuvia Raviv—that we would conduct a holding operation, containing the expected Egyptian advance." Sharon made it clear that he was unhappy with these orders. "For me, this was not the time to sit back and allow the Egyptians to build up their bridgeheads . . . We should be pushing them, probing them for their weak points, looking for openings to exploit." He told the brigade commanders that even while they were defending and containing, "I expected them to use their initiative . . . They should watch for any opportunity to recover the ridgeline positions we had given up the previous day."

In the morning, Reshef executed one of the most breathtaking operations of the war, rescuing thirty-three survivors from the strongpoint of Purkan under the noses of the Egyptian infantry. Sharon had urged their commander, Major Wiezel, to break out under cover of darkness and head for Hamutal, where he would send tanks to pick them up. Reshef himself led the rescuing force, and though many of its vehicles were hit and disabled, one tank made the rendezvous. "With all thirty-three of them clinging to its hull," Sharon wrote, "the tank emerged out of the maelstrom looking like something from an alien world."

Sharon now asked Gonen's permission to strike out along Akavish Road toward the beleaguered strongpoint of Matzmed.* He also told Gonen, quite without foundation, that "Talik's invention"—the steel

---

* Unbeknownst to Sharon and his brigade commanders, Matzmed had in fact fallen earlier that morning.

rolling bridge—would be ready that day. (In fact it would not be ready until the twelfth or thirteenth.) He urged the CO to let his division approach the canal at Matzmed rather than Adan's. "You didn't let us yesterday. So let us this time. We know the terrain very well."[26] An hour later, Chief of Staff Elazar issued a formal and categorical order to Gonen not to get into tank battles and not to approach Matzmed. Gonen transmitted the order to Sharon. He phoned Reshef directly and stressed there must be no further attacks that risked IDF lives.[27]

Raviv's and Reshef's brigades nevertheless engaged in pitched tank battles during the afternoon in order to retake Machshir and Televizia, second-line fortifications northeast of Matzmed that had fallen to the Egyptians the day before. Gonen repeatedly ordered Sharon to stop. He flew by helicopter to Sharon's forward headquarters and ordered him personally to stop. But still the battles continued, the Israeli forces losing tanks but taking a heavier toll of the enemy and nudging steadily west. "After this incident," Herzog writes, "Gonen telephoned the chief of staff asking for Sharon to be relieved of his command."

By evening, Reshef's brigade faced the "Chinese Farm." Reshef ordered the divisional reconnaissance battalion to probe gently forward. "I ordered the probe; Sharon took the credit," Reshef recalled without rancor. "I told him I'm moving the battalion forward, westward, and he said okay." The unit moved gingerly to the southwest, reaching the bank of the Great Bitter Lake and then turning north and driving silently up the bank, until close to the point where the canal feeds into the lake at Deversoir, where Sharon had prepared his "yard." It was a definitive moment. "The probe had revealed the boundary between the Egyptian Second and Third armies," Herzog affirms, "and the soft underbelly of the Second."[28]

"Here if anywhere was a situation that begged to be exploited," Sharon writes.

> The Egyptians had not noticed the reconnaissance unit's penetration. The path to the Canal beckoned—wide and open. At 6:30 p.m. I contacted Gonen to tell him that we were on the water. "Shmulik, we are near the canal," I said into the phone. "Shmulik, we can touch the water of the lake" . . . We were in a position to start bringing assault rafts down from Baluza and preparing the bridging equipment. Right now we could begin organizing for our own crossing. In parallel with Adan's division, we could grab the whole area and push across. Why just sit back and wait for the Egyptians to discover the seam and close it up?

Elazar by this time was following Sharon's operations closely. When he learned of the recon battalion's position and of Sharon's proposals, he exploded. "Get him out of there!" he shouted. "I say he is not to cross. Not to cross! Not to cross!!"[29] At dawn the next morning, Reshef made his reluctant way back to the division.

To Sharon, this reaction to Reshef's remarkable breakthrough reinforced his worst suspicions. "They" would never allow him and his division to cross the canal. "They" were reserving that honor for Bren, one of their own. "They" were determined to link Bren's name, not his, to the hoped-for victory.[30] To judge from the records of the cabinet consultations cited above, however, these suspicions seem groundless, indeed almost paranoid, at least at this stage of the war. Golda, the ministers, and the generals all clearly assumed in those meetings that when and if there was a crossing, Sharon would be the man to make it.

For Elazar at any rate, the overriding concern at this stage was the fact that the main body of Egypt's armor, the Fourth and Twenty-First Armored Divisions, had not yet crossed into Sinai. Better, the chief of staff reasoned—and Haim Bar-Lev fully concurred—to wait patiently for the Egyptian armored divisions to cross, defeat them in battle in Sinai, and only then abruptly shift the focus of the war to the other side.

Sharon's own senior officers also broadly agreed with that military logic, despite their commander's fulminations. "I thought the considerations of the High Command were totally correct," Reshef said. "I didn't feel we were ready to cross," Gideon Altschuler recalled frankly. "I was a product of the British army, where things were done in proper order. Arik would talk to Dayan . . . would try to exert influence so that we'd cross earlier than the chief of staff wanted. I wasn't comfortable with that."[31] Even Abrasha Tamir, who, as we have seen, was entirely at one with Sharon in his conspiracy theory regarding *who* was to cross, was on Bar-Lev's side over *when* to cross. "I thought Bar-Lev was right," Tamir recalled. "What opened the way to our successful crossing was our destruction, effectively, of the Twenty-First Armored Division on October 14. I recognized at the time that Bar-Lev was right and I told Arik as much."[32]

Both Reshef and Jackie Even, the deputy commander of the division, maintained, moreover, that—despite his fulminations—Sharon himself did not seriously intend or attempt to cross before everything was ready and before the High Command gave its assent. Even insisted that Sharon's talk on the ninth of the rolling bridge being ready was pure bluster. "I was his deputy. I was in charge of this business. And I got no order at all from him throughout that day regarding the bridge or other crossing equipment. He clearly did not have any serious intention of crossing then. He was trying to stabilize a defensive line as ordered. He didn't talk to me about any crossing; we both knew there was nothing to cross on. The idea of crossing on Egyptian bridges was nonsense, delusional nonsense."

For his senior officers, the best proof that Sharon was not swept along by his own bluster came a day later, on the tenth. "Sharon presented us three brigade commanders with a plan for attacking the Third Army and trying to drive it off the east bank," Reshef recalled. "I objected outright, and so did Haim Erez. What is Sharon's greatness? He knows we object, yet he takes us with him in the helicopter to Dvela to present the plan. When Arik submitted the plan to Bar-Lev, Bar-Lev asked, 'What do the brigade commanders think?' I said straightaway that I opposed the plan because it would be like banging our head on a wall. I'd already lost a hundred men killed in the brigade. I thought it would be wrong to court more casualties now. Haim Erez also spoke against it."

"Bar-Lev then turns to me," Jackie Even said, continuing his account. "I had worked on the plan together with Sharon and agreed to it. I look at Bar-Lev. I look at Sharon. And I say, 'What I'm hearing from my comrades the brigade commanders is that they're not ready for this assignment. So I say to you, we're not ready.' " Bar-Lev thereupon ruled against Sharon's plan and sent the 143rd Division back to its original assignment, so unloved by its commander: containment and waiting. Sharon was furious, but he swallowed it. "He didn't speak to me for twenty-four hours," Even recalled. "He could have thrown me out for a thing like that. But . . . nothing."

Gonen and Bar-Lev, not disposed like Sharon's admiring officers to discern between his bluster and his obedience, would still have been happier to get rid of him. But Dayan, vacillating and unassertive about so many decisions in the war, stood firm on this one. "I have to admit," he told Elazar, in response to Gonen's demand on the ninth to fire Sharon, "I prefer Arik's pressures and initiatives tenfold to the hesitations and excuses of other divisional commanders."

On the twelfth, Bar-Lev tried his hand. He, too, urged the chief of staff to fire Sharon. Elazar, after all, had specifically asked his "personal representative on the southern front" to make a recommendation on this fraught matter. But Elazar would not act on his own authority. Once again, he took it to Dayan, knowing, presumably, what the response would be. And sure enough, Dayan demurred. In Chaim Herzog's words, "Dayan said that such a move could create political problems."[33] Bar-Lev, never one to ventilate his emotions, took this expected rebuff in stride. His biographer has him going off to sleep at one point during this waiting period, with the explanation that "a tired general is a stupid general," and leaving orders "to wake me only if Arik makes trouble."[34]

During the four days that now followed of relatively low-key warfare on the southern front, from October 10 to 13, the Egyptian infantry pushed forward time after time in local attacks, backed by armor and artillery. Each time they were driven back, often with heavy losses. They made no further territorial gains.

As the IDF regained its balance and its confidence, Dayan's idea of a strategic withdrawal to the passes finally receded. The cabinet and the High Command waited anxiously for the Egyptians to commit their main armored strength to the battle for Sinai. Time was becoming critical. If the two superpowers jointly resolved to impose a cease-fire, their client-protagonists would hardly be able to balk. The Syrians certainly had nothing more to gain from an extended war. Their forces had been pushed back beyond the prewar line, and Israeli long-range artillery threatened the suburbs of their capital, Damascus. Israel, too, could not long go on hemorrhaging the blood of its young men.[*] The home front, laboring under near economic paralysis, had yet to assimilate the true figures of dead and wounded sustained thus far.

Yet without a turnabout on the canal front, the war in the south, if it ended now, would end as a defeat. It would be Israel's first-ever battlefield defeat—with all the psychological and political ramifications that that could entail. On October 12 in Tel Aviv, the top ministers and military commanders convened to grapple with this quandary. As good luck would have it, the first intelligence reports of an Egyptian crossing started to come in while their meeting was still in progress. Units of the Fourth and Twenty-First Armored Divisions were beginning to move across the canal. There were indications that they intended to mount a major attack and try to strike deeper into Sinai. Presumably, Anwar Sadat was acting to take the pressure off his Syrian ally, now reeling under IDF counterattacks. This was the news the cabinet had been waiting for.

Both divisions in central Sinai, the 143rd and the 162nd, now braced to take on the Egyptian armored columns. This occasioned a

---

[*] Among the fatalities during this waiting period was General Mandler, killed by artillery fire on his command vehicle on October 13. Kalman Magen was immediately appointed in his place to command the southern division.

visit by Bren to Arik's headquarters, where, he writes primly, he was "reminded that 'civilization' still continued to exist." First, Amnon Reshef talked him into taking a shower at the empty base camp of the Fourteenth Brigade nearby. "I'd gotten used to the dirt and the unshaven cheeks," Bren writes, "and had almost forgotten there were showers in the world." Then, as he waited for Chief of Staff Elazar to arrive at Sharon's bunker at Tasa, "one of Sharon's officers turned to me and said it was time to taste some of the delectable cheeses. And, indeed, there was a rich and impressive assortment to choose from."[35]

The great armored encounter, when it finally came on October 14, was "one of the largest tank battles ever to take place in history," according to Herzog, "with some 2,000 tanks locked in battle across the entire front." Once again, Reshef's brigade was in the thick of the fighting. But this time the tide of battle was unmistakable. Deployed on higher ground in front of Hamadia and waiting patiently until the vast Egyptian armored column rolled into range, Reshef's tanks culled dozens of the enemy armor. He used the divisional reconnaissance battalion, reinforced by additional tanks, to hit them from the flank. By the end of the engagement, the Egyptians had lost more than a hundred tanks to Reshef's three. The First Brigade of the Twenty-First Armored Division was effectively destroyed.

To the north, Bren's division made major gains, too, blocking and crushing Egypt's Twenty-Third Mechanized Division. In the south, another Egyptian armored brigade, advancing toward the Mitle, was ambushed by armor and infantry forces under Magen, while the Israeli Air Force, beyond ground-to-air missile range in that theater, pounded them from above. "Within two hours," Herzog writes, "some sixty Egyptian tanks and a large number of APCs and artillery pieces were in flames." Bar-Lev telephoned Golda. "It's been a good day," he reported. "Our forces are themselves again and so are the Egyptians."[36] For Dayan, the final tally of some 260 Egyptian tanks was still lower than he had hoped. Not all the top-of-the-line Egyptian forces had yet been committed. But the IDF had shown that it was finally learning to deal with the Egyptian infantry's antitank missiles, particularly the wire-guided Sagger, which had been deployed to such devastating effect in the first days of the war. Israel's own infantry, moreover, was proving effective with its SS11-type antitank missiles.

The cabinet convened that evening for what everyone present understood would be a fateful meeting. Dayan, previously hesitant, now unequivocally recommended approving "Noble Hearts," the plan for an Israeli crossing at Deversoir. Some of the ministers were still worried by the thought of a sizable Israeli force being stranded on the far side of the canal. Elazar said the issue of bridges was still the weak point. Could they be gotten there in time? How would they survive Egyptian bombing and shelling? But they would have more than one bridge, he assured the ministers. "My best analysis of all the facts tells me the prospect of failure is very low and the chances of success are good."

The cabinet sat and pondered till long after midnight. In the end, taking Prime Minister Meir's lead, almost all of the ministers voted in favor. But what precisely did Noble Hearts, in its current form, envisage? More specifically, how many divisions were to cross? One or two? If two, then when? And in what order? These key questions were not unequivocally and explicitly answered. Elazar told the cabinet on the night of the fourteenth that "in the first stage only one division will cross, and if it carries out its assignment successfully it will open the way for the second division."[37]

The discussions on the fourteenth, both in the cabinet and within the army command, seemed to assume a one-divisional crossing—by the 143rd Division. But even before the first soldier had set his boot down on "Africa," the commander of the front, Bar-Lev, suggested vaguely that perhaps both the 143rd and the 162nd—Arik and Bren—should take part in the operation, with Bren's division crossing the canal while Sharon's division broadened and defended the eastern bridgehead.

This obfuscation, as we shall see, became the cause of friction, suspicion, and jealousy for the remainder of the war and long thereafter. Sharon, his senior officers, and his political "hinterland" back home accused the High Command, and especially the Labor Party minister Bar-Lev, of deliberately holding him back and pushing Bren forward in order to deny him, the Likud politician, the glory of the victory. Conversely, Sharon's rivals accused him—the Likud politician—of deliberately pushing himself forward and attempting to deny Bren his rightful place in the roll of honor.

OCTOBER 15–16

At Tasa the next morning, Sharon went over his plans with Bar-Lev and Gonen:

> My division would break through the Egyptian lines, secure a corridor to the canal, and establish a crossing point at Deversoir on the

east bank—at precisely the location where the reconnaissance unit had penetrated six days earlier. Meanwhile, rubber assault boats would be brought forward to ferry Danny Matt's paratroop brigade to the west bank. Once the paratroops had secured the area, a pontoon bridge would be laid across the canal and Haim Erez's tank brigade would cross. The great reconstructed rolling bridge would also be towed into place and pushed across.

On the northern edge of the opening, two east-west roads ran to the water line . . . One, code-named Akavish, connected Tasa with the shore of the Great Bitter Lake. About five miles to the east of the canal another road started and ran parallel to and north of Akavish. This road, code-named Tirtur, had been especially laid out for towing the 600-ton steel roller bridge to the canal. Its terminus on the water line was just above the enclosed yard I had prepared in May as the staging area for a crossing. These two roads, Akavish and Tirtur, would constitute our corridor to the canal. Along them we would have to move two divisions and all the crossing equipment.

Directly south of Akavish was the undefended seam between the two Egyptian armies, so we had plenty of maneuvering room on that side. But on the northern edge of the seam, Tirtur Road skirted the perimeter of the Second Army bridgehead, and this perimeter was very heavily defended. Here the Egyptians had established a major fortified base known as "Missouri," whose southwestern anchor was an area we called the "Chinese Farm"—an agricultural station set up with Japanese equipment years earlier. This Chinese Farm . . . sat on the Tirtur Road and on the junction of Tirtur and Lexicon, the communication road that ran parallel to the canal bank. The deep irrigation ditches and the mounds of dirt thrown up when they were excavated made this a natural defensive site where machine guns and anti-tank weapons could dominate the field.

The strange, slightly comical code names—*akavish* means "spider," *tirtur* means "clatter"—were to become etched on the Israeli public mind like Antietam and Monte Cassino, with all the pride but also all the grief and the heart searching that those names evoked among the victors of those terrible battles. The technical, euphemistic term that Sharon uses, "secure a corridor," was to translate into bloody and costly fighting in the nights and days ahead.

My plan . . . was to attack at dusk and fight the main battle during the night. Tuvia Raviv's tank brigade would assault Missouri from the east, a head-on thrust that would appear to the Egyptians very much what they expected. But in fact Tuvia's attack would be a diversion, meant to draw their forces and attention. At the same time, Amnon Reshef's brigade would execute a hook to the southwest through the unoccupied gap between the Egyptian armies, then north into the rear of the Egyptian base area. Here his missions were to secure the yard as a crossing site, push the Egyptians northward, and open up Tirtur and Akavish from west to east—that is, from behind. With the roads clear, Danny Matt's paratroop brigade would move into the yard along with the assault boats and cross the canal. Once the paratroop bridgehead was secure, engineers would push the bridges across.

It was a brilliant plan, reminiscent in its daring and complexity of the multipronged nighttime attack on Abu Agheila in the Six-Day War. And despite every form of snafu and misfortune, the glaring lack of battlefield intelligence, and the yawning gaps that opened, perhaps inevitably, between the plan and the reality, in essence it worked. By dawn of the sixteenth, the paratroopers were across, fortifying their eerily peaceful bridgehead. So were Haim Erez's tanks, foraging as deep as eighteen miles into the countryside, overrunning missile batteries and radar sites, cutting a swath of Israeli control through the Egyptian rear.

But as Sharon outlined his tactics on the morning of the fifteenth, speaking with fluent confidence, the unresolved dilemma lurked into focus.

SHARON: The order of crossing will be 421 (Erez), and then 600 (Tuvia) and then 14 (Reshef).
BAR-LEV: Just a minute. How's that? How's that?
SHARON: 421's at the bridge already . . .
BAR-LEV: No, no. You're not transferring three [brigades]?!
SHARON: No, no. I'll leave [forces] here. I suppose I'll leave a battalion of tanks. It depends . . .
BAR-LEV: No, no. You'll leave a brigade.
SHARON: Okay, then I'll leave 600 Brigade.

Sharon continued talking, assuring his superiors that the operation is "complicated but doable." He talked about the rolling bridge and the self-propelled rafts and the Gilowa amphibious tugs cum rafts, and the need to get the forces across to the west bank "on whatever is available" as soon as they reached the canal shore. But Bar-Lev, as slow speaking as Sharon was fast, hauled him back to the east bank again.

BAR-LEV: Now, regarding the brigade that remains here . . . who secures the bridgehead?

SHARON: 600 does the containment.

BAR-LEV: And what infantry remains here to secure the bridgehead?

SHARON: I'll leave a battalion of paratroopers . . .

BAR-LEV: Have they got those LOW [antitank] missiles?[38]

The contours of the looming dispute are already discernible: Who crosses? Who stays to defend the eastern bridgehead? Who breaks out to the west and cuts off the enemy army? The war against Egypt was about to be turned around. It was a great martial triumph for Israel. But the triumph was marred—some claim actually diminished—by the "war of the generals" that seethed within the Israeli camp.

October 15 was the fifth day of the eight-day Jewish festival of Sukkot, or Tabernacles. "As we headed toward the front," Sharon writes, "we passed dozens of jerry-rigged Sukkot huts. Traditionally these huts are made of branches and foliage and are hung with the season's harvest. Often they are elaborate and elegant. But for this Sukkot in the Sinai, ammunition cases and packing crates were the main building material, supplemented by an occasional scraggly bush the soldiers had managed to dig up from the desert."

Amnon Reshef's much-mauled brigade had been beefed up for this operation with additional units. He had four tank battalions under him and three more of mechanized infantry. "We knew they had two divisions at Missouri, the Sixteenth Infantry and the Twenty-first. But they were just large eggs on our maps. We didn't know precisely how and where they were deployed. I hoped to slide through like a knife, from the rear, where we were least expected."

The reconnaissance battalion slid through, the sound of its clanking treads drowned by the din of battle raging to the north where Raviv's 600th Brigade had launched its diversionary attack on Missouri. The battalion swung out wide, crossed Tirtur, and headed on toward the canal shore at Matzmed, ready to assist the paratroopers' crossing. Reshef himself, with two other tank battalions, now also crossed Tirtur from the south, also without incident, and hurried north to engage the Egyptian positions in Missouri. The next battalion, however, the 184th, suddenly found itself under murderous fire as it followed north. "I'm with half the brigade," Reshef recalled, "and we're in a major tank battle north of Akavish. Tanks are exploding and burning all

Map of Suez Canal Crossing

October 15-16, 1973

- Town
- Road, Axis
- ▲ Idf Strongpoint
- ○ Areas of strategic importance
- → Sharon's Division
- ⇢ Egyptian Army
- Freshwater canal

Kantara

Milano

Mifreket

Artillery Road

SINAI

Hizayon

Suez Canal

Lexicon Road

Artillery Road

Egyptian 2nd Army

○ Machshir

Ismailia

Purkan

Lexicon Road

Hamutal ○

Artillery Road

Talisman Road

Televizia ○

Tasa ▲

Missouri

Akavish Road

"Chinese Farm"

Hamadia ○

Suez Canal

EGYPT

Tirtur Road

Lexicon-Tirtur crossroad

Akavish Road

Kishuf ▲

to Cairo

Deversoir

"The Matzmed Yard"

Lakekan

Egyptian 3rd Army

Great Bitter Lake

Um Hashib ("Dvela")

Botzer ▲

Little Bitter Lake

Gidi Pass

0   10   20 km

to Suez

Lituf ▲

Mitle Pass

around. I'm looking at Egyptian tanks from a range of two meters. I'm looking at dozens of Egyptian soldiers."

"Unknown to Reshef," Chaim Herzog explains, "his force had moved into the administrative center of the 16th Egyptian Infantry Division, to which the 21st Armored Division had also withdrawn after being so badly mauled on October 14. His force found itself suddenly in the midst of a vast army . . . Pandemonium broke out in the Egyptian forces. Thousands of weapons of all types opened fire in all directions and the whole area as far as the eye could see seemed to go up in flames."[39]

Behind Reshef and his troops, the Tirtur-Lexicon crossroad was blocked by intense and sustained Egyptian fire. Efforts by Reshef's infantry battalions to open Tirtur from west to east resulted in repeated, costly failure. The reconnaissance battalion, fighting to free up the crossroads, also sustained mounting casualties.

"From 9:00 p.m. to midnight we fought like madmen," Reshef continued:

I was shooting nonstop, and every one of my men likewise. From Sharon—hardly a sound. This was his greatness. If he trusted someone, he'd let them get on with it and didn't pester. Once or twice, pleasantly and politely, he would say to me over the radio that it was really important that we opened Tirtur. And I'd say, "It'll be all right, Arik. I'm working on it." And he said, "I always know that with you there everything will be all right." He heard how we were fighting, at ranges of half a meter. It was like inside hell. Thousands of men fighting for their lives.

At one juncture, Reshef, in his command tank, believed he was joining one of his own companies when suddenly, at a distance of fifty meters, he saw they were enemy tanks. "I knocked out all five of them," he recalls matter-of-factly.

"Did you contact Sharon and tell him?"

"I told him I'd knocked out three."

"What was his reaction?"

"He was pleased. I told him in order to boost his morale."[40]

Morale, that intangible but all-important substance, was what decided the 143rd Division's battle that night, and with it the war. As Reshef and his brigade fought their vastly more numerous foe, Sharon himself, just a few miles to the south, led Danny Matt's paratroopers into the "yard." "Unnoticed," Sharon recalls in *Warrior*, "we entered into the protection of the yard's sand walls. Though we did not know it, behind us the reconnaissance battalion was dying in a barrage of Sagger missiles and tank fire. By 1 a.m. lead elements of the paratroopers had started crossing to the west bank in their rubber assault boats. On the other side of the canal the troopers found the area almost deserted. We had taken the Egyptians utterly by surprise. As they established their beachhead, the paratroopers radioed back the code word Acapulco—Success."

By this time, the first Gilowas were lumbering into the yard. With the traffic backed up for miles on the road from Tasa and only one of the two access roads to the canal open, Sharon had ordered his deputy, Jackie Even, to have these amphibious tugs* "jump the queue."

Inside the yard the bulldozers had been unable at first to breach the wall, until I pointed out the red bricks that marked the specially thinned area. Now they were digging fiercely at the ramparts, while the engineers had already started wrestling with the bridging equipment. A unit of antiaircraft machine guns had taken up positions on the walls ready for the air attacks that we knew would come in the morning. Elements of Haim Erez's tank brigade were also crowding into the enclosure, waiting to join the paratroopers on the other side. Akavish was open; it was along that road that the paratroopers, rafts, and tanks had made their way into the yard. But Tirtur—crisscrossed by the Chinese Farm—was still shut tight.

Tirtur was extremely important. It was only along this road that the giant rolling bridge could be towed to the canal, while the extension of Tirtur to the canal bank itself had been especially prepared as a launching site for the bridge . . . But as Amnon's units hammered all night at the Egyptians in the Chinese Farm, it became clear that we simply did not have the strength to dislodge them from Tirtur itself. For the moment, at least, we would have to rely on Akavish to conduit men and armor toward the crossing site.

The morning of October 16 dawned on the most terrible sight I had ever seen . . . As the sky brightened, I looked around and saw hundreds and hundreds of burned and twisted vehicles. Fifty Israeli tanks lay shattered on the field. Around them were the hulks of 150 Egyptian tanks plus hundreds of APCs, jeeps, and trucks. Wreckage littered the desert. Here and there Israeli and Egyptian tanks had destroyed each other at a distance of a few meters, barrel to barrel. It was as if a hand-to-hand battle of armor had taken place. And inside

---

* See above, p. 88.

those tanks and next to them lay their dead crews. Coming close, you could see Egyptian and Jewish dead lying side by side, soldiers who had jumped from their burning tanks and died together. No picture could capture the horror of the scene, none could encompass what had happened there. On our side that night we had lost 300 dead and hundreds more wounded. The Egyptian losses were much, much heavier.

. . . At almost the same moment . . . the bulldozers broke through the last of the ramparts, opening the yard to the canal. And now, directly in front of us across two hundred yards of water was Egypt . . . On our side everything was barren sand and dust. On theirs the palm trees and orchards grew in lush profusion around the Sweet Water Canal. From where we stood it looked like paradise.

During the night we had managed to get Danny Matt's entire paratroop brigade to the western side of the canal. Now they were quickly joined by a number of APCs and twenty-eight of Haim Erez's tanks, which were ferried over on rafts. As soon as they landed, Haim's armor raced westward, destroying the surprised Egyptian units and positions that had the misfortune to be in their path. By nine o'clock they reported they had eliminated five ground-to-air missile sites, tearing a gaping hole in the Egyptian anti-aircraft umbrella that had effectively closed this area to Israeli jets. Now they were marauding at will, picking off the last Egyptian units in the area. Nothing stood in their way; the region west of the canal was virtually empty. Haim's voice came over the radio: "We can get to Cairo" . . .

Inside the yard and in the canal opening, engineers were working like mad, directing traffic, widening the breach, getting tanks, men, and supplies onto the rafts and across to the other side. A race was on. The Egyptians were still not aware of what we had done. They were not trying to interdict the crossing, and as yet there was no pressure on the yard itself.

It was right in the middle of this frenzy of activity that an order came through from Southern Command that was so outrageous I at first refused to believe it. All crossing activity, it said, was to cease immediately. Not a single additional tank or man was to be transferred. According to them, we were cut off, surrounded by Egyptian forces.[41]

The next battle in the "war of the generals" was shaping up, threatening to dull the heroism and sacrifice of the night's titanic struggle.

· · ·

The rolling bridge, or "the 600-ton monster lying on its belly," as the 143rd Division's deputy commander, Jackie Even, dubbed it, was a doubly beached whale that night. Tirtur, the ruler-straight access road forking off from Akavish, remained closed. And the tank battalion detailed to drag it along was neither trained nor qualified to do so. "We were Pattons," Even explained. "American M60s. The tanks originally trained to drag the bridge were British Centurions from the Seventh Brigade. But they had been sent to the Golan before the war to reinforce positions there."

During the morning, Sharon kept hurling the remnants of Reshef's brigade at Tirtur, bolstered by battalions from the 600th and the 421st. But to no avail. Even when Reshef finally took the crossroads at Lexicon, the road east remained impassable, at the mercy of the Egyptian artillery and armor deployed in Missouri to the north. He suffered still more casualties. Sharon asked for reinforcements from Bren's division.

By now, the High Command had decided on a radical change to Noble Hearts: Sharon's division would not be crossing the canal; Bren's would instead. Sharon's division would be tasked with widening the eastern bridgehead and defending it. For the moment, Bren's division would help with this while preparing to cross.

In the late afternoon, Reshef and Sharon, both bone tired and both at once exultant over the initial crossing and devastated over the casualties, met on the battlefield, overlooking the crossroads. It was a moment of profound emotion and of intense comradeship. It remained engraved on Reshef's memory, despite the subsequent vicissitudes in their relationship—and despite the incongruity of the gourmet feast they consumed amid all the carnage and destruction:

> We're sitting on the tank engine. His guys bring us food. Arik had two four-by-four Wagoneers. One for milk and one for meat! Because you mustn't mix swiss cheeses with Hungarian horse-meat sausages! It's not kosher!! Anyway, he had two separate vehicles full of food. It was Lily's doing really.
>
> They hand up the food . . . all sorts of delicatessen, and the two of us are talking and eating. He talks, and I fall asleep. I talk, and his head lolls. Somebody comes and tells us that they're sending in the 890th Paratroop Battalion—attached to the 162nd Division—into the Chinese Farm, attacking on the east side of it. He was pretty astonished, I think. He couldn't understand it. But both of us were too tired to analyze it anymore. We didn't have the facts.

Reshef said he wanted to cross, too, and Sharon said he wanted him to as soon as possible, as soon as his brigade was relieved. "In the end, it took several days—because they didn't let our division cross," Reshef recalled, dredging up the old recriminations decades later.

They transferred the other division first. Arik wanted us to cross first. He believed in us. He wasn't going to send me across in defiance of his orders, but he wanted me to be relieved so I could cross. And so did I. I'd taken a sort of oath: I was the one who tried to stop the original Egyptian onslaught on Yom Kippur, and now I wanted to cross over first into Egypt. Yes, Erez had crossed already. But Erez was our comrade, from our division. I wasn't jealous of him. But I wanted to be next in line after him. Yes, someone's got to fight against Missouri. But I'd been doing that since the first day of the war.[42]

The paratroop attack on the Chinese Farm that night, which Sharon and Reshef spoke of but failed to take action to prevent—it was under Bren's command—became, for Israelis, one of the most famous and tragic battles of the war. The heroism of the men of the 890th Battalion under Yitzhak Mordechai* furnished books, songs, and legends for a generation and more. The battalion was cut to pieces. Forty of its men died in fourteen hours of incredible tenacity against hopeless odds. A hundred more were injured. Historians and old soldiers still pick over the records, trying to understand what went wrong. The core mystery centers on the informational lacunae. How was it possible that word of the 143rd Division's desperate battles there the night and day before, involving both armor and infantry—including paratroopers—apparently failed to reach the 162nd Division, deployed nearby?

It was a near-suicidal assignment, probably superfluous, and plainly conceived in profound error. But it could justly be crowned a success, indeed a historic victory. While the paratroopers fought and died to try to free up Tirtur, just behind them on Akavish a convoy of uni-float rafts† was being tenaciously dragged and pushed toward the canal. Together they would form the bridge on which, the next day, the 162nd Division crossed into Egypt, thus finally clinching the turnabout in the war. The blood of the paratroopers had not flowed in vain.

It was a disaster nevertheless, and Sharon's officers had no hesita-

---

* He rose to become a general and, later, minister of defense (1996–1999).
† See p. 87.

tion in bad-mouthing Bren for it. After all, he had assumed overall responsibility for securing the roads to the canal. The episode brought the underlying tensions and recriminations among the generals into even sharper relief. The order that morning, so hateful and misguided in Sharon's eyes, to stop the crossing had come from both Gonen and Bar-Lev. "As long as there's no bridge, there's no crossing" is how Jackie Even remembered Bar-Lev's fiat. "I'm not transferring the IDF aboard those Gilowas!" Chief of Staff Elazar reacted in the same way—increasingly so during the day as the strength of the Egyptian resistance at Missouri/Chinese Farm became clearer. "As long as we do not have a safe and stable bridge, we will hold on to the west bank with limited forces only," he ruled.

Elazar was angry that the situation at Missouri was not made clear to him in real time. He was bitter and furious at what he felt was glib and inadequate reporting by Sharon's division—both about the true state of the roads and about the true intensity of the resistance they had encountered. He was even angrier to hear that Sharon was vociferously criticizing the order to stop the crossing until a bridge was up. Sharon's officers were saying that a whole division could have crossed on the Gilowas—had the High Command not wasted this crucial day with its overcautious hesitations.[43]

To Sharon, Elazar and Bar-Lev were indeed squandering the military opportunity that his division had paid much blood to create. The whole strategy of crossing, he argued, was designed to throw the enemy off balance and recapture the initiative. He had successfully plunged through the gap between the two Egyptian armies. Surprise had been total—and was still in effect. Despite Haim Erez's vigorous rampage on the western shore, the bridgehead on both banks was still amazingly quiet and peaceful. This was the time to exploit the breakthrough by pouring more and more armor and supplies over to the other side. Granted, there was no bridge yet, and no real prospect of getting one up soon. But the Gilowas were doing the job.

OCTOBER 17–22

"October 16 could have been the day of our real triumph," Sharon writes.

But it was not. Instead, after the previous night's immense efforts, the advance was halted. That day and more than that day were wasted . . . That night, exhausted and morose, I went to sleep on the warm engine cover of a tank. Early on the morning of the seventeenth I was awakened by the sound of self-propelled rafts being towed into the yard. They were a welcome sight. With enough of these rafts on hand we would now be able to assemble the bridge. Once that was done, we might finally be able to change some minds about getting our forces across fast, even though by this time surprise was no longer with us.

That last assessment was now violently confirmed with a sudden and intense artillery bombardment of the yard.

Almost simultaneously MiG fighters swarmed over the yard in an attack that turned the compound into an inferno . . . Suddenly I felt a smashing pain on my forehead. But an instant later my eyes opened and I realized that whatever had hit me was just a glancing blow. Though my head was bleeding heavily, nothing else seemed wrong . . .

I felt I had to get the command vehicles out of there. The fire was so heavy that our aerials were taking hits and we were in danger of losing radio control. So I ordered them to the gate area . . . As I looked I realized that while inside the yard we were under artillery fire, outside the vehicles were being hit by direct flat-trajectory tank fire . . . Through my binoculars I looked toward the road junction several hundred yards away and was shocked to see an Egyptian counterattack of tanks and supporting infantry coming directly toward us. It was an absolutely critical moment. These Egyptians were about to close the yard behind us. The only force I had under my hands at that instant was the command APCs, those five M113s.

Sharon described how they charged the junction, all their machine guns blazing, and somehow held off the advancing Egyptians for a few precious minutes until a rescuing force of Israeli armor swung into view and drove them off.

His forehead swathed in bandages and his heart racing from this narrow escape, Sharon was now summoned to a consultation at a point several miles back from the canal.

When we got to the co-ordinates on the dunes, I saw waiting for me Moshe Dayan, Haim Bar-Lev, David Elazar, and Avraham Adan. As I approached, nobody said a word—except Dayan, who greeted me with a normal, friendly "Shalom, Arik." I hadn't seen any of them since the fourteenth. Since that day virtually the entire crossing battle had been carried out by my division alone. But now there was not a single word or an outstretched hand. Just silence.

Then Bar-Lev said, very quietly and deliberately, "The distance between what you promised to do and what you have done is very great." At that moment I felt tired to death . . . I knew there was only one thing to do. I had to smack Bar-Lev in the face. I felt I just had to do it.

To this day I do not know how I kept myself from hitting him. Instead, I simply clamped my mouth shut. After a moment more of silence, a short discussion took place and they decided to do what they should have done two days earlier. Very soon the pontoon bridge would be completed. Now we could proceed across the canal. My division would hold the yard, secure the corridor, and proceed north on the west bank of the canal toward Ismailia, and westward twenty-five to thirty kilometers in the direction of Cairo. Adan and Kalman Magen would cross the bridge and would proceed southward around the shores of the Great Bitter Lake to the rear of the Egyptian Third Army. It was a brief exchange. When it was over, Gonen, Bar-Lev, and Elazar got into their helicopter and flew off. Adan mounted his APC to go back to his division. I was there alone with Moshe Dayan . . . He asked me about my head. It was, at least, a human interaction.[44]

Perhaps it was the sight of his head that momentarily dehumanized the others. Perhaps they realized that the bloodstained bandage, with Arik's telltale gray locks peeking out from on top of it, was about to become one of the iconic images of this war—in Israel and throughout the world. With one superficial head wound, Sharon had dealt his rivals a mortal blow in the public-relations race for glory.

The "war council on the dunes" should have been the moment of greatest gratification, when the principal commanders paused to rejoice together as they finally set about turning the tables on the enemy. Instead, they could barely speak a civil word to one another. In the days that followed, as the military situation improved, their relations continued to deteriorate. The cease-fire with Egypt and Syria, on October 22, ushered in an even more public and acrimonious round in the "war of the generals."

Dayan, at any rate, remained with Sharon for a couple of hours and visited with him in "Africa." He could scarcely have failed to sense the outpouring of love and adulation for the divisional commander wherever they went. The simplistic but evocative sobriquet "Arik, king of Israel,"* was already making the rounds of the division. Within days it would be on all the soldiers' lips and on makeshift banners hung from their tanks.

Dayan, describing the "war council on the dunes" in his own memoirs, supplies the recognition and appreciation that the other generals could not bring themselves to utter. "Sharon's division had fought with total self-sacrifice," he writes.

> It had suffered very heavy casualties, but it had not wavered from its assignments. Its soldiers had conquered the bridgehead on the eastern bank in devastating armored battles. All of the men—from Arik and his staff to the last field unit—were under constant bombardment. In the battles for the eastern bridgehead the division had lost some two hundred men. In Amnon Reshef's brigade all the senior commanders were killed and replaced twice over. The company commanders were now the "third generation." Dozens of the brigade's tanks had been hit and left burned out and destroyed at Lakekan, at Matzmed, and at the Chinese Farm.

Within hours of the "council on the dunes," tensions were running high again, this time over what Sharon and his staff regarded as Bren's sluggishness—unpardonable in the circumstances, they maintained—in crossing the canal *even once the bridge of rafts was up*. "At 1600 the bridge was ready," Jackie Even recalled, "and nothing happened! Total silence. I'm screaming at Bren on the radio that we're open for business, and no one comes. For seven hours no one came."

Bren's division had been fighting all day against a determined Egyptian effort to break out of Missouri and cut off the Israeli eastern bridgehead by severing both Akavish and Tirtur. In the afternoon, a separate Egyptian attack, by the Third Army's Twenty-Fifth Armored Brigade, was mounted from the south. Reshef lay in wait for the Egyptian column, and he was supported by two of Bren's brigades, the 217th under Natke Nir and the 500th under Arieh Keren. It was an important battle and ended in a huge success for Israel with more than eighty Egyptian tanks knocked out.

Regrouping, refueling, and reorganizing after these battles naturally took Bren's brigades hours, and it was nearly midnight by the time the 162nd Division began its crossing.

---

* The original slogan, millennia old, applied to the biblical king David.

Even recalled:

At last, Bren arrives with his command unit and another brigade. And Natke Nir also begins arriving. The Egyptians must have twigged what was going on, and a bombardment from hell opens up on us. The whole area seems to be burning. It's midnight, but it's light like day. I say to myself, "Whether you die or not, if this operation doesn't succeed, everything is lost." After Bren and the first brigade are across, the bridge is hit and breaks apart. A tank on a raft is hit and sinks with its crew inside. Gilowas—now ferrying Bren's tanks across—are hit and several sink. I'm in the middle of the bridge, on my own with no engineer officers. Our people are being killed and wounded all around me. I maneuver a bridging tank into position to span the break in the bridge—and the division continues to cross . . . The cries of the wounded mingle with the crashing of shells, but I say to myself, "We've won the war." Getting the 162nd over to the other side, to join the force already over there, was the event that won the war. I had this feeling of sudden, total relief. We'd won.[45]

The next day, in hard battles against Egyptian reinforcements rushed in from around Cairo, the 162nd Division broke out of the west bank bridgehead and surged west, intent on swinging down the coast of the Great Bitter Lake to the south and cutting off the Third Army from the rear. It was joined later by elements of Magen's division, striking out farther to the west and then sweeping south. Together in the days ahead they would advance down the coast and cut the Cairo–Suez road that was the Third Army's vital supply route. An attempt to take the city of Suez itself ended in costly failure.

"Of course," Sharon writes bitterly, "by the time Adan broke out of the bridgehead the Egyptians had managed to concentrate forces opposite him. And what could have been done so easily on the sixteenth and even on the seventeenth became a hard and costly job on the eighteenth."[46]

Back in Tel Aviv, Dayan batted away renewed efforts by Gonen and Bar-Lev, working through Elazar, to engineer Sharon's removal. With the end of the war in sight, the defense minister told the chief of staff, it simply wasn't going to happen.

Sharon, meanwhile, was preparing to send Reshef's brigade across the canal at last, to join Erez. Crossing was no longer a problem: the huge roller bridge was finally dragged to the canal, and on the morning of the nineteenth it spanned the two banks about half a mile north of the pontoon bridge made from the self-propelled rafts. Reshef and

Erez, together with Danny Matt's paratroopers, were to press north toward Ismailia. But Gonen still wanted the bulk of the 143rd Division to stay on the east bank and keep attacking Missouri in order to widen the bridgehead and push the Egyptian artillery out of range.

Sharon argued, more and more vehemently, that attacking Missouri would be costly, misguided, and unnecessary. "On the contrary, the most effective thing to do would be to move northward along the west bank of the canal, behind the Egyptian positions. As we moved up behind them toward Ismailia, the Egyptians would be so menaced themselves, they would not even begin to think about threatening our lines of communications." But he was ordered to bring back forces from the west bank to beef up the projected assault. Sharon kept dragging his feet. On the afternoon of the nineteenth, Gonen once again asked Elazar to fire Sharon on the grounds that he was defying Southern Command's orders.

These were not without logic. The area of the bridgehead was still under constant, heavy shelling, and the toll on IDF lives was unbearable. October 19, Dayan writes, was the worst day of the war in terms of casualties, with one hundred dead and more than four hundred injured, most of them in the bridgehead area.

But Dayan himself was becoming increasingly disenchanted with Southern Command's adamant insistence on attacking Missouri. The Egyptians, now seriously alarmed at their situation, had begun urgently lobbying their Soviet patrons to procure a cease-fire. Henry Kissinger, the American secretary of state, seemed inclined to go along with it. Prime Minister Meir believed they had three days left before the two superpowers, working through the UN, issued a joint ukase bringing the war to an end. The priority now, Dayan advised her, must be on shaping the cease-fire lines.

"We need to focus on our offensives west of the Canal," Dayan told the prime minister. "We need to push northwards and southwards, and try to reach Ismailiya and Suez."

Nevertheless, Dayan was still not prepared to intervene directly on Sharon's behalf in his struggle against the order to attack Missouri. "I fought it," Sharon writes.

I railed against it. I tried every way I knew to get the order rescinded. It would be a useless gesture, an absolutely needless waste of lives. But at the end I was not able to change it. On the twenty-first I obeyed the order.

The morning of the attack I stood on a rampart on the western bank and watched Tuvia's tanks and APCs rush the Egyptian positions. I saw them penetrate deep into the defenses, and as they did I saw them hit by a torrent of RPGs, Saggers, and tank fire. One after another Tuvia's vehicles stopped and burst into flame. It was a sight that sickened all of us who were watching . . .

That evening Southern Command ordered me to attack again . . . to take forces from the western side of the canal . . . and transfer them back to the east to take part in a battle that should never have been fought in the first place . . . It was generalship of the worst kind. But I am afraid that it was more than just bad generalship . . . To this day [sixteen years later] I cannot free myself from the feeling that one of the reasons they were pressing me to attack the Sixteenth and Twenty-first divisions on the east side of the canal was not because they considered the corridor too narrow, but because they wanted to keep my troops on the eastern side. They would allow me to proceed north, but they did not want me to have sufficient forces to do it effectively. These are hard things to say. But my strong impression then was that the antagonisms of years between myself and those in command (Bar-Lev and Elazar), augmented now by political considerations, played a considerable role in the military decisions.[47]

"Do you intend to reinforce Tuvia?" Gonen yelled at Sharon on the radio that night.

"No way," came the laconic reply.

"So I say reinforce!"

"No way!"

"You should know—this is insubordination."

"Oh come on, leave me alone with that kind of talk."

Bar-Lev got on the radio and gave Sharon a specific order to transfer forces back to the east bank and to attack Missouri again in the morning. Sharon transferred five tanks. But now, at last, Dayan stepped in. Sharon called him to appeal Bar-Lev's order. Dayan called Yisrael Tal, the deputy chief of staff. "An appeal like that from Arik can't just be ignored," he said. He asked Tal to review the arguments and "issue appropriate orders." "Fifteen minutes later," according to Chaim Herzog, "Tal phoned Gonen to transmit an order from the minister of defense not to attack Missouri."[48]*

---

* According to Elazar's biographer, it was Elazar who in fact rescinded the order to attack. Tal awoke Elazar before dawn, Bartov writes, and briefed him on the crisis. Elazar sided with Sharon. "There's a limit to how often you can tell a senior commander who's in the field and thinks he can't do it and thinks he'll have casualties," Elazar explained later. "That morning—I thought, enough is enough!! And so Tal called Gonen and told him to call off the attack" (Bartov, *Dado,* 313).

Dayan, having exercised his waning authority at last, did not make do with that. At dawn he flew down to Sharon's division, heard his side of the story, flew on to the Southern Command headquarters, and poured out his wrath on Gonen (Bar-Lev was not in the war room). "You told him to take Missouri. That is scandalous. Attacking Missouri is suicidal. There is a conditioned reflex in this Command against every suggestion from Sharon."

GONEN: Arik is conducting his own private war.
DAYAN: There are those who say that it's this war room that has been infiltrated by political considerations.[49]

By now, the cease-fire was imminent. Sharon's division had the Ismailia–Cairo road within its gun sights, but Sharon wanted the town itself, and he pushed his armor forward. The column was stopped by two battalions of Egyptian commandos dug in around a sewage plant on the southern outskirts. A desperate battle developed. The cease-fire hour agreed to by Israel, Egypt, and Syria, 18:52 on the twenty-second, came and went, but the fighting outside Ismailia raged on until close to midnight as the Israelis sought to evacuate all their dead and wounded.

"It wasn't till the last night that the Command allowed us to attack Ismailia," Abrasha Tamir recalled.

What can you achieve in an attack that you mount helter-skelter at the last minute? I'm not saying Arik's behavior all through the war was right, his tantrums, his not answering on the radio, and so forth. But the fact is that Southern Command forbade us to transfer more of our forces to the west bank and forbade us to go onto the attack against Ismailia until the twenty-second. It wasn't because Bar-Lev and Gorodish really thought the eastern bridgehead needed widening. They simply didn't want *us* to attack! They wanted the only attack to be accomplished by Bren and Kalman, while we stayed with the bridgehead . . . All in order that Arik shouldn't strut around as though he were the victor.[50]

Tamir's judgment was shared, to a greater or lesser extent, by other key figures on Sharon's staff. "If you've decided to cross, then cross!" said Yehoshua Saguy, the divisional intelligence officer.

Arik was there on the canal bank with the Gilowas [on the morning of the sixteenth]. They should have tasked Bren's division with clearing the area of the approach roads. And let Arik cross.

They stopped Haim Erez and turned him around. And soon enough, of course, the Egyptians recovered and built a new defensive line with vast minefields and reinforcements. Instead, we should have continued advancing westward toward Cairo with two divisions. I'm not saying we should have entered Cairo. I'm not saying the Great Powers would have allowed us to approach Cairo. But that would have meant decisive victory. If the powers had intervened to stop us, that means we have achieved a decision in this war. As it was, the war ended indecisively.

The contrary viewpoint is perhaps best expressed by Asher Levy, the brigadier-general who fought the war first in Bren's division and then in Southern Command headquarters. Best expressed—because Levy, at the end of the day, is among those who believes passionately that without Sharon there would have been no crossing of the canal. But as regards what came later, he says,

It was because of his character, the bad traits in Arik's character. He saw that he was left behind while Bren began to sweep ahead, down the coast of the lake toward Suez. Not because [Bren] was such a great general, but because things went well for him. The IDF was back to its old self. The plans for racing down southward were good, and all went fantastically—until Suez. All the glory was over there. And Arik's sitting over here . . .

He was wrong about Missouri. It was vital to ensure at all costs that the eastern bridgehead stay open. That was Southern Command's most crucial task, and they assigned it to Arik. But he didn't like it, because the glory wasn't there. The plan was that he takes care of the bridgehead and Bren crosses. But he wanted to cross. And Haim Bar-Lev wouldn't let him. He said, Bren crosses and you broaden the bridgehead. And Bar-Lev was 100 percent right.

And so he decided that we've got to conquer Ismailia. The Command were against it. They said it would be too great an effort, and they were opposed to making another such effort at that stage of the war. But Arik dragged them into it, and many men were killed there.

It is that sort of scathing and forthright criticism of Sharon—Levy, it will be recalled, is similarly unbiased about the events of October 8—that gives cogency and conviction to Levy's ultimate verdict on Sharon's war record. "The fact that Arik Sharon was there meant that despite all the setbacks and difficulties and despite the fact that the bridge hadn't arrived, Arik Sharon with his tenacity and perseverance determined that Israel crossed the canal. No one can take that away from him, ever. Whoever denies it is simply not telling the truth."[51]

Levy's appraisal, shared by every last soldier in the 143rd Division, has long become a part of the national ethos. It is not assailable in the collective public mind. Sharon, whatever the subsequent—and previous—controversies surrounding him, has his place assured in the Israeli pantheon on the basis of that one night's battle.

In a way, that makes the "war of the generals" that followed all the more pointless and perverse. If, as Sharon and his friends say, Bar-Lev was trying to rob him of the glory, he failed. If, as Sharon's many enemies say, Sharon was obsessively and selfishly pursuing the glory on the west side of the canal, he didn't need to. He'd got it already. As far as Israeli history is concerned, Arik Sharon crossed the canal. As soon as the first paratrooper on the first rubber dinghy touched down on the west bank at 1:32 a.m. on October 16, that was the story: Sharon had crossed. When Haim Erez's tanks were trundled over five hours later, it was sealed in the nation's annals.

Even if nothing more had happened in his life after the Yom Kippur War, that war alone would have imprinted Ariel Sharon's name indelibly into Israel's history. The surprise attack by Egypt and Syria on October 6, 1973, sent a jolt of existential terror through the nation. Suddenly the survival of the Jewish state seemed to hang in the balance again. People feared for their lives as the front lines gave way and enemy armies poured across the 1967 borders. In days and nights of desperate fighting, the Syrians were stopped and then pushed back across the Golan Heights. Ten days into the war, a wave of relief swept through the country with the news that Israeli troops had crossed the Suez Canal and were counterattacking on the Egyptian mainland. "Arik" was on everyone's lips. "Arik, king of Israel," the general who had led the crossing and turned defeat into victory of sorts, however costly and incomplete.

If Yom Kippur was Israel's Pearl Harbor—though even more traumatic because so much closer to the heartland—Sharon was its MacArthur: arrogant, swashbuckling, manipulative, loved or hated, always controversial, master of self-promotion, contemptuous of his superiors. It was his image that everyone associated with the national deliverance.

Events veritably conspired to produce his moment of triumph. Sharon had only recently doffed his uniform—but not so recently as to be held responsible for the debacle on the Suez front. He had been forced out of the army, as he claimed, by the very men who *were* now held responsible for the disastrous war and were forced by a commission of inquiry and a public outcry into ignominious retirement. Though forced out of the regular army, moreover, he had been left with a reserve command that placed him at the very heart of the maelstrom and allowed his great gifts as a general to shine through.

He was a general again, for the duration, but he was already a frontline politician—running an election campaign against the government, which, as it now suddenly turned out, had led the country into catastrophe. Party loyalties and military tactics blurred and clashed in the heat of battle as Sharon vied for the glory that was rightfully his and his rivals, as he saw it, conspired to rob him of it. He was supported and protected, as so often in his stormy military career, by Moshe Dayan. The minister of defense was himself mortally weakened by the war. But he was still strong enough to prevent Sharon's adversaries from removing him, as they sought repeatedly to do.

In the final analysis, it was Sharon's generalship that won the day, won Dayan's backing, and won him the nation's adulation. No amount of manipulative self-promotion could manufacture that battlefield reality—just as no amount of bad-mouthing by his many detractors could ultimately obscure it. A good general needs luck, Napoleon famously observed. But he also needs to be a good general. Sharon was a superb general in 1973, not only in the eyes of his own men in the 143rd Division, but also in the view of more dispassionate observers. "He was our outstanding field commander," says Ehud Barak, subsequently chief of staff, prime minister, and minister of defense, whose tank battalion was attached to Sharon's division. "I saw it at the time, and I saw it again later when I studied all the battle logs and debriefings of that terrible war."[1]

After the war, despite the battlefield successes, the nation sank into the blackest despondency. It was not just the endless military funerals and the hospital wards teeming with wounded soldiers and besieged by anxious families. It was the nagging, relentless sense that all this need not have happened, that the tragedy could have been avoided or at least greatly diminished. In 1948 there were more dead and wounded and fewer families who emerged from the war unscathed. But people shared in the joy of victory. The overwhelming mood was of optimism and confident determination. The dead, it was felt then, had not died in vain.

From the moment the guns fell silent now, the war became the stick with which the Likud opposition beat the government. Menachem Begin's sonorous, theatrical voice filled the Knesset chamber: "Why did you not deploy the tanks? Why did you not mobilize the reserves?" For months, he never changed the script and never relented, until there was barely a child in Israel who could not intone those searching accusations.

Sharon, poised to resume his war-delayed entry into political life, saw his role as twisting the knife into the bowels of the Labor establishment. The black mood that gripped the nation would be the catalyst, he believed, for achieving his vaunted purpose in political life: bringing about a change of government for the first time in Israel's history.

The election, originally scheduled for October 21, had been postponed with the outbreak of the war. It was now to take place on December 31. Sharon would no longer be the Likud campaign manager; he declined to leave his division and doff his uniform until the last possible moment. But he led the electoral charge no less effectively from the west bank of the canal. "Israeli General Assails Superiors," *The New York Times* blared forth on November 9. "The general who led Israeli forces across the Suez Canal," correspondent Charles Mohr began his first report, "says he believes that his superiors were too slow to reinforce and exploit his breakthrough, losing the chance to achieve a decisive victory over Egypt."

In minute detail, in two long articles illustrated with maps and photographs, Mohr laid out Sharon's version of the war in the south, replete with all of his complaints about how it had been run and how he had been stymied and constrained at every turn. "The most arresting assertion," Mohr wrote, "was that higher Israeli headquarters delayed for 36 to 48 hours in pushing reinforcements across the canal bridgehead that General Sharon's troops had seized." An even more arresting assertion, for Bar-Lev and Elazar and their political bosses, was the broad and brazen spin that permeated Mohr's entire text: the canal crossing was Sharon's own exclusive stroke of strategic genius.

"To comprehend the debate that General Sharon's remarks will surely provoke," Mohr wrote, "it is necessary to understand something of *the canal-crossing he planned and evolved*. The plan was complex . . . General Sharon said that during his four years as southern area commander *he had realized that it might be necessary someday to make a canal crossing* and had made preparations for one . . . Of his plan General Sharon said: 'The main problem was how to reach the water and establish the bridgehead in the same night . . . It worked,' General Sharon said in his faint, husky voice, 'but it was complicated.' "

The "war of the generals" now merged into the election campaign, and *The New York Times* account became, in effect, a part of the Likud platform. The other side had tried to stop it. "Officials in Tel Aviv had apparently attempted to prevent General Sharon from telling his story and voicing criticisms," Mohr wrote at the end of his second piece. "On the day on which the general was finally reached, an order had been given in Tel Aviv that a journalist who knew the general from the 1967 war was 'not to be allowed to go to Arik.' But this obstacle was overcome. As General Sharon poured cognac in his trailer that night he began to order arrangements made so that two guests could stay overnight. A press liaison officer protested that this was not possible because it was against orders. With a smile General Sharon said, 'You are a major. I am a major general. They stay.' "

The other side hit back as best it could. The plan to cross the canal "did not belong to any individual," Haim Bar-Lev retorted in an interview with *Yedioth Ahronoth,* also prominently carried in *The New York Times.* "It was IDF doctrine since the Six Day War . . . The Command decided on the time and the place."[2] Chief of Staff Elazar issued an official castigation of "biased and one-sided descriptions and interviews . . . which serve no constructive purpose but only personal enhancement." Sharon's reserves command was revoked; this time Dayan made no effort to block the decision.

The election results were a disappointment for Sharon. The Likud did fairly well, increasing its representation from 32 seats to 39 in the 120-seat Knesset. But the Labor Alignment still held firmly to the reins of powers with an invincible plurality of 51 seats—a drop of only 5 from the previous Knesset. Labor's allies—the National Religious Party (10 seats, down from 12) and the Independent Liberals (stable at 4 seats)—made their mathematical calculations and slid back into the familiar postelection mode of negotiating a new coalition with Labor.

But the new political arithmetic did not fully articulate the public mood. The people had preferred Labor to the Right, but they did not want the prewar leadership to continue in office. They wanted new men to head the new Labor government. Lone demonstrators back from the front lines attracted angry throngs. The streets seemed to seethe with resentment. Sharon, newly elected to the Knesset and about to take his seat, contributed to the gathering storm with a parting order of the day to his 143rd Division. The canal crossing, he wrote, carried out by their division had won the war. It had been achieved "despite blunders and mistakes, despite failures and obstacles, despite hysteria and loss of control." Now, he continued, the war was over, and talks were taking place with Egypt. "I feel the need to fight on another front . . . That is why I am leaving. I want you to know that I have never before served with fighters like you. You are the finest of them all . . . If we have to come back and resume our fight—I promise you that I will be with you."*

---

* In a final act of pettiness, General Avraham "Bren" Adan, now CO of Southern Command, declined to provide a helicopter to take Sharon back up north. "Frankly, I was shocked," Sharon's deputy, Jackie Even, recalled. "In the end we

That same afternoon, Sharon called a news conference at the press center in Tel Aviv. No longer in army fatigues but still striking a photogenic pose in a black turtleneck and leather jerkin, he blasted the disengagement of forces agreement just concluded with Egypt.

Under the prodding of the U.S. secretary of state, Henry Kissinger, Israel had agreed to withdraw from the west bank of the canal, and Egypt had agreed to pull back most of its forces from the east bank. Some lightly armed Egyptians were to remain on the east bank in a narrow "limited forces zone." An adjacent strip of desert would be held by a UN Emergency Force, and a third strip was designated another "limited forces zone" in which IDF troops would be restricted to light arms.

To Sharon and the Likud, this was "the retreat of a victorious army, led by a defeated government." Sharon poured scorn on Dayan's assertion that Anwar Sadat, the Egyptian leader, seriously sought to make peace with Israel. If Dayan was mistaken, "it could cost us thousands

---

smuggled him up on a plane." A generation later, with David Elazar (1976), Shmuel Gonen (1991), and Haim Bar-Lev (1994) all dead, the "war of the generals" still raged between Adan and Sharon unabated.

"At the end of the war," Bren told *Yedioth Ahronoth* in 1999, "I was sure Arik felt like shit. He hadn't succeeded in *anything.* He hadn't crossed the canal properly; he hadn't gotten to Ismailia; he had been embroiled in arguments all the time. I felt that our division, on the other hand, had had enormous achievements. After some time I began to realize that people believed the opposite . . . During the war, I thought it was immoral to spend time briefing journalists, holding press conferences. Big mistake! The journalists went to Arik."

INTERVIEWER: But wasn't it important in terms of morale that Sharon drove forward and reached the other side of the canal?

BREN: That was a contribution in terms of morale, no doubt about it. But he only appeared to be driving forward. In fact, he crossed the canal on three light motorized barges that could hardly transport two whole divisions. In other words, there was a bridgehead on both sides of the canal—but no bridge! When Sharon's division tried to move large forces forward, it was unable to do so. The troops were taking hits. A crisis developed. Then my division went into action. First thing, I sent a battalion to defend Sharon from the north, and this battalion knocked out sixty Egyptian tanks. My deputy, Dovik [Tamari], handled the retrieval and concentration of all the rafts, and by Sisyphean effort he brought them to the canal. Meanwhile, our brigades under Natke Nir and Arieh Keren smashed an Egyptian brigade moving up from the south in an ambush that I planned and laid.

On the seventeenth we started bridging the canal together with an engineering battalion from Arik's division. We crossed the canal; we took Egyptian positions on the other side, and we destroyed Egyptian missile bases one after another.

of lives. We've just ended a terrible war caused by the government's mistake . . . You can't base a disengagement accord on one side's sudden belief that the other side wants peace."[3]

From the press conference he drove on to a massive antigovernment demonstration nearby. Begin, Yitzhak Shamir, and he were the main speakers. Afterward, he was mobbed by well-wishers. "Arik, king of Israel," was on everyone's lips.

Despite the fulminations from the Right, the disengagement with Egypt was not unpopular. It ended the desultory exchanges of fire along the cease-fire lines that had continued since the war, and it enabled many thousands more reservists to be demobbed at last. (On the Golan, a mini-war of attrition rumbled on until April, when, again after persistent shuttle diplomacy by Henry Kissinger, a separation of forces agreement was signed there, too.)

But popular outrage over the war itself did not abate; the returning soldiers gave added impetus to a swelling tide of disaffection. "It was not just my resignation or Dayan's that was being called for in that storm of protest," Golda Meir recalled in her memoirs. "It was a call to eliminate from the scene everyone who could possibly be held responsible for what had happened and to start all over again with new people, younger people, people who were not tainted by the charge of having led the nation astray. It was an extreme reaction to the extreme situation we were in, and therefore, though it was very painful, it was understandable."[4]

She hoped to fend it off, nevertheless. In March, she presented her new government to the Knesset. Dayan had offered to quit, but she insisted that he serve again. However, she was on borrowed time, and it ran out in less than a month. On April 2, the commission of inquiry that the government had appointed to examine the lead-up period to the war and the first two days of fighting submitted its interim report. The five-man panel—Chief Justice Shimon Agranat, another justice of the Supreme Court, the state comptroller, and the former chiefs of staff Yigael Yadin and Haim Laskov—recommended the dismissals of Chief of Staff Elazar, Chief of Intelligence Zeira, and other intelligence officers. It severely censured the CO of Southern Command Gonen and recommended that he be suspended pending its final report. The commission cleared Golda and Dayan of "direct responsibility" for the intelligence blunder and the delay in mobilizing and deploying the troops. As for their indirect responsibility, the commission said it would not pass judgment on the accountability of the civilian leadership because ministerial responsibility was a matter for parliament and the electorate.

These findings were tantamount to an invitation to the political opposition, and, more important, to the extra-parliamentary opposition that was daily growing on the streets of the cities, to redouble their pressure for the government to go. The commission stoked the public anger, moreover, by its ruling exonerating Dayan of direct, personal responsibility for the debacle. This was bitterly and publicly attacked by Elazar in his resignation letter. "In fact and in practice," he wrote, "the minister of defense was the level of authority above the chief of staff."

The commission's report and the public response sealed Dayan's and Golda's fates and brought down the weeks-old government. "On April 10, I told the party leadership that I had had enough," Golda wrote. "My decision is final, irrevocable," she said. "I beg of you not to try to persuade me to change my mind. It will not help."

Labor quickly set about choosing its "new people, younger people" to lead a new government. While Golda stayed ostensibly above the fray, her finance minister and close ally, Pinchas Sapir, threw all his considerable weight behind Yitzhak Rabin, the Six-Day War victor who had just recently entered politics after his stint as ambassador in Washington. During the war, Rabin had put on his uniform, toured the fronts, and sat in on the key meetings. He appeared in many of the photographs, looking glum and smoking incessantly. But he was not involved in the "war of the generals," nor was he tainted by the prewar negligence and arrogance that had brought on the disaster.

He was, however, tainted by rumors that as IDF chief of staff he had suffered a nervous breakdown before the Six-Day War—rumors that were now given new credence by his then deputy, now a hawkish and vindictive Likud figure, Ezer Weizman. Weizman urged Labor central committee members to prefer the rival candidate, Shimon Peres. Rabin, he advised them, could not be relied on to stand firm under pressure.

Rabin desperately needed a military figure of equal military prestige and comparable nationalistic credentials to step forward and defend him before Weizman's allegations hit the headlines. Arik Sharon, who remembered how Rabin had saved his career in 1963 when he was in the deep freeze, did not hesitate. He called around to every national newspaper, offering his unequivocal confidence in Rabin's leadership qualities.[5] On June 3, Rabin's government was sworn in. Reluctantly, but unavoidably given his rival's clout in the party, Rabin named Peres minister of defense.

Sharon, watching from the Likud benches while the Labor leaders took their places around the cabinet table, was almost visibly chafing in his seat. As long as Golda and Dayan had hung on, there was enough adrenaline coursing through the political system to make life in the opposition bearable. There was a real prospect of forcing new elections. But once Rabin took over, the postwar waves of political pandemonium abated. The vista of four more years of Labor rule and Likud speech making was too arid for Sharon to contemplate. Yet his path back to the professional army was effectively blocked now by the appointment of Mordechai Gur—another general untainted by Yom Kippur; he had been serving as defense attaché in Washington—as the new chief of staff in place of Elazar. Sharon and Gur were enemies from the time of the paratroopers' revolt back in 1957.

Sharon tried to get his reserves command restored. Labor ministers and members of the Knesset (MKs) were vociferously opposed to this, but Rabin insisted. They responded, though, with a draft amendment forbidding senior officers with field commands to serve in the Knesset. There were other MKs serving as officers in the reserves, but only Sharon had—and now sought again—a field command. In December 1974, the cabinet endorsed the measure. Sharon, always courting victimhood, naturally saw the legislation as aimed specifically at him. This time he was probably right. But he had not been enjoying backbench life much anyway, nor been fully engaged in the Knesset, though he did chair an important and top secret subcommittee that supervised defense spending. He announced his resignation from the House.

The Likud faction convened for a requisite outpouring of outrage at the government's arbitrary injustice and grief over losing Sharon. "If I'd known how much you all love me," Sharon said archly, "maybe I wouldn't have resigned."

As for Labor, "they've achieved exactly the opposite of what they intended," wrote Yoel Marcus in a *Haaretz* column. "They wanted to stop him becoming a general again and to stymie his political career by gagging him. But now he'll be both: three days a week an officer, and the rest of the week a public statesman. Forcing him to quit the Knesset was the biggest favor. If he had stayed there, he'd have slowly sunk under the gray grind of party politics, which he is totally not cut out for."[6]

In another turn of good fortune, Sharon was able to project himself to the public as vindicated, indeed extolled, by the Agranat Commission over the grave and politically devastating charge of insubordination in the face of the enemy. As part of his postwar, pre-politics media blitz a year before, Sharon had told the newspaper *Maariv* in January that he regretted obeying the High Command's orders to attack

Missouri on October 21.* "I should have disobeyed an order I knew was wrong," Sharon said. "I should have disobeyed and accepted a court-martial for my disobedience."[7]

This triggered a firestorm of criticism and controversy. The Agranat Commission, whose remit effectively ended on the third day of the war, was asked nevertheless to take up this crucial question of obedience in wartime. "When is it permissible for a commander, of whatever rank, to disobey orders?" Sharon was asked bluntly by Justice Moshe Landau, a commission member.

Sharon replied that as a basic rule all orders must be obeyed. But special situations could arise, and October 21 was one.

> You're in the field, and no more senior commander is with you, and you receive an order which you know that, if executed, will result in the deaths of a great many of your men but will produce only the most negligible gain. If you have no one to address your arguments to, then perhaps you need to take a decision yourself. Such situations are very rare indeed. But I was in such a situation at that time, although I did carry out the order. But to this day I believe I should not have done so. It indeed resulted in very heavy casualties and in virtually zero gains. In my view this was the classic case in which a commander needs to say, "We are not carrying out this order, no way."[8]

In February 1975, in the published section of its final report—the vast bulk of which remained secret[†]—the Agranat Commission effectively exonerated Sharon, though at the same time did not endorse his rationale.

Whatever Justice Agranat and his four colleagues had said or had meant to say about Sharon's alleged insubordination, their comments were vindication enough for Prime Minister Rabin to be able to do what he had probably been planning to do for some time: hire Sharon as his adviser. The original job definition, "defense adviser to the prime minister," quickly fell prey to the animosity between Rabin and Peres. So Sharon was called just "adviser."[9] Peres hired Sharon's old

---

* See pp. 131–33.
† The report was classified for thirty years, but in 1995 the High Court of Justice lifted the restrictions on all but forty-eight pages of the findings, which remain under wraps. In 2008, the military censorship waived restrictions on many of the testimonies, but not those of Prime Minister Golda Meir and the head of Military Intelligence, Eli Zeira.

friend, comrade, and rival Yisrael Tal as *his* defense adviser, although of course, as defense minister, he had the entire General Staff to advise him.

Sharon understood that in part at least he was being used as a weapon in the escalating duel between Rabin and Peres. This did not deter him, though it would complicate his relations with Peres over the years. What did worry him, though, as he considered Rabin's tempting offer of a role at the heart of power, was the prospect of his rightist credentials being compromised by his perceived association with the Labor government's peace policy.

Under relentless pressure from Kissinger, Rabin was negotiating an ambitious "interim agreement" with Egypt. Under its evolving terms, Israel would withdraw some thirty miles from the canal to a line east of the Mitle and Gidi passes. The UNEF buffer zone separating the two armies under the original postwar cease-fire and separation arrangements, and the two limited forces zones that flanked it, would all shift eastward. The proposed withdrawal meant that Israel would also cede the lucrative oil field at Abu Rodeis, farther down the Gulf of Suez coast. Israeli cargoes, though not Israeli ships, would be allowed through the Suez Canal.

An important new element in the agreement was a hands-on American surveillance role. The United States would set up watch stations in the UNEF buffer zone, to be operated by two hundred American civilian personnel. Israel and Egypt could also each set up a surveillance station in the zone. In addition, U.S. planes would carry out daily surveillance flights over the area and would supply the data from them to Israel, Egypt, and UNEF.

Washington sweetened the pill for Rabin by significantly upgrading the quality and quantity of weaponry it undertook to supply to Israel, including F-15 and F-16 warplanes, M60 tanks, hydrofoil naval boats, and intelligence-gathering equipment.[10]*

Rabin, having balked at a similar proposal earlier in the year—and having incurred an ominous public "reassessment" of Washington's policy toward Israel—now recommended the Interim Agreement package to the Knesset as a step toward peace with the largest and most powerful Arab state and a major enhancement of the relationship with Israel's superpower patron.

For the Likud and its allies, progress to peace meant progress to withdrawal from the remainder of Sinai, and perhaps from the other

---

* The United States also increased civilian economic assistance and guaranteed Israel's oil supplies to compensate for the loss of Abu Rodeis.

occupied territories too. Meanwhile, they argued in the Knesset, Israel was trading tangibles for paper promises. As a Knesset member, Sharon, too, had spoken of the critical danger, as he insisted, of withdrawing from the Mitle and Gidi passes. Now, as Rabin's adviser, his chief concern was to keep a low profile in the hope that people would not dig up his previous pronouncements.

Privately, though, as the Interim Agreement evolved, Sharon kept up a barrage of detailed and specific criticism that Rabin found both constructive and honorable. "It was my adviser, Arik Sharon, who recommended, contrary to other views, that the Egyptian early warning station be inside the passes, as close as possible to our forces," Rabin recalled later in his memoirs. "In general, I drew encouragement from Arik's approach. He said, 'I disagree with your position and strongly oppose the Interim Agreement. But as long as I'm your adviser, I'll give you the best advice possible in the context of your policy.' In this way, Sharon demonstrated both loyalty and decency."[11]

Rabin went on to contrast Sharon's "loyalty and decency" with the behavior of one of Peres's advisers, Professor Yuval Ne'eman, "who, while serving in his official position, turned his house into a meeting place for key people from Gush Emunim, the religious settler movement, who sat there and planned harsh attacks on the prime minister ... The comparison between Sharon and Ne'eman exposes the difference between decency and hypocrisy. It was no coincidence that Ne'eman worked for Shimon Peres and Arik Sharon worked for me."[12]

This passage is evidence of the depth of Rabin's antipathy toward Peres. But it also reflects Rabin's naïveté—or was it willful blindness, or indeed hypocrisy?—toward Sharon's own vigorous dalliance with Gush Emunim during his period of service as the prime minister's adviser. Gush Emunim (Bloc of the Faithful), then in its infancy, rose to prominence after the Yom Kippur War and spearheaded Jewish settlement campaigns in the biblical heartlands of "Judea and Samaria," as the Right pointedly termed the West Bank. Emunim balked at the policy of the Labor-led governments since 1967 limiting Jewish settlement to the Jerusalem area and the Jordan River valley.

Naïveté, blindness, and hypocrisy have characterized the attitudes and actions of a long series of Israeli leaders toward Gush Emunim and its relentless drive to build Jewish settlements throughout the Palestinian territories. Labor "hawks" clandestinely encouraged still-small and inchoate groups of religious-nationalist would-be settlers immediately after the Six-Day War. Men like Yisrael Galili, Golda Meir's close confidant, and Yigal Allon, her deputy prime minister, hankered for "the integrity of Eretz Yisrael." Moshe Dayan and his followers in the Labor Party also opposed relinquishing the West Bank.

Under Rabin, the contradiction deepened: on the one hand, the government fought Gush Emunim's settlement efforts; on the other, collusion increased between Labor ministers and the young religious activists. Each group thought it was using the other. The ministers thought they could harness the religious zeal and nationalist fervor of these youngsters to create new Jewish settlements in places they considered strategically necessary. The religious youngsters believed they could harness the ministers' support in order to create settlements everywhere. Their purpose was twofold: to do God's will by settling the entire land, and to preclude the return of the territories to Arab rule (which, too, they believed was doing God's will).

As an opposition backbencher protected by parliamentary immunity, Sharon had joined Gush Emunim's first foray to an intended settlement site in the heart of Samaria, near Nablus, just days after the Rabin government took power. As soldiers moved in to dismantle the encampment and forcibly removed the would-be settlers, Sharon physically shielded the elderly spiritual leader of the movement, Rabbi Zvi Yehuda Kook. "Don't touch him," he shouted, shoving the soldiers away. "And don't touch me." He urged the young men and women settlers to hug the rocks and refuse to budge.

Rabin was tough with the would-be settlers on this occasion, but in fact he had already signaled significant weakness on the crucial question of the West Bank and its future. Presenting his new government for the Knesset's endorsement on June 3, he gave a solemn undertaking to call new elections before concluding any agreement with Jordan that involved territorial concessions. He noted, rightly, that Golda Meir had given the same commitment when she set up her last, short-lived government three months earlier. It had been squeezed out of her by her coalition partner, the National Religious Party (NRP), and now it was being squeezed out of Rabin in the same way. The NRP, Labor's longtime political ally and traditionally a dovish party, was steadily being dragged to the right by its young generation of activists who were closely affiliated to Gush Emunim.

Sharon, while still in the Knesset, zeroed in on this political weak point at the heart of government policy. "What is this talk of 'priorities'?" he challenged Rabin in a debate in July 1974. "The government purports to uphold the right of Jews to settle everywhere in the homeland, but in accordance with 'political and security priorities.' What are these priorities? These priorities are designed to pave the way for restoring Samaria to Jordan. Let's talk straightforwardly. Tell the truth, why don't you. The truth is that you want to hand this territory back to Jordan. Say so openly! Say: 'We have decided to hand this territory to Jordan.' Don't talk to us about the right to settle in all parts of the homeland, but the need to do so according to priorities."[13]

As adviser to the prime minister, Sharon could hardly maintain that level of strident political polemic against his boss. But he did keep up his intimate contacts with Gush Emunim.

The Sharon-Emunim nexus, interacting with the Sharon-Rabin bond, was to stamp an indelible imprint on Israel's history, as well as on the personal futures of the prime minister and his adviser cum critic. In December 1975, during the festival of Hanukkah, Gush Emunim mounted its eighth attempt—the army had dispersed the previous seven—to found a Jewish settlement in the heart of Samaria. The site chosen was Sebastia, an abandoned Turkish railway station. The timing of this eighth effort was especially propitious: the UN General Assembly had recently passed a resolution defining Zionism as a form of racism. The Israeli ambassador, Chaim Herzog, famously tore up the resolution at the podium. The government convened a gathering of world Jewish leaders in Jerusalem to demonstrate solidarity with Israel. Rabin was loath to give the order for yet another forcible eviction while this conference took place in Jerusalem. He postponed the showdown—a tactical mistake that encouraged more and more sympathizers to stream to Sebastia and bolster the settlement attempt.

The result, eventually, was a compromise, and Ariel Sharon, the prime minister's adviser and the settlers' champion, was instrumental in securing it, shuttling busily between Sebastia and Jerusalem. Thirty settler families were to move in to the nearby IDF artillery training base, Camp Kadum, "pending a cabinet decision" in their case. This ostensibly provisional solution was in fact a huge victory for Gush Emunim and an ignominious defeat for the government. The temporary lodgings at the army base steadily grew into a sizable civilian settlement, which eventually dwarfed the base. It was subsequently named Kedumim. It was the forerunner of many other settlements throughout the populated Palestinian heartlands of Samaria and Judea.

When the deal was concluded, at Minister of Defense Peres's office in Tel Aviv on December 8, the settler leaders pulled out a bottle of brandy and drank toasts. Rightly, they saw this outcome as a watershed: the Labor government's policy restricting Jewish settlement had been breached. Back in Sebastia, a thousand young men danced and sang in fervent rejoicing.

By the same token, Sebastia represented a fateful moment of irresolution by Yitzhak Rabin. Recriminations flew between the Prime Minister's Bureau and that of the minister of defense over who had been weak and offered concessions. It seems clear that the original idea of moving a group of the settlers to an army base was Sharon's.[14] He, after all, had been the driving force in situating these army bases in the West Bank in the first place. "For this alone," Sharon reportedly said at Sebastia after the deal was done, "my service in the Prime Minister's Office has been worthwhile."[15]

Sharon nurtured the hope that his time with Rabin had somehow rekindled his candidacy for army chief of staff but found himself rebuffed yet again. It was always a vain hope, certainly as far as Rabin was concerned. "As long as I've got a say, Arik won't be chief of staff," the prime minister was quoted as saying in the left-wing paper *Al Hamishmar*. He explained that Sharon's previous high-profile political activity made him ineligible.

Sharon accordingly turned back to politics. A bizarre interlude ensued during which he haggled with the Likud leaders and at the same time engaged in vigorous flirtations with well-known figures on the dovish left with a view to creating a new party under his leadership. He was to have a hard time living down this not-so-brief spell of political promiscuity once he finally gave it up and reverted to the nationalist fold. His subsequent years are peppered with lame denials and mealymouthed prevarications, but they never quite allayed the suspicions that this dalliance aroused among the religious settlers and the hard-core ideological Right. When he eventually did change his political outlook, as prime minister, his detractors pointed to this inconstancy long ago as the first telltale sign of ideological deviance.

And indeed, Sharon at this time was less concerned with ideology than with the unsettling thought that he might find himself left out of government again after the next election. He saw that Labor under Rabin was losing popularity: the government was beset by a series of economic scandals involving prominent Labor Party figures. There was also a pervasive feeling that Labor had not been sufficiently punished for the Yom Kippur catastrophe. Nevertheless, Sharon did not believe that the Likud could successfully capitalize on the ruling party's growing weakness as long as Menachem Begin stood at its head. He frankly doubted that Begin, whom he saw as remote and detached from the public despite his rousing oratory, could win an election after seven consecutive defeats over twenty-nine years.

Since unseating Begin as the Likud leader was not really a practical proposition, the alternative, he thought, might be to create a third party, between Likud and Labor, to siphon off disaffected Labor voters. But first he went through the motions inside the Likud, baldly proposing that the party hold a primary to choose its candidate for prime minister and hinting that he would run against Begin.

Sharon continued desultory negotiations over his future in the Likud through the summer of 1976. Matters came to a head in September at a tête-à-tête with Simcha Ehrlich, the Liberal Party leader and thus Begin's partner at the helm of the Likud. The two met in the coffee shop of the Waldorf Astoria hotel in New York, where both were attending a Zionist conference. "Simcha," Sharon began bluffly, "let's forget the past." "As far as I'm concerned," the mild but canny Ehrlich replied, peering out through horn-rimmed glasses, "the past begins this morning."

SHARON: Let's talk like a couple of horse thieves.

EHRLICH: Well, I've never actually tried horse thieving. But you talk and I'll adjust to your style.

SHARON: You have to understand, I can't leave the Likud twice. You have to guarantee me a majority in the Likud.

EHRLICH: But in a democratic society there's no guaranteed majority.

SHARON: I'm thinking of running at the head of an independent party. That way I can be in government whoever wins. I'll partner the Likud if it forms the government, and I'll partner Labor if it does.

EHRLICH: You may end up a mere breakaway fragment . . . We'll attack you mercilessly. We know your weak points.

SHARON: If I don't get the conditions I've asked for, I'll run as an independent.

EHRLICH: First of all, we've accepted your various conditions. And second, don't talk to me in ultimatums. Don't forget that since 1973 there's been a devaluation not only of the Israeli lira but also of Arik Sharon . . .

By November, there was nothing more to talk about. Sharon announced the creation of his new party, to be called Shlomzion, and Ehrlich provided the above embarrassing account of their conversation to *Haaretz*.[16] As good as his word, Ehrlich attacked him mercilessly. "Arik can't work in a team. His personal ambition is what drove him to leave the Likud. That, and his political volatility. He is not a man of principle. For him, tactics take priority over principles."

In a letter written the following April and published only after his death in 1983, Ehrlich was even more damning. "In 1973, I said that

I admired those who prevented Arik from becoming chief of staff, because he would have been a disaster. I see him as a danger to democracy and free society. If he were in power, he would be capable of setting up camps for political prisoners. He is a man without principles, without human feelings, and without any moral norms whatsoever."[17]

Sharon for his part proclaimed that he would never return to the Likud "even if the election results are disappointing and Shlomzion emerges as a small party. I have never abandoned my comrades on the field of battle—and I'm not about to do so now."[18] He was spending his mornings at the Tel Aviv home of his new comrade Amos Keinan, a multitalented writer, playwright, sculptor, and prominent intellectual of the Left.* Keinan had lived for years in Paris and had met there with Palestinian activists. Sharon wanted to meet with Yasser Arafat, the chairman of the Palestine Liberation Organization. Shlomzion, he proposed, should call for the creation of an independent Palestinian state. He himself had long believed that "Jordan is Palestine," in other words, that King Hussein's Hashemite monarchy, a colonial creation of the British, ought eventually to disappear, leaving the Jewish republic of Israel and the Palestinian republic of Jordan to resolve their territorial differences over the West Bank.†

The dream of Shlomzion began to come unstuck, according to Keinan, when polling data showed a distinct disconnect between its bold thinking on the Palestinian issue and the much more hawkish inclinations of Sharon's grassroots admirers. Sharon summarily dumped his leftist friends, Keinan recalled, "and swung 180 degrees rightward," packing Shlomzion's list of Knesset candidates with his personal friends and old army buddies.

The Rabin government collapsed prematurely in December 1976 when the National Religious Party refused to support the prime minister in a vote of confidence. Election Day, originally scheduled for the fall of 1977, was brought forward to May 17. Then, out of the blue, Rabin himself was forced to resign in March 1977 when the attorney general, Aharon Barak, decided to prosecute his wife, Leah, for a currency violation. Leah had been exposed by *Haaretz* as holding a (relatively small) account in a U.S. bank, which was forbidden under

---

* Shlomzion was the name of Keinan's elder daughter, after a Second Temple–era queen of Judea, Salome Alexandra.
† Keinan was less focused on the Hashemite Kingdom of Jordan across the river than on the need, as he saw it, for Israel to come to terms with the Palestinian people in Palestine. He wanted Shlomzion to call for a demilitarized Palestinian state on the West Bank. Sharon, he recalled in later years, was broadly if vaguely agreeable.

Israel's then-still-draconian currency restrictions. Everyone did it, but she was caught, and Barak threw the book at her—and vicariously at her husband. Shimon Peres took over as party leader and acting prime minister, and Labor slid steadily down in the polls.

On the Likud side, Menachem Begin was struck by a heart attack and spent much of the election campaign in the hospital.

Sharon realized that his own election battle had been reduced to getting past the threshold—1 percent of votes cast—and making it into parliament. The joke doing the political rounds was that his grand pretensions were all now condensed into the hope that the men of his Yom Kippur War division would come out and vote for him.

He telephoned Begin in the hospital and humbly pledged that Shlomzion would merge with the Likud after the election. Really, he would have preferred to join before and receive an assured if humiliating entry ticket to the new Knesset. Begin, who still bore warm affection for the all-sabra war hero, asked Ehrlich and Yitzhak Shamir to arrange it—and the two old foxes managed to fudge and stall till the deadline passed and the lists were closed.[19]

In the event, Sharon scraped in with two seats—his own and his No. 2, a little-known teacher from Tiberias named Yitzhak Yitzhaki. Some thirty-four thousand people voted for Shlomzion, 1.9 percent of the votes cast. The overall results were a political earthquake for Israel. Labor plunged from 51 seats to just 32, and the Democratic Movement for Change (DMC), a new, centrist movement, won an astounding 15 seats. The Likud gained 4, up to 43. The arithmetic was compelling: Labor, for the first time ever, had effectively lost the capacity to lead a coalition. Menachem Begin would be prime minister. Moreover, together with the religious parties and Shlomzion, Begin could build a coalition of 62; he didn't need the DMC to govern.

Sharon wasted no time. At 5:00 a.m. on May 18, as the new era dawned over the country, he telephoned to congratulate the jubilant Begin and was enormously relieved to hear the words "Your place is with us." "How do I make that happen?" he asked ingratiatingly. "Write a conciliatory letter to Ehrlich." Sharon immediately sat down at the kitchen table of an aide's home in Tel Aviv and wrote, with all the pathos and contrition he could conjure up. Shlomzion's two seats were the Likud's to command, he assured the Liberal leader.[20]* He sent off his missive by messenger to Ehrlich's home and sat back to contemplate life in a Begin cabinet.

---

* Ehrlich blocked Sharon's way back to the Liberal Party, but he could do nothing to prevent the two Shlomzion men's merger into Begin's Herut.

CHAPTER 5 · HIS WILL BE DONE

The political earthquake of the election was quickly eclipsed by its dramatic and unpredicted aftershock. No sooner had he been sworn in than Menachem Begin, the inveterate extremist and warmonger in the eyes of his rivals, authorized secret peace talks with Egypt. These were conducted by the new foreign minister, whose accession to the Likud government itself triggered sharp political reverberations—the lifelong Laborite Moshe Dayan.

In November, the secret burst upon a bemused world and an incredulous Israel. President Sadat announced that he would fly to Jerusalem and address the Knesset; Begin immediately responded with a formal and courteous invitation. On Saturday night, November 19, the enemy leader was received with flags and fanfare at Ben-Gurion International Airport. "Aha, it's you," Sadat said, smiling, when he saw Sharon alongside the red carpet. "I hoped to capture you on Egyptian soil in October '73." "I'm glad I managed to avoid you," Sharon replied.[1]

It is hard now to re-evoke the feelings that swept the country then; so much has soured since. But for the crowds that poured onto the streets of Jerusalem to wave their welcome to Sadat, for the millions who watched and listened spellbound as he spoke in the Knesset, for the whole euphoric nation, it was a dreamlike moment that seemed to hold out new worlds of hope. After thirty years of hermetic regional isolation and implacable Arab enmity, and only four years after the trauma of Yom Kippur, the president of the strongest Arab state had come to make peace. "No more war" was the pledge on both Sadat's and Begin's lips. If that were enshrined in a treaty, with solid security safeguards, the existential threat that Israel had always lived with would hugely diminish.

The euphoria of the visit was followed by more humdrum diplomacy. Quickly, though, this ran aground. A second Begin-Sadat summit at Ismailia, on the Suez Canal, on Christmas Day 1977, ended in

deadlock. Begin signaled that he was ready for far-reaching concessions in Sinai but not in Judea and Samaria.* Sadat, already accused
of betraying the Arab cause by seeking a "separate peace," demanded
a meaningful Israeli commitment regarding the Palestinians' future.
The United States stepped up its involvement, to keep the process from
stalling. More fitful negotiating followed, but the radiant optimism of
the original breakthrough seemed in danger of fading amid a welter of
disputes, recriminations, and misunderstandings.

For Israel under Begin, the historic breakthrough with Egypt bared
a deep contradiction at the core of its policy making. Begin was genuinely committed to peace with the states of the Arab world but not
with the Palestinians. Of course he wanted Israel to live at peace with
the Palestinian people, too; but not as equals, not as two nations living side by side in a Palestine partitioned into two states. For him,
Palestine belonged to the Jews alone. The Palestinians, or the "Arabs
of Eretz Yisrael," as he insisted on calling them, could have autonomy,
but not sovereign independence. By the same token, he would not hand
back the Palestinian territory to Jordanian sovereignty.

Begin was not the first Zionist leader conflicted between the desire
for peace and the burning belief that Israel must govern all of Palestine. Parts of the Zionist Left, too, especially in the immediate
pre-state period, were loath to accept the compromise of partition
proposed by the international community and accepted, reluctantly,
by Ben-Gurion.

After 1967, that ambivalence resurfaced, prompting key Labor
ministers like Moshe Dayan and Yigal Allon to advocate and support Jewish settlement in parts of the West Bank while at the same
time professing to seek peace and a repartition of the land. They, at
least, contended that their limited settlement plans would not prevent
repartition. Begin and Sharon, when they came to power, proclaimed
unequivocally that *their* settlement plans were intended precisely to
achieve that end: preventing the repartition of Palestine between Israel
and Jordan or the rise of an independent Palestinian state on the West
Bank.

But Begin, complicating the contradiction, did not annex the West
Bank. This would have been the natural and logical consequence of
his lifelong ideology. He solemnly renounced annexation when Dayan
made that his condition for becoming foreign minister.[2] Begin most

---

* One of the Begin team's first instructions when it came to power was to the Israel
Broadcasting Authority to stop referring to "the West Bank" (implying the area
was part of Jordan) and use instead the biblical designation "Judea and Samaria."

likely would have forgone annexation anyway, with or without Dayan. To annex the occupied territories would have confirmed all the world's worst fears of this onetime terrorist leader. It would have forfeited American support and turned Israel into a pariah. Begin's decision not to annex was a clear signal that he sought legitimacy and acceptance in the international community.

But of course—another facet of the same contradiction—occupation and settlement precluded legitimacy and acceptance. This was doubly the case now that the prospect had opened of real peace with the Arab world. For Begin and Sharon, perversely, the opening to peace made it all the more urgent to sprinkle settlements all over the Palestinian territories. Sadat's visit, Sharon blithely explained as though this were the obvious logic, "added immensely to the pressure to get the Samarian and Judean settlements established quickly."

Compounding that perversity, President Jimmy Carter, who regarded the settlements as both illegal and an obstacle to peace, soft-pedaled his objections to them during this key period for fear of provoking Israel to backtrack on the peace with Egypt. The years between Camp David in 1978 and the final Israeli withdrawal from Sinai in April 1982 were the period of the most relentless and determined settlement building by Begin and Sharon.

Thus encouraged, Begin believed he could have it all: peace (with Egypt), peace and occupation (with the Palestinians), occupation and legitimacy (with the rest of the world).

To sustain these contradictions, Israel under Begin followed a policy of prevarication. Begin nurtured the quintessential inconsistency that informed his government's words and deeds. All the ministers were complicit, but none more so than Sharon. Begin was the architect; Sharon was the master builder.

Happily for Sharon (and for the settlers), inconsistency and disingenuousness were the very attributes with which Sharon's personality was bountifully endowed. This fortunate confluence enabled Sharon to achieve an ever-higher profile within the government.

His first sally into this realm of settlement building and prevarication, however, ended up a much-ridiculed fiasco. He argued that now that peace talks with Egypt were under way, Israel must build more settlements in northeastern Sinai (the Rafah Salient*) as fast as possible. He discussed his thinking with Dayan, who had been trying to get the Egyptians to agree to let the Israeli settlements in Sinai remain under Israeli rule. Sharon and Dayan talked vaguely about extending

* See p. 82.

water pipes and other infrastructure from the existing settlements into as-yet-unsettled tracts. Begin gave his "enthusiastic consent."[3]

On January 3, 1978, Sharon presented his plan to the cabinet, and Begin quickly called a vote. Within days word leaked out of the cabinet decision and of new earthmoving work in Sinai. Predictably, a storm erupted in Israel and around the world. This seemed the ultimate proof that Begin was negotiating in bad faith. Israel's state radio made matters worse by reporting that Israel was in fact building twenty-three *new* settlements in the Rafah Salient. Begin immediately issued a denial, and at the next cabinet meeting he forcefully repeated it. There would be no new settlements, he declared, only an increase in the population of the existing ones.

Sharon saw red. By his own account, he lashed out at the prime minister.

> "I did not come on January 3 just to get a decision for the protocol. I came to get it implemented. It seems strange to me that someone who was party to the decision thought I wouldn't implement it . . . What should I do right now—give orders to dismantle the water drilling rigs, send back the tractors, stop the pipeline builders? Should I instruct them all to come back?"
>
> "We heard your question," Begin said. "You'll get an answer!"[4]

The crisis was defused, and Sharon's righteous posturing punctured, when the Israeli media began pointing out that the new settlements were not in fact settlements at all but rather just dummy facades, a couple of hastily erected water towers and a few uninhabited old buses. There was method in this piece of vintage Sharon madness, the media explained: once the "new settlements" were up, Israel would offer to take them down—in exchange for Egypt's agreement to let the old (genuine) settlements remain. Begin and Dayan, and indeed the whole cabinet except for the defense minister, Ezer Weizman, had gone along with this silly charade. The media exposé, at any rate, lampooning the government's transparent ruse, put paid to the "new settlements," and the negotiations with Egypt reverted to haggling over the old ones.

The embarrassing episode is instructive because it points up the atmosphere of duplicity that attended settlement building under Begin. During the Mandate, new Jewish settlements sometimes went up overnight, behind the backs of the British authorities, as the pre-state Yishuv, through the kibbutz movements, staked out its territory. Gush Emunim, the religious-nationalist zealots, purported to revive that Zionist tradition and turned it against the Zionist state, giving the government and the army the runaround time and again as they mounted their clandestine drives to settle at their chosen sites. In Sharon's comical, covert operation the government was caught duping its own ministers, dodging the Israeli press and public, misleading both the new partners in peace and the wider international community.

Sharon was single-minded from the outset about his intended role as master builder in Menachem Begin's settlement-building government. On the morning after the election, having sent his groveling letter to Ehrlich (who was going to get the powerful Finance Ministry in the new cabinet), Sharon hosted at his Shlomzion campaign office the secretary of Gush Emunim, Zvi Slonim, and another prominent settlement leader, Hanan Porat. Together they pored over a future map of the West Bank. "It is incredible," said Slonim, looking back in 2003, "how identical that map was to the map of Israel today."[5] Their map contained dozens of prospective settlements, dotted all over the West Bank. By 2003, indeed long before, virtually all of them had become reality.

Sharon led the settlement-building boom during Begin's first government in his dual capacity as minister of agriculture and chairman of the ministerial settlement committee. Even though most of the new settlements in the territories were not agricultural, the Ministry of Agriculture naturally had budgets, contacts, and expertise at its disposal that were all helpful in planting new villages on virgin soil. The Ministry of Agriculture, moreover, had always worked closely with the settlement department of the World Zionist Organization (WZO) building kibbutzim and moshavim around the country. As part of the policy of obfuscation surrounding the West Bank settlement project, it was the WZO rather than the government itself that was tasked with much of the infrastructure work for the new settlements.

Lily, the boys, and eighty-year-old Vera gazed down with pride from the visitors' gallery as Sharon took his oath of office in the Knesset. "I thought for a long moment about my father—an agronomist, a farmer, a pioneer in his field. I knew exactly how he would have felt had he been alive to see his son named minister of agriculture. And as I looked at my mother, I was sure she was thinking the same thing."[6]

Three months after the government took office, Sharon had his comprehensive settlement plan ready for presentation to the cabinet and the Knesset. The key departure from the Allon Plan that had guided settlement policy during the Labor years was the new government's determination to build on the hills of Samaria overlooking the heavily populated Israeli coastal plain. Sharon sketched out a chain of "urban, industrial settlements on the ridges" that, he claimed, would give Israel critical strategic depth and "keep the dominant terrain in our hands now and in the future so that it could never be used militarily by anyone else." This meant expanding the old, cramped pre-1967 borderline eastward. But in addition, the new government would broaden the line of settlements that Labor had built flush along the Jordan River, building westward into the hills overlooking the Jordan.

So the West Bank was to be squeezed from both sides. It would also be crisscrossed with "several east-west roads along strategic axes, together with the settlements necessary to guard them." And East Jerusalem, which the unity government had formally annexed to Israel immediately after the Six-Day War, would be ringed by "a horseshoe [of Jewish settlements] that would run about ten to fifteen kilometers outside of the center, from Gush Etzion and Efrat in the south to Ma'aleh Adumim in the east to Givat Ze'ev and Bethel in the north. If we could develop a greater Jerusalem along these lines that would eventually include a population of a million people or so, then the city would be secured into the future as the capital of the Jewish people."[7]

Carved up and colonized, the Palestinian lands would thus be prevented from ever sustaining a unified, contiguous Palestinian political entity. Yet Sharon and Begin maintained that they did not intend to drive the Palestinians off their land and insisted that none of the settlement building was being done at the expense of the individual Palestinian farmer. For Begin particularly, this purportedly humane and law-abiding approach accorded with the pristine Revisionist doctrine whereby the Muslim and Christian inhabitants of Palestine could live dignified and prosperous lives under Jewish rule. Moreover, by not confiscating private Palestinian land for Jewish settlement building, Begin and Sharon believed they could keep on the right side of the Supreme Court, which exercised jurisdiction over the government's activities in the occupied—or, as they were sanitarily called in official usage, the "administered"—territories. The settlements, Begin ruled, were to go up on state land, not on privately owned land.

In practice, this meant political duplicity dressed up as legalistic propriety. The government purported to protect the individual property rights of the Palestinians (though in practice these, too, were often infringed). But it ignored their collective right not to be occupied by another state.

There was an interesting ideological twist here. The previous Labor-led governments had expropriated private Palestinian lands on occasion to build settlements, justifying their action in court on security grounds. Begin believed in settlement not only on security grounds but on national grounds—on the grounds that it was the Jews' right to settle everywhere in Eretz Yisrael. "We will approve settlements everywhere," he ruled, "on condition that they are built on state land and no one, Arab or Jew, is deprived of his private land."[8]

After spring and summer of 1978 had passed in desultory and increasingly frustrating negotiations between Israel and Egypt, President Carter decided on a bold gamble and invited Begin and Sadat with their teams to a secluded summit at the presidential retreat at Camp David in September. For two weeks Egyptians and Israelis wrestled with the substance of their decades-long conflict. Carter and his team served at once as referees, mediators, and demanding spectators, doggedly prodding the protagonists to overcome their deep-rooted inhibitions and make bold decisions that would change history.

Two draft agreements were hammered out. The "Framework for the Conclusion of a Peace Treaty Between Egypt and Israel" laid down the outlines for a bilateral accord between the two countries, with elaborate security arrangements in Sinai. The "Framework for Peace in the Middle East" provided the basis for an autonomy scheme for the Palestinians for "a transitional period" of five years. Both agreements would require further negotiation to flesh them out. The peace treaty was to be concluded within three months (it took six). The autonomy talks, everyone understood, would take longer.

The summit was kept remarkably leakproof, and despite massive media interest held at bay by frequent but vacuous briefings, the public was unaware of the substantial progress that had been made. The agreements were set to be signed at the White House in a ceremony that—if it took place—would surprise and electrify the world. But as the end of the summit approached, both agreements were still bogged down, mainly over the issue of settlements.

Before the summit, Begin had publicly and repeatedly pledged that he would not abandon the Israeli settlements in the Rafah Salient and the new township of Ophira, at Sharm el-Sheikh in the south. But Sadat remained adamant: he would not make peace without getting back every inch of Sinai. He was prepared for extensive demilitarization and limitation of forces zones, but he insisted that all the land, including the settlements, be returned to Egypt.

It was Sharon who persuaded Begin to relent. Abrasha Tamir, Sharon's longtime comrade who was at Camp David as the defense minister Weizman's military aide, arranged a phone call to Sycamore Ranch at Weizman and Dayan's behest. The two of them were convinced there would be no deal without this concession. They thought Sharon, the champion of the settlements, could talk the prime minister into making it.[9] Begin went back to Carter and said he was prepared to bring the issue to the Knesset. He would not make a recommendation one way or the other, he said. But both he and the Americans knew that there would be a substantial majority in the Knesset in favor of ceding the Sinai settlements.

Sinai, at the end of the day, was not Eretz Yisrael. It was not the biblical homeland, nor indeed was it modern-day Palestine as delineated in the British Mandate. Begin was breaking a political promise; he was not betraying an article of faith. But as the summit moved to its climax, he was squarely confronted with the contradiction at the heart of his peace policy. All the complexity—and the inherent artifice—in his statesmanship came to the surface. On the last night, with success or failure still hanging in the balance, Carter pressed Begin for a commitment to suspend settlement building in the West Bank and Gaza for the duration of the peace talks. Carter maintained ever since that meeting, which went on long past midnight, that he received from Begin an open-ended commitment not to build new settlements for the duration of the Palestinian autonomy negotiations. Begin insisted that he agreed only to a three-month freeze—the anticipated period of the Egyptian treaty negotiations.*

The ceremony went ahead. National Security Adviser Zbigniew Brzezinski briefed journalists in Washington that night, giving the U.S. understanding of what had been agreed. Begin briefed Jewish leaders in New York the next day, giving his interpretation of the agreement.

The news from Camp David left Gush Emunim bitterly disillusioned with Begin. He had promised them before the summit that he would "pack up and come home" if pressured to cede the settlements. "I will not lead a government that agrees to uproot settlements," he vowed. Sharon, too, with that phone call from Camp David, had seri-

---

* Carter's understanding "certainly made sense," the U.S. ambassador to Israel, Samuel Lewis, observed years later. "Certainly in Carter's mind he was talking about a settlement freeze of indefinite length through the period in which you were negotiating over autonomy. And that's what [U.S. secretary of state Cyrus] Vance thought they were talking about. [Nevertheless,] my hypothesis to this day is that it was a genuine misunderstanding, not a deliberate double cross by Begin. Carter thinks the opposite. He thinks Begin lied to him at Camp David. And he was there" (Sam Lewis interview, Jerusalem, February 2, 2009).

ously undermined his standing even among those settlers who were prepared to forget his preelection political meanderings.

Would the peace with Egypt now weaken the government's commitment to settle Jews all over the West Bank? To ensure it didn't, Emunim launched a provocative settlement venture two days after the summit, in the heart of Samaria. Encouraged by the aged rabbi Kook, yeshiva students, would-be settlers, and hundreds of supporters made their way to a barren hilltop near Nablus and proclaimed there the settlement of Elon Moreh.*

The site was unauthorized and the settlement consequently illegal. With Begin's approval from the United States, the acting premier, Yigael Yadin (the leader of the Democratic Movement for Change), ordered the army to evict the settlers and their supporters by force. But as with Sebastia, one lost round didn't mean the fight was over. In December, the Elon Moreh group set forth again. They pitched camp off the Nablus–Kalkilya road, where TV footage of runny-nosed children out in the wet and the cold soon had the intended effect, and the cabinet decided "in principle" to recognize the group and help them settle in Samaria.

Sharon immediately began searching for a site and alighted on a privately owned tract near the village of Rujaib. Yadin, Dayan, and Weizman all objected, but Emunim's lobbying was stronger. By June the cabinet majority had approved the settlement, and the local military commander had signed an order sequestering the land "on security grounds." Within hours, a triumphant procession of cars, trucks, trailers, bulldozers, and the other paraphernalia of settlement was en route to the site, accompanied by Sharon and his comrade-in-arms from far-off days, Meir Har-Zion.

There was an apparent hiccup later in the year when the High Court of Justice upheld the pleas of seventeen Palestinian farmers and ordered the settlement dismantled. The case was closely followed and celebrated—briefly—in anti-occupation circles at home and abroad as proof of the Israeli justice system's equity. "There are judges in Jerusalem," Begin was famously reputed to have responded,[10] purportedly reflecting his abiding respect for the rule of law.

The upshot was redoubled efforts by Begin and Sharon to encourage Emunim's settlement energies but to channel them to sites on "state land." "A large Jewish settlement will surely arise near Nablus," Sharon told the Knesset on December 12, following the high-court ruling.

---

* The name appears in the Bible (Gen. 12:6).

"This is essential in terms of security, of policy, and of national interest." The government would obey the Supreme Court ruling, but the settlement drive would continue.

He wished, Sharon said, that he could "explain to hundreds of thousands of our citizens the importance of our holding the high ground in Judea and Samaria." He was confident that "the day will come, very soon," when people would hear his message, "the truth of Eretz Yisrael," unmediated by the biased media.[11]

The day did come soon. Within a year, and with elections on the horizon, Sharon set up We're on the Map—the media dubbed it "Sharon Tours"—a program offering voters, almost for free, a picnic day touring Jewish settlements on the West Bank. The funding, he told a suspicious press, came from donors abroad, not from the taxpayer. It was all legal and didn't violate the election financing rules.[12]

> Buses with trained guides drove voters up into the mountains, where they could actually look down on their homes and envision for themselves the strategic consequences of giving up the line of western settlements I had built . . . And they could understand how precarious the Jordan Rift communities were without the line of eastern settlements I had planted on the dominating high ground behind them. By the time the campaign was over more than 300,000 people had made the trip.[13]

Sharon's intervention at Camp David had shown that he was by no means a marginal figure in the Begin government, despite the Shlomzion episode. As time passed, he grew increasingly more central both in the cabinet and in the party. This was due in large measure to the removal from the scene of the two most senior and most charismatic ministers—Dayan, who resigned in October 1979, and Weizman, who followed him in May 1980.

Both quit in despair over Begin's disingenuous interpretation of the Camp David "Framework for Peace in the Middle East," reflected in his approach to the Palestinian autonomy negotiations. He appointed an unwieldy Israeli negotiating team of six ministers (including Sharon), presided over by the minister of interior, Dr. Yosef Burg, the head of the National Religious Party, to negotiate with the Egyptians. Plainly, their mandate was to drag their feet and get nowhere. An urbane and moderate man himself, Burg was weak and wholly in the thrall of the NRP's settler wing.

Dayan did not even bother to attend the talks. "After four months," he wrote to Begin in his letter of resignation, "I feel that the negotiation is for the most part bogus." Weizman, when he finally stormed out of the cabinet seven months later, tore a peace poster off the wall of the prime minister's office, shouting, "No one here wants peace."[14]

Begin and his legal advisers had the small print on their side. The five-year transitional period was not to begin until the terms of the autonomy were agreed on to Israel's satisfaction.

It is against that backdrop that Carter's demand for, and Begin's rejection of, a settlement freeze for the duration of the autonomy talks need to be seen. For Carter, and vicariously for Sadat, the freeze was to be the tangible, cogent sign that Israel intended real autonomy for the Palestinians, winding down the occupation and leading eventually to some form of independence. That, after all, was the plain meaning of the "Framework for Peace," the spirit of the text before Begin's lawyers parsed it into meaninglessness. The transitional period was designed to build mutual confidence. Begin, the Americans hoped, would be able to relinquish his ideological inhibitions, or else his successor would.

"The agreement provides a basis for the resolution of issues involving the West Bank and Gaza over the next five years," Carter told Congress the day after the Camp David Accords were signed. "After the signing of this framework and during the negotiations concerning Palestinian self-government, no new Israeli settlements will be established in this area."

Begin, however, digging in behind his denial of the settlement freeze and his legalistic exegesis, could dismiss that plain reading and keep building his settlements as the tangible, cogent sign that he would never accede to Palestinian independence. Begin's aides hinted that Sadat was "in on" this twisting of the plain meaning of the agreement. For the Egyptian leader, they nudged and winked, the "Framework for Peace" was merely a fig leaf covering what was in effect a separate Israeli-Egyptian peace. That, indeed, is how much of the Arab world saw Camp David. Egypt found itself largely ostracized and had to give up the leadership of the Arab League, which it had traditionally held. Inside Egypt, too, opposition forces regarded the peace with Israel as a betrayal of the Palestinian cause.

Sharon enthusiastically endorsed the most restrictive interpretations of Israel's commitment to the autonomy. He loudly and repeatedly demanded a thorough debate in cabinet on this issue. Begin resisted, knowing that that would inevitably exacerbate tensions between the senior ministers. But that was precisely Sharon's intention. He wanted to shore up his Eretz Yisrael credentials with the settler camp and at the same time keep hitting at Weizman, whose job he coveted and whom he saw as the chief obstacle on his path to the conquest of the Likud.

Weizman made it easy. He was genuinely undergoing a profound change of heart, from aggressive Herut hard-liner to ardent peace advocate and positive-minded negotiator. And he brought the same uninhibited extroversion to his new political persona as he had to his previous one. He criticized Begin openly and called him behind his back "the late," a cruel reference to the prime minister's frequent illnesses and bouts of depression.*

Although Weizman himself staunchly denied it then and thereafter, his dramatic departure was interpreted by some pundits as designed to catalyze the government's collapse and Begin's replacement.

But Begin flatly refused to appoint Sharon as defense minister. He approached Minister of Foreign Affairs Shamir, who declined to swap jobs. He tried Moshe Arens, a U.S.-raised aeronautical engineer who served as chairman of the Knesset Foreign Affairs and Defense Committee. But Arens turned him down, too, on the grounds that the new defense minister would have to supervise the evacuation of the Sinai settlements and he was not prepared to do that.[15] Begin finally decided to keep the post for himself; he would serve as both prime minister and defense minister, as Ben-Gurion had done.

Begin was heard muttering to the finance minister, Simcha Ehrlich, that if Sharon were defense minister, he might well send tanks to surround the prime minister's office. He had to apologize for that, explaining to Sharon that it had been "men's talk . . . just a jocular moment."

For Sharon, Begin's hawking the defense post to Shamir and Arens when he was eagerly available for it was a searing insult and, he charged, an act of irresponsibility to the nation. For Begin then to

---

* "From the moment the peace treaty was signed," Weizman wrote in his memoir *The Battle for Peace,* immediately after his resignation,

> Begin . . . turned his back on this chink of hope that had opened for Israel after thirty years of bloodshed. More than anyone else, Begin turned the peace into something banal, something not to be proud of. Instead of surging forward to lead Israel into a new age, Begin preferred to sink back into his fanciful dreams. Perhaps he didn't truly understand the historic significance of the moment. Perhaps because of conflicts with his lifelong ideological beliefs . . . It sometimes seemed that the very prospect of peace was depressing him. An air of depression wafted through the corridors of power and spread throughout the land.

keep it for himself was downright charlatanism. "The Defense Ministry is not some political boon or payoff," he hurled at Begin across the cabinet table on June 1, 1980. "Prime Minister, you are assuming very grave responsibility indeed if you do not appoint the man most suited for the job."

BEGIN (outraged): There are countries where former army commanders are barred by law from becoming minister of defense.

SHARON: Only a charlatan would fail to create the best resources to fight terrorism. Defense is above such constitutional considerations.

YADIN: Never!

(Sharon stomps out of the cabinet room but soon returns.)

BEGIN: Well, have you leaked everything to the press already?

SHARON: This is pure vindictiveness! If anyone thinks he can hurt me, he's wrong!

BEGIN: Don't raise your voice.

SHARON: Don't provoke me. I'm not like the last defense minister, who just sat quietly when he was attacked. I hit back.[16]

It hardly helped that Weizman, before his resignation, took to referring to Sharon as *wazir al-bandura*—Arabic for minister of tomatoes.[17] This was a slighting reference to Sharon's frequent visits to Egypt to supervise an Israeli show farm at Sadat's home village and other projects in agriculture and irrigation.*

In his time as minister of agriculture, Sharon left two momentous marks on the history and geography of his country. One, the Jewish settlements all across the Palestinian areas, was a fateful national blunder that he finally understood and set out to correct toward the end of his life. The other, a network of Jewish villages spread across the hilltops of the Galilee, became a popular success story. It aroused controversy among Israeli-Arabs—its declared purpose was to "Judaize" this part of the country—but enjoyed broad praise in the Israeli Jewish mainstream. By Sharon's count, twenty-two new kibbutzim

---

* On one such visit, Sharon was taken to the Temple of Karnak in Luxor. Gazing up at the huge pillars and listening to the guide explain the hieroglyphic annals of the ancient pharaohs, he asked his close aide: "Do you think I'll be written about too, in the annals of Jewish history?" The aide replied, "It depends what you do," but remembered thinking how the determination to leave a lasting mark was such an essential part of Sharon's being (Eli Landau interview, Herzliya, October 30, 2007).

and moshavim and another thirty-four *mitzpim** were founded during the years 1977–1981.[18]

"I didn't come here to change the demographic balance," a long-time resident of Mattat, the first *mitzpeh,* said, looking back. "I'm an individualistic type, and I wanted to live in a place where I don't have to be in close contact with other people. Our motivation was to live this sort of life; the motivation of the authorities was 'to Judaize the Galilee.' The two ideas melded together and the State of Israel benefited."[19] In Klil, another early *mitzpeh,* the nine founding families built their homes in 1979 on two and a half acres each. They were rugged, eco-friendly types, into organic agriculture and sheep rearing. "I remember riding my horse to a meeting at the first house we built," one member recalled. "Sharon came to visit . . . We asked him from where to where, in his opinion, we could build our *mitzpeh.* Arik, being Arik, replied, 'From the Mediterranean to the Kinneret.' But we didn't really need all that."

"One can only imagine what would happen if the American government announced that it was worried about the demographic situation in New York because there were too many Jews living there and too few Gentiles," Arab Knesset member Talab el-Sana observed. "When forty Jewish families want to set up a *mitzpeh* in the Galilee, they get all the licenses at once, because they're 'Judaizing the Galilee.' The Arabs have to build houses in the fields—and then they get them demolished by the local authorities because they're 'illegal.' "[20]

In part, Israeli Jews were broadly receptive to the strategic thinking behind Sharon's *mitzpeh* program because of a traumatic jolt the whole country experienced on March 30, 1976, when protests over Arab land grievances in the Galilee escalated into a bloody standoff with the police and the army. Six Arab citizens were shot dead. It was a moment when the fabric of coexistence between majority and minority threatened to tear apart. There were fears expressed that parts of the Galilee could become permanent no-go areas for Jews. In the Israeli-Arab community, Land Day has been marked ever since with marches, demonstrations against discrimination and land requisitioning, and commemorative events.

---

* Singular: *Mitzpeh,* or lookout post, the name given to these hilltop villages. By 1999, the number of *mitzpim* had grown to fifty-seven, and Sharon took the credit for all of them. In the 2001 election campaign for prime minister, he spoke of settling another half million Jews in the Galilee, all in the existing towns and villages. There was no need, he declared, to build any more places, just to bring in more people ("The Target: Half a Million More Jews in the Galilee," *Haaretz,* January 18, 2001).

• • •

Begin's firm refusal to give Sharon the Defense Ministry was tempered over time by his need for and reliance on Sharon's support for his decision to bomb Iraq's nuclear reactor before it became operational. Secret arguments within the cabinet and the defense establishment over whether to bomb or not to bomb began in the months before Weizman's departure in May 1980 and did not cease until the operation took place, in May 1981.

Saddam Hussein was working feverishly to complete his reactor, the ministers were told during early 1980. He had an agreement with France to supply weapons-grade uranium and contracts with Portugal and Niger for further quantities of raw uranium.

Weizman himself, the celebrated air ace, was flatly against an Israeli Air Force operation, chiefly because of its possibly catastrophic effect on the peace process with Egypt. The head of Mossad, the head of Military Intelligence, and the deputy prime minister, Yigael Yadin, were also all against bombing. The naysayers pointed to intelligence assessments that Iraq would not have a bomb available for years. They maintained that close cooperation with Western intelligence agencies would ensure that Saddam Hussein never reached that point, or at least that Israel had full information in real time. But Begin was unconvinced. For him, Saddam's bombastic threats to destroy the Zionist state raised all the Holocaust associations. Sharon strove mightily to manipulate this ongoing drama to his advantage.

In October 1980, Begin convened the full cabinet to argue his case. He gravely listed all the reasons not to strike but said they were outweighed by the dangers of doing nothing until it was too late. Iraq's war with Iran had forced Saddam to suspend work at the reactor for the moment, he disclosed. That meant an Israeli attack would not risk radioactive fallout over a wide area. Begin asked for a decision in principle in favor of bombing and won a majority vote.

Still the raid was delayed. "Raful, why don't we carry out the distant, sensitive matter?" Sharon wrote in a note to Chief of Staff Rafael Eitan at a cabinet meeting in March 1981. "Everything's ready," Eitan replied. "You've got to keep pressing." Sharon accordingly wrote to Begin: "Prime Minister, why don't we carry out our decision to hit the 'distant and sensitive target'? Best, Arik." "Arik," Begin wrote back, "I'll talk to you about it. Best, MB."[21] Three weeks later Sharon wrote again. "Prime Minister, week after week goes by and we're still delaying . . . It's a matter of life and death. I can't understand these delays." The next day they spoke by phone. "I can't sleep at night," Sharon said. "Believe me," Begin answered, "your words are not without influence on me."

At the beginning of May 1981, Begin asked the cabinet defense committee to formally approve the Israeli raid taking place later that month. The general election was scheduled for June 30, he noted, and if the Likud lost, he did not believe that Shimon Peres, the Labor Party leader would be capable of ordering the attack. Meanwhile, a shipment of enriched uranium had reached Iraq, and the reactor was due to start working again in September. The ministers agreed to empower a small committee—Begin, Minister of Foreign Affairs Shamir, and Chief of Staff Eitan*—to determine the precise date. "Prime Minister," Sharon wrote fulsomely, "this is the historic decision that you faced. I congratulate you on your success in taking it . . . No more delay. Best, Arik."

But there was more delay. On May 10, with the Israeli warplanes poised for takeoff, Begin received a letter from Peres urging him to postpone the operation. The newly elected, not-yet-installed president of France, the Socialist François Mitterrand, should be given the opportunity to stop supporting Iraq, as he had promised, Peres argued. Begin was not persuaded, but realizing that the secret had leaked to the opposition and fearing that the operation could be compromised, he ordered the air force to stand down.[22]

The air strike finally went ahead on June 7. It was an unqualified success. The nuclear plant was destroyed. There was no significant radioactive fallout. Just one French technician among the foreign scientists was killed. All the Israeli planes returned safely. There was an international outcry, as expected, but it was mitigated both by a widespread feeling of relief in many countries that Saddam had been defanged and by the unmistakable impression that Washington's heart was not in its upbraiding and punishment of Israel.

The verdict of history was similarly sympathetic. The first Gulf War, when a beleaguered Saddam hurled (conventional) missiles nightly at Tel Aviv, and the subsequent unearthing of his chemical and biological stockpiles by UN inspectors made the danger of his nuclear program retrospectively unarguable.

In Jerusalem, ministers waiting anxiously with Begin at his home broke into shouts of relief when word came through from Chief of Staff Eitan. Begin walked over to Sharon and embraced him.[23] Two days later, though, reporting to the Knesset Foreign Affairs and Defense

---

* According to some subsequent accounts, Sharon and not Eitan was the third man on the committee. Either way, Sharon clearly stayed intimately involved.

Committee, Begin pointedly denied press reports that Sharon's threat to resign had forced his hand.

He denied, too, with all the oratorical pathos at his command, the whispered suspicions that he had ordered the raid with the polls in mind. "Would I send Jewish boys to risk death, or captivity, which is worse than death, for elections?! Would I send our boys into such danger for elections?!!"

Begin was at his rhetorical best in this campaign, seizing on an ethnic slur by a pro-Labor popular entertainer to stir up furious resentment among his largely Sephardic constituency. "Is some ham actor hired by Labor to stand on a platform and defile the name of the Sephardic communities?! Sephardim are among the most heroic of the IDF's fighters. The bravest Israelis. They crossed the canal with Arik Sharon. Under his command they fought on the other side."

Though Labor managed to woo back almost all of its supporters (from thirty-two seats in 1977, it pulled back to forty-seven), Likud was up, too, from forty-three to forty-eight, and with the renewed backing of his religious allies Begin had no difficulty forming a new government.

PEACE AND WAR

"There are rumors that Arik is pushing me into war," Begin told the cabinet in May 1981, just before the election, when tensions with Syria were running high. "I have stated that I am not easily pushed."[24]

Not all the ministers were convinced. Simcha Ehrlich and Yigael Yadin, who had warned Begin against giving Sharon national security responsibilities back in 1977, warned him again in 1981. Moshe Dayan, gravely ill with cancer, went to Begin to voice his trepidation. "I hear Arik's going to be minister of defense in the new government. I am seriously worried that if he gets the job, he will embroil us in a war in Lebanon. I know him." Begin tried to allay the sick man's concerns. The whole cabinet, he pointed out, not the defense minister alone, was constitutionally responsible for the army. Moreover, he himself would make sure to stay in close touch with the chief of staff. "What!" Dayan retorted. "Raful? He's no better!"[25]

The most eerily accurate of the real-time admonishers was the former chief of staff and longtime Sharon foe, Mordechai Gur, now a senior Labor figure, who delivered his message in a newspaper interview. "I've sat with Sharon in dozens of meetings about Lebanon, and his mantra has always been 'We've got to march into Lebanon and smash the Syrians!' When people asked him what we do after smashing the Syrians, he had no answer. This man mustn't become minister of defense."[26]

Why did Begin, strengthened by his election to a second term, weaken now in the face of Sharon's pressure and agree to appoint him defense minister, despite all the warnings and reservations? Lebanon was certainly part of the prime minister's thinking, though it was not yet front and center in the Israeli public's mind in the summer of 1981. As Begin began his second term that summer, the main challenge on his horizon was carrying out the final, painful phase of the peace treaty with Egypt by the following spring and pulling out of Sinai. Begin needed Sharon, above all, to evict the Sinai settlers.

"He genuinely feared that settler resistance could lead to bloodshed," his cabinet secretary, Arye Naor, explained years later. "And he believed that the only man who could, perhaps, carry out the evacuation without triggering a violent confrontation was Sharon . . . because the settlers had faith in Sharon. And so Begin reconciled himself to appointing Sharon [defense minister]. And the upshot indeed was an evacuation without bloodshed. There were protests and barricades . . . but no serious, violent confrontation."[27]

For the settler ideologues and activists at the head of Gush Emunim, Begin and Sharon's impending, treacherous evacuation of Yamit, a township of some 1,750 people, and of the other, smaller settlements in northeastern Sinai, needed to be carved into the Israeli consciousness as a national trauma never to be repeated. The greater the trauma, they reasoned, the greater its deterrent effect. They and their supporters descended on the Rafah Salient in large numbers, moving into the settlement homes as some of the original settlers moved out to new farming villages built for them inside sovereign Israel, or took cash compensation and left.

The newcomers were determined to confront the troops, hopefully to fend them off, more likely to be dragged out kicking and screaming and pushed into waiting buses. The less messianic among them knew this battle was ultimately doomed. Begin had solemnly pledged to hand back Sinai settler-free, and Sharon was committed to make that happen. But the Emunim activists wanted maximum media coverage of "the trauma," and maximum resonance in people's minds, so that no such "expulsion" was ever contemplated for the West Bank and Gaza settlements.

Ironically, Sharon himself, having carried out the evacuation smoothly and with relative ease, joined enthusiastically in the "post-trauma," "never-again" brainwash. "In Sinai, in Yamit we have reached the end of our concessions," he declared in his order of the day on April 25, 1982, the date Israel completed its withdrawal from Sinai under the peace treaty.

A dozen years on, he was publicly beating his breast over the evacuation of the Sinai settlements. "When I see how it's exploited to weaken Israel's position regarding the Golan and Judea and Samaria, I think it was a mistake. We should not have agreed to evacuate the settlements, no matter what. I rejoiced over the peace and supported it. But I made a mistake when I agreed to evacuating settlements."[28] He professed his regret, too, over his famous phone call with Begin at Camp David. "Let's be accurate: It wasn't I who phoned him; it was he who phoned me. And I didn't say evacuate the settlements. I just said I'll support you whatever you decide. But anyway, today I say it was a mistake on my part. Everyone makes mistakes and regrets them. I regret this one."[29]

In point of fact, stripped of the spin and the hype (including Sharon's), the evacuation of the Sinai settlements was a trauma only for the settlers themselves and their supporters. The country at large looked on bemused, visibly untraumatized. Moreover, viewed in the perspective of Sharon's dramatic and hugely more ambitious and significant evacuation of the Gaza and North Samaria settlements as prime minister in 2005, the Sinai evacuation appears not merely as *not* a traumatic deterrent against further evacuation but actually as Sharon's own precedent-setting paradigm for effective, nonviolent evacuation of settlements. All his key tactical decisions in 2005 had their antecedents in Sinai in 1981–1982, and Sharon proved the diligent student of his own success.

The IDF had evacuated "its brothers and sisters not with violence but with love," he wrote in his April 1982 order of the day, "not with indifference but with empathy." In Gaza and North Samaria twenty-three years later, the directive to all the evacuating forces, army and police, was essentially the same. The guideline was "With determination and with sensitivity," and it was rehearsed countless times, from Prime Minister Sharon down to the most junior platoon leader.

In 1982, Attorney General Yitzhak Zamir demanded at cabinet that hundreds of Gush Emunim settlers and sympathizers from Judea and Samaria who had illicitly infiltrated into the Sinai settlements be arrested and prosecuted. But Sharon urged Begin to cool Zamir's ardor and leave him to handle the infiltrators by patient persuasion. He insisted that normal life continue in the Sinai settlements until the very last possible moment. The remaining indigenous settlers, who would mostly go quietly when the time came, deserved at least that, he explained. As for the newcomers, most of whom were armed, he was not prepared to believe, he said, that they would ever use their weapons against IDF soldiers. "Lots of people in this country have weapons for self-defense. My mother sleeps with a rifle under her bed. That doesn't mean she intends to use it, certainly not to attack anyone."[30]

He adopted precisely the same approach in the much more complex 2005 disengagement. Then, too, he refused to be rattled by the infiltration of thousands of West Bank settler families and yeshiva students into the Gaza settlements. The newcomers were led by many of the same Emunim rabbis and lay activists who had "reinforced" the Rafah settlements, now gray bearded and with children and grandchildren in tow.

In 1982, as the moment of evacuation approached, Sharon flooded the Rafah Salient with fifteen companies of frontline IDF troops and auxiliary units of medics and firefighters and a strong police contingent. The last holdouts, mainly rightist students and Emunim youngsters, battled the evacuating forces from the rooftops of Yamit. They hurled an assortment of nonlethal objects at soldiers trying to climb up scaling ladders. They succumbed, in the end, when cell-like cages were deposited on their rooftops by crane and they were hustled inside. Threats of suicide by bombs and gas proved so much empty posturing.

The scenes of destruction that followed the withdrawal also presaged the disengagement of 2005. With the last of the protesters out, Israeli bulldozers began systematically demolishing Yamit (though not the agricultural settlements, which were handed over to Egypt intact). "The infrastructure we had built there," Sharon explained, "could serve to transform the place very quickly into a population center of 100,000 . . . It was important that we not have Egyptian centers of population near our borders."[31]

Finally, the Sinai withdrawal served as a precedent for the Gaza disengagement—but this in the negative sense—in the way that state compensation for the settlers grew and grew until it reached wholly inflated and inequitable dimensions. Sharon was not solely to blame, but he was more to blame than anyone. "Arik could refuse them nothing," the director general of the Ministry of Agriculture, Avraham Ben-Meir, recalled.

Sharon was now at the zenith of his brief, bizarre, and ultimately disastrous term as minister of defense. It was a bizarre term because, drunk on his own success and more arrogant than ever, he seemed to lose touch with his own place and his country's place in the reality of world affairs. But he did not lose touch with Begin; the prime minister was right there beside him, stoking the same dangerous fantasies.

On an official visit to Washington with Begin in September 1981, the prime minister asked President Ronald Reagan if Sharon might brief the American side "with some ideas that might give form to the relationship" between the two countries. Sam Lewis, the long-serving U.S. ambassador to Israel, provided a graphic recollection of what followed:

> Reagan agreed; so Sharon stood up with a set of maps of the Middle East and proceeded to give an absolutely hair-raising description of the ways the Israeli Defense Forces could be of assistance to the U.S. in contingency situations. It would have taken Israel as far east as Iran and as far north as Turkey. I could see [Secretary of Defense Caspar] Weinberger blanch visibly . . . Everyone on the American side was shocked by the grandiose scope of the Sharon concept for strategic cooperation. It even included use of Israeli forces to assist the U.S. in case of uprisings in the Gulf emirates.[32]

The formal purpose of Begin's visit was to begin discussions on a memorandum of agreement on strategic cooperation between the two countries. Sharon at this period made a tour of several African countries, and he wove his experiences in Gabon, Central African Republic, Zaire, and South Africa into the ongoing strategic dialogue with the Pentagon. Israel, he suggested, could be helpful in Africa too, in combating Libyan subversion, in countering Soviet influence. Weinberger's team remained unimpressed. Begin, monitoring the talks from Jerusalem, ignored the American lack of enthusiasm. For him, in Lewis's words, "that signed piece of paper was much more important than the content. He wanted a symbol of the alliance."

Eventually, a document was drawn up, lean in practical content. Sharon and Minister of Foreign Affairs Yitzhak Shamir, visiting Washington together in November 1981, attended the signing ceremony, which Weinberger contrived to hold in the basement of the Pentagon, without media coverage.

Despite the American cold shoulder, Sharon maintained that the memorandum was significant. "Though not a vehicle for joint Israeli-American activities of the kind I had been recommending to [Secretary of State Alexander] Haig and Weinberger, it did acknowl-

edge explicitly the threat of Soviet-inspired military activity in the
region and provided channels for closer military and intelligence coordination between the two countries."[33] He never tired of unfurling his
maps and delivering his briefings on Israel's role as a regional superpower and as America's strong and willing surrogate. Foreign statesmen, Israeli politicians, military men, academics, and journalists—all
were treated to his sweeping presentations during this period.

One far-fetched scheme, which was kept out of the briefings,
involved two Israeli businessmen-friends of Sharon's and their Saudi
Arabian partner who were to supply large quantities of American
arms to Sudan. These were to serve the son of the exiled Shah of Iran
to mount a revolt against the ayatollahs who had taken over his country. The arms would also be useful to foment rebellion against Libya's
Muammar Ghaddafi. There was a clandestine meeting—Sudan and
Israel had no formal diplomatic relations—in May 1982 in Kenya,
between Sharon and Lily and the Sudanese leader, Jaafar Numeiry.
Also present were the two Israeli businessmen, the Saudi partner, and
the director general of the Israeli Foreign Ministry, David Kimche,
who had recently resigned from the Mossad. Perhaps it was fortunate
that the Lebanon War intervened before this particular piece of mega-
lomania could get off the ground.[34]

No African adventures or Asian wars actually resulted from Begin's
posturing and Sharon's strategic bombast. They are important,
though, as indicators of the two men's shared mood as they conceived
the Israeli strategy that led to the Lebanon War. They both reveled in
Israel's military power and potential, recovered now after the Yom
Kippur setback. They both regarded Israel as an outpost of American
power in the global confrontation with the Soviet bloc and its Arab
satellites. And they were both convinced that the Reagan team, funda-
mentally, saw things the same way.

Did they both, in their exhilarated assessment of Israel's capabilities and America's sympathies, conceive a sweeping military move
designed not only to defeat the PLO and the Syrians in Lebanon and
install a pro-Israel government there but also to drive the Palestinians
from Lebanon to Jordan, where they would overthrow the king and
set up their own state? Sharon, as we have seen, had long believed that
regime change in Amman was the key to solving the Palestinian problem. Some of his critics suspected him of harboring this undeclared
agenda when he launched the Lebanon War.

Lewis was one of them. But "Begin and Sharon had the same
goals," he insisted. "The basic strategy was shoving the PLO out of
Lebanon . . . maybe back into Jordan. I believe Begin and Sharon had

the same strategic goal. Their strategic hope was that Jordan would become the Palestinian state. They never intended giving up any of the West Bank."[35]

This is an important perspective from a key observer who was at the heart of the unfolding drama. Begin, in years to come, was to deny Sharon's claim that as prime minister he supported and encouraged the "Jordan is Palestine" thesis that Sharon openly espoused. Begin's apologists argued that Begin could never uphold that thesis because he still believed, at least theoretically, in the Revisionist Zionist doctrine that both banks of the Jordan belong to the Jewish people. Lewis, familiar with all this, nevertheless asserted that Begin "no longer really held ideologically that Jordan is Israel. He thought it was the place where the Palestinians ought to be."

Having achieved his cherished U.S.-Israel Memorandum of Agreement, Menachem Begin was beside himself with rage when Lewis called at his home on December 20, 1981, barely a fortnight after it was signed, to inform him that it was suspended.

Washington was infuriated by Begin's sudden decision to effectively annex the Golan Heights.* Begin had slipped in the bath the previous month and broken his hip, a painful injury that laid him up in the hospital and then convalescing at home for several weeks. Worried by the gathering storm within his political constituency over the Sinai settlements, and angered by some intemperate rhetoric from Syria's president, Hafez Assad, that he heard on the radio, Begin came up with the Golan annexation as a dramatic political palliative. He got the cabinet to approve it on December 13. Then, from a wheelchair, he rammed the legislation through its three Knesset readings on one day, and the annexation became law.

Lewis was ushered into the prime minister's bedroom, where he found Sharon and Shamir flanking the prime minister, his face gaunt with pain and indignation. After terse pleasantries, Begin launched into a seventy-minute diatribe, which, he said, was his "message" to President Reagan. "Do you think that we are teenagers to be punished, slapped on the wrist? Do you think Israel is a vassal state of the United States? Are we just another 'banana republic'? Let me tell you,

---

* The legislation provided that "the law, jurisdiction, and administration of the State of Israel" should henceforth apply to the Golan Heights. This is the same language that Israel used when it annexed East Jerusalem in 1967 and is tantamount to annexation, though the word "annexation" was not used.

Mr. Ambassador, that this is not Israel!" Lewis was allowed five minutes at the end to make his remonstrances, then was ushered out. As he walked down the stairs, he was intrigued to see the entire cabinet and top army brass assembled in the reception room for what was clearly going to be an important cabinet meeting.

Begin was then carried downstairs, with Sharon and Shamir attending, and took obvious satisfaction in recounting to his ministers how he had proudly upheld the dignity of their country in the face of the condescending superpower. He then proceeded to acquaint them, for the first time, with his plan for the invasion of Lebanon.

The IDF, he said, must go into Lebanon and clear out all the terrorist bases. The invasion was necessary because the PLO, despite an American-brokered cease-fire in south Lebanon the previous July—after months of cross-border rocket and artillery exchanges—was relentlessly attacking or trying to attack targets elsewhere in Israel and Jewish targets abroad.

He wanted a decision in principle from the cabinet authorizing the proposed operation. He asked Sharon and Chief of Staff Eitan to present the plan in greater detail. They said the invasion by armor and infantry would extend up to the outskirts of Beirut. Amphibious units would land at the Christian-controlled port of Jounieh, north of Beirut, and link up with the Christian militias. Sharon said they did not want war with Syria and hoped the cease-fire between Israel and Syria could be preserved. But the army would be ready to fight back if need be against any Syrian intervention. The proposed operation was code-named Pines.

The ministers were gobsmacked. They had not previously been exposed to Begin and Sharon's planning, much less to the army's detailed preparations. But Ehrlich, Burg, and some of the other moderates quickly assimilated the scene: Begin dangerously euphoric, Sharon assiduously egging him on, Shamir silent but approving, the army zealous for a new war to excise the trauma of Yom Kippur. They put up a spirited resistance. One after another, they spoke against the plan, emphasizing the complications that could arise from an invasion and trying, albeit deferentially, to cool the prime minister's ardor. Begin, suddenly deflated, realized he would not have a majority. Abruptly, he ended the discussion without putting his proposal to a vote and had himself carried back upstairs.[36] "You see," he was heard explaining to Sharon and Eitan, "it's not yet ripe for a decision."[37]

Though genuinely taken aback by the scope of Begin's war plan, the ministers could hardly pretend to be surprised by the prime minister's preoccupation with Lebanon. Lebanon, and specifically the

Mayflower man: Grandfather
Mordechai Scheinerman

A nicer childhood than he admitted to:
Arik (left) and his sister, Dita,
in Kfar Malal in 1933

Busy farmyard

Fussily turned out: with Avigail,
Samuil's sister

Family portrait to send home to Russia?
Father Samuil and Mother Vera with
Arik, Dita, and Vera's brother, Joseph

Defending the property: no annexation here

Rare respite: Samuil with
his two children at the
Tel Aviv beach

Stories from Petrograd:
with Miriam and Dita

Seder night at the Scheinermans, 1935: bare boards but fine wine.
Left to right: Aunt Avigail with cousin Natana, Uncle Sholem with Arik,
Vera with Dita, Grandmother Miriam, Samuil.

A plump, clear-eyed boy, 1937

"Neck-deep in it and fighting":
January 1948

Reprisal operation: with "Israel's finest soldier,"
Meir Har-Zion, April 1954

Spirit of 101: "hostile takeover" of the paratroopers

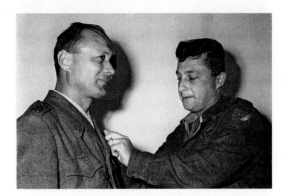

"Awarding wings" to Chief of Staff Moshe Dayan,
1955: a complicated lifelong relationship

"Ate from the same mess tin": Sinai War, October 1956

At the Mitle Pass, October 31, 1956. Rehavam Ze'evi
(center) warns; Arik (left) laughs. Who directed
the pointless battle that followed?

Special affection: with David Ben-Gurion in 1957

"He really was a lovely boy." Gur with Arik,
Lily, and Vera, December 1963.

May 1967: digging in on the Egyptian border

With Yael Dayan, war correspondent,
legend debunker

The Six-Day War winning team, June 1967:
Generals Tal, Sharon, Gavish, and Yoffe.

On our side? Arik and Ze'evi pray together with Chief
Chaplain Shlomo Goren, March 1968. An IDF reprisal
force was pinned down across the Jordan border.

Bereaved father, bereaved brother:
Arik with Omri, May 1968

With Chief of Staff Haim Bar-Lev (left) and
Dayan (right) on the Suez Canal. Israel's
initial defenses were "amateurish."

"I really like the Bedouin." With General Avraham
Yoffe, visiting Negev neighbors.

Not up to the job: transferring Southern Command
to General Shmuel Gonen, July 1973

"The situation was catastrophic. He was focused, businesslike, constructive." With Colonel Amnon Reshef at the start of the Yom Kippur War, October 1973.

October 8: Gonen tracks Arik down in the desert

Grappling with the monster. Tanks drag the 180-meter-long rolling bridge toward the canal.

Amphibious bridging tugs put the first Israeli tanks across

On the dunes with Haim
Bar-Lev, October 17. "I kept
myself from hitting him."

Command vehicle: M113
armored personnel carrier

Monster in place: the rolling bridge viewed from the Israeli side of the canal

With Dayan and Abrasha Tamir (top right). The superficial head wound dealt his rivals a mortal blow in the race for glory

With iconic wartime singer Yafa Yarkoni, in "Africa," days after the canal crossing

"King of Israel": reservists of the 143rd Division after the cease-fire

Together, in lockstep, for decades: with Yitzhak Rabin,
prime minister, 1976

Ministerial repast, 1978; lifelong yearning for falafel

"Aha, it's you." Egyptian president and
peacemaker Anwar Sadat.

"A large Jewish settlement will surely arise near Nablus."
February 1981: the minister of agriculture and chairman of the
cabinet settlement committee shows Prime Minister Menachem
Begin and Interior Minister (and Palestinian autonomy
negotiator) Yosef Burg (directly behind Begin) the site of
Elon Moreh. Right, Gush Emunim leader Benny Katzover.

November 1981:
now minister of defense,
with young settlers at
Maon in the Hebron hills

Going over the ground: with Egyptian officers near the canal
during an official visit as defense minister

In pain, but in control:
Begin with his defense minister, March 1982

Guard of honor:
with South Lebanese
army commander
Sa'ad Hadad

Allies at war: Begin and Hadad, June 7, 1982

Costly conquest:
Beaufort, June 7, 1982

King again? With IDF reservists
in Lebanon, June 1982.

"Those who say he duped
us and misled us are simply
distorting." Cabinet briefing
in Lebanon, June 21, 1982.
Yitzhak Shamir, foreign
minister, in the foreground.
Behind him, Mordechai
Zippori, general turned
minister, a persistent
critic of the war.

Rabin (second from right),
still supportive: August 1982
near Beirut. Chief of Staff
Rafael Eitan is on the left;
General Abrasha Tamir
is in the center.

PLO's activities there, had been on this government's agenda since the beginning of its first term in 1977. Always Israel's quietest frontier, the Lebanese border had gradually become a hotbed of terrorist violence in the early 1970s, following the forcible eviction of the PLO's forces from Jordan in September 1970 and the relocation of many of them to south Lebanon. In 1975, civil war broke out in Lebanon as the long-dominant Christian communities lashed out at the other, increasingly assertive confessions—Sunni Muslims, Shiite Muslims, and Druze. The PLO fanned the flames. It claimed to speak for, and protect, the more than 200,000 Palestinian refugees, many of them second- and third-generation, living in refugee camps around the country.

Israel traditionally maintained discreet ties with the Christians; Ben-Gurion back in the 1950s had seen them as potential allies. In 1976, Syrian forces entered Lebanon and joined the fighting on the Christian side. Soon, the Syrians were deployed across much of the country and were dominating its politics.

Yitzhak Rabin regarded Syria's intervention as essentially a favorable development from Israel's standpoint and willingly acceded to U.S. requests that Israel not interfere. Rabin believed that the Syrian army would now be extended across two fronts, the Golan Heights and Lebanon, making it more vulnerable and less threatening should war come. Together with U.S. diplomats, he drew a "red line" across southern Lebanon that, by unwritten understanding with Damascus, was to mark the limit of Syrian deployment acceptable to Israel. Rabin always insisted that the serious threat to Israel's security was from Arab regular armies—Egypt, Syria, Iraq, and Jordan. The PLO, he maintained, was a nuisance, albeit a painful one, but not an existential military challenge. Rabin and his defense minister, Shimon Peres, began arming and funding local Christian and Shiite militias in the border area of south Lebanon to serve as a counter to the growing PLO presence there.

In March 1978, with Begin now in power, a group of nine Palestinian terrorists reached Israel from Lebanon by boat, killed a young woman swimmer, hijacked two buses, crammed all the passengers into one of them, drove it down the coast, and were eventually halted in a murderous firefight outside Tel Aviv in which thirty-five of the passengers were killed and another seventy-one injured. All nine terrorists were killed. The IDF, under Minister of Defense Ezer Weizman, launched a swift sweep into south Lebanon, Operation Litani, aimed at killing or capturing PLO fighters or driving them north out of the border zone. It was a success and ended with the deployment of a UN force in the area. Israel withdrew most of its troops from Lebanese soil but retained what it called a "security zone," patrolled by a local Lebanese militia commanded by a Christian officer, Major Sa'ad Hadad, in close liaison with the IDF.

Gradually, the PLO filtered back into the south, and a guerrilla war developed between the Palestinian fighters and the south Lebanese militia and IDF forces. The PLO's Soviet-made Katyusha rocket launchers and 130-millimeter cannon could fire from north of the "security zone" and hit Israeli towns and kibbutzim across the border. Weizman kept the Israeli response to pinpoint reprisal raids. But after his resignation in 1980, and with Begin now the defense minister, Chief of Staff Eitan steadily escalated the situation with repeated IDF attacks and air strikes against Palestinian bases north of the "security zone."[38]

In April 1981, when Christian militia forces in the mountains to the east of Beirut found themselves hard-pressed by Syrian forces—the Syrians had meanwhile switched their support from the Christians to the Muslims—Begin sent in warplanes to shoot down a pair of Syrian troop-transport helicopters in a signal to Damascus to back off. The Syrians stopped their attack, but they deployed ground-to-air missiles in the Beqáa Valley, threatening Israel's aerial ascendancy.

For Begin, the Lebanese Christians were more than a strategic ally; their plight was a test case for Israel's most profound moral and historical mission as he understood it. The Syrians had turned against them, and they faced a coalition of hostile Muslim forces inside their country. "Yigael," Begin admonished his deputy prime minister, Yigael Yadin, his voice thick with drama and pathos. "Yigael, the danger of annihilation hangs over them. They are our allies. We will not behave toward them the way Chamberlain and Daladier behaved." Yadin, citing intelligence reports and backed by the deputy defense minister, Mordechai Zippori, and the chief of Military Intelligence, Yehoshua Saguy, warned Begin that the Lebanese Christian politicians were a feckless and self-serving bunch who "mean to drag us into their war. What interest do we have in supporting them?"

By the summer of 1981 the IDF was taking increasing casualties. The north of Israel was close to paralysis. Begin, in his campaign speeches that summer, declared, "Watch out, Assad, Raful and Yanosh are waiting for you." (Raful was Chief of Staff Rafael Eitan; Yanosh was CO of Northern Command Avigdor Ben-Gal.) The crowds loved it. But Begin's words rang increasingly hollow after the election as the border war intensified. Israeli warplanes bombed PLO bases in the refugee camps around Beirut, taking a heavy toll. But the Katyushas and artillery shells continued raining down across the border.

The Americans rushed in their top Lebanon expert, the veteran diplomat (and scion of a Lebanese-American family) Philip Habib, to negotiate a cease-fire. Sharon, the new defense minister, and Eitan urged a massive ground operation. But Begin bowed to the American pressure and overruled them. A cease-fire—Begin refused to use that term since it implied equality between the two combatants; he referred to a "cessation of hostilities"—went into effect on July 24, 1981. The border war immediately subsided. "I strenuously opposed the cease-fire," Sharon recalled. "No doubt the PLO would reduce its activity along the Lebanon border in accord with the letter of the agreement, but . . . it would step up its activities elsewhere." In the months that followed, Sharon cited every terrorist incident at home and abroad to bolster his case.[39]

The cabinet meeting at Begin's home on December 20 ended with a vague instruction from the prime minister to the generals to come up with an alternative, impliedly less sweeping plan. But Sharon proceeded in the confident expectation that the original one would eventually "ripen" to approval. On January 12, he flew secretly to Jounieh to meet with Bashir Gemayel, leader of the Christian Phalange Party and commander of the Lebanese Forces militia. The handsome young Gemayel drove his Israeli guest around Beirut incognito. Sharon was impressed by Gemayel's obvious popularity. He met his wife, Solange; his father, the veteran Lebanese Christian leader Pierre Gemayel; and Pierre's longtime ally cum rival Camille Chamoun, a former president of Lebanon.

" 'In case there is a war,' Bashir asked, 'what would you expect of us?' 'The first thing you should do is defend your borders here,' Sharon replied. 'We will not be able to come to your rescue if you lose ground little by little. Second, that hill over there, the defense ministry hill [in the Beirut suburb of Ba'abda]. That hill is vital. If there is a war, take that hill. [The hill was vital because on its slopes ran the Beirut–Damascus highway.] Third, Israel will not enter West Beirut. That's the capital, the government, the foreign embassies . . . West Beirut is your business and the business of the Lebanese Army.' "[40]

Sharon reported to Begin and the inner cabinet on his talks in Lebanon. Clearly, the idea of IDF forces linking up with the Christians, and, presumably, helping Gemayel in his bid for the Lebanese presidency, was still very much alive despite the cabinet's reservations over Operation Pines. Begin himself met with Bashir Gemayel in Jerusalem on February 16.

On April 3, 1982, an Israeli diplomat was shot dead by a terrorist in Paris, and the inner cabinet decided that from now on any such attack would bring an Israeli response against the PLO. On April 21, just days before the Sinai handover, Israeli warplanes were sent to bomb Palestinian targets in Lebanon, for the first time since the July cease-fire, following a mine explosion inside the south Lebanon "security zone" that took the life of an Israeli officer. The PLO did not retaliate; the Americans reportedly warned it that to do so would be to trigger an IDF invasion.[41]

On May 7, following terrorist attacks in Ashkelon and Jerusalem, the air force bombed again in Lebanon. This time PLO guns and Katyusha launchers responded, but all their hundred-odd shells fell wide, and it was clear the Palestinians were trying to avoid escalation.

It was clear, too, that as far as Israel was concerned, the war was just a matter of time. No evidence was adduced linking the explosive charges laid in Ashkelon and Jerusalem to the PLO in Lebanon. The shooting in Paris, too, could not be pinned directly on Yasser Arafat's PLO. The specific provenance of specific acts of terrorism was plainly irrelevant. Israel was determined to act against what it saw as the chief source of Palestinian terror: the PLO in Lebanon.

How extensive would the Israeli military operation be? There had been a certain scaling back of the military planning in the wake of the December 20 cabinet meeting. Among those in the loop, there was vague talk of "Small Pines" as opposed to "Big Pines." But as meeting followed meeting of the inner cabinet and the full cabinet, that key question was still unresolved.

On May 16, Eitan submitted a more limited plan to the cabinet, and Begin asked for an approval in principle, with the precise timing still to be settled. But while both Sharon and Eitan spoke in terms of clearing south Lebanon of PLO artillery, the maps displayed before the ministers were essentially those of Operation Pines, showing the IDF columns striking north toward the Christian-controlled areas. Sharon did not speak explicitly of linking up with the Christian forces. He did say, though, that the Israeli operation would have an influence on affairs inside Lebanon. He also said the IDF incursion would last only twenty-four hours.[42]

The ministers knew, of course, that Begin and Sharon's original plans called for a deeper penetration and presumed it would take considerably longer. Yitzhak Modai, minister without portfolio (and Sharon's friend and erstwhile fellow officer), asked: "Given that there are always unexpected developments on the battlefield, would the cabinet be asked for approval of movements farther north?" To this Begin responded that the cabinet could be called to meet at any time such a question came up.

Begin, in a passionate speech, said Israel's problem was not one of three miles or ten miles but of the interpretation of the cease-fire. The PLO had announced that it would continue its attacks inside Israel. "They are declaring war on the people of Israel, that they will make every form of trouble, massacre and assassination of men, women, and children, all over Israel . . . Every nation would react to that."

Sharon now flew to Washington to make essentially the same presentation to Secretary Haig and, hopefully, get a green light from the Americans to proceed. At least now Washington's fear of Israel not withdrawing from Sinai had been laid to rest.

The question of what color light, green, yellow, or red, Sharon actually received from Haig has been exhaustively discussed over the years. The two men themselves, as might be expected, both denied there was any green light. "They [the Americans] were against. Totally against. I have to admit that," Sharon said in an interview with the Italian journalist Oriana Fallaci during the war. "There was no collusion," he insisted in a later interview. "The most one could say is that Haig understood our situation better than others in Washington."[43]

Sharon's report to the cabinet when he returned gave the ministers the distinct impression that the United States would be sympathetic when the IDF struck.[44] Haig, probably apprised of this, wrote to Begin on May 28 urging "complete restraint." To this the prime minister replied, "Mr. Secretary, the man has not been born who will ever obtain from me consent to let Jews be killed by a bloodthirsty enemy."

CHAPTER 6 · THROUGH THE MIRE

A bloodthirsty enemy struck in London on June 3, 1982. His Jewish victim was the Israeli ambassador to the U.K., Shlomo Argov, shot through the head by a lone assailant as he left a dinner at the Dorchester hotel. The injury left him mentally and physically incapacitated for the rest of his life.

The attack was perpetrated by the Abu Nidal group, headquartered in Baghdad. Abu Nidal, or Sabri al-Bana, broke away from the PLO years before and was a virulent foe of Yasser Arafat, the PLO chairman, whom he called "the Jewess's son" and had tried in the past to assassinate.[1] But none of that was of any interest to the cabinet, which convened in emergency session the next day. "Abu Nidal, Abu Shmidal," Chief of Staff Eitan retorted to the intelligence briefings. "They're all PLO. We need to f—k the PLO."[2] He was out of line, but he perfectly expressed the sense of the meeting.

Prime Minister Begin preferred not to grace Palestinian terrorists with any name or initials. They were all *hamenuvalim,* the swine. No country on earth would fail to respond to an attack like that, he said. Israel had desisted for long enough from hitting the PLO in Lebanon. To continue to desist would be absurd.[3] But Begin did not propose the invasion of south Lebanon at this stage. His decision was to bomb PLO bases and depots in south Lebanon and in the Beirut suburbs. The PLO's response would determine whether Israel would make do with that or launch its long-planned ground assault.

The Israeli warplanes hit nine targets, including a sprawling sports center in south Beirut that served the Palestinian fighters as a training camp. The PLO "signed its own death warrant," in the words of Ambassador Lewis, by responding with a massive artillery barrage all across the Israeli border zone. Interestingly, neither Arafat nor Sharon was involved in this preliminary round of hostilities. The PLO leader was in Jeddah, on a mediating mission to end the Iran-Iraq War.[4] Sharon was on a discreet official visit to Romania.

When the cabinet met again, on Saturday night, June 5, in Begin's official residence, Sharon was back, and the shelling in the north had continued unabated for twenty-four hours. Begin made it clear that he would ask the ministers to approve the ground assault. "It is our fate in Eretz Yisrael to fight and sacrifice. The alternative is Auschwitz." He asked the minister of defense to take them through the details of the proposed operation once again, "as though for the first time." Sharon and Eitan described a short, multipronged incursion designed to clear the entire border region of the PLO. The army would advance some forty to forty-five kilometers, they said, the farthest range of the PLO's artillery. "What about Beirut?" the always-skeptical Ehrlich asked. "Beirut's out of the picture," Sharon replied.

Begin acknowledged Ehrlich's question by saying, "In war, you know how it begins, but you never know how it ends. But let me state very clearly: nothing will be done without a cabinet decision." Ehrlich was unconvinced and abstained, as did his fellow Likud-Liberal the energy minister, Yitzhak Berman. "You know Sharon," Ehrlich whispered, as they walked out together. "He'll dupe everyone. He'll take us much farther than 40–45 km."[5] The communiqué, meticulously edited by Begin himself, informed the waiting world that

1. the cabinet has decided to instruct the IDF to place all the civilian population of the Galilee beyond the range of the terrorists' fire from Lebanon, where they, their bases, and their headquarters are concentrated;
2. the name of the operation is Peace for Galilee;
3. during the operation, the Syrian army will not be attacked unless it attacks our forces; and
4. Israel continues to aspire to the signing of a peace treaty with independent Lebanon, its territorial integrity preserved.

This language, and the fraught exchanges leaked from inside the cabinet room, were immediately subjected to the most intense parsing and speculation by Israeli and foreign commentators. Did the reference to the PLO's "headquarters"—everyone knew they were in Beirut—mean that the IDF was headed for Beirut after all? And what would happen if the Syrians did attack "our forces"? Would there be war between Israel and Syria? What was the reference to a "peace treaty with independent Lebanon"? Did that mean Israel would stay and intervene in Lebanese politics in order to install its ally the Maronite Christian leader Bashir Gemayel as the country's new president? There was no explicit mention of the forty- to forty-five-kilometer line that ostensibly was the limit of the IDF's intended advance.

In many ways, this ongoing exegesis was a microcosm of the months to come and indeed of the years of political and historical argument that followed. The same questions resounded: What did Sharon say? And what did he conceal? How much did Begin know? Were the ministers misled?

For Sharon, Begin's state of mind was crucial. If the defense minister left the prime minister out of the loop, then he was guilty, in effect, of a sort of putsch. If, on the other hand, Sharon acted in close concert with Begin, then the awareness or understanding of the other ministers at any given point was less important in terms of constitutional propriety. In wartime, after all, a small cabal of ministers led by the prime minister always runs things, to the exclusion of others.

Moshe Nissim, who was minister of justice under Begin, insisted years later that the ministers were fully informed at all times. "I've got a very great deal against Sharon," said Nissim, who was to become a bitter political foe of Sharon's in the decade following the war. "But those who say he duped us and misled us are simply distorting. They're trying to justify themselves, to escape criticism, to pretend they didn't know or didn't see when things began to go wrong. I was actually among the few who opposed the war that first Saturday night. I spoke against it. I said the casualties would be too high. But I said, 'I can see there is a large majority in favor, so I will vote in favor, too, though with a heavy heart.' "

The critics claimed that Sharon presented the cabinet, time after time, with faits accomplis on the ground and then argued that unless additional forward movements were approved, the troops would be in danger. Nissim did not deny this dynamic. But he insisted that the ministers, himself included, were open-eyed participants in it, not blind dupes. They visited the battlefields or studied the maps. "Let's be honest . . . I'm not going to change my tune to the media's rhythm, to the media attacks on Sharon."[6]

Begin's attitude during the buildup to the war was, as we have seen, implacably belligerent toward the PLO and expansively supportive of the Christians. There is overwhelming evidence that this remained the case throughout. Once again, as so often in his career, Sharon was the executor of the policy; despite his new eminence, he was not its conceiver or its instigator. Begin's apologists, however, among them his son, Benny, subsequently charged Sharon with misleading Begin, and Sharon fought them for years after to clear himself of that charge.

From the start, Israeli ground forces were never able to bring their considerably superior firepower fully to bear.* Four IDF armored columns streamed across the border into Lebanon. In the west, the Israeli tanks and artillery pushed up the heavily populated coastal strip toward Beirut, battling entrenched and determined PLO defenders all the way. At first, the advancing columns swung around the coastal towns of Tyre and Sidon and the large Palestinian refugee camp at Ein Hilwe near Sidon. Palestinian forces there were to be mopped up subsequently. But the "mopping up" proved tougher and much bloodier than had been envisaged. Civilian casualties mounted; fleeing refugees clogged the roads.

The world media, fed by the Palestinians—the IDF ill-advisedly barred reporters from covering the battles from the Israeli side—relayed horrific accounts of mass death and dislocation in perennially war-torn Lebanon. The figures widely quoted—Anthony Lewis, the noted columnist, cited them in *The New York Times*—10,000 killed and 600,000 made homeless, were later debunked. There weren't 600,000 people living in the entire area that the IDF had taken at this time. But the damage to Israel was deep and lasting. As the war dragged on into the summer, few in the world's chanceries were disposed to listen to Sharon's or Begin's justifications.

In the east, two divisions fought together as a corps under the command of Avigdor "Yanosh" Ben-Gal. An initial advance on the first day drew Syrian fire. PLO artillery embedded within the Syrian lines was also firing sporadically across the border onto Israeli villages.[7] Sharon ordered the army to prepare an advance along the west of the Beqáa Valley, in a movement demonstratively designed to outflank the Syrian deployment in the valley. This, he told the cabinet that night, would hopefully persuade the Syrians to withdraw northward—and take the PLO with them. Begin extolled this tactic as a "Hannibal maneuver."

During the night, meanwhile, the crack reconnaissance company of the Golani Brigade succeeded in storming the most symbolic strong-

---

* The IDF force deployed in the central and eastern sectors comprised some 35,000 men and 800 tanks. Another 22,000 men and 220 tanks fought in the west. Syrian forces in Lebanon on the eve of the war, according to Bregman, numbered some 30,000 men, 600-plus tanks, and 300-odd artillery pieces. More troops were brought in after the fighting began. The PLO had 15,000 full-time fighting men and additional militiamen recruited from among the refugees. They had only 100-odd tanks but 350 artillery pieces.

hold in south Lebanon: the ruined Crusader castle of Beaufort. Towering over the surrounding country, this fortress for years had given PLO gunners an unrivaled view toward their targets across the border while affording them, with its massive stone walls and underground chambers, effective protection from even the most furious Israeli bombing.

Sharon and Eitan's critics argued that the advancing armored units could have skirted the Beaufort and left it to fall later without a fight. In the event, the PLO defenders put up a spirited fight, and six Golani men died, including the company commander. To make matters much worse, Begin and Sharon, who arrived by helicopter on Monday afternoon and clambered about the fortress while the television cameras whirred, were not properly briefed on the battle and, in Sharon's words, "expressed our happiness that there had been no losses. In so doing we inadvertently caused great pain to the families of the soldiers killed in this battle."

This macabre episode fed a by-now-nagging feeling of discomfort among the few skeptical ministers about the way the "twenty-four- to forty-eight-hour, forty- to forty-five-kilometer operation" against the PLO in south Lebanon was being conducted. It already seemed to be evolving into running battles between sizable armored formations of the Israeli and Syrian armies. Sharon's "Hannibal maneuver" did not succeed. Not only did the Syrian units in the Beqáa fail to withdraw, but other units were quickly brought in from the north to confront the Israeli armor advancing gingerly along the narrow, winding mountain roads. During Monday, large-scale battles developed at several points across the central and eastern sectors.

The sense of unease deepened and spread in the wake of Begin's speech in the Knesset the next day, Tuesday, June 8. By the time he spoke, Israeli units converging on the strategic mountain town of Jezzine were engaged in pitched battles with the Syrian defenders. Yet Begin proclaimed, "We do not want war with Syria," employing all his rhetorical theatricality. "From this rostrum, I call on President Assad to instruct the Syrian army not to harm Israeli soldiers, and then nothing will happen to them. We do not want to harm anyone. We want only one thing: That no-one harm our settlements in the Galilee any more . . . If we achieve the 40 kilometer line from our northern border, the job is done, all fighting will cease. I make this appeal to the Syrian President."

The Syrian president and his soldiers in the field must have been bemused if they were listening. The Israeli prime minister was plainly out of touch with events on the ground. As the day wore on and the true situation emerged from the battlefield fog, awkward questions began to surface among Israeli politicians and pundits. Did the prime minister know what was going on in real time? Were Sharon and the army keeping things from him? Did he understand the risk of a full-fledged war with the Syrians, a war that might spread from south Lebanon to the Golan Heights?

Sharon, to his credit, spoke without Begin's glib certitude. "I cannot say to the cabinet that there will not be a clash with the Syrians," he warned on Saturday night. "There is that danger, because of the terrain in Lebanon and the proximity of the various forces and lines. But we will make every effort, and we will tell the Syrians that we harbor no hostile intention against them."[8]

The critics, whose numbers grew as the war dragged on, accused Sharon and Begin of deliberately courting the fight with Syria as part of their plan to install Bashir Gemayel as Lebanon's new president and weaken the Syrians' hold over his country so that he would sign a peace accord with Israel. Sharon and Begin insisted that these were not their war aims but only ancillary benefits that might accrue from the principal war aim, which was to uproot the PLO from the south.

Begin did have an additional war aim that he did not conceal, though neither did he proclaim it publicly as an "official" part of his policy. The war in Lebanon, he believed, would heal the nation from the trauma of the Yom Kippur War.[9] Yom Kippur had been "a darkening of the lights," Begin told Eitan when he visited the chief of staff's forward headquarters on Monday, June 7, before they flew on together to the Beaufort. "But that was a long time ago," the prime minister continued, waxing euphoric. "We are coming out of that trauma. Now [with this war] we are coming out of it."[10] Two days later, he asserted proudly that "in Operation Peace for Galilee the nation of Israel has overcome the trauma of the Yom Kippur War."[11]

To be fair, Begin delivered that exultant verdict on Wednesday, June 9, at the moment of Israel's undeniably momentous success against the Syrians—and at the moment before the war in Lebanon began to go grievously wrong.

On Tuesday, one Israeli column advanced north, to within striking distance of the Beirut–Damascus road. If the road were cut, the Syrian force in Beirut, some seven thousand men, would be effectively cut off. With the Christian Phalange's Lebanese Forces holding the territory north of Beirut, moreover, the Palestinian fighters holed up in the city and all those fleeing there from the fighting in the south would find themselves trapped. Israel's paramount interest in reaching and cutting the road was now both strikingly evident and tangibly feasible.

But the Syrians were not done for yet. They had their anti-aircraft missiles, deployed thickly in the Beqáa. On the basis of the Yom Kippur War experience, the Syrian commanders were confident that the SAM-6s and SAM-3s gave their ground forces reliable protection against the Israeli Air Force. In early dogfights over the border region the Syrians had lost six MiGs. The IAF was intact. But now the fighting was moving toward the areas covered by the missile umbrella. Sharon urged the cabinet to approve a concerted aerial attack on the missile batteries. His rationale, as so often in this war, was unarguable: soldiers' lives were on the line.

At 2:00 p.m. on Wednesday, June 9, the IAF struck. Within an hour, nineteen of the twenty-three Syrian batteries were smoldering wrecks and the other four badly damaged. The IAF was still entirely intact. The Syrian commanders sent up, by their own account, a hundred MiGs to challenge the Israeli warplanes. Twenty-nine of them were downed before the day was over. Israeli losses were still nil.[*]

For the IAF, it was "a sensational triumph, one which can be compared only with its successes on the morning of 5 June 1967 . . . or its successful bombing of the Iraqi nuclear reactor on 7 June 1981."[12] The Israeli success against the Soviet-supplied missiles prompted discreet jubilation among intelligence experts and aerial and electronic warfare officers in Washington and serious ripples of concern in Moscow.[13] For Syria, the results of the air battle may have influenced its decision not to extend the land engagements to the Golan Heights.[14]

Despite the aerial victory, the land battles with the Syrians over the next two days were tough, and the IDF sustained painful losses. In the central sector, the Israeli armor ran up against strongly entrenched units of Syrian commandos equipped with antitank missiles and fighting hard to prevent the tanks breaking through to the road. Syrian attack helicopters joined the fray, to deadly effect.

On the night of June 10, an Israeli tank battalion, apparently losing its way, found itself entrapped in a narrow defile near Sultan Yakub, fired on from all sides by Syrian infantry dug into the hills. Due to administrative snafus and lapses in communications, the large IDF forces in the area were not directed to relieve the hard-pressed battalion. Finally, under cover of artillery fire, the surviving tanks and APCs retreated to the IDF lines. Twenty Israeli soldiers died at Sultan

---

[*] Air battles continued sporadically until the end of the week, and the Syrians lost another 51 planes, bringing the total to 87, all frontline fighters: MiG 23s, MiG 21s, and Sukhoi 22s. The IAF tally of air losses in the war was two helicopters and a Skyhawk jet downed by PLO rocket fire (Herzog, *Arab-Israeli Wars*, 338).

Yakub, and another thirty were injured. Six more were left on the battlefield.*

All in all, during the first week of the war the Syrians lost close to three hundred tanks compared with barely over a tenth of that figure on the Israeli side. On paper, then, especially when joined with the destruction of the ground-to-air missiles and the totally lopsided outcome of the aerial dogfights, Israel had scored a convincing victory over Syria. Nevertheless, the stinging defeat at Sultan Yakub, exacerbated by the lingering uncertainty surrounding the MIAs, cast a pall for Israelis even over this relatively brief, relatively successful part of "Operation Peace for Galilee."

In the west, too, the first week's fighting against the PLO had proved harder and more costly than had been anticipated. Calls by the IDF to civilians in Tyre and Sidon to flee to the beaches were heeded in part, but the numbers of dead and wounded among noncombatants were still very high, and damage to civilian buildings and infrastructure was extensive. As they labored up the coast toward Beirut, the Israeli columns encountered ever tougher Palestinian resistance. Palestinian boys barely in their teens wielded rocket-propelled grenade launchers to devastating effect. IDF casualties mounted daily. At the village of Sil, just south of the capital, Syrian commando units took part in the battle alongside the PLO fighters. From Sil, part of the Israeli force veered east, toward the suburb of Ba'abda on the southeastern edge of Beirut, where the Lebanese Ministry of Defense and the official presidential residence were situated.

On the morning of Thursday, the tenth, Sharon explained to the cabinet that IDF forces from the west and from the center would try to reach the road at Aley and cut it there. It was hard going, Sharon stressed, not a picnic at all. The roads were steep and narrow and frequently mined. The advancing columns came under attack from close range.†

The troops would be close to Beirut, Sharon continued, but were

---

* One died, and his body was subsequently returned by the Syrians; another was captured by the Syrians and eventually returned; a third was captured and returned three years later as part of the prisoner deal with Ahmed Jibril's Popular Front for the Liberation of Palestine–General Command. Three more, Zechariah Baumel, Zvi Feldman, and Yehuda Katz, disappeared and were never found.
† In *Warrior,* Sharon wrote of "serious tactical mistakes and poor staff work" in the army that had resulted in episodes such as Sultan Yakub and had led to the "failure to keep the planned timetable" and reach the road before the Friday cease-fire.

Legend:
- Israeli Attack
- The 40-45 km line
- The Israeli Front line June 6-11, 1982
- Stream
- Road
- International Border
- IDF seaborne forces
- Siege of Beirut, June-September 1982

LEBANON

Jounieh

Beirut   Port

Bikfaya

Zahle   Riyak

Lebanon Mt.

Sabra
Shatila

Airport
Sil   Ba'abda   Aley   Beirut-Damascus Road

Bhamdoun

JUN. 23-25

Barr liyas

JUN. 9   JUN. 11

Damour

Rushmieh

Mediterranean Sea

JUN. 8

Shouf Mt.

JUN. 8

JUN. 10

Sultan
Yakub

Awali River

JUN. 10

Beirut-Damascus Road

Beqaa Valley

Sidon

Lebanon Mt.

JUN. 10

Jezzine

Karaoun

JUN. 10

Zaharani River

Aramta

JUN. 9

Rashaya

JUN. 7

JUN. 9

Ein Ata

Nabatiyah   JUN. 7

Litani River

Hasbaya   JUN. 9

JUN. 6

Litani River

Marjayoun

Beaufort

Khiam

Hermon Mt.

SYRIA

Tyre

Sayda

JUN. 6

Kiryat
Shmona

Tibnin   JUN. 7

JUN. 6

Kuneitra

Bint Jbeil

ISRAEL

0   km   40

Nahariya

Safed

explicitly instructed not to advance into the city itself. Dealing with Beirut, as he put it, would be better left to the Lebanese government and the Lebanese army. As to the IDF linking up with the Christian Phalange forces, "We won't initiate it, but if they approach us, we won't reject them out of hand."[15]

This last was blatantly disingenuous: a Phalange liaison officer was already stationed with the IDF forward command post at Ba'abda. Bashir Gemayel himself had visited Northern Command headquarters at Safed on June 8, the third day of the war, and conferred there with Eitan.[16] But the Phalange forces' involvement in the war thus far had been peripheral and ineffective. Their leader, carefully nursing his presidential ambitions, made it clear to the Israelis that he must avoid the perception of being in cahoots with their invasion of his country.

By this time, the Soviets' concern for their Syrian client was producing anxious Soviet pressure on Washington. The situation was growing "extremely dangerous," Leonid Brezhnev wrote to Ronald Reagan, and was rife with "seeds of escalation." The United States itself was growing hourly more anxious over the fate of Lebanon and the repercussions of the widening war throughout the Arab world. Vice President George Bush and Defense Secretary Weinberger had urged tough measures from the outset to rein in Israel. But Secretary of State Haig, traveling in Europe with the president, had held, with Reagan, to a more sympathetic line. The U.S. special envoy Habib rushed back to the region at the outbreak of the war. He tried to convey Begin's message of reassurance to Hafez Assad in Damascus. Now he was urging stern U.S. diplomacy to procure a cease-fire.

"As for Begin," Haig recalled, "he was not inclined toward a cease-fire until Israeli objectives had been achieved. But what were these objectives? Were they the ones we had heard earlier in the war or were they now the more ambitious goals of the Sharon plan?" In fact they were the latter, and always had been.* Begin was entirely supportive as Sharon explained to the ministers that the army needed a little more time to take the road. He warded off direct demands from Reagan to put a cease-fire in place on Thursday. Finally, with the

---

* Eitan insists in his memoirs that the maps presented to the cabinet at the Saturday night meeting had arrows pointing clearly to the road. "We presented the 'big plan,' and the cabinet approved it. The plan explicitly included capturing a stretch of the Beirut–Damascus Road." Eitan adds that the forty- to forty-five-kilometer line was "never part of the cabinet decision or the instructions of the General Staff to the commanders in the field . . . Everything was clear, and the ministers fully understood it."

troops close to Aley, although not there yet, he could resist no longer. He ordered the end of hostilities at midday on Friday.

Had the cease-fire held, Habib might have succeeded at this stage in peaceably negotiating the PLO's withdrawal from Beirut. The United States supported this Israeli demand. The deal would presumably have entailed Israel's withdrawal, too. "Habib was trying to work out an arrangement which would have the PLO evacuate Beirut and would have brought the conflict to an end," Sam Lewis recalled.[17]

But the cease-fire collapsed and, though reinstated, continued to collapse again and again as all the while IDF units pushed steadily forward until they reached the road and clamped tight their ring of steel around Beirut. Instead of peaceable negotiations, seventy days of siege ensued, amid incessant bombardment and hardship for the people of the city—and deepening opprobrium for Israel in the world—until a deal was finally struck and Yasser Arafat and his men were evacuated under the close protection of American, French, and Italian troops.

The casualties that the IDF sustained—some three hundred soldiers dead and more than fifteen hundred injured by the end of this period—and the enormous damage to the American relationship and to Israel's international standing clearly outweighed any benefit obtained from driving the PLO from Beirut. All that was true, moreover, *before* the massacre at Sabra and Shatila in September. But neither Begin nor Sharon had the statesmanship to break out of the vortex of their own swirling, arrogant ambitions. Together they were sucked down into the morass of murderous Lebanese strife.

On June 22, with Begin on a visit to Washington (and Ehrlich standing in as acting prime minister), the IDF launched a concerted attack eastward along the road, supported by artillery and airpower. Sharon was determined to broaden Israel's grip on the road, making the siege of the city impermeable. The Syrians fought back hard with their antitank commando units, and it was only after sixty hours of battle that the stretch of road from Bhamdoun to Aley was clear of them. The cost to Israel of that battle alone: another 28 soldiers killed and 168 wounded.[18]

In the cabinet, ministers demanded of Ehrlich that he put a stop to the renewed fighting. Ehrlich admitted that he had had no prior knowledge of it. Again, Sharon and Eitan resorted to their soldiers-in-danger and enemy-violations arguments. But increasingly these were losing their credibility. Ministers were being assailed by complaints from relatives and friends in the reserves who felt the war was dragging on needlessly, at mounting cost in life and limb. Some brought reports depicting Sharon, on the front lines, mocking his cabinet colleagues. "In the morning I fight the terrorists," he was heard to say, "and in the evening I go back to Jerusalem to fight in cabinet."

Begin appeared to emerge from the White House more or less unscathed, despite a deepening distrust and animosity toward him and Sharon among many senior U.S. officials. "Reagan Backs Israel" was *The Washington Post* headline the next morning. "Reagan and Begin Appear in Accord," *The New York Times* reported. But the newspapers were reading it wrong, as was Begin himself. "The President's anger with Begin, fed by the greater anger of Weinberger (who was reportedly exploring ways to cut off military deliveries to Israel) and others, seemed to grow by the day," Alexander Haig wrote. And with Haig himself about to leave office, Israel's war aims would lose their only advocate in the Reagan administration.

Haig believed with Begin and Sharon that sustained, relentless Israeli pressure in Lebanon would bring about the PLO's departure. The secretary designate, George Shultz, was not convinced.

Begin, however, relished the moment. Addressing the Knesset on June 29, he insisted that the IDF was "near Beirut . . . at the gates of Beirut" but absolutely not *in* Beirut. "I've said all along that we don't want to enter Beirut, neither west Beirut nor east Beirut. We totally didn't want to. And we still don't want to today. But, for God's sake, you are all experienced people; I appeal to you as a friend to friends, as a Jew to other Jews. . . . [A]s a result of developments . . . we are deployed today alongside Beirut, and the terrorists are trapped within. . . . Mr. Speaker, happy and fortunate is the nation that has such an army; happy and fortunate is the army that has such a general as Raful as its commander; and happy and fortunate is the state that has Ariel Sharon as its defense minister. With all my heart I say this."[19]

Habib was working on a package that was to include a U.S. Marine presence in Beirut to ensure—and also protect—the PLO's departure. Sharon inveighed against this on the grounds that even after the evacuation some PLO men would be left behind and would need to be flushed out. But the marine presence would prevent or impair that necessary activity.[20]

The PLO for its part, gradually acquiescing in the eventual likelihood of its being forced out, demanded Israel's withdrawal, too, and the deployment of a multinational force in Beirut to defend the Palestinian communities living in the sprawling refugee camps in the south of the city after the fighters had left.*

A cabinet communiqué at the end of July proclaimed that "Israel is willing to accept a cease-fire in Lebanon, with the explicit condition that it be absolute and mutual." With breathtaking chutzpah, it went on to announce that "the Government of Israel is of the view that measures should begin, through the Lebanese government, to provide accommodation for refugees in Lebanon, in preparation for the winter months," and that "the cabinet decided to establish a ministerial committee . . . to elaborate principles, ways and means for a solution of the refugee problem in the Middle East through their resettlement. The committee will be aided by experts and will submit its recommendations to the cabinet."

By the first week of August, Israel was facing the full fury of an American president who felt his friendship had been betrayed. On August 2, in the Oval Office, a somber foreign minister Shamir listened while Reagan railed over television footage from Beirut "of babies with their arms blown off." The previous day, Israel had bombed the southern suburbs of Beirut for ten straight hours. " 'If you invade West Beirut, it would have the most grave, most grievous, consequences for our relationship,' the president told Shamir and added, 'Should these Israeli practices continue, it will become increasingly difficult to defend the proposition that Israeli use of U.S. arms is for defensive purposes.' "[21]

The crisis escalated further that same night when Habib called the State Department, as Shultz recalled,

> screaming in rage . . . [that] the IDF shelling was the worst he had seen in eight weeks of war . . . Begin was calmly denying that any shelling was taking place; this had just been confirmed by Defense Minister Ariel Sharon . . . The United States was being fed hysterical, inflated reporting, Begin said.
>
> [Charles] Hill [a foreign service officer] relayed this to Habib. "Oh, yeah?" Habib said, and held his tacsat earpiece out the window so that we could hear the Israeli artillery firing. Hill counted eight shells

---

* Relations between Sharon and Habib steadily deteriorated. "As time wore on," Sam Lewis recalled, "[Habib] became . . . increasingly an Israel critic, influenced no doubt by the continual Israeli shelling of Beirut. He must have been shaken at the continuing sight of smoke plumes from artillery shells and bombs from planes . . . The pattern of an anguished Habib reporting at great length to Washington, followed by some kind of démarche delivered either in Washington or in Jerusalem, began at the end of June and continued through the summer until the PLO finally withdrew."

within thirty seconds from IDF artillery batteries located just below Habib's position . . . Meanwhile, back in Israel, Ariel Sharon was on the phone to Bill Brown [the deputy chief of mission], heaping scorn on our reports: they are false, hysterical, unprofessional; the IDF has done nothing like what is being claimed, Sharon said.[22]

Sam Lewis picks up the story. "Shultz's U.S. Marine Corps background kicked in at that point; his face turned almost purple as he told Shamir just what Habib was personally watching; he also told him to set the Prime Minister straight and see to it that the bombardment ceased forthwith." Reagan wrote to Begin warning that the relationship between their two nations hung in the balance.

Begin's gushing reply, comparing Arafat holed up in West Beirut to Hitler in his bunker in 1945, left Reagan cold. Begin for his part was heard to mutter in regard to the American president, "Jews bend the knee only before God."[23]

IDF troops were dispatched to Jounieh on August 8 deliberately to harass and disrupt the landing of the first units of the multinational force (MNF), which was to comprise American, French, and Italian troops. American helicopters tried to ferry the French troops ashore, but Israeli jeeps raced around the designated landing pad to prevent them from doing so. Presumably, this was Sharon's way of underscoring his continued objection to the MNF deploying in Beirut before the PLO had left.

Habib had managed to find safe havens for the PLO men in Tunisia and several other Arab countries. On August 10, Israel received a draft of Habib's proposed "package deal" for finally ending the war. In a compromise between Israeli demands and Palestinian fears, it provided for the evacuation by sea of part of the PLO a few days before the deployment of the MNF. After that, the remainder of the PLO and the Syrian troops in Beirut would be evacuated from Lebanon under MNF supervision. The PLO was to be allowed to carry its small arms, but heavy weapons would be handed over to the Lebanese army. The MNF would remain in Beirut for one month.

Sharon was unhappy with the timetable and wanted assurances that if the evacuation stopped, the MNF would be withdrawn. The cabinet decided to accept the package "in principle." But in defiance of the cabinet's decision in principle, the air force was ordered to prepare another massive bombardment of Beirut. In addition, large forces of long- and medium-range artillery were deployed around Beirut. They were instructed to prepare to lay down a "rolling screen of fire" on the Palestinian southern suburbs, a bombardment more concentrated and devastating than even the air force could deliver. On August 12, this vast firepower began to rain down on the city. The IAF flew more than a hundred bombing sorties. Civilian casualties mounted by the hour.

Reagan called Begin and spoke, deliberately, of a "holocaust." Begin instinctively bridled. Reagan did not back off and gave Begin an "ultimatum" to stop the bombardment forthwith. Begin reported back to the president that the bombing had stopped at 5:00 p.m. The cabinet had also decided, he said, that any further use of the air force would require the prime minister's personal approval. Sharon was no longer empowered to bomb Beirut.

Begin's public clipping of Sharon's wings reflected a bitter debate inside the cabinet room, the angriest and bitterest since the war began. Minister after minister accused Sharon of deliberately seeking to upend the American-mediated package deal.

There had been earlier signs of a weakening in Sharon's all-powerful position. On July 30, the housing minister, David Levy, pointedly asked Begin at cabinet if he knew about certain troop movements around the Beirut airport, and Begin replied: "David, I always know about everything. Some things I know about before, and some things after." Sharp-eared ministers discerned a note of exasperation in his voice.[24]

A week later, Minister of the Interior Burg asked Begin about the call-up of a reserves paratroop brigade (his son's) at short notice. He feared it meant the army was preparing to storm West Beirut, with the inevitably high loss of life that that would entail. He warned the prime minister that his party, the National Religious Party, would leave the coalition if that happened. Begin said he knew nothing about the call-up and hadn't approved it. He called Sharon, who readily confirmed that he had approved it. After all, he explained, the two of them had discussed the prospect of storming the city, albeit as a last resort if the diplomacy failed, and calling up reserves for this eventuality was "obvious." "Obvious? What do you mean obvious? How can you do that without [my] approval? So many people know and the prime minister doesn't know!" Sharon apologized profusely.[25]

Outrage over the bombings put paid to any lingering solidarity in the Labor opposition with the government at war. Yitzhak Rabin, Labor's premier defense spokesman, had supported the siege of Beirut, including the cutoff of water, much to the chagrin of his own party doves. Now the doves called for Sharon's dismissal and for a commission of inquiry to be set up to investigate the war.[26] Sharon for his part began accusing the opposition of cynically exploiting the war for political ends. Labor was "marshaling all its great media strength and international resources . . . to unseat the government—and all this while

Israeli forces were in the field in mid-battle. It was unprecedented and, to anyone with a sense of Israeli political history, unbelievable."[27]

On August 21, the evacuation of Beirut began. It lasted for twelve days, and by the end 14,298 armed men had been ferried out of the city. More than 8,000 of them were PLO men and the remainder Syrian soldiers. Another 664 women and children were evacuated with them. Some 8,150 of the evacuees were taken out by sea, to Tunisia and seven other Arab countries (Syria, North Yemen, South Yemen, Algeria, Sudan, Iraq, and Jordan). The rest went overland, along the Beirut–Damascus road, with Israeli soldiers shouting obscenities at them from the hillsides.

Whether the Israeli military pressure or the dogged American diplomacy was the primary reason for Arafat's agreement to go, Sharon felt vindicated. "This mass expulsion was an event whose importance could hardly be exaggerated. Here was the first step in what I saw as a process that would lead to a peace treaty between ourselves and the new Lebanese government. Hardly less significant, the PLO's defeat [opened] the possibility of a rational dialogue between ourselves and Palestinians not dedicated to our destruction."[28]

Even the evacuation occasioned a furious altercation between Israel and America, an altercation that, incredibly, almost turned violent. The casus belli was a number of jeeps that the departing Palestinians had loaded onto a ferry that was part of the evacuation fleet. Sharon ordered the evacuation stopped until the jeeps were off-loaded: the agreement permitted personal weapons, not jeeps.

"Sam Lewis approached Begin about it," Shultz writes, "and the prime minister exploded: 'They are not an army! They are rabble! Let Bourguiba [the president of Tunisia] take them in and buy them Cadillacs.' We told the Israelis that the ship was going to leave . . . The Joint Chiefs of Staff instructed our naval assets in the area to prepare to defend the car ferry, and themselves, against Israeli attack . . . Lewis told Begin we would give the order to sail, and we hoped that Israel would not try to block the ship's departure . . . The ship sailed."*

---

* Secretary of Defense Weinberger was far less cooperative with Shultz and Habib when it came to deploying the U.S. Marines on land. "The Palestinian forces under Syrian command wanted to turn over their positions to the Americans, not to the Lebanese army," Shultz writes. "They feared that the Lebanese army would not be strong enough to stand up to the Khataeb, the Christian militia; they were afraid that the Khataeb would take over the PLO positions and attack the Palestinian civilians left behind . . . The Defense Department . . . did not want American

On Monday, August 30, Arafat embarked on a Greek freighter, escorted by the Greek warship *Croesus*. The Sixth Fleet provided air cover. Israeli marksmen stationed on nearby rooftops had the PLO chairman in the sights. But Begin was personally committed to Reagan to let him sail unharmed.

Meanwhile, on August 23, Bashir Gemayel was elected president of Lebanon by the parliament. He made a point of declaring, both before and after his election, that he had not colluded with the Israeli invaders and that he did not propose to sign a peace treaty with Israel.[29] This left the Israelis still divided along the lines that had evolved over the previous two years. Many of the army commanders had little faith in Gemayel and his Phalange. They felt their view was amply borne out by the Christians' stolid reluctance to take any serious role in the fighting over the past three months or even to say anything publicly that would sound like support for the Israeli goals (which were, after all, their own goals, too). Key members of the Mossad, however, as well as Begin and Sharon and Chief of Staff Eitan, continued to believe that once Gemayel was firmly installed, he would conclude a formal peace accord with Israel that would have important political and economic repercussions throughout the Arab world. They suspected that the Americans, and specifically Habib and his deputy, Morris Draper, were advising Gemayel to avoid openly friendly relations with Israel.[30]

Begin's—and Gemayel's—painful awakening came on the night of August 31, in the northern border town of Nahariya, where Begin and his wife were briefly vacationing in a pointed demonstration of how quiet and peaceful the border area was now. Gemayel arrived for a meeting with the prime minister at a nearby military base. It ought to have been an occasion for mutual congratulation and heartfelt, if discreet, celebration. Instead, the president-elect encountered a cold and sullen Begin, who barely returned his embrace and immediately launched into a grudging congratulatory speech replete with heavy hints about the need now to pay outstanding bills.

They then retired to a separate room, with only a handful of advisers on each side. But Begin's tone and tenor did not change. "Where do we stand regarding the peace treaty?" he began truculently. Gemayel tried to answer discursively, explaining that he absolutely did want

---

forces exposed to danger in a situation of mixed command. 'The U.S. Marines can't just sit on their ass all the time,' Habib howled." Sharon wanted the MNF troops, and especially the U.S. Marines, confined to as narrow and brief an assignment as possible. Shultz could not overcome what he calls this "Sharon-Weinberger co-veto," even though Habib warned ominously of the dangers ahead.

"real peace, in the long term" but that he wasn't the sole decision maker. There was a government and a parliament. It would not do to rush things, either politically or militarily.

Gemayel spoke about an "order of priorities" that he had discussed with the Americans. The main thing now was to get the Syrians and the Palestinians out of the Beqáa and out of the north of the country. Begin interrupted. He wanted a firm deadline for signing a peace treaty. He suggested December 31. Gemayel balked. He would need at least a year, he said.

"From the moment Gemayel was elected," Yitzhak Shamir recalled years later, "he no longer wanted to be an ally. He evaded and equivocated, and ever since then Begin was not the same man. It was a grievous blow for him to see that after all our help, the man was disloyal."[31]

Both Sharon and Eitan (separately) visited Gemayel during the following fortnight in an effort to patch things up. Sharon dined at the Gemayel family estate at Bikfaya on the evening of August 12. "The atmosphere was especially warm," he wrote. "I knew the first item of business was to allay the hard feelings that had developed between Bashir and Begin at . . . Nahariya. The chemistry that night had not been good." It was different now. "Bashir and his wife, Solange, were happy and obviously excited about the inauguration, and a feeling of intimacy pervaded the room as Bashir and I sat down to talk over the steps he planned to take as president."

The ironic truth is that it wasn't Gemayel's extreme caution—not to say his pusillanimity, or even infidelity—that blackened Begin's mood on that fateful night in Nahariya. That had occurred earlier in the day, in a terse meeting with Ambassador Lewis, who arrived in Nahariya to deliver in letter form and verbally an entirely unexpected American plan for Israeli-Palestinian peace. The bottom line was that Israel must eventually cede much of the West Bank and Gaza and in the meantime must stop its settlement building. "It was as if he had been hit in the solar plexus with a sledge hammer," the Foreign Ministry director, David Kimche, recalled, describing Begin's reaction.[32] Begin himself muttered through clenched teeth, "The battle for Eretz Yisrael has begun."

Almost as if to mock Begin, or to take revenge on him, the American plan stressed repeatedly that it sought to build on "the opportunity" offered by the Lebanon War. The war had demonstrated two key things, Reagan wrote:

First, the military losses of the PLO have not diminished the yearning of the Palestinian people for a just solution of their claims; and, second, while Israel's military successes in Lebanon have demonstrated that its armed forces are second to none in the region, they alone cannot bring just and lasting peace to Israel and her neighbors . . .

Palestinians feel strongly that their cause is more than a question of refugees. I agree. The Camp David agreement recognized that fact when it spoke of "the legitimate rights of the Palestinian people and their just requirements . . ."

The United States will not support the use of any additional land for the purpose of settlements during the transitional period. Indeed, the immediate adoption of a settlement freeze by Israel, more than any other action, could create the confidence needed.

This, ironic perhaps in terms of American politics, signaled Reagan's endorsement of the plain, straightforward reading of the language of Camp David, the reading of his unloved predecessor, Jimmy Carter. And now—most ironic of all in hindsight—Reagan offered his solution: no Palestinian state; no Israeli annexation; but Palestinian self-rule under Jordan. The irony lies in the sad fact that a Likud-led government in Israel today, let alone a more dovish government, would grab at these terms with both hands—if only they were still available.

Begin rejected them with both hands. He cut short his holiday and convened the cabinet for a somber session ending with a bitterly truculent communiqué. "The positions conveyed to the Prime Minister of Israel on behalf of the President of the United States consist of partial quotations from the Camp David agreements, or are nowhere mentioned in that agreement or contradict it entirely . . . Were the American plan to be implemented, there would be nothing to prevent King Hussein from inviting his new-found friend, Yasser Arafat, to come to Nablus and hand the rule over to him."

Instead of concocting this casuistry, designed to perpetuate the occupation of the West Bank and Gaza, a more farsighted leader would have been devising urgent plans to end the IDF's occupation of Lebanon, and most especially of Beirut. As Chaim Herzog writes, the terrible and tragic events that were now to take place in Beirut

totally overshadowed [Israel's] achievements in the war, which had ended with the PLO and the Syrians ousted from Beirut. If the government of Israel had had the good sense to leave Beirut after the evacuation of the terrorists was completed Israel would have avoided sinking into the mire of Lebanese politics, it would not have entered west

Beirut and it would thus not have become involved in any way with the massacre of Palestinians by the Phalange. The IDF's remaining in Beirut after the [PLO's] evacuation proves the validity of the ancient rabbinic adage: "Grab too much—and you grab nothing at all."[33]

A wholly different view of the war thus far, predominant by now in opposition circles but also troubling some of the ministers, was that the drawn-out hostilities had been, on balance, a disaster for Israel—in terms both of casualties and of the international (including American) opprobrium. Ousting the PLO in no way counterbalanced those setbacks. As for the Syrians, while they had been forced out of the Lebanese capital, they were still firmly entrenched in the northern Beqáa. The hope, moreover, of a peace treaty between Israel and Lebanon had been roughly crushed at the Begin-Gemayel meeting in Nahariya.

From that—negative—assessment of the war, too, the sensible thing for Begin and Sharon to do once the PLO had left was to cut Israel's losses and get the IDF out, too. But Begin and Sharon were not ready to leave. "Even after the [Begin] meeting with Gemayel," writes Begin's biographer,

> Sharon had no intention of giving up his aim—clearing out West Beirut, in other words destroying the arms stores hidden there and removing the Palestinian militants who had remained there, particularly in the refugee camps. Because of the heavy price in blood that Israel had already paid in this war, Sharon wanted the Phalange to finish this job, and he sent senior IDF officers and Mossad operatives to coordinate with them. Begin backed him ... Sharon did not deviate from the guidelines that Begin laid down. When Begin read intelligence reports, after the PLO's evacuation, which said that thousands of terrorists had remained in the city, he told the Knesset Foreign Affairs and Defense Committee that Israel still intended to drive out the "hostile elements" that had remained in West Beirut. Once again, Sharon acted to execute the policy goal that Begin determined.[34]

The intention, then, was for the IDF to stay put while the Lebanese—the Phalange forces, perhaps with the national army, too—cleansed West Beirut of remaining PLO men. But was that the true and full extent of the Israelis'—and Gemayel's—intention? Or did they envisage, condone, and essentially encourage a much broader ethnic cleansing of Palestinians from Lebanon to be perpetrated, by the Lebanese Christians, by violent means?

The IDF chief of intelligence, Yehoshua Saguy, redoubled his warnings that the Phalange was likely to commit acts of revenge against the Palestinians and its other domestic enemies now that the Syrians and most of the PLO were gone from the capital. For this reason, he urged, the IDF would do well to distance itself from the scene.

On September 14, that option was finally, fatefully rejected. "I was driving toward Tel Aviv," Sharon writes, "when I received word on the car radio to telephone the defense ministry as soon as possible. Stopping at an army base along the way, I phoned in and was told that an explosion had taken place in an East Beirut building. Our information was that Bashir Gemayel had been inside." Eight hours later, with the death of the president-elect now confirmed, Begin, Sharon, and Eitan decided that the IDF must take over West Beirut forthwith.

Sharon's purpose in ordering the IDF into West Beirut—and he confirmed this in his testimony to the Commission of Inquiry into the Events at the Refugee Camps in Beirut (the Kahan Commission)—was to ensure that the remaining PLO men were cleared out in the days ahead by the Lebanese Forces (the Phalange) as had been agreed before the assassination.[35] In his conversation with Begin, though, on the night of the assassination, the stress was on the need for the IDF to prevent chaos in the city. Begin said to Eitan, too, on the phone that Muslims must be protected from the Phalange.[36]

Later that night, Eitan went to the Phalange headquarters at Karantina, where he explained to the stunned and grieving commanders that their leader's assassination—which everyone attributed to Syrian agents—"had the potential of sparking a new round of violence" and that it could signal a Syrian-PLO effort to reverse the results of the war and get back into Beirut. "I asked them if their forces would be prepared to assist us, and, to my surprise, received an immediate affirmative answer. I asked . . . that they prepare to capture the Palestinian camps Sabra, Shatila and Fakahani."[37]

Was the IDF's entry, then, designed to ensure the "cleansing" of the Palestinians or to ensure their protection? An official announcement the following day reflected this ambivalence: "IDF forces entered West Beirut to prevent possible grave occurrences and to ensure quiet."[38]

At dawn on the fifteenth, IDF troops took over key buildings, road arteries, and intersections in West Beirut, encountering scattered opposition. Sharon flew up later in the morning and met with Eitan and the other senior IDF commanders at a forward command post on a rooftop overlooking Sabra and Shatila. He discussed the plans to send in the Phalange "under the IDF's supervision." Then he, too, went to Karantina to talk to the Phalange officers and on to Bikfaya to offer his condolences to the bereaved father, Pierre Gemayel, and to his younger son, Amin.

The next day, Thursday, September 16, CO of Northern Command Amir Drori personally briefed the Phalange officers due to lead the assault on the Palestinian camps. "They were instructed to be careful in their identification of the PLO terrorists," Sharon recalled. "The mission was only against them. Civilian residents, they were specifically instructed, were not to be harmed." Brigadier Amos Yaron, the divisional commander, made the same point to Elie Hobeika, the Phalange intelligence chief, who came up to his rooftop command post for final coordination.[39]

In Jerusalem, meanwhile, Morris Draper, Habib's deputy, and Sam Lewis were remonstrating vigorously but vainly with Sharon and Eitan over Israel's cavalier violation of its solemn commitment not to enter West Beirut. Israel had undermined its own credibility, Draper said. Sharon replied there were between two and three thousand Palestinian terrorists left in the Beirut camps—"we've even got their names"—and the IDF had taken the western city in order to get them out. The day before, Draper had been treated to the other tack in Israel's ambivalent—in fact, contradictory—explanation of its decision to enter West Beirut. Israeli forces had been ordered to make some minor positional adjustments—"limited and precautionary," Begin told him, according to Secretary Shultz's account. "This was in the interest of security in the city . . . Specifically, the Israelis said they wanted to prevent the Phalange militia from raiding the Palestinian refugee camps south of the city to avenge Gemayel's death."[40]

By the time the cabinet convened, at seven o'clock on Thursday evening, the Phalange units had entered Sabra and Shatila. "While I was speaking," Sharon recalled, "a note came in that the Phalangists were now fighting inside the neighborhoods, and as I described this development, there was no negative reaction from any one of the assembled people."[41]

This was a remarkably silly lie, given that almost every child in Israel knew by the time it was written, following the Kahan Commission Report, that Minister of Housing David Levy had voiced his grave concern. "When I hear that the Phalangists are already entering a certain neighborhood," Levy said, "I know what the meaning of revenge is for them, what kind of slaughter. Then no one will believe we went in to create order there, and we will bear the blame."[42]*

---

* Eitan, in his memoirs, acknowledges that there was "one inquiry" at cabinet "about the possibility that the Phalange would seek revenge. I responded that they

Levy's warning went unheeded. The ministers—including the skeptical ones, not just the nodding heads—were more concerned about why the army had been sent into West Beirut without the cabinet's knowledge, let alone approval, than about David Levy's pontifications about oriental vendetta lore. The cabinet communiqué, drafted by Begin, rehearsed the ambiguous Israeli line: "In the wake of the assassination of the President-elect Bashir Gemayel, the IDF has seized positions in West Beirut in order to forestall the danger of violence, bloodshed and chaos, as some 2,000 terrorists, equipped with modern and heavy weapons, have remained in Beirut, in flagrant violation of the evacuation agreement."

The next day, Friday, was Rosh Hashanah eve, the saddest day of the year for Sharon. With Lily and the boys, his mother, and a few friends, he held his annual graveside memorial ceremony for his dead son, Gur. Then he drove to Jerusalem and, together with Shamir, met again with Draper. "I pressed Draper to use his influence to get [the Lebanese government] to order the Lebanese army into the Palestinian neighborhoods."[43]

In the Palestinian neighborhoods, meanwhile, unarmed people were being butchered. No IDF personnel had accompanied the Phalangists into the camps, and there was no direct line of vision from the forward command rooftop into the warren of streets and alleys below. But the Phalange operation had proceeded through the night by the light of illumination shells thrown up by an IDF mortar unit, at the request of the Phalange liaison officer.[44]

And IDF intelligence was not entirely in the dark. One intelligence officer, according to the Kahan Commission, "received a report that the Phalangists' liaison officer had heard via radio from one of the Phalangists inside the camps that he was holding 45 people. That person asked what he should do with the people, and the liaison officer replied, 'Do the will of God,' or words to that effect."[45] Another offi-

---

[the Phalangist soldiers] appeared to be motivated to fulfill the objective of their mission, and that they had never displayed a tendency toward misconduct." This, of course, was also a lie at the time it was purportedly said, and an even sillier lie at the time it was published, years after the Kahan Commission Report that condemned Eitan (inter alios) for precisely this disingenuousness.

What Eitan in fact said at cabinet, according to the stenographic account published by the Kahan Commission, was that sooner or later, in the wake of the assassination, there would be "an eruption of revenge" on the part of the Phalange. "It makes no difference if we are there or not." In his testimony to the commission, and in his memoirs, Eitan insisted that he was referring in this last remark not to the Phalange force that entered Sabra and Shatila that night but "to other militias that had less direction and were not tightly structured."

cer, Lieutenant Elul, "heard a Phalangist officer from the force that had entered the camps tell Elie Hobeika (in Arabic) that there were 50 women and children, and what should he do. Elie Hobeika's reply over the radio was: 'This is the last time you're going to ask me a question like that, you know exactly what to do'; and then raucous laughter broke out among the Phalangist personnel on the roof."[46]

Despite these early indications, it took the whole night and half of the day of unhurried paper pushing between Beirut, Northern Command, and Tel Aviv before the senior IDF officers finally decided that, in General Yaron's words to the commission, "something smelled fishy." Drori phoned Eitan at noon to say he would end the Phalange operation. "He informed me that they were mopping up houses without removing the civilians," Eitan writes in his memoirs, "and were shooting at people randomly. I immediately notified the minister of defense* and left my home for Northern Command. I was extremely upset."

But not upset enough to ensure the operation was shut down at once. "I reached the Phalange headquarters at 3:30 . . . When I asked for an update on their progress in the camps I was told that all was well and that they had completed the capture of Sabra and Shatila. They told me they had suffered several wounded and killed and requested that we provide them with tractors, so they would be able to destroy the tunnels and trenches they had discovered."[47]

Sharon went back to his ranch to celebrate the festival-eve meal quietly with his family. "At 9 p.m. I received a call from Raful Eitan. He had just returned from Beirut, he told me, and there had been problems. During the operation the Phalangist units had caused civilian deaths. 'They went too far,' he said."

Sharon went to bed early, but at 11:30 an Israeli television journalist (and colonel in the reserves), Ron Ben-Yishai, phoned him with a fuller account of what had been going on. As initial rumors of the carnage filtered out, journalists stationed in Beirut began filtering into the camps. Soon, their reports, television footage, and still photographs started flooding the airwaves. The world's media were swamped with coverage and with commentary, almost all of it unreservedly condemnatory of Israel. All the criticism—of the initial invasion of Lebanon, of the killing of civilians and destruction of property in the coastal towns, of the months-long siege and bombardment of Beirut, of the blatant manipulation of Lebanese domestic politics, and, beneath all

---

* The Kahan Commission accepted Sharon's testimony that no such notification reached him.

this, of Israel's occupation of the Palestinian territories and denial of Palestinian rights—fed a great wave of fury and revulsion against Israel, against Begin, and most especially against Sharon.

President Reagan voiced horror, too, and demanded that Israeli forces withdraw from West Beirut immediately. "We also expect Israel thereafter to commence serious negotiations which will, first, lead to the earliest possible disengagement of Israeli forces from Beirut and, second, to an agreed framework for the early withdrawal of all foreign forces from Lebanon."

Begin's initial, instinctive reaction was the usual mix of forensic polemics and defiant self-righteousness. "A blood libel was plotted against the Jewish state and its government, as well as against the IDF, on Rosh Hashanah," the cabinet pronounced after an emergency meeting on the night of September 19. "In a place distant from an IDF position, a Lebanese unit entered a refugee camp where terrorists took shelter, in order to arrest them. That unit attacked the civilian population, resulting in many losses of lives . . . All the accusations—direct or hinted—claiming that the IDF has any responsibility whatsoever for the tragedy in the Shatila camp are groundless. The Cabinet rejects them with disgust . . . No one will preach to us values of morality and respect for human life."

The government won a vote of confidence in the Knesset. But the confidence was a splintering facade. Inside the coalition itself there was a growing realization that the opposition's demands were inescapable: a judicial inquiry would have to be established, and Sharon would have to go. The alternative, political pundits wrote, was that the government itself would implode. One minister, Yitzhak Berman, didn't wait. He voted in the Knesset in favor of the opposition motion and announced his resignation the same day.

On Saturday night, September 25, Kings of Israel Square in downtown Tel Aviv was thronged with protesters in what the organizers—Peace Now and other groups—claimed was the largest demonstration ever held in Israel: 400,000 people. There had been earlier, smaller protests against the war in the same square during the summer. Naturally, those were seen as associated with the opposition. This one, despite its provenance, was simply too big for such comfortable categorization.

Sharon tried, nevertheless. "We've got nothing to hide," he fulminated on television the following night. "Nothing! Let everything be investigated! Let everyone be investigated! We didn't want to harm the civilian population. We don't fight civilians. We weren't involved."

Israelis needed to understand that behind the calls for an inquiry were "far-reaching political aims. Certainly there is anti-Semitism involved. And there are certain plans that people are trying to impose on us. They're not after Sharon's head or Begin's head. What they're after is Jerusalem! They're after Hebron! They're after Beit-El, they're after Elon Moreh! And I say this without any intention whatsoever of covering up or minimizing the ghastly outrages that were perpetrated. But we have to understand: We're up against the whole world."[48]

It was a desperate attempt to depict the crisis in political hues and thereby rally the Right. But when the president of the state, Yitzhak Navon, hinted that he would resign if the government did not set up a commission of inquiry, Begin realized the fight was lost. He tried one last wriggle, sending the justice minister, Nissim, to the president of the Supreme Court, Yitzhak Kahan, with a proposal that Kahan personally investigate the massacre rather than appoint a full-fledged commission of inquiry with statutory powers to subpoena witnesses and order discovery of documents. Kahan dismissed that gambit out of hand.[49]

Begin was able to convince the commission that he did not know in advance that the Phalange forces were being sent into the camps. This proved the key to his exoneration by the commission, which presented its report on February 8, 1983.

The tasks of the Prime Minister are many and diverse, and he was entitled to rely on the optimistic and calming report of the Defense Minister that the entire operation was proceeding without any hitches and in the most satisfactory manner.

As for David Levy's warning at cabinet,

According to the Prime Minister's testimony, "no one conceived that atrocities would be committed . . . simply, none of us, no minister, none of the other participants supposed such a thing . . ." The Prime Minister attached no importance to Minister Levy's remarks because the latter did not ask for a discussion or a vote on this subject. When Minister Levy made his remarks, the Prime Minister was busy formulating the concluding resolution of the meeting, and for this reason as well, he did not pay heed to Minister Levy's remarks.

The commission rejected Begin's claim that he was "absolutely unaware" of the danger inherent in sending the Phalangists in. After all, Begin himself had explained that the decision to send the IDF into West Beirut was "in order to protect the Moslems from the vengeance of the Phalangists."

> The Prime Minister's lack of involvement in the entire matter casts on him a certain degree of responsibility . . . It is sufficient to determine responsibility and there is no need for any further recommendations.

In effect—an acquittal, albeit Begin said when he first read the report that he felt he ought to resign. But he was quickly talked out of that idea by Minister of Justice Nissim and the cabinet secretary, Dan Meridor. The two of them focused Begin on the real political hot potato that emerged unequivocally from the report: the need to fire Sharon.[50]

> The Minister of Defense bears personal responsibility. In our opinion, it is fitting that the Minister of Defense draw the appropriate personal conclusions arising out of the defects revealed with regard to the manner in which he discharged the duties of his office—and if necessary, that the Prime Minister consider whether he should exercise his authority under Section 21-A(a) of the Basic Law: The Government, according to which "the Prime Minister may, after informing the Cabinet of his intention to do so, remove a minister from office."

Sharon's guilt was that he should have known.

> Responsibility is to be imputed to the Minister of Defense for having disregarded the danger of acts of vengeance and bloodshed by the Phalangists against the population of the refugee camps, and for having failed to take this danger into account when he decided to have the Phalangists enter the camps. In addition, responsibility is to be imputed to the Minister of Defense for not ordering appropriate measures for preventing or reducing the danger of massacre as a condition for the Phalangists' entry into the camps.

Sharon claimed, like Begin, that no one had imagined that the Phalangists would perpetrate a massacre. And, as with Begin, the commission dismissed that contention as implausible, even specious. Sharon could not claim, as Begin had, that he did not know the Phalangists were being sent into the camps, because it was he and Eitan who decided to send them.

The commission reached essentially the same conclusions regarding

Chief of Staff Eitan. In addition, unlike Sharon, it found him guilty of failing to put a stop to the killings as soon as he became aware of them. The commission made it plain that it would have recommended Eitan's dismissal had he not been at the end of his term as chief of staff anyway. It recommended that Yehoshua Saguy, the director of Military Intelligence, "not continue as director" and that Amos Yaron, the divisional commander, "not serve as a field commander" for at least three years. The Mossad, which had nurtured the alliance with the Phalange, got off scot-free.

No one on the Israeli side was found guilty of direct responsibility for the massacre, only of indirect responsibility. The sole direct perpetrators of the heinous crime were the Phalangists. The "hints and even accusations" that IDF personnel were present in the camps during the massacre were "completely groundless and constitute a baseless libel." The charges of collusion were similarly specious the commission held.

Sharon demanded that the government reject the commission's recommendations. When the cabinet convened on the evening of February 10 to discuss the report, the police had to force a path from Sycamore Ranch for Sharon's car, which was beset by angry demonstrators, many of them from local kibbutzim. In Jerusalem, though, pro-Sharon loyalists were holding a raucous demonstration outside the prime minister's office when he arrived for the cabinet meeting. "As I stopped for a moment to greet them, I was engulfed by a thousand hands reaching out to shake mine and a thousand expressions of warmth and encouragement. But these supporters were not alone. At the same moment another demonstration came marching through the streets, this one composed of Peace Now people yelling at the top of their lungs, '*Sharon rotzeach* (Sharon the murderer),' their shouts mixing with 'Arik, Arik, Arik' from my supporters."

In the tense debate, with the noise of the demonstrations wafting through the windows, Sharon warned his colleagues that if they accepted the commission recommendations, they would be "branding the mark of Cain on the foreheads of the Jewish people and on the State of Israel with your own hands." If, on the other hand, they had the courage to reject the recommendation, which would mean new elections, the Likud would win its greatest victory ever.

By 16 votes to 1, Sharon's, they voted to accept the recommendations. That meant either that Sharon now resigned or that Begin fired him. Sharon writes that the ministers had seemed upset and jealous at the "gigantic, spontaneous crowd of Likud supporters . . . It was such an irony, I thought, that these loyal people who had gathered there to help were in fact sealing my fate."

Incredibly, in an omission more telling than any of the hyperbole, Sharon makes no mention in his book of the fact that a rightist fanatic (not one of the demonstrators in his support) threw a hand grenade into the Peace Now march, killing one prominent activist, Emil Grunzweig, and wounding seven others.

Grunzweig's death, as well as the dramatic funeral the next day attended by many thousands, was in some way a fitting, tragic, traumatic end to the tragic national trauma of the Lebanon War. Grunzweig himself had served, dutifully if reluctantly, as a reservist in Lebanon.

That same day of the funeral, Friday, Sharon told Begin he had decided to resign. The attorney general had ruled that he could stay on in another ministry or as a minister without portfolio.[51] " 'When do you want to do it?' Begin asked. 'I'll do it on Monday,' I answered. 'Why,' he said after a pause, 'should it take so long?' "[52]

One effect of Sharon's removal from the Defense Ministry was that Israel softened its stance in the ongoing, desultory negotiations with Lebanon—now under the presidency of Bashir Gemayel's brother, Amin—over a much-watered-down draft peace treaty between the two countries. Sharon's demand for IDF surveillance stations on Lebanese soil was dropped. Toward the end of April 1983, the U.S. secretary of state, George Shultz, embarked on a Kissinger-style shuttle to try to clinch a deal. Israel continued to dig in its heels over the future status of the South Lebanese Army (SLA), the Israeli-backed, mostly Christian militia under Major Sa'ad Hadad.* The Israeli negotiators insisted that the integrity of this force be maintained, even if it was formally incorporated into the Lebanese army.

Judicious arm-twisting by Shultz eventually persuaded "the Israelis, grudgingly, and the Lebanese, fearfully," to sign, on May 17, 1983, an "Agreement on Withdrawal of Troops from Lebanon." The title was deliberately unbombastic. Not a peace treaty, as Israel had originally

---

* In January 1984, Major Hadad died of cancer. In April, General Antoine Lahad took over the SLA. He was a Maronite Christian and a retired general in the Lebanese army. Under his command, the SLA grew to 2,500 men. Most of the soldiers were Shiites; most of the officers were Christian. All of the arms and equipment were Israeli. Being in the SLA often meant that members of one's family were allowed into Israel daily to work in factories and kibbutzim in the Galilee. In 1996, Lahad was tried in Beirut in absentia for treason and sentenced to death. After Israel's final withdrawal from south Lebanon in 2000, he lived for a time in France, then moved to Tel Aviv, where he opened a Middle Eastern restaurant.

wanted, but a more modest agreement that the Lebanese parliament could allow itself to ratify without incurring the wrath of Syria and the scorn of other Arab hard-line states. Israeli forces were to withdraw from Lebanon "within 8 to 12 weeks . . . consistent with the objective of Lebanon that all external forces withdraw from Lebanon." This was as explicit a reference as could be made, given Lebanese sensitivities, to the unarticulated core of the agreement: that Israel would withdraw when Syria did, or at least when Syria had credibly committed itself to do so.

The two signatories undertook "to settle their disputes by peaceful means" and to create a "Security Region" in south Lebanon. They affirmed that neither would allow itself to be used as a staging ground for hostile activity against the other. Neither country would intervene in the internal affairs of the other or propagandize against the other.

It was a far cry from the full "normalization" that Israel had initially proposed, with embassies, open borders, and trade ties. But it was an undeniable move away from the official boycott of Israel that Lebanon, along with most Arab countries, had maintained until then. And the agreement held out the hope of a further thaw.

Press and public in Israel had not followed the negotiations with much interest. Expectations from the agreement were low, cynicism sky-high. This assessment was quickly vindicated when Syria, and also the Druze community in Lebanon, rejected and condemned the agreement. President Hafez Assad of Syria made it clear that he did not intend to withdraw his troops. President Amin Gemayel's request that he do so was invalid, he argued. Only the Arab League could legitimately ask him to go. The Soviet Union's strong backing of Syria meant that this was unlikely to happen.[53]

The agreement remained on paper only—and in fact not even that, for though it was ratified by his parliament, President Gemayel never actually signed it into law. The inter-confessional civil war gradually resumed in all its bloody and bewildering complexity, with the various armed militias in constantly changing alignments with each other and with the Syrian forces. The Lebanese army seemed powerless to impose the state's authority. The multinational force had neither the mandate nor the political will to help it do so. Israeli troops, still deployed deep in Lebanon, sustained ever-mounting casualties, sometimes without knowing which of the local militias was shooting at them or why. Diplomats and Mossad emissaries maintained their largely fruitless contacts with the different factions.

The Druze began to make life difficult for the U.S. troops stationed in and around Beirut as part of the multinational force. Druze forces, based high in the Shouf Mountains, started drizzling fire onto the Lebanese army units and American marines on the coastal plain below. Israeli forces in the Shouf also came under attack from Druze guerrillas. An anomalous situation developed in which Israel wanted to withdraw unilaterally from the Shouf, while the Americans pressured it to stay.

Compounding the problem for Israel was the government's reluctance to admit that it was delaying the withdrawal—and sustaining further pointless casualties—in deference to American demands. On September 4, the eve of Rosh Hashanah, the Israeli army was withdrawn from the Shouf Mountains and from the whole of the Beirut area, regrouping along the Awali River.

On October 23, 1983, a truck packed with dynamite rammed through the inadequately guarded fence of the marine compound in Beirut and blew up, killing 241 American servicemen. That same day, 58 French soldiers serving in the MNF were killed in another suicide attack. Reagan insisted he would not be driven out by terror. The marines were replaced, and American forces—including the aged battleship *New Jersey*, anchored off Beirut—started firing back at their various shadowy attackers. But Washington's heart was no longer in this Lebanese misadventure. Weinberger wanted out, and Shultz did not have sufficient clout to gainsay him. Early in the New Year the U.S. Marines left. By March, the French and the Italians had gone too, and Lebanon was left to its internecine war.*

Israel made a second unilateral withdrawal in June 1985. The IDF pulled back all the way to the border, save for a lingering presence, varying over the following fifteen years from dozens to hundreds of soldiers, who operated alongside the South Lebanese Army militia in a narrow security zone.

Sharon blamed America for the failure of the treaty. "They don't want to give Israel its full achievements from the war," he told a party audience in Tiberias in April 1983, days before Shultz's arrival on his shuttle mission. But he blamed Israel, too. "No nation can survive," he pronounced, "if it kowtows to others; even to a superpower."

At cabinet, where he now sat in the empty role of minister without portfolio, Sharon attacked his successor at Defense, Moshe Arens, for climbing down over the surveillance stations. When the draft agree-

---

* The civil war was eventually brought to an end in 1991. By this time the balance of power in Lebanon had greatly shifted, with Syria wielding untrammeled influence and Hezbollah, the fundamentalist Shiite militia, a growing force both in Beirut and in the south.

ment with Lebanon came up for approval, Sharon let loose such a stream of vituperation—"treachery" and "cowardice" were the milder epithets—that even the depressed Begin summoned the strength to upbraid him. He lashed out at General Abrasha Tamir, formerly his close military aide, who headed the Israeli military team at the talks with Lebanon. "You are bringing disaster upon this country," Sharon shouted. Tamir ignored him. The cabinet voted 17 to 2 to endorse the agreement. Later, Sharon attacked the government for acceding to American requests that Israel delay withdrawing from the Shouf.

When Yitzhak Rabin, as defense minister in the 1984–1988 Likud-Labor unity government, proposed the June 1985 withdrawal, Sharon attacked again. The army should stay where it was on the Awali, he maintained, though with fewer troops. "Look Who's Talking" was the columnist Yoel Marcus's headline:

One might have expected Messrs. Shamir and Sharon to stand, heads bowed, tears in their eyes, at the funerals of the latest Lebanon victims. One might have expected them to do what Begin never had the guts to do—take a day in the week to comfort the thousands of disabled soldiers who gave their arms, legs, eyes to this war. But these two gentlemen don't like standing face-to-face with the living or dead evidence of their acts and omissions . . . They stand on the ruins of their pointless, pathetic pipe dream, and they have the nerve to be dissatisfied with the efforts that Rabin and Peres are making to get us out of there.[54]

CHAPTER 7 · ON THE FARM

T his is the only country in the world," Sharon often said ruefully during the months that followed his ouster from the Defense Ministry, "in which the minister of defense is sent home to drive his tractor because of what the Christians did to the Muslims." That was spurious, of course. There *was* no other comparable country that had got itself into a situation in which its duty was to keep blood-crazed Christians and helpless Muslims apart and had woefully failed to discharge that duty.

But just as Sharon's self-centered lament was bound to deepen the shame and loathing for him on the left, it was calculated to elicit sympathy in the center and to shore up support on the right. The words deliberately harked back to the bitter remark, also disingenuous but arresting nevertheless, attributed to Begin soon after the massacre (he denied its accuracy), "Goyim [non-Jews] killed goyim, and we are held to blame."*

Sharon was calibrating the catastrophe for anyone who would still listen to him, putting it "into proportion," as he said—both in terms of Israel's history and international standing and in terms of his own interrupted career. His traducers had wickedly exaggerated. They were wrongly condemning Israel and him. The Kahan Commission

---

* On September 22, Amnon Rubinstein, MK (Shinui), said in the Knesset: "When these things happen to Palestinian children, to Arab children, the only thing he [the prime minister] has to say is that goyim kill goyim. This is outrageous. It will be quoted; it will be recorded and held against us in the annals of history. It is intolerable. Regardless of party affiliation, all of us should regard it as such." Begin's reply was that his words had been misquoted. "Dr. Rubinstein . . . has reached a hair-raising conclusion: that I said—of course this was an inaccurate leak, but never mind—'goyim murdered goyim' " (The Need to Set Up a Commission of Inquiry into the Massacre at the Refugee Camps in Beirut, *Knesset Record*, September 22, 1982).

had perpetrated a terrible injustice "against the Jewish people and against me personally."[1] It wasn't time, yet, to do battle against this injustice. But that time would come. "This is something that I believe must be dealt with in the future."

Meanwhile, he was back at the ranch, ostensibly doing what he always said he wanted to do. When he was still in uniform, Lily had often said she looked forward to the day when she would tell callers, "He's out in the fields, riding his horse; he'll be back for suppertime."[2] Sharon writes in his book, "The next day [after his ouster] I was out in the fields on the tractor, looking down on the crops, on the sheep and lambs." He proudly records how he crossed indigenous Awasi sheep with imported merino ones. "The resulting crossbred ewes combined the Merino's propensity for twins and the Awasi's milk production and excellent maternal behavior. Experimenting with hormones, we developed techniques of inducing three births every two years rather than the usual one a year."

In later years, Sharon would insist that he was wrongly perceived as driven by politics and the pursuit of power. He was philosophical, he claimed, almost fatalistic, about his chances of ever making it to the top. "My secret weapon," he was fond of saying, "is that I'm actually much less ambitious than people think."[3] He could afford to be, he explained, because, unlike so many of his colleagues and rivals, he had a rich life waiting for him beyond politics, after politics. If he were ever pushed off the greasy pole, he would not undergo a single day of suffering or remorse. "The next day I'd be out working on the farm, and truly enjoying it . . . I've never had enough time for all the things I want to do. Experiments in agriculture, for instance. And travel to the many places I've never visited. Meeting people I've always wanted to meet; and reading all the books I've never had time to read."[4]

It wasn't from the world of politics that he drew his strength, he insisted. "People don't understand the source of my strength," he told an interviewer for the popular women's magazine *La'isha*. "Hard, physical work, agriculture, flowers, trees, the farm animals, and the fields—those are the source of my strength . . . People don't know that if I'm not a politician, I won't be miserable. I'll look after an injured bird, a nest of chicks. My strength doesn't come from politics. It comes from the land."[5]

But for all these paeans to bucolic bliss—and they were not entirely insincere—Sharon suffered pangs of frustration and boredom during his exile at Sycamore Ranch. "I was now minister without portfolio," he writes. "But without a portfolio there was nothing for me to do . . . I was completely isolated in the government. Work of any sort was kept out of my hands, even the kinds of projects that are ordinarily given to ministers without portfolio . . . I used to sit in on the cabinet meetings, then go to my office, which was in an unused government building—an empty office in an empty building."

Important political figures in Israel had sometimes wound up as ministers without portfolio, but they usually served as intimate advisers to the prime minister, sharing some of the burden of his office. There was no more intimacy between Begin and Sharon, and he was effectively frozen out. The people around Begin were pleased and relieved to be rid of him and fully intended for him never to return to a position of influence.

Sharon's strategy for a return would entail a dogged, single-minded march along three parallel tracks. First, he resolved to hang on to his ministerial status, however reduced. By his own account, his loyal and loving aide Uri Dan played an important role in his decision not to quit but to stay on in cabinet as a demeaned and reviled junior minister. Dan had famously assured reporters on the day Sharon resigned that "those who didn't want him as chief of staff got him back as minister of defense; and those who don't want him as minister of defense will get him back as prime minister."[6] This prophecy achieved instant immortality in Israeli popular annals. People laughed at it, but they remembered it. Dan persuaded Sharon that as long as he was in the game, his fortunes could rise again, but if he cashed out, the ranks of pushy politicians would close behind him, and he would quickly be forgotten.

Second, Sharon began assiduously to build his own political base within the Likud. Here, much of the credit goes to a young student leader with a sharp eye and political pretensions of his own. "I sat at the ranch with Arik and Lily," Yisrael Katz recalls, "and I kept saying, 'Arik, you don't understand the first thing about politics. Let me help you build a camp . . .' He was fuming, but Lily said, 'Listen to him. What have you got to lose? He means it for your good.' "

The third track toward rehabilitation opened up the very day Sharon left the Defense Ministry. *Time* magazine, in a rambling cover story on the Kahan Commission findings, asserted that Sharon, the day before the Sabra and Shatila massacre, had discussed with the Lebanese Phalangists "the need to take revenge" for Gemayel's assassination.[7] Here, too, a young adviser, the lawyer Dov Weissglas, who had represented him before the commission, was key in Sharon's decision to sue the magazine and in the epic legal battle that followed.

• • •

Sharon was not present at the tail end of a long cabinet meeting on August 28, 1983, when Begin, without warning, announced that he was resigning "for personal reasons . . . I cannot do this job any longer."[8] Sharon had stormed out of the cabinet room earlier, slamming the door behind him, after vehemently attacking his successor at Defense, Moshe Arens, over policy in Lebanon. Begin, who took little part in the proceedings before delivering his bombshell announcement, showed no reaction to Sharon's antics. Two days later, at the meeting of the coalition leadership with Begin, Sharon took the floor to advise his colleagues "that we put things in proportion." With all the deep regret that they all felt at Begin's decision, it did not mean the Likud was disintegrating or losing its way.

The Likud, and with it the whole political community, were naturally seething with rumor and speculation over why Begin had quit, and much of it focused on Sharon. Increasingly, people were saying that Begin felt he had been led, or perhaps misled, by Sharon into disastrously dragging out what should have been a brief border war into a long, costly, and ultimately unsuccessful campaign. There were more than five hundred* IDF dead at that point.

Begin had been sinking into a deep depression, not for the first time in his life. In the weeks prior to his announcement he hardly went to the office at all, receiving ministers and officials at his home. After his announcement, he stopped going out altogether. Even his formal resignation letter to the president of the state was delivered by the cabinet secretary. Begin, it was explained, had developed a skin condition that prevented him from shaving, and he would not appear before the presi-

---

* At the first cease-fire the number of IDF fatalities was 214. By the end of the siege of Beirut the figure had risen to some 300, with another 1,500 injured (Morris, *Righteous Victims,* 705). All told, from June 1982 to June 1985 the IDF suffered 650 dead and nearly 3,000 injured (ibid., 521). Two explosions, one an accident, the other a terror attack, accounted for 103 of the Israeli dead. On November 11, 1982, a gas leak caused an explosion at the Israeli security offices in Tyre that brought down the entire building, killing 75 Israeli servicemen and 15 Lebanese prisoners. Almost exactly a year later, also in Tyre, a car packed with explosives blew up outside the IDF headquarters. This killed 28 Israelis and 31 Lebanese. The bombing came two weeks after the similar attacks on American and French forces in Beirut that took the lives of 241 U.S. Marines and 58 French paratroopers. All three attacks were attributed to Imad Mugniya, later leader of Hezbollah's military wing and a senior officer in the Iranian Revolutionary Guards Corps. He was eventually killed in a car bombing in Damascus in February 2008, an assassination widely attributed to the Mossad.

dent unshaven.[9] For the next eight and a half years, until his death in March 1992, he hardly ever appeared in public, rarely spoke on the telephone, and met with only a handful of his closest relatives and aides.

Sharon had his own theory as to why Begin went into seclusion, but he had the political good sense not to publicize it. Privately, he said that Begin had recoiled, terminally, in the face of his (Sharon's) anguished accusation in the wake of the cabinet's decision to accept the Kahan Commission Report. "Menachem, you are handing me over," Sharon had cried. The words he used, deliberately, were loaded with terrible meaning for the old man. *Ata masgir oti* (you are handing me over) sent Begin's mind reeling back to the traumatic pre-state days, to the Haganah's *saison,* or hunting season, against Begin's Irgun men when they tracked them down and handed them over to the British police. This was seen on the right as the most despicable act of national treachery.

On September 1, the foreign minister, Yitzhak Shamir, easily defeated the ambitious minister of housing, David Levy, in a leadership contest at Herut's central committee. As prime minister designate, Shamir quickly renegotiated the coalition agreement with the parties that had partnered Begin in government. In the new cabinet Sharon served, once again, as minister without portfolio, with nothing to do but carp and criticize. The Prime Minister's Bureau continued to emit toward him the same cold disdain. If anything, it was colder. Shamir, the hard-bitten former underground leader and onetime Mossad operative, never entertained the admiration for Sharon that accounted for half of Begin's ambivalent attitude to him.*

There was a lower nadir still to come. The Jewish Agency, which had been the government in the making before Israel was set up but bizarrely continued to exist thereafter, retained responsibility for immigration, or aliya. The post of chairman of the Aliya Department fell vacant in January 1974. By dint of the political agreements that carved up the Jewish Agency between the Zionist parties, it was a Herut Party fiefdom.† Sharon wanted it. He could be both a minister and an agency department head, he argued. After devoting himself for years to defense and then to settlement, he wanted now to devote him-

---

* During the Lebanon War, foreign minister and defense minister had barely been on speaking terms. Shamir's director general at the Foreign Ministry, David Kimche, whom Sharon had come to know in his previous capacity as deputy head of the Mossad, served as the preferred channel of communication between the two senior ministers (Kimche interview).
† Herut and the Liberal Party, though joined in the Likud, still maintained separate structures at this time.

self to aliya. But the Labor Zionists reacted with predictable horror, as did many of the philanthropists in the United States and elsewhere whose largesse kept the Jewish Agency afloat, and Sharon was defeated by 59 votes to 48 in a secret vote in the Zionist General Council.

Apart from this misguided sally into the arcane and essentially trivial world of Israel-Diaspora intrigue, Sharon, guided by young Yisrael Katz, was assiduously cultivating the members of the Herut central committee. Increasingly, this 850-man behemoth was becoming *the* arena that mattered in Israeli public life, the pulsating heart of the party in government, the thriving bourse of power and patronage.

Sharon's basic problem, insisted Katz, who rose to become a Knesset member and a minister, was that he thought like a military man. "He was always looking upwards, towards the commander, towards Begin, whom he naturally regarded as the font of authority and power. But in politics you need to look constantly downwards, to the party activists who are the real base of the leaders' power. That's what I had to instill in him." [10]

Sharon learned how to call central committee members when they were sick, to send a bunch of flowers, to call again to make sure they were recovering. "I cried with emotion," one small-town party activist recalled with gushing appreciation, remembering how Sharon had telephoned after his son was injured in school. "I told him it wasn't really serious, but the next day Lily phoned to see how he was getting on. People say he's a tough general, with no interest in the troops. But who am I? An ordinary guy, a factory worker." [11]

In local elections in November 1983, Sharon crisscrossed the country, making speeches before small audiences with no chance of attracting national media attention. But the Herut candidates for local councils and the party grassroots activists took note. The other ministers rarely bothered to roll up their sleeves and pitch in. Sharon, by contrast, claimed an endless curiosity to see and learn how people lived. He loved to visit their homes, he said, and share their occasions, joyous or sad. Heartfelt or not, he convincingly carried off this new, ubiquitously solicitous persona.

He was lucky, too. Shamir's government effectively collapsed because of the defection of a small coalition ally, and the major parties agreed on an early general election in July 1984. Neither David Levy nor Sharon stood a realistic chance of dislodging Shamir, who, though initially seen as a stopgap appointment, had taken a firm hold of Herut and headed a large and loyal camp of followers. Announcing his decision not to run, Levy publicly proposed that Sharon follow suit and close ranks behind Shamir. But Sharon saw his chance. Confounding the pundits who were unanimously predicting he would barely make double digits, Sharon scored a whopping 42.5 percent of the central committee votes. After the results were announced, the old war chant "Arik, king of Israel," rose up in a roar from the floor of the hall. Uri Dan did the rounds of the journalists, reminding them of his fantastic, eccentric prediction just thirteen months earlier. It didn't sound quite so eccentric now. With just another fifty-four votes, one commentator pointed out, Sharon would have become the Likud's candidate for prime minister right there and then.*

The national election, on July 23, 1984, was inconclusive. The Labor Party emerged with 44 seats, the Likud with 41, in the Knesset of 120. Each side's first business was to ensure that the other couldn't form a government by allying with enough of the smaller parties to reach a "blocking majority." To this end Sharon appointed himself the Likud's plenipotentiary to the ultra-Orthodox parties. It was important work. He was shoring up the covenant between the Right and the religious that was the essence of Begin's political legacy. It was the bedrock of the Likud's consolidation, first under Begin himself, then under Shamir, and later under Benjamin Netanyahu, as the natural party of power, the leader of the "national camp."

Likud politicians were not, by and large, religious. Shamir loved his seafood, Sharon his spareribs, and neither tried to hide it. But the Likud, and especially its Herut component, seemed to feel an easy empathy with the religious, and with the religion, that was conspicuously lacking on the Labor side. Sharon's particular formulation, which he never tired of rehearsing in conversations with Jew and Gentile alike, was that he was "a Jew first—and then an Israeli." He would quickly volunteer that he was not himself religiously observant, sometimes adding that he regretted that. The set piece—his aides as prime minister knew it virtually by heart—went on to bemoan the ignorance of the tradition among secular Israeli youth, a growing apathy among young Diaspora Jews, his envy of the Orthodox, who knew "where their grandchildren would be" in decades hence.

Having blocked each other's hopes of going it alone, Shimon Peres and Yitzhak Shamir resorted to the alternative option, thoroughly distasteful to both of them, of going it together. As Peres recounts it, they would have gotten nowhere without Sharon.

---

* In the subsequent months Sharon took particular pleasure in pulling up aides who referred to "the 42 percent." "Er, hm . . . point five," he would hector, mock didactically. "Forty-two point five. Don't let's forget the point five."

We met for three straight days, just the two of us, in the royal suite of the King David Hotel in Jerusalem. The idea was to sit and to talk until a deal emerged. If I tell you that Shamir uttered ten sentences during the whole three days, I'd be exaggerating. He just sat there, silent. And I kept having to think of things to talk about, and to keep talking.

Finally, [the businessman] Azriel Einav phoned me up. "Sharon wants to meet with you, at my house." I said okay, and we met. I told him what had been going on and that I was getting tired of talking. Arik asked, "What do you propose?" I suggested an evenly balanced inner cabinet (five Labor Party ministers and five Likud) with the prime ministership rotating halfway through the fifty-month term. He said, "Okay, I'll fix that up." He went off to Jerusalem, sat with Shamir, and Shamir agreed to everything. Didn't change a thing. Shamir was dead scared of Arik. We know that . . .

That's how the government of national unity was created. With Shamir alone it would never have happened. Not a chance in the world. Arik, in this, was first-rate. Absolute straight shooter. Whatever we agreed was agreed.[12]

One of the things that was agreed with Sharon that Peres forbore recalling, presumably out of an *omertà*-like discretion that bound these old-timers despite their decades of political rivalry, was that Sharon would be minister of industry and trade. Formally, the job wasn't Peres's to offer. He was supposed to appoint the ministers of his own Labor Party, and Shamir those of the Likud. But Sharon, aware of how dearly Shamir and his people would have liked to leave him out, made sure to cut his own deal with the leader of the other party. In return, Sharon vigorously supported Peres's demand to serve as prime minister for the first twenty-five months, even though virtually everyone in Likud believed the much-distrusted Peres would renege on the deal when the time came to "rotate" and would somehow engineer new elections.

In terms of the greasy pole, Industry and Trade was about halfway up. For Sharon at this time, rehabilitation meant his eventual return to one of the three senior ministries: Defense—which was unavailable for the foreseeable future, given the Kahan Commission's verdict—Foreign Affairs, or the Treasury.[13] But he knew that he would need to amass more power in his own party and more popularity throughout the national camp before he could claim one of those three.

The new government, battling against the raging inflation that threatened to engulf the economy, instituted a price and wage freeze that was expanded, in June 1985, into a draconian Economic Stabilization Plan. Price controls are the purview of the Ministry of Industry and Trade. They need inspectors to impose them. Yisrael Katz, acting for Sharon, made no bones about his quest for loyal Herut men in need of a job to sign on as inspectors. He searched hard and successfully filled all fifty-odd positions with Herut activists.

Sharon urged Katz to make sure the appointments resonated throughout the party. And sure enough, says Katz, they duly impressed not only the favored fifty and their families and friends but the entire rank and file, who took note of the fact that Sharon was a minister who looked out for the party faithful and most especially for his own loyalists.

Allegations of more insidious activities by the minister's bureau began sloshing around the Ministry of Industry and Trade almost from the start of Sharon's tenure. A persistent one concerned the appointment of party activists as commercial attachés in embassies overseas that created fierce resentment among career ministry staffers who had been waiting and hoping for years for one of these plum positions. In 1987, the long-entrenched staff petitioned the High Court of Justice against the appointment of two of Sharon's political aides as overseas attachés.

By then, Sharon's stewardship at Industry and Trade had become tainted by persistent allegations of conflict of interest, political but also personal. Sharon and his aides were accused of abusing the ministry's powers to advance the business interests of party cronies and family friends. In at least one case, the minister was suspected of reaping direct and substantial profit for Sycamore Ranch from a policy decision he rammed through. Ran Cohen, a Knesset member of the opposition Meretz Party, petitioned the high court to order the police to open criminal inquiries.*

Courts, comptrollers, police, and prosecutors—they were all to become an awkwardly familiar presence in Sharon's public life over the next two decades. But in January 1985, two years into his quest for rehabilitation, he could justly allow himself a moment of grim gratification from a singular judicial victory. Sharon, still balking at the Kahan Commission's condemnation of his perverse disregard of the obvious danger of allowing the Phalange into the camps, had decided to contest *Time* magazine's far more heinous accusation that

---

* See p. 269.

he had actually encouraged the massacre. *Time*'s report claimed that the unpublished part of the Kahan Commission Report contained the incriminating evidence against Sharon.

In the Israeli media, Sharon's case, which rested on the critical distinction between passive negligence and active incitement, was widely recognized as just—but still dismissed as disingenuous. Instead of sympathy for his cause, the press devoted its column inches and its ire to the money that the drawn-out proceedings in New York were costing the taxpayer. Who was footing the lawyers' fees and the other legal costs? Sharon, Lily, aides, guards, and sometimes Omri, too, crisscrossed the Atlantic, stayed in upmarket Manhattan hotels, ate in chic restaurants. The media, and in their wake the politicians, dissected these doings with increasingly jaundiced eyes.

Sharon began discreetly tapping rich American supporters for help in the summer of 1983. He bolstered his fund-raising efforts with an application to the Exemptions Committee, headed by a retired high-court judge, which considered requests from elected officials and civil servants to earn income outside their official positions. Sharon requested, and received, a green light to lecture abroad for money.

At the suggestion of the New York judge, the parties agreed that Justice Kahan himself be asked to address the core question of whether the unpublished parts of his report provided a factual basis for *Time*'s allegation. "In none of the documents or testimony," Kahan replied unequivocally, "is there any evidence or suggestion that Minister Sharon had any discussion with the Gemayel family or with any other Phalangist, at Bikfaya or elsewhere, in which Minister Sharon discussed the need to avenge the death of Bashir Gemayel."

On January 16, 1985, after two days of deliberation, the jury gave its first verdict, on the defamation question, saying that *Time* had indeed defamed Sharon. "We find that the paragraph in context states that, in permitting the Phalangists to enter Sabra and Shatila, Minister Sharon consciously intended to permit the Phalangists to take acts of revenge extending to the deliberate killing of non-combatants in the camps."

The jury held against *Time,* too, on the question of falsity—the second of the three verdicts that the federal judge Abraham Sofaer instructed it to render. Sharon made the most of the moment, sensing, perhaps, that it would be the zenith for him. "What has been proved now is that *Time* Magazine lied . . . They libeled not just a blood libel against me but against the state of Israel and against the Jewish People. We showed clearly that we spoke the truth, and *Time* Magazine lied . . . Had I not fought it, their terrible lie would have become unchallenged fact . . . That is why I see in the jury's second decision a great moral success for all of us." He told reporters he would be going home straight after the third verdict, regardless of what it was. If he won on malice and was eventually awarded pecuniary damages, they would all go to a fund to protect Jewish rights around the world. He had not sued to make money and would not keep any of it if he won any.

But on the issue of malice, the jury came down on *Time*'s side. "To the question, 'Has the plaintiff proved by clear and convincing evidence that a person or persons at Time Incorporated responsible for either reporting, writing, editing or publishing the paragraph at issue did so with actual malice in that he, she or they knew, at the time of publishing any statement we have found was false and defamatory, that the defamatory statement was false or had serious doubts as to its truth?' To that question, we find: The answer is no, plaintiff has not so proved by clear and convincing evidence."*

Sharon put the best face on it, repeating the words of gratification he had voiced after the second verdict. He could draw encouragement from Begin, who, from his seclusion, issued a generous statement: "Ariel Sharon has won a complete moral victory. The issue was never one of monetary consideration, as I believe and as Sharon himself said. From the moral viewpoint, there is no doubt, in my view, that Sharon won an absolute victory."

American law's requirement of actual malice in libel cases involving public officials is not shared by most other legal systems, including Israel's. Sharon's suit against *Time* in Tel Aviv, therefore, given the New York court's verdict on defamation and malice, became at last the slam dunk that he had hoped for when the saga began. *Time* agreed to an out-of-court settlement, paying Sharon $200,000. This was ten times more than the highest sum of damages ever awarded for libel in Israel to date. This time there was no talk of a fund for the Jewish people; Sharon kept the lot.

---

* For a fuller account of the Sharon against Time Inc. trial, please see www.arik-davidlandau.com.

CHAPTER 8 · WARS OLD AND NEW

For much of the decade after the Lebanon War, Yitzhak Shamir served either as prime minister or as vice prime minister. He was finally defeated in 1992 by Yitzhak Rabin, and Labor replaced Likud as the party in power. Three days later, in an uncharacteristic lapse into momentary candor, Shamir admitted to an interviewer that he had always intended to drag out peace negotiations indefinitely while vigorously expanding the Jewish settlements in the West Bank and Gaza.[1] Later he denied having said it, but everyone, at home and abroad, believed the original story rather than the denial.[2] President Reagan and Secretary of State Shultz and President Bush and Secretary of State Baker all tried hard to prod things along. But Shamir was rocklike in his intransigence. After Desert Storm, Baker managed to drag him to Madrid, where a Middle East peace conference offered a glimmer of hope for the future of the region.

For the "peace camp" in Israel, Shamir's decade was a lost decade, a decade of diplomatic disappointments that brought on the Palestinian intifada, or uprising. For the "national camp," it was time well spent, building up and consolidating the network of settlements that Begin and Sharon had spread across the Palestinian territories during the Likud's early years in government.

For both camps, the decade was one of intense, unremitting struggle over their very different visions for the future of the country. A remarkable paradox held sway in public life: Likud-Labor unity governments ruled for years (1984–1990), yet beneath that formal, fragile facade there was no letup in the ideological battle that divided Israeli society. If anything, the divisions deepened and widened. They reflected not only politics but religion, culture, and class, too. Increasingly, the "peace camp" represented the better-off, better-educated Ashkenazi middle class and intelligentsia. The "national camp," led by the Likud, succeeded in bringing together under one political roof groups that felt themselves excluded from "the elite": the mainly poor, mainly Sephardi working class in run-down city suburbs and small provincial towns; the growing ultra-Orthodox sects; the large modern-Orthodox community whose leaders had abandoned their historic alliance with Labor and whose ideological vanguard, the West Bank settlers, now provided ideological fervor for the whole "national camp."

For Sharon, it was a decade of frustration and fury. The first five years were suffused with bitter recrimination in the aftermath of a war that refused to reach closure. In his relentless pursuit both of rehabilitation and of renewed political power, Sharon exploited the sharpening polarization of Israeli public life. He cast himself as the wounded champion of the Right, unfairly brought down by the Left. Relentlessly, he rammed the controversy around the Lebanon War into that Left-Right, dove-hawk mold. Albeit Begin, the historic leader of the hawks, had ultimately abandoned him, forcing him out of the Defense Ministry, but that was an aberration, engineered by a cabal of closet doves who surrounded the former prime minister. Some of them, Sharon maintained, continued to influence the new Likud leader, Yitzhak Shamir. He, Sharon, was the authentic, reliable, and unswerving leader of the hawks. That was why he had been brought down; that was why he must rise again.

But the Lebanon War and its interminable aftermath reinforced Sharon's image in the minds of many Israelis, even in the "national camp," as a warmonger, and not a very astute or successful one at that. Sabra and Shatila added a dimension of monstrosity and of abiding shame. For all their deprecation of this judgment of him, Sharon's party rivals never balked at using it against him. He was, they snidely opined, unelectable. His unremitting attacks on Shamir, displaying both disloyalty and extremism, made their opinion all the more persuasive.

Sharon's constant accusation was that he had been betrayed by his political enemies and allies alike, and that in betraying him, they were betraying the most fundamental interests of the state itself. By stabbing him in the back, his detractors were unraveling the fiber of national solidarity. By accusing him of leading the army into an unnecessary war, they were courting the risk of every future war being branded unnecessary by men who lacked the patriotism to fight it.

In a television appearance after the massacre, he steered the conversation away from events at the camps to an earlier, hitherto-unpublished episode: his decision during the war, together with Chief of Staff Eitan, not to mobilize an entire reserve infantry brigade because of mutinous murmurings within its ranks. The interviewer was aghast; this could undermine the whole ethos of the citizen army. That was precisely the point, Sharon said. Criticism was all well and good. He was all for it. He absolutely wanted the massacre to be investigated. All the way. Leave no stone unturned. "Our strength as a nation is our ability to speak freely. I believe in that. But! But there have to be limits. Everything has to have limits. We face a hostile world. We're still sitting on a powder keg. And I want you to know that this thing makes me tremble. The fact that I had to sit with the chief of staff and decide not to mobilize a reserve brigade of the IDF."

There, then, was the real danger: the enemy within. A straight line led from criticism to mutiny. From criticizing him to endangering the very survival of the nation. So what to do? asked the interviewer. Ban all criticism? "Criticism is legitimate," Sharon replied. "But there is a limit to what a nation can take, a limit to what it can accuse itself of. A nation must understand that. It must understand that it has to survive. If we want to keep on living, then, alongside the moral thing—to prevent reprehensible things from happening—there must be a unified stand. We must all stand together. People among us must not help our enemies to destroy us."[3]

Part of the "enemy within" was, of course, the media. "You all know what the media are; I don't need to tell you," Sharon roared to a crowd of young rightists in downtown Jerusalem in September 1983. "PLO! PLO!" came the answering roar. He told them, nevertheless. The media were "hypocrites, champions of self-destruction, corroders of the nation, suppliers of fuel to anti-Israeli and anti-Semitic machines from Damascus to Moscow." The Kahan Commission was another of his regular targets. It had "put weapons into the hands of Israel haters throughout the world," he told the Jerusalem crowd. "A terrible injustice has been done to the Jewish people, to the State of Israel, and also to me personally."*

---

* Sharon had given vent to an "enemy within" vilification at least once in the past, although less publicly. Yossi Sarid tells of a trip around the West Bank that General Sharon persuaded the powerful minister of finance, Pinchas Sapir, to take with him one Saturday in 1968. Sarid was Sapir's aide:

The conversation got around to [Minister of Foreign Affairs] Abba Eban, when suddenly Sharon says, "Abba Eban is a spy." We thought we weren't hearing right. Or perhaps he was speaking metaphorically: that Eban's dovish views made it seem to him, Sharon, that he was a metaphorical spy. But Sharon insisted that he was speaking literally.

"He was simply paranoid. There's no other word for it." Yossi Beilin, who served as cabinet secretary for Shimon Peres's half of the rotating prime ministership (September 1984 to October 1986), looked back bemused at "the kind of friendship" that developed between Sharon and himself during that peculiar government, which Sharon had been so instrumental in creating:

> He used to drop into my office almost every week, before the cabinet meeting, sit down, and immediately start slagging off other people. "Yossi, you should know, so-and-so is dangerous. He's out to get you. He'll stab you in the back . . ." It was a friendship grounded in his unshakable conviction that everyone was against him. People were against me too, he explained. But I was too naive to understand, and he, because of our friendship, would warn me and try to protect me. I came to see him as a haunted man. A haunted man. Convinced that the whole world was plotting against him, that he must fight them, constantly fight them.

At cabinet, he always fell asleep after half an hour and awoke only when food was brought in. "He would write me cute notes, 'Yossi, did I miss anything important?' The subtext, of course, was that in his eyes nothing was important if he wasn't involved in it, preferably running it. When the food came, however mediocre it was, it focused his entire attention. He would reach out a huge hand and load up with sandwiches or cookies, whatever was on offer, and proceed to eat it all down with deliberate concentration. 'Eat something. Why don't you eat?' he would whisper to me, an expression of his friendship."[4]

Three times during Peres's twenty-five months as premier, Sharon provoked the Labor prime minister into almost sacking him. Presumably, he thought this tightrope trick scored him points inside the Likud. Arguably, he was right. But unarguably, it weakened him in the country, reinforcing his image as an obtuse and foulmouthed extremist. Since Sharon was not obtuse but highly intelligent, and not naturally foulmouthed but polite by instinct and education, a certain mystery hangs over this behavior. Surely he and his advisers understood that at

---

Sapir went pale. "What's he saying? What's he saying?" he kept asking. I replied, "He's saying Abba Eban is a spy." "A spy?!" Sapir shouts. "Yes, a spy," Sharon calmly replies. He explained that Eban had been seen in various places, among them the top floor of the Hilton hotel in Tel Aviv, with a pair of binoculars, looking at things and writing notes. For years afterward, Sapir and I would have a private joke: "Abba Eban, the spy."

the end of the day the Likud would not vote in as its leader a man who was seen as rude and extreme and therefore unelectable as prime minister? Where was the sophistication behind this strategy of extremism? Or were the periodic explosions of spleen not wholly under his own or his political counselors' control?

In August 1985, Sharon decided to share his impressions of the cabinet room with a group of Irgun veterans. "You cannot imagine the hatred for the settlers in Judea and Samaria that comes through at cabinet meetings," he told the rightist old-timers. The government, which was trying to stop settlers from taking over more houses in the center of Hebron, was conducting a "white paper policy," he declared. The reference was to Britain's infamous White Paper of 1939 drastically limiting Jewish immigration and land purchase in Palestine, just on the eve of World War II. There could hardly be a more infuriating comparison for this audience, indeed for any Zionists. But Sharon had more. "Peres and his gang can jump as far as I'm concerned," he asserted, using a Hebrew sexual vulgarism.

Labor ministers urged Peres to fire Sharon. Shamir warned that would trigger a full-blown cabinet crisis if he did. Sharon delivered a wishy-washy apology of sorts. Peres proclaimed that such unbridled attacks made it impossible to continue with the unity government. But he did continue—until three months later, when Sharon struck again, this time blasting Peres's peace efforts as underhanded and pusillanimous. The cabinet was being kept in the dark. He, Sharon, had demanded that Israel insist on the removal of the PLO offices from Amman as a precondition for talks with Jordan, "but I was answered with cynicism." It was "no accident" that Peres did not explicitly rule out the PLO as a negotiating partner. Peres's weak-kneed policies were also endangering the peace with Egypt.

Peres drafted a formal letter of dismissal and leaked a facsimile of it to the press. Shamir again threatened to bring down the unity government, but this time Peres called his bluff. Now it was Sharon's turn to sweat. "I find it appropriate to clarify," he meekly announced, "that if things I said were interpreted as a personal insult against the prime minister, I hereby apologize to him." But he insisted on his right to hold his views "on critical policy issues." Not good enough, said Peres's bureau. Sharon duly added, live on camera: "I support the government's policy as outlined in its Basic Policy document. Of course, I regret the harsh expressions that I used." Still not good enough. Peres informed a special cabinet meeting of his decision to dismiss Sharon. Behind the scenes, Peres drew up the text of an apology that he wanted Sharon to sign. One key sentence expressed Sharon's "confidence" in

Peres. Sharon said it was "demeaning." But his support in cabinet was growing noticeably ragged. Nobody wanted to lose their jobs, and risk elections, over Sharon's lip. Sharon wrote another letter, almost groveling.

A year later, on the eve of the rotation, and with many in Labor openly urging Peres to seize on Sharon's latest insult and bring down the government, Shamir was worried. The Likud must "deal with" Sharon's words, the soon-to-be prime minister told his Likud cabinet colleagues. Sharon's words this time were particularly vicious. On Saturday, September 6, Palestinian terrorists had killed twenty-two worshippers in an Istanbul synagogue. They shot them indiscriminately with automatic weapons and later tried to set their bodies on fire. That same night, Sharon issued a statement asserting that "this terrible pogrom is the Palestinians' answer to Israel's peace entreaties and Israel's concessions. [Our] concessions to the PLO . . . have been interpreted as weakness and have spurred Palestinian terror, backed by Libya and Syria . . . The incessant pursuit of chimerical peace plans . . . has contributed to the undermining of Israel's defensive shield."

At cabinet the next morning Sharon had his slick letter of apology ready. "It would be absurd to attribute to me any intention. . . . [etc.]" But Peres was not having it. He wouldn't negotiate, he said. Sharon had effectively blamed the murders in Istanbul on the government. He wanted a complete and categorical retraction, and nothing less would do.

The Likud ministers made it clear to Sharon that he was on his own this time. If Peres fired him, they would not resign. Perhaps Shamir and his aides hoped Sharon would dig in and they would be rid of him. But he quickly drew back and signed an apology cum capitulation penned by Peres's people. "I hereby clarify that there is no connection between our constant and sincere striving for peace and the murder of Jews," his statement averred.

Bizarre though it sounds, and despite this baiting of Peres, Yossi Beilin says unhesitatingly that "Sharon was one of our guys." There were ten men in the inner cabinet, the body that Peres and Sharon had created in their secret conclave to run an evenly divided country.

It was supposed to be five and five, but in practice it was six and four. Not in terms of policy, but in terms of atmosphere. Labor's five were either generals or aides to David Ben-Gurion, or both. Shimon was a virtual general, nurturing all the derring-do memories of the BG years. Rabin, Bar-Lev, and Weizman were real generals. And Yitzhak

Navon was BG's secretary. Sharon felt comfortable as one of the six. He didn't like any of his four Likud colleagues. He disliked [Moshe] Arens. He had contempt for Moshe Nissim. He had the mother of contempts for David Levy! And he didn't like or respect Shamir.

Each of the Labor men had his own long and complicated relationship with Sharon. "They all went back a long time," says Beilin. He felt like one of the *hevra* (the good old boys). With most of them it was love-hate. With Bar-Lev it was pure hate, but they kept it in check, radiating coldness at each other but rarely baring their fangs. "It was clear to me that Peres and Rabin didn't see in Sharon what I and my generation saw in him: the father of the settlements, the unprincipled cynic, the epitome of the ugly Israeli. That doesn't mean they liked him or that they didn't understand he was a dangerous man. But they saw him as he saw himself—as one of the *hevra*."

By 1985, Sharon was developing his attitude of aggrieved and aggressive victimhood into a comprehensive narrative of the Lebanon War and of his role in it. He published three lengthy essays in *Yedioth Ahronoth,* the largest-circulation newspaper by far, reexamining the Lebanon War and concluding that it had been a major triumph. But then came the stab in the back.[5]

Between the outbreak of the war and the massacre at the camps, "the Israeli Left, with Labor at its head," cast aside consensus, preferring instead an opposing doctrine "that might best be called, in the language of our times, 'nowism.' " This of course was Sharon's slighting reference to Peace Now, the dovish ginger group that had spearheaded protests against the war culminating in the huge demonstration in Tel Aviv after Sabra and Shatila. " 'Nowism' means: peace—now, concessions—now, withdrawal—now . . . It is the product of non-Zionist Jewish leftism, a conflation of cosmopolitanism, communism, and self-hate . . . It totally rejects Jewish nationalism and fights against it while giving blind support to Arab nationalism and snivelingly kowtowing before the worst of its leaders."

The Zionist Labor movement had always rejected "nowism," Sharon continued. But now Labor had betrayed itself, its past glory, and its ideological heritage because that was the only way it could attack and malign those who were conducting the war, oust them from power, and get back into power itself.

In his second essay, Sharon turned to the accusation that he had led the country into a "war of choice" (Hebrew: *yesh breira*) in Lebanon, whereas all of Israel's previous wars had been wars of no choice (*ein breira*). This was sometimes put in terms of Lebanon having been a "political war" while all the others were wars of national defense. This spurious distinction, Sharon argued, was a deliberate perversion of Israel's history, indeed of all history. Clausewitz himself had determined that war was in essence an extension of policy.

The Left had simply brainwashed public opinion into believing, or at least mouthing, an assertion that wasn't true. The truth was that 1982 was a war of *yesh breira*—and so were the wars of 1948, 1956, 1967, and 1973. "The only war of *ein breira* was the war in the Warsaw Ghetto, where the war aim was to prove that Jews can die fighting." In all the subsequent wars fought by the State of Israel, there had been a choice, between fighting for political goals and forgoing those goals. That was the choice that confronted the leadership under Ben-Gurion before Israel's declaration of independence in 1948. And, indeed, "the precursors then of today's nowists" had advocated deferring the declaration or even making do with something less than statehood.

With the *yesh breira* canard set straight, by his lights, Sharon now took issue with the gravest charge against him—that he had misled the government and the nation. Another vicious calumny, he asserted in the third and last essay. "Operation Peace for Galilee was the first and only war in which everyone knew, in advance, in full and in detail, what its declared aims were. Everyone understood what the military and political advantages were that we hoped to achieve. Anyone claiming to have been misled (unless he was a complete idiot or completely out of touch) is simply lying."

But that, of course, begged—and fudged—the key question. Was the war aim what the government declared or what "everyone understood"? Sharon's fine distinction seemed to be that Israel didn't *want* to extend the war beyond the forty-kilometer line, but it *anticipated* that that was what would happen, and it made its preparations accordingly, using long pre-laid plans.

"With the removal of the terrorists from Beirut, Israel achieved a strategic success on the order of significance of the Six-Day War . . . The defeat of the PLO produced most favorable consequences in Judea, Samaria, and Gaza and among hostile elements within the Israeli-Arab community . . . Our real strategic and political situation—that based on sober assessments, not on the fads of hostile media—has vastly improved."

But the success had starkly eroded, "and the tragedy is that we've done it to ourselves. Operation Peace for Galilee succeeded. But it has been made to fail. The blame for this erosion, as for the drawn-out siege of Beirut, as for the demoralization within the army—all that blame rests on the shoulders and on the consciences of the leaders of the Zionist Left." After the brief period of political consensus at the start of the war,

> the Zionist Left began making common cause with extremist fringe groups. The mass demonstrations they staged, long before Sabra and Shatila, were Yasser Arafat's one ray of hope. These caused him to stiffen his position, and the result was that the siege went on for longer . . .
>
> Collaborating with an unprecedented campaign of slander by the world media, and relying on domestic media that were either bought or cowed, the Zionist Left organized an unprecedented brainwashing campaign against its own government and army. Apart from actually calling on soldiers to refuse to fight, the Left did almost everything possible to undermine the soldiers' motivation and their belief in the justice of their cause.*

---

* Sharon invested his stab-in-the-back thesis with historical, quasi-academic import. But it was never solely cerebral. In February 1986, he leveled the accusation at two leftist Knesset members, Yossi Sarid and Ran Cohen, who complained to the police on behalf of an (Israeli-) Arab hunter who had allegedly trespassed on Sharon's land sixteen months earlier. "I was in my car in an unfenced, uncultivated area," Feisal Tawfiq Younis attested in his somewhat lurid affidavit,

> when suddenly a jeep drew up and a young man identified himself as a security man working for Sycamore Ranch. Soon, Mr. Sharon himself arrived . . . I explained that I had committed no offense and had not violated the conditions of my hunting license. After I gave Mr. Sharon my rifle, he asked me to step aside with him "so that we're not standing next to the child." I walked a few steps with him, and he suddenly landed me the most massive punch on my left eye, smashing my glasses and causing a deep cut in my eyelid. While I was shocked and dazed from this blow, Mr. Sharon delivered an extremely forceful kick to my testicles. Mr. Sharon tried to plant another kick in my testicles, but I was able to ward this off with my left hand, whereupon he said, "I will finish you off."

Sharon's office said the man and his friends had been illegally hunting on Sharon's private land and had refused to turn over their weapon to the security man. This had made it necessary for Sharon to take it himself. Sharon had not filed a complaint with the police because the hunters had begged him not to.

And now came the stab in the back: "More than a year after the event, the hunters have complained, egged on by two leftist politicians, shortly before the Herut Party conference is due to convene."

· · ·

Two years later, in the summer of 1987, Sharon decided to try once again to persuade the establishment and the intelligentsia, if not to see the war his way, then at least to concede that his narrative of it was legitimate. At a lecture marking the fifth anniversary of the war, at the Center for Strategic Studies at Tel Aviv University, Sharon spoke for three straight hours, reading from a prepared text and referring to large maps he had brought with him. The audience included top army brass, past and present, politicians, academics, and journalists.

His text purported to be, in large part, his own campaign diary, recording day by day the unfolding of the war and showing how military necessity—and not a nefarious plot—had turned a forty- to forty-five-kilometer, forty-eight-hour incursion into a long and costly war that was still not entirely over. His subtext was an attempt to show that Begin, far from the depressed and introspective hermit he had now become, was fully and vigorously in control throughout the war.

Sharon was focusing, rightly from his perspective, on what had become by then his critics' central thesis: that he had duped not only the cabinet but Begin, too, into expanding and extending the war. Begin's sad decline in the months after the war, the loss of his beloved wife, and his subsequent reclusive retirement and long, poignant silence, all conspired to dramatically improve his retrospective standing in the eyes of the largely dovish intelligentsia. Decades of opposition to all he stood for gave way to sympathy for his personal plight. He shared, it was felt—and indeed suffered—the pain and shame of an unnecessary war.

And as Begin's stock rose, Sharon's fell ever lower. He alone bore the sin of the accursed war, and of the accursed occupation of the Palestinians, too. Begin's role as the inspiration and the architect of the Likud's policies seemed to fade, whereas Sharon, who was still on the national stage, albeit not center stage, became "the father of the settlements," as though Begin were merely their doddery old grandfather, and the sole villain of the Lebanon debacle, as though there had been no prime minister above him, urging him forward or reining him in.

Twelve times in his lecture Sharon referred to Begin's decisive role before and during the war. In February 1982, he disclosed, Begin had hosted Bashir Gemayel in Jerusalem. " 'It [war] could happen any day,' " Sharon quoted the prime minister telling the Phalange leader. " 'We won't be the ones who start.' There would have to be a provocation 'that will be clear to the whole world. We have to be sure that the U.S. will support us internationally. For your information, I met yesterday with Mr. Shimon Peres, the leader of the opposition, and we reached a near consensus. If we go into Lebanon, we will have the backing of 105 out of the 120 members of the Knesset. If this does happen, we will advance northward as far as possible.' This is what Begin said." Sharon paused to make his point. "And then Begin continued: 'If your existence is in danger, we will fight . . . We will act to defend you. I have a consensus with Mr. Peres to this effect, and we have told Secretary of State Haig.' "

On Saturday night, June 5, at the fateful cabinet meeting, Begin had said:

> Today, as the defense minister has said, the intention is to roll back the bastards and to destroy their weapons to a distance of forty kilometers so that no artillery piece of theirs can hit any village of ours. If it becomes necessary to conquer Beirut, the cabinet will decide on it. We must, in this operation, ensure once and for all complete tranquillity for the northern towns and villages.

This statement by Begin, at this crucial moment, was powerful corroboration of Sharon's contention—the leitmotif of his lecture—that Peace for Galilee, with its forty-kilometer limit, was understood by all concerned, and certainly by Begin, to be a first stage in what might develop into a wider war, "Rolling Pines," as he now termed it.

Sharon highlighted other key interventions by Begin in the running of the war. On June 10, Begin had complained at cabinet about "people hostile to us" who were accusing the government of cheating over the forty-kilometer line. "It is so typical," Begin said. "We're Jews—so we cheated. Whom did we cheat?! What is this nonsense? What do they want? Can you measure a battlefield with a ruler?" Much later, on August 1, after long weeks of siege, Sharon quoted Begin telling the cabinet, "If there's no choice, we will enter Beirut. It is absolutely wrong for us to say that we will not [enter Beirut]."

Sharon's lecture triggered an outpouring of predictable reactions. It was criticized for tendentiousness and selectivity. All the old arguments resurfaced, but this time on the back of a version that Sharon himself had carefully crafted. This was pretty much as he had planned and hoped. A resurgence of the debate would help his long-term rehabilitation: it would remind people that he had a case, that it wasn't all black-and-white. The whole burden of a war that went terribly wrong could not be dumped exclusively on him. There was a powerful prime minister above him. There was a cabinet. And there was the army, too, which had unfortunately not succeeded in carrying out all its operational plans, certainly not in the time originally allotted by the prewar planning.

What Sharon neither planned nor hoped for was the duel that developed, in the wake of the lecture, between him and one of his most implacable foes, Menachem Begin's son, Benny. This was particularly galling for Sharon, because the former prime minister himself, pressed on the phone by reporters the day after Sharon's lecture, had declined to comment on it. "The time has not yet come for me to say my piece about the war. I am not yet ready for that. When I'm ready, I'll respond."[6] No denial, no rebuttal. No criticism.

Benny Begin built his attack solely on the cabinet communiqué of June 5 and on his father's statements to the leaders of Labor and to the Knesset the next day, all of which referred to the forty-kilometer line. He failed to take up any of Sharon's references in his lecture to Menachem Begin's detailed discussion, before, on, and after June 5, of the broader war aims. He did not grapple with the prima facie impression that these references to Begin provided—of an active, informed, and aggressive war leader. In Benny Begin's version of the war, there was no war leader, no prime minister, just Sharon, duping "the government," misleading the nation and the world.

Although Menachem Begin himself said nothing, Ze'ev Schiff, the preeminent military analyst, observed in *Haaretz* that it was unlikely "that Benny Begin said what he said . . . without his father's agreement and consent."[7] But if Sharon read that at the time, four years later he apparently forgot it. On July 11, 1991, out of a clear blue sky, Sharon filed suit for libel against Uzi Benziman, a journalist, for writing in *Haaretz* that he had duped Begin in the Lebanon War and that Begin knew it. *Haaretz* was sued as co-defendant. The lawyer, once again, was Sharon's now-longtime confidant Dov Weissglas.

There had been over the years—as the defendants pointed out during the trial—846 instances in which journalists and authors had made the same or similar allegations in print. Why Benziman? Mibi Mozer, a leading libel lawyer who acted for both *Haaretz* and Benziman in this case, had no doubt there was personal animosity involved. Benziman had published a hostile biography of Sharon in 1985, titled (in Hebrew) *Does Not Stop on Red,* and innumerable articles critical of him. "Our sense was that Sharon had an agenda: to catch Benziman out."

Sharon filed suit in the Jerusalem District Court, claiming half a million shekels ($208,000) in damages. The two sides sparred over whether Begin should be called to give evidence early, before the case was ready to go to trial, because of his advanced age and ill health. Before that was resolved, Begin died, on March 9, 1992.

In his book on the trial, *Nothing but the Truth,* published in 2002, Benziman describes how his disappointment gradually turned to despair as source after source declined to provide him and Mozer with signed affidavits and begged, citing all manner of reasons, not to be called to give evidence in court. "Public figures, politicians past and present, and senior officers in the reserves all banded together in a conspiracy of silence over the Lebanon War. They did not want to get involved in giving evidence. They would rather that the deception that had taken place in the war, and that they knew about from up close (some of them had even discussed it in the media), remain unchallenged. Israel's political and military elites are full of cowards who are afraid to tell the truth about the Lebanon War so as not to come into conflict with Ariel Sharon." Dan Meridor, the cabinet secretary and close Begin confidant, said he didn't want to testify and that anyway his testimony wouldn't help the defendants. "On the face of it, I had good reason to be angry with Meridor," writes Benziman. "He knew that what I had written was true."

Benny Begin came to Benziman's rescue. He was reluctant at first but eventually supplied an affidavit that, in Benziman's own words, "was everything I could have dreamed of. It was a complete confirmation of what I had written and a dramatic description of how, for the first time, he had heard his father speak in a way that made it clear that Sharon had indeed deceived him."

"I showed my father the relevant passages in Sharon's [1987] lecture. He responded with shocked disbelief . . . He recalled forcefully that he had informed the opposition, the Knesset, and the president of the United States of the limited aims of the operation. 'Did I then deceive them with my statements?' he asked. He was greatly agitated and kept repeating, 'These things are completely untrue.' "

But was it not possible, Mozer asked Benny Begin, that Sharon and his father had been in cahoots? Together they had planned the expanded war, and together they had concealed it from the cabinet? No way, he replied, describing again his father's reaction to Sharon's lecture and to his own articles published in response: "It's just not possible that Arik planned from the outset to reach Beirut," the elder Begin had remonstrated.

The judge in the Tel Aviv District Court, Moshe Telgam, declared himself impressed by the "sincere and knowledgeable tenor of Dr. Benny Begin's evidence." He held against Sharon both on grounds of fair comment and on grounds of truth.

The Supreme Court swept this away on appeal. It took another five years, but eventually Sharon achieved, if not victory, then at least a

backhanded affirmation from the highest court in the land that the
historical facts of the Lebanon War were not quite as straightforward
as Benziman and Benny Begin made out. Sharon lost the case in the
Supreme Court, too—but solely on grounds of fair comment. All three
justices held that Judge Telgam should have confined himself to this
defense of fair comment, which was adequate to decide the case. The
presiding justice in the Supreme Court, Eliahu Matza, was elaborately
careful not to take sides on the historical issue. "It must not be deduced
that I accept, or do not accept, in whole, or in part, the lower court's
findings. For my part, I prefer to ignore them, not only because of my
usual desire to avoid unnecessary obiter dicta, but also, and mainly,
because of the nature of the historical argument. As far as I am concerned, determining historical truth is best left to historians."

The second justice, Eliezer Rivlin, joined with Justice Matza in ticking off Judge Telgam. "The means at the judge's disposal could not
enable him to find his way through the thickets of the factual questions that he chose to grapple with." The third justice, Ya'acov Turkel,
was the most censorious. "A judge should curb his desires and confine
himself—in his judgments and not only in his judgments—exclusively
to the issues that he is duty-bound to rule on in order to reach a decision in the case before him."

Turkel concluded with a one-sentence "final comment" that gave
Sharon's side cause for gratification. "To remove any doubt, the
dismissal of this appeal does not imply endorsement of the district
court's conclusion that the defendants are protected by the defense of
truth—about which we have said what we have said."

Benziman, in his book, reacted with bad grace, suggesting that the
Supreme Court took account of the fact that Sharon was now prime
minister. Ironically, though, his own honest reporting in the book
provided abundant reason why the justices would have been uncomfortable to rule for either side on the historical issue. Benziman even
confided to his readers that Mozer, his lawyer, tended to believe at one
stage that Sharon and Begin conspired together, behind the cabinet's
back. Benziman reported, too, that several leading journalists held
that view and tried, therefore, to persuade him to drop his suit. And he
reported at length the categorical testimony of Begin's longtime close
aide and friend, Yechiel Kadishai, that Begin did take into account the
possibility that the war would extend beyond the original forty kilometers and that he said so explicitly to a number of people. Kadishai
testified that he himself had told Begin, early in the war, of the rumors
already then circulating that Sharon was deceiving him—and Begin
brushed them aside.

On the strength of my deep and intimate knowledge of Menachem Begin over many years, of his opinions, his positions, and his reactions, and in consideration of the close relations that prevailed between us, I assert categorically that if he had thought that Sharon deceived him, I would have known.*

NEW WAR, OLD WARS

After five years, "stab in the back" was wearing thin as the platform from which Sharon proposed to storm his way back to national leadership. However cogent his arguments seemed to be, in his own mind at any rate, they suffered from the inherent political weakness of casting other people's minds back to the Lebanon War. While Sharon felt he had convinced at least some of the public that the war was not his responsibility alone, he could hardly claim to have persuaded many Israelis that it was a success, as he continued doggedly to assert. It was fortunate for him, therefore, if to be cynical, that the first Palestinian intifada, or uprising, broke out when it did, at the end of 1987. The intifada breathed new life into the frustrated general, who seemed to be fading away as a frustrated politician. It was, after all, a new war, and he was an acknowledged master of the art of war. Better yet, it was nothing like the Lebanon War.

Granted, his contention that driving Arafat from Lebanon would render the Palestinians of Palestine placid and compliant had been debunked long ago. The incidence of violence in the occupied territories had not fallen off, even at the height of the war, and it had remained fairly stable in the subsequent years. Stones were frequently thrown at army and civilian cars; more rarely, Molotov cocktails.

But that was small beer compared with the mayhem that erupted throughout the territories after an Israeli truck plowed into a group of Palestinian workers in the northern Gaza Strip on December 8, 1987,

---

* There was another witness with unique insight into the Sharon-Begin-cabinet nexus whom the court in *Sharon v. Benziman* did not hear, because Weissglas neglected to call him. The then minister of justice, Moshe Nissim, as we have seen, denied the claim that ministers were uninformed or misled during the war. He vehemently rejected the notion that Begin was duped. "Begin talked to me more than to any other person. He would pour out his heart to me . . . I don't care what Benny Begin says. Those who say, 'We didn't know, we didn't hear,' they are distorting." Why, then, did Nissim not testify in the Benziman case? "Nobody asked me to" (Nissim interview, Tel Aviv, January 9, 2008).

killing four and injuring ten. By all accounts, then and later, it was an accident. But the fifty thousand Gazans who marched from the funeral that evening to the gates of a nearby army camp, hurling rocks and abuse, were not prepared to believe that. The next day, rioting spread like a brush fire up and down the Strip; days later it had broken out all over the West Bank and East Jerusalem. In the twenty years of Israeli occupation there had never been anything even remotely comparable in scope to this spontaneous, countrywide rebellion, led by youths with stones and slingshots. Quickly, the movement grew a grassroots political leadership. Local committees formed in the Palestinian towns. When members were arrested, others took their places. On the Israeli left, some could say they had warned that a Palestinian uprising was ultimately inevitable, that there was no such thing as "enlightened occupation."

By February 1988, after just two months of intifada, there were 48 Palestinian dead. By late 1991, the figure was 787. Some 750 of them had been killed by the army, among them 159 minors, and another 37 were thought to have been shot by settlers. Israel lost 13 dead soldiers and another 13 civilians during this period. By July 1993, the Palestinian death toll topped 1,000. Another 503 Palestinians had been killed by their own people as collaborators. The Israeli death toll, from attacks in the territories and inside Israel proper, stood at 165.[8]

The intifada caught the Israeli government and army wrong-footed. They had not seen it coming, despite the extensive intelligence network that the Shin Bet security service maintained throughout the territories. Yitzhak Rabin took his time to speak out—and, when he finally did, provoked a worldwide wave of revulsion. He ordered the army to "break their bones," which some of the troops proceeded to do with gusto. Rabin and his aides tried repeatedly to explain that what he had said, and the wooden nightsticks that had been issued to the troops in the territories, were not intended as a license to maim. He had meant club rather than shoot, and then only to put down violent rioting, not to punish. He had been misquoted. Officers or soldiers found abusing their powers would be tried and punished. There would be no sadism in the Jewish army.

Sharon, quick-footed and smooth-tongued, saw his chance and moved with alacrity. He had been planning a festive housewarming for his and Lily's new town house: an apartment in the heart of the Muslim Quarter of the Old City of Jerusalem. It was a publicity stunt planned to coincide with the winter festival of Hanukkah. Now it could coincide with the raging intifada, too, making it dramatically more topical. More than three hundred politicians, businessmen, and assorted glitterati of the Right made their way through the tightly guarded alleys of the Old City, braving the catcalls of Peace Now demonstrators, to watch Sharon, in a big black yarmulke, kindle the Hanukkah lights and nail a mezuzah to the doorpost of his new home. His Muslim neighbors had been ordered by the police to stay indoors, behind closed shutters.

Sharon and Lily, elegantly dressed and sparkling with energy, effusively greeted Prime Minister Shamir and the Likud cabinet members. Peres and the Laborites stayed demonstratively away. Yossi Sarid, the left-wing firebrand now in Meretz, best evoked the feeling in the peace camp. "The country is burning," he cried, "and the emperor Nero goes up to the roof of his new house in the Muslim Quarter of Jerusalem and plays his fiddle. With Sharon-Nero on that roof were three hundred toadies, hypocrites, arse-lickers, opportunists and adventurers, deluded dreamers and lunatics."*

For Sharon, the party celebrated not merely the new house—which he barely used thereafter, though its police protection cost the taxpayer 1.25 million shekels a year—but a new lease on political life. "I've moved to the Old City of Jerusalem," he asserted at cabinet, "because you, Shimon Peres, wanted to hand the Old City to King Hussein. I've moved there to stop you."

On television, Sharon explained that "the deteriorating security situation in Jerusalem" was what prompted him to move into his new home. Many more Jews would follow him to the Muslim Quarter, he believed. He had never asked to be guarded; he had spent most of his life guarding others. Menachem Begin had telephoned to congratulate him, he added. What needed to be done now in Jerusalem was to shut down and drive out the PLO-linked political agencies operating there. Years ago he had shown in Gaza how to deal with terror. He had also submitted proposals on how to solve the Gaza refugee problem. But no one listened to him. There was no serious political leadership in this country, capable of making decisions.

The message was unmistakable: make him minister of defense instead of Rabin, and the intifada would quickly be crushed. Sha-

---

* In the Knesset on March 23, 1988, Charlie Biton, a colorful Jerusalem social activist and Knesset member for the largely Arab Hadash communist party, asked as follows: "Was the cost of the minister's housewarming borne by the state? 1. If so, how many people took part in the housewarming dinner in the Muslim Quarter? 2. What exactly was on the menu? 3. Is it correct that the dinner was prepared by the chef of the Jerusalem Plaza Hotel? 4. What was the cost of the event?" Sharon's reply, "not read out, but submitted to the protocol," as the official *Knesset Record* notes, was "No."

ron's new agenda turned him into Rabin's most relentless critic. When Sharon lambasted Rabin at cabinet over the state of security on the roads, both in the territories and inside Israel, Ezer Weizman, now a Labor-affiliated minister in the unity government, lashed back, terming Sharon's purported panaceas "cheap demagoguery . . . He's got a glib tongue, and he's good at arguing. That's what makes him so dangerous." On another occasion, Weizman stood up and, red-faced, stormed around the table to Sharon, shouting, "Shut your face. I will chuck you out of the government" (which of course he couldn't do).

> SHARON: One must be sensitive to human lives . . .
> WEIZMAN: *You're* talking!!? What about the 650 [IDF fatalities in Lebanon] . . . ?
> SHARON: You called me "murderer."*

Sharon's rift with Rabin was the more traumatic given their long and close relationship. After one stormy cabinet meeting Sharon was heard phoning Lily. "I've had it with that man!" he bellowed, angry but sad, too. "Our special friendship is over forever."[9] It wasn't over, but it was never quite the same again. Sharon was directly challenging the credentials of the man who in the eyes of the peace camp was the nation's unrivaled specialist in all matters of defense and security. "Jewish lives are at stake," Sharon asserted in June 1988. "If the minister of defense is not capable of acting to defend them, he should be replaced."[10]

After elections in November 1988, which the Likud won by a whisker, Sharon demanded to be made minister of defense in the new government. He urged that it be a narrow-based rightist-religious coalition and not another alliance with Labor. But Shamir preferred to renew the national unity partnership with Labor, partly to keep Sharon out of Defense. Back at Industry and Commerce, Sharon stepped up his sniping at Rabin, harping now on his penchant—which everyone knew and no one talked about—for drinking large quantities of whiskey. Thus, at one cabinet meeting:

> SHARON: You are not fit to serve as defense minister because of your failure in handling the terror in the territories and your failure to defend Jewish lives.

---

* Yet two months earlier, at a party, Ezer put his arm around Arik's shoulder and proclaimed for all to hear: "Listen, fatty. Only you and I can pull this country out of the mud. Only we two can do it."

RABIN: You had better be careful with what you say. To date, only one defense minister has ever been removed from office by a commission of inquiry. The Lebanon War and its failure strongly point to your need to be careful about what you say.

SHARON: I don't want to relate to the style of Rabin's remarks. This happens to him sometimes. Mainly when he's not sober enough. When he loses control of himself.

RABIN: Your words barely reach the tip of my ankle.

Sharon's own proposals for defeating the intifada, which he never tired of repeating, included tightening controls on money transfers from the Arab world, barring men from violent Palestinian villages from working in Israel, and outlawing political and charitable organizations suspected of ties to the PLO. But above all he advocated deportation—peremptory deportation, and not just of the offenders themselves.

"That is the biggest single sin of this government," he told an audience of government spokesmen in March 1988:

That it hasn't brought in urgent legislation enabling the deportation of all the rioters, immediately and without delay. Let me remind you that when I brought order to Gaza, there was serious rioting at first. What did we do? We took hold of twenty-five Arabs, cousins and brothers of youngsters who had been rioting, we gave each of them a little money, a hat, a loaf of bread, and a water bottle, and we drove them to the Arava. There we showed them the way to Jordan. After that, total peace and quiet descended on Gaza. Only the sound of the weeping of the riotous youngsters could be heard from afar. No, we didn't do anything to them. It was their families who beat them, as punishment for having caused their relatives to be deported. That's what we should be doing now . . . Believe me, I've got experience.[11]

Sharon's "bringing order" to Gaza in 1970, it will be recalled, included a more brutal aspect that led, after much controversy, to the Strip being taken out of his hands. He constantly urged the same kinds of aggressive initiatives, using elite commando units, now, too. Armed militants must be hunted, smoked out, ambushed, captured, or killed. The army needed to take the fight to them. Again, the message was simple: I did it then; I can do it now; let me do it.

. . .

Rabin became an easier target for Sharon to attack as the intifada dragged on because his defenders were themselves growing increasingly uneasy with his performance. Rabin talked of weeks, but the intifada went on for months that eventually became years. His initial self-confidence—he was in America when the intifada broke out and refused to cut short his visit and hurry home—began to grate. Much worse, the criticism surrounding his "break their bones" line, whatever its true context, mushroomed into a huge and anguished controversy over the morality of the army's actions—and the patent immorality of some of its excesses.

Rabin, despite his years in diplomacy and in politics, always remained something of the gruff and honest soldier. He explained to his Labor Knesset faction that "nobody dies" from the kind of "aggressive action" the army was taking to disperse demonstrations and restore normal life. He was aware, he said, that "any confrontation between soldiers and civilians looks bad on camera." But he preferred such footage to scenes of shooting, of Molotov cocktails and burning tires.

Both kinds of scenes proliferated. Random incidents of IDF cruelty were caught on camera, bringing down on Israel, especially in Europe, a new outpouring of deprecation reminiscent of the Lebanon War. The most ghoulish episodes occurred in the early months. The army's instinctive reaction to the unanticipated uprising was that it must be quelled fast. Orders were unclear and confused as they filtered down from Rabin to the units in the field. In one case in February 1988 in a Gaza Strip refugee camp, five soldiers from the Givati infantry brigade beat and kicked a forty-three-year-old man to death. They jumped on him, smashing his ribs and banging his head on the ground—all this in front of his twelve-year-old son. In the same month in Nablus, soldiers beat and kicked several young Palestinians whom they had arrested during rioting. One soldier pounded at one of the prisoners with a rock, deliberately trying to break his shoulder, then went at another, trying to break his arm. The whole sequence was filmed by a CBS crew and broadcast around the world. Again in February 1988, also near Nablus, a group of soldiers used a bulldozer to bury four young Palestinians up to their necks in wet earth, as "punishment" after a riot.

In the media, and among soldiers and their families, there was both widespread repression and enormous ambivalence. People preferred or pretended to be ignorant of what was going on. They were also ashamed, but angry too—at themselves, at their sons or brothers in uniform, but also at the Palestinians who were confronting the army with challenges it had not been trained or equipped to confront. Why it was not trained or equipped, why after twenty years of occupation, with no land-for-peace deal in sight, did it not occur to anyone in government that a popular Palestinian uprising was inevitable, or at least likely—that question goes to the heart of Israeli attitudes to the Palestinians and to the conflict. It was never directly addressed, let alone answered, even after the intifada had subsided.

Sharon was careful not to be seen as siding too uncritically with soldiers and officers who had committed brutal offenses. At the same time, it was important to him to sympathize publicly with the fighting men and to score points off Rabin. "Soldiers Need Backing," Sharon headlined an article in *Yedioth Ahronoth* in March 1988. The episodes cited above were mostly still unpublished then. But rumors abounded, and Sharon himself knew broadly what had been happening on the "front lines" of the intifada. "There is nothing that weakens the military more than the fighting soldiers' sense that the top echelons are not giving them the backing they need," he wrote. "There is nothing more destructive to an army's operations and to its motivation than the soldiers' feeling that . . . they are scapegoats for the incompetence of higher echelons."

When courts-martial finally began to be held, the sentences handed down for acts of savagery usually entailed no more than a few months behind bars. The military judges wrote ringing condemnations of the brutal acts recounted before them and warned in their judgments that pillars of the national ethos were in danger of erosion. But they made a point of stressing, too, how hard and frustrating these young soldiers' conditions of service had suddenly become, cursed, insulted, and stoned as they were, day in and day out, by Palestinians of both sexes and all ages. The courts often agreed to plea bargains in which charges of aggravated assault were reduced to mere conduct unbecoming, with the punishments similarly mitigated.

In June 1988 a soldier was sentenced to one year's imprisonment and another two years on probation for fatally shooting a Palestinian in Saja'iya, Gaza, at point-blank range. "I told him to stand still and put his hands up, but he refused and cursed me and my mother. I walked up to him and stuck my rifle into his belly. He looked at me. My whole body shook, and I pulled the trigger." The military judges had harsh words for the army's induction system, which had not weeded out this recruit, who was clearly unfit to serve. The case highlighted nevertheless the unconscionable fact that the IDF was pitting soldiers trained to shoot and kill against rioters who were in the main unarmed (though there were many armed attacks, too, and instances of shooters mingled in with stone throwers and unarmed demonstrators). Israeli propaganda harped on the killing propensities of stones, which could indeed be lethal if large enough or if fired with sufficient force from slingshots. The soldiers were not permitted, in theory at least, to fire live ammunition at stone throwers unless they felt themselves in serious danger.

In order to reduce fatalities, soldiers were issued rubber-coated bullets. These are fired in volleys from regular rifles and, unless used from very close range, are intended to hurt but not to penetrate. But there were mishaps. In June 1988, a nine-month-old baby lost an eye to a rubber-coated bullet. She was lying in her mother's arms inside their home in Jabaliya, Gaza, when the bullet came through the window and hit her. In August 1988, the IDF began issuing plastic-coated bullets. These are fired singly and at a much greater velocity than the rubber ones. Within six months, the plastic bullets had accounted for forty-seven Palestinian fatalities.

By early 1991, 154 officers and men had been court-martialed. Hundreds more had faced disciplinary action within their units. During the same period 75,000 Palestinians had been arrested and 45,000 of them charged before military courts. Sharon joined more than fifty coalition ministers and Knesset members who supported a private member's bill providing pardons for all IDF soldiers (but not officers) who had carried out illegal orders during the first three months of the intifada. The bill's sponsors argued that the soldiers, suddenly transformed into untrained policemen, had no mens rea when they stepped beyond the bounds of legality. The bill was opposed by Minister of Defense Arens and by Minister of Justice Dan Meridor and never became law. In practice, generals were commuting any severe sentences and making sure no soldier stayed in jail for too long.

CHAPTER 9 · JORDAN IS PALESTINE?

The intifada was the palpable proof that forcible occupation could not be sustained indefinitely. Eventually, that realization led to the Oslo Accords between Israel and the PLO, which were signed in 1993, and the creation of the Palestinian Authority (PA) in the West Bank and Gaza. But Israel, both its rightists and its leftists, balked for long years before finally, reluctantly, agreeing to go down that road. In the eleven years between the Likud government's rejection of the Reagan Plan in 1982 and the Labor government's acceptance of Oslo, both parties tried, separately and together, to avoid making a deal with the PLO.

The Likud, under Yitzhak Shamir, sought to avoid making a deal with anyone. Ariel Sharon, though hardly a loyal subordinate or favorite colleague, was an important collaborator throughout Shamir's years of prime ministerial intransigence. As minister of commerce and trade, Sharon helped ensure the settlements thrived. As minister of housing after 1990, he made sure they grew and multiplied and did his best to frustrate American peacemaking efforts.

But his special contribution during the decade was his unflagging advocacy of "Jordan is Palestine." This was Sharon's own exclusive ax that he never stopped grinding until Yitzhak Rabin and King Hussein signed a treaty of peace between their two countries in 1994. Only then, and reluctantly, was Sharon finally prepared to set aside his dream of the Hashemite house being displaced by a Palestinian republic, presumably under Yasser Arafat's PLO, which would then somehow cut a deal with Israel over the West Bank.

This thesis and his dogged devotion to it always singled Sharon out from the dogmatists of the Right, and, back to the days of the short-lived Shlomzion Party, it piqued interest on the far left, where there was always vague embarrassment over Israel's de facto alliance with Hashemite Jordan, a colonial creation if ever there was one.

"Jordan is Palestine" was mortally discredited by being implicated in the Lebanon War, that is, by the widespread suspicion that beyond "Big Pines," which plotted regime change for Lebanon, there lurked in Sharon's secret scheme of things a "Very Big Pines," which envisaged his long-hoped-for revolution in Jordan, too. The Palestinian refugees in Lebanon, fleeing that country in the wake of the PLO's defeat by Israel and the Phalange's seizure of power, would force themselves on Jordan, reuniting with the Palestinians living there and sweeping out the Hashemite monarchy.*

While the possible place of Jordan in Sharon's war strategy remained opaque, Sharon left no uncertainty throughout the postwar decade as to his unequivocal belief in "Jordan is Palestine" as the right, indeed the only, long-term strategy for Israel. The PLO, he wrote in July 1985, had succeeded

> in downplaying, distorting, and concealing the fact that for the past sixty years an independent Arab state has existed in Palestine. More-over, even if one accepts that the "Palestinian people" comprises only those originating from west of the river Jordan—even by that defini-tion this state has long become a Palestinian state. I am referring, of course, to the state of Jordan. Some 70 percent of its people are Pales-tinians, and the Arabs of Judea and Samaria are citizens of Jordan too, and have an outlet for their political aspirations by electing representa-tives to the Jordanian parliament. This is a political, geographical, and demographical fact that cannot be changed or denied . . . The Arab world invented the artificial distinction between "Jordan" and "the Palestinians" because its true purpose is not, and never was, to pro-vide the "Palestinian entity" with political self-expression, but rather to remove Israel and the Jewish people from the map of the Middle East . . . Why should we in Israel be dragged along after the PLO and the Arabs and accept their position as though it were self-evident?[1]

Sharon's incessant efforts to subvert Jordan's Hashemite regime in the Israeli public mind were especially galling to Shimon Peres and the Labor side of the unity government. For them, peace with Jordan, based on some form of sharing the West Bank with King Hussein, was the central pillar of all their political plans and hopes. The "Jordanian option" had been for the best part of two decades Labor-speak for resolving the Palestinian problem without acceding to the creation of a separate Palestinian state under the PLO.

---

* See pp. 174–75.

The Labor Party leaders regarded Yasser Arafat's organization as an implacable foe that could never become a pragmatic partner in a peaceful accommodation. It was not just the terrorism, though, that induced profound loathing. It was the professed ideology of the PLO, which rigidly rejected the principle of a sovereign Jewish presence in Palestine. In addition, Peres always insisted, on the basis of intelligence assessments, that Arafat was "not serious," that is, not capable of making the hard decisions that a revolutionary leader needs to make in order to transform his revolutionary movement into a sovereign state. He held to his contemptuous view of Arafat even after the PLO softened its ideological stance in 1988 and only relented when the secret negotiations in Oslo, initiated by Yossi Beilin, were well under way.

Before the peace with Egypt in 1979, the hopes of an agreement with Jordan had anyway been somewhat hypothetical since Hussein always made it clear he could not be the first Arab leader to sign a peace treaty with Israel. Now, though, Egypt had made the breakthrough. But the Likud, still committed to "Greater Israel," was not prepared to contemplate any concession in "Judea and Samaria." Peres applied his fertile mind to squaring this circle, while Shamir's purpose was to keep it unsquared.

"King Hussein's position," Peres wrote in his memoirs, "was that he was prepared to negotiate a peace treaty, but only in the context of an international conference on peace in the Middle East that would bring together the Great Powers and all of the regional protagonists. He was supported in this by the Soviet Union, France, Britain, and, with some hesitation, the United States. Shamir flatly rejected the idea of an international conference. He argued that such a conference would try to impose a solution on the parties."[2]

Reduced to vice prime minister and foreign minister after the "rotation" in November 1986 and champing at the bit, Peres arranged a secret summit between himself and King Hussein in the home of a London lawyer, Victor Mishcon, in April 1987. They sat all afternoon and eventually hammered out a document that would have been a momentous success and very possibly changed the face of the region—had it gotten past Shamir. It provided for an international conference, under UN auspices, that would "invite the parties" to negotiate bilaterally between themselves. Crucially, on the Palestinian question the Hussein-Peres "London Agreement" provided that negotiations would take place between Israel and a "Jordanian-Palestinian delegation."*

---

* The key points in the London Agreement were (1) the international conference will not impose any solution or veto any agreement arrived at between the par-

In other words—no PLO, or certainly not in a lead role. And, very probably, if the envisaged Jordanian/Palestinian-Israeli negotiations had ever transpired, some form of condominium between Israel and Jordan, with autonomy for the West Bank and Gaza perhaps evolving into Palestinian independence within an Israel-Jordan-Palestine confederation.

But it was never to happen. Peres sent Yossi Beilin to Helsinki, where George Shultz was visiting, to brief the secretary of state's top aide, Charlie Hill. He himself reported to Shamir, whom he had told of the meeting with Hussein ahead of time. He read him the agreement but, probably ill-advisedly, refused to leave the famously discreet prime minister a copy of the text on the grounds that it might leak. Shamir said nothing but immediately dispatched Moshe Arens, then a minister without portfolio, to Washington to abort the nascent accord. Shultz, discerning the state of discord in Jerusalem, quickly drew back—and let the agreement die. In retrospect, this was probably an egregious error of American diplomacy.

Sharon lashed out both at Peres for making the agreement and at Shamir for not stopping him before and not punishing him after. It was "one of the greatest deceits of all time," he said, to depict the London Agreement as providing merely for an international "opening" or "umbrella." Peres and Hussein had agreed on a full-fledged international conference, Sharon asserted, at which the substantive negotiations were to be conducted. The agreement also paved the way for the PLO to take part, he maintained. Moreover, Peres had agreed to Soviet participation in the conference without insisting, as a condition, that Moscow permit free Jewish emigration and without demanding that it restore diplomatic relations with Israel.[3*] As for Shamir, his letting Peres get away with it betrayed a total "lack of leadership," Sharon asserted at a steamy Herut central committee meeting in July. Peres was still going around the world persuading people to support the international conference. Why didn't Shamir fire him?

---

ties; (2) the negotiations will be conducted in bilateral committees directly; (3) the Palestinian issue will be dealt with in the committee of the Jordanian-Palestinian and Israeli delegations; (4) the Palestinians' representatives will be included in the Jordanian-Palestinian delegation; (5) participation in the conference will be based on the parties' acceptance of UNSC Resolutions 242 and 338 and the renunciation of violence and terrorism; (6) each committee will negotiate independently; (7) other issues will be decided by mutual agreement between Jordan and Israel.

[*] The Soviet Union and all its satellites save Romania severed diplomatic relations with Israel at the time of the Six-Day War in 1967.

Shamir himself dubbed the international conference "a mirage," "a nightmare," "a slaughter," "a surrender," "a suicide," and "a trap." As long as Likud was in government, it would never be convened, he vowed. But still, he made it clear that he wanted Peres and Labor to stay in the government alongside Likud, under his prime minister-ship, and to continue with their strange partnership despite this latest hiccup.

Sharon, speaking at a Likud rally against the London Agree-ment convened in the Samaria settlement-township of Ariel, called on King Hussein, "who is a brave leader," to enter into negotiations with Israel. But, he told his audience, there were some things Israel would not concede. Jerusalem was one. And other areas in Judea and Samaria and Gaza were not open to negotiations either. And security would have to remain in Israel's hands forever. And Jewish settlement throughout the territories must remain free and unfettered. And not a single Jordanian soldier, or policeman, or even civilian official would be allowed anywhere in the territories. "Even so," he proclaimed, straight-faced as far as is recorded, "there remains a great deal to be negotiated about."[4]

While the United States declined to side with Hussein and Peres against Shamir, Shultz made it clear that he favored in principle the idea of a peace conference. Shamir played along, negotiating for long months with the Americans over the format for a conference he had no wish to attend.

Shamir, too, met secretly with King Hussein in England. He sent an upbeat account of their meeting to the U.S. secretary of state.

Hussein came away thoroughly disheartened. For him, Washing-ton's shortsighted dismissal of his London Agreement with Peres sig-naled the end of the road. In July 1988 he announced that the West Bank was no longer part of Jordan, either legally or administratively. "We respect the wishes of the PLO, the sole legitimate representative of the Palestinian people, to secede from us in an independent Palestin-ian state."

The PLO now saw its opportunity. At a session of the Palestine National Council, the PLO's parliament, in Algiers the follow-ing November, Arafat proclaimed an independent Palestinian state "with holy Jerusalem as its capital" and hinted at recognition of Israel. After further verbal to-and-fro, he produced a statement, in the dying days of the Reagan administration, that explicitly fulfilled long-standing U.S. conditions for dialogue with the PLO: acceptance of Israel's right to exist; acceptance of negotiations under UN Security Council Resolution 242; and a permanent commitment to desist from terror.

Shultz hardly rejoiced at this development (unlike others in Washington, who saw it as a breakthrough). But he bit the bullet and instructed the U.S. ambassador to Tunisia to begin official talks between the United States and the PLO. Shamir, horrified, could only reiterate lamely that Israel would never have truck with the organization. But his protestations rang increasingly hollow. In a sop to the new Bush administration in Washington, Shamir submitted a new plan for elections in the Palestinian territories that he had jointly formulated with Minister of Defense Yitzhak Rabin. Israel would then negotiate with the elected, indigenous Palestinian leadership over an interim self-government regime.

For Sharon, too, this chain of events presented an opportunity—to deprecate all the policy makers. He railed at Shultz. "I can't believe that the U.S. would bring the PLO into the process. If that happened, it would only show how little one can rely on signed American commitments."[5] As for Labor, it was "koshering the rat." Labor, he asserted, was prepared "to negotiate over our future with the greatest Jew murderers of our time, whose whole raison d'être is the destruction of the State of Israel . . . I never believed a day would come when I would have to level such a serious accusation against Peres, the man I knew in the 1950s . . . and against Rabin, under whose command I fought in the Six-Day War."

He demanded that Israel immediately annex those parts of the West Bank, sparsely populated, that Yigal Allon, the Labor minister, had approved for Jewish settlement back in the 1960s and 1970s. The Allon Plan was hardly his dream, he wrote. "But, given the current sense of erosion in our national will and purpose, I embrace it now." Sharon presented his new ideas to the cabinet in a long lecture, aided as always by large colored maps, this time purportedly representing the Allon Plan.

It sounded good, but it was shot through with disingenuousness. Israel had committed at Camp David not to annex any of the occupied territories but to negotiate a Palestinian autonomy for them. Sharon's "enhanced Allon Plan," moreover, proposed to annex all the settlements that had been built since 1977, with all the Palestinian population in the areas surrounding them. This was no enhancement of Allon but a perversion of it.

WAR OF WORDS

President George H. W. Bush and his secretary of state, James Baker, were hardly bowled over by the Shamir-Rabin proposal for Palestinian elections. But they decided to give it a chance, despite what they immediately discerned was the Israeli leader's distinct lack of enthusiasm over the plan that bore his own name.

Confirming the Americans' suspicions, hampering their efforts from day one, and seriously souring relations between the two governments was the old irritant of settlement building. Bush quickly concluded that Shamir "was not being straight with him in this regard," Baker writes in his memoirs. "At first, Shamir had suggested that this was strictly an internal matter and not the business of the United States. 'You have things that concern you, we have things that concern us,' he said. 'Don't let it concern you.' Given the fact that at the time American taxpayer–financed assistance to Israel amounted to more than $1,000 per Israeli citizen per year, this was not a brush-off George Bush was prepared to accept."[6]

For Sharon, it was "1938 all over again." No less. "They want to do to us what they did to Czechoslovakia in 1938: they sacrificed her in order to prevent war." The proposed elections would lead inexorably, he warned, to the creation of "a second Palestinian state, after Jordan, which in essence *is* the Palestinian state."

Baker presented an easy target for Sharon and the group of rebel ministers that was beginning to form around him, by publicly giving vent to his frustrations in refreshingly plain English. He chose the annual conference of the American Israel Public Affairs Committee, or AIPAC, the powerful pro-Israel lobbying organization, to declare in May 1989, "For Israel, now is the time to lay aside once and for all the unrealistic vision of a Greater Israel . . . Israel should forswear annexation . . . stop settlement activity . . . reach out to the Palestinians as neighbors who deserve political rights."

In Tel Aviv, Sharon had a field day. The cause and blame for this "slap in the face," he wrote in the newspaper *Hadashot,* was the government's so-called peace plan and the pusillanimity it betrayed. Israel's failure to suppress the intifada had led to the Reagan-Shultz decision to talk to the PLO. And the same weakness had now produced Baker's "unprecedentedly blunt and harsh public statement . . . America's attitude to us will be determined above all by the question whether we are weak or strong."

Sharon organized a series of meetings at his home in East Jerusalem for Likud Party activists and elected officials who felt, or could be persuaded to feel, as he did about the Shamir-Rabin plan. The venue, he explained, was intended to dramatize his conviction that if the plan were implemented, it would lead to the repartition of Jerusalem. His strategy was to try to get the plan rejected by the Likud central committee, which was due to convene in July.

By July 1989, Sharon's hard-line ginger group had gelled. Its members were himself, David Levy, and Yitzhak Modai. They drew up a list of six "constraints," or, literally, hoops, as around a barrel: no negotiation with the PLO; no Palestinian state; no limitation of settlement building; no foreign sovereignty west of the river Jordan; no votes for East Jerusalem Palestinians; the intifada must be brought to an end before any negotiation with any Palestinians.

The sting was in the tail. The first five points were motherhood and apple pie for Shamir, too. But the prime minister, under sustained American pressure, had signaled that he was prepared to start informal talks without insisting as a prior condition that the intifada end. Kids with stones, the Americans argued, could not be allowed to dictate the future of the Middle East. Once the talks began, the violence would subside. No formal negotiation would take place until it did.

At a session of the Likud central committee, which with the final merger of Herut and the Liberals had grown to three thousand members, Sharon and his two allies appeared to have the upper hand. Shamir announced that he accepted the list of constraints. The central committee, relieved to have avoided a bruising showdown, immediately endorsed the prime minister's statement unanimously. Sharon, Modai, and Levy stood on the platform flashing V signs to their supporters.

But Shamir was not contemplating his own political demise quite yet. The committee's endorsement prompted unexpected resistance: threats from Labor to secede and exhortations from Washington forced Shamir to demand, and obtain, a re-endorsement of the original plan by the full cabinet, with an addendum, for what it was worth, declaring that the new decision committed all the ministers.

In the months that followed, speculation grew that the prime minister had had all he could take from Sharon and was considering firing him. Shamir himself hinted at a thought that had clearly been exercising him privately for some time: the Likud would do well to skip a generation in its leadership stakes, moving on from him to the group of bright young "princes" who surrounded him.[7] These included Dan Meridor and Ehud Olmert, whose fathers had been Herut Knesset

members; Ronni Milo, who was related by marriage to the Begins[8]—
Shamir made all three of them ministers in his 1988 government;
Benny Begin, son of the now-reclusive leader; and Benjamin Netanyahu, a brilliant young diplomat then serving as ambassador to the
UN. Skipping a generation would mean passing over Moshe Arens,
perhaps the Likud's most competent and most widely respected politician. But Arens, who grew up in America, seemed to lack the fire in
the belly that fuels unquenchable political ambition. Shamir was sorry
to sacrifice him, but the upside was irresistible: sidestepping David
Levy, whom he despised, and Sharon, whom he loathed.

A *High Noon*–type showdown with Sharon, full of political drama
and personal venom, shaped up for February 12, 1990, the next
scheduled session of the mammoth Likud central committee. Sharon,
as chairman of the central committee, sent out three thousand invitations at the beginning of February, embossed with the logo of the
Ministry of Industry and Trade. Shamir's people, unhappy with the
wording and suspicious that Sharon was planning some sort of procedural ambush, printed up their own invitations in the name of the
prime minister and party leader and sent them out the next day. They
also busily planted stories in the media to the effect that Sharon's dismissal was both inevitable and imminent. The prime minister himself
told party stalwarts that things had to come to a head. "The central
committee must decide to endorse my speech or to reject it, and to vote
confidence in me for the past and for the future."

Shamir would demand a yes-or-no vote on his policy and on his
prime ministership. If he lost, he would step down, and that would
very likely trigger new elections. He was confident that the central
committee members, confronted by that sobering scenario, would
give him their backing. At least half of them had jobs in government
or local authorities, held directorships in state-owned companies, or
held lucrative or prestigious (or both) positions on public commissions.
These would all be in danger if the government fell.

Sharon demanded a vote specifically on the "constraints." He
wanted the central committee to choose between Shamir's policy and
his own. If Shamir lost, as he was likely to do under that procedure,
and brought the government down, then so be it. The Likud could
set up a narrow-based government with the far-right parties and the
Orthodox, as it should have done, in Sharon's view, straight after the
election sixteen months before.

On the day itself, Sharon was back in his element: a general at war.

He ordered his loyalists to arrive hours ahead of time and pack the front rows. Sharon, true to his military tactics from the earliest days of Unit 101, had prepared, in addition to his battle ranks, a feint designed to throw the enemy off balance. He opened the proceedings as chairman, urging members to maintain dignity and decorum and thus bring honor to their movement, in Israel and throughout the world. He would say a few words, then Shamir would make the keynote speech, then a policy debate would take place in which twenty-five members would take part, representing the positions of both sides. Then there would be a vote.

Members were digesting this, looking for a catch, when they thought they heard Sharon go on to say he had sent a letter of resignation to Shamir. "What's that he said?" Modai asked the man next to him. Even "the constrainers" were taken totally unawares. Sharon read on. The hall broke into bedlam and then slowly subsided into total silence.

> Mr. Prime Minister, I hereby tender my resignation. I have decided to resign from the government so that I can continue the struggle for the national goals that are in danger under the policy of the present government. I will continue as a Knesset member and as chairman of the party central committee.
>
> Under your government Palestinian terror is raging throughout Israel . . . Jewish lives have become cheap. I can no longer be party to this . . . Your diplomatic proposal has put Israel on the road to the creation of a Palestinian state . . . I do not leave with a light heart. But there are moments when a man must stand up and start to shout. There are moments when one must awaken and fight with all one's strength before disaster strikes. This is perhaps the last moment to do so. May you all be blessed.

Shamir, next up, said he was as surprised as everyone else. But he deflated Sharon's attempted coup by saying that he had not received Sharon's resignation letter and would react only once he had studied it. He then resumed his prepared speech, a forty-five-minute review of his diplomatic efforts thus far and of his government's domestic policies:

> I am conducting a difficult struggle against many different parties abroad in defense of our principles and our positions. I have to sustain huge amounts of animosity and vituperation from many quarters. That does not weaken my resolve to stand and fight for the things I wholeheartedly believe in. But I am sick and tired of this impossible situation in which I am viciously attacked from without and at the

same time attacked by comrades from within who treat me to a daily barrage of insults.

I think I have the right therefore, morally and politically, to ask for your endorsement. People at home and abroad are entitled to know if I speak for our movement or not. The public in Israel needs to know who represents the Likud: I or my traducers.

He then read out the text of the resolution that he was submitting: "The central committee endorses the content of the prime minister's policy statement. The central committee expresses its confidence in the prime minister and chairman of the party." And he then did precisely what Sharon suspected he would do: he asked for a show of hands.[9]

A sea of hands went up. But Sharon, his alacrity belying his girth, was on his feet and at *his* microphone at the other end of the platform, reading out *his* resolution and asking for the members' support. "Who is in favor?" he demanded, in his high but booming voice. "Who is in favor of eliminating terror? Raise your hands. Who is opposed to letting deportees participate?* Raise your hands. Who is in favor of eliminating terror? Who is in favor of eliminating terror?" Over and over. *Mi be'ad chissul haterror?* The question instantly entered Hebrew usage, and has firmly remained there ever since, as an expression of the quintessence of disingenuousness.

"I have won by massive majority. His statement has no significance," Shamir shouted into his microphone, which by now had mysteriously lost its resonance. The thousands of hands were still up, but for what resolution? The serried ranks in the front kept up a chorus of "Arik, Arik." Shamir delivered a final, hoarse shout into his microphone: "I thank the members of the central committee for the confidence that you have placed in me. In view of the disorder in the hall, I hereby close this session of the central committee. Any resolutions passed hereafter will have no validity." Upon which he and his entourage swept out of the hall, followed by all the ministers loyal to him. Sharon, unperturbed, droned on, reading the "constraints" one by one

---

* A "deportee" meant a Palestinian political activist, usually a prominent loyalist of the PLO, who had been deported from the country in the past and subsequently allowed back. Minister of Defense Rabin proposed, and Secretary of State Baker accepted, that to admit such a person into the peace negotiations as a member of the Jordanian-Palestinian delegation could be a way of accommodating the Palestinians' demand that their diaspora be represented. Rabin similarly proposed that the dispute over East Jerusalem Palestinians be finessed by admitting a "dual addressee"—a Palestinian who lived in the territories but maintained a second residence in East Jerusalem. The "constrainers" opposed both of these devices.

and asking for a show of endorsement for each of them. At the end he announced that all of them had duly been endorsed.

"So, Arik Sharon, an own goal?" asked the well-known television interviewer Dan Shilon, kicking off a conversation with the ex-minister for the weekend issue of *Yedioth Ahronoth*. As though to rub it in, he added: "Since your resignation I haven't met a single person who believes in the sincerity of your professed motives." Sharon's reply was classic: "That is one of the sad things that has happened in our public life. People find it difficult to believe that someone can get up and leave his cabinet seat over a matter of principle." As for "the night of the microphones," Shamir had tried "to steal the vote," Sharon said, leaving him no alternative but to intervene. Shamir was "a dangerous man." Shamir's concessions were feeding terrorism and increasing the danger of war. "I am not prepared to return to a government headed by Yitzhak Shamir."

Four months later, he returned, as minister of housing in a new government headed by Yitzhak Shamir. The new government was the narrow-based, rightist-religious coalition that Sharon had long demanded. Baker had decided to force the issue—and was delivered a resounding rebuff. The secretary tried to fuse Shamir's original proposal together with a proposal from Egypt's president, Mubarak, and with American ideas into one simple and direct question: "As regards the participation in the Israeli-Palestinian dialogue, would the government of Israel be ready to consider on a name-by-name basis any Palestinian who was a resident of the territories?" To say yes would implicitly admit deportees and dual addressees. Shamir said no. Shimon Peres, believing he could form a Labor-led narrow government with the help of the ultra-Orthodox parties, engineered the collapse of the unity government in a Knesset vote on March 15, 1990.

"I felt battered, beaten, and betrayed," Baker writes. "From the outset, I'd tried to give Shamir the benefit of the doubt . . . In the end, Shamir wasn't even willing to embrace his own plan."

But if Baker felt battered, Sharon felt buoyed, and justly so. He did not claim to have foreseen, when he resigned his cabinet seat, for just how short a time he'd be enjoying the bucolic life again. The government, after all, had two and a half years still to run. But he did now claim retrospective victory for the "constraints": Shamir had defied the Americans over precisely the terms that Sharon and his allies had demanded that Israel reject. Shamir had "stopped at the edge of the precipice," Sharon asserted triumphantly. "The drama surrounding my resignation perhaps catalyzed that welcome development."[10] More likely it did not, and Shamir would have refused Baker without any histrionics from Sharon. His and Arens's endless foot-dragging was only good so long as they had room to maneuver. Once Baker decided to corner them, they reverted to the rigid rejectionism that was the true underpinning of their policy.

At any event, Sharon now urged all his party colleagues to set aside the frictions of the past, however raw and recent, and unite to defeat Peres's attempt to form a government that would throw any constraints to the wind and rush headlong into a chimerical peace with the PLO. A Peres government would be dependent, worse yet, on the votes of the Arab parties, which, Sharon insisted, were simply PLO surrogates in the Israeli parliament. Shamir was their leader, Sharon assured his colleagues. No one was challenging that. They must all work to ensure that he had "a decisive, national government" to lead.

Shamir was of the same mollifying mind. He pointedly invited Sharon to attend the Likud ministerial caucuses and encouraged him to pick up his contacts with the *haredi* rabbis and their political lieutenants. Sharon needed no encouragement. "We must restore the rightist-religious alliance between us and the Orthodox," he said.

Shimon Peres pinned his hopes for forming a Labor-led government on the three ultra-Orthodox, or *haredi,* parties, Agudat Israel (five seats), Degel Hatorah (two), and Shas (six). Doctrinally cool to the whole concept of secular Zionism, most *haredi* rabbis preferred the relative moderation of Labor to the more assertive nationalism of Likud. This was particularly true of the "Lithuanian," or anti-Hasidic, rabbis who ran Degel Hatorah and also held considerable sway over Shas. It was an unexpected and devastating blow to Peres, therefore, when, on the night of March 26, Rabbi Eleazar Schach, the ninety-two-year-old doyen of the anti-Hasidic rabbis, told a Tel Aviv sports stadium packed with his supporters that Labor were "rabbit-eaters who have severed themselves from the Jewish people . . . There are kibbutzim that don't know what Yom Kippur is. And they raise rabbits and pigs there," he added, referring to animals whose consumption is forbidden under Jewish dietary laws. "And this is called the Jewish people?"[11]

Peres refused to be deterred. He believed he had the five men of Agudat Israel firmly in his camp. He was confident that once he had a government up and running, Rabbi Schach would see the upside, and Degel Hatorah and Shas would join, too. He informed the Knesset that he would present his government for swearing in on April 15.

But only after Peres and his ministers arrived at the Knesset, all decked out in their Saturday best and with their families in tow, did they discover that two of the Agudat men, vital for their majority, would not be attending. Sharon had gotten to them. One of the two, Eliezer Mizrachi, was in hiding, protected by bodyguards hired by Sharon. The other, Avraham Werdiger, phoned Peres ahead of time to say he could not vote for a dovish government.

The crestfallen Peres could only apply sheepishly to the president for an extension of his coalition-making mandate. But that, too, proved fruitless, and in the end it was Shamir who presented a new government to the Knesset, on June 11, 1990. It was the farthest right, most religious coalition Israel had ever had, an amalgam of the Likud, the National Religious Party, the three *haredi* parties, and three ultranationalist parties. None was omitted. Even Moledet, which advocated the "transfer" of the Palestinians out of Palestine, was in; its leader, Rehavam Ze'evi, became a minister.

Peres's effort went down in Israeli history as "the stinking ploy," a phrase coined by his inveterate rival, Yitzhak Rabin, who soon displaced him at the head of Labor. It involved not only wooing the *haredim* but also trying to winkle away individual Likud members with promises of perks and preferment for them and their supporters. The Likud fought back, Sharon in the forefront, with blandishments of its own to the same for-sale backbenchers.

BOGEYMAN

"The telephone number is 1–202–456–1414. When you're serious about peace, call us." James Baker, testifying in Congress two days after the new Israeli government won Knesset approval, minced no words. Bush backed his secretary of state with a polite but firm letter to the new-old prime minister, Yitzhak Shamir. "What I need to know from you," he wrote, "is whether you are prepared to go forward without new preconditions on the basis of acknowledging—privately at first, if need be—that you will meet with a delegation of Palestinians from the territories that include a few individuals who fit the deportee and dual-addressee categories." Shamir, through diplomatic channels, replied that he wasn't. American peacemaking efforts seemed effectively over, pending, as Baker writes in his memoirs, "a new Israeli Prime Minister and another Secretary of State."[12]

But the real trouble between the two governments was only just beginning. There had been a hint of it earlier in the year when Shamir told the Knesset that the anticipated immigration of hundreds of thousands of Jews from the imploding Soviet Union would require "a big Israel." The Soviet mass aliya, plus the new Israeli government's no-holds-barred settlement policy in the Palestinian territories, plus its request from the United States for guarantees for the huge loans it needed to absorb the new immigrants—all these together made for a combustible mix. The invasion of an Arab state by half a million American soldiers and assorted European and Arab armies, plus Israel getting rocketed by Iraq but still staying out of the war at Bush's insistent request, plus a truculent Ariel Sharon building those settlements as fast as he could, thumping on the drums of war, provoking and insulting all and sundry—all these dramatically enhanced the volatility. It is a tribute to Bush and Baker that out of this dangerous brew they nevertheless did eventually orchestrate a lurch forward toward peace at the Madrid Middle East Peace Conference in October 1991.

With Labor now out of the government, the Americans feared a splurge of land confiscation and settlement building. Worse yet, in terms of Arab world sensibilities, they feared Israel would channel its abundant new infusion of Jewish immigrants into the Palestinian territories. But they had—or they hoped they had—a means of leverage: Israel had asked for $400 million in loan guarantees. The request would subsequently grow to $10 billion. Bush and Baker took the position that they would not fund, even obliquely, the expansion of Jewish settlement on Palestinian land. Shamir and his government, girding themselves with righteous outrage, insisted that the "humanitarian" issue of immigrant absorption never be linked to—much less conditioned on—the "political" question of the territories.

Sensing the strength of feeling on the American side, and aware of the serious financial need on their own side, the Israelis tried at first to fog and fudge. Minister of Housing Sharon declared in June 1990 that there would be no deliberate encouragement of the immigrants to make their homes in the settlements. The State Department said this statement was encouraging and "a step in the right direction." But the spokesperson Margaret Tutwiler noted that Sharon's statement had been reported in several different versions, and Washington awaited clarity.

But clarity was one commodity that would be hard to come by in everything to do with settlement building and settlement policy during the next two years. In July 1991, the newspaper *Davar* disclosed that would-be settlers could obtain parcels of land free from the government to build their homes on. In addition, easy mortgages were made available in the settlements, and infrastructure—water, sewerage, and electricity—was laid for free.

There was a pall of unclarity, moreover, surrounding the number of homes that were being built in the settlements. They were, after all, a small part of a vast, countrywide building program presided over by Sharon and designed to provide every newcomer from the former Soviet Union with a roof over his head. American diplomats on the ground, and, Israel assumed, satellites in the sky, kept trying to tally the houses and trailers in the settlements as they went up. Leftist Knesset members, aided by Peace Now, published their own count—for which they were excoriated by Sharon as snitches and traitors. In fact, construction in the settlements quadrupled during 1991. In the first nine months of that year, according to official Israeli figures collated much later, 6,435 new houses (most single-family, some multiple-family) were begun in the settlements, compared with 1,820 during all of 1990 and 1,410 in 1989. In October 1990, Baker announced that he was postponing a visit to Israel by U.S. officials tasked with wrapping up details of the loan guarantee.

D esert Storm provided something of a hiatus in the gathering tempest with Israel over the settlements and the loan guarantees. The war against Iraq generated tensions of its own in the U.S.-Israel relationship, but the sides were aligned differently. The president and the secretary of state persuaded Shamir that his country's deepest interest lay in staying out of the conflict and not responding militarily to the Scud missiles that began falling on Tel Aviv once the American attack on Iraq began. The Americans feared that any Israeli involvement would disrupt their coalition of Western and Arab armies. "There is nothing your air force can do that we are not doing," Baker assured Shamir. "If there is, tell us and we'll do it."[13]

Arrayed against Shamir's policy of restraint were Sharon, Modai, and other hard-line ministers who demanded that the IDF act, and also Minister of Defense Arens, who was eager to order Israeli air and ground attacks, but only in coordination with the U.S.-led allied forces.

In all, thirty-nine Scuds hit Tel Aviv, Haifa, and other Israeli cities during Desert Storm. They wrought considerable damage to property but directly caused only one death (several deaths during this period were attributed to missile-induced heart attacks and to asphyxiation from wrong use of gas masks) and left some three hundred injured (from assorted causes, some related only indirectly to the rockets),[14] also a relatively low figure. This was, however, the first time in Israel's history that the Jewish state was attacked and failed to respond. As such, it produced a major national trauma, over and above the huge dislocation of civilian life as large numbers of Tel Avivans and Haifaites sought refuge each night in less targeted areas of the country.

Arens kept up a solid front of loyalty with the prime minister throughout the nearly two months of conflict. The Americans knew that Arens's incessant pressure for an air corridor to western Iraq, and for the allied air forces to "deconflict" while the IDF engaged, could always be deflected by a direct appeal to Shamir for yet more forbearance and gritting of teeth. Arens let none of his reservations leak out to the depressed Israeli public, many of whom never stopped worrying till the very end that Saddam Hussein might tip a Scud with a chemical warhead.

Sharon had no such inhibitions. Within days of the outbreak of the war, the whole country knew that Sharon was urging IDF action to silence the Scud launchers and to punish Iraq and that the elderly, overcautious Shamir didn't have the stomach for it. Sharon had no compunction over disloyally tongue-lashing the government's passivity as he posed for the cameras clambering around the ruins of homes hit by the Scuds.

At cabinet, Sharon advised that the air force be instructed to send aircraft over western Iraq on photography missions without obtaining prior American consent. "Notify them and fly!" was Sharon's prescription. Five days later, he broadened it: Israel should land commando units in western Iraq to search and destroy the Scud launchers, simply informing the Americans "that we are carrying out an operation there, and that for the following three days the area is under Israeli responsibility." But Shamir did not waver, and the majority of the ministers sided with him. That remained the policy—despite Arens's persistent efforts to change it—until the end of the war.[15]

King Hussein of Jordan seriously damaged his relations with Washington by publicly sympathizing with the Iraqi dictator before and during the war. For Sharon, contemplating the Middle East peace conference that Secretary Baker quickly began organizing on the back of America's victory, Hussein's bad bet was added reason why Israel should use the occasion to explain to the world that Jordan is Palestine.

During a six-week period of intensive shuttle diplomacy in the region in April and May 1991, laying the groundwork for the conference, it seemed to Baker that Sharon announced a new settlement in the territories every time his plane touched down in Tel Aviv. "I am not happy with these statements [of Sharon's]," Baker recalls Shamir assuring him. " 'I'm not asking you to adopt our position,' I countered.

'But I *am* asking you to keep this man from throwing land mines in the way of peace.' 'I don't want to involve you in our internal politics,' Shamir demurred . . . 'I will deal with it.' By now, of course, I felt that he wouldn't—and he never did."

That testimony is important because, as with the Likud government's original settlement drive after 1977 and as with the Lebanon War in 1982, it sets in proper perspective the relative roles of the prime ministers of the day—then Begin, now Shamir—and the minister charged with executing their policy: Sharon. There was no question in Baker's mind that Shamir was Israel's ultimate policy maker, on settlements as on everything else, regardless of his mealymouthed excuses, which the secretary had long stopped buying. Shamir was very different from Sharon. He was amicable, conciliatory, and soft-spoken.* But at the end of the day Shamir chose to acquiesce in Sharon's settlement provocations because the two of them were of one mind in regard to the settlement issue and in their determined resistance to Bush and Baker's efforts to impose a settlement freeze using the loan guarantees as both the stick and the carrot.

Baker flew indefatigably from capital to capital wooing regional leaders to attend a peace conference (both the word "peace" and the word "conference" were the subjects of prolonged and bitter argument among the invitees) that would launch two tiers of negotiation: bilateral talks between Israel and each of its neighbors, and multilateral talks on key issues affecting the entire region. Baker termed his exhaustingly long sessions with President Hafez Assad in Damascus "bladder diplomacy." Shamir was hardly less obstreperous, but in the end even he realized that he could drag his feet no longer without jeopardizing the foundations of American support for Israel. He carried his decision by a comfortable vote of 16 to 3 in the cabinet. Sharon was the only Likud minister to oppose it.

The conference took place at the end of October 1991 in Madrid. It was a triumph for American diplomacy and a moment of new hope for the Middle East. After all the delays and nitpicking—the protagonists were wrangling over the shape of the table till the morning the conference opened—the bald and remarkable fact was that Israelis and Arabs sat together, in front of the whole world, and pledged to embark on peace talks. Presidents Bush and Gorbachev opened the

---

* When Baker was informed during one of their meetings that his mother had died, Shamir flowed over with sympathy. At their next meeting, he gave the secretary a certificate attesting that trees had been planted in her name in the Jerusalem hills. Baker wept.

proceedings with appropriately momentous speeches, and even though the spell was broken by some crude rhetoric from the Syrian foreign minister, everyone present felt that a window of promise had opened up. Shamir, wary of too exuberant momentum, resorted to Menachem Begin's tactics after Camp David: to slow things down, he put trusted hard-line aides at the head of Israel's negotiating teams in the talks with the Syrians and with the Jordanian-Palestinians that now began. Suffice it to say that ten weeks later, the Jordanian/Palestinian-Israeli negotiators were still sitting in the corridor *outside* the negotiating room in Washington, arguing about whether the Jordanians and the Palestinians were one delegation or two.

In Israel, Baker's pre-conference shuttles had been darkened by the resurgent dispute over the loan guarantees. In April, coinciding with a Baker visit, a new settlement, Revava, was founded on the West Bank, and Sharon's Housing Ministry announced plans to build twenty-four thousand homes for settlers in the territories over the next four years. In May, Sharon visited Washington. Baker refused to see him. "I intervened with the President to block a meeting between Sharon and Secretary of Housing and Urban Development Jack Kemp at Kemp's office. The meeting . . . was held at the Israeli embassy . . . Like his settlements policy, Ariel Sharon was an obstacle to peace."

The dispute grew more personal with the passing months. Bush was increasingly portrayed on the Israeli right as unsympathetic and his secretary of state as downright hostile. Shamir was seen by Bush as devious and by Baker as straight and honorable but implacably extreme. Sharon was the chief focus of the Americans' ire. Bush was said to be distressed at the thought that if the United States withheld the loan guarantees and Shamir was damaged politically, Sharon would benefit, whereas if the United States relented on the loans and the settlement building still continued, Sharon would benefit from that, too.

The antipathy that Sharon had generated in U.S. government circles during the Lebanon War, and his infamy in the American media, had been marginally mitigated by the verdict in the *Time* trial. But he had kept up his transatlantic sniping throughout the decade, bolstering his chosen political image at home as an unbending nationalist who would not countenance seeing Israel be pushed around by its superpower patron. Thus, for instance, in the highly embarrassing and potentially disastrous "Pollard affair" involving an Israeli spy in the heart of U.S. intelligence, Sharon lashed out at Peres, Shamir, and Rabin for cooperating too readily with Washington—and made sure his strictures became public knowledge. Sharon made much play of having been kept out of the loop while Jonathan Jay Pollard, an intelligence analyst for the U.S. Navy, was transmitting reams of raw intelligence to Tel Aviv. He was similarly kept in the dark while Israel scrambled to contain the damage after Pollard's arrest, in November 1985, outside the Israeli embassy in Washington.

Sharon was not in fact completely in the clear, because Pollard was recruited by the Bureau for Scientific Liaison ("Lekem" by its Hebrew acronym), a shadowy organization over which Sharon, as defense minister, had installed an old friend and sleuth, Rafi Eitan, as director. But he berated the top troika with gusto and vilified the United States for its vindictiveness toward an ally. He warned at cabinet that Israel's decision to send back the voluminous product of Pollard's espionage was tantamount to ensuring a life sentence for the young Jewish spy. In the event, that is what Pollard received.*

Inevitably, the U.S.-Israel spat over the loan guarantees became entangled in Washington's pre–Madrid conference discussions with Arabs, too. The Americans feared that to award the guarantees might deter Arab states from attending, while to refuse them might deter Israel. The administration asked Israel to defer its request until after the conference. This triggered a huge confrontation with Israel's supporters in Washington, marshaled by the lobbying organization AIPAC. Memorably, at the height of the battle, Bush referred to himself as "one lonely guy" fighting "powerful political forces."

In the event, the administration won a 120-day postponement, until after the Madrid conference. When it ended, Baker suggested a compromise, originally proposed by Senator Patrick Leahy of Vermont, whereby the guarantees would be conditioned on a ban on any new

---

* In 1987, in advance of a report into the affair by an Israeli board of inquiry, Sharon demanded at cabinet that Peres resign, triggering an almighty slanging match between the two of them. Sharon asserted that Peres was to blame for Pollard getting a life sentence. Peres hit back with the hundreds of Israeli soldiers who had gotten a death sentence in the Lebanon War. Sharon, inevitably, retorted that in the Yom Kippur War thousands had died because of the Labor government's ineptitude. Peres was a minister in that government.

PERES: You're to blame for Pollard.
SHARON: When Pollard was recruited, I'd been back at the ranch for a year and a half. I sat at home as a result of the demonstrations that *you* instigated against me in order to help the PLO.
PERES: You're not the pope! You're a lousy tenth-rate politician.
SHARON: I can't compete with you in offensiveness.

settlement construction and reduced by the amount spent by Israel to finish construction of settlement homes already begun. This immediately ran up against the problem of an Israeli smoke screen. How many homes were under construction in the settlements? Baker maintained that according to his information there were 6,000. Some Israeli officials said 13,000. Sharon claimed there were 22,000. But it made no difference, because Shamir rejected the proposed settlement freeze out of hand. No compromise was possible, and Israelis went to the polls on June 23, 1992, in the knowledge that their Likud-led government had been denied the vitally needed loan guarantees because of its settlement policy.

They responded by kicking the Likud and its allies out of office, after fifteen years in power. Shamir miscalculated the Russian immigrants' reaction to his steadfastness, and that was part of his undoing. The newcomers pouring into the country from the disintegrating U.S.S.R. were indeed hard-line on the whole: they wanted Israel big and strong and had little sympathy for the Palestinians, long backed by the Soviet regime. But essentially they were pragmatists. The messianic sentiments of the Emunim settlers were alien to them. They looked askance at the worsening relationship with the United States, especially as it threatened the funding for *their* housing and absorption. In significant numbers, they voted for Yitzhak Rabin's Labor. Bush and Baker finally recommended to Congress to award Israel, under Labor rule, the $10 billion in loan guarantees.

HOUSING BOOM

For Sharon, the vicarious battle against Bush and Baker was just one bruising fight among the many that filled his two frenetic years as housing minister. Challenged with a sudden, hugely welcome, but also hugely daunting influx of Soviet immigrants, Sharon fought against building regulations, he fought against planning laws and zoning commissions, he fought accusations of cronyism and political preferment, he rode roughshod over budgetary restraints and fought the minister of finance and his mandarins who held the purse strings—and in the end he fought a bitter, ugly brawl with the state comptroller, Miriam Ben-Porat, a stern ex-judge charged with supervising proper governance and administration.

By now Sharon had become something of a fixture in the annual state comptroller's reports, just as he was a regular target of newspaper investigations, of parliamentary questions, and of criminal complaints to the attorney general and to the police. Stories of pork-barrel politics blurred and fused with allegations of personal malfeasance.*

In countless allegations against him over the years, his line of defense was that contrary to the suspicions about him he had acted solely in the public or the national interest. He or his aides would usually bolster this defense by asserting that those impugning his motives or besmirching his actions were themselves politically motivated.

Time after time, Sharon emerged from his legal scrapes unscathed, having been granted the benefit of the doubt. Public reaction ranged from admiration to disgust. Many Israelis came to associate Sharon with corruption. A leading academic jurist, looking back, said he loathed Sharon for single-handedly undermining the ethics of Israel's public life. In his youth, this professor admitted, Sharon was his idol. Others, perhaps less starry-eyed about Sharon earlier, and certainly less starry-eyed about Israeli public life, tended to conclude that Sharon did what other politicians did—only more so.

Sharon evoked this full range of reactions in his constant tussles over political appointments as minister of industry and trade. With his disarming forthrightness, he said it was in the public interest to see Herut people appointed to top jobs in government companies, because they had been discriminated against in the past. Apart from directorships and top jobs, a solicitous political patron like Sharon, installed in a powerful ministry, could also help clients, supporters, and other favorites with more oblique forms of preferment. Thus, for instance, in late 1985 two newcomers suddenly surfaced among the select coterie

---

* An exchange between Sharon and Ben-Porat's predecessor, Ya'acov Maltz, in 1987 in many ways typifies this side of Sharon's public life. The issue was possible conflict of interest. His friend and benefactor Meshulam Riklis, who had lent him $200,000 back in 1973 to help buy Sycamore Ranch, was now involved, with his partner and Sharon's close friend Arie Genger, in the purchase of Haifa Chemicals, a partially state-owned company that the government had decided to privatize. State Comptroller Maltz wrote to the minister of industry and trade asking if it was true that he had been personally active in the government's handling of the sale, and specifically in the purchasers' application for a $10 million soft loan from the government. Sharon replied: "Mr. Riklis, an old friend, did indeed make me a personal loan 14 years ago, which I finished paying off in October 1985. That said, I did indeed see great public interest in extending as much help as I could, within my ministerial authority, to a group of overseas investors which has invested more than $50 million in an Israeli company. I faithfully assure you that I was guided solely by these legitimate considerations." In that case, the comptroller wrote back, "you should have declared your private interest . . . and transferred all further conduct of this matter to a ministerial committee."

of iron importers, and both, according to newspaper reports, were devoted Herut Party activists. "These particular licensees don't seem to have any knowledge of the iron business at all," an opposition Knesset member observed. "The only thing they know how to do is to sell their iron licenses to someone else. The licenses are worth $150,000."

Sharon asserted, "These licensees are not close to me personally, and quite frankly I don't even know if they're close to me politically . . . I don't even know these people."[16]

Some of the allegations cut closer to the bone. Sycamore Ranch was one of the country's largest producers of mutton and lamb. Muslims particularly like to eat mutton or lamb for the *iftar,* the meal eaten at sunset after a day of fasting during the holy month of Ramadan, and during the three-day feast of Eid al-Fitr at the end of Ramadan. The price of mutton and lamb regularly rose by some 25 percent during this period. To keep it from rising even more, governments in the past had always permitted the import of up to a thousand tons of frozen lamb ahead of Ramadan. In September 1986, *Haaretz* noted that Sharon had forbidden such import ever since he became minister of industry and trade, and this despite repeated appeals from importers. The director general of the ministry, Yehoshua Forer, was quoted as saying, "There's nothing to talk about. The minister won't allow any lamb import."

In January 1987, Forer's successor, Yoram Belizovsky, was quoted as admitting privately that Sharon had vetoed an interministerial committee's proposal to permit the import of six hundred tons of lamb. Unnamed mandarins in the Treasury volunteered that the decision would profit Sycamore Ranch to the tune of $60,000 for each Ramadan season. Sharon had already been in office for three Ramadans. The Meretz Knesset member Ran Cohen went to State Comptroller Maltz and to the police.

The police were reluctant to open a criminal inquiry against Sharon. Cohen petitioned the high court. Not good enough, said the justices. "There's got to be meat on it." This attempt at humor signaled to Sharon that once again he was off the hook. He redoubled his attacks on the "petty political foes" who had latched onto his beloved sheep and lambs in order to impugn him.[17]*

The sheep were back under public scrutiny three years later. This

---

* He would sometimes pose for photographers nuzzling a sheep or cradling a lamb in his arms. While his love for them did not extend to forgoing their eventual slaughter, he never offered guests roasts prepared from his own flock. "We don't eat friends," he observed in a television interview in February 2005.

time the issue was milk. The Milk Council, which carefully controlled production across the country, allotted a generous 33,000-liter quota of sheep's milk to Sycamore Ranch for 1990. Other, more veteran sheep farmers wanted to know why, especially since they had had their own annual quotas cut back by the council because of a surfeit of sheep's milk and sheep's cheese flooding the Israeli market at the time.

The Milk Council, it turned out, had been pressured by the director general of the Ministry of Agriculture, Yehezkel Zakai, who just happened to have been given a guided tour of Sycamore Ranch by the owner shortly before the decision was made. Zakai explained that Sycamore's sheep dairy was so well run that the ministry wanted to hold it up as a model for the industry.

All these dubious episodes were small potatoes compared with the vast budgets that Sharon was accused of squandering and the huge contracts that he was suspected of channeling to political supporters when the gates of the Soviet Union suddenly burst open and hundreds of thousands of Jews flooded into Israel, needing to be housed. He was accused of casting to the winds every principle of basic good administration, with the resulting wastage of taxpayer millions. Stories of mismanagement on a massive scale blended with tales of misfeasance by the minister and his acolytes as hundreds of new housing projects went up around the country. None of the accusations and suspicions against Sharon himself gelled into a criminal investigation, much less an indictment. He brushed them all off as vicious and petty, leveled by small-minded people with chips on their shoulders, people incapable of rising to the historic occasion of the miraculous, unanticipated Soviet aliya.

He had a point: the dramatic reemergence of the huge Soviet Jewish Diaspora, after decades of isolation behind the Iron Curtain, was an event of sufficient import for Israel that even hallowed zoning laws and building regulations might be bent a little in the rush to house them. And he was probably right, retrospectively, in that he couldn't have known in 1990–1991 that the huge wave of immigration would actually peak in 1991 and fall sharply the following year.* No one knew at that time how many Jews there actually were in Russia and its satellite states, let alone how many of them wanted to leave, or how

---

* Some 184,000 Soviet Jews landed in Israel in 1990 and 147,000 in 1991. In 1992 the figure dropped to 65,000. It remained at about this level for the rest of the decade (Government of Israel, Central Bureau of Statistics).

many of those wanted to come to Israel, or indeed how many of those who did come would want to stay.*

He had only himself to blame, though, for the almost instinctive suspicion among many Israelis that he was exploiting these lofty goals for his own base purposes. His incessant brushes with the law enforcement agencies over the years now fed a widespread presumption that if Arik was embarked on a splurge of construction, a lot of hangers-on would be making a lot of money on the side, and he himself would be amassing, if not money (though some whispered that he was), then naked political power. His political enemies were aghast at the thought that the thousands of new arrivals might come to regard him as their savior and their champion.

Sharon's task on assuming his new post in the new government, in June 1990, was compounded by a rash of tent cities that sprang up around the country at this time, populated by homeless young families. Many of the tent dwellers were unemployed, but even those in jobs found it hard to get a mortgage and harder still to keep up the interest payments on it. Almost all were Sephardic, whereas almost all the Soviet Jews now beginning to pour in were Ashkenazic[†]—a fertile furrow for ethnic tension to grow. Sharon, in a series of sweeping statements, undertook that everyone would have a roof over his or her head before the winter. He set his ministry officials to renting two- and three-star hotels and youth hostels in kibbutzim. These were to provide temporary accommodation pending the arrival of thirty thousand trailers and prefabricated homes that he proceeded to order from producers around the world. At the same time, tens of thousands of new apartments would begin to be built by private contractors, to government specifications, at government-selected sites around the country.

The Treasury mandarins insisted that imported trailers and prefabs would cost too much foreign currency. And the prefabs would wilt under strong Israeli sun and rain and turn into instant slums. At a stormy cabinet meeting in August they got the order reduced by one-third. But the fight went on. The Treasury warned importers that it would not pay for the foreign homes if the Housing Ministry did not ensure they met official Israeli building standards. The same would apply to domestic construction companies, Minister of Finance Modai ruled.

---

* An internal government assessment in 1990 anticipated 200,000 Soviet immigrants a year for the next five years (State Comptroller's Report No. 42, 242).
[†] The exceptions were Jews from the central Asian republics, many of whom belonged to ancient oriental Jewish communities.

By this time, would-be importers and would-be constructors were flocking to the trough, sensing the rich profits to be made from the imminent splurge of government contracts. Some were neither importers nor contractors; they were small-time artisans—plumbers, plasterers, electricians—looking to get into the big time. In place of knowledge or experience, they deployed their membership in the Likud central committee, or their links to friends or relations who were members, to further their candidacies for the ministry tenders now pouring out. Quick-witted political aides became builders overnight, or, if not builders, then at least middlemen, arranging deals between builders and the ministry.[18] Many of the large and established construction companies elbowed their way forward, too, determined to take their rightful place in Israel's biggest-ever building bonanza.

"The Treasury is not letting me work," Sharon complained in an interview in September 1990. The officials there were willfully undermining his efforts, he said. They were phoning the builders and the importers and warning them that they wouldn't get a penny. All he was trying to do was to shorten processes, cut through red tape, side-step bureaucracy. But the petty bureaucrats were fighting him.

Sharon scored a significant victory in November, when the cabinet approved "closed tenders" for the construction projects. This put unprecedented power in the hands of the Ministry of Housing. It could henceforth limit tenders to selected companies or, in some cases, forgo tenders altogether and decide on one particular company for a specific project.

It was a bonanza without risk. Sharon undertook on the government's behalf that every apartment built in "the periphery"—that is, the north and south of the country—which the contractor failed to sell would be bought back by the government at its full market value. Here, too, he ran into vehement opposition from the Treasury, which warned, rightly, as it turned out, that he would saddle the state with a huge inventory of unsold homes. The key to the intelligent selection of sites for immigrant housing was jobs, the civil servants argued. Sharon was building in the wrong places. There was no point building in the periphery if employment prospects for the Soviet newcomers were all concentrated in the center, around the Tel Aviv megalopolis. The immigrants could hardly be forced to live in the boondocks, and as a result the homes built there would remain empty.

But Sharon refused to see this issue from a purely economic perspective. Israel would hopefully increase its population by 20 percent over the next few years, he pointed out. It was important to use this opportunity to build up the outlying areas of the country. He charged around the country in his ministerial Volvo sedan, from building site to building site, welcomed at each site by foremen in hard hats and architects with maps and technical drawings. They spread them out on the hood of the car, or on wooden trestle tables, like in the army. Sharon and his aides pored over them. The ministry's PR photographers clicked and whirred. Ben-Gurion had dreamed of the Negev as the great industrial and technological powerhouse; this was the chance to make that dream happen. The Galilee had become an area where Arab citizens outnumbered Jews; now was the time to redress that balance. Sharon had long argued for a string of new towns and villages to be built along the length of the pre-1967 border, where a major new highway was planned; the Soviet newcomers could be encouraged to live in these new places.

A close aide, looking back, said Sharon was consumed at this time with the consciousness that, once again, destiny had sought him out and placed in his hands the future of the country. "He kept repeating that this was a unique opportunity not only to change the demography of the country but to change its geography. And he did what he said. Beersheba in the south literally doubled its population as a result of his policy. Towns in the north like Carmiel, Safed, Upper Nazareth, grew beyond recognition in those two years."[19]

By November 1991, Treasury officials were threatening to prosecute Housing Ministry officials for signing contracts that had not been approved by the Treasury budgets department, and Sharon was sounding the way he did in the Lebanon War. "All the projects were submitted to the cabinet for approval," he insisted. "Every one of them was marked on a map, and the map was appended to the cabinet's decision." The Treasury was a place of "insensitivity, evil, and jealousy." Moreover, there was no glut of unlived-in homes. Quite the contrary.

Nevertheless, by the year's end even Sharon could not completely ignore the shrinking projections for immigration, and he reluctantly agreed to a reduction of the home-building target in the 1992 state budget from forty thousand to fifteen thousand. Burdened but unbowed by a whopping budget deficit, Sharon and his ministry braced for a special report from the state comptroller on their efforts to house the immigrants.

It was published in April 1992, just weeks before the election. "The ministry did not seriously examine the financial creditworthiness of the companies it was considering for construction contracts," the comptroller wrote. "It awarded sizable contracts to companies with negligible paid-up share capital . . . to companies that did not meet its own criteria . . . to companies whose ability to honor such contracts was patently dubious, even in the ministry's own opinion." The report did not explicitly allege political preference, but that was the obvious implication.

For Sharon, all this stickling for bureaucratic propriety was part of the petty-mindedness. But the comptroller went on to hoist him with his own petard. Even by his lights, his accelerated building policy had been a woeful mess. Time and again, by offering the construction companies tempting incentives, he had got them to complete the apartment blocks in record time—only to find that the ministry had neglected to coordinate all the requisite infrastructure work. As a result, the homes were not ready to be lived in, despite the speed with which they had gone up. The state had paid over the top for the construction, but it might as well have saved the money.[20]

Worse yet, the quality of the building was often inadequate or downright shoddy, even though the ministry had a veritable army of inspectors in its pay whose job it was to ensure that the standards laid down in the regulations were met. Here, again, as with the fly-by-night construction companies, the allegation was between the lines: the inspectors owed their jobs not to any professional qualifications but rather to their political connections. In one case of a "repairs coordinator," the comptroller wrote, inquiries by her office had established "that the repairs coordinator had no previous experience whatsoever, either in work in general or in repairs work in particular. He had just recently graduated from university in political science and sociology." He was, however, "an active member of the Likud Party branch in Jerusalem and regularly attended party conventions."

A similar saga of departmental incompetence had blighted the vastly expensive importation of trailers and mobile homes, the comptroller continued. At the end of the day, many of these units remained unlived in, because the ministry had failed to orchestrate all the planning and administration required for their proper installation. They were ordered and shipped over at top speed, with scant attention to their price or to regulations regarding quality—and then "languished on the outside of building sites or in storage centers" for months on end. "The lesson of all this," the comptroller concluded—and her words resounded through the media—"is that ends do not justify means. There is no justification for a government ministry, using government money, to flout laws and regulations."

CHAPTER 10 · BACKWOODSMAN

If you go to them, you become their leader! Grab the leadership, it's yours for the taking." This urgent exhortation, from Ariel Sharon's political adviser, came within moments of the television exit polls predicting the Likud's devastating defeat in the June 1992 election at the hands of Yitzhak Rabin. The outgoing minister of housing spent the evening quietly in a suite at the Tel Aviv Hilton, watching the results on television. The party faithful—central committee members, campaign workers, grassroots activists—were assembled not far away, at the Tel Aviv exhibition grounds, hoping for the best but fearing the worst. Their mood quickly plummeted to one of profound depression.

Yitzhak Shamir, an underestimated politician if ever there was one, had managed to hold on to the prime ministership for longer than any of his predecessors apart from Ben-Gurion. But after Shamir lost the election, his term as leader of the Likud was now clearly over. "Whoever gets there first will take the party. Go there; show leadership. That was my advice to Arik," the adviser recalled. "But he didn't take it. He blew the opportunity. Why? To this day I don't know. He always used to say, 'For me, politics is an option, not an obsession.' Bibi Netanyahu instinctively understood the situation. He acted cleverly and quickly. Our people were knocked flat. He helped them up. He lifted their spirits. Later I told Arik, if you run against Bibi, it'll be over my dead body. You've got no chance. Bibi's conquered the Likud."[1]

Realistically, Sharon was not the ideal candidate for the defeated party to choose as its bright hope for the future. He was sixty-four, though that in itself was not necessarily a drawback. Rather, after a decade of sniping at his own party leader, Sharon was regarded as too extreme. *Hishuka'ut,* or constraining, no longer seemed so cool. The other two "constrainers," David Levy and Yitzhak Modai, had been working assiduously to soften their images, leaving Sharon alone in his pristine rejectionism. That hardly seemed an election-winning platform, especially as the next election would be fought under a new, reformed system in which the candidates for prime minister would be voted for directly, like American presidents.* In addition, he still bore what he himself called his mark of Cain from the Lebanon War, despite all his ceaseless efforts to erase it.

The British have a word for the kind of political profile Sharon appeared to be contemplating. They call it the Tory backwoodsman. He is typically a red-faced, tweed-clad country squire, comfortably ensconced in his safe parliamentary seat, a justice of the peace and (until recently) master of the hounds, who descends infrequently on London to thump and blather his far-right fulminations before a bored but tolerant House of Commons. There was something of that same faintly amused forbearance in the Knesset for the periodic eruptions of the formerly all-powerful minister who was now, as all thought, finally on his way to political extinction. Sharon, philosophically unflustered about his present reduced political circumstances and dim future prospects, and always game for mordant parliamentary cut and thrust, joined in the fun.

"Mr. Speaker, I've got a little problem," he observed straight-faced as the house broke into a cacophony of catcalls following some particularly provocative rhetoric from him two weeks into the new term. "Mr. Speaker, there are so many new members. Who is that screecher over there? I can't seem to identify him."

(Laughter in the chamber.)
MR. SPEAKER EDRI: I'm sorry, Knesset Member Sharon, I'm going to have to ask you to withdraw that remark.

---

* The new election law had been passed on March 18, 1992, the last day of the previous Knesset. It was to go into effect in 1996. Under its provisions, voters would cast two ballots, one for prime minister and the other for the party of their choice. The intention was to strengthen the big parties, whose leaders were naturally the prime ministerial candidates, at the expense of the smaller parties. Advocates of the reform assumed that most voters would vote the same ticket for prime minister and for party. But it backfired badly. Many people apparently felt that having cast one vote for a prime minister who was the leader of a big party, they could allow themselves to cast their other vote for a small party. The result, in 1996, was a shrinkage of Likud and Labor, the two big parties, and a surge among the smaller parties, like Shas, a Sephardic-Orthodox party, and Yisrael B'Aliya, a Russian immigrant party. The Likud had voted against the measure, but Benjamin Netanyahu broke ranks and sided with its proponents—a wise choice, since the new system brought him to power.

(Heckling.)

ARIEL SHARON (LIKUD): I am ready to withdraw it. I just want to know who he is.

MR. SPEAKER EDRI: His name is Knesset Member Professor Less. I now instruct that the remark by Knesset Member Sharon be struck from the record. Thank you.

(Heckling.)

ARIEL SHARON (LIKUD): I myself request that the remark be struck out. Mr. Speaker, honorable members can calm down: I request that it be struck out. It's just that I never imagined that a professor could screech like that. It simply never occurred to me.

(Heckling.)[2]

He had the good sense and good fortune to develop a regular relationship with *Yedioth Ahronoth,* the tabloid-format, middlebrow paper that was then at the apogee of its success. It was printing some 400,000 copies on weekdays and 660,000 on Friday—this in a country with, at that time, a total population of 5.5 million, of whom a million-odd were Arabic readers and had their own newspapers, another three-quarters of a million were Russian readers and had *their* own papers and magazines, and many other, smaller groups still preferred to read newspapers in their various mother tongues rather than in Hebrew. *Yedioth*'s penetration of the Hebrew-reading public, therefore, was probably unsurpassed by any newspaper in the free world.

"There was always a dearth of good writers on the right," the paper's then editor, Moshe Vardi, explains. "Arik was a good writer." Sharon would usually send his copy from the ranch, by fax, carefully penned in longhand. "People didn't believe he wrote the pieces himself," said Vardi. "But he absolutely did. I know, because sometimes I would ask him for a short, quick piece for the next day's paper—and half an hour later his fax would arrive." Sometimes they would discuss politics on the phone, Sharon would voice a thought, "and I'd say, Arik, write it. Don't just talk it, write it. 'You think so?' he'd ask. He was actually easy to work with."

Other politicians, especially on the right, were jealous when they realized that Sharon was becoming a fixture in Friday's *Yedioth* and thereby reaching two-thirds of the newspaper-reading public. "Is the fat man writing again?" Vardi recalls one particular rival asking snidely. When the paper offered space to other politicians, they would want to know if their article was to appear before or after Sharon's in the weekend lineup.[3]

The articles and his Knesset speeches, which he prepared with great care, often overlapped. Sharon would borrow phrases, paragraphs, sometimes whole passages, from one to use in the other. If he felt a speech had not been listened to in the chamber, or had not been paid adequate attention by the parliamentary correspondents, he would repeat it or elaborate on it in his newspaper column. He sent the ones he thought were especially important to *The Jerusalem Post,* where they appeared in English translation.

The new columnist's first article appeared ten days after the election, while Rabin's coalition building was still under way. "The real political turnabout in the State of Israel," Sharon wrote, "the truly significant one, took place not in the election of 1977 but in the election of 1992. In 1977, the Likud's ascent to power merely replaced one Jewish political bloc with another Jewish political bloc. In 1992, however, something entirely different took place, something shocking and perturbing. For the first time in the state's history, it is the Arab minority, and more precisely the anti-Zionist part of it, that will determine who rules this country and who shapes its future."

In the election, Labor under Rabin had won 44 seats to the Likud's 32. Labor's ally, Meretz, won another 12. The largely Arab Hadash Party won 3, and the wholly Arab "Arab Democratic Party," 2. This gave Rabin's leftist bloc an unassailable "blocking bloc" of 61. The rightist and religious parties, led by Likud, could muster only 59 between them and could not therefore form a government. In the event, after the usual postelection haggling, Rabin was able to woo Shas, the Sephardic-Orthodox party with 6 seats, over to his side. He set up a government comprising Labor, Shas, and Meretz. The two Arab parties did not seek to be part of it, nor did Rabin offer them to be. But Rabin could count on their support "from the outside" against attempts by the Right to torpedo his peace policies.

The full impact of the Arab voters had been even more decisive, as Sharon calculated it. Votes in Arab areas, he wrote, had provided more than 4 seats to Labor and Meretz, and just 2 to the Likud and its allies. He went on: "The correct and meaningful result of the election, reflecting the true balance of forces within the Jewish sector—is not 61 against 59, but around 57 for the Right against 51 or 52 for the Left.

"It's democracy," he continued, "but it is also the beginning of the road to the gradual dissolution of the State of Israel as the state that was created, according to its Declaration of Independence, as 'the Jewish state in the Land of Israel.' "

For Sharon, this article was no slip of the pen. It laid out what was to be a consistent and recurring theme in his writing and speaking throughout the Rabin years: the government, which had come into being thanks to Arab voters, lacked the legitimacy to negotiate concessions on the part of the Jewish state. In May 1993, Sharon grabbed the headlines at the Likud's national convention by baldly proposing that Arab citizens not be entitled to vote in any election or referendum on the future of the West Bank or of the Golan Heights. "It is inconceivable," he declared, "that such fateful questions should be decided by the votes of the Israeli Arabs who regard themselves as part of the Palestinian nation. Their criterion is the interests of their nation, not those of the Jewish people . . . The question whether to withdraw from the Golan Heights, or the decision regarding the future of the historic heartlands of the ancient kingdoms of Judah and Israel—these are questions of life and death for the Jews. They must therefore be ours alone to answer."[4]

In his newspaper column that weekend, headlined "Democracy and the Jewish State," he took issue with

> those who brand me an enemy of democracy on the basis of distorted and partial quotes from my remarks at the Likud convention. What I said was: "Our parents and grandparents did not come here to create a democracy. It's a very good thing that a thriving democracy has been created. But—remember this!—they came here to create a Jewish state" . . . I don't think Yitzhak Rabin's true assessment of these [Palestinian-Israeli] supporters of his is fundamentally different from mine. But I fear that his weakness, or his political ambition, has smothered his assessment and his misgivings. But giving the Israeli Arabs or their representatives the right to determine the fate of the State of Israel and the Jewish people is too great a price even for ensuring the survival of the Rabin government.

Sharon was not just lashing out wildly. While Rabin's "true assessment" of the Arab parties was certainly different from his, it was not all that different. Rabin would never have said the things Sharon had said and written, calculated as they were to deepen interethnic divisions and fan the flames of hatred. Such statements were beyond the realm of decent political expression in Israel at that time, and some in Sharon's own Likud Party squirmed uncomfortably to hear them. But Rabin had agreed to unpalatable concessions to the ultra-Orthodox Shas, in order to have *"a Jewish majority"* for the peace moves he intended to make. "Jewish majority" was not a phrase coined by Sharon or the Far Right. It was coined—or at any rate uninhibitedly used in everyday political life—by the Labor prime minister and his closest allies.[5] Rabin wanted a majority of Jewish Israelis to support his pol-

icy. Indeed, he wanted an Orthodox Jewish component in that majority. The Arab parties were good for blocking, not for governing.

Another key theme that suffused Sharon's rhetoric and writing in
the period following the 1992 election was "Jordan is Palestine." He
was nothing if not consistent. And he had never given up on this thesis, however exotic or quixotic it seemed to others. The fact that Israel
had been negotiating since Madrid with pro-PLO West Bank Palestinians (under the gossamer guise of a "Jordanian-Palestinian delegation") made "Jordan is Palestine" more anachronistic than ever. Not
to Sharon. "We should negotiate with the Palestinian state, Jordan,
whose ruler, as far as we're concerned, can be King Hussein or someone else—that's for them to decide."[6]*

With Begin now dead, Sharon allowed himself a freedom of expression that he had never been bold enough to adopt while the old man
lived. Begin's autonomy had been nothing but a "fig leaf," he wrote,
"to enable Egypt and us to sign our peace treaty. The Egyptians needed
this document in order to demonstrate their 'concern' for the Palestinian cause. We for our part had the deepest interest in signing the peace
treaty with Egypt and precious little interest in any change of the status quo in Judea, Samaria, and Gaza."

This, of course, had been the unwavering conviction of the peace

---

* Sharon's depiction in this article of the dangers of withdrawing from the Gaza
Strip was eerily identical to the arguments used against him by the settlers and the
Right when he ordered the disengagement from Gaza in 2005. (They would say it
was eerily prescient.) "The too-hasty among us proclaim, 'Gaza first,' " he wrote.

> There are some of them in our own camp. [Sharon was referring to Moshe
> Arens and Ronni Milo, two senior Likud figures who urged Shamir before the
> 1992 election to get out of Gaza.] "Get out of Gaza," they say. "Who needs
> Gaza?" Well, not to mention the inherent perversity of volunteering to cede
> a part of the national homeland, which no normal nation would do, I would
> like to ask them to explain how they think it will be possible to live without
> a Jewish cordon sanitaire between the Gaza Strip, with its 700,000 hostile
> Palestinians, and Sinai, an incessant source of weaponry and terror. Without
> the bloc of Jewish settlement [Gush Katif, in the southern Gaza Strip], who
> is going to block that traffic? They say: "We'll put up a fence, we'll mine the
> border, we'll dig canals, we'll set up barriers and roadblocks. The main thing
> is to get out." Well, first of all, it is just not possible to seal off a territory
> hermetically. In the past, bands of terrorists have infiltrated from Gaza and
> reached as far as the suburbs of Tel Aviv. But to attack southern Israel, they
> wouldn't have to leave Gaza at all. A Katyusha rocket deployed on Falastin
> Square in central Gaza will easily hit Mohammed V Square (remember the
> sad national farce of that name?) in central Ashkelon. It will hit Kiryat Gat,
> Sderot, Netivot, and dozens of kibbutzim and moshavim. What will we do?
> How will we respond?

camp in Israel since back in the late 1970s, when it became clear that Begin intended to fudge and drag his feet about his Camp David commitments on Palestinian autonomy while building—through the assiduous agency of Ariel Sharon—as many settlements on the West Bank and Gaza as he could.

Sharon's point, of course, was that with Rabin's election at the head of a government genuinely committed to peace, the fudging and foot-dragging might stop, and Israel might actually agree to a genuine autonomy regime that would set the Palestinians on the road to eventual independence. "Autonomy in the days of Rabin and the Left is not the same thing at all as autonomy under Mr. Begin and the Likud," he warned.

This being the case, he wrote, the only way to rescue Israel now from the specter of eventual Palestinian independence, and the armed irredentism that would inevitably go with it, was to limit the autonomy to carefully circumscribed enclaves. These would center on the main Palestinian towns and their immediate hinterlands. The enclaves would be isolated from each other by large, contiguous tracts of countryside that would remain under full Israeli military control. The settlements, with their separate roads linking them, would crisscross this whole area, ensuring that the autonomous Palestinian enclaves remained isolated. Sharon attached a map, which *Yedioth* spread over a whole page, displaying the enclaves, seven of them on the West Bank and four more in the Gaza Strip.

All together, they accounted for barely 30 percent of the territories. This proportion was to grow in subsequent presentations of the plan. But for Sharon's detractors, both Israeli and Palestinian, then and thereafter, the proposal became known, and deprecated, as "Sharon's Bantustans." The allusion to South African apartheid was used advisedly, and it stuck. It was meant to accentuate the effects of the separated enclaves on the Palestinians' freedom of residency and of movement.[7] In later elaborations of his plan, Sharon suggested an elaborate network of roads, bridges, and tunnels to link the Palestinian enclaves.

OLD SOLDIERS

"Eitan, we both raised our voices. We shouted at each other." Eitan Haber, Yitzhak Rabin's longtime bureau chief, recalled his boss emerging from long, one-on-one meetings with Arik Sharon in the aftermath of the Oslo Accords. "He would be red-faced with anger after Sharon left, visibly agitated." Why, then, did the prime minister inflict on himself these tongue-lashings from a bitter political foe? "He always had a soft spot for Sharon. Don't forget, they went back decades together. 'Ate from the same mess tin,' as old soldiers say."

Sharon agreed. "Our relations are built on a completely different background [from politics]; they come from another world. In that world, too, there were clashes between us. But we marched together, in lockstep, over decades, on tough missions and in life-and-death situations. My assessment now is that on key national issues Rabin has completely reversed his positions. I consider this reversal dangerous. But that doesn't affect our relationship."[8]

The turnabout in Israel's diplomatic direction, in the fall of 1993, was indeed breathtakingly sharp. For years and years, the focus of its policy and public advocacy had been directed at how to spurn the Palestine Liberation Organization and all it stood for. And now Rabin of all people was extending a hand of peace to the PLO leader, Yasser Arafat, the man a generation of Israelis had been taught to hate and fear as a cunning and vicious terrorist.

True, on the left, and even among moderate Likudniks, beneath the public facade of rejection—the law of the land had until recently made it a criminal offense to meet with a PLO official*—many talked privately of the inevitability of an Israel-PLO deal. This was the case before King Hussein turned his back on the West Bank in 1988, and all the more so thereafter.

Nevertheless, when the turnabout came, it took everyone by surprise. Peres and Rabin succeeded in keeping the months of talks in Norway secret.† The initial agreement, signed on the White House lawn and sealed with that famous handshake—Rabin reluctant, Arafat eager, Clinton fairly forcing them to clinch—was called "Declaration of Principles on Interim Self-Government Arrangements." The aim was to put in place an "elected Council for the Palestinian people

---

* In January 1990, Prime Minister Shamir learned that Ezer Weizman, then his minister of science and technology (and later the president of Israel), had met in Geneva with the PLO representative to the UN agencies there, Nabil Ramlawi. Shamir wanted to fire him on the spot but acceded to Rabin's plea that he merely evict him from the inner cabinet. Sharon, then at the height of his "constraint" campaign against Shamir, said in a speech to party loyalists that the fact that Weizman had not been properly punished was "just as serious" as his offense itself.
† They were begun by two academics on the Israeli side, working under the loose aegis of Yossi Beilin, who served as Peres's deputy at the Foreign Ministry. Abu Ala (Ahmed Qureia), a senior PLO official, headed the Palestinian delegation.

in the West Bank and the Gaza Strip, for a transitional period not exceeding five years, leading to a permanent settlement based on Security Council Resolutions 242 and 338."[9]

The five years were to begin "upon the withdrawal from the Gaza Strip and Jericho area." The two sides would negotiate an "Interim Agreement" providing for a "transfer of powers and responsibilities from the Israeli military government . . . to the Council." "Permanent status" negotiations were to begin "no later than" the third year and were to cover "issues, including: Jerusalem, refugees, settlements, security arrangements, borders, relations and cooperation with other neighbors."

The declaration was accompanied by an exchange of letters between Rabin and Arafat. The PLO recognized "the right of the State of Israel to exist in peace and security," committed itself to resolve "all outstanding issues through negotiations," renounced "the use of terrorism and other acts of violence," and affirmed "that those articles of the Palestinian Covenant which deny Israel's right to exist . . . are now inoperative and no longer valid." Rabin wrote simply, in response, that "Israel has decided to recognize the PLO as the representative of the Palestinian people and commence negotiations with the PLO within the Middle East peace process."

Sharon never ceased excoriating Oslo as a historic mistake of monstrous proportions. For him, Arafat was and would always remain a base murderer, an unreformed terrorist, an inveterate liar, implacably committed to Israel's destruction. Nevertheless, the gradual transfer, under the Oslo Agreement, of parcels of territory to Arafat's Palestinian Authority offered, in Sharon's mind, an opportunity to advance his own ideas on the shape of Palestinian-Israeli peace. Thus, while protesting vehemently in speech and in print against the initial "Gaza-and-Jericho First" phase of the Oslo process, Sharon was also boasting, "In Gaza, Rabin is basically implementing my plan. What he's done is pretty close to what I've been proposing."

Sharon meant that Israel's military withdrawal from the Gaza Strip and the establishment of Arafat's rule there had left all of the Jewish settlements in the Strip intact and undisturbed. They sat on nearly 20 percent of the land.[10] They would continue to be protected by the army. The newly formed Palestinian Authority was to exercise its self-rule, for the time being, over the remainder of the Strip. Sharon wanted that "time being" to go on indefinitely. And more important, he wanted the same sort of arrangement to pertain in the West Bank.

He wanted to input his ideas with Rabin regardless of their formal

status on opposite sides of the political divide. Rabin, never too busy
for Sharon, would hear him out, time after time, just the two of them,
in meetings from which even the prime minister's closest aides were
excluded. For Rabin, Eitan Haber explained, "it was a way of reexamining his own positions, by submitting them to the rigorous criticism
of someone with mirror-image views, but with experience and detailed
knowledge that he really respected . . . Sharon would say, 'Why are
you giving them this hill? It's higher than the next hill. Give them
that.' He knew the map like the back of his hand."[11]

The agreement on Gaza and Jericho was signed on schedule, on
May 4, 1994, in Cairo. On July 1, Arafat arrived in triumph in Gaza.
His long exile seemed over. A new era of peace seemed to have dawned.
Later that month Israel and Jordan signed a joint declaration in Wash-
ington proclaiming their intention to conclude a full peace treaty. The
Israel-Jordan peace treaty itself was signed in October at a colorful
ceremony on the Arava border, with President Clinton affixing his
signature as witness.

But the negotiations with the Palestinians over the Interim Agreement dragged on for a further sixteen months. The atmosphere was
poisoned by an unprovoked massacre of twenty-nine Muslim worshippers in the Ibrahimi Mosque* in Hebron in February 1994, perpetrated by an American-born settler-doctor, Baruch Goldstein, from
nearby Kiryat Arba, and by a series of Palestinian terror attacks,
including suicide bombings, perpetrated mainly by Hamas, a fundamentalist organization that opposed any accommodation with Israel.
Buses were blown up in Afula (April 1994), Hadera (April 1994), and
Tel Aviv (October 1994). In January 1995 a double suicide bombing took the lives of twenty-two off-duty Israeli soldiers waiting at a
bus stop at Beit Lid, near Netanya. More bombings followed in Kfar
Darom (April 1995) and Jerusalem (August 1995).

The Rabin government blamed Arafat and his various security
forces, which were supposed to have taken full control over Palestinian life in the Gaza Strip, for failing to rein in Hamas. The parties
of the Right blamed the Rabin government. They pointed out that
under Oslo hundreds of Hamas militants whom Rabin had deported
to Lebanon in 1992 had been allowed back home to Gaza. These men,
the Right alleged, had learned the ghoulish trade of suicide bombing
from the Lebanese Hezbollah.

---

* Known to the Jews as the Cave of Machpela. Both faiths believe their forefather
Abraham lies buried there.

The Interim Agreement, or Oslo II, as it was called, was finally signed, in Washington, in September 1995. Israeli forces would withdraw from the six major cities on the West Bank, and these would become "Area A," under full Palestinian civil and security control. A special regime would be negotiated for the city of Hebron, with the enclaves of Jewish settlement there remaining under IDF protection. Other densely populated areas of the West Bank would become "Area B," where the Palestinians would have civil and police control but Israel would retain "overall security authority to safeguard its citizens [that is, the settlers] and to combat terrorism." The third and largest, but least populated, area would be "Area C," where Israel retained civil and security control.

The natural assumption throughout the region and around the world was that the Oslo process would culminate in the creation of an independent Palestinian state. Arafat, in his every public utterance, insisted that this would be so and that the capital of his state would be Jerusalem. Rabin, it is worth noting, never committed himself publicly to this outcome. The five-year transitional period was explained by Rabin government officials as a testing and confidence-building period during which the two sides would learn to live together. These officials explained that in Rabin's view the Israeli public needed to be conditioned gradually to the idea of a Palestinian state. The trauma of the turnabout on recognizing and negotiating with the PLO was about as much as the public could take at one time. A second trauma, of swallowing eventual Palestinian independence, would have to be administered gradually.

Interestingly, the original Israeli architect of Oslo, Yossi Beilin, was among the first to understand that the process he had devised harbored within it the danger of its own demise. He realized that by deferring the "permanent status issues" to later, Israel and the Palestinians were essentially proposing to leap over a chasm in two steps, a surefire formula for plummeting to destruction. During 1994–1995, Beilin entered into a series of intensive discussions with the key peacemaker on the Palestinian side, Mahmoud Abbas (Abu Mazen), and together they drafted the outline of a permanent status agreement. It provided for the establishment of an "independent State of Palestine." Two national capitals, Yerushalayim and al-Quds, would exist within one undivided city of Jerusalem. The border issue was to be resolved by land swaps. Beilin and Abbas completed their text in late October 1995. Beilin, though close to Peres, decided to submit it to Rabin. But Rabin was assassinated on November 4.[12]

• • •

Throughout this period, political discourse in Israel was debased on occasion by outright incitement and was sullied more frequently by borderline rhetoric that gave rise to heated debate as to the legal limits of inflammatory language in a democracy. Sharon walked the borderline—uninhibited by his private friendship with the prime minister. Ostensibly, he condemned the incitement against Rabin and Peres, but he himself engaged in it. Moreover, he seemed to justify or at least condone it by holding himself up as the victim of similar incitement. "The ministers complaining today," he asserted, "are the very same people who stood at demonstrations under signs saying, 'Begin—Murderer,' 'Sharon—Murderer,' in the middle of a war, after Christian Arabs killed Muslim Arabs in Sabra and Shatila."[13]

Instead of the chants of "Rabin—traitor," he said, he himself would prefer "silent demonstrations, protests that cry out in their stillness." To this end, in August 1995, he joined a small group of rightist Knesset members and political activists who pitched two tents in the park opposite the prime minister's office in Jerusalem and declared a hunger strike against Oslo. For eight days, he subsequently claimed—though he hardly looked the worse for it—he subsisted solely on mineral water, which a solicitous Lily brought with her on her exhortative visits.

The trouble was that apart from Lily and other relatives and friends of the fasters, their sacrifice of body mass somehow failed to attract the masses, and the days passed in relative solitude. Sharon tried to take command, arranging cell phones, radios, and televisions for the fasters. "We must all stay on message," he urged. The message was "Wipe out terror" and "Think again about Oslo." It was to be delivered by "a shout of silence." Sharon hoped the protest would reach out to a broad public, well beyond the settlers and their national-religious hinterland. But the couple hundred well-wishers who turned up to demonstrate their solidarity each day were mainly young men in crocheted *kippot* and girls in long denim skirts—hard-core settler gear—and a smattering of black-clad Jerusalem *haredim*.

But any pretension to dignified, silent protest was giving way by this time to a culture of rabid, violent incitement. It all came spewing out at a huge demonstration organized by the parties of the Right at Zion Square in downtown Jerusalem on October 5, 1995, to protest the signing of the Oslo II accord the week before. Amid a crowd estimated at more than 100,000, Rabin was not merely called a traitor. His photograph was held up on placards dressed in the uniform of an

SS officer. The leaders, haranguing the crowd from a balcony, did not react. Later, after Rabin's murder, some of them claimed they had not seen the offensive signs.

Sharon, the last speaker, accused the government of "double collaboration—once with a terrorist organization led by a war criminal, and once against Jews. Never in history has a country freely ceded a part of its historic homeland. They are doing it in their own names, not in ours."[14]

Some of the demonstrators then marched toward the Knesset, attacking official government cars as they went. Rabin's car, without Rabin in it, was vandalized, its lights smashed, and its bodywork dented and scratched. The Knesset Guard, a highly trained force usually deployed for ceremonial purposes, took up positions on the perimeter fence to protect the seat of Israel's democracy. The police, on the streets outside, were pelted with stones and burning torches. They waded into the crowd and arrested dozens.[15]

The buzzword "collaboration," with all its emotive undertow, was no slip of the tongue on Sharon's part. He had compared Rabin and Peres to Marshal Pétain in an interview in *Penthouse* several months earlier. Now he dug up the French national hero turned collaborator again in an interview with the *haredi* magazine *Hashavua*. "Their [Rabin and Peres's] action is even graver than what Pétain did," he said. "It's hard to speak of treason in connection with Jews, but the essence of their action is no different [from treason]. They sit with Arafat and plot with him how to deceive the citizens of Israel. And I am choosing my words carefully."

He chose similarly scurrilous words in an interview at this time with another *haredi* magazine, *Kfar Chabad*. "Rabin and Peres are a couple of collaborators," he said, "who in any normal country would be put on trial." Now, though, he moved from Nazi collaboration to Stalinist provocation. The reports appearing in the media about purported rightist threats to assassinate the prime minister and other ministers were deliberate provocations, he asserted. They were like the alleged threats against Stalin published in Russia in the 1930s. Stalin used them to destroy his enemies.

Compounding his inflammatory references to terrible chapters from history, Sharon added an ancient and uniquely indigenous component. The government was becoming a *mosser,** he wrote in June 1995 in an article addressed specifically to the settlers. The govern-

---

* *Mosser:* one who hands over Jews.

ment, in its withdrawal policy, proposed in effect "to hand over the settlers to gangs of armed Palestinians . . . They've handed over Jews to non-Jews before," he continued, alluding to the pre-state *saison*. "Being a *mosser* and a snitch is part of the spiritual ethos of the Israeli Left. Don't forget for a single moment that the members of Peace Now and its various metastases are closer in their souls to the PLO murderers than they are to you."

Here, though he may not have precisely intended it—what he did intend was reckless and pernicious enough—Sharon came close to fanning the burning core of fanatical religious incitement that was later held directly responsible for Rabin's murder. The term *mosser* had its origins in the religious law, or halacha, of the Jewish Diaspora, where it meant to hand over Jews to the Gentile authorities. That could spell cruel death, and so medieval rabbis ruled that, where possible, the *mosser* himself should be executed. Settler-rabbis on the West Bank seriously weighed during the summer and fall of 1995 whether the ancient law of *mosser* applied to Yitzhak Rabin. If it did, the halachic implication was that he must be put to death. It is unclear to this day to what extent, if at all, the young religious assassin Yigal Amir was influenced by these religious deliberations. There is no doubt that many in the settler community and its political hinterland knew of the deliberations.

Sharon assiduously cultivated the settler community during his wilderness years. He could no longer direct bulldozers and budgets at their behest. But he was eager to establish himself, though in the opposition, as their leading champion in the public arena and as their dependable bulwark of consolation and encouragement as they absorbed the body blows of Oslo with increasing trepidation.

He took credit, as we have seen, for Rabin's retaining all of the settlements in Gaza intact and handing over only the balance of the Strip to Yasser Arafat in the Gaza and Jericho First phase of the Oslo process. There were mutterings on the left over this decision. Some felt it betrayed weakness or, worse, fear of the settlers. Rabin spoke of them disparagingly in private and sometimes in public. But the fact was that since his first government's climbdown at Sebastia* he had avoided another head-on clash with them. Under his long stewardship at Defense during the 1980s, some restriction was imposed on the creation of new settlements, but the existing ones grew and flourished.

The pressure on Rabin to confront the settlers came to a head after Baruch Goldstein's massacre of Muslim worshippers in the Ibrahimi Mosque in Hebron in February 1994. The Hebron settlers could not

---

* See pp. 148–49.

in all fairness directly be blamed for Goldstein's wholly unpredicted crime. The man was a doctor by profession and had until the day of the murder discharged his Hippocratic oath toward Palestinian patients in exemplary manner. But these Hebron settlers, or some of them at any rate, were vicious, provocative, and insidious in their relentless efforts to make life miserable for their Muslim neighbors. Even their little children were mobilized in this battle of dispossession: they would be sent to spread thumbtacks on the carpets of the mosque (which doubles as a synagogue), when the Muslims prayed barefoot. Rabin was urged, indeed implored, immediately following the massacre to seize the moment of national outrage and shame and physically, forcibly, remove the couple hundred Jewish Israelis who had made their homes in the heart of the fundamentalist Muslim city. He considered the proposal but rejected it.

Faced with this possible threat to the Hebron settlers, Sharon weighed in with gusto. In a television interview he called on "all the citizens of Israel" to come to Hebron and offer passive resistance to any attempt at evacuation. He vowed that he himself would be there, at the head of the resisters.[16]*

---

* Unlike the Begin government after Sabra and Shatila, the Rabin government needed no pressure to set up a commission of inquiry into the massacre at the mosque. The president of the Supreme Court, Meir Shamgar, headed it, and another two justices (one Jewish and one Arab), a former army chief of staff and an academic, sat alongside him. Within a week, they began to hear evidence.

Sharon wasted no time either. For him, massacre plus commission spelled an opportunity to ratchet up his own unending battle against the verdict of the Kahan Commission ten years earlier. "I am writing to you," he wrote in a bitter and cynical open letter to Justice Aharon Barak in March, who was widely thought to have been the moving spirit behind the Kahan Commission's determinations and recommendations, "in order to save Prime Minister and Minister of Defense Yitzhak Rabin and the chief of staff and his generals from the danger of 'indirect responsibility' for the massacre in the Cave of Machpela. They face that danger as a result of the 'principle of indirect responsibility' which you laid down when you served as a distinguished member of the commission of inquiry into the murder of Muslims by Christians at Sabra and Shatila."

The Shamgar report found much disorder and sloppiness within the IDF and the police and a "totally unsatisfactory" level of coordination between the two. It found laxity and remissness in the way the law was enforced against the settlers. But it apportioned no responsibility for the massacre, direct or indirect. "We do not believe that anyone can be blamed for not having foreseen the fact that a Jew would plan and carry out a massacre of Muslims in the Tomb of the Patriarchs." Sharon celebrated this as "a ringing slap in the face to the false standards which guided the Kahan/Barak Commission . . . The responsible report of Justices Shamgar, Zouabi, Goldberg, and their colleagues is the first nail in the coffin of the Kahan/Barak Report."

The talk of evacuating settlements in the Palestinian territories, even though hypothetical at that point, and the separate start of negotiations on the Syrian track, inevitably rekindled the memory of the only settlements that Israel had actually evacuated—Yamit and the Rafah Salient. Sharon took the opportunity of a pro–Golan settlements rally in July 1995 to publicly recant over that episode. He wanted to apologize, he told the crowd, for his shameful membership in a government that had agreed to hand back the Sinai settlements to Egypt. He was sorry to have done it, and it must not in any way serve as a precedent.

A month later, he urged the settlers to "seize the hilltops" in the face of the Oslo process. In an interview, with the author and a colleague on *Haaretz,* Sharon described a spate of minor landgrabs by settlers on the West Bank as a "mere warm-up exercise" in preparation for "the real struggle." He explained:

SHARON: The settlers in Judea and Samaria today number 150,000. By the end of the year, when they have completed all the building plans that I initiated, they will number 160,000. They are not going to leave their settlements when the army pulls out. In order to survive and thrive, they will have to seize the hilltops around their settlements. It is inconceivable, after all, that when the army pulls out, the Jews allow the Arabs to sit on the hills around them and to shoot down at them. They will therefore seize the hills around the settlements and create territorial contiguity between the settlements, and from the settlements to Israel proper . . . So the real struggle for these hills is still ahead of us.

QUESTION: Will you recommend them to do this?

SHARON: The Jews in the settlements know exactly what they need to do in order to keep living there. And they know my views on the subject.

QUESTION: You're saying this on the basis of firm information that the settlers have given you?

SHARON: I know it because I know these people. Twenty years ago, in 1976, when the episode at Sebastia began, I was working with Rabin, and he asked me, "Who are these Gush Emunim people?" I replied, "They're like we were forty years ago, only more serious."[17]

But he did not really know them. In his continuous swirl of cynicism and extremism he turned a blind eye to the ominous inner dynamic at work among Orthodox settler ideologues. He did not comprehend where their religious and political hatred for Rabin was leading the most violently fanatical among the settlers. He did not "know these people." Yet he, more than anyone, had the duty and the responsibility to know.

For every Israeli, the assassination of Yitzhak Rabin was an indelible trauma. People compare the moment they heard of it to the shock of the siren that sounded the onset of the Yom Kippur War. For Sharon, Rabin's death was a personal bereavement, too. He saw himself as a protégé and a friend of the slain leader. For Rabin, too, their relationship was an intimate web of professional patronage and personal friendship that transcended their political rivalry. In the months before the murder, his daughter Dalia Rabin recalled, "Arik said the most terrible things. He incited no less than Bibi. We have all the speeches collected here [at the Rabin Center for Israel Studies in Tel Aviv]. And then, in the evening, he would phone up or come around to my father, and they would talk. Where to draw the lines and how to redeploy the troops. My father would never mention the speeches of the daytime. Never. Arik told me himself: 'We talked topography.' "

Dalia, a lawyer, had a brief career in Labor Party politics and served as deputy minister of defense (2001–2002) in Sharon's first administration. "Arik had a really warm spot for me. I was invited to every meeting of the 'kitchenette,' every late-night consultation at the prime minister's residence. He never apologized publicly for the things he said against my father. But privately, to me, he did concede that 'there were things said that shouldn't have been said.' "[18]*

RIGHT IN, LEFT OUT

As after the shock of Oslo, so too, mutatis mutandis, Sharon was quick off the mark in assimilating and countering the political trauma of

---

* Dalia Rabin recalled:

While I was deputy minister, cabinet secretary Gideon Sa'ar ordered the removal of photographs of the Oslo process from the walls of the prime minister's office. I wrote a very long and very strong personal letter to Arik. I wrote that you can't change history like that. If you take these pictures off the wall of the prime minister's office, in a way you're giving legitimacy to the assassination. He didn't reply. Not a word. When I resigned, he invited me in for a private chat. He tried to persuade me not to quit the Knesset. We discussed politics and many things, and then, at the end, as I stood to leave, he said, out of the blue: "And as regards the pictures—you were right." But he still didn't put them back up.

Rabin's assassination. Potentially, this heinous act was devastating for the standing and respectability of the "national camp," especially of the religious Right, which was the crucible of the assassin Yigal Amir's murderous mind-set. In the first week or two after the assassination, *kippa* wearers were verbally and sometimes even physically abused. There was little patience for the claim that Amir was a "wild weed," an unintended excrescence of the settlers' zealotry. The broader Right was indicted with him. It had furnished, after all, the political hinterland for the settlers and their fanatical rabbis with their pernicious dogmas of hatred.

And indeed, those dogmas and the religious Zionism that spawned them had become, in effect, the only real ideology of the whole Right. The old-style, secular Revisionism of Begin and Shamir had been swallowed up by the rampant messianism of Gush Emunim and its settler cohorts. They set the tone for the whole of the "national camp," and that camp, therefore, could not wash its hands of the responsibility for Rabin's blood. Time and again, the balcony scene was replayed in the media and in people's minds.

Netanyahu was spurned and humiliated by Leah Rabin at the funeral. Sharon could have exploited the party leader's discomfiture to his advantage. He did not do so. Instead, reassured by the acceptance of his own condolences, he pushed back for the Right, rallying the disconcerted troops and throwing his support behind the embarrassed and endangered Bibi. "The struggle for Eretz Yisrael must go on," Sharon urged the Likud leadership the day after the funeral. "Any weakness on our part will spell disaster." The media were inciting against the entire Right, he warned.

Netanyahu, in a statesmanlike act, announced that his party would not stand in the way of the formation of another Labor-led government, under Shimon Peres. "Governments in Israel are changed by the ballot, not the bullet," he told the Likud executive on November 19. When elections came, the Likud would win. Meanwhile, they would stand firm against the baseless allegations being leveled against them. He dwelled on the revelation that the Shin Bet had had a mole among Yigal Amir's small circle of ultraradical friends who appeared to have functioned more as an agent provocateur than as a covert source of information. He demanded a full inquiry. Democracy was in danger.

Speaker after speaker echoed this sentiment. Sharon said the story was typical of the way the Left had conducted itself for decades. An unwonted spirit of unity pervaded the party. Netanyahu was hugged and warmly applauded. In New York a fortnight later, prompted apparently by this same spirit, Sharon protested vehemently over a memorial event for Rabin organized by American Jewish leaders at Madison Square Garden, to which the Likud leader had pointedly not been invited.

Before the year's end Sharon announced that he was following this line to its logical conclusion and shelving his own pretensions to the party leadership. This statement was particularly welcome and timely for Netanyahu, because new rumblings had begun in the party after the assassination about possibly replacing him with Dan Meridor. Internal polling showed Netanyahu's popularity plummeting. The fear was that he had been irreparably tainted on that balcony. But Sharon's contempt for Netanyahu (most of the time) was surpassed by his loathing for Meridor, Begin's cabinet secretary and Sharon's enemy from the days of the Lebanon War. He called on the Likud to unite behind Netanyahu and urged the other parties of the Right to do so, too.

In January 1996, Israeli agents killed Yihye Ayash, Hamas's most notorious bomb maker in Gaza, by setting off an explosive device planted in his cell phone. Ayash, "the Engineer," was held personally responsible for some of the worst terror outrages that had hit Israel during the previous year. Peres was to regret giving the go-ahead to eliminate him. A series of revenge bombings by Hamas took a terrible toll of Israeli civilians in the months leading up to the election in June.

Hamas struck back first on February 25. Twenty-six people died on a No. 18 bus in Jerusalem and 44 more were injured. On the same day, a woman soldier was killed and 34 other passengers injured on a bus in Ashkelon. Both explosions were suicide bombs. The next day, a woman was killed and 23 others injured when a terrorist in a car deliberately plowed into a queue at a bus stop in Jerusalem. A week later, again on Sunday morning, again a suicide bombing on a No. 18 bus in Jerusalem, 18 died, and 7 were seriously hurt. The next day, March 4, the festival of Purim, 14 died in a suicide bombing near Dizengoff Center in the heart of Tel Aviv, and 157 were injured.

Suddenly there was only one issue in the election campaign. And Peres was no longer the certain victor. Sharon nevertheless called for the creation of an "emergency government of national unity," even if this meant postponing the election for a year. He, as the leading expert on security, in his own eyes at least, presumed he would be minister of defense. His colleagues in the Likud saw this as a transparent attempt to bypass Bibi and get back to where he wanted to be. Peres, in any event, turned Sharon down.

· · ·

For Peres, things seemed to go from bad to worse. This second premiership of his, born in tragedy, had not gone well from the start.
He seemed depressed and sluggish compared with his usual frenetic
self. Friends and aides urged him to hold snap elections in the wake
of the assassination. By all indications, he would have won a landslide
had he done so. But he was obsessed with the need to be his own man
rather than merely inherit the mantle of his slain rival. He wanted to
notch up successes of his own before going to the polls. He took over
the Defense Ministry together with the prime ministership, as Rabin
had, and as had Ben-Gurion, his mentor.

The Conference of Peacemakers held at the Egyptian resort of
Sharm el-Sheikh on March 13 was a bald effort by leading figures
in the international community to help Peres ward off the growing
challenge from the Right. President Clinton and President Mubarak of
Egypt hosted twenty-nine world leaders, among them Russia's Boris
Yeltsin. They stood for photographs alongside Peres and Arafat, and
all pledged their best efforts to fight against terror. But Israeli voters
were unimpressed, and the gap between Peres and Netanyahu kept
steadily narrowing as Election Day, May 29, drew near.

Peres seemed jinxed. In April, responding to an escalation of rocket
fire across the Lebanese border, he launched Operation Grapes of
Wrath, a massive bombing and shelling campaign by the IDF designed
to drive the villagers of south Lebanon to flee north toward Beirut.
The mass flight, it was thought, would bring irresistible pressure to
bear on the Lebanese government to send its army south and rein in
the Hezbollah guerrillas who were firing the rockets. This strategy
was deemed sophisticated by some Israeli policy makers, but others
found it both cynical and far-fetched. Sharon was an enthusiast. The
army should take the opportunity to extend Israel's "security zone"
up to the Litani River, he proposed expansively during a tour of the
border region on April 17. The next day, Operation Grapes of Wrath
was peremptorily terminated, amid much international outrage and
domestic embarrassment, when an errant shell fell on a UN shelter in
the village of Qana, killing more than a hundred civilians.

During April, two more suicide bombs, one in Hadera, north of
Tel Aviv, the other near a settlement in the Gaza Strip, took a further heavy toll of Israeli civilian lives. Peres's hopes of progress on
the Israel-Syria track were also fading. Two rounds of talks between
Israeli and Syrian officials at the Wye River Plantation conference cen-

ter outside Washington in December and January were businesslike but did not produce a breakthrough. Meanwhile, Netanyahu's figures were steadily creeping up.

The final push came in the form of a hugely visible, hugely energetic nationwide campaign launched by the New York–based Chabad-Lubavitch Hasidic movement three days before the elections. Every crossroads, every public space in Israel, was plastered with the slogan "Netanyahu is good for the Jews." Thousands of black-hatted Hasidim and *kippa*-clad settlers fanned out across the land to spread this pithy, pointed message. Its corollary, of course, was that good Jews should vote Netanyahu, who, moreover, would be not so good for the Arabs—in other words, would not cede any of the Holy Land to them.

If indeed, as many pundits believed, this last-minute effort by fervent groups of Orthodox believers swung the election to Bibi, then Sharon had every right to take the credit for it. It was he who, two weeks earlier, initiated a secret meeting at the dead of night with a leading rabbi of the Israeli branch of Chabad, Yitzhak Aharonov. They met in a girls' school at Kfar Chabad, a village wholly peopled by Chabad Hasidim not far from Tel Aviv. Sharon spoke of the danger hovering over Eretz Yisrael if Peres remained in office. Bibi, he said, would guard the land. Aharonov, well versed in political affairs, wanted to hear the pledge from Bibi himself. Sharon telephoned, and soon Bibi arrived and launched into a passionate speech of his own about the land and his loyalty to it.

Chabad Hasidim were his special forces in the election battle. But Sharon paid diligent heed to the other *haredi* communities, too, visiting their rabbis, touring their neighborhoods, and reminding them all of his prodigious home-building efforts for their communities, as minister of housing, on both sides of the green line. This was the first election to be held under the reformed voting system. Voters would cast two ballots, one for prime minister and one for the party of their choice. With the two candidates for prime minister running neck and neck, the disciplined phalanxes of *haredi* voters would be crucial.

Under Sharon's dogged wooing of their leaders, almost all of them voted for Netanyahu. Some rabbis had toyed with the idea of instructing their flocks to cast blank ballots for prime minister; after all, why should they take sides? Sharon talked them out of any such foolishness, persuading them that the return of the Likud to power would mean more state-built homes for their young couples and more state budgets for their yeshivas.

• • •

Netanyahu won by a whisker. On election night, it looked as if he had lost. Peres went to bed thinking he would still be prime minister in the morning. The final figures were 1,501,023 votes for Netanyahu, 1,471,566 for Peres: a margin of 29,457 votes, or just under 1 percent of the valid votes cast. In the vote for the parties, Labor beat Likud by 34 seats to 32.

Netanyahu owed his victory, in no small part, to Sharon. But it quickly emerged that the new prime minister did not intend to repay his debt. As the coalition making went ahead and the names of the prospective ministers began to leak out, Sharon's was not among them. Demeaningly, Sharon found himself fighting for a job in the new government. Netanyahu planned to leave him out entirely or offer him a junior portfolio, knowing he would refuse it, which amounted to the same thing. Sharon insisted that he had been explicitly promised one of the top three posts: Defense, Finance, or Foreign Affairs. Netanyahu did not contradict him; he just ignored him. Years later, he explained that Sharon brought disharmony to the work of a cabinet. He did not fear him as a contender for the leadership, Netanyahu insisted. "In those days Arik was not considered a threat to leadership. He was a threat to government."[19]

Sharon did the rounds of the *haredi* "courts" again, ostensibly to thank the rabbis for their votes, in fact to solicit their help to get him into the new government. They tried their best. Their key supporters, wealthy businessmen in Israel and abroad, lobbied with Bibi for Sharon to be named finance minister.

At half past three on June 18, Netanyahu's spokesman announced to waiting reporters that a seventeen-man cabinet was to be sworn in. That meant Sharon was still out. David Levy, the foreign minister designate, stormed into Netanyahu's room. "I won't be part of a government that Arik Sharon's not part of. We've come a long way together. If he's out, I'm out!"

"David, what are you doing to me?!" Netanyahu cried, sweating. "In ten minutes' time I've got to present my government, and now you tell me you're out." "Sharon's got to be in," Levy replied stolidly. "You know I'm trying to fix it," Netanyahu wailed. "Give me a few more days."

Netanyahu, reluctantly, had been trying to fix it. He came up with a new creation, the Ministry of National Infrastructures, and began the thankless task of harvesting a basket of departments and functions from other ministries that he had already manned. The new incumbents were unsurprisingly grudging. A package pulled together by Minister of Justice Ya'akov Ne'eman, one of Netanyahu's closest advisers, included the defense industries (transferred from the Defense Ministry); the Public Works Department (from the Housing Ministry); the powerful Israel Lands Authority (from the Prime Minister's Office); the Electricity Corporation (from the Energy Ministry); sewerage (from the Interior Ministry); the railways (from the Transport Ministry); water infrastructure (from the Ministry of Agriculture); and assorted other projects. But Sharon wanted more. He wanted the ports, the airports, oil and gas refining. Even his sympathizers in the Likud began to mutter about his appetite for budgets and power, which seemed to grow with the swallowing.

On July 3, David Levy struck again. At a meeting of the coalition executive, open to the press, he rose and turned to Netanyahu. "The manning of the government is not yet completed," he boomed in his sonorous bass. Sharon sat stony-faced as Levy thundered on. "I want to say this to the prime minister: There is one dear colleague, a colleague who did his very best so that this coalition should come into being but who has yet to find his proper place at the cabinet table. This situation cannot continue." Levy looked around slowly and continued: "So, if it is not resolved before the prime minister flies to Washington next week, I myself will bring relief to ministers who are not prepared to give up departments in their ministries on behalf of the Ministry of Infrastructures. I will vacate my own ministry and thus free up one cabinet seat. No doubt, there will be those who interpret my words as a gimmick. But I am not weak. I do not need to resort to gimmicks."

For Netanyahu, there was no more wiggle room. Years later, he looked back with disarming frankness:

NETANYAHU: It wasn't a particularly insightful thing of me to do. If you don't want to appoint him, don't appoint him.

QUESTION: So why did you?

NETANYAHU: Well, because essentially I had no coalition [without David Levy, who led a three-man faction].

QUESTION: And when you said to David Levy, look, you've been in cabinets a long time, you know it's impossible to work with this person—what did he say?

NETANYAHU: I didn't say that.

QUESTION: You didn't?

NETANYAHU: No.

QUESTION: But Levy must have asked you, why are you taking this position, why can't you give him a job?

NETANYAHU: He didn't say that either.

QUESTION: He must have. There must have been a rational conversation between you two.
NETANYAHU: There was no rational conversation. This is Israeli
politics.[20]

In the Knesset on July 8, Netanyahu took the rostrum to introduce
the new ministry and explain why it would make the work of governing smoother and more efficient. As he stepped down, sarcastic cries
went up from the Labor benches: "Sharon! What about congratulat-
ing Sharon?!" "Three weeks you've been torturing him." Netanyahu
turned and climbed back onto the podium. Sharon's accession to the
government, he said, would be beneficial "not only in developing those
important areas over which he will be in charge, but also in the areas
of defense and foreign policy, where he has much experience." He
stepped down again, walked over to Sharon, and shook his hand.

That handshake was the minimum that good manners and basic
parliamentary etiquette required. It signified nothing. Sharon
headed for the members' dining room, where aides and friends laid on
an impromptu party to celebrate his appointment. "I want to thank
one man in this government who has shown there's really such a thing
as true friendship," Sharon gushed. "This man stood up tall and firm
at the critical moment . . . It has been a demonstration of friendship
in the deepest meaning of the word." Levy beamed. "We'll work as a
team," he said, "in loyalty and harmony."[21]
Within a year, the two were at daggers drawn. The first crack in
their lovefest came inside of a month. In August, Netanyahu asked the
full cabinet's consent for the creation of an inner cabinet—the Hebrew
sobriquet was "kitchenette"—comprising himself, Levy, and Minister
of Defense Yitzhak Mordechai. Sharon, who sat almost opposite the
prime minister at the center of the long cabinet table, could hardly
contain his fury. Without looking across at Netanyahu, he said, "This
is inconceivable. This is what I've joined the government for. I'm the
most experienced man here. I'm not prepared to receive reports on
defense and foreign policy in chance conversations in corridors." "It's
what I've decided," Netanyahu replied coldly. "And it's what's going
to be." Levy said nothing.
But Sharon's cup of mortification had not yet brimmed over. The following summer, Netanyahu effectively forced Dan Meridor to resign
as minister of finance, which seemed to open up a promotion for Sha-

ron to one of the top three cabinet posts. Sharon's condition: a seat in the "kitchenette." Levy called a snap press conference to propose that the prime minister scrap the inner cabinet altogether. Its very existence caused tension among the ministers, he explained piously. The prime minister's aides let it be known that there was no way Netanyahu would let himself be pushed around by Levy. The finance post was Sharon's. The next day, Netanyahu announced he was giving it to his longtime lawyer and political consigliere, Ya'akov Ne'eman.

This episode combined the two themes that would dog and dominate Sharon for the remainder of his political life: his profoundly conflicted relationship with Netanyahu, and his indefatigable striving to attain—and then to retain—a central role in shaping the most fateful policies of the country. If he could somehow thrust Bibi aside and replace him as prime minister, then so much the better. But, at nearly sixty-nine and serving under an energetic party leader aged forty-eight, he was under no illusions. The chances of his vaulting back over the younger man, who had vaulted over him and his generation of political aspirants, were slim at best. But that hardheaded assessment did not dim his zeal to get back into the heady realm of defense and foreign policy. He had done his time, he felt, after Sabra and Shatila, winning neither pardon nor remission for good conduct. Ten years as a middle-ranking minister and four more on the opposition benches had earned him a comeback to the senior echelons of decision making.

Not getting the Treasury, and getting publicly ridiculed by Netanyahu to boot, was reminiscent of his mortifying rejection as head of aliya at the Jewish Agency back in 1984. Then, it was American Jewish philanthropists who turned their noses up. This time, anonymous officials in the Clinton administration and in European chanceries voiced fears that Sharon as Israel's finance minister would squander the country's treasure on the West Bank settlers.[22] From this last indignity, Sharon's political fortunes began to surge, first slowly and then dramatically. But the younger man's shadow never quite lifted from over him, until the end.

"Sharon's attitude to Bibi was always one of contempt and revulsion, but it was always blended with admiration and with fear," says a senior Likud figure who was very close, at different times, to each of the leaders. "It was a complex attitude—and an attitude of complexes. He admired abilities that Bibi had and that he knew he didn't have. Like his rhetorical skill. Sharon always warned the people around him:

Don't make light of Bibi; don't take him for granted. Yet he himself, during the '90s, would always refer to Bibi as 'the male model.' He had a basic lack of trust in him, of confidence, of credence."

In the halcyon days of their relationship before the 1996 election, Netanyahu promised Sharon that if they won, he would appoint him minister of defense. Neither man ever explicitly confirmed this in public, and one wonders how the High Court of Justice would have responded to arguments that the Kahan disqualification was for life. But a senior Likud figure, a man with a long record of credibility, insists that he himself heard from an unimpeachable source that the commitment was indeed made. His account underscores the enormity of Bibi's post-victory betrayal. Not only did he break his word; he tried to reduce Sharon from defense designee—the apogee of his rehabilitation—to nothing. And even when that plan failed, he vindictively kept his former defense designee out of his inner cabinet, where matters of defense were decided.

But Netanyahu was learning the art of survival. As crisis followed crisis, his staying power seemed to strengthen. The British ambassador spoke of him as "a drunk who lurches from lamppost to lamppost."[23] But Sharon was closer to reality when he urged his own supporters in the Likud to "stop all this talk" of dumping the prime minister. "I am hardly suspected of being his friend or close political ally," he declared in June 1997. "But this is the prime minister whom we all worked so hard to get elected. Now—let's everyone get on with his job, and let's let him get on with his."

Granted, Sharon's words of allegiance came the day after the finance portfolio opened up, and he was to voice very different sentiments about Netanyahu when he was not appointed to it. Nevertheless, the speech marks an acknowledgment, however grudging, that this nervy and jumpy prime minister was digging in and would not be so quickly or so easily dislodged. Better, then, to join him than to expend fruitless energy on beating him. "Let's show a little bit of restraint," Sharon advised his loyalists, whose anti-Netanyahu catcalls threatened to drown out his speech. "Let's stand behind the government, change and improve what needs to be changed and improved. But let's all stop whining from morning to midnight."[24]

Sharon's opportunity to put his new loyalty into practice came in September, when Netanyahu blundered into his largest and most painful lamppost yet.[25] A Mossad team, working undercover in neighboring, friendly Jordan, botched the assassination of Khaled Meshal, a prominent leader (in exile) of Hamas, the Palestinian Islamist movement. Two agents smeared a powerful poison onto his neck, and he duly lost consciousness, but they then got involved in a street brawl with his bodyguard and, subsequently, with a Jordanian policeman, who arrested them. A backup team of four other agents bolted to the Israeli embassy in Amman. King Hussein, feeling outraged and betrayed, threatened to sever relations with Israel.

Netanyahu quickly ordered the Mossad to provide the Jordanian health authorities with an antidote to the lethal smear. A doctor had accompanied the hit team to Amman. The Mossad director, Danny Yatom, rushed to Amman and met with King Hussein, and as a result the doctor was enabled to inject the antidote into Meshal and thus arrest his advancing demise.[26]

King Hussein, just a few days earlier, had called in a senior Mossad official and communicated to him an offer from Hamas to negotiate a thirty-year *hudna,* or truce, with Israel. The king had not received any reaction whatsoever to the proposal when the abortive Mossad attempt took place on that Thursday morning.

Efraim Halevy, who had left the Mossad two years earlier as deputy director and was now serving as ambassador to the European Union, was rushed home to handle the crisis. He proposed that Israel offer to free the spiritual leader of Hamas, Sheikh Ahmed Yassin, as its gesture of propitiation toward Jordan. The king, in return, would quickly and quietly release the Mossad men. The sheikh, almost blind and a quadriplegic, was arrested in Gaza in 1989 and had been in prison since then. He, like Meshal, an ostensibly political figure unconnected with Hamas's terror wing, was accused by Israel of direct responsibility for some of Hamas's most murderous terrorist attacks. To release him would inevitably stir up controversy. Politically, it would be risky. Netanyahu balked at first, but eventually he gave Halevy the green light to go to Amman and open negotiations. The veteran spymaster met with the king and returned with the four agents who had been holed up in the embassy. This was Hussein's royal intimation that his wrath might be abating.

At midnight on Sunday, September 28, a contrite Netanyahu helicoptered from Jerusalem to Amman to meet with Crown Prince Hassan, the king's brother, and General Batikhi, the head of the Jordanian security service. His delegation of ministers and officials included Sharon, who, if he had any reservations about the wisdom of Netanyahu's original decision to approve the operation, kept them to himself. Seeing Sharon, Prince Hassan wondered acidly if the hit on Jordanian soil had been Israel's way of weakening or perhaps destroying the Hashemite house.

The negotiations got bogged down in the following days, and

Halevy returned to his post in Brussels.* Netanyahu now asked Sharon to lead the Israeli team, which the minister of infrastructures did with aplomb and to the evident gratification of the royal court in Amman (and to the unconcealed disgruntlement of Minister of Defense Yitzhak Mordechai, who felt that by rights he should have been put in charge of this business). Sheikh Yassin was freed to Jordan, from where he returned to Gaza a week later to an ecstatic welcome from thousands of local people.[27] The two Mossad would-be assassins were duly released, too. On October 4, Sharon dined alone with King Hussein at the royal palace in Amman. Four and a half hours of feasting and flowing conversation left him, as he said later, enchanted by Hussein's blend of "desert magic and British manners."

It was all a far cry from his frustrating years of deprecating and disparaging Netanyahu, and an even farther cry from his decades of denigrating the Hashemite house and insisting ominously that "Jordan is Palestine." Sharon was now effusive in his praise for the prime minister's handling of the crisis. "He displayed both leadership and self-control," he told journalists who were used to hearing long and caustic laments from him over Netanyahu's lack of precisely those two qualities. Netanyahu's people, in turn, briefed with newfound bigheartedness of their own. Sharon, they said, may have been troublesome and unconstructive in the past, in relatively minor disputes. But when the national interest was seriously prejudiced, he had set aside any petty scores and performed superbly. Jordanian officials told an Israeli reporter that Sharon was someone they could do business with and that he "delivered."

The change in Sharon's standing in Amman was particularly striking in view of the fear and loathing his name had evoked there for so many years. A series of Knesset speeches and newspaper articles during the Rabin years, finally acknowledging the demise of "Jordan is Palestine," were the first phase of this process of personal and political conciliation, which culminated in that intimate dinner with the king. The second phase had evolved, fortuitously, during the months that preceded the Meshal fiasco and took the form of an act of generosity by the Israeli minister of national infrastructures in regard to that most precious of regional resources: water. "I knew he was going to give in to them," recalls Meir Ben-Meir, the then water commissioner, "when he didn't take me with him to meet Hussein and his minister of water at Aqaba in May 1997. 'Where's your company commander?'

---

* Temporarily. Netanyahu asked him to head the Mossad in place of Yatom. He agreed and served as director until 2002.

the king asked. He knew that Sharon and I had been officers together in the 1948 war. 'I've left him at home,' Sharon replied. He came back and told me he had signed over to Jordan another twenty-five million cubic meters a year."[28]

The water talks between the two riparian owners of the upper Jordan River were anchored in their peace treaty of 1994. Rabin had agreed to allocate fifty million cubic meters per year to Jordan from Lake Kinneret (the Sea of Galilee).[29] The water "belonged" to Jordan, inasmuch as it had flowed down the river and into the lake during the rainy season. But Jordan has nowhere to store it, and storage is the key problem of water supply in this semiarid area.

Other government departments were outraged at Sharon's largesse. The Treasury made it clear that there was no money for a desalination scheme that Sharon had also promised. It would have to be raised abroad—a difficult proposition. Until it was, though, the additional twenty-five million cubic meters per year would keep flowing.

The flowering of his friendship with Ariel Sharon came late in life for King Hussein. It produced a poignantly memorable tableau. The king, pallid and bald from anticancer drugs, received Sharon and Lily in October 1998 in his suite at the Mayo Clinic in Rochester, Minnesota. It was the eve of an Israeli-Palestinian negotiation convened by President Clinton at Wye Plantation, outside Washington. "Stay strong," Sharon urged the king. "We need your courage, your experience as the most veteran statesman in the Middle East, and your help in promoting and achieving a stable peace in the region." For sensitive Israeli ears, the subtext was clear: it takes one to know one. For by then Sharon himself was basking in the role of statesman—he was now foreign minister—and man of peace.

I believe there will be peace. There has to be peace, in my view. We have to make every effort to bring peace about. I have always been depicted as an enemy of peace. But I have never been an enemy of peace, because I witnessed the horrors of war. I believe in peace, and I believe that the day will come when peace will prevail. Thank you."[1]

Sharon's transformation during this period from man of war to man of peace was neither complete nor consistent. He did not become a born-again peacenik, now or later. His detractors, still legion, mocked the intimations of change as a cynical stunt. It was designed, they said, by his admen friends to make him more eligible for promotion, to get him into the kitchen cabinet at last. The talk at the top, in the region and in Washington, was of progress to peace. To get there, therefore, Sharon had to talk the talk. That didn't mean he would walk the walk.

Still, talk, however disingenuous, is not just talk. Talk is the stuff of politics. Talk makes the political man. In June 1997, Sharon invited Mahmoud Abbas (Abu Mazen), Yasser Arafat's deputy in the Palestinian Authority, for a long private talk at Sycamore Ranch. It was leaked two weeks later, probably by Sharon himself. "This meeting," wrote Shimon Shiffer, a veteran political commentator, "is one of the most important developments that has happened in the process of reconciliation between the two nations." In an article headlined "Sharon Has Crossed the Lines," Shiffer wrote that Sharon now recognized the realities that had given rise to the Oslo Accords and that in effect he, too, now recognized the PLO as the authentic representative of the Palestinian people.[2]*

---

* Immediately after Oslo, Sharon urged that the Likud and its allies "proclaim before the whole world that when the Likud returns to power, it will not abide by agreements that endanger the very existence of Israel." In the Knesset a week later he was less definite: the agreement was terrible; it could yet be improved, especially

Cynical or significant, Sharon's meeting with Arafat's longtime lieutenant intrigued the Knesset, and most especially the doves, both Jewish and Arab. The quotation at the beginning of this chapter was Sharon's extemporaneous closing flourish, at the end of a lengthy statement and subsequent exchanges with members. The deputy Speaker, Professor Naomi Chazan of Meretz, granted him extra time to make his replies. "We're all riveted," she said, without sarcasm. "Don't worry," Sharon said, with plenty of sarcasm on his part, "nothing's happened to shake my views about our right to Eretz Yisrael. I've heard so many worried voices here in the debate. Let me assure all the worriers: they've got nothing to worry about!" But then he seamlessly switched into his new, conciliatory vein. "I just think we must find a solution that everyone can live with . . . I believe that Jews and Arabs can live together in peace and must live together in peace. And I believe that day will come."

He had met with Abu Mazen, he said, in order to lay out in a straightforward and unvarnished way "what Israel can and can't do."

He did not deny reports in the press that he had given Abu Mazen to understand that he accepted, or at least did not dismiss, the Palestinians' principled demand for an independent state. Even if we set aside for a moment the impossibly narrow borders that Sharon envisaged for the Palestinians, his very countenancing of Palestinian statehood, however hypothetical, was still anathema at that time to much of the Israeli Right (and heresy to the religious Right). This was probably the first time (apart from his ideological swerves during the Shlomzion episode, which he subsequently denied) that Sharon intimated pub-

---

its security provisions; a Likud government would—or might, there was some deliberate obfuscation here—abrogate it. As time wore on, Sharon's obfuscation deepened. In August 1994 he said a Likud government would honor agreements signed by Rabin. It would not try to turn the wheel back, but would rather focus on ways of preventing further concessions. And later that year, in a wide-ranging interview in *Penthouse,* Sharon implicitly conceded that Oslo was no longer wholly reversible. Arafat was back, in Gaza at least, to stay. In December 1995, after the signing of Oslo II and the murder of Rabin, the irreversibility had broadened: Sharon told the ultra-Orthodox magazine *Hashavua* that it would be both impractical and irrational for Israel to abrogate the Oslo Accords, especially now that the Interim Agreement was being implemented on the ground. "I would not now demand that areas which have been handed over to them should be taken back by us."

The Likud, in its manifesto for the May 1996 election, declared, "The government will recognize the facts that have been created under the Oslo agreements and will act to minimize the dangers that flow from these agreements for the future and the security of Israel." Sharon said he was "not happy" with the party's stand, but since the majority of his colleagues had approved it, he, too, would accept it.

licly, albeit by insinuation, his pragmatic thinking on this touchstone political issue.

In a way, acceptance of Palestinian independence was less of an ideological leap for Sharon than for the others in his camp and for many in the Labor Party, too. After all, he had always favored Palestinian statehood—but centered on Jordan, not on Palestine. That was the essence of the "Jordan is Palestine" doctrine that he had espoused for so long, in defiance of the political orthodoxy. He therefore did not need to shake off the dogmatic Israeli denial of Palestinian national aspirations that constricted Israel's policy thinking under both Labor and Likud. He had never donned that particular piece of political and intellectual corsetry.

But while the Palestinians stressed that Abu Mazen had visited Sharon's home with Arafat's blessing, Sharon insisted that his attitude to Arafat was unchanged and that he would continue to boycott him. "We know that in war civilians get killed, and we all regret that. But the purpose in war is not to kill civilians. Arafat ordered the killing of civilians—of children, women, old people. That is why I refuse to speak to him."

He made a point, too, of telling the Knesset that Abu Mazen's visit was fully coordinated with the prime minister, who was "very interested" in it taking place. That was a cruel rubbing of salt into the wounded ego of David Levy, who had vociferously protested being left out of the loop, even though, as foreign minister, he was supposed to be running the negotiations with the Palestinians. The dynamic of Levy's discomfiture and eventual displacement by Sharon was already under way.

A month later, in August 1997, Sharon met with the U.S. peace envoy, Dennis Ross, in Jerusalem, at the specific request of the prime minister. The envoy briefed the minister on the state of ongoing interim negotiations, and Sharon talked about his ideas for the permanent status negotiations. But more important than the substance of their talk was the fact that it took place at all. It was the first time for years that a high-ranking American official sat opposite Sharon, the bogeyman of the Bush-Baker era (and no special favorite of the Clintonites either). More than anything, it signaled that he was on his way back to the heart of the matters that mattered. In November, he was in the White House, sent by Netanyahu to expound to the national security adviser, Sandy Berger, and other key officials on his ideas for eventually parceling the West Bank between the two nations.

He knew full well, he told his American hosts, that his original "enclaves" scheme was no longer relevant, in the wake of the Oslo

Accords. He knew the Palestinians needed contiguity, and he believed that he could provide it, with tunnels, bridges, and overpasses. He knew above all, he said, that a Palestinian state was inevitable. He wanted, therefore, to reach "strategic understandings" with the United States on the size and nature of the security zones that Israel would need to keep, and also on key issues like water resources. An unnamed senior American official was quoted in the Israeli press as saying that Sharon had left an impression in Washington of "moderation and pragmatism."[3]

He was working hard, mainly on himself, to create the same impression in the eyes of the political community back home. "In the past, he was often to be heard voicing uncomplimentary comments on the prime minister's performance," wrote Yossi Verter, *Haaretz*'s political reporter, with his customary understatement. "Not anymore."[4] But Sharon could still not resist an occasional swipe even in his new role as Bibi's loyal and devoted elder minister. "A few days ago," he told delegates at the Likud Party conference in November, "the prime minister said to me, 'There'll be a tough fight at conference. I'll need your help.' And I replied, 'That's a bit difficult, because I don't know whether to help your right hand or your left hand.' " The audience roared with laughter. The ministers on the dais smirked and guffawed. The reporters on the side chortled. Only Netanyahu seemed nonplussed and grinned awkwardly. The phrase became an instant perennial, still trotted out whenever Netanyahu's famous indecisiveness is up for discussion.[5]

"Bibi confided to me his view," wrote Dennis Ross, the American peace envoy, "that a leader can never afford to give up 'his tribe'—those who are fiercely loyal to him, who identify with him because of shared roots, long-standing ties, and emotional connections. Bibi never figured out how to reconcile his ambition to be a historic peacemaker with the reality of his political tribe, which did not believe peace with the Palestinians was possible, and were certainly not prepared to pay the price that a test of peace might entail."[6]

Some would say that was too charitable a reading of the tribe and of the leader who strung along the Americans for years and ultimately chose the shortsighted pretensions of this tribe over the nation's crucial long-term interests. Sharon, at any rate, became his prime minister's close ally during 1997–1999, both in stringing along Ross and his bosses in Washington and in trying to have it both ways with the Likud's political base back home.

The Americans understood that Netanyahu's preference was to cede nothing and play for time. They hoped, nevertheless, that they could engage the other side of his conflicted political persona, the side that craves success. After the Meshal affair, the Clinton administration was intent on seeing Netanyahu pursue the implementation of Oslo II, the Interim Agreement, which Rabin had concluded and Netanyahu had ratified but which remained a dead letter in regard to its provision for three further redeployments (FRDs) by Israel on the West Bank. The second of these FRDs was due to have been carried out in September 1997, but the first remained unimplemented.

Coincidentally, and conveniently for Sharon, the timing coincided with David Levy's resignation from the Foreign Ministry. Levy had been moving steadily leftward on both domestic and foreign policy and increasingly chafing at Netanyahu. Now he chose to quit over an evolving state budget that he found far too tough on low-paid working people. Netanyahu made no immediate move to replace him at the Foreign Ministry, but Sharon quickly became the leading candidate, at least in his own eyes. He stepped up his public praise of Netanyahu.

There now followed a long period of months during which Sharon performed the most elaborate minuet, dancing between the ostensibly—but only ostensibly—irreconcilable positions of loudly opposing a double-FRD from 13 percent of the West Bank and quietly intimating that he could in fact live with it, *if* he became the foreign minister who negotiated it. Thirteen percent became the line behind which the Americans decided to dig in, after being pushed steadily back by Netanyahu from the original 20 to teens and then to low teens. It was fairly arbitrary, but they had lined up the Palestinians beside them, and they did not intend to budge.

The crunch came in the fall of 1998, when the Americans issued invitations to the two sides to attend a summit conference in order, at last, to wrap up the FRDs. The hard Right in Netanyahu's coalition threatened open rebellion. The government was in imminent danger of collapse. Netanyahu finally played his ace: Sharon would be foreign minister. He would be responsible henceforth for the peace process with the Palestinians. And, as a fast-working analgesic for the hard-liners' angst, Sharon would join the Israeli delegation to the conference. Sharon for his part was still publicly proclaiming his opposition to 13 percent. The implication was that he would carry the fight to the summit. "Tie us up, hand and foot!" he demanded of the cabinet.

On October 14, 1998, the day before the summit was to begin at the Wye River Plantation conference center in Maryland, Sharon's appointment was formally approved by the cabinet. He flew off after the prime minister to the United States, first to visit King Hussein at the Mayo Clinic, then on to Wye, where he arrived near midnight on the fourth day of the conference. President Clinton asked to meet with him alone, and they sat until nearly two o'clock in the morning. It was the first time they had met, and plainly the American side hoped that Sharon, now that he had achieved his ambition to get back into the center of policy making, would prove an asset in the negotiations.

Sharon's foremost concern at this relatively early stage of a conference that was to distend into a nine-day marathon was to impress upon the public back home the firmness of his determination not to shake hands with Arafat. No requirements of pomp or protocol attaching to his new office would weaken his resolve. This ultimately non-substantive issue consumed him, and the Israeli media, to an obsessive degree—given, after all, that Sharon had pressed so hard, and for so long, to get into the room where decisions were made and where Arafat sat and talked with Israel's leaders.

Talking, as distinct from shaking hands, was kosher in the new foreign minister's book. The very next evening he participated in a dinner that Clinton gave for the senior delegates and held forth expansively to the Palestinian leader on farming and animal husbandry. This, however, as the Israeli press breathlessly reported, was after he had demonstratively ignored Arafat's gesture of greeting as he entered the room—"General Sharon," Netanyahu announced to the assembled company by way of introduction—and dexterously contrived to shake the hands of Abu Mazen, Abu Ala, and Nabil Shaath while avoiding that of Arafat.

The Palestinians, in their briefings, grandly dismissed Sharon's antics. The *rais*'s gesture, they said, far from obsequious, was intended to convey the thought that Sharon had tried to crush him in Beirut, yet here he was, sixteen years later, the American president's honored guest—and Sharon's negotiating partner.[7] Beneath the posturing, though, Arafat was hurt, and he harped on it long after in conversation with his intimates.[8] Arafat's own behavior had been the opposite of churlish. Sharon had asked Arafat, through a reliably discreet middleman, not to overly decry or condemn his appointment as foreign minister and not to boycott him. And sure enough, the Palestinians' public reaction to Sharon's appointment was the least strident of all the Arab states. Arafat himself made do with an anodyne observation that this was an internal Israeli matter. In private conversations with the Americans, the Palestinians pointed to the potentially favorable effect of Sharon's appointment, if indeed he and Netanyahu intended to push through the FRDs. "The time for moderate leaders will come later," the Palestinians told their American interlocutors.[9]

"The Wye River Memorandum," as it was called, provided for a 13 percent first-and-second FRD. All of it was to be from Area C to Areas A and B, as the Palestinians and the Americans had insisted. "Everyone was euphoric," Dennis Ross wrote, recalling the predawn moment when the draft was finally approved. But it didn't last. "The President and Bibi were sitting alone; no smiles, only stern looks. They were barely talking, and Bibi looked positively stricken." The hiccup that seriously threatened to choke the euphoria was Jonathan Jay Pollard, the U.S. Navy analyst turned Israeli spy who had now served thirteen years of his life sentence. Earlier in the year, Netanyahu had formally recognized—he was the first prime minister to do so—that Pollard had spied for Israel. Now he wanted the president to pardon the spy as part of the Wye package, which included Israel's release of 750 Palestinian prisoners. Clinton's CIA chief urged him to resist.

In the event, Netanyahu caved. Sharon was around throughout this frantic eleventh-hour drama. Some reports later said he thought Netanyahu should hold out for Pollard even at the expense of the accord.[10] But the bottom line is that over Pollard, as over the accord itself with its 13 percent FRD, Sharon at the end of the day acquiesced and gave the prime minister his political support.

Yet even in this long-desired position in the prime minister's intimate proximity, Sharon still managed to keep dancing his two-directional minuet. He was foreign minister, he had been a key negotiator at Wye, he advocated and defended the accord, yet now he urged the settlers to move swiftly and unilaterally to seize lands adjacent to their settlements as a way of warding off the dangers of Wye. In point of fact, only three disused outposts were to be dismantled under Wye. Yet Sharon told a group of settlement leaders on November 15 that they should push out the boundaries of their settlements without asking or waiting for official approval.

They needed no further encouragement. In the months that followed, spurred on by Sharon, by their determination to thwart Wye, and finally by their sense that the rightist government was about to fall, the settlers grabbed "hilltop after hilltop . . . Within a few weeks, new settlements were established, one after another, unhindered. Netanyahu was fighting for his political life and needed the settlers' votes. The settlers scorned the IDF Civil Administration officials who tried to enforce the law. 'You will not be able to stop us; we have help from on high,' they said. In at least four cases, Netanyahu ordered that

Civil Administration inspectors who came to evacuate the settlements be stopped."[11]

Sharon hosted Mahmoud Abbas (Abu Mazen) at the Foreign Ministry in Jerusalem for what was billed as a first preview of the permanent status negotiations. Sharon brimmed with bonhomie, his aide Tomer Orni recalled. The Palestinians, he said, must "jump ahead" economically. It was completely untenable—and made peacemaking veritably impossible—that the Palestinian GDP per capita was a mere fraction of Israel's. He suggested that the two of them, together, visit the model Israeli high-tech industrial park at Tefen in the Galilee, near Abbas's birthplace at Safed. Sharon himself was looking into a vast desalination project in the sea near Gaza. Why didn't he and Abbas go together to the United States to seek funding? They must meet frequently to promote these ideas, to create economic interdependency between Israel and the PA and thus deepen both sides' stake in peace.[12]

The brilliantly gifted literary critic Yoram Bronowski, who wrote subtle and cruel television reviews for *Haaretz,* seized on Sharon's facial tic, long a favorite prop of Israeli comics and cartoonists, to illustrate the inconsistency of his positions at this time. In a television interview soon after Wye, Bronowski noted, the whole comportment of the foreign minister seemed to broadcast the "inner conflict in which he finds himself. Thus, the 'best' agreement is also a 'dangerous' agreement. He didn't 'applaud Arafat,' he merely 'stood up and clapped, like everyone else.' As he said these things, his nose seemed to move, like in children's stories, in the opposite direction from his mouth. For a moment, it seemed to be growing longer, or at least to be denying its owner's words . . . Is it possible that his lips will vote in favor, while his nose, or his ears, vote against?"[13]

In the event, the Knesset vote went smoothly, and the first phase of the Wye Agreement was duly implemented on Friday, November 20, 1998, in the area around Jenin. Territory comprising 2 percent of the West Bank was transferred from Area C status to Area B, and a further 7.2 percent from Area B to Area A.

The next phase of the withdrawal was scheduled for December 14. It did not happen. As November ended, Palestinian demonstrations in the West Bank and especially in East Jerusalem in favor of prisoner release grew daily more violent. On December 2, Netanyahu and his inner cabinet—by now seriously beleaguered by rightist political allies turned critics—resolved that further withdrawal would be conditional on Arafat calling off the prisoner campaign, taking effective action against incitement, and committing not to issue a unilateral declaration of independence. The Palestinians balked. None of this was in

Wye, they said. It was all pretexts dredged up by Israel to avoid with-drawing and to provoke a crisis just as Clinton was due to visit Gaza and make a historic appearance before the Palestinian parliament. Ministers still loyal to Netanyahu, meanwhile, feeling their cabinet seats increasingly wobbly beneath them, began muttering about why Clinton needed to come in the first place. His visit would only deepen the fissures within the coalition. Sharon was hastily dispatched to Washington to try, somehow, to hold things together.

The irony of the former persona non grata now reappearing in the U.S. capital on a mending mission was not lost on either side. In an unscheduled meeting with Clinton himself, Sharon turned on all his charm and effusive good manners to while away the time on anything and everything—other than the scheduled next withdrawal. He had brought with him a tasteful gift for the president, which he spent pre-cious minutes elaborately bestowing. "If Clinton asked himself after-ward what happened," a senior Israeli diplomat recalled, "he would have answered that Sharon set out to avoid the issue—but he'd have had to admit that he did it elegantly!"[14]

By the time Clinton arrived in Gaza on December 13, 1998, at the head of a large delegation, both the Israeli coalition and the Wye Accords were in parlous condition. Netanyahu and Sharon tried to confine their bickering with the Americans to whether the Palestin-ian parliament needed to vote for the abrogation of the PLO Charter or whether an acclamation would suffice. But in the end they had to admit to Clinton that they would need "a brief respite" before proceed-ing with the next withdrawal, even if the session in Gaza passed off satisfactorily. There were many other issues, they claimed, on which the Palestinians were not living up to their Wye commitments. Sec-retary of State Madeleine Albright argued back; the president barely shrugged. Plainly, he had given up the ghost as far as this Israeli gov-ernment was concerned.

The meeting of the Palestinian parliament in Gaza proved an emo-tional and memorable event. The members, duly responding to Arafat's request, approved almost unanimously his letter to Clinton abrogating the offensive provisions of the Palestinian National Covenant. Clin-ton's sensitive and finely honed rhetoric moved everyone present and the millions who watched on television. The Palestinians, he declared, were "free to determine their own destiny on their own land." He spoke of the Palestinian "history of dispossession and dispersal" and praised the parliament's act of abrogation. His appearances in Israel, especially at a school in Jerusalem, elicited an outpouring of warmth from the public there, too. But the diplomacy remained paralyzed.

Once Clinton left the region, the collapse of the coalition quickened. Rumors swirled around Sharon again: Would he bid for the leadership? At a low-key and unhappy session of the Likud central committee on December 26, Sharon proclaimed categorically, "I don't want to be prime minister . . . I object to these incessant attacks on the prime minister that haven't let up from the day he took office . . . I myself always knew when to stop. I always stopped when the government was in danger of falling." Two days later, Likud and Labor jointly announced a date for elections: May 17, 1999. The 140-day limbo period, plus the time it would take to form the new government after the election, was in line with the Israeli political tradition, where governments take a very long time between their death and their burial.

MINGLING

For Ariel Sharon, it was to be time well spent. Few people today, even inside Israeli politics, remember that he served as foreign minister; he left no lasting mark on this prestigious but often overrated portfolio. He hardly could, given that for his entire tenure he represented a government collapsing or collapsed. But it left its mark on him.

Eytan Bentsur, a long-serving professional diplomat whom Sharon kept on as director general of the ministry, was subsequently to develop deep reservations over Sharon's policies as prime minister and profound distaste for his ethical conduct and for the coterie of friends and advisers who surrounded him.* Nevertheless, Bentsur was full of praise for Sharon's performance at the Foreign Ministry. "He was a man you could talk to. He would encourage everyone to speak freely. There was no dogmatism about him. And he was really easy, pleasant actually, to work with. He didn't throw his weight around."

According to his chief of bureau, Tomer Orni, Sharon took his appointment as foreign minister with great seriousness and embarked on a round of briefings and conversations with policy experts from across the spectrum, scribbling furiously in his little orange notebooks as though their analyses of the conflict and the region were all new to him. "He saw the Foreign Ministry as his preparation for the prime ministership—regardless of the slender political prospects, as he and everyone knew, that he would ever actually make it to prime minister."

Despite the diplomatic chill, Sharon did manage to set up one

---

* See p. 366.

lengthy, unpublicized meeting with Abu Ala, the senior PA official who negotiated the Oslo Accords. It took place at his ranch in late January 1999. Abu Ala drove down from Jerusalem incognito. Sharon had a log fire blazing in the hearth, Lily served cookies, and the atmosphere was relaxed and friendly. The host let the guest into a home truth. "For making war," Sharon explained, "Israel needs a left-wing government. But for making peace, there has to be a nationalist government." The election campaign was by no means over, he said, and the shape of the new government was unpredictable. Abu Ala said the PA had resolved to do nothing that could be perceived as intervening against the Likud. That was his message from Arafat. The *rais,* he said, respected Sharon as a man of his word.

What they should do, Sharon continued, was to forget the elections and get on with the peace process. Let's take a specific issue, he suggested, and work on it. For instance, the "safe passage" route that was to link Gaza and the West Bank. Abu Ala said the Palestinians wanted that to be extraterritorial. Sharon said Israel would never agree. Abu Ala recounted his own humiliating experiences at Israeli army roadblocks. Sharon voiced anger at the soldiers' behavior and sympathy for the Palestinians. He spoke of the danger of terrorism triggering a cycle of violence that could engulf the region. Abu Ala said he, Abu Mazen, and Arafat himself were potential terror targets. The dialogue flowed back and forth with ease. Abu Ala contributed to the ambience by making no mention of Sharon's call to the settlers to grab the hilltops.

Sharon had returned the night before from a trip to Russia, the first of three he was to make there during his short spell as foreign minister. The frequency of his flights to Moscow raised eyebrows, especially in light of an ill-advised visit he had made to Russia as minister of infrastructures in June 1997 that had since mushroomed into the latest of his uncomfortable brushes with the law. That indiscretion (at best) involved his relations with one of the businessmen who accompanied him: Avigdor Ben-Gal, chairman of the government-owned Israeli Aircraft Industries (IAI), director of the government-owned Tahal water company, would-be entrepreneur, former army general, longtime critic of Sharon's running of the Lebanon War, and, by coincidence or not, a witness soon to give evidence for the defendant in Sharon's libel suit against *Haaretz.*[*]

Ben-Gal took part in meetings between Sharon and high Rus-

---

[*] See p. 236.

sian officials where a projected pipeline project was discussed that would transport natural gas from Georgia to Turkey and on, under the Mediterranean, to Israel. Ben-Gal made no secret of his desire to be involved in this lucrative venture. Sharon, despite their years of strained relations, introduced him as the IAI chairman and a military hero. A fortnight after they returned to Israel, Ben-Gal testified in the trial. He said that a lecture he had given ten years earlier, in which he accused Sharon of misleading Begin in the war, had been "nonsense and rubbish," based on information he had since learned was completely groundless. Lawyers for *Haaretz* lodged a criminal complaint against him, alleging a gas-for-evidence bribery deal.

The attorney general ordered a police inquiry. In the months that followed, Sharon, Ben-Gal, and many others spent long hours in police interrogation rooms. On April 30, 1999, almost two years after the events, and, as so often in Sharon's corruption cases, just days before the election, reports leaked out that the police were recommending that Sharon be indicted for bribery, perjury, suborning a witness, and a string of lesser charges. In the event—after the election—Attorney General Elyakim Rubinstein and State Attorney Edna Arbel decided to close the file for lack of evidence. "In a case based solely on circumstantial evidence," Rubinstein wrote, "the test is whether the evidence leads to only one logical conclusion. This case, in our opinion, does not pass the test."*

In the end, no pipeline was built, and Israel continued to buy its natural gas from Egypt and, later, from its own offshore fields. But Sharon's drive to expand Israel's relations with Russia was undaunted by this disappointment, or indeed by the waves of ugly speculation that now accompanied his sallies to Moscow. "Russia is a superpower," he told Minister of Foreign Affairs Igor Ivanov on the January visit. "I have no doubt you will overcome your present difficulties and resume the global role which is properly yours." He portrayed himself to his hosts as a proud and consistent Russophile with a fair knowledge of the language—he made a point of correcting the interpreters—and a love for the culture that he had absorbed from his mother.

Plainly, he had one eye on the large ex-Soviet immigrant constituency at home. He would make a point of beginning his diplomatic meetings, and especially those in Russia, with the declaration: "I am a Jew. First and foremost a Jew. That to me is the most important thing."

---

* The judge in the libel action was less finicky. In his judgment for *Haaretz*, given in November 1997, he described Ben-Gal's appearance on the witness stand as "a sorry sight about which the less said the better."

"On his first visit to Moscow in January," Orni recalled, "he began in this way with the president of the Duma, Gennadiy Seleznyov, and added: 'I have come here to talk about the Jewish people.' " There had been some ugly instances of anti-Semitism in the parliament, and he waded in straightaway. "With the defense minister, Marshal Igor Sergeyev, he made the same 'Jewish' opening and went on to praise the Red Army's role in 'destroying the Nazi beast' and spoke of the many Jews who fought with distinction in its ranks." To Prime Minister Yevgeny Primakov, Sharon asserted that the million Russian immigrants in Israel were "a bridge of friendship" between the two countries. He had called on the Jews in Russia to continue to immigrate to Israel, he said, and he hoped to see a million more. Primakov replied diplomatically that they necessarily differed on this matter, since Russia was a multicultural society and, from his perspective, there was no need for the Jews to leave. However, he added, the government would "not interfere with anyone who wants to go, though we won't encourage it either."

Bentsur, the director general, also emphasized Sharon's "extraordinary sensitivity to the Jewish dimension" of Israeli policy making. "One time, for instance, I was asked to fly to Vienna to meet representatives of the Hungarian Jewish community. They seriously feared an explosion of fascistic anti-Semitism in their country. I remember Sharon phoned me in Vienna to ask for details. I felt his concern was totally sincere. He would expound on the themes of Jewish suffering and Jewish rights in every diplomatic conversation. He saw Israel, and indeed he saw himself, as the guardian of Jewish interests worldwide."[15]

While Iran, the Israel-Palestine conflict, and anti-Semitism were the issues that took up most of the talks, it was Sharon's maverick stance on the Balkan conflict that attracted most attention, both at home and in Washington. Sharon stood out in his unconcealed preference for the Serbs, who were backed by their traditional ally—Russia. Urged by his professional staff at the Foreign Ministry to join his voice to worldwide condemnation of the Serbs, he agreed only to a general and vaguely worded condemnation of all aggression against innocent persons. "Today bad things are being done to the Albanians; not long ago bad things were done to the Serbs."

Sharon's reasoning was complex. First, there was the memory, still very much alive among some Israelis, of the Serbian people's support for persecuted Jews during the Nazi Holocaust, a distinct rarity among the nations of Europe. Then there was his basic belief that

Israel needed to improve its relations with Russia. Beyond that, Sharon urged Israeli policy makers to look to the future: if armed intervention by outside powers to enforce a solution to a regional conflict was legitimate in one part of the world, it would be legitimate in other parts of the world. Israel could become a future victim of such legitimacy.

Netanyahu tried to stand behind Washington while at the same time not falling out with Sharon on the eve of the election. His office formally announced that Israel supported the NATO bombing. Sharon still tried to have it both ways. "As loyal friends of the U.S.," a Foreign Ministry statement said, "we expect U.S. and NATO forces to do everything to end the sufferings of innocent people and bring about a resumption of negotiations between the parties as soon as possible." But the Americans were in no mood to appreciate minor ameliorations in what they saw as Sharon's treacherous position. Secretary Albright made him sweat when he visited Washington in March 1999. "It makes me wonder," she observed sarcastically, "that Israel is not fully supportive of the United States in Kosovo. To tell you the truth, I'm shocked."

Unbowed by this drubbing, Sharon flew on to Moscow, where he basked in the glow of his self-arrogated status of global fixer. He assured Prime Minister Primakov that he had spoken in Washington on Russia's behalf to Stanley Fischer at the International Monetary Fund and to James Wolfensohn at the World Bank, and he hoped a loan would be forthcoming. As for Mrs. Albright, "you will be happy to know that she really likes you. It made me almost jealous."

Primakov praised Sharon for his position on Kosovo, "which is not like that of Netanyahu." Sharon, at his most statesmanlike, suggested that the Americans wanted Russia's help in reaching a solution in Kosovo. "They're pushing us into a corner," Primakov replied grumpily. Sharon said Russia could improve its international image and standing if it would only speak out publicly against the atrocities. "Women are raped there daily, and you don't say anything. It's not my business. I'm just telling you my impression."

Plainly, Sharon enjoyed his time as foreign minister. He was cold-shouldered by some world statesmen; Britain's foreign secretary, Robin Cook, was one notable example. But others were cordial enough, and with one in particular, Germany's foreign minister, Joschka Fischer, Sharon built a warm relationship. His enjoyment was clouded, however, by the start of Lily's battle with cancer. She was diagnosed in February 1999. Sharon devotedly accompanied her to examinations and treatment in Israel and the United States.

· · ·

Sharon's last trip to Moscow as foreign minister was originally scheduled to coincide with a visit to the Russian capital by Hafez Assad, the president of Syria. As it happened, Assad canceled due to ill health. Sharon urged his Russian hosts to work urgently in order to bring Israel and Syria to the negotiating table—at least according to Ze'ev Schiff, the respected defense analyst. Writing in *Haaretz* during Sharon's visit, Schiff asserted that the foreign minister was proposing to the Russians an immediate mediation that would lead to Israel's withdrawal from the Golan Heights in two stages in return for a full peace treaty with long-term security arrangements on the Heights.[16] Sharon flatly denied Schiff's report. The story, he insisted, was a complete fabrication.

Schiff, who died in 2007, was not one to fabricate stories. Soon after the 1999 election, he exposed in *Haaretz* in elaborate detail a long and intricate pattern of secret talks that Netanyahu had conducted with Syria, through middlemen, almost throughout his term. An EU envoy, an Omani minister, and the American Jewish businessman and public figure Ronald Lauder had all shuttled assiduously between Netanyahu and Assad in separate back-channel efforts to broker a deal.[17]

Three days after this account appeared, Sharon asserted, in a speech to the Likud Party branch in the West Bank settlement town of Ariel, that it was actually he who had prevented Netanyahu from relinquishing the Golan Heights. It was his vigorous intervention, Sharon asserted, that thwarted Netanyahu's intention to send Assad, through the middleman, a detailed withdrawal map.[18]

The most intensive mediation effort, through Lauder, apparently took place during August–September 1998.[19] It was this effort that Sharon claimed to have thwarted. Netanyahu, however, vehemently denied it. His voice thick with contempt, he insisted that Sharon played no role at all:

> QUESTION: Sharon claimed the credit for stopping you from signing away the Golan Heights.
> NETANYAHU: That's false. We had a series of contacts with Hafez Assad that actually Sharon didn't even know about.
> QUESTION: When he became foreign minister?
> NETANYAHU: No, I don't think he knew about them. I don't think he knew. He was not involved in any of the negotiations. It was done between me and the Defense Ministry and that's it. I don't remember ever bringing him to the conversations.[20]

Both Netanyahu's version and Sharon's are disputed in every particular by the then defense minister, Moshe Arens, who was appointed to the post (this was his third stint) in January 1999.

ARENS: I had my suspicions about [Sharon] because when I got into Bibi's government, [I learned] that these guys had been maneuvering to make a treaty with Hafez Assad. There was only one way to make a treaty with Hafez Assad, right?

QUESTION: Give back the Golan.

ARENS: Give back the Golan!

QUESTION: Bibi claims that Sharon never knew, right to the end.

ARENS: Not true. That's not true. And it wasn't Sharon who stopped him.

QUESTION: Who stopped him?

ARENS: Well, first of all he never got to sit down with Hafez Assad. Anyway, I could see that Sharon was in on this deal.

QUESTION: Sharon was in on this deal?

ARENS: I knew he was. Of course he was . . . When I got into the government, he knew about it. Bibi couldn't do a thing like that without Sharon knowing it. Sharon was a very dominant figure. Sharon talked to me about it. I said giving up the Golan is a crazy idea. But he wasn't totally averse to it. He didn't sound dead set against it. He asked me what I thought.

QUESTION: Bibi said he never knew.

ARENS: Of course he knew. It's a lie.[21]

CHAPTER 12 · SUMMIT

The hope of peace for us Israelis lies in the principle of separation between the Palestinians and ourselves. I feel it is my solemn duty to warn my country at this time: If, heaven forbid, Israel fails in the coming years to implement this crucial principle of separation from our Palestinian neighbors—preferably by agreement, otherwise unilaterally—then it will be putting in mortal danger not only the security of its citizens but its very essence as a Jewish and a democratic state."

Ariel Sharon's investiture as prime minister, on March 7, 2001, was such a captivating political and human drama that the packed Knesset had no mind for the parting words of his discomfited predecessor. Yet within three years, Ehud Barak's message would ring prophetic. It seemed to have portended Sharon's momentous act of unilateral disengagement from the Gaza Strip. Did Sharon recognize the man he ousted as a source of his inspired if ham-fisted lunge at implementing the "principle of separation"? If he did, he certainly never articulated such recognition. Probably he never articulated it even to himself.

But there had been something so uncharacteristically considerate and respectful in Sharon's relationship toward the soon-floundering and desperate Barak through the nineteen tortured months of his magnificent but mad prime ministership that the tempting conclusion is that he, at least, was listening to the younger man. Listening, and thinking hard. Otherwise, how to explain his constant striving, as leader of the Likud opposition, to enter a national unity government under the Labor prime minister who was single-mindedly trying to dump the Golan Heights, the Gaza Strip, and almost all of the West Bank—all the occupied territories that the Likud has sworn to keep? Would Menachem Begin have countenanced a unity government under this Labor Party leader, whose policies had become those of the hated and despised Peace Now? Would Yitzhak Shamir? They would have tongue-lashed Barak as a military hero turned political coward. Granted, Sharon, too, tongue-lashed him. Granted, too, Sharon insisted that if there were to be a unity government, it would have to be under different policy guidelines. But how different? Sharon's own evolving ideas of what might be an acceptable unity platform seemed increasingly remote from the Likud's pristine doctrines.

Granted, politicians and pundits all knew that the autocratic Labor prime minister and the ersatz, temporary, fortuitous, short-term leader of the Likud—for that is how everyone saw Sharon—both never took their eyes off Bibi. The polls all told the same story: during the early months of Barak's prime ministership, Netanyahu was the only rightist politician who could have given him a reasonable fight. As Barak's popularity declined, Netanyahu alone was shown beating him while all other Likud possibles still lost to him. Only toward the end of Barak's tumultuous term, when it became clear that Netanyahu would not run against him, did Barak begin to lose to Sharon in the polls.

The stop-Bibi theory behind the Barak-Sharon axis was much too strong to deny. And yet it was not strong enough to fully account for the political behavior of Barak and Sharon, individually and as a mutually desired, never consummated unity partnership. Barak, his ego as vast as his ambition—and as his political and interpersonal ineptness—swept into power determined to make peace at one fell swoop with Syria and Lebanon to the north and with the Palestinians to the east (the West Bank) and west (Gaza). He believed he could do it and brusquely dismissed anyone who thought he couldn't.

Sharon thought he could. Almost fatalistically, Sharon, now leader of the opposition, anticipated Barak negotiating a peace treaty with Syria and running with it for reelection. He was convinced during the Camp David summit (July 2000), and then during the negotiations that followed its collapse, that Barak would eventually sign a permanent status accord with Yasser Arafat, the Palestinian leader, and that the majority of the Israeli public would support it. Sharon did not believe he could prevent it. Rather, as with Rabin's Oslo Accords, he believed his historic task was to improve it, to mitigate damage and avert danger by helping negotiate the details and the implementation—even while maintaining, rhetorically at least, his fundamental opposition to the far-reaching concessions on which these agreements were to be founded.

On the face of it, the Sharon-Barak relationship lacked the special intimacy that fueled the Sharon-Rabin connection. The two of them had not, after all, "eaten from the same mess tin." And yet, in a way, they had, despite the generation gap. "Ehud Barak is a courageous soldier," Sharon made a point of saying, not once, but many times in the course of their relatively brief political rivalry. And Barak had served under Sharon's command in the Yom Kippur War.* Barak's courage was an objective fact. He was the IDF's most decorated soldier. But Sharon was not usually generous with his compliments to politicians, especially in matters that he really cared about, like battles and bravery. There was a special relationship here, too, and it transcended the political divide.

In the crowded Knesset that afternoon in March 2001, Barak continued with his meticulously prepared parting speech: "An Israel that controls a little less territory but that has clearly defined borders, and lives within those borders with a solid Jewish majority and with confidence in its character, its purpose, and the justice of its cause—an Israel like that would be stronger and more secure than an Israel which continues to bleed in steadily worsening demographic chaos, and in steadily deepening international isolation."

If he had talked like that to the Israeli public, boldly and honestly, when he was prime minister and people were listening to him, Barak might still have been prime minister. But that was pointless hand-wringing over profound character flaws in a leader who never really understood the political process in a parliamentary democracy, then or later. The "peace camp," the taste of missed opportunity acrid on its tongue, braced to face life under the man it had deprecated and feared for decades. The Knesset Speaker, Avrum Burg, a leading dove who was injured by the grenade that killed Emil Grunzweig in the anti-Sharon demonstration in 1983, did signal service to the country that day when he declared: "I address the leaders of the world, in the name of the Knesset of Israel, which represents all of the people of

---

* Barak says Sharon was directly responsible for his promotion to general, against the wishes of the then chief of staff, Rafael Eitan.

He virtually imposed it on him. How do I explain that? It was to do with how he first came across me, back in 1962. I was a second lieutenant in Sayeret Matkal [the elite IDF commando unit]. One of the things the Sayeret used to do by way of training was to infiltrate IDF bases without getting caught. We would try to penetrate the operations center of a heavily guarded military installation, or to raid the commanding officer's quarters, break into his safe, remove the contents, and leave without trace. One of my first assignments was Training Camp No. 3, near Netanya, commanded by Colonel Arik Sharon, then still "in exile" after the 1956 Mitle Pass saga. With a small squad of men I headed for the commander's office, slipped in, cleared out the safe—and left a note in handwriting to his bureau chief, a girl I knew. Arik was pretty gobsmacked in the morning. He wanted to meet the guy who did it, and that's how he first got to know me. (Ehud Barak interview, Tel Aviv, July 2006)

Israel, and I say: From this moment forth, let the world know, and let us know—this is the legitimately elected prime minister of Israel. Right or wrong, he is our prime minister, and no man other than he will henceforth decide who rules in Jerusalem and who speaks for Israel in the capitals of the world." For Barak, though no friend, Burg had sage words, too. "History," he said, "will without doubt render a more generous judgment than the voter has just done."

The excitement was so great in the house that not only did the outgoing prime minister's prophetic words go unnoticed but Sharon's speech, too, barely impacted on the collective consciousness of the members and guests. Peace, he said, was going to involve "painful compromises on both sides." The new government, which would be a Likud-Labor unity partnership (but with Likud's rightist partners in it, too, and without Barak, who was quitting public life), would seek "realistic arrangements" with the Palestinians on the way to that final, painful peace. He had used the same word—"painful"—during the election campaign. It was hardly vintage Sharon and was vaguely disturbing for the hard-line Right. But it sounded noncommittal enough for them not to worry about it unduly.

Twenty-two months earlier, on May 18, 1999, Ofir Akunis would have bet his bottom dollar that that scene in the Knesset would never, ever be enacted. "I wasn't 90 percent sure that Bibi would be back," the young Likud Knesset member, then the party's spokesman, recalled. "I was 99 percent sure. So were all of us. And if it wasn't to be Bibi, for whatever reason, then there were younger-generation figures who were jostling for attention. Silvan Shalom, Limor Livnat, Tzachi Hanegbi. All of them looked more likely candidates than Sharon." That near-certain assessment, Akunis explained, was what moved the stricken party leaders on the day after the election defeat and the scene at the Hilton hotel to offer Sharon the temporary leadership.

Sharon's chief advantage, in the eyes of his ambitious comrades, was his age. By the time the next election was held—presumably, given the size and confidence of Barak's coalition, in 2003—he would be seventy-five, hardly the age for a first run at the prime ministership. This comfortable calculation led the Likud leaders to a seemingly logical deduction: Sharon wouldn't want to run in the primaries for permanent chairman of the party and prime ministerial candidate.

The comrades should have sensed that something was amiss in their calculations when it quickly became clear that their temporary chairman was indeed contemplating the prospect of running for permanent chairman, or alternatively of somehow extending his temporary chair-manship into a permanence-like limbo. The nineteen members of the sadly reduced Likud Knesset faction,* convening on June 1 to discuss "lessons of our election defeat," were surprised and bemused to hear from Sharon that he would probably compete in the primaries. Wasn't he a bit old, somebody ventured bravely. Sharon rounded on him, at his most caustically sarcastic. "I don't suggest," he growled, "that we run in the primaries waving our birth certificates. In general, it's not a good idea to wave one's birth certificate. Rather, I say—wave your certificates of achievements."[1]

Despite Sharon's repeated protestations that his grandmothers lived deep into old age and that the genes therefore were on his side, age became a key theme in the race. To parry the crass ageism emanating from his two younger rivals, Ehud Olmert (fifty-three) and Meir Shee-trit (fifty), Sharon proposed, and managed to push through the central committee, a resolution that the Likud would hold another leadership primary before the next general election. The main task of the leader elected now, therefore, would be to rebuild the party after its defeat. Rebuilding needed internal peace and harmony. Sharon, solid and experienced, was the man best capable of providing them.

Sharon had another advantage: his warm personal relationship with Barak. Granted, Olmert was on good terms, too, with the Labor prime minister. But the Sharon-Barak nexus was different. Sharon, it was felt within the still shell-shocked party, might well lead the Likud into four years of partnership in a unity government under the seemingly unas-sailable Barak. Sharon, it was said, might be minister of finance in this scenario. What remains incontrovertible, at any rate—and needs to be stressed over and over in view of what unfolded less than two years later—is that, whatever Sharon's own inner aspirations, no one else in the party, or indeed in politics in general, seriously contemplated the possibility that Sharon might become prime minister.

Sharon spent most of the primaries campaign on the road. In his large, worn-out Cadillac, the candidate and his aides, sometimes with a journalist in tow, would be out early. "On Monday, he began his day at 5:00 a.m.," wrote Danny Ben-Simon[†] in *Haaretz*.

He toured the far north, stopping in Ma'alot, where he spoke to a group of Russian-immigrant writers and artists, then on to Beit Jan,

---

* Down from thirty-two in the previous election.
† This prominent journalist and social commentator later became a politician him-self: he was elected to the Knesset in 2009 as a member of the Labor Party.

a Druze village near Yokneam, then a meeting with supporters in Migdal Ha'emek, and finally a wedding in the family of a Likud activist. He got back to his ranch after midnight. After four hours' sleep, he was back in his car for another day of hard labor. "Age?" he says, wounded to the quick. "This is the age to begin! What do people want from me? When one sets out to win, age doesn't matter at all."

Everything was going well, until Omri and Uri Shani, the campaign manager, let their hair down—of all places in an interview with a leading *Yedioth Ahronoth* journalist—and said that the armored Cadillac "makes a huge impression on the Indians." There were other pearls in the same genre: "All the Likud activists really care about is jobs and money," and so forth.[2] Senior figures in the party demanded that Shani be sacked. They could hardly demand the same for Omri, but clearly he had fouled the nest. Touring the Mahane Yehuda market in Jerusalem, a famous stronghold of Likud support, later that week, Sharon and his entourage were greeted by large signs: "Indians and Proud of It." The visit was not a success, the renditions of "Arik, king of Israel," less than lusty. Sharon published a statement saying he had "sternly upbraided" the two offenders. "They claim to have said what they said in jest. That, too, is serious. Such sentiments are alien to the Likud, even in jest."

The crisis passed, and Sharon won comfortably, on the first round, with 53 percent of the vote, against 24 percent for Olmert and 22 percent for Sheetrit. "His victory was almost entirely grounded on the support of the Bibi camp," Ofir Akunis recalled. He described a sweaty celebration in the Independence Hall, on the ground floor of the Likud's rather down-at-heel headquarters building in Tel Aviv, Metzudat Ze'ev.* Smiling and relaxed, Sharon reveled in the congratulations of supporters and opponents alike. Lily was there with him, and she, too, was warm and gracious, but she kept fending off well-wishers who tried to kiss or embrace her. She was under treatment for her cancer and had to beware of infection.

It is hard, in light of how fast he fell, to recall how high Barak seemed to be riding when he came into office in 1999, directly elected with a solid popular majority and seemingly myriad possibilities of putting together a stable and cohesive coalition. He was Israel's golden boy. Kibbutz-born, a dashing military career, with brain as well as brawn, just four years in politics and already at the summit, commit-

---

* Literally, Ze'ev's Fortress, after the founder of the Revisionist Party, which eventually evolved into the Likud, Ze'ev Jabotinsky.

ted to making peace, he seemed unstoppable. On election night, a huge crowd gathered at Rabin Square in Tel Aviv, where the man Barak regarded as his mentor had been murdered. Now Barak proposed to take up his bloodstained mantle. People wept openly as he declared, in sonorous tones, with his familiar, not unattractive lisp, "This is the dawn of a new day."

Many in the crowd chorused back at him, "Just not Shas." Shas had become a byword for sleaze. Its leader, Arye Deri, had been convicted of bribery and fraud a month before and sentenced to four years in prison. The trial and conviction, far from deterring voters, had become Shas's election platform. The slogan was "He's innocent!" The result was seventeen seats, by far the highest tally Shas had ever attained.

But Barak, like Rabin before him, recognized the crucial need to include at least one religious party in his peacemaking coalition. The national-religious community had become almost homogeneously hard-line, intimately tied to the settlers. The National Religious Party joined the government at first but was certain to secede as soon as serious peace negotiations began. But the ultra-Orthodox, growing rapidly because of their young marriages and large families, were conflicted between their xenophobic anti-Arabism and the instinctive political moderation of their rabbis. Rabbi Ovadia Yosef, the spiritual leader of Shas, had ruled back in the 1970s that withdrawal from the biblical territories was permissible if it saved lives. Barak was determined to have him at his side as he set out to make peace, as Rabin had when he embarked on Oslo.

Like Rabin, too, Barak proposed to seat Shas ministers at his cabinet table alongside their most strident foes: Meretz. Rabin, hardly a political charmer, had worked overtime to keep that strange couple together. He managed to do so until after Oslo. Barak, socially gauche and an unconcealed misanthrope toward politicians of every stripe, managed to put both parties' backs up almost from the start and eventually lost them both. He started, in fact, with the two ultra-Orthodox parties in his mammoth seventy-five-seat coalition,* but lost the five members of United Torah Judaism that first summer in a gratuitous fight over transporting a large electricity turbine to a power station on the Sabbath.

Barak's political maladroitness might have been mitigated had

---

* Barak's government initially comprised One Israel (Labor), 26; Shas, 17; Meretz, 10; Center Party, 6; National Religious Party, 5; United Torah Judaism, 5; Yisrael B'Aliya, 4; One Nation, 2. In addition, it could count on the votes of the 10 Arab MKs in support of its peace moves.

the new prime minister surrounded himself with politically savvy, smooth-talking aides and used them effectively. He had these in abundance, gifted young people devoted to him, but he managed to set them, too, at each other's throats. The blood on his office carpet never seemed to dry, and he seemed to take peculiar pleasure in shedding more and more of it. The rumor mills began feeding the political gossip columns, and eventually even the languid torpor and sense of resignation enveloping the Likud and its leader began to give way to a vague consciousness that all was far from well on the other side of the aisle.

All the gossip, of course, and all the seepage of political strength would have been stanched had Barak's main order of business—making peace—proceeded satisfactorily. Tragically, though, despite his frenetic activity from the get-go, his grand ambitions on the peace front crashed, too. Ariel Sharon, as his luck would have it, was on hand to pick up the pieces.

"Barak's peace strategy was simple, at least on paper," writes the historian Ahron Bregman. "He would first strike a deal with Syria, then get Israeli troops out of [south] Lebanon . . . then—and only then—turn seriously to the conflict with the Palestinians."[3] Regarding the Palestinians, moreover, Barak proposed a radical change from the incremental strategy of peacemaking prescribed by the Oslo Accords, in which the hardest problems were left till last. Instead, he wanted to achieve a final, comprehensive peace agreement in one fell swoop. "We don't need to waste our time on little issues," Barak told Yasser Arafat when the two leaders met at the Erez checkpoint on the Israel-Gaza border, just days after the new Israeli government was sworn in. The "little issues" were Israel's fulfillment of the Wye agreement.

Such out-of-the-box thinking, although refreshing after three years of Israeli foot-dragging under Netanyahu, set warning bells tinkling among the disappointment-hardened Washington professionals. But Bill Clinton bubbled with enthusiasm. "I'm eager as a kid with a new toy for the meeting I'm going to have with the new Israeli prime minister," he told a Democratic fund-raiser in Florida on July 13.

They met alone in the Oval Office for two and a half hours, without even note takers present. Clinton unhelpfully swelled Barak's ego by telling him, "There are only two people in the world who I know are capable of thinking of the third, fourth and fifth steps, it's you, Ehud, and myself. But you do it better than I do."[4] Later, they flew with their wives to Camp David and stayed up there talking till nearly 3:00 a.m. "It was a night full of hope," Clinton recalled.

An intensive spate of diplomacy unfolded between the frenetic new Israeli premier and the ponderous Syrian president, who had held power in Damascus for more than three decades and whose health was now visibly failing. The difficulty was apparent right from the start: Barak told Clinton he was not prepared to withdraw to the June 4, 1967, line, as Syria demanded, if Syria insisted that that line ran right along the shore of Lake Kinneret.

Clinton tried to narrow the gaps both on the line and on security arrangements. In October, at Barak's urging, Clinton wrote to Assad saying he believed the gaps were bridgeable and stressing that an Israel-Syria agreement would mean a new era in America's relations with Syria. In December, Assad told Secretary Albright in Damascus that he was ready for immediate, high-level talks with Israel without preconditions and was delegating Minister of Foreign Affairs Farouk Shara as his representative. Barak decided that he himself would represent Israel. The talks were set for December 15 at Blair House, the official guest residence opposite the White House.

On December 13, in a hushed and expectant Knesset, Ehud Barak declared with appropriate pathos that peace with Syria and with the Palestinians would be "the apex of the realization of the Zionist vision." He spoke empathetically of the eighteen thousand Israelis living on the Golan. They would face uncertainty as the negotiations went ahead and the pain of sacrifice if the two countries reached agreement. He promised to submit the agreement to a plebiscite. He was confident it would be approved.

The opposition, led by Ariel Sharon, duly performed its constitutional role. But it was a perfunctory performance. "The Golan is not lost," Sharon said, winding up his speech. "Our fight for it is just, and therefore we will prevail. I call from here to all the citizens of Israel who fear for the future: Join our struggle. Together with you we will triumph. Thank you."

Party members knew of Lily's illness and Sharon's long and difficult hours at her side through trips to New York and treatments. "He gave her a lot of time," Akunis recalled. "He was very preoccupied. But beyond that, I had the feeling he was sluggish. The truth is the whole Likud was pretty soporific as an opposition at that time. Sort of groggy, on the ropes."[5]

Another Likud source who sat in on the faction meetings during this period remembers the MKs delicately ignoring Sharon's frequent snoozing. "They weren't troubled," he says, "because they were all basically waiting for Bibi to come back. They didn't really regard Arik as their leader."[6]

As if to dramatize this low, sad period in his life, on December 19 his beloved Sycamore Ranch burned half down to the ground. There was no question of terror or arson; a bird's nest near the chimney top caught fire from sparks flying upward. The roof and upper floor were gutted. A lot of the couple's belongings were lost. They moved into the adjacent home of their son Omri while the long job of rebuilding began.

Despite Barak's still-undented aura of supreme confidence and the sense of resignation that seemed to hang over the Likud, Sharon's expressions of tenacious opposition to withdrawal from the Golan seemed to capture a shift of popular sentiment. Public opinion polls, both those published in the media and those commissioned privately by Barak's bureau, showed that a referendum was by no means a foregone conclusion, after all.

The polls apparently accounted for Barak's exasperating assertion to the Americans, on the eve of the Washington meetings of December 15–17, 1999, that he could focus only on "procedural issues" at this stage and would not agree to meet alone with Shara. "I cannot afford to discuss substance," he explained lamely to Dennis Ross. "The risk of leaks is too great . . . I may be undercut politically and rendered incapable of making the decisions necessary for agreement."[7]

"Barak now had a really serious attack of cold feet," Bregman records. The two delegations reconvened after the Christmas–New Year break at a secluded conference center belonging to the U.S. Fish and Wildlife Service outside Shepherdstown, a small town in West Virginia.

Three days after the conference Akiva Eldar published in *Haaretz*, word for word, an American draft peace treaty submitted to the two sides at Shepherdstown in the strictest secrecy. The document referred in detail to provisions for normalization and security between the countries—the two areas in which Israel had pushed for Syrian concessions—but it fudged the critical borderline question, the key question for Assad that Barak was not prepared to answer. A number of other issues still in dispute were rendered in alternative bracketed texts, one reflecting the Israeli position (I), the other the Syrian (S). The leak of Syria's concessions to Israel without concomitant Israeli concessions, in an Israeli newspaper to boot, confirmed all Assad's suspicions that somehow the Americans and the Israelis were in cahoots. He told Clinton he would not send representatives to another round of talks.

Barak hoped the Israeli public would have learned from the reports out of Shepherdstown that he was driving a tough bargain. But for at least 150,000 demonstrators, gathered on a chilly night in Rabin Square in downtown Tel Aviv just after Shepherdstown ended, that was not the lesson learned. Their placards and their chorused chants made it clear they still felt Barak was about to sell out. Two of Barak's ministers, Natan Sharansky of Yisrael B'Aliya and Yitzhak Levy of the National Religious Party, sat on the dais, alongside opposition politicians and Golan mayors. They had both abstained in the Knesset on December 13. But that was a passive demonstration of displeasure. This was an open act of defiance.

The Palestinian track was also demanding attention. The deadline for implementing the next further redeployment was fast approaching. At a meeting early in January, Arafat asked Barak to include three villages close to Jerusalem among the territories that were to become Area A—that is, wholly Palestinian controlled—in the imminent FRD. The villages were effectively suburbs of the holy city. One of them, Abu Dis, was the site of the Palestinian parliament building, still under construction. Barak didn't say no, which for Arafat was as good as saying yes. In the Knesset, Sharon accused Barak of "lying and cheating, not to the enemy, God forbid, but to our own loyal citizens."[8]

On March 26, Clinton, encouraged by Barak, met with Assad in Geneva. He assured the Syrian leader that Israel now accepted the June 4 line, but Barak wanted to be sure "that Israel retained sovereignty over the water of the Sea of Galilee and the Jordan River and therefore the borderline should not touch either one." Assad, wan and sickly looking, replied: "Then they don't want peace . . . The lake has always been our lake; it was never theirs . . . There were no Jews to the east of the lake."[9] Clinton later recalled Assad saying, "Look, you and I are friends, but there's not gonna be a deal if I don't get to run my feet in the lake." There was no further reason to sit and talk, and after barely an hour the meeting ended.

Sharon followed some of this from his temporary home alongside the fire-ravaged ranch house. Lily was in bed now most of the time, venturing out almost only to go to the hospital for treatment. "A man gets used to living in a beautiful house for twenty-five years, with her touch all over it," he told Amira Lam in Yedioth Ahronoth on March 10. "Every plant and vase, the pictures on the piano, the embroidered towels in the bathroom, the table napkins lovingly folded. I would come home, and the music that we both loved was always playing. I would sit in my armchair, and Lily would pour me a drink, and when I still used to smoke, sometimes she might light me a cigar, and we would sit and talk. We don't have that now, and I really miss those moments."

The interview made poignant yet somehow uncomfortable reading. Poignant, because Lily was lying upstairs as he spoke with the reporter, sinking to her death. Uncomfortable, because he was so frank and almost maudlin, but also because he seemed to be parading, not to say exploiting, his personal sadness on the magazine cover of the country's largest-circulation newspaper. On the other hand, he was leader of the opposition at a crucial time for the country; he legitimately needed to show that he was functioning despite his burden of worry and grief. "I know there is all kinds of talk in the party, that this is affecting my work," he said.

I admit it's hard. But it is not impairing my ability to function. I live between concern and hope, but that doesn't affect my performance.

It was a pretty hefty blow [when Lily was diagnosed with lung cancer]. But we got ourselves together at once. We went abroad. We started treatment there. I never allowed myself to break down even for a second. One must not break down, especially when there are tough decisions to be made . . . I've seen the greatest victories and the most terrible disasters in my life, and I've never broken down. But if you ask me if tears didn't choke my throat when I spoke to the doctors, then that's not true: they did. And how they did. And now, too, every so often I have a kind of crisis when I see her, this girl with inexhaustible energy, fighting, suffering . . . But I haven't lost my confidence. And I do not acquiesce, not for one minute, in her being in this condition.

I told her this morning that at the very first opportunity I want us to go back to the concert hall, to our own seats, which it took us so many years to get to. We started with one ticket in the gods, behind a pillar. Then it was two, slightly lower. And we gradually made our way down. Now we sit in row five. I told her the first thing I'm going to do is take out a subscription to the new concert series.

On March 24, the temporary home became a house of mourning. The entire political community, regardless of affiliation or ideology, turned out for Lily's funeral on a hilltop near the ranch or for a consolation visit during the seven-day shiva period of mourning. They all knew her personally, because she had always been at her husband's side. Even during her illness, she had made the effort to be there for him. Shimon Peres spoke for many of them when he said, "Lily was a wonderful woman who fought her illness with uncommon courage and with the same devotion and determination with which she stood by her husband's side through every one of his battles."

"You fought till the last moment, with fortitude, with serenity, with dignity," Sharon said in his eulogy at her graveside. "You left our world loving and enveloped in the love of all your family and friends. They will love you forever." She was just sixty-three.

During the shiva mourning period Sharon made it clear, as he had in the interview, that Lily's absence would not end his political career. But there was more than that. Though cut off by his bereavement, Sharon discerned that the Geneva denouement might mean that Barak was weakening faster than anyone had expected. To a group of party activists who came to comfort him, Sharon said: "Carry on, carry on—and in the end you will breach the wall."

"I really liked that," Ofir Akunis recalled. "I remember it to the present day. Sharon had been party leader for the best part of a year, but this was the first time I felt he was seriously exhorting us to action. The 'wall' was Ehud Barak, and the message was, if we keep attacking, we can defeat him. Sure enough, politics seemed to come back to life in the following months as Barak's popularity continued to drop."[10]

Another Likud member, who had feared that Lily's death would leave Sharon suddenly old and lonely, found himself wondering at the speed and feistiness of his resurgence. "There were more important things to do than to mourn Lily . . . so he did them," this man recalled, drily. "Arik dearly loved Lily. He would stroke her hand and gaze into her eyes. But did he love her for herself or out of his overwhelming love of himself? I remember later someone suggested that Arik was so egocentric that apart from his sons he couldn't actually love another person. He loved to have her with him, because she loved him and spoiled him. When she was no longer around, she was no longer around."[11]

Within days of the Geneva letdown, Barak gave orders—no tactic this, but a momentous, if impetuous, decision—to have the army out of Lebanon long ahead of his original July deadline. Since there was to be no agreement with Syria, the withdrawal would be unilateral. He sent a stern warning to Damascus not to interfere as the Israeli troops pulled out.

At the same time, he resolved to travel to Washington to present his plans to Clinton. He spoke of a three-way summit with Arafat in the summer. He would bring a comprehensive peace plan, he promised the president.[12]

The clearest indication that Barak was serious was his appointment of two unimpeachable peaceniks as his envoys to a series of discreet Israeli-Palestinian negotiations that now got under way, first in the region and later in Sweden. The purpose of these talks, at least in Barak's mind, was to prepare the ground for the make-or-break tripartite summit, along the lines of the Carter-Begin-Sadat summit at Camp David in 1978. Shlomo Ben-Ami, a professor of history whom Barak had incongruously appointed his minister of internal security, had long argued for sweeping Israeli concessions on the West Bank and in Jerusalem. Alongside him, Barak appointed a former army officer and now a successful lawyer, Gilead Sher, also a confirmed dove.

The interaction in the months ahead between Barak and these two gifted but difficult men was to bring Israel to the brink of peace, much, much closer than any previous leaders had ever dared to go.

On May 8, Barak and Arafat met at Abu Mazen's home in Ramallah. Their negotiators then enplaned for Sweden, where, courtesy of the prime minister, Göran Persson, they held relaxed, secluded conversations at a remote government guest complex. Ben-Ami indicated that the three "settlement blocs" that Israel wanted to keep would require annexation of 8 percent of the West Bank.[13] This was unacceptable to the Palestinians. But it was already a far cry from the double-digit annexation being bandied about in public. And the concept of land swap, a political unmentionable in Israel until then, was firmly on the table at the Swedish guesthouse.

This hopeful beginning was soon disrupted when serious violence broke out in the Palestinian territories around May 15, Naqba Day in Palestinian parlance, the anniversary of the creation of Israel. Barak ordered the negotiators home.

In the north, the IDF's unilateral withdrawal from Lebanon was gathering pace but increasingly looking like an undignified flight. Thousands of Lebanese civilians, marshaled by Hezbollah, were marching southward, sweeping through the crumbling lines of the South Lebanese Army, Israel's mainly Christian militia ally in the "security zone." Barak gave orders to speed up the pullback. SLA men and their families desperately but fruitlessly clustered at the border fence demanding to be let through, too.

The constant toll of military deaths in the unending guerrilla war with Hezbollah would now, hopefully, end. A wave of visceral relief swept the country. The withdrawal, moreover, had been accomplished without any further loss of Israeli lives. But the abandonment of the SLA gnawed at the national conscience. And Hezbollah trumpeted the Israeli retreat as a great victory for its Shiite fighters and a shining example to the Palestinians of what armed resistance could achieve.

Barak pointed to the unilateral withdrawal as a bold act of leadership and the honorable discharge of a solemn electoral commitment. Sharon tried to tap into the public's ambivalence. "It's a very good thing that we've gotten out of Lebanon," he told the Knesset on June 5. "It was the right decision, though it should have been taken earlier. But while getting out was right, the way it was done was absolutely wrong." The "erosion of the IDF's deterrence" in the eyes of the Arab world would make Arafat even more intransigent. "He wants to achieve what the Hezbollah ostensibly achieved . . . to the last centimeter." Unbeknownst to Sharon, that logic was shared by the Palestinian negotiators who were working with Ben-Ami and Sher on ideas for compromises. "What have you done to us with this crazy withdrawal from Lebanon?" Abu Ala (Ahmed Qureia) complained.[14] Mohammed Dahlan, the head of the Palestinian Preventive Security Forces and a powerful political figure in the PA, said the Israeli withdrawal "gave our people the message that violence wins . . . the message from Barak was that he would move under pressure . . . that he would withdraw only if forced to."[15]

Barak's unilateral withdrawal from Lebanon provided double closure for Sharon. By bringing back the army to the international border, Barak finally stanched the hemorrhaging of IDF blood that began in June 1982 and had never really stopped for eighteen years. Moreover, by briefly reopening the national debate over Lebanon, Barak showed that time, and perhaps Sharon's own incessant battles with his critics, had had their effect. The burden of Lebanon no longer made Sharon unelectable.

Buoyed by the public's support for the Lebanon withdrawal, and with the Syrian track in indefinite abeyance following the death of Hafez Assad on June 10, Barak now swung all his energies behind his push for a tripartite summit. Arafat was reluctant, fearing that if the summit failed, Clinton would line up with Barak to blame him for it. Clinton promised him that whatever happened, he would not point fingers afterward, and he invited the two leaders to come to Camp David on Tuesday, July 11.

Like the abortive Geneva summit between Clinton and Assad, Camp David has been subjected to a good deal of twenty-twenty hindsight analysis by participants and pundits. Clinton did go back on his word and blamed Arafat for the summit's lack of success. Others faulted the U.S. president for allowing himself, as they saw it, to be cajoled by Barak into holding the summit in the first place. Clinton made no determined effort, moreover, once the summit got under way, to break down Barak's high-handed decision not to deal with Arafat directly and to leave the negotiating to their subordinates. There was no substantive dialogue between the two leaders, even though Barak's logic for pressing Clinton to host the summit had been that the end-game must be conducted by the principals themselves.

Barak decided early that there was no chance of a breakthrough until the eve of Clinton's scheduled departure, on the eighth day of the summit, for a meeting of the G8 in Okinawa. That naturally became a self-fulfilling prophecy, and the first week was spent treading water. On the night before Clinton left, Barak asked to meet with him alone and presented him with a proposal that both gobsmacked and delighted the Americans: the partitioning of the Old City of Jerusalem. The Palestinians would have sovereignty over the Muslim and Christian Quarters, Israel over the Jewish and Armenian Quarters. The Temple Mount, or Haram al-Sharif, would be handed by UN resolution to the joint custodianship of Palestine and Morocco, the nation that chaired the Islamic Conference's Jerusalem Committee. The Palestinians would have sovereignty over all the outer Arab neighborhoods of the city, and there would be shared sovereignty in the inner neighborhoods. Barak whittled down his demands to control the Jordan River border, now suggesting an IDF presence in a small area for a period of years. He spoke of some land swap as compensation for Israel's annexing up to 9 percent of the West Bank for its settlement blocs. There would be a "satisfactory solution" to the refugee question.

The idea of sharing Jerusalem, including the Old City, between Israel and the Palestinians has since become so commonplace, at least among pro-peace advocates, that it is instructive to rehearse here the U.S. ambassador to Israel Martin Indyk's words to Bregman in *Elusive Peace*: "The idea that half of the Old City would be under Arafat's sovereignty was completely unthinkable to any American at Camp David, and any Israeli, other than Ehud Barak himself." Bregman adds: "This was a generous, even stunning offer . . . that had never before been proposed by an Israeli prime minister."

Even those superlatives are inadequate to express the change that Barak wrought in more than thirty years of Israeli dogma. "United Jerusalem," in the distended city limits that Israel unilaterally imposed after 1967, was an axiomatic and virtually consensual tenet of Israeli policy. It was rehearsed by politicians of the Right and of the Left—apart from the Far Left—in almost every speech, like a catechism. "The united city, never to be divided again." Audiences would applaud automatically. Suddenly all this was challenged, opened to rational reexamination.

But when Clinton took the offer to Arafat, the Palestinian leader demurred. Custodianship was not sovereignty, he pointed out. He did not have the right to cede sovereignty over the Haram. He insisted, too, on exclusive Palestinian sovereignty over the Palestinian suburbs adjacent to the Old City (the inner neighborhoods). He remained impervious to the combined pressures and blandishments of the president, the secretary of state, and the national security adviser. He managed to infuriate Clinton still more by insisting that the ruins of the ancient Jewish temple were not in Jerusalem at all but in Nablus, blithely nullifying thereby important parts of the Old and the New Testaments.

Clinton returned to Camp David on July 23 and plunged back into the discussions with renewed energy. But Jerusalem remained the crucial deal breaker. That is how the president himself assessed the summit on the morning of July 25, after trying one last time, and failing, to move Arafat on this issue. Shlomo Ben-Ami agreed. The considerable progress made on borders and security "was only hypothetical," he wrote later, "because in the Palestinians' working assumption it was conditional on Israel's accepting the fundamentalist Palestinian positions on two key issues: Jerusalem and the refugees."

Writing as a historian as well as a politician and negotiator, Ben-Ami saw in the religious zealotry prevalent in the Muslim world on the issues of Jerusalem and the refugees the factor that furnished the deeper reason, or pretext, behind Arafat's position. He noted that both the imam of al-Aqsa and the mufti of Jerusalem, the second an Arafat appointee, spoke out during Camp David forbidding on religious grounds any concession on sovereignty.[16]

Tragically, this analysis can be applied to Ben-Ami and Barak. They, too, were influenced by the religious fundamentalism on the Israeli side regarding the Temple Mount. They, too, were swayed by this fundamentalism to advance a position at Camp David that made a pragmatic compromise on Jerusalem effectively unattainable. In a cynical and ultimately hopeless effort to win support from zealot circles in Israel, Barak and Ben-Ami proposed that a synagogue for Jewish prayer be built on a tiny area of the Temple Mount. This drew outraged rejection from Arafat and his top aides.[17]

Back in 1967, Moshe Dayan vested administration of the Mount/

With Lebanese presidential candidate Bashir
Gemayel at his headquarters near Beirut,
August 1982: collusion now, peace later

September 15, 1982, the day before the massacre: Arik and Raful
at the IDF command post on a rooftop overlooking Sabra and Shatila

Honor guard for dishonorable departure:
February 1983, leaving the Ministry of Defense

Arik's courtroom victory in New York over *Time* magazine
was not unanimously welcomed back home.

Made his mark on the geography:
with unfurled maps in 1984

"Let me help you build a camp":
with political adviser Yisrael Katz
in 1985, starting the hard climb
back up the greasy pole

With Lily at a Likud Party meeting, 1986:
"by her husband's side through
every one of his battles"

Guest of honor at a Druze feast

The "constrainers": left to right: Arik, Yitzhak
Modai, David Levy. (Behind Arik is Ehud Olmert.)

"Who is in favor of eliminating terror?"
Tel Aviv, February 1990,
"Night of the Microphones."

Minister of housing, 1990: a splurge of building—
and of settlement

From Russia, with votes

Sycamore Ranch soiree, 1991

Ousted: election night, 1992

"Where's your company commander?"
With King Hussein of Jordan, 1997: flowering
of a late friendship. (Prime Minister Benjamin
Netanyahu is in the background.)

"Tie us up, hand and foot!" With
Netanyahu at Wye River Plantation, 1998.

"We don't eat friends." With Yonatan,
on Sycamore Ranch.

"The hope of peace for us Israelis lies in the principle of separation." With outgoing prime minister Ehud Barak in the Knesset Speaker's office, March 7, 2001, moments before Arik is sworn in as prime minister.

On the Temple Mount, September 28, 2000: unintelligent gimmick that changed history

Reuven Adler: saccharine text, slick footage. "No, we weren't duping the voters."

Prophetic portrait: election night 2001.
With (left to right) Uri Dan, Cyril Kern, Arie Genger.

Grand old coalition

"I can't even have my own secreta[
With Marit Danon. "He's not
the man you think he is."

With Mayor Rudolph Giuliani at Ground Zero. "You don't understand what happened to us," the U.S. ambassador berated Arik.

Unambiguous evidence: arms haul from the *Karine A*, January 2002. Left, Chief of Staff Shaul Mofaz; right, Minister of Defense Binyamin Ben-Eliezer.

...y 2002: slinking would not be good enough for ...s. "Teaching you where the fish pees from" is a ...quely Israeli idiom meaning humiliation. Arik's ...lass here comprises Shas members, with their leader Rabbi Yosef visibly sweating.

A bus bombing in Jerusalem, June 2002. Mothers trembled and wept as they sent their children to school.

Reading his thoughts even when he hadn't yet thought
them? Dov Weissglas, attorney, friend, adviser,
and finally bureau chief.

"Arik and I, I and Arik." November 2002:
veteran poll reader Netanyahu concedes
to the prime minister's popularity.

With Michal Modai: "Complete poppycock . . .
of course he kissed me." Behind Arik is Uri Shani.

Comfortable, confident, enjoying the job

Comfortable, too, in the Oval Office

Aqaba, June 2003. Abbas: "It is time to bring all this suffering to an end." Sharon: "A viable Palestinian state."

Aqaba: "The president liked Ariel Sharon."

With Mahmoud Abbas (Abu Mazen), then
Palestinian prime minister, July 2003: he constantly
and publicly opposed the intifada's violence.

A more jaundiced view of Sharon's peace diplomacy:
"First, my best wishes for the Eid festival."

With grandson Rotem, Gilad's son, at an air force
graduation ceremony, June 2002

Purim at the prime minister's office: reading the Scroll of
Esther with Yitzchak David Grossman, a favorite rabbi

An ignoble act: with Likud Knesset member
Naomi Blumenthal, in better days

With Dan Halutz (middle), the new IDF
chief of staff, who carried out the disengagement, and (left) Moshe Ya'alon, the
old chief of staff, who balked at it

Omri in the Knesset: vicarious political power

With Minister of Justice Tommy Lapid: "Today may be
the start of a real peace process with the Palestinians, even
though the move we've decided on is unilateral."

Celebrating the Festival of Tabernacles
with the Four Species: Was Arik *etrogized*?

Youngsters at the Gaza Strip settlement of Atzmona, 2001:
"What have we got to look for there?"

Crawford, Texas, April 2005: "Mr. Prime
Minister, welcome to my home."

Disengagement, Morag,
August 17, 2005:
no match for massed
phalanxes

Phony war, phony trauma:
melodrama at Kfar Darom,
August 18, 2005

"He did not wish to hurt others."
Omri goes to jail, February 2008.

Hanukkah, December 2005:
between two strokes

Haram in the Muslim *waqf,* or religious authority, and banned Jewish prayer there. Jews, like anyone else, were free to visit this sacred site. But only Muslims were allowed to pray there. Happily, as Dayan knew, this edict coincided with the provisions of the Orthodox Jewish law, the halacha, which forbade observant Jews to set foot on the Mount until the Temple was restored in God's good time. Orthodox Jews had meticulously observed this prohibition for centuries. After 1967, the chief rabbinate of Israel solemnly reaffirmed it.

For many years, pressure to pray on the Temple Mount came from a marginal group of ultranationalist but not especially Orthodox Jews in Jerusalem, the Temple Mount Faithful. They would make periodic set-piece attempts to enter the precincts with prayer shawls and would be carted off by the police. The Muslim authorities, though forever warning of nefarious Jewish plots to take over the Mount and destroy the mosques, were well aware of the Israeli government's strictly enforced ban on Jewish prayer there.

The Muslim warnings, however, turned out not to be wholly without foundation when a Jewish underground was discovered by the Shin Bet security service among Jewish settlers on the West Bank and the Golan Heights in the mid-1980s. Among its plans was one to plant explosives beneath the mosques. Although the underground group was excoriated by the settler leadership, in the wake of this episode the blanket religious ban on ascending the Temple Mount began to fray. One prominent plotter, released from jail after five years, began agitating in favor of sacrificing the Paschal Lamb on the Mount. Settler rabbis searched for ways of ritually purifying people so as to enable them to tread on the Mount without defying the age-old Orthodox halachic ban. Others ruled that the ban did not apply to certain parts of the precincts, and they began exhorting religious Jews to visit those areas of the holy site.

Barak and Ben-Ami's synagogue proposal fed into this dangerous trend within the settler-based community. It also contributed to the breakdown of Camp David, providing Arafat with proof for his suspicions that Israel was ultimately bent on taking over the holy site. In the wake of the failed summit, political attacks on the government were suffused with religious jingoism centering on Jerusalem and the Temple Mount. Even though the synagogue idea faded from the negotiations after Camp David, it remained a part of the backdrop to Ariel Sharon's ill-advised visit to the Temple Mount in September 2000, which preceded—some say triggered; some say caused—the outbreak of the Palestinian intifada.

Sharon's action, too, was designed to feed the jingoism, which he

had been busily fomenting throughout the summer. His perverse provocation must be seen in this broader context of political and religious
ferment.

"Mr. Speaker, no prime minister has the right to make concessions
over Jerusalem," Sharon proclaimed in the Knesset on July 24, while
Camp David was still in progress.

> Jerusalem is the birthright of the entire Jewish people. Our generation
> had the honor of liberating Jerusalem and uniting it, and we must
> preserve it in precious trust for future generations. Arafat says, and
> I must say I really admire him for this . . . that in the matter of Jeru-
> salem he needs the approval of the Arab and Muslim world. Barak,
> on the other hand, doesn't understand that before he signs any-
> thing, before he agrees to anything even verbally, he must have the
> consent and approval of the entire Jewish people, in Israel and in the
> Diaspora.[18]

A week later, with Barak now back, the controversy raging, and the
coalition floundering, Sharon lambasted the prime minister. "Eighteen
times in your election broadcasts you promised not to divide Jerusalem. You promised it would remain united forever. You have broken
every promise you made. You say you speak in the name of your supporters. But they no longer support you, Mr. Barak. They've changed
their minds, like you changed your promises."[19]*

Barak had already lost Shas, the National Religious Party, and Yisrael B'Aliya. The three coalition partners bolted on the eve of Camp
David. David Levy, who had switched sides and become Barak's foreign minister, now announced his resignation, too. The government
no longer commanded a Knesset majority. That made the regular business of governing difficult. But Barak could still rely, just about, on the

---

* In a formal statement that day in the Knesset, required by protocol, Speaker
Avrum Burg announced that Sharon was leader of the opposition. New legislation had been passed recognizing the leader of the opposition as an official state
officeholder, with attendant rights and privileges. "I have the honor of informing
the Knesset that, in accordance with Section 11 of the Knesset Law, the Likud faction, which is the largest opposition faction, has informed me that Ariel Sharon,
MK, is leader of the opposition. Wherefore I hereby announce that Ariel Sharon, MK, is leader of the opposition. My congratulations, sir, on your maiden
speech." Sharon replied with grace, laced with his usual irony. "Mr. Speaker, I
thank you. Even though it will only be for a short time, I am happy to hold this
title" (Speaker's announcement, *Knesset Record*, July 31, 2000).

"blocking bloc" of Jewish and Arab MKs that precluded an alternative, Likud-led government.

On August 15, Sharon attacked the synagogue scheme: "Barak has agreed to cleave in two the heart of the Jewish people: the Old City of Jerusalem . . . He is ready to concede on the Temple Mount. He is trying to soften the blow by demanding that Arafat recognize the Jews' right to pray. This very proposal, that Arafat recognize our right to pray at the holy of holies of the Jewish people, is in itself debasing and only goes to show to what depths our side has sunk."[20]

The holiness of Jerusalem, he continued, was "many times more meaningful for the Jewish people than it is for the Christians and Muslims." The Jewish people "were the only pioneers in the annals of the Land and of Jerusalem who transformed the rocky and . . . barren scrubland into green and arable terraces. They did this by hard work and sweat; no other people were creative in the same way. The Jewish people were the first who built a glorious temple in Jerusalem, which was the font of holiness for the entire nation and the entire land."

Sharon was a thoroughly secular Jew. But this confused exposition on "holy" and "holiness" reflected more than the modern, secular Jew's grappling with the significance of a unique, religion-based national identity in today's world. It was also a politician's shameless milking of these emotive terms for whatever populist advantage he could get from them. But, as we have seen, politicians on both sides of the Israeli divide were engaged in this dubious pursuit.

At the UN Millennium Summit in New York in September, Clinton and Arafat discussed vesting sovereignty over the Temple Mount/ Haram in the Organization of Islamic States. Barak was encouraged, although for his part he spent much of his time in New York persuading world leaders that the outcome of Camp David proved that Arafat was not a serious partner for peace. Negotiators for the three sides continued batting ideas about. Clinton's presidency was running out, but he still hadn't given up hope of pulling off a peace deal in the closing weeks of his term.

Back home, in an unwonted gesture of conviviality, Barak invited Arafat and his top aides to dinner at his home in Kochav Yair. He sent an army helicopter to bring them over. Nava, his wife,[21] radiated good cheer and plied her guests with good food. Barak and Arafat strolled arm in arm through the French doors and sat alone in the garden, without note takers. They seemed to get along fine. Their aides wondered why they hadn't tried this simple technique of talking to each other at Camp David. Clinton, apprised ahead of time, phoned in to exhort them. They confirmed to the president that their negotiators would be leaving for Washington that same night for further intensive talks.

There was an elephant in the room, but no one seemed to notice it. According to Gilead Sher, "Nobody mentioned the imminent visit by Ariel Sharon, the leader of the opposition, to the Temple Mount."[22] The dinner took place on September 25. Sharon's visit was scheduled for September 28. Shlomo Ben-Ami, the minister of public security, was effectively doubling as foreign minister (the only job he really wanted: he was formally appointed foreign minister on November 2, 2000, and held both portfolios until the end of the Barak administration). He was to fly out to Washington later that night at the head of the Israeli negotiating team.

In the garden, the visit did come up. "Why didn't Sharon visit the Haram when he was defense minister or foreign minister?" Arafat complained to his host. "That's our democracy," Barak replied. "I can't prevent the leader of the opposition from visiting the site."[23]

In any event, any disturbing thoughts about the impending visit did not cloud the upbeat atmosphere at the dinner or at the talks that opened in Washington a day later. These talks were intended as a final refinement of the parties' positions, and a final attempt at narrowing the gaps between them, before the United States presented its own package of proposals designed to bridge or resolve all the remaining points in dispute.

Ben-Ami took time out from the talks on September 27 to be briefed over the telephone by his commissioner of police, Yehuda Wilk, as to what was expected the next day on the Mount. "He told me that on the basis of intelligence assessments he recommended allowing the visit to go forward," Ben-Ami recalled. "He said he had a contingency plan in place to get Sharon out fast if serious violence erupted." The minister for internal security spoke by phone, too, with Jibril Rajoub, the PA's head of preventive security on the West Bank. "Rajoub told me that if Sharon did not enter the mosques themselves, he believed there would not be any rioting, and whatever demonstrations did take place would be kept under control."[24]

INTIFADA

In Israel, September 27 was a busy day, too. In the afternoon, the radio broadcast the propitious announcement that Benjamin Netanyahu had long been waiting for with great and mounting trepidation. He was not going to be prosecuted for bribery, fraud, and breach of public trust. And his wife, Sara, was not going to be prosecuted for theft. This was good news indeed. His political career would not be hobbled for months or years, perhaps even forever. The couple's conduct in relation to a longtime family retainer was, in the words of the attorney general, "dismal and worthy of the most stringent criticism." But that was veritable music to the Netanyahus' ears. For in the next paragraph of a lengthy report, Attorney General Elyakim Rubinstein explained that however reprehensibly they had behaved, their actions and omissions did not meet the criteria for a criminal prosecution. He therefore ordered the files against them closed for lack of evidence.*

Netanyahu issued a string of suitably contrite statements. His loyalists could barely contain their exultation. He would come roaring back now, they confidently predicted, to sweep away the debris of Barak's collapsing coalition and restore the Likud to its rightful place of power. They mocked recently renewed talk of a unity government as the Canute-like last-gasp efforts of the failed prime minister and the over-the-top Likud stand-in leader to turn back the irresistible tide of Bibi's return in triumph.

That same morning, the reporter Yossi Verter accompanied Sharon on a tour of a bellwether bastion of Likud supporters, the Mahane Yehuda outdoor market in Jerusalem. The stallholders were friendly, but their chorused advice to their visitor was "Arik, step aside for Bibi." "That simple call," Verter wrote in the next day's *Haaretz,* "encapsulates the condition of Sharon, of Bibi, and of the Likud."[25]

---

* Netanyahu's brush with the criminal law involved a removals contractor cum handyman cum political activist, Yigal Amedi. He had been performing various removals assignments and other odd jobs for the Netanyahus ever since their return from Bibi's service as ambassador to the UN in 1988. But he had never been paid. When Netanyahu lost the election, Amedi submitted a bill to the Prime Minister's Office for close to half a million shekels ($125,000).

The suspicion was that Amedi's various attempts over the years to wheedle from the Netanyahus various job placements and recommendations for his relations and friends were his reason for not asking to be paid. Amedi turned state's evidence and poured out a tale full of bitter recriminations to the police. In the course of the investigation it also turned out that he and Sara had hauled off hundreds of valuable gifts given to Netanyahu in his official capacity (and therefore the property of the state) and had stored them in a warehouse.

There was not much evidence that the Netanyahus had actually helped Amedi. Still, the Israeli law of bribery incorporated the principle enshrined in Ecclesiastes 11:1: "Cast thy bread upon the waters, for after a long time thou shalt find it again." This meant that no specific act of give-and-take had to be shown, as long as a general criminal intention could be proven. But in the Netanyahus' case it could not, the attorney general ruled.

· · ·

By the time most *Haaretz* readers digested this analysis the next morning, Sharon was on the Temple Mount, and history was changing, though the protagonists did not yet realize it.

Flanked by half a dozen members of the Likud Knesset faction—a pretty poor showing, the electronic media were quick to note—and by phalanxes of police, Sharon spent forty-five minutes on the Mount. He looked over a recently refurbished underground hall that the *waqf* had inaugurated as an overflow mosque. Some Israeli archaeologists had loudly protested this quasi-excavation, and the academic dispute quickly morphed into a political controversy. Sharon steered clear* of the two Muslim shrines, the Mosque of al-Aqsa and the Dome of the Rock, as Jibril Rajoub had requested. And as Rajoub predicted, the visit passed without serious violence. The police kept a rigorous separation between Sharon's group and a thousand-odd Palestinian demonstrators, mostly youngsters, who hurled stones and curses at the Butcher of Beirut.† Also prominently present were several Israeli-Arab MKs. They were seen chatting and even joking with their Likud Knesset colleagues, but as soon as the television cameras panned onto them, they let loose a tirade of invective.[26]

The demonstrations and stone throwing continued after Sharon and his party left. The police fired tear-gas canisters and rubber-coated bullets at the stone throwers. Rioting spread to other parts of the Old City. The Jerusalem police chief, Arye Yitzhaki, asked the Knesset member Ahmad Tibi and Palestinian *waqf* officials to help persuade the rioters to disband. Some thirty policemen and a dozen demonstrators were reported hurt, none seriously. Sharon issued a press statement that he was sorry about the injured policemen, "but it is the right of every Jew to visit the Temple Mount and I was right to do so." A Labor Party spokesman said it was a miracle that "Sharon's exhibition of counterfeit patriotism had not ended in bloodshed."

All in all, Sharon was pleased with himself. The idea—it was a gimmick really—to visit the Mount had not been unanimously popular with his friends and advisers in his informal "ranch forum."[27] Omri thought it was "not intelligent" and declined to accompany his father. Gilad went instead, while Omri drove to the cemetery outside Tel

---

* Or the police steered him clear; this point was never clarified.
† The proximity of the anniversary of that event exacerbated Palestinian resentment over the visit, both in the Palestinian press and in the street.

Aviv to ensure that all was ready at his brother Gur's graveside for the annual family memorial gathering the next day.[28]

By afternoon, the Likud was fully preoccupied again with Netanyahu's exculpation and the looming leadership contest. The morning's escapade was fading. Sharon had sent a message of congratulation to both the Netanyahus, adding the hope, at once unctuous and ironic, that Bibi would henceforth "be able to join us in the struggle against . . . the Barak government." Now, at a pre–Jewish New Year toast at party headquarters in Tel Aviv, he was in fighting fettle. "No gifts!" he proclaimed. "There'll be no gifts here." If people expected him to make way for anyone else, they were going to be disappointed. The gifts metaphor was not lost on his audience. None of the three leading newspapers made Sharon's visit their lead story the next morning. *Yedioth Ahronoth* wondered whether Sharon had hoped to rob Netanyahu of the limelight on his day of exoneration and celebration.[29]

In Jerusalem and Washington, too, officials allowed themselves to breathe easy as the ominous fallout of Sharon's visit seemed to die quickly away. Warnings by a lone police officer in Jerusalem, Nisso Shaham, and by a lone former security officer then in Washington, Yisrael Hasson, that more and worse trouble was yet to be expected fell on strangely desensitized ears. Intelligence reports that pointed to a possible eruption of violence after prayers on the Mount the next day, Friday, resulted in an almost routine decision to reinforce the regular police presence there. Even the murder, at dawn on that Friday morning, of an Israeli officer by his Palestinian comrade on a joint patrol near Kalkilya set no alarm bells ringing.*

Ben-Ami flew home overnight. From the airport he made his way straight to national police headquarters in Jerusalem—not, however, with a view to taking personal control over a potentially explosive situation, but rather to announce his choice of the next police commissioner. He had written a speech on the plane explaining to the assembled senior officers why he had decided to appoint Shlomo Aharonishki, commander of the Tel Aviv region. The Jerusalem commander, Yitzhaki, grievously disappointed, left at once for the Mount, where some twenty thousand worshippers had gathered and where the young men among them were reported to be piling up stones, bottles, and other projectiles.[30]

Yitzhaki was one of the first to be hit. Despite his helmet, a stone

---

* The killer turned himself in to the Palestinian authorities, who immediately announced that he was of unsound mind.

caught him on the back of the head. He passed out. Blood streamed from the wound. He was evacuated, and rumors started to spread among his men that not only had he been unfairly passed over for the commissionership but he was dead. (He was not, nor badly hurt.) Stones rained down meanwhile on Jewish worshippers at the Western Wall plaza below the Temple Mount plateau. Yitzhaki's deputy ordered his men to charge the rioters. Police sharpshooters began firing live ammunition. Other policemen shot rubber-coated bullets from close range. The result was seven Palestinian dead and more than a hundred injured. Blood spattered the flagstones of the holy site. Only the advent of Mickey Levy, the levelheaded and authoritative police commander of the West Bank, brought a modicum of calm. He made contact with *waqf* officials and with Jibril Rajoub, and together they worked out a "cease-fire": the police would withdraw from the Mount, and the Palestinians would rein in the rioting and stone throwing. By mid-afternoon the Mount was quiet.

But the morning's events had been carried live on Voice of Palestine, the PA radio, and screened on Al Jazeera. The sermon was always broadcast on a Friday; this time it had become a running commentary on the carnage. Grief and outrage swept Palestinian communities on both sides of the green line.

What should have happened next was that the police, under their minister and senior commanders, should have assessed that the wave of protest could spread through the Israeli-Arab community and lead to riots and acts of violence inside the country. They should have ensured, above all else, that their units were deployed at likely flash points in sufficient force and properly equipped with nonlethal riot-control gear as befits a civilian police force preparing to confront demonstrating citizens of its own country almost certain to be unarmed.

What should have happened, too, was that the army under its minister, Ehud Barak, and chief of staff, Shaul Mofaz, should have anticipated that the protests could spread from the Mount to engulf the occupied territories in a torrent of raging violence.

What should have happened long before the bloody riot on the Temple Mount was serious thinking and planning in the army for how to confront mass popular unrest in the territories. After all, that had been the nature of the first Palestinian intifada (1987–1993), which the IDF, under Yitzhak Rabin for much of that period, had such great difficulty combating and curbing in a humane way. The state comptroller, in his 2000 annual report, severely criticized the fact that the IDF had made no serious attempt to develop nonlethal or less lethal methods of riot control.

Ideally, too, after thirty-three years of occupation, the IDF should have trained special units for riot control, instead of assigning whatever infantry or armored regiment—conscripts trained to fire rifles or guns—happened to be deployed in the specific area at the specific time of a riot. When the entire West Bank and Gaza were swept by violence, as they were now, virtually all units deployed there were pressed into these police duties, for which they were both unsuited and unprepared.

On the day after the Friday deaths on the Temple Mount, the army, confident in its preparations for a low-grade war, gave battle to the young Palestinian rioters who massed at road junctions and outside military bases across the territories. There was some sporadic shooting at the Israeli troops. And that night, gunmen in Ramallah opened fire on the outlying houses of the nearby Jewish settlement of Psagot. The army's response in many of the clashes, with sharpshooters and sometimes other soldiers, too, firing large quantities of live ammunition,[31] inevitably felled unarmed rioters alongside the gunmen. At least six Palestinians died on the West Bank that first day and four more in Gaza. More than a hundred were wounded.[32] A twelve-year-old boy, Mohammed al-Dura, was filmed by a French television cameraman caught with his father in the center of a vicious firefight at the Netzarim junction in Gaza. They ducked behind a barrel. The father tried to shield him with his own body. To no avail. Mohammed's death was screened throughout the world that night; instantly it became the iconic image of an intifada that was taking scores of young Palestinian lives for hardly any Israeli ones.*

The next day, the serious violence reached the Israeli-Arab sector. Rioters blocked a major highway to the north. They burned banks and government offices and vandalized other public property. Thirteen Arab men and youths, all but one of them Israeli citizens, were killed by police gunfire on that Sunday and Monday. The outbreaks of violence did not finally subside until a week later.

The death of a dozen citizens at the hands of the police was a national trauma. But even more traumatic, and with farther-reaching effects, were the widespread horror and fear that pervaded Jewish Israel in the wake of the Israeli-Arab rioting. For the first time since the creation of the state—and this unblemished record included all the various wars and the first intifada—the Israeli-Arab minority appeared to be rising

---

* The IDF appeared to accept responsibility at the time. But an Israeli government inquiry concluded in May 2013 that Mohammed was not in fact shot in the incident. In France, a media analyst was convicted of defamation in June 2013 for accusing France-2 TV of staging the death of Mohammed.

up in rebellion, out of solidarity with the Palestinians beyond the sovereign borders of the state. The unrest even reached Jaffa, the mixed Arab-Jewish part of Tel Aviv where the two communities had lived for decades in reasonable harmony. These were days of near panic. The unspoken but ever-present nightmare of Arab irredentism seemed to be unfolding. The intensity of this trauma experienced by the Jewish majority inside Israel increased the level and intensity of lethal violence employed by the army—and condoned by the public—against the Palestinians across the green line during those early days and weeks of the intifada.

Two arguments broke out in Israel immediately: Had Arafat planned the intifada in advance? Did Sharon cause it by his visit to the Temple Mount? On the face of it, the two positive propositions seemed mutually exclusive: if Arafat had planned it, Sharon didn't cause it. But that immediately begged the important question, what was "it"? Sharon could incontrovertibly be said to have caused the fairly minor fracas that occurred during and immediately following his visit. But did he "cause" the next day's tragic events on the Mount? Could those events have been avoided, or at least mitigated, by greater moderation on the part of the police? And even after the deaths on the Mount on Friday, could Barak and Mofaz and Ben-Ami have contained the spiraling violence by a more judicious deployment of the army and the police—even if Arafat or lower-level Palestinian figures were avidly fanning the flames of this, their preplanned intifada?

The official Israeli position, from the outset, was that Arafat had been plotting for months to unleash another round of violence in the territories if he did not get his way at the negotiating table. Sharon's visit, it therefore followed, was not the cause of the intifada; at most it served as a trigger or a catalyst by provoking public outrage that the Palestinian leadership cynically latched on to as a pretext to launch the preplanned violence. By the same token, Arafat could have stopped the violence or at least reduced it, just as he started it.

Barak and Sharon both subscribed to this narrative. For Barak, it explained why the talks had failed: Arafat was not negotiating in good faith. It exonerated him, moreover, for not preventing Sharon's visit to the Mount. Even if he had prevented it, that would not have prevented the intifada. And it put the lopsided death toll in a more palatable light, at least for the Israeli public. Arafat had deliberately brought on the Palestinian fatalities. He veritably reveled in them; they were his political goal.

For Sharon, of course, this version of events minimized the adverse import of his visit to the Mount. Not that he ever expressed regret or remorse for it. "I find it totally unacceptable that your spokesman was quick to make a false statement that my visit to the Temple Mount 'may have caused tension,' insinuating that it ignited the riots," he wrote to Secretary of State Albright on October 2. "Your spokesman has been swayed by slanderous propaganda on the part of the Palestinian leaders and media."

In an interview months later to his longtime acolyte Uri Dan, he contended that his ascent to the Mount "would have remained a political gesture—part of my fight against the concessions that the government was preparing to make—if the Palestinians had not deliberately used it as a pretext to unleash their campaign of violence and terror that was in the works since the Camp David summit."[33]

Ben-Ami agreed. Writing four years later as a historian again, he professed "no doubt at all" that without Sharon's visit, which was "the perfect pretext," the Palestinians would have found another springboard from which to launch their intifada. He cited a speech by Arafat in Nablus on June 25 warning of a possible return to armed struggle. That was the decision that Arafat had made as soon as Camp David ended in failure.

That did not mean, though, Ben-Ami wrote, that Israel was blameless. He listed the settlements, the settler-only roads, the blockades and sieges, the Netanyahu government's rejectionism, "and the ambivalence of the Barak government, too, especially in regard to the settlements," as valid accumulated cause for the Palestinians' burning resentment.[34] He did not list his own performance as the minister in charge of the police.

"No countries and no media subscribe to the Israeli version of events," France's president, Jacques Chirac, said, railing at Barak on October 4 at the Élysée Palace in Paris. "The whole world shares the same feeling . . . Sharon provoked these incidents and he did so with the consent of your government."[35]

Chirac certainly spoke for much of the world. "It is hard to believe," wrote the British newspaper *The Independent,* "that Mr. Sharon, perhaps the Israeli politician most detested by the Palestinians, did not expect trouble—trouble that, as he is an opponent of further concessions by Israel, can only serve his aims." At the UN Security Council, Israel was lambasted by delegate after delegate for Sharon's provocation and for the army's subsequent use of disproportionate force against the Palestinians' protests. The Friday fatalities on the Mount were largely elided between Sharon's visit on Thursday and the splurge of violence across the West Bank that began on Saturday. Sharon was the villain, with Barak and Ben-Ami in supporting roles. Arafat's part, if he had one, was seen as that of victim.

But some world opinion, even in the first few days, was more nuanced. *The New York Times,* for instance, though asserting that Sharon's "provocative and irresponsible visit" had been the "precipitating incident," warned on October 3 that "now the fighting has taken on a life of its own."

Israeli public opinion, too, reflected the complexity of what was happening. "Pride and provocation—no matter what. Those were the hallmarks of the visit," *Haaretz* editorialized on October 2. Yoel Marcus, the paper's leading columnist, asserted that Sharon had "caused the conflagration that has led thus far to dozens dead and hundreds injured."[36] But the Palestinians were blamed, too. "The territories are burning, and Arafat is doing nothing to extinguish the flames," wrote *Maariv*'s Oded Granot. "Sharon's visit . . . provided the Palestinian Authority with the excuse it needed to ignite the battlefield."

Sharon's action was quickly subsumed into the broader crisis. The broader crisis, moreover, rendered his action, even in the minds of his critics, retrospectively less pigheaded and pernicious than it initially appeared. Even moderate Israelis began to think that the Palestinians had shown by their subsequent behavior that perhaps Sharon had a point. "These events prove that we must not cede sovereignty over the Temple Mount to the Palestinians," wrote Ron Ben-Yishai, the veteran defense analyst of *Yedioth Ahronoth* and the reporter who first confronted Sharon on the telephone with the horrors of Sabra and Shatila (and subsequently testified against him before the Kahan Commission).* Sharon had acted unwisely this time, too, Ben-Yishai wrote. But the violence on the Mount and beyond had been instigated by the PA's own security forces. "The man whose security chiefs deliberately ignite a firestorm on the holiest site to Islam and to Judaism is plainly not fit to have the sovereignty over that site vested in him."[37]

By the month's end, *Haaretz*'s Ze'ev Schiff added his authoritative endorsement to official Israel's accusation that the intifada had been preplanned. Ironically, Schiff wrote, Israel owed Arafat a debt. "He has brought us back to recognize our strategic reality: Israel is still a nation at war, and it needs to behave like one when it weighs its options and considers the limits of its concessions.[38]†

---

* See p. 205.
† "And another thing," Schiff added, "a nation at war cannot be run by mothers' organizations." That was the veteran defense analyst's somewhat sour reference

Another violent shock for Israelis came on October 12. Two reservists driving in a civilian car mistakenly entered Ramallah. They were set upon by a mob, dragged to a police station, and beaten to death. One of their assailants leaned out of a window and held up his hands, dripping with blood, for the mob to see and cheer. Another phoned one of the men's wives on his cell phone and announced, "I've just killed your husband."

The country was swept by a paroxysm of anger and impotence. These feelings were not relieved when Barak ordered air force helicopters that night to bomb and strafe the Ramallah police station and other PA offices in the West Bank and Gaza but to give sufficient advance warning so that in practice the attacks were on empty buildings. In a less flamboyant but more effective response, Barak gave orders to the security services that every Palestinian militant involved in this bestial outrage be brought to justice or killed.

B arak had rejected the PA's demand for a UN inquiry into the Temple Mount episode. In effect, he was protecting Sharon's action, and his own failure to prevent it, from what he presumed would be a sweeping international condemnation. The most he would agree to was a carefully selected inquiry commission headed by an American, and eventually, after much negotiating, this was appointed. Its chairman was George Mitchell, the former Democratic majority leader of the U.S. Senate who had won kudos around the world for his role in brokering the peace in Northern Ireland.*

The creation of the Mitchell Commission provided the backdrop

---

to a women's group called Four Mothers that had lobbied vigorously in favor of withdrawal from Lebanon. The unilateralism of that withdrawal and the undignified way it was carried out still rankled with many in the defense community, and Schiff was reflecting this. The northern border had been basically quiet following the pullout in April. But on October 7 a Hezbollah raiding party crossed into Israel and kidnapped three soldiers patrolling in their jeep. Barak, embroiled in the intifada, massed forces in the north and laid the blame on Syria. In the event, though, there was no Israeli military response.

* The commission worked for five months and presented its findings and recommendations in April to the new president of the United States, who passed them on to the new prime minister of Israel.

For Ariel Sharon, they were worth waiting for. "The Sharon visit did not cause the "Al-Aqsa Intifada," the panel wrote. It was not a blanket exoneration. There was plenty of criticism of Sharon and of Barak, and indeed of Arafat. The commission did not buy the Israeli line that Arafat had preplanned the intifada, but it accepted that Arafat did nothing to curb the violence once it had erupted.

conducive for yet another attempt to create a Barak-Sharon unity government. Barak tried to persuade his party ministers, meeting on October 22, that Sharon was much more moderate than he appeared. If he joined a unity government, that wouldn't spell the end of the peace process. The Sharon of today was not the Sharon of old, Barak asserted. The ministers were unconvinced. So were Sharon's comrades. Of the nineteen Likud members, fourteen spoke against a unity government at a faction meeting the next day. This was quickly leaked, and it reinforced the opposition on the Labor side. Sharon wasn't even master of his own house, the Labor doves jeered.

A week later, at a Knesset session marking the anniversary of Rabin's murder, Sharon spoke of his "yearning for a leadership figure projecting stability and reliability, radiating a deep understanding of events, an ability to analyze and to draw conclusions, and above all to take responsibility."[39] But he still didn't mean himself. Even at this late date, he was still admonishing the younger man and urging him, in effect, to take him into his government as his deputy.

But Barak, and indeed Sharon, were no longer calling the shots. The Knesset was about to dissolve itself. It could by law do so if 61 of its 120 members raised their hands in favor. Shinui, a small, anti-Orthodox party that broadly supported Barak's peace policy, joined now with the parties of the Right to ensure that absolute majority. Dissolution meant new elections; Netanyahu looked a shoo-in.

But now Barak suddenly announced that he was resigning as prime minister. Since the dissolution of the Knesset had not yet been approved on three readings, Barak's resignation overrode it. Instead of general elections for both the prime minister and the Knesset, there would be an election for the prime minister alone. It would be held in exactly sixty days from the date of Barak's resignation. That would be February 6, 2001. By law, only sitting MKs would be eligible to run. Netanyahu was not a sitting MK.

Sharon insisted he was as surprised as everyone else. No, there had not been any collusion between him and Barak to keep Bibi out, he retorted angrily to the many Likudniks who claimed that there had.

Netanyahu's supporters drafted an amendment to the existing legislation to enable a non-MK to run for prime minister. Sharon immediately announced that he would support it. Netanyahu, confident that it would pass, called a press conference in Jerusalem where he formally announced his candidacy for leader of the Likud and for prime minister. Two days later, on December 12, the Likud central committee endorsed the party's support for the "Netanyahu Law" and voted to hold the party's leadership primary a week later, on December 19. Sharon, in a speech laced with sarcasm but also with a bitter, between-the-lines recognition that this might well be his swan song, pointedly ignored the probability that Netanyahu would displace him. He would run against Barak, Sharon told the rowdy hall, and he would beat him. "After the elections, there'll be a country to govern," he kept repeating. The delegates got the point and roared their displeasure.

Netanyahu made a hero's entrance into the crowded hall, hugging and kissing ecstatic delegates as he progressed slowly to the podium. "You don't know how much I've missed you," he began his speech. Their adulation was almost palpable. He spoke like a candidate confident of triumph. But there was a vaguely discordant note, which the rapturous delegates did not pick up. There ought to be general elections for both the prime minister and the Knesset, Netanyahu remarked. "The present Knesset is fractured, divided, splintered."

On December 18, the day before the Likud primary, the Knesset voted. By a majority of 65 to 45, it passed the "Netanyahu Law" enabling a non-MK to run for prime minister. The bill was rushed through all three readings and the committee stage in one afternoon. The proceedings stopped briefly while members crowded around television screens to watch Netanyahu, at an impromptu press conference, inveigh against the law bearing his name and insist that he would not run even if it were passed. They ignored his fulminations, all presuming he himself would ignore them, too.

The prime ministership was his for the taking, but he declined to take it. True to his word, and dumbfounding backers and critics alike, Netanyahu confirmed that he was standing down. "I will not stand as a candidate in elections that . . . offer the winner the title of prime minister but deny him the tools to effectively lead the country," he declared.*

---

* "You'll have to wait for my book," Netanyahu replied, when asked in an interview for this book to explain his decision not to run against Sharon.

Omri Sharon insisted later that throughout these dramatic weeks his father never ceased to hope and even to expect that Netanyahu would withdraw in the end rather than stand and fight. But Yossi Verter of *Haaretz,* writing at the time, described Sharon as a man on a roller coaster. "Talking to him a few days ago, after the 'welcome' he received from the Likud central committee, one encountered a bitter and frustrated leader. Everyone was lining up with Bibi; Sharon was alone and abandoned, staring defeat in the face. Yesterday, he was a different man. 'I kept telling you all that it would be me who runs against Barak,' he crowed. 'But I saw out of the corner of my eye the pitying shrugs or malicious grins that my words elicited.' " Sharon, wrote Verter, was "like a mortgage defaulter about to be evicted from his home who suddenly wins the lottery."

Barak still had one potential trump card in his hand: the peace process. Right up to the last minute, Sharon continued to believe—and to fear—that Barak and Arafat would reach a deal. The territorial issue had now narrowed to around 5 percent of the West Bank, with swaps, and both leaders gave Clinton to understand they were "in the ballpark."[40] Dennis Ross quotes the veteran Saudi Arabian diplomat Prince Bandar, responding to a briefing on the state of the negotiations on December 19: "If Arafat does not accept what is available now, it won't be a tragedy; it will be a crime."

On December 23, in a last-ditch effort, Clinton presented U.S. bridging proposals to negotiators from the two sides. On territory, he suggested "a solution that provides between 94 and 96 percent of West Bank territory to the Palestinian state with a land swap of 1 to 3 percent." On Jerusalem, the "Clinton Parameters" followed "the general principle that what is Arab in the city should be Palestinian and what is Jewish should be Israeli; this should apply to the Old City as well." On the Temple Mount, the president proposed "Palestinian sovereignty over the Haram and Israeli sovereignty over . . . the Western Wall and the space sacred to Judaism of which it is part. There would be a firm commitment by both not to excavate beneath the Haram or behind the Western Wall." On refugees "our guiding principle has to be that the Palestinian state will be the focal point for the Palestinians who choose to return to the area, without ruling out that Israel will accept some of these refugees."

The Israeli negotiators Ben-Ami and Sher, diligently transcribing the president's words, found the time to exchange furtive glances and scrawled notes in Hebrew. "We can live with this," they both wrote. Ben-Ami noted worriedly, though, that their Palestinian negotiating partners were looking glum.[41]

The Barak cabinet voted on December 27 to accept the Clinton Parameters. There were reservations, but they were "within the parameters, not outside them," in Ross's words. Arafat, on the other hand, "was never good at facing moments of truth," Ross writes caustically. He came to Washington but rejected the president's proposal.

Like Clinton and Ross, Martin Indyk, the U.S. ambassador to Israel, lays the main blame on Arafat for the failed peace process. He calls him "the artful dodger." Indyk writes: "President Clinton formally offered Arafat Palestinian sovereignty over the Haram al-Sharif as one of the parameters for the final agreement. If that is what he had been holding out for at Camp David, why did he turn down Clinton's offer? The answer, to my mind, is straightforward: rather than breaking through into a new world, he clung to what he knew best—the ways of the old Arab order." It needed courage, Indyk adds, for Arafat to tell the Palestinian refugees "that they would not be going back to the homes of their forefathers, few of which existed anymore, even though they had known that in their hearts for a long time . . . Arafat was too scared to tell them the truth."[42]

Even with Clinton gone, Barak sent Ben-Ami and Sher, boosted by the dovish ministers Yossi Beilin, Yossi Sarid, and Amnon Lipton-Shahak, for a week of negotiations at Taba beginning January 21. Ben-Ami in his book writes of Israeli intelligence assessments in January that Arafat was suddenly and belatedly waking up to the prospect of Barak losing to Sharon on February 6 and the new Bush administration turning its back on the Middle East peace process. Hence his urgent instruction to Abu Ala to get an agreement at Taba. Sadly, the Israeli foreign minister adds, the new instructions were not accompanied by serious new flexibility.

In the months before this final denouement, Barak had been working fitfully on an alternative policy option: unilateral separation. Separation, that is, between Israel and the Palestinians, or, more accurately, separation by Israel from the Palestinians. If there was "no partner" on the Palestinian side for the foreseeable future, given Arafat's obduracy and the mounting violence, then Israel must act alone in its national interest by separating itself from the Palestinians along the lines of the agreement that the Palestinian leader was rejecting now but that his successors, it was to be hoped, would be prepared to negotiate at some time in the future.

The tangible expression of this new unilateralism was to be a security fence, a barrier of barbed wire and, in places, concrete wall, dotted with watchtowers and flanked by a patrol road. The IDF, no longer reliant on or desirous of cooperation with Palestinian security forces, would deploy this barrier as its bulwark against terrorist incursions from the West Bank.[43]* The fence was to incorporate the settlement blocs along the pre-1967 border, which Israel intended to annex in an eventual peace agreement with the Palestinians. This would mean

---

* Israel built a security fence around the Gaza Strip in 1994, at the insistent instigation of the IDF general then commanding the southern front, Matan Vilnai, who had since left the army and become a Labor Party politician. That fence, erected precisely along the pre-1967 borderline, proved effective throughout the intifada in preventing terrorist incursions from Gaza.

enclosing some Palestinian areas that Israel would ultimately not wish to annex. They would be "returned" in negotiations that would one day resume. Similarly, Israel would unilaterally designate the whole of the Jordan valley as a security zone for the foreseeable future, with the understanding that this arrangement, too, would end once a negotiated final agreement came into sight again.

With each new crisis in the post–Camp David negotiations, Barak would return to these still-inchoate ideas. As elections began to loom, he tried to project them to the public, to demonstrate that Arafat's intransigence and the intifada violence would not leave Israel powerless. "Us here; them there" was his slogan. His campaign strategists' difficult job was to inject this unilateralism into the national debate while at the same time leaving room for a dramatic return of "bilateralism," should the final, frenetic negotiating efforts yield an agreement after all.

There was a logical flaw in this: In practice, there was no prospect of the fence being built and the new separation policy going into effect unless the miraculous happened and Barak won the election.[44] But such a miracle was only conceivable if the negotiations produced a last-moment agreement—in which case the unilateral solution would no longer be necessary . . .

As leader of the opposition, Sharon opposed all the Barak government's proffered concessions in the negotiations with the Palestinians. But he regarded the process as unstoppable. And in a vicarious but significant way, reminiscent of his complex relations with Rabin during the Oslo process, he underwent together with Barak the experience of having those concessions rebuffed by Arafat and the slide into violent confrontation. Together with Barak, despite the continuing differences between them, he drew dramatic conclusions from Arafat's intransigence. Both men concluded that the collapse of bilateral negotiations in the Israel-Palestine conflict pointed to unilateralism as Israel's sole way forward. Both saw the demographic danger to the Jewishness of Israel inherent in indefinite occupation of the Palestinians. Both believed the United States and the international community would not countenance ongoing low-grade war and diplomatic stalemate. Thus, when Barak lectured Sharon in the Knesset, in his final act as prime minister, on Israel's existential need to achieve unilateral "separation" between itself and the Palestinians, he was nurturing a seed that had already been planted and was growing.

Barak's belated unilateralism as expressed in the planned fence—and its conceptual rationale, the demographic threat—were both still ideological anathemas to the Israeli Right. A fence meant partitioning

Eretz Yisrael. Even if it were purportedly erected as a temporary step for strictly security reasons, it would become a permanent political reality, the Right warned. Israel would be back on or near the 1967 line, and all the settlements beyond the fence would wither or be forcibly dismantled. As for the so-called demographic threat, with more than a million ex-Soviet immigrants having unexpectedly poured into the country over recent years, only Israelis of little Zionist faith could still brandish that cowardly old canard.

In the Likud, and even more so in the settler movement, there was a vague but uncomfortable sense that Sharon was wobbling. Why did he persist in proclaiming, even after Netanyahu had withdrawn from the race, that his goal after the election was a national unity government with Barak as his minister of defense? Granted, the Knesset arithmetic would make it hard for him to form a coalition. But why Barak? Likud loyalists demanded. Barak was the man who still, even at this eleventh hour, was trying to sell out on Jerusalem and the Temple Mount. And what was this vague but troubling talk by Sharon of "painful concessions," a phrase Sharon began to use in late December? Apart from anything else, this was hardly the way to fire up party activists and get them out on the streets in the weeks before the election.[45]

Sharon for his part, and his campaign managers, assumed the settlers and their supporters, whatever their doubts about him, would come out and vote for him. On the "Russian front," Sharon's team felt confident of crushing victory. Both Avigdor Lieberman, leader of the mainly immigrant party Yisrael Beiteinu, and Natan Sharansky, head of the older and now declining Yisrael B'Aliya, urged their followers to vote for Sharon. His sloganeering in this sector was unsubtly different from the general line. In Russian, the candidate was "a strong Sharon for a strong Israel" rather than the only man who would bring peace.

The Sharon camp remained anxious, though, over the danger that another large and important constituency, the *haredim*,* might not

---

* The *haredim* numbered an estimated 10 percent of eligible voters in the 2001 election. It is hard to be precise about the size, especially in electoral terms, of the various groupings that make up Israel's highly sectorized society. Not every "settler" or "Russian" or *haredi* or Israeli Arab necessarily votes with his sector, and these classifications themselves are not airtight. Among most self-defined *haredim*, though, voting "discipline" is strong—the rabbis choose the candidates—and there are relatively few deviants. The 2001 election was to be particularly noteworthy in this respect: whereas the average nationwide turnout was 61.2 percent (the lowest ever in an Israeli election), turnout in *haredi* areas topped 90 percent, meaning that the effective *haredi* proportion of the vote was around 15 percent. *Haredi* political power looks likely to grow: in 2009, 30 percent of Jewish first-grade children attended *haredi* schools.

turn out to vote at all. No one could confidently dismiss that prospect. There had never been an election solely for prime minister in Israel. The *haredim* had never before been required to go to the polling stations solely in order to vote for a Sabbath-desecrating, unkosher-eating candidate to lead the Zionist state. Granted, they had voted once before (in 1996) under the new electoral system for a secular prime minister (an overwhelming majority of them voted for Netanyahu in that impressive show of *haredi* political clout). But then, elections for the Knesset and for the prime minister were held simultaneously. The justification for voting in both was obvious to any Talmud student: We *went* to vote for our *haredi* party, which is our religious duty. Once *in* the polling station and handed two ballot slips, we voted for the (unfortunately secular) prime minister, too.

The key, as always, was in the hands of the rabbis. They had sanctioned—indeed, they had ordered—the vote for Bibi in 1996. Sharon needed them now to extend that Talmudic logic just a little bit further. For many years, he had been well enough liked in their councils. Barak, moreover, was positively disliked, having proclaimed in the fall of 2000 that he was planning a "secular revolution" that would dismantle many of the hallowed status quo arrangements between synagogue and state. But Sharon, too, had queered his pitch by voting and speaking in the Knesset, in July 2000, against the Tal Law, a controversial bill that sought to enshrine in statute the ad hoc exemption from army service granted by the state to yeshiva students. Sharon ensured that the rest of the Likud faction voted against the bill, too, despite mutterings in the ranks.

The original exemption had grown out of an agreement between David Ben-Gurion and the ultra-Orthodox parties in 1948. Back then, it affected a couple hundred yeshiva students. Each year it was extended by the minister of defense for another year. Now their number had risen to tens of thousands, to the seething resentment of those who did serve three years in the regular army and decades more in the reserves.

Sharon would have to eat his words if he wanted the votes of the *haredi* rabbis. He proceeded to do so with the best grace possible.

It worked. On January 27, Rabbi Ovadia Yosef, the Shas sage, gave orders to his followers to take to the streets and campaign for Sharon. It would be a sin, he ruled, for anyone not to vote for him. The aged Ashkenazi rabbis who ruled the United Torah Judaism party required more wooing, but eventually they, too, came around. On Election Day, February 6, the Council of Torah Sages published a formal letter in the *haredi* press instructing their flock to vote for "the candidate who, it is

to be hoped, will not lend his hand to destroy the status of religion."
It was a grudging, unenthusiastic endorsement. It pettily avoided men-
tioning Sharon's name. But it was good enough. Rabbi Yosef Shalom
Eliashiv, the senior non-Hasidic rabbi, let it be known that he himself
intended to go and vote. The rebbe of Vishnitz, doyen of the Hasidic
sages, said he would, too, if his health permitted. Sharon breathed easy.

While Sharon's strategy with the *haredim* was to persuade them
to come out and vote, his purpose with another large and potentially
crucial constituency, Israel's Arabs,* was to encourage them to stay at
home. Their various political leaders were urging them to do so as a
deliberate act of retribution against Barak in the wake of the October
police shootings. Barak hoped that his appointment of a commission
of inquiry into the shootings would mollify Arab opinion and lead
to a rescission or at least partial relaxation of the boycott. But that
had not happened. Now the Barak camp pinned its hopes on Sharon's
long-established image, from Kibbiya through Sabra and Shatila, as a
cruel and indiscriminate killer of Arabs. Surely that would persuade
Arab voters to swallow their anger and come out to vote?

The Sharon campaign could only soft-pedal the candidate's military
past in its television broadcasts and hope not to arouse painful memories among the Arabs. Happily, this tactic perfectly dovetailed into the
campaign's broad election strategy. This was essentially two-pronged:
to say as little as possible, and to project a reassuring aura of empathy
and sagacity. Saying little was simple enough: the campaign media
chief, Eyal Arad, simply declined almost all requests for interviews, on
air or in print. On the rare occasions when he did speak, the candidate
visibly strained to confine himself to unprovocative platitudes. The
message was peace, security, and unity, and he kept on message.

In television campaign broadcasts, the image of the grizzled old
warrior was not completely airbrushed out; there were still the heroic
scenes from the Yom Kippur War, with Sharon in his bloodstained
head bandage. But that was no longer the predominant impression.
Rather, viewers took away with them an oft-repeated scene of the
white-haired, portly, but spry grandfather-farmer striding through
his fields in gum boots, two young children running toward him. He
stoops and, strong but gentle, hoists his beloved grandson into the air.
He hugs him to his breast. The cows look on, in sympathetic bovine

---

* Arabs accounted for 12.3 percent of eligible voters, according to Central Bureau
of Statistics figures. As with the *haredim,* this figure was significantly lower than
their overall percentage of the population, because of the relatively high proportion
of children in the Arab and *haredi* communities.

placidity. String instruments play subtly patriotic music in the background. "Ariel Sharon—leader to peace" is the slogan sung softly but with conviction by a choir of girls.

In unused footage, some of the farm animals are seen turning and trotting away as he approaches. "If they're going to run off, people will say I frighten even the cows," Sharon jokes into the camera. The chief goal was to portray him as strong but not frightening. Middle-of-the-road voters were to be subtly weaned of their long-ingrained fear of him.

It was probably one of the more brilliant makeovers in advertising history. It succeeded, in part at least, because the scene of rural domesticity was not false. Sharon's home and family had always been integral parts of his life. Especially after the death of Lily, he sought out the company of his grandchildren and loved to live alongside them on the ranch. The task of Reuven Adler, his adman friend and now his campaign manager, was to project that aspect of the candidate's persona, less familiar to the general public, and eclipse, though not entirely erase, the image of the tough old general. Old generals never die, and this one, the TV clips beamed, was still fighting fit and would know how to handle the terror and violence of the intifada. "I will bring peace that will protect us," a sober-looking Sharon declares to the camera, now in a solid blue suit and conservative tie. The unseen girls' choir chants that line, too, in a sentimental jingle. The mature and loving Sharon offered much more to the voter than military know-how. He offered experience, moderation, reliability, statesmanship.

In a deeper sense, beneath the saccharine texts and slick camera work, the makeover was the climax of two decades of dogged, infinitely patient work—by the admen and other advisers, but above all by the candidate himself. Sharon's comeback began the day after he was ousted from the Defense Ministry by the Kahan Commission in 1983. Circumstance and fortune helped him to stay on the slippery pole and keep clambering relentlessly up it. But his chief mainstay was his own iron determination to recast his appeal to the broad swath of the Israeli mainstream, no longer as a swashbuckling extremist with a vicious streak and a big chip on his shoulder, but as a seasoned yet mellowed leader whom the country could rely on.

Sharon, then, was no mere actor reading his lines. He was part of the plot. Indeed, his new image *was* the plot. But was it all political strategy, or was it substance, too? And where is the line between them? Plainly, this windfall election was a defining moment for Sharon. Was the change in his image all slick campaigning, or did it reflect changes taking place "inside him," in his understanding of what was required of Israel's leader? Was his sole concern achieving popularity—first in the election, then in the job of prime minister, and finally in the history books? Or did his newfound moderation express a genuine embrace of pragmatic positions not only because they were popular but also because he was coming to believe in them?

The two advisers closest to him, who effectively ran his campaign, are divided over how to read this defining moment. For Uri Shani, the veteran aide whom Sharon had brought in to revitalize the half-moribund Likud when he took over as chairman, the election campaign was just that: a campaign. Scripted and directed by cynical professionals, it sought solely to harmonize the candidate, to the greatest extent possible, with the needs and desires of the voters. The candidate, in Shani's narrative, was as cynical and professional as the rest of the team—at that point. Sharon did definitely undergo a dramatic and genuine change of perspective, says Shani. But it came later, when he was prime minister. Sharon's oft-repeated line as prime minister, "What you see from here, you don't see from there," was literally true. Once ensconced in the Prime Minister's Office, he began seeing things differently.

Shani recalls the moment he noticed the change creeping over his boss. "I saw him become prime minister in the real sense; no one else did." In July 2001, now director of the Prime Minister's Bureau, Shani was riding alone with Sharon in a motorcade speeding the Israeli leader from an Italian military airport toward Rome, on an official visit.

> It was a lovely sunny day. There were the shiny limousines, the uniformed outriders, the helicopters above. I must have said something about how nice it all was, when suddenly he says, "Don't get too enthusiastic: they exiled us from Eretz Yisrael." I honestly didn't know what he was talking about. "Who exiled us?" "The Romans," he says. "What's that got to do with this?" I asked. "It's the same thing . . ."
>
> This was a serious conversation; not some kind of charade or joke. It was the first time that I saw he was looking at things differently. Later I was to see it again, with the Americans and in other diplomatic encounters. He was looking three thousand years backward and thousands of years forward. He was looking at himself as just one link in the chain of Jewish history. His task was to carry it through his term and hand on the burden. He felt it on his shoulders. For me, it was completely unexpected.

Reuven Adler, the advertising executive and personal friend, was never part of Sharon's official entourage and did not watch him function as prime minister on the international stage as Shani did. But Adler maintains that he, as campaign manager and copywriter par excellence, was profoundly in tune with the process of change and maturation that had been going on in Sharon for years before he became prime minister. For Adler, the 2001 election campaign was the confirmation of that process and the unambiguous signpost to what lay ahead. The slogans, which he authored, were not manipulative or cynical: they said what the candidate meant.

"I knew for sure that everything was changing with him when he approved the slogan 'Only Sharon will bring peace.' He sat here, in this room," Adler recalls, looking around the bright corner office from where he directs his large advertising agency.

I told him the slogan. He looked at me for a long moment; he didn't say anything. I was alone with him. And then he said, "Go with it." I asked him if he was sure he knew what it entailed. He said, "I know. Go with it."

No, we weren't duping the voters. Israelis were looking for hope. The situation was beyond despair. Arafat was the demon, which helped Arik enormously. But basically the people don't want endless war. The Jewish dream in Eretz Yisrael is to bash the Arabs and to give back the territories! That was my point of departure. Only a strong and charismatic leader can deliver that dream. He's a huge leader, and if he believes in it—and in my heart I believe he wants peace—that's what the people want: a leader who can bring them peace and quiet. Now, that's a message you can express in a hundred pages, or you can say it in five words. I knew it would raise eyebrows, and I knew some people would dismiss it as merely cynical. I'm an image person myself, not an agenda person. But I am saying absolutely unequivocally that when we discussed the significance of the image-changing slogan "Only Sharon will bring peace," it was entirely clear to me, and to him, that this was not just an election slogan.[46]

CHAPTER 13 · POWER FAILURE

David Rubinger, an award-winning press photographer, had been taking intimate and memorable pictures of Ariel Sharon for decades. On election night, inside Sharon's hotel suite, his victory tableau seemed suffused with prophetic insight: a one-frame promo of the five tempestuous years to come. On the left, smug and beaming, is Uri Dan, the sharp-penned journalist whose much-scorned prophecy had now come true.* Dan had been Sharon's spokesman, amanuensis, friend, and indefatigably adulatory apologist since the 1950s. Now he confidently anticipated a position of prominence and influence in the Prime Minister's Office. He would be rudely shunted aside.

Dan's arm is draped around the shoulders of another jubilant Sharon associate of fifty years' standing, an ex-British, now–South African textile merchant named Cyril Kern. Kern came to fight as a young volunteer in the 1948 war. A wartime comradeship grew into a lasting friendship between the two men and their families, sustained by Cyril's frequent visits to Israel and stays at Sycamore Ranch. He was entirely unknown to the general public. Two years later, embroiled in allegations of shady political funding for Sharon, his name would become a household word.

Next in line, thrusting a smiling face between Cyril and Arik, is another longtime friend and funder, the ex-Israeli, now-American businessman Arie Genger. He is about to embark on a brief but not insignificant career as unofficial messenger between the prime minister of Israel and the White House. He was assisted on this mission by

---

* "Those who didn't want him as chief of staff got him back as minister of defense; and those who don't want him as minister of defense will get him back as prime minister." See p. 216. Dan's 1983 prediction had since entered Hebrew idiom as a byword for hubristic, revenge-filled fantasy.

the happy coincidence of being on friendly terms back from his student days, as he proudly told Sharon's aides, with Lewis "Scooter" Libby, powerful chief of staff to the powerful new vice president, Richard Cheney.[1]

And last in the group, Sharon himself, fixing the camera with a relaxed, composed, but distinctly non-exultant look. In the following days, reporters began to comment on how restrained and almost solemn Sharon appeared after his election triumph. He had reached the apex of his political life, but he hardly seemed to be rejoicing, at any rate not outwardly. With time, this behavior would become the hallmark of his increasingly popular leadership: coolness, restraint, an aura of mature unflappability and gravitas.

Behind the front line in Rubinger's composition is a group of laughing, chattering, plainly euphoric Likud Party activists. Sharon, turned away, seems to be almost pointedly ignoring them. That, too, would prove prophetically significant as his prime ministership unfolded. Omri Sharon, who had run the campaign and would run his father's relations with the party faithful, is seen in another frame, bending down to embrace the new prime minister.

Omri's partner in the campaign, Uri Shani, who would now become the all-powerful director of the Prime Minister's Bureau, was typically invisible but undoubtedly present behind the scenes. One celebrant discreetly not in the room was Muhammad Rashid, Yasser Arafat's financial adviser. He had spent much of the earlier evening with Omri at the offices of the Sharon family lawyer Dov Weissglas, watching television coverage of the voting. Why the three were together, why they continued to meet and talk over the next few weeks, and why Rashid seemed to welcome the election outcome that the Arab world, and indeed much of the wider world, mourned and feared—these questions fueled rumor and speculation as the new team prepared to take over.

Rashid was the Palestinian Authority's representative on the board of the hugely lucrative Oasis Casino in Jericho, which had drawn thousands of Israeli gamblers each evening in its heyday but now stood silent and empty because of the intifada. Weissglas represented the PA's partner in the enterprise, Martin Schlaff, an Austrian Jewish businessman and friend of the Sharons'. Once the television exit polls were in, Rashid phoned Arafat. "I told you, he's won big-time," he said, and immediately set about trying to broker a meeting between the two old enemies. Sharon did not say no. He insisted, though, that a meeting would have to be conditional on a major move by the Palestinians to suppress the rampant violence of the intifada.[2]

Only Omri and a very few others in Sharon's coterie were privy to these early diplomatic feelers. For much of the outside world, and certainly for the defeated and dispirited Israeli peace camp, Sharon's triumph exacerbated a nightmare that had begun on the Temple Mount and was now threatening to engulf all of Palestine in bloody conflict. There seemed no prospect or hope of any meaningful diplomacy. *The Guardian* put it baldly:

Sadly, Mr. Sharon needs no introduction. From his infamous role in the 1982 Lebanon invasion to his deliberately provocative, personal intrusion into Arab East Jerusalem last September, the ex-general and Likud leader has been a consistently prominent foe to peace, a confrontational rejectionist to match the hardest of Hamas or Hizbullah hardliners.

Israeli doves were devastated. People uninhibitedly gave voice to their moral and political despair and, in many cases, their physical fear for their own and their children's futures. Some spoke openly of looking to leave the country and build their lives elsewhere. Remembering him as the builder of the settlements, the instigator of the Lebanon War, and, most recently, the provoker of the Palestinian uprising, they expected only the worst from Sharon as prime minister. The speed and starkness with which Barak's policies and promises had all collapsed were driven home now by the huge margin of his defeat. Sharon swept home with a 62–38 majority.* Every middle-of-the-roader, every floating voter, seemed to have turned his or her back on the Labor Party leader, on the Oslo process, and effectively on peace with the Palestinians.

For Marit Danon, the dread and desperation posed an immediately practical problem. "I was in panic," she recalls. "Both because of my political views and because I was frightened of what would happen. I'd been reading up about him. One night I had to get Barak to sign some documents, and I let it out. 'Prime Minister, I won't work with that man . . . I don't sleep nights . . . I can't stay here . . . My conscience won't allow me to.' "

Danon had worked as the private secretary of Prime Minister

---

* The final figures were 1,698,077 votes for Sharon, or 62.38 percent; 1,023,944 votes for Barak, or 37.62 percent; the margin—674,133 votes, or 24.67 percent. Voter turnout was the lowest ever in an Israeli election: 62.28 percent, compared, for instance, with 78.7 percent in 1999. But this was the only ever Israeli election just for prime minister, not for the Knesset.

Yitzhak Shamir as well as of the politically more palatable Rabin, Peres, and Barak. "Barak slammed his fist down on the desk. I think this was the first time he raised his voice at me. 'You're not leaving this place! He's not the man you think he is . . . Listen to me. This is a man who reads, who loves music and art. He's not what he looks like from the outside.' Back home, I thought to myself that I'd had a good working relationship with Barak and he wasn't going to dupe me deliberately. I'd give it a chance."[3]*

In the world's chanceries the reactions to Sharon's victory were similarly horrified or at best ambivalent. Statesmen mouthed the requisite diplomatic congratulations through clenched teeth. In Washington, Secretary of State Colin Powell issued an "impassioned plea" for restraint. Leaders in the region should "recognize the absolute importance in controlling the passions, in controlling the emotions," Powell said. This made predictably little impact in Syria, where officials described Sharon as a racist, a war criminal, and a terrorist and predicted his election probably meant war. In neighboring Lebanon, too, the newspaper *Almustaqbal,* owned by Prime Minister Rafiq al-Hariri, ran the headline "Israel Has Voted to Reject Peace." In Egypt, though, the state-owned Cairo Radio urged the Arab world to give Sharon a chance. Here, Begin's return of the whole of Sinai had been a dramatic change of policy and ideology that gave hope, however slender, that Sharon, too, might change his thinking.

Sharon was eager to set about proving that the fears and trepidation about him were misplaced, the dredged-up detritus of times long gone. He was determined to build the closest possible relations with the United States. He had been effectively decreed persona non grata in Washington under the first Bush. A first friendly phone call from George W. Bush was encouraging. The president recalled his heli-tour of Israel as Sharon's guest back in December 1998. Neither of them had thought then they would meet next time as heads of their respective countries, Bush joked.[†]

---

* Four months later, Marit Danon walked into Sharon's room and "apologized 'for the terrible opinion I had of you.' I didn't blame the media or anything. I laid it on myself. I said, 'Prime Minister, I need to make a confession.' I felt I had to do it; it was really weighing me down. Because he'd been beyond the pale for me. Absolutely beyond the pale. He was dumbstruck." Her eyes mist over as she recalls this scene. In the 2003 election, though, she says, she voted, as always, Meretz.

† Particularly encouraging for Sharon to recollect was then governor Bush's reaction to the view from the air of pre-1967 Israel's ten-mile "waistline." According to

Sharon had not waited for the election to make contact with Arafat. Toward the end of January, he dispatched Omri, Dov Weissglas, and Eytan Bentsur, his director general back at the Foreign Ministry, on a discreet mission to Vienna, where they spent a long evening at Martin Schlaff's home together with Muhammad Rashid.

They were not, however, discreet enough. A report of their trip was broadcast the same evening on Channel 1 (state-owned) television. It said they had flown to see Schlaff. Weissglas was quoted as saying they would meet with "a Middle Eastern personality" who happened to be in Europe. The trip, he insisted, had nothing to do with Schlaff's business affairs. This immediately triggered speculation, much of it pejorative, about the Sharon family's rich friends, about kickbacks and corruption in the Palestinian Authority, and about possible connections between the two.

Weissglas, flying back into the storm, denied the Jericho casino had even been mentioned at the talks in Vienna. But the Labor campaign hammered away at the attorney's multitasked role as Schlaff's business representative, Sharon's libel lawyer, and now Sharon's political emissary to . . . Schlaff and Rashid, the casino partners. "Sharon's world blurs between business interests and policy considerations," Labor accused.

But no one could produce any hard proof of bribery—then or later. Sharon himself claimed the meeting in Vienna had been Arafat's idea and was intended for Rashid to learn firsthand about Sharon's policies. It had nothing to do with the casino. "I don't gamble with the fate of the country the way Barak does," Sharon quipped. On the Palestinian side, Minister of Information Yasser Abed Rabbo complained the leak helped Sharon contend he was in dialogue with the Palestinians. "We want to prevent this criminal and murderer from attaining power," he thundered. But he did not deny that the meeting had taken place.

Allegations of corruption dogged Sharon virtually throughout his term. It was almost taken for granted that Sharon's family finances and his political funding were shot through with conflict of interest, at the very least. In tens of thousands of Israeli homes that weekend, people lectured each other knowingly about Sharon's vast (for Israel) ranch, and where had he got the money for it? And what did he owe the rich men who helped him buy it? And all his other rich friends in America and Europe, and Israel? But this pervasive presumption of

---

Mel Sembler, a Republican activist who organized the 1998 trip for Bush and three other governors, Bush remarked: "We've got driveways in Texas longer than that" (Miller, *Much Too Promised Land,* 324).

impropriety seemed to have little or no effect on voters—not at the 2001 election, which took place ten days after the Vienna story broke, and not in the 2003 election, which, as we shall see, was also preceded by seriously uncomfortable media disclosures.*

Barak himself led Labor in intensive negotiations with Likud for a fortnight after the election, then suddenly announced that he was taking a break from politics after all, as he had originally announced on election night, and would not serve as defense minister or as any other minister. The Labor top echelon, with undisguised reluctance, gathered in late February to elect Shimon Peres interim leader in place of Barak, pending a party-wide leadership primary later in the year. Peres wasted no time in agreeing to Sharon's terms for the unity government. Labor made a last, feeble effort to get the Treasury instead of Defense. But Sharon was adamant: the purse strings stayed in the hands of the Likud. He earmarked Silvan Shalom, a hungrily ambitious Likud figure, for that post—and only then telephoned Netanyahu, who was in New York, ostensibly to ask him to join the government. "What position?" Netanyahu asked. "Come home and we'll talk about it." Netanyahu got the message. "There's no need to talk," he said. "I wish you every success." Peres took the Foreign Ministry; his Labor colleague Binyamin Ben-Eliezer got Defense.

Sharon's treatment of David Levy was breathtakingly shabby. Levy had led his three-man faction out of Barak's coalition, hastening its collapse. "I'm sorry, David," Sharon told him, blithely ignoring the enormous debt he owed the man from Beit She'an for single-handedly preventing Netanyahu from leaving him out of his government in 1996, "I don't have a department for you." He suggested that Levy become a minister without portfolio, which the onetime deputy prime minister, foreign minister, housing minister, and absorption minister

---

* Bentsur insisted, in an interview for this book, that there was no impropriety in the Vienna meeting, at least at the session in which he participated. "The casino never came up. We were trying to weave channels of communication so we could start working together as soon as Sharon came into office. It was entirely proper, and in fact quite promising." But Bentsur did not dismiss a friend's subsequent suggestion, purportedly based on an intelligence source, that he was taken along as a front to cover separate talks of an improper nature. "I think Omri and the others are corrupt from head to foot," he said of Sharon's close advisers. Bentsur was the first of several high-ranking public officials—we shall encounter the head of the Mossad and the army chief of staff later—who left the government service after clashing with Sharon's staff and became outspoken critics of Sharon's alleged corruption, though without being able to adduce smoking-gun evidence to clinch their accusations.

indignantly spurned. "I'm not going to sit there just to warm a chair," he told reporters outside Sharon's office.

A month for cobbling together a coalition is considered, in Israel, almost lightning speed. On March 7, Sharon stood proudly on the Knesset podium to read out his list of twenty-six ministers. "I could have formed a more compact and more homogeneous government," he said, meaning a rightist-religious alliance. "That would have been easier to run the country with. But I fear the price we would have had to pay to keep it going would have been too high." That same day, he demonstrated the advantage of leading a broad-based government and not being held in thrall to a bevy of little parties. The Knesset, led by the two biggest parties, Labor and Likud, voted to abolish the direct election system for prime minister and restore the old method whereby the voter cast one ballot only—for the party of his choice. This was an impressive show of consistency: Sharon had always opposed the direct election reform that was enacted nine years earlier, and he continued to oppose it, even though it had brought him to power so convincingly.

The peroration of his inauguration speech was taken from Lincoln's Gettysburg Address, which prompted Tamar Gozansky, a much-liked Hadash (communist) MK, to call out: "He freed the United States from slavery. It's time you freed us from the occupation." Sharon ignored that and concluded, to a hushed house: "It is Lily's birthday today. Lily was at my side and supported me through all the hard times and the happy times, and in all my struggles. At this moment I and my family miss Lily very much. Thank you all."

By the time of the inauguration, Sharon's aides, working quietly, had negotiated a draft cease-fire accord with Arafat's men. Sharon himself, despite his vaunted distaste, had spoken twice on the telephone with the *rais*, in English and without interpreters. He said he would send a trusted emissary to meet with him and his people in Ramallah. He had sent the most trusted of all: Omri.

This could only be interpreted as a positive gesture toward Arafat. Omri went together with Yossi Ginossar, a former Shin Bet man now in business with Palestinian partners who had served both Rabin and Barak as a discreet messenger to the PA. They had two meetings with Arafat, who was attended by Rashid and other aides. Subsequently, Arafat's deputy, Mahmoud Abbas (Abu Mazen), and the chief Oslo negotiator, Abu Ala, now Speaker of the Palestinian parliament, visited Sharon at the ranch. Sharon proposed a temporary Palestinian state on 42 percent of the land—effectively Areas A and B. This was rejected, unsurprisingly. But on February 28, the draft cease-fire was concluded to end the current violence and resume formal peace negotiations. It would have ended the intifada right at the outset of Sharon's term.*

The draft was never signed. A senior Palestinian official hinted privately to the Israelis that Arafat had backed away at the last minute. Rashid, the chief go-between, disappeared for several weeks, and when he finally surfaced, he, too, confirmed that "the *rais* rejected my plan."⁴

Sharon, meanwhile, was preparing for his first visit to Washington. The president invited him to come on March 20, barely a fortnight after he took office. That looked like a friendly sign, but it also seemed to indicate that the administration wanted early confirmation of its own assurances to other governments of Sharon's newfound moderation and perspicacity.

The visit laid the foundation for a remarkable—because so unexpected and seemingly incongruous—empathy between George W. Bush and Ariel Sharon (though it is unsurprising that Bush 43 shrugged off warnings and pejorative depictions of Sharon from members of the Bush 41 administration). For all new Israeli prime ministers, their first visit to Washington is almost an extension of their election victory celebration. For Sharon—and especially given the name and provenance of his host—it was the very acme of his long-yearned-for rehabilitation.

The Israeli press punditry pointed out that the U.S. administration had yet to define detailed policy goals in the region beyond the broad aim of crushing or at least containing Saddam Hussein's Iraq. Hence, according to the pundits, Sharon had been allowed to drone on about the dangers of terrorism worldwide (he mentioned bin Laden), about

---

* Published only years later, the draft provided that

- Israel was to pull back its troops within four weeks to their pre-intifada positions;
- final status negotiations would resume by the end of April;
- a Sharon-Arafat summit would be held in March, to be followed within three days by security coordination talks on various levels;
- Israel would carry out the still-unimplemented third further redeployment (FRD);
- Israel would refrain from unilateral actions in Jerusalem and from building new settlements; and
- the PA would commit to fight terror and prevent attacks; Arafat would denounce terror and violence; as a goodwill gesture, Israel would release forty Palestinian prisoners.

Arafat's inadequacies, and about Israel's security needs, without Bush pushing him harder on the nitty-gritty issues of the occupation and the intifada.*

But for all of Bush's broad sympathy with his Israeli guest, the private meeting was not all declamatory. Sharon surprised the president, in the deepest confidence, with a remarkably far-reaching catalog of the areas he would be prepared to cede, and the settlements he would be prepared to dismantle, in the context of an end-of-belligerency agreement with the Palestinians. This would be less than full peace but a substantial interim step on the road to eventual peace (which, in Sharon's view, could take fifty years to reach). Bush for his part made Sharon promise that despite his loathing for Arafat, and despite the president's own barely veiled contempt for him, Israel would not physically harm the Palestinian leader.

The violence at home, meanwhile, was steadily escalating. In March 2001, Palestinian suicide bombers attacked civilian targets inside the green line. There had been a spate of such attacks inside Israel during the mid-1990s, but in the "al-Aqsa Intifada" thus far suicide attacks had been confined to the occupied territories, targeting soldiers and settlers. (There had been car bombings and other forms of terror attacks inside Israel.) Israeli Military Intelligence saw the change as a calculated strategic decision and attributed it directly to Arafat. He had given the Islamic organizations the "green light," Sharon was told.

Shaul Mofaz, then IDF chief of staff and subsequently Sharon's minister of defense, recalled a clandestine report that reached him on February 11 of a meeting between Arafat, his security chiefs, and key Hamas leaders at which the *rais* asked, "Why do the Jews not have more deaths?" And he added: "You know what to do." "That was the day," said Mofaz, "when he unleashed the wave of suicide assaults inside Israel that grew more and more devastating until it climaxed in the Passover seder attack in the hotel in Netanya a year later."[5]

---

* Indyk recounts how Bush pulled him aside and asked, " 'Why didn't Arafat take the [Clinton] deal?' I responded that there was enough blame to go around. However, if I had to give the most important reason, I would say it was lack of leadership on Arafat's part. 'That's exactly right. No leadership,' said the president. '. . . Now there's nothing to be done because Arafat already rejected an offer that Sharon is not going to repeat . . . There's no Nobel Prize to be had here.' He obviously felt he had it figured out" (Indyk, *Innocent Abroad,* 379). Aaron David Miller, another Clinton Middle East man, conveys the same presidential wisdom more graphically. "Colin Powell summed up the president's view best for me: 'I don't want to do what Clinton did because it takes a lot of time. The prospects of success, rather than fear of failure, are really quite low . . . and I got two wars going on. Why am I going to fuck around with these people?' " (Miller, *Much Too Promised Land,* 324).

When Arafat asked his question, the Palestinians had sustained more than three hundred dead in the intifada and Israel around sixty. Not all intelligence experts concurred as to the hierarchical nature of the intifada and the measure of blame and responsibility that should be attributed to Arafat. When the suicide bombings multiplied, some argued that individual motivation, especially revenge over the killing or wounding of a close relative, needed to be factored in alongside ideological and organizational aspects to fully analyze and understand the spectacular growth of this ghoulish form of terror.[6]

Sharon roundly blamed Arafat for everything on the Palestinian side of the intifada, including the suicide bombings. His preoccupation during these early months was over the growing mood of help-lessness among the public as the bombings took their arbitrary toll of Israeli civilian lives. But above all, he was concerned about the army's ability to fight back and win. "In my day, we didn't know how to do these things," he observed caustically when treated to a state-of-the-art computer presentation by senior IDF officers early in his term. "But I'll tell you what we did know how to do. We knew how to fight."[7]

He seriously feared that despite the almost immeasurable disparity of military power, the army was incapable of defeating the Palestinian armed uprising. "He felt the army, for all its might, was helpless," Uri Shani recalled. "Something had gone seriously wrong. The main prob-lems, as Sharon saw it, were unsuitable commanders and inadequate training. The elite units were brilliant, but the regular forces deployed in the West Bank and Gaza—he wasn't sure they had the capacity to defeat the intifada. For years, Lebanon had been seen as a fighting front, whereas the Palestinian territories were a policing assignment."[8]

The prime minister's concerns were not just tactical. "He felt the IDF, in addition to its operational weaknesses, lacked a basic under-standing of the ripple effect of losing . . . of the need to demonstrate effective military strength if you were going to show flexibility on the diplomatic front."

In June 2001, after a ghastly Friday night suicide bombing at the Dolphinarium discotheque on the Tel Aviv seafront that left 21 teen-agers dead and 132 injured, Sharon ordered the army to prepare to enter the *casbas,* the Palestinian inner cities, in pursuit of terror cells. Chief of Staff Mofaz noted that the soldiers' lives would be in danger because there weren't enough ceramic bulletproof vests to go around. Sharon retorted that the emergency stores were full of these vests, so much so that Israel had been supplying them to neighboring Jordan.

Mofaz replied that these stores were intended for war. "Kaplan* and I exchanged glances," Shani remembered. "We knew what was coming. 'This *is* war, in case you haven't understood till now,' Sharon thundered. 'We are at war!' "

Sharon did not see the hardy and usually aggressive Mofaz as his problem, but rather the echelon of field commanders below the chief of staff. His solution was to take to the field himself. "There were dozens of visits to units in the West Bank," said Arnon Perlman, Sharon's close aide and spokesman. "He focused on the colonels and the lieutenant colonels, the men who commanded the brigades and battalions. He would spend hours with them, going over ideas, poring over maps. He would come away feeling the army was not prepared, conceptually, for winning this war. That he needed to shake it up himself."[9]

Sometimes he would invite groups of field officers to his office in Jerusalem. He would regale them with accounts of the exploits of Unit 101 in the 1950s and of his anti-terror operations in Gaza in the 1970s. His message never varied: surprise the enemy; throw him off balance; come at him from an unexpected angle; attack, always attack.

"RESTRAINT IS STRENGTH"

For all his nostalgic, blustering exhortations to the officer corps, Sharon as prime minister was a very different, much more cautious commander than the brutal major of the 1950s, the ruthless general of the 1970s, or the intemperate defense minister of the 1980s. "He consciously allowed himself to be restrained, by me, by others," Minister of Defense Binyamin Ben-Eliezer recalled years later. Sharon ranted and bellowed in fury after particularly heinous terror attacks, demanding instant and massive retribution. "Kill the dog" was his mildest demand, often screamed into the telephone, usually in reference to Arafat. But by the time the first meetings took place with the defense minister and senior IDF officers, the prime minister's wrath was subsiding and cooler councils prevailed.

Moshe Kaplinsky, who was appointed military secretary to the prime minister in July 2001, said he "quickly discovered that Sharon as prime minister was very different from his image . . . much more

---

* Sharon's military secretary Moshe Kaplinsky, later CO of Central Command and then deputy chief of staff.

realistic and controlled. He understood that not everything was military force. Yes, I thought restraining him would be part of my job, to the extent that a military secretary can restrain a prime minister. But in intimate consultations I saw how he thought about the ramifications of every move. I saw this was a complex man; not the simplistic advocate of brute force that one had been led to believe."[10]

International diplomacy had moved into high gear with the publication of the Mitchell Report on April 30. As we saw, the commission declined to lay the blame on Sharon for triggering the intifada with his visit to the Temple Mount. Nor did it give succor to the Israeli contention that Arafat had preplanned the uprising. But it also spoke movingly about the need to stop the violence and offered a blueprint for a way forward. This included

- an immediate end to the violence;
- an immediate resumption of security cooperation;
- "the Palestinian Authority [should] make a 100 percent effort to prevent terrorist operations and to punish perpetrators";
- "the Government of Israel should freeze all settlement activity, including the 'natural growth' of existing settlements";
- "the GOI should ensure . . . non-lethal responses to unarmed demonstrators";
- "the PA should prevent gunmen from using Palestinian populated areas to fire upon Israeli populated areas and IDF positions"; and
- "the GOI should lift closures, transfer to the PA all tax revenues owed, and permit Palestinians who had been employed in Israel to return to their jobs."

The PA announced on May 15 that it accepted the report and supported its immediate implementation. Sharon for his part said Israel accepted the report, too—with two reservations and one condition: it rejected the settlement freeze; it objected to the criticism of the IDF; and it demanded seven days completely free from violence before implementation could begin.

The Mitchell proposals became the basis of American and international diplomacy, with efforts focused on getting the parties to translate their ostensible acceptance into tangible action. Sharon stuck to his seven-day demand, which, given the chaotic situation in the territories, he could confidently assume would not be met. This conveniently enabled him to ignore the initial requirement from Israel in the Mitchell Report: the settlement freeze. In late May 2001, though, in response to mounting international pressure, he proclaimed a unilateral cease-fire, "save for life-threatening instances." The IDF stopped initiating operations in the territories and tightened its open-fire regulations. The Americans were to procure parallel steps from Arafat, but the most he would agree to was a resumption of meetings between officers for security coordination. This initial, tentative upturn was blown to smithereens at the Dolphinarium discotheque on the Tel Aviv promenade that Friday night in June.

On the following Sunday evening, Sharon visited the injured youngsters and their families at the Ichilov Hospital in Tel Aviv. He was not a frequent visitor at hospitals or at gravesides or at the scenes of terror attacks. His aides explained that the security phalanxes around him made such visits burdensome. Not all commentators were convinced. Some recalled pointedly that as defense minister, too, during the Lebanon War, he generally steered clear of hospitals and funeral parlors.

He was visibly moved by the self-discipline of some of the injured Russian immigrant kids, biting back their pain, summoning up a determined smile when the prime minister swept in trailed by a bevy of cameras. "Restraint, too, is a component of strength," he proclaimed at an impromptu press conference at the hospital. "We are waging a very hard battle indeed. The behavior of the injured boys and girls is truly admirable, as is the behavior of their families, dignified behavior by people who have only recently come to this country."[11]

There was nothing impromptu in Sharon's choice of words. The phrase "restraint is strength" instantly became an aphorism, as its author, Reuven Adler, knew it would. It came to articulate what was seen as the quintessence of the new Sharon: prudent, calm, long-suffering, conscious of the complexities of Israel's predicament. Sharon enhanced the effectiveness of the phrase by appearing to apply it both to himself and to the young patients smiling through their pain. "When will it all end?" Larissa and Victoria, both encased in plaster, asked him as he walked slowly between the beds in the orthopedic ward. "It's gone on for a hundred years," he replied. "Only peace will end such attacks," one of the girls ventured. "I am trying all I can to bring that about," the prime minister quietly answered her.

" 'Restraint is strength' worked," Uri Shani said, looking back, both as a slogan and as a policy, though it was not popular with the Israeli public at the time. Israel did not strike back then. But when it did lash out nine months later, invading the Palestinian cities in Operation Defensive Shield, it enjoyed the broad support of the (post-9/11) Bush administration. "The fact that we restrained ourselves brought us political strength. The image of schoolchildren blown up at a beachfront club touched the world."[12]

The upshot was that within months of his coming to power, the visceral fear of Sharon in Israel and around the world largely dissipated. The many Israelis who were convinced, and terrified, that his advent would inevitably mean a drastic escalation in Israel's response to the intifada, with the concomitant dangers of igniting a regional war, recognized that that wasn't happening.

Abroad, too, leaders and commentators who had excoriated Israel under Barak for its disproportionate and indiscriminate use of military force against the Palestinians, and had warned direly that Sharon's election would bring a bloodbath, began to concede that they were wrong. The overall level and intensity of Israel's military activity remained essentially unchanged for the first year of Sharon's premiership. Targeted assassinations of Palestinians increased. But the overall rate of Palestinian fatalities never returned to the peaks of October and November 2000, while the number of Israeli victims rose toward the end of 2001 and soared in March 2002.

For many mainstream Israelis, the initial fear morphed into an uneasy distrust. This distrust was never fully to fade. Sharon's intentions, and even more so his motives, would always be impugned by his detractors and suspected, or at any rate questioned, by the broader public. But the distrust was to be increasingly tempered by two other attitudes that gradually embedded themselves in people's minds: reliance and, however grudging, admiration. Sharon as national father figure was an image that many people contemptuously eschewed in 2000. Five years later, almost incredulously, they were embracing it.

For Ariel Sharon to preach, and even more so to practice, "restraint is strength" was every bit as dramatic a reversal of his lifelong policies and lifelong image as the disengagement from Gaza four years later. The drama was less apparent at the time, and is perhaps less easy to pinpoint in retrospect, because, unlike the disengagement, it consisted of omission rather than action. Even when he did finally unleash the army, in Operation Defensive Shield in April 2002, he did so with restraint—relative to the IDF's real strength and relative, too, to the initial fears and dire prognostications about what he would do. This reversal of the whole flow of his public life until then led to a surge in his popularity. It would contribute significantly to the support he enjoyed in the broad center and even on the left of the Israeli spectrum when he eventually embarked on the disengagement from Gaza three years later. "Restraint is strength" paved the way for the disengagement.

From Shani's perspective, "restraint is strength" was also the culmination of his own makeover of Sharon during the previous two years, working closely with Sharon's son Omri. Though a true expression of the prime minister's policy, it was also a slogan, an extension, in a way, of the sophisticated sloganeering of the election campaign.

Marketing or reality? Image or substance? For Shani, the etymology seems inextricably blurred.

> I'm not talking about marketing. When a man says, I want to be prime minister, and I'm prepared to change my behavior in order to achieve that goal . . . I won't be the same man. I'll behave differently. I'll consult with people and listen to what they have to say—that's not just marketing.
>
> Right at the outset I said to him, if you want to be prime minister, you need to have 60 or 70 percent of the people supporting you. If you're seen as extreme right-wing, you don't have a chance. If you plonk down settlements all over the place . . . Omri kept saying: There is a chance. I wasn't sure. I was sure, though, that he was prime ministerial timber. That he was a man who could take decisions. I said, every time he talks extreme, or thinks extreme, we've got to pour a bucket of cold water over him. Like if you have a child who's hyperactive, you've got to give him Ritalin, and give him a balanced diet, and give him a calming environment, because at the end of the day he's a brilliant child. But if you allow noise and hullabaloo around him, then he'll be crazy. I'm trying to construct a colorful metaphor. This is Arik Sharon. When he was surrounded by people who worshipped him, who told him all day long, You're the greatest; you're a howitzer, you're the leader of Israel, which he wasn't, and they boosted the extremist side of his character, of his behavior, of his policy thinking . . . Look at his relations with the U.S. when he was defense minister—he didn't give a damn for them—compared with when he worked with us, before he became prime minister and as prime minister.[13]

What Shani depicts as his and Omri's successful effort "to bring out the inner Arik" was seen by some of Sharon's old retainers as a veritable kidnap. "After Lily got ill, Arik started to change," a former aide recalled sadly. "She was his compass; that's how he regarded her. Without her, Omri started to run riot. He took control of his father. He took his father to bad places. He sent himself as emissary to Arafat. He said to his father, 'Let me handle it' . . . The most painful moment was after the Dolphinarium. We'd got carte blanche from the

U.S. to act. Here in Israel there was total consensus that we've got to act. And . . . nothing!"

In this aide's pained, nostalgia-filled reading, the radical change that took place in Sharon's policy thinking was brought about by the overwhelming influence of Omri. " 'Restraint is strength'? I'm trying to explain to you this joke . . . The closeness of that family is difficult to describe and impossible to exaggerate. 'All for one and one for all' is a gross, gross understatement of their sense of solidarity. They trusted no one but each other, relied only on themselves."

Omri, the ousted aide conceded, may genuinely have changed his own views on the conflict with the Palestinians. But Arik—never.

> When Arik was minister of infrastructures, I once said to him, "Why don't you say you've got no problem with the Palestinians having a state? What do you care if they call themselves a state, as long as they don't have an army and an air force and we control their borders?" He nearly threw me out of the window! As prime minister, I once said to him on the phone, "Why don't you dismantle Netzarim [an isolated Jewish settlement in the Gaza Strip]? We need two battalions to defend it. Soldiers are getting killed there. Civilians are getting killed. Take it down . . ." I nearly dropped the phone from the decibel level of his shouts! And then he went and dismantled all the settlements in Gaza.[14]

Omri listened impassively to an account of this bitter indictment and said only, "I was an easy target. Whoever wanted to attack him attacked me." He phoned later to say, "You're overdoing my role, my influence, my views . . . I wasn't him."[15]

Omri's diffidence is closer to the truth than Shani's arrogance or than the spurned aide's bitter refusal to stomach his adulated leader's change of heart. "To say that Sharon was an instrument in the hands of Uri and Omri and Reuven Adler is an exaggeration," Avi Gil, a close aide to Shimon Peres, confirmed. "He was very dominant, very opinionated. Politicians aren't puppets." Gil was both an insider and an outsider during the formative period of Sharon's prime ministership. As Peres's man, he was not a member of Sharon's close coterie. And yet the coterie embraced him almost as one of their own, using his professionalism in their diplomatic activities and his interpersonal savvy in helping to keep the Sharon-Peres relationship running smoothly.

There was an informal atmosphere around the prime minister, Gil said, and people were encouraged to bat ideas around. Sharon felt enormously grateful to the people who helped him present an image of himself to the public that made him prime minister. "And they continued to be around him—Uri and Omri and Adler and others. But I do not believe that Sharon was dramatically influenced, in cardinal issues, against his will. He was clever and cunning and endowed with a healthy sense of humor so that he didn't really care if someone claimed to have influenced him. He could live with it."[16]

Another astute insider-outsider perspective came from Binyamin Ben-Eliezer, the defense minister during this first phase of Sharon's rule:

> Sharon was still totally preoccupied with defense, as he had been his whole life. But as prime minister he saw things differently. If anything, I was the one who wanted to hit out harder, particularly against the suicide bombers and the people behind them. He was for more careful, gradual, and considered actions. Yes, he went into a storming rage after terror attacks. But he knowingly let himself be restrained. He shouted and screamed, "Kill them," "Assassinations," "Bomb Arafat." But then he calmed down, and things were decided differently.
>
> As time went on, he continued to change. I'd known him for many years, in the army and in politics, and I felt it clearly. It was the effect of how he was impacting on the outside world and how the world impacted on him. From a persona non grata he became a legitimate leader and eventually an admired leader. Arik had been through a lot in his life. I'd almost go as far as to call this a brainwash. By Western leaders. By Bush, mainly. By Blair; he liked Blair. By others. They learned his weak points. They saw the gulf between his image and his sensitivities. He was a tough guy—the world likes tough guys—but he was talkable to. By his second year he felt he was being made welcome. This had a fantastic effect. You saw his eyes light up when he talked about Bush or even Mubarak.

It was the effect of his experience as a player on the world stage, Ben-Eliezer believes, that principally accounted for Sharon's subsequent further transformation, from settlement builder to settlement remover. "I knew he was totally determined to carry through this move. It began long before, with the security fence. Once he'd internalized the need for something, he would go for it, to the end. He was always like that. He had the feeling that the world expected something from him, and from him alone. To make the breakthrough."[17]

• • •

While Uri Shani's boasts—and the old loyalist's accusation—about Shani's influence on Sharon's mind need to be substantially discounted, Shani can justly take credit for running a tight ship at the Prime Minister's Bureau, imposing iron discipline on everyone, including his boss. The prime minister's other aides all attribute Sharon's eventual success and popularity, in no small degree, to the smooth functioning of the bureau, in terms both of its quiet efficiency and of the remarkable—indeed unique in Israeli prime ministerial annals—absence of interpersonal quarrels and rivalries among the close advisers. Years later, still all singing from the same hymnbook, they say of themselves and of each other: We all had big egos; we all left them at the door when we came to work for Sharon; Uri Shani was our model and mentor in this respect.

Even Marit Danon, who faults Shani for overstating his influence on Sharon, praises him as "a very, very good manager. Everything worked. There were no snafus. How does that come about? First, everyone is punctual. Things happen precisely when they're scheduled. Then there's the personality of the leader and his relationship to his staff. And finally, the team spirit. This was a very cohesive bureau. None of Sharon's close aides was sitting there with one eye on his future Knesset career (apart from Gideon Sa'ar, the cabinet secretary). To the present day, we're almost like one family."[18]

Danon's own presence on the team was due to Shani's diktat, as he tells it:

> When Sharon first came into the bureau, we had a quarrel over the secretary. I'd been there for two weeks ahead of time, organizing things. I decided we want Marit and not Arik's longtime secretary, Sara Shema. He approved of my other arrangements but balked at that. "What," he said, "I can't even have my own secretary?" I said simply, "No, you can't. You're the prime minister. You're not the manager. You're here to take the political decisions, the military decisions. You don't run the office." He agreed. I believed, and still believe, that prime ministers rise or fall on the way their bureaus operate. Of course that's not 100 percent of the story; but it's 60 percent at least!

Shani's despotism extended to the highest officials in the land.

> I resolved from the outset that this prime minister would not meet alone, "four eyes only," with anyone. Not the head of Mossad; not the head of Shin Bet; not the IDF chief of staff—no one. I and the military

secretary, or I and the policy adviser, or one of them alone, plus a tape recorder, would be present at every meeting.

Once, after "Gandhi's"* murder in October 2001, he was sitting with the head of Shin Bet, [Avi] Dichter, together with me and the military secretary and the tape recorder, and the head of Shin Bet says to him, "I'd like to talk to you four eyes only." The military secretary jumps up and leaves the room. After all, this is the prime minister and the head of Shin Bet. I said, "Sorry, there's no four eyes." Arik says to me, "Excuse me, yes?" I say, "*You* excuse *me*. There's no four eyes, Arik. I know what he wants from you in four eyes, and it's not going to happen." He went ballistic. He banged on the desk. "I demand to sit with Dichter!" I said, "Look, I'm sorry to have to remind you, but remember Sabra and Shatila? Remember the commission of inquiry? If I leave the room, that'll be precisely the point on which you won't be covered at a commission of inquiry. I'm not leaving. Think carefully. If you want me to leave—order me out of the room." All this in front of Dichter. Arik subsided, and they continued the meeting as though nothing had happened. Arik was crafty; he understood, despite his rage, that I knew something he didn't know, and wanted only to protect him.

Dichter, in the "six eyes conversation," asked Sharon to issue a statement explaining that he, as prime minister, had approved the Shin Bet's not having guarded Ze'evi. Ze'evi had refused to have a close Shin Bet escort, 24/7.

In other words, Dichter was saying, "Give me a rope and I'll hang you!" I didn't wait for Arik to answer. I said, "The prime minister will not do that. But I will help you, because you are an excellent head of Shin Bet and we're in wartime. If we were at peace, Dichter, I'm looking you in the eyes and saying quite frankly, you'd have to go, because the Shin Bet screwed up and a minister was murdered. What do you mean, 'He didn't want to be guarded'?! You screwed up. But we're at war. So you and I together will deal with this thing and fix it. But it won't touch the prime minister." Arik just listened. We got up and left the room. I issued a statement in my own name. It was the first I'd ever issued. And there was no commission of inquiry into how and why Gandhi was murdered, which is remarkable when you come to think of it.[19†]

---

* Rehavam Ze'evi, tourism minister and leader of the ultranationalist Moledet Party, was assassinated by Palestinian gunmen in October 2001.
† Shani was ruthless in winnowing out people he didn't want—including people to whom Sharon had promised jobs. Eytan Bentsur was one. The veteran diplomat

. . .

After the Dolphinarium, Sharon's efforts and his time were devoted almost entirely to fighting "the war" and conducting the diplomacy surrounding it. The U.S. administration sent the head of the CIA, George Tenet, to negotiate an immediate cease-fire and implement the Mitchell proposals. After hours of argument, he handed out a "working paper" and demanded a yes-or-no answer.

Sharon said yes. Tenet spent hours with Arafat in Ramallah, lying on the floor of the *rais*'s office with crippling back pains and haggling with him from this supine position. In the end, Arafat said yes, too, though he wrote Tenet a letter emphasizing the linkage between the Tenet Paper and the Mitchell Report, particularly the section of the report that required an Israeli settlement freeze.

On June 13, the two leaders each announced to his own people a new cease-fire and his acceptance of the Tenet Paper. Arafat's staff contacted a few of the key Fatah-linked activists and instructed them to hold their fire. Orders were transmitted to the Tanzim youth movement and the al-Aqsa Brigade cells across the Palestinian territories. But the PA did nothing to impose the cease-fire on Hamas and Islamic Jihad, the Islamist militias. In the ten days following the joint announcement, six Israelis were killed in shootings and bombings in

---

claimed later that he saw that the Sharon team were "amateurs and boors"—and walked out. Shani claimed he showed Bentsur the door because he was "not a team player." The man appointed foreign policy adviser was Danny Ayalon, a relatively junior Foreign Ministry man on reassignment to the Prime Minister's Office.

That was just the start of Ayalon's lucky streak. "I advised Peres not to accept any candidate put up by Sharon for ambassador to Washington who was not a professional diplomat," Peres's senior aide and Foreign Ministry director general, Avi Gil, recalled.

Block every proposed political appointment, I said, and then, once they're exhausted, let's present them with a list of Foreign Ministry candidates. That's what happened. There was a big lunch at the prime minister's residence, and Peres said, "Arik, let's make a really nonpolitical appointment from among our professional diplomats." Sharon said, "Whom do you have in mind?" and I immediately produced a list of twelve senior diplomats. Arik started discussing some of the names. He didn't rule them all out. Just then Danny Ayalon walks in with some document for Sharon to sign. Peres was feeling so triumphant that he exclaims, "Every Foreign Ministry man can be a candidate. Even Danny Ayalon." Ayalon, needless to say, was not one of the twelve names on the list. But Sharon, like a shotgun, banged his hand down and said, "We've got an ambassador!" He'd come to know Ayalon, apparently, and he liked him. I started whispering frantically to Peres, but it was too late. (Gil and Ayalon interviews)

the territories. Within weeks, Tenet's effort had sunk into oblivion, and the country was in the throes of a new wave of escalation.

Behind the scenes, the Bush administration was under heavy pressure from the Saudis to toughen its stance against Israel's repression of the Palestinians. Crown Prince Abdullah sent the president a stern letter, calling in question the entire American-Saudi relationship.[20] In his response, Bush committed himself, for the first time, to a "viable independent Palestinian state." In the State Department, too, work was under way on a major Middle East policy speech by Secretary of State Colin Powell, later in the fall, that would signal a more energetic and more evenhanded American approach to Middle East peacemaking.

For Sharon, says the then U.S. ambassador, Dan Kurtzer, this Saudi-U.S. exchange exacerbated his constant anticipation and fear of vigorous U.S. diplomatic intervention in the conflict. This was the ambassador's explanation of the Israeli leader's bizarre, provocative—but somehow ultimately canny—behavior in the period following 9/11.

Like every head of government, Sharon put in a condolence call to the president on watching the fall of the Twin Towers. He was called back about twenty-four hours later. He offered his sympathies and solidarity. Bush thanked him and said that now more than ever the United States understood what Israel is up against in its fight against terror. "Then," Kurtzer recalled, "Bush says, listen, you can do me a favor. I know you've authorized Shimon Peres to go meet Arafat. Well, this would be a good time to do it. Sharon says no, I'm not ready to do this now. He gets off the phone, and now you have a split screen: In the Oval Office, they're pissed, because Sharon is the first person in the world to say no to the president after 9/11, on something that they don't think is very cosmic. Sharon is pissed because the truck seems to be coming down the highway at him faster than ever."

The next day, Sharon held a conference call with members of the Conference of Presidents of Major American Jewish Organizations. "His anxieties and the anxieties of some of the people on that call fed off each other," Kurtzer recalled.

> I heard about it and asked to see him alone. I'd only been here two months, and we didn't yet have a relationship. But this is what ambassadors do. I tried to explain to him American politics and life after 9/11, which is my job. I told him, you understand what happened to us intellectually, but you don't understand it emotionally. Because you're a country that's been attacked. You've been at war for sixty years. We were attacked once, in 1941 . . . three thousand people is

huge. It's not like anything happened to us, but everything happened
to us. And in that context, I said to him, for you to say no to Bush on
anything . . . If he asked you for the moon, the answer had to be yes.
Well, he got angry at me, and the answer was no. And this built up
and built up and built up to his Munich speech.[21]*

In the weeks between 9/11 and the Munich speech, both Bush and
Sharon made public statements voicing their support for the eventual
creation of an independent Palestinian state. Sharon, aware that this
was the thrust of Bush's letter to Crown Prince Abdullah, made his
statement on September 23 to a gathering of teachers at Latrun, the
site of his 1948 brush with death in the bloody, failed battle against
the Jordanians. "Israel wants to give the Palestinians what no one else
gave them—a state. Not the Turks, the British, the Egyptians, or the
Jordanians gave them this possibility."

In hindsight, this speech was the harbinger of the transformation
to come. "His end goal was clearly partition," says Avi Gil. "That's
why he accepted publicly the principle of a Palestinian state." But the
speech made little impact at the time. No one in Jerusalem or in Washington took Sharon's declaration too seriously because it was assumed
that the borders he was contemplating would be rejected by the Palestinians as inadequate and the security conditions he proposed to
demand of them would be unacceptable. No one was thinking at that
time in terms of unilateral action. On the far right, nevertheless, the
speech deepened suspicions. When Bush spoke, a week later, some of
Sharon's hard-line critics blamed his Latrun speech for the president's
public espousal of Palestinian national aspirations.

Bush's "vision" of an independent Palestine living at peace alongside Israel was articulated at a press conference in the Oval Office on
October 2. "The idea of a Palestinian state has always been part of a
vision, so long as the right of Israel to exist is respected," the president
said. That was doubtless true, at least since the United States began a
dialogue with the PLO in the late 1980s. But it had never been spelled
out before so explicitly. The administration was at pains to stress that
the new policy pronouncement had been in the works before 9/11. The
pundits all presumed, nevertheless, that the decision to go public now
was linked to Washington's efforts to garner Muslim world support
for the imminent military assault on Afghanistan.

---

* Sharon's no quietly turned into a yes, and Peres and Arafat met on September 26, the day before Yom Kippur, at the Dahaniye Airport, close to the Gaza-Egypt
border.

Then, on October 5, Sharon lashed out at Bush with a pathos and ferocity that left the world aghast. "I appeal to the Western democracies," Sharon proclaimed in prepared remarks to journalists in Tel Aviv, "and first and foremost the leader of the free world, the United States: Do not repeat the terrible mistake of 1938. Then, the enlightened democracies of Europe decided to sacrifice Czechoslovakia in return for a temporary, comfortable solution. Do not try to appease the Arabs at our expense. We will not be able to accept that. Israel is not Czechoslovakia. Israel will fight against terror." He went on to review the failed cease-fire efforts and ended: "We can rely only on ourselves. And from today onward, we will rely only on ourselves."[22]*

Washington was livid and demanded an immediate retraction. Within a day, Sharon's office sensibly issued a statement explaining that his words had been misinterpreted. Sharon himself bawled out Ambassador Kurtzer on the phone. "It's *your* fault. *You* stirred things up in Washington. *Your* reporting of the speech shaped their thinking." When he finished, Kurtzer replied coldly: "Mr. Prime Minister, *you* created this crisis. I didn't even hear your speech, let alone report it."

In the Munich speech, Sharon's near-compulsive apprehensiveness over American diplomatic involvement in the conflict seemed to sweep aside all other considerations. His own aides were aghast. "He wrote the speech alone," one staffer recalled, "in his own hand, and sent it by fax from the ranch. As soon as I read it, I started sweating. I rushed over to Shani, but he said that Sharon was insisting. I phoned him and got shouted at: 'That's what I'm going to say, and that's all there is to it!' "

But Sharon read Bush right. Their relationship soon pulled out of this trough and developed into a closeness rarely achieved between leaders of the two countries. "That the president liked Ariel Sharon wasn't the point," Aaron Miller explained. "When it came to fighting terror, seeking peace, and promoting democracy, Israel was on the right side of the line. Arafat and the others had chosen the wrong side."[23]

Arafat moved with desperate speed not to be caught wrong-footed by 9/11. Initial outpourings of joy in the West Bank and East Jerusalem were quickly smothered, on his orders, by the PA's security forces.[24]

---

* Danny Ayalon, then still in Jerusalem as Sharon's policy adviser, blames Sharon's unofficial emissary to Washington, the businessman Arie Genger, and also the long-serving director of the Conference of Presidents of Major American Jewish Organizations, Malcolm Hoenlein, for whipping up "a sincere but unfounded sense that the Americans were going to dump us after 9/11 in order to cozy up to the Arabs. Genger usually read the American scene accurately. But this time he was way out. And Hoenlein, who saw molehills as mountains, nagged him incessantly. A professional diplomat would not have fallen into that rut."

He called in TV crews to film him giving blood in a Ramallah hospital for those injured in the al-Qaeda attacks. That same evening, a close aide met with three prominent Hamas figures in Gaza to deliver an unequivocal message from the *rais*. "From now on, you must do nothing that can damage the Authority. If Sharon succeeds in portraying us as terrorists, no one on earth will support us." The Fatah-linked Tanzim, too, was sternly warned to rein in its men. "We all heard," the Gaza Tanzim boss, Sammy Abu Samadana, recalled later. "But everyone went back home and did as he pleased."[25]

The Popular Front for the Liberation of Palestine (PFLP) certainly did. On October 17, two of its activists trailed the Israeli minister of tourism, Rehavam "Gandhi" Ze'evi, to his hotel room in Jerusalem and shot him dead. It was an act of revenge for the assassination by Israel of Abu Ali Mustafa, the PFLP leader, ten weeks earlier, and it was a great coup. Ze'evi was not merely the highest-ranking Israeli to be assassinated by Palestinians; he was a symbol and spokesman of the most extreme anti-Palestinian sentiment in Israeli political life. When Sharon, in the run-up to the election, had sent a greeting card to Arafat for the Muslim festival of Eid al-Fitr, Ze'evi commented that he, too, "would have sent Arafat an envelope, but not with a greeting card inside."[26]

"The era of Arafat is over," Sharon declared after Ze'evi's death, laying the blame on the *rais*.* The Shin Bet caught two members of the assassination squad and tracked down the others, including the man who masterminded the plot, Ahmed Saadat. They were holed up in Ramallah. Israel gave precise information to the PA and the United States. Arafat ignored the demands that he arrest them.

Sharon's relentless assault on Arafat's credibility with Washington was hugely assisted by the saga of a small cargo ship called the *Karine A,* which Israeli intelligence had been shadowing for weeks toward the end of 2001. Flying a Tongan flag of convenience and commanded by a Palestinian naval officer, the ship had taken on fifty tons of arms and ordnance at the Iranian island of Kish. The weapons were paid for, according to Israeli intelligence, by Fuad Shubaki, head of finance in the PA and Arafat's confidant.[27] When the ship turned toward the Suez Canal, intent on unloading its cargo off the Gaza coast, Israel decided to act. Chief of Staff Mofaz commanded the interception per-

---

* This was not far-fetched: the PFLP, though independent, was not an opposition force within the PA. Abu Ali Mustafa's office in Ramallah, where he was killed by a helicopter-launched rocket, was only a few hundred yards from Arafat's *muqata* headquarters.

sonally on the night of January 3, 2002, from an air force Boeing 707 command-and-control plane high above the Red Sea.

The first person Sharon told about the combined ops success was a man who he knew would appreciate its finer points: the former U.S. Marine Corps general Tony Zinni. "I asked Sharon if I could break the news to Arafat," the general writes in his memoirs. "I wanted to see the look on Arafat's face when I told him about it."[28] Zinni had been appointed in November U.S. special envoy to the region. He confronted Arafat with the *Karine A* on the first day of his second trip. " 'That is not true,' Arafat shot back. 'This was not our ship. It's an Israeli plot. This is an Israeli setup.' "[29]

Sharon sent Mofaz to Washington with detailed and unambiguous evidence of Arafat's personal involvement in the illicit (under Oslo) arms purchase. Condoleezza Rice, the national security adviser, saw the Israeli chief of staff as soon as he arrived. She took the evidence to the president that same evening.[30] Arafat made matters worse for himself by writing a letter to President Bush strenuously denying any link to the ship. It was transparently untrue, and Bush took it as a personal insult to his intelligence. "The president wrote him off after that letter," an American diplomat recalled.

By this time, the intifada violence had spiraled to new heights.

On November 27, a Palestinian disguised as an Israeli soldier sprayed bullets around the bus station in the northern town of Afula, killing 3 and injuring 30. Two days later, a suicide bomber on a bus killed 3 passengers at Hadera. Two days after that a double suicide bombing in the center of Jerusalem left 11 dead and 180 injured. On December 2, the following day, 15 died in a suicide bombing on a bus in Haifa. Hamas claimed responsibility for both of these attacks. On the fifth, an Islamic Jihad bomber apparently detonated his suicide belt prematurely on a street in Jerusalem; several passersby were injured. On the ninth, again in Haifa, a suicide bomber exploded himself at a busy junction, injuring 30. On the twelfth, two suicide bombers injured Israelis traveling in two cars to a settlement inside the Gaza Strip. And on the same day, on the West Bank, 10 bus passengers were killed and 30 injured in an attack outside the settlement of Emanuel. Within hours of this last outrage, the Israeli Air Force had bombed Arafat's headquarters in Gaza and destroyed his fleet of three helicopters.

Arafat, under intense American pressure, issued orders on December 16 for "a complete halt to all operations, especially suicidal operations." He vowed to "punish all those who carry out and mastermind such operations." A lull in the violence followed. Any hope of it lasting was dashed, though, by Sharon's decision, in mid-January, to authorize the assassination of a prominent and popular Tanzim militant, Raed Karmi. That, at any rate, is how many critics of the prime minister interpreted the even bloodier escalation in the violence in the early months of 2002.

The twenty-seven-year-old Karmi, formerly a PA intelligence officer, had become the undisputed boss of Tulkarm and the surrounding area. In the early months of the al-Aqsa Intifada, Karmi was answerable, at least nominally, to the senior Fatah figure in Tulkarm, Dr. Thabet Thabet, a dentist by profession and a man with many friends in the Israeli peace camp. These friends continued to maintain later that Thabet had remained a moderate and had done his best to rein in the swashbuckling Karmi. But the Shin Bet insisted that Thabet actively instigated attacks by Karmi and his men on settlers and soldiers in the West Bank. Ehud Barak accepted this extrajudicial indictment cum conviction, and Thabet was assassinated outside his home on December 31, 2000, by an army sharpshooter.

Thabet's killing divided Israelis. But Karmi's act of brutal revenge united them and marked him as a doomed man. Two young Tel Avivans were espied in a Tulkarm restaurant on January 23, 2001. They had come, with an Israeli-Arab friend, to buy provisions for their own restaurant on Sheinkin Street, Tel Aviv's trendy downtown drag, a million light-years from the intifada. Karmi and his thugs kidnapped them at gunpoint, drove them out of town, and shot the two Jews dead. They sent the Arab home to tell the tale.

Karmi was arrested by PA police and briefly jailed in Ramallah. But he easily escaped. For the whole of the next year he evaded Israeli hunter-helicopters and undercover hit teams while continuing to take his toll of Israeli lives, mainly on the West Bank roads but also inside Israel. In January 2002, with the new cease-fire spreading a partial and precarious quiet,* the Shin Bet tracked Karmi to his latest paramour and found that he was carelessly visiting her at the same time every morning, when her husband was out of the house. In his terrorist activities, the Shin Bet told the prime minister, Karmi was blithely ignoring the cease-fire, even though he had assured his Fatah superiors and an EU diplomat sent to pacify him that he would abide by it. He had two suicide belts ready for use and could send them on

---

* By IDF figures, Palestinian shooting attacks were down 75 percent. The Palestinians said the IDF had nevertheless killed twenty-one people in the three-week period following December 16, demolished dozens of homes, and made multiple incursions into Area A (Harel and Isacharoff, *Seventh War*, 185; *Economist*, January 31, 2002).

deadly assignment at any time. He was a "ticking bomb" and thus a legitimate target for elimination. Senior IDF officers and Minister of Defense Ben-Eliezer opposed Karmi's assassination at this time. They argued it would trigger a wave of reprisals. They believed that Arafat had been so weakened by 9/11 and compromised by the *Karine A* that the cease-fire might hold this time and perhaps be widened into a general pacification. But Sharon preferred the advice of the Shin Bet's chief, Dichter, and Chief of Staff Mofaz, and the order went out: kill him.

The means chosen was a roadside bomb, hidden in a wall. Israel was to feign ignorance; such devices were used in internecine feuds among the Palestinian militants. But someone in the Prime Minister's Bureau was indiscreet, and within hours the true story was out. Marwan Barghouti, the best-known Fatah-Tanzim leader on the West Bank, responded at a press conference in Ramallah: "If there is no security for the people of Tulkarm, there will be none for the people of Tel Aviv. The cease-fire is dead. Sharon has opened the gates of hell."[31]

Three days later, on January 17, a young Palestinian walked into a bar mitzvah celebration in Hadera, just across the green line from Tulkarm, pulled out an M16 assault rifle, and emptied two magazines into the celebrants. Six died and dozens were wounded. The assailant was finally shot dead. In Tulkarm, militants rejoiced on the streets, firing their rifles in the air. The cease-fire collapsed. Following Raed Karmi's killing, the al-Aqsa Brigades attached to Fatah threw off any previous inhibitions about crossing the green line. A grisly rivalry developed with Hamas and Islamic Jihad over which organization could send more successful suicide bombers into Israel proper.

Sharon's prime ministership was approaching a critical point; many of the key players were still not resigned to his durability as the long-term national leader. He was losing height in the polls, week after week. After a suicide bombing on December 1 in downtown Jerusalem, crowds had gathered on the hosed-down pedestrian mall, chanting "Sharon, go home" for the first time. "They're right," he told his aides in his New York hotel, preferring to hear the literal meaning of the ominous mantra. He ordered his U.S. visit cut short and his plane readied to return home at once.[32]

The sharpest slippage in his standing was happening within his own rightist constituency. "You keep shouting, and I'll keep fighting terrorism," he told an unruly gathering of the Likud central committee some months before. The committee members didn't like his talk of restraint being strength. They applauded politely when the prime minister came into the hall but exploded into a paroxysm of cheering and chanting when Netanyahu made his entrance. Netanyahu spoke of the "three years of relative quiet" under his government. He was at his most disingenuous when he voiced his ostensible approval for the three tenets of Sharon's policy: "No negotiations under fire." "But there are!" the audience bayed back, as he knew they would. "No negotiations under terror." "But there are!" they shouted. "Jewish blood shall not be cheap." "But it is. It is!"[33]

On his left flank, too, Sharon's situation was not reassuring. Labor had gone through an ugly primaries process, replete with accusations of fraud and vote rigging, and had eventually installed Defense Minister Ben-Eliezer as its new leader. That was good from Sharon's standpoint: the other candidate, Knesset Speaker Avrum Burg, had pledged to take the party out of Sharon's coalition. But Ben-Eliezer would be awaiting the right opportunity for Labor to secede, if not over defense policy, then over domestic issues. The party could hardly go into a general election as the docile junior partner in a government run by Arik Sharon.

The attack in Hadera was followed later in January by a suicide bombing in Jerusalem. The bomber was a young woman, carrying more than twenty-two pounds of explosives on her body. During February the attacks intensified. On the tenth, two soldiers were killed in a bold assault on the main gate of the IDF's Southern Command headquarters at Beersheba. On the fourteenth, Hamas militants set off a massive 420-pound charge under an Israeli tank in the Gaza Strip. Five days later, six soldiers were shot dead by two Fatah al-Aqsa Brigades assailants who calmly walked up to their roadblock west of Ramallah, pulled out rifles from under their jackets, and opened fire.

On March 3, seven reservist soldiers and three civilians were killed at another West Bank roadblock. On March 14 in the Gaza Strip, the same armored corps regiment sent out another of its tanks to patrol the same road, and once again Hamas was lying in wait. The charge, 220 pounds of high explosives, tore through the Israeli-made Merkava, killing three of its crew. The pain and shame felt nationwide were exacerbated by resentment toward the settlers. Army officers had complained about the poor positioning of the West Bank checkpoint, but the settlers insisted on having it just there because it "gave them a sense of security." The tank's mission had been to scour the road ahead of a school bus from Netzarim, the Gaza Strip's most isolated settlement, which required three whole army regiments to protect it.

For the Palestinians, the roadblocks, like the tanks, were iconic symbols of their occupation and suffering. The suicide bombers were their "strategic weapon," their answer, as they insisted, to the disparity of firepower between the IDF and their own guerrilla forces.

By March 2002, suicide bombings, interspersed with shooting attacks, were an almost daily occurrence, not only in Jerusalem and the other Israeli cities near the green line, but in Tel Aviv and Haifa, too. On March 9, Café Moment, literally around the corner from the heavily guarded official residence of the prime minister in Jerusalem, was blown up by a Hamas suicide bomber, leaving 11 dead and 54 injured. On March 20, a suicide bombing on a bus in the north killed 7. Another in Jerusalem the next day killed 3 and injured 80.

Israel's main cities took on the aspect of ghost towns. Half-empty buses plied half-empty streets. Car drivers steered clear of them, in case they exploded. Shopping malls and markets echoed eerily to the footsteps of the few hardy customers who still ventured into them. Restaurants and cafés, those that stayed open, were mostly empty; many of them were now patrolled by uniformed civilian guards. Hotels were empty, too, as tourism dried up to a wartime trickle. Businessmen arranged their meetings with overseas partners and clients in nearby Cyprus. Foreign airlines also took to flying over, empty, to Cyprus to spend the night there and return briefly to Tel Aviv in the morning to pick up the few customers who were still flying. International sporting fixtures took place abroad: no teams would come to Israel. The economy was reeling. But, more seriously, so was the people's confidence that this plague of indiscriminate carnage could be defeated.

Not since the terrible first days of the Yom Kippur War did such a pall of depression descend on the nation. Back then, Israelis faced an existential threat as two large and well-equipped armies broke through Israel's lines and seemed poised to advance toward the heartland. Now, with the Jewish state much stronger and more populous, small and relatively weak Palestinian paramilitary groups posed what on paper ought to have been a policing problem. And yet the fear and uncertainty that gripped ordinary families were making for an ominous corrosion of national resilience. Mothers trembled and wept, literally, as they sent their children to school in the morning. The ubiquity and unpredictability of the suicide attacks were turning ordinary urban life into Russian roulette. The impossibility of deterring on pain of death someone who was determined to die imbued all the precautions and protective measures with a sense of despair.

Preventive intelligence, moreover, seemed increasingly useless as the "profile" of the suicide bomber morphed from the young, male, religious fanatic to a broad and inclusive swath of Palestinian society.

Male and female, religious and secular, illiterate and intellectual, poor and well-to-do, unemployed refugee camp dweller and yuppie—all were represented among the bombers and would-be bombers. Intifada activists, both Islamist and secular, were swamped during this period with people clamoring to be strapped up with a suicide belt and sent out to die. Their motivations were as varied as the candidates' backgrounds. Religious zeal and an entrancement with death and heaven still inspired many youngsters to volunteer. But increasingly, experiences of personal injury or humiliation of the bombers or their close relatives at the hands of Israeli forces furnished the fury that drove them to kill and die. Often, of course, motives were mixed and confused.

Suicide bombings accounted for barely one half of 1 percent of the violent attacks on Israelis during the intifada. But they accounted for almost half of the deaths incurred in those incidents. They accounted, too, for Sharon's plummeting popularity in March 2002 and for the sense in Jerusalem that the long-predicted invasion of the West Bank towns and military takeover of the entire territory were now inevitable and imminent.

URBAN WARFARE

Despite the escalating violence, talks led by the U.S. peace envoy, Tony Zinni, were succeeding in narrowing gaps. On March 24, the tough-talking general presented the two sides with what he called "the Zinni Bridging Proposals." These were designed to secure an immediate cease-fire and then move to implementation of the Tenet Paper.

The Israeli reply to Zinni was delivered at 2:00 a.m. on March 27, straight from Sharon's office. The two IDF negotiators, Major General Giora Eiland and Brigadier General Eival Gilady, had asked to see Sharon. They were ushered in at midnight. "Sharon made us work very hard," Eiland recalled later. "What if, what if, what if?" But the two officers persuaded him not to unpick any particular provision but to accept the whole package. Eiland was ready to wait with the good news till the morning, but Gilady said, "We've kept the prime minister busy till two a.m. Let's get Zinni busy as well." They phoned the American envoy, and Gilady formally announced: "The state of Israel accepts your proposals and we are ready to implement them from tomorrow." Zinni, half awake, replied, "You've got to be kidding. You accept it?" He ordered his State Department aide, Aaron Miller, "to push as hard as you possibly can with the Palestinians."[34]

Miller, however, ran into a wall of Palestinian procrastination. "Now under 'house arrest' in his compound in Ramallah, Arafat was focused much more on trying to get the Israelis to let him out than he was on saying yes or no to Zinni's ideas."[35] Zinni faulted Sharon for making "a hero, a martyr, and a victim out of Arafat. The American government pressed him to let Arafat go, but the gut hatred between those two is so bad he couldn't bring himself to do it. Of course, this enhanced Arafat's stature on the street."

Zinni and Miller were at a Passover seder at the home of an Israeli official when the upshot of Arafat's dithering and Sharon's vindictiveness struck home. "During the meal," Zinni writes, "news came of a horrific suicide bombing at a Passover celebration in a hotel restaurant, with heavy casualties. This bombing had a tremendous effect on the people of Israel. It was their 9/11."[36]

For Israelis, Yom Kippur and the Passover seder are the most widely observed religious rituals of the year. But Passover eve is more than a religious time. It is the time when families get together. They bond through eating, drinking, singing the ancient hymns, and talking. For Israelis, the suicide bombing at the Park Hotel in Netanya on Passover eve, which took 28 lives and left 140 injured, was a national trauma. "I knew immediately we had come to the end of our road," Zinni writes. For Sharon, as all his aides instinctively knew, it was the end of his first period as prime minister. "Restraint is strength" would not be abandoned, but both sides of the equation would now be adjusted: there would be less restraint and much more strength.

Operation Defensive Shield, the IDF invasion of all the major West Bank towns apart from Jericho and Hebron, and many of the major refugee camps, was decided on that same night. The operation should be limited to the West Bank, the army proposed, since the fence encircling Gaza was proving almost hermetically effective against terror incursions from there. The inner cabinet met and quickly endorsed the army's plans. Orders went out to start preparations. Sharon knew he had the nation behind him.

At the full cabinet the next night, Sharon added his voice to those of the ministers like Silvan Shalom and generals like Mofaz who demanded that Arafat be deported and never allowed back. Peres argued against this. "I don't want another Jesus story on our shoulders," he said. "Arafat outside could be no less effective than Arafat inside . . . Arafat is also a political leader, not just the leader of a former terrorist organization."[37] The heads of the Mossad, the Shin Bet, and Military Intelligence also all spoke against expelling Arafat. They warned he might resist and be hurt, or even take his own life, if Israeli soldiers tried to capture him. Sharon finally relented, as he may well have intended to do from the outset. His original promise to Bush had not expired, and Powell now phoned to remind him of it. The cabinet's eventual decision was to declare Arafat (though not the PA) an "enemy" who would be "isolated" in his *muqata* compound "at this stage." The last three words were added by Sharon to imply the threat of further action later.

That same night, IDF armored columns began trundling toward Ramallah and Bethlehem, and emergency call-up notices went out to more than thirty thousand reservists.[38] It was the biggest mobilization since the Lebanon War. "We are at war," Sharon declared in a television broadcast. "A war for our home." Israel had done everything possible to attain a cease-fire, "and in return we have got only terror, terror, and more terror." Arafat, he said, was "an enemy of the free world and a danger to peace in the region."

The reservists' response to the sudden summonses was dramatically better than the usual turnout for reserve duty, when shirking and bellyaching are fairly widespread. The tanks and armored personnel carriers were "oversubscribed" in many units, and soldiers literally scrambled for a place on board. The army encouraged media coverage; the reservists interviewed all sounded positive about the operation despite their own natural apprehensions and discomfort. Some sounded outright jingoistic. If any further spur were needed, it came in the form of another ghastly suicide bombing, on March 31, this time in a busy restaurant in Haifa. Fourteen people died and forty were injured. Again, as at Netanya, Hamas claimed responsibility.

Invading the zones ruled by the PA was not in itself a wholly new departure for IDF ground forces. They had been making incursions into the Palestinian towns for several months, in pursuit of suspects or in the wake of a terror attack. Usually, these raids focused on a specific building or cluster of buildings where militants were thought to be hiding. Shin Bet men accompanied the troops, and the initial purpose was to arrest the suspects, though the raids often ended in firefights. The operations were usually wound down at dawn or, at most, extended for a couple of days. If they went on longer, admonitions from Washington helped expedite the withdrawal.

Defensive Shield was different. Beyond its sheer size, it was open-ended; it embraced the refugee camps as well as the towns; and the initial American reaction was mild, though it got tougher later. The formal goals were vaguely worded. IDF Central Command was to make war on terrorists and those who sent them on their missions. It was to dismantle infrastructures of terror, to hit at terror activists and suspects, and to "levy a price from the Palestinian Authority." It was unclear from this wording whether the purpose was to bring about the total collapse of the PA and a return to direct Israeli administration of the West Bank. In any event, that did not happen.

The nighttime raids had never ventured into the hearts of the densely built refugee camps. Run by the various militant groups, which often clashed with each other, they had been virtual no-go areas even for the PA police. At the end of February, however, a month before Defensive Shield, a decision was made to raid simultaneously two important camps, Balata near Nablus and Jenin camp, near the town of Jenin. The two crack infantry brigades, Golani and the Paratroopers, carried out the operation, which went far more smoothly than had been feared. There was armed resistance in both camps. The IDF lost two. The Palestinians lost dozens. "Collateral" killing, the euphemism for civilian casualties, was relatively light.

To avoid explosive booby traps that the defenders had planted all around the likely access routes, the soldiers advanced *through* the houses instead of along the streets. This involved drilling or sometimes blasting holes through the walls of people's homes. A week later, the army surrounded the refugee camp at Tulkarm, trapping some fifty armed militants within. With the memory of Balata and Jenin still fresh, they were persuaded to give in without a fight. They filed out stripped to the waist and holding their weapons above their heads, as television cameras captured the moment.

This experience and these tactics served the IDF in many of the incursions that made up Defensive Shield. In the words of a UN report, "The operation began on 29 March with an incursion into Ramallah, followed by entry into Tulkarm and Qalqilya on 1 April, Bethlehem on 2 April, and Jenin and Nablus on 3 April. By 3 April, six of the largest cities in the West Bank, and their surrounding towns, villages and refugee camps, were occupied by the Israeli military." In many of the actions, Palestinian resistance was scattered, disorganized, and ineffective.

Ramallah fell without much of a fight. By midnight on the night of the twenty-eighth, Israeli infantry had taken over the radio station in the center of town. By dawn, the muzzles of IDF tank barrels were pointing at Yasser Arafat from virtually under his office window. The tanks had smashed down the main gate of the *muqata* complex. The soldiers first swarmed over the prison wing, where the PA was ostensibly holding the killers of Minister Rehavam Ze'evi; the man who sent them, Ahmed Saadat; and Fuad Shubaki, who Israel believed was behind the *Karine A*. But they had been spirited away to Arafat's own suite just minutes ahead of the invading force. The Israelis freed twenty-six men held in the prison cells as collaborators, then blew up the building. They shelled and bulldozed other buildings in the compound and shut off water and electricity supplies to the central block where Arafat and some four hundred aides and guards were holed up, effectively under siege. Sporadic shooting continued for four days, until a group of Israeli and foreign peace activists managed to slip through the army's lines and join the beleaguered *rais* and his motley forces. Their presence deterred further gunfire.

Bethlehem also fell easily, but there, too, the IDF was dragged into an extended siege situation. Due to a snafu by a heli-borne commando unit that was to have surrounded and sealed off the Church of the Nativity, more than two hundred Palestinian militants, retreating before the invading force, were able to take refuge inside the ancient Christian shrine. Thirty-nine days of complicated negotiations followed, accompanied by sporadic exchanges of rifle fire that took its toll of the venerable stonework. The church, with its web of subterranean chapels, suffered other damage and desecration, too. The Greek, Latin, and Armenian monks who share the shrine according to rigid, time-encrusted rules tried to continue their sacred rites despite the siege. Some donated food to the hungry militants; others surrendered it less willingly. The Israelis allowed in some food, sometimes. Palestinian civilians managed to boost supplies by throwing packages from the surrounding rooftops into the church precincts. European and American diplomats labored to bring the episode to a bloodless end.

If the Palestinians holed up in the church showed disregard for its historic treasures, some Israeli forces displayed callous contempt, and in some cases outright covetousness, for the property of Palestinian civilians caught up in the fighting. The couple dozen indictments filed in military courts after Defensive Shield hardly did justice to the widespread looting and vandalism that some units, particularly reservist units, left in their trail. Tanks in some cases made no effort to avoid crushing cars, electricity pylons, and water hydrants under their treads.

In Nablus, the largest city in the northern West Bank, the IDF scored its smoothest military success. The old *casba* of the town was seen as a formidable militant stronghold, and the IDF pitted against it top-flight infantry regulars backed by tanks. Over four days of street fighting, the Israelis pushed hundreds of militants into a small area of the *casba* where, on April 8, they eventually surrendered. Just one IDF officer was killed in the fighting and more than seventy Palestinians. Most of the dead were fighters, but the figure included a family of eight, wiped out by a stray tank shell.

In nearby Jenin refugee camp, meanwhile, the Israeli operation was anything but smooth. Hamas and Fatah activists set aside their ideological differences to fight together under the command of a former PA officer, Abu Jendal. He divided the camp into small zones and sowed each of them with mines and booby traps. His fighters, operating in small, well-coordinated groups, put up dogged and effective resistance to the cumbersome advance of an IDF reserve division. The Israelis called in attack helicopters, but their daily forward movement was still slow and labored, and they were taking casualties.

With Defensive Shield still in train, Arafat in palpable peril, and Jenin still unvanquished, Bush began to signal that his forbearance was running out. He had been unequivocal in his initial, sympathetic support of the operation and had made it clear that for him the Israeli action was part of the global war against terror that he had declared after 9/11. But now he had an announcement:

I've decided to send Secretary of State Powell to the region next week to seek broad international support for the vision I've outlined today . . . an immediate and meaningful cease-fire, an end to terror and violence and incitement; withdrawal of Israeli troops from Palestinian cities, including Ramallah; implementation of the already agreed upon Tenet and Mitchell plans, which will lead to a political settlement.

Tony Zinni, still in the region, went to see Arafat ahead of the secretary's arrival. "Sharon didn't object. So my security guys saddled up in their SWAT gear—black helmets, Kevlar, the whole deal—and off we went . . . By then, Arafat's Muqata headquarters had been turned into Berlin in the spring of 1945." The Americans had to clamber over rubble and file into the beleaguered headquarters one by one, under the rifles of nervous Palestinian guards. "The place smelled bad," Zinni recalled. "Things were grim. I met Arafat in a dimly lit little room; there was a semiautomatic weapon by his side. All his aides looked like drowned rats, stressed out and beaten; but he was in his glory, upbeat and animated, more alert and fired up than I had ever seen him. The siege had brought out the fighter in him. 'I am under siege,' he announced dramatically, enjoying the hell out of the moment."[39]

Sharon made it clear to the secretary of state that the reoccupation of the towns was not going to be indefinite. "But there are some objectives that still have to be achieved."[40] One of these objectives was taking Jenin refugee camp, where the Israeli reservists were still being held off by the well-organized defenders. On April 10, the IDF took its worst casualties in the campaign when an infantry unit was ambushed in the heart of the camp and suffered thirteen dead. After that, the army used armored bulldozers to smash its way through wide swaths of densely populated alleys and courtyards. Helicopter gunships and tanks rained fire on the defenders.

The battle reached its inexorable end during Powell's visit. Most of the Palestinian fighters surrendered. Abu Jendal, their commander, died fighting. But the Palestinians, defeated by overwhelming force, briefly threatened to turn the tables on Sharon as they had done in Beirut twenty years before—with a world-shaking accusation of massacre. For several days, the region and the world were once again engulfed in allegations that Israeli soldiers under Sharon's command had been responsible for the deaths of hundreds of innocent Palestinians. Moreover, unlike at Sabra and Shatila, the Israelis were not just vicariously responsible; they had actually shot, bombed, and bulldozed the victims to death.

This time, though, there was no massacre. In fact, despite the length and intensity of the fighting and the scale of the destruction in the center of Jenin camp, there were relatively few fatalities. Fifty-two Palestinians died, according to UN figures, and twenty-three Israeli soldiers. Most of the Palestinians were armed fighters, though some were innocent civilians caught in the imbroglio. Most of the inhabitants of the camp managed to flee to the neighboring town of Jenin before the fighting began.

The massacre canard had many fathers, among them the Palestinian negotiator Saeb Erekat, who spoke on television of war crimes and five hundred dead, and the UN envoy Terje Larsen, who went into the camp on April 15 and told reporters, "I am shocked at the sight and smell of corpses and destruction . . . This is horrifying beyond belief." But the Israelis themselves carry much of the blame for their own discomfiture. The IDF spokesman, Ron Kitri, spoke of an estimated two hundred Palestinian dead. Worse yet, he and his bosses sealed off the whole Jenin area from local and foreign press coverage for several days. The IDF and Shin Bet commanders on the scene made matters still worse by taking large numbers of Palestinian men away from Jenin for questioning and then releasing them miles from home with no means of communicating with their beleaguered families.

For Yasser Arafat, beleaguered himself in Ramallah, Jenin was his "Stalingrad," as he put it, a victory of Palestinian arms and honor. But when Powell came to see him twice at the *muqata,* much against Sharon's wishes, he gave the secretary nothing with which Powell could push back in Washington against the neocons, the pro-Israel lobby, and the powerful conservative Christian forces within the Republican constituency that were becoming increasingly vocal against the Palestinian leader. Arafat claimed he had been effectively neutralized by the Israeli attacks on the PA. But Powell said, "You still have influence and authority . . . and that's what we're looking for you to use."[41] He left the region after ten frustrating days, and with nothing to show for them. He spoke vaguely of a possible peace conference and his intention to return, but the administration was not behind him.

The charge that Israel used disproportionate force in Defensive Shield was powerfully reinforced by the scenes of destruction at the camp, and it resulted in a UN Security Council resolution on April 19 calling for an inquiry into "recent events in the Jenin refugee camp." Israel initially went along with the UN demand. "We've got nothing to hide," said Sharon's spokesman for the foreign media, Ra'anan Gissin. The U.S. delegation drafted the Security Council resolution. But soon after, senior army generals persuaded Ben-Eliezer, and together they persuaded Sharon, that they could not afford to cooperate with a UN inquiry for fear that this process might end up with Israeli officers facing charges in an international court.

The upshot was a convenient trade-off: the Americans engineered the quiet demise of the UN inquiry; Israel lifted the sieges in Ramallah and Bethlehem. Some creative diplomacy by Britain gave Sharon a sufficiently face-saving solution to his demand that the wanted men besieged in the *muqata* and in the Church of the Nativity not be released. Tony Blair had tried to persuade Sharon back in November that Arafat could never agree to hand over Ahmed Saadat, Fuad Shubaki, and the others but that he might agree to British monitors assisting in their Palestinian imprisonment. "Is that offer still on the table?" Sharon's aide Danny Ayalon now asked the British ambassador in Tel Aviv, Sherard Cowper-Coles, in an out-of-the-blue telephone call.[42] A week later, Andrew Coyle, a former governor of the famously austere Brixton Prison, waited outside Sharon's office door at midnight while Cowper-Coles and Dan Kurtzer, his American counterpart, argued within over the conditions under which Saadat, Shubaki, and the four others would be held in a PA jail in Jericho, with Coyle supervising. "He wants to see you," Cowper-Coles came out and told the tough ex-warden. "Tell him exactly what it's like in Brixton for an IRA prisoner." It was not going to be quite like that for the Palestinians. But Sharon was apparently satisfied by Coyle's no-nonsense mien and agreed.[43]

The siege in Bethlehem ended a week later, after complicated negotiations involving Muhammad Rashid for the PA, the Tel Aviv CIA station officer for the Americans, and a former British MI6 agent, Alastair Crooke, representing the EU. Thirteen Palestinians with Israeli "blood on their hands" were deported to Cyprus aboard a British RAF plane; twenty-six more were exiled from the West Bank to the Gaza Strip; and the remaining eighty-four Palestinians in the church (a hundred-odd had been allowed to leave earlier) were released to their homes.

Defensive Shield was over. Some 260 Palestinians had been killed,* thousands injured, and close to two thousand arrested. Most of the Palestinian dead were armed men, but there were many innocent deaths and injuries and widespread damage to property. The Israelis had lost 34 soldiers, 23 of them in Jenin. Another 60 Israelis had been killed in terror attacks during the period of the operation. One of the bloodiest, on May 7, was a suicide bombing in a gaming club in Rishon Lezion, near Tel Aviv. Fifteen people died, and 55 were injured in that attack; Hamas claimed responsibility.

Still, the surge of terror deaths seemed to be receding. April's figure was lower than March's, and May's would hopefully end lower than April's. Clearly, Defensive Shield had not "solved" the problem. But it had salved the pernicious spread of helplessness and despair within Israeli society. It might not have been a military masterstroke. Perhaps no such stroke is possible in a regular army's struggle against armed militants. But by seizing the initiative, it restored Israelis' confidence in their state and their army and, by extension, in their prime minister.

This restored confidence, which showed dramatically in the polls, stemmed both from the massive deployment of military power and from a notable moderation in its use. This was Sharon's only war as prime minister, as it turned out, and he ran it very differently from his past military campaigns. With tens of thousands of soldiers under arms and on the move, the death and devastation in the Palestinian territories could have been of an entirely different dimension. Given the firepower he had mobilized, he unleashed relatively little of it. For all his banging on the table and barking at his generals, he kept Defensive Shield within the confines of his new, prime ministerial weltanschauung: restraint is strength.†

Arafat marked his release from five months of siege with a stately

---

* Harel and Isacharoff, *Seventh War*. Miller cites a figure of 300 Palestinian dead.
† Sharon declined, moreover, to open a second front in the north, despite strenuous efforts by Hezbollah and Palestinian groups in Lebanon to provoke him into doing so.

progress by helicopter and car through the battered towns of the West Bank on May 13. He met with bereaved families, embraced orphans, spoke words of encouragement to injured people. But the public at large was largely absent from the streets. The *rais*'s return was far from triumphal. Commentators put this down to the unpopularity of the deal he had struck in Bethlehem, especially the deportation of some of the men trapped in the church. One place where enthusiastic crowds did gather was the Jenin camp. But Arafat, apparently fearing local Islamic radicals, declined to leave his car. His convoy swept past the battered camp. In the months that followed, Arafat did not leave the *muqata* much. He did not go abroad, or even visit Gaza, apparently for fear that Israel would not let him return.

Arafat owed his freedom above all to Crown Prince Abdullah. He was effectively the Saudi ruler; King Fahd, his half brother, was elderly and not really functioning by this time. Abdullah had flown to Crawford, Texas, on April 25 and virtually threatened Bush with a major rupture in relations if Arafat continued to be besieged by the Israelis.

Abdullah had recently proposed peace and normalization between Israel and all the Arab countries in return for the creation of a Palestinian state in all of the West Bank and Gaza, with Jerusalem as its capital. The key issue of Palestinian refugees was "to be agreed upon in accordance with UN General Assembly Resolution 194." "Agreed" meant Israel could not be forced. It signified Arab recognition that most of the refugees and their descendants would not return to Israel. Commentators presumed the plan was floated to curry favorable sentiment in the West following 9/11, in which most of the hijackers had been Saudi citizens. Nevertheless, this was the first time the Saudis had expressly held out the prospect of Israel's full acceptance into the Arab region. In normal circumstances, Prince Abdullah's plan would have had a powerful impact on Israeli public opinion. In fact, it was barely noticed. It was submitted to and approved by the Arab Summit in Beirut on the very day of the suicide bombing at the hotel in Netanya. Instead of a wave of hope and encouragement, Palestine was swept by a new wave of violence. Sharon gave the plan a cautious and perfunctory welcome.

For the Palestinian president, Defensive Shield had been a heavy, though not a mortal, blow. Ironically, the IDF's attacks on the PA security forces and its ransacking of government buildings vindicated Arafat's claim that he was powerless to impose his authority on Hamas and the other militant groups. The Israelis, however, were past caring, having effectively given up on any security cooperation with the *rais* and his multiheaded security apparatus.

In many of the towns and refugee camps, street power now passed to the militants, with armed gangs of al-Aqsa Brigades and others roaming around uninhibited, brandishing their weapons, and meting out summary and brutal justice to alleged collaborators with Israel. Ramallah and Jericho were the last redoubts of PA military control. Much of the PA's civil administration managed to continue functioning, though—schools, hospitals, municipal services. But without effective policing, law enforcement and tax collection faltered. Daily life deteriorated. Freedom of movement, which had been hampered by Israeli roadblocks since the start of the intifada, was now even more severely constrained. Roads between villages, even between neighborhoods in the same town, were severed by mounds of earth or concrete cubes piled up by army bulldozers. The effect on the economy was direct and disastrous. Tens of thousands of working people joined the lists of the unemployed. Many of them turned to the Hamas-affiliated welfare agencies for material help.

By forcibly reopening the whole of the West Bank to IDF and Shin Bet control, Defensive Shield contributed in time to the suppression of the intifada, and in particular to the detection and prevention of suicide bombings. Nevertheless, Defensive Shield gave Israelis, both soldiers and civilians, pause for thought about the limits of military power deployed against a nation in revolt. Despite the show of force, despite the killing and capturing of militants, among them senior figures in the various armed organizations, despite the deployment of the army and the Shin Bet throughout the West Bank, terror attacks continued. More and more influential Israelis now joined the growing clamor among the public for a "security fence," a barrier between the West Bank and Israel that would physically block the suicide bombers on their way to murder and death. Barak had ordered staff work on the fence toward the end of his term, but when Sharon swept him from office, the idea seemed to have been swept out with him.

Sharon's popularity surged after Defensive Shield, but so did support for the fence. In a *Maariv* poll published in June 2002, 69 percent of those questioned favored building a fence, and only 25 percent opposed it. "Perhaps this is the secret of the fence's broad popularity," wrote the analyst Chemi Shalev. "It's both a physical barrier and a symbolic, emotional bulwark, an opaque screen behind which people feel they can push the Palestinians and all the grief they bring with them and, as far as most people are concerned, the settlers too."

Sharon could no longer ignore the public demand. On June 23, the cabinet formally approved plans for the first stage of the separation fence. It would stretch for seventy miles, from Salem on the northwestern tip of the West Bank south to Kassem, opposite Netanya. It would hug the old green line on parts of its route but would periodically belly into the West Bank to encompass major Israeli settlements. Some of this bellying would take in Palestinian villages, too. Two other small stretches of fence were also approved, north and south of Jerusalem, both of them on West Bank land. The Defense Ministry announced the creation of a new department that would supervise construction of this first stage and prepare for the subsequent stages that would eventually seal off the entire West Bank.

For Sharon, the decision to build the fence was his first substantive break with the settlers and with the pristine dogma of "Greater Israel." This was not mere talk of a hypothetical Palestinian state arising from a hypothetical negotiation at some vague time in the future; it was the tangible and immediate consequence of unilateral action that the government was taking. It would mean that farther-flung settlements that Sharon himself had deliberately located in the Palestinian heartland would find themselves on the wrong side of a fence. Sharon and the ministers could contend all they wished that the fence was solely a security barrier with no political significance. No one believed that, least of all the settlers who would be crossing through it each day on their way to and from work in Israel.

The long struggle on which Sharon now embarked—against the Palestinians, against the Americans, against world opinion, and against Israel's own high court—over the precise route of the separation fence was itself the most convincing proof that he understood full well that the fence would become the baseline for a future border. Arguably, Sharon's decision to build the fence was no less momentous or historically significant than his later decision to disengage from Gaza and dismantle the settlements there and in the northern West Bank. The two decisions, in fact, need to be seen as an integral progression along a path of unilateralism that Sharon was steadily adopting as his overarching strategy toward the conflict.*

Unilateralism could exist and flourish, however, only to the extent that the international community, and especially of course the Americans, forbore to insist on bilateralism—that is, on a credible peace negotiation between Israel and the Palestinian Authority. As his good luck would have it, the very next day after the fence decision by the cabinet in Jerusalem, Sharon and the world received public and formal

---

* Haim Ramon interview, Tel Aviv, September 2009.

confirmation from Washington that as far as George W. Bush was concerned, negotiation with Yasser Arafat was no longer a viable option.

"Peace requires a new and different Palestinian leadership," the president declared in a long-expected, meticulously drafted statement on the Middle East. With Secretary of State Powell, Secretary of Defense Donald Rumsfeld, and National Security Adviser Rice at his side in the Rose Garden of the White House, Bush called "on the Palestinian people to elect new leaders, leaders not compromised by terror. I call upon them to build a practicing democracy, based on tolerance and liberty." Bush's message was starkly clear: as long as Arafat stood at the head of the Palestinian people, the United States would not be promoting or supporting their claim to statehood.

Bush reiterated his "vision of two states living side by side in peace and security." But he immediately added—and this was critical in Sharon's eyes—"There is simply no way to achieve that peace until all parties fight terror." The order of business, then, was to be: first fight terror, and only then make progress toward peace. "Today, Palestinian authorities are encouraging, not opposing, terrorism. This is unacceptable. And the United States will not support the establishment of a Palestinian state until its leaders engage in a sustained fight against the terrorists and dismantle their infrastructure." Even the short-range American demands, that Israel pull back its troops to the pre-intifada line and cease settlement building, were preceded by "As we make progress toward security . . ." The president added that the PA was tainted by "official corruption. A Palestinian state will require a vibrant economy, where honest enterprise is encouraged by honest government.

"When the Palestinian people have new leaders, new institutions and new security arrangements with their neighbors," Bush continued, "the United States of America will support the creation of a Palestinian state whose borders and certain aspects of its sovereignty will be provisional until resolved as part of a final settlement in the Middle East." As for the eventual full realization of his two-state vision, "The final borders, the capital and other aspects of this state's sovereignty will be negotiated between the parties as part of a final settlement."

"Dismantle their infrastructure," whatever that meant, was a recognizably Israeli phrase. And small wonder: Sharon and his top aides had been intimately involved in the American drafting process, offering language and arguing about the wording almost till the moment of delivery. The Israeli input began during Defensive Shield, when Efraim Halevy, the outgoing head of the Mossad, brainstormed with his senior staffers with a view to offering Sharon a forward-looking exit strategy once the fighting was done. The Mossad men came up with a plan called "An Alternative Leadership for the Palestinian People."

Unbeknownst to Halevy and the Mossad, the IDF planning branch under Giora Eiland had been brainstorming, too, and it came up with very similar ideas. Halevy and Eiland were invited separately to Sharon's residence in Jerusalem for breakfast on the same morning. Halevy attests that the prime minister's appetite at his breakfast—the second—gave no hint that he had already eaten once with the army general. Both were invited to the ranch the next day for further discussion. Sharon instructed them to go together to Jordan and Egypt and then to Washington and other friendly capitals to sell their idea.

In the Roosevelt Room at the White House, the Israeli officials made their presentation to assembled Brahmins from several departments of the Bush administration. "Why Arafat is not capable of becoming a viable partner for a peace negotiation," Halevy began reading from a lengthy document he had prepared in English. "He does not *really* want to establish a Palestinian state at this time." In London, Halevy recalled, he sat on the carpet explaining it to Tony Blair and his adviser David Manning in the residential part of 10 Downing Street. "I cannot recall why we were sitting on the carpet, but we were." From London he went on to Moscow. Reading from his document, Halevy assured his interlocutors that "significant persons in the PA will cooperate in an intelligent and sophisticated plan of action designed to elevate Arafat to the position of 'symbolic' leader."

The Palestinians, who sent a senior minister, Nabil Shaath, to Washington at the last moment to influence the drafting, were aghast at the content of the president's speech. But Arafat gave stern orders to welcome it and not display their dismay in public. Sharon, in mirror image, made sure there was no crowing from his side.

The transition in the Prime Minister's Bureau from Shani to Dov Weissglas, Sharon's longtime personal lawyer, was unexpected and unexplained. But the bureau weathered it without serious disruption. "One Friday midday," Marit Danon recalled, "I get a call from Uri Shani, who tells me he's leaving. He didn't say why, and I didn't want to pry. I was in the supermarket later, standing at the checkout line, when the prime minister phones. 'Everything's going to stay exactly the same,' he says. I was worried but couldn't speak too freely with all the other shoppers around, so I just said, 'I hope so.' This needled him. 'I tell you everything will be the same! You'll see.' He seemed to feel he needed to persuade me."

With Shani gone and the gregarious, easygoing Weissglas in his place, someone else was going to have to run the bureau if it was to retain the style and standards of crisp efficiency that Shani had maintained. That someone was Danon. With the tacit consent of everyone from Sharon down, she now became the fulcrum around which the disciplined working of the office revolved. Weissglas made the decisions; Danon made sure they were implemented. By now, fifteen months into his prime ministership, Sharon was visibly more comfortable and confident, sometimes even relaxed in his job, which he clearly had begun to enjoy. But he was rarely happy.

Every night, says Danon, before he left the office, no matter how late it was, Sharon would pause for a moment at the photographs of Lily that he had hung on the wall opposite his desk. He would stand and look at them and then walk on through the door.

> He was an elderly widower who lived with his family. On Sunday mornings I'd sometimes ask him how his weekend had been, and he would reply, "Marit, I'm a lonely man." That's what he'd answer. I'd say, "Prime Minister, how can you say that? You're surrounded by your lovely grandchildren, your family . . ." He needed married life. But I'm not sure if after Lily's death he was open to it anymore. He spoke of Lily very frequently, of the deep friendship between them. Clearly she had been his pillar of support and at the same time his mouth and eyes to the world. He wasn't a man for small talk; she fulfilled that side of him.
>
> There was a picture of Gur on the wall, too. None of Margalit, though he'd speak of her, too. He spoke of her with respect and admiration, as a strong and very able, competent woman. She had risen very young to become a top psychiatric nurse. Of Gur he spoke with great pain. It was hard for me. Awkward. Sometimes I had to control myself not to cry in his presence.

Sharon took his loneliness home to the prime minister's official residence, a modest stone house in the suburb of Rehavia, surrounded since Rabin's assassination by high walls and watchtowers. "He didn't like it," says Danon.

> The residence radiated coldness as far as he was concerned. He'd use it for official events. And for midday naps. But he could never feel warm there like he did at the ranch, with Gilad's family. The ranch was enveloping, embracing. The children, the farm, the animals, the

ground itself. I've never known anyone who loved the land so much. Loved the clods of earth.

He had a little button under the cabinet table which connected him straight to me in the office downstairs. Many times in the middle of cabinet meetings he would buzz, I would go running upstairs in my high heels, and he would give me a little note: "Please call Gilad and ask how many millimeters of rain have fallen at the ranch." Or "Please call Gilad and find out how many ewes have given birth." He was very verbal, incredibly verbal for a man. He used to say to me, when it rained, "What I would like now is to be lying in front of my burning hearth, wrapped up in a coarse blanket . . ." In the last two years he rarely slept in Jerusalem. Even if his day ended at 2:00 a.m., he would go back to the ranch. By helicopter or by car, whichever the security detail decided.

Meirav Levy started working for Sharon before the 2001 election as his makeup artist, applying white powder to his scalp to make his famous forelock look even more striking and a touch of rouge to his cheeks. By the time he became prime minister, she was in constant attendance. She, too, witnessed his aversion to the official residence. During the first term, Omri would sometimes come and sleep over. But after the 2003 elections Omri became a member of the Knesset, and that ended. Sharon was very alone. He would wake up alone in the morning and come home at night—alone again. The kitchen staff would arrive at 6:30–7:00, but he would be up from 5:00, with nothing to drink. He didn't make coffee himself. He would stay in his room, listening to the radio, listening to reports from his military staff, listening to Ra'anan Gissin's press survey over the phone. He could not look out of the windows: they were kept closed and curtained for security reasons. At the ranch, an aide recalled,

when he drew back the curtains, he'd see a rolling landscape. Here—just bulletproof glass and a courtyard . . . And at the ranch he'd see the children. They'd come into his room and give him a good-morning kiss. That would make his day.

When he was alone in Jerusalem, he wouldn't have much for breakfast. He'd try to diet. He'd invite his driver, Gilbert, or the security guards to join him. They'd have slept in the house; they had little rooms downstairs . . . By 7:00 he'd be on the road to the office. If he was at the ranch, he'd leave at 6:30. He liked to invite people for breakfast sometimes, and then he'd lay on a nice spread.

This is something of an understatement. Sharon's breakfasts, both at the ranch and at the residence, were famous for their rich variety of fishes and cheeses, eggs and vegetables, breads and honeys and other delectables with which he would assiduously ply his guests. He himself was known to partake of two or even three breakfasts, one at the ranch, one at the residence, and one at the office, in the course of a morning. In one instance, attested to separately by his spokesman Perlman and his military secretary Kaplinsky, he moved seamlessly from breakfast to lunch without any diminution of appetite. "One day," Perlman recounts,

> there was a huge breakfast at the ranch, and we ate and ate and ate. At midday, Kaplinsky and I slowly and heavily made our way to the car and drove up to the office in Tel Aviv. Arik meanwhile gets himself organized and flies up by helicopter. At about one o'clock he sees us in the corridor. "Er, come in for a moment, would you?" So we come in. No sooner had we sat down than one of the kitchen staff walks in with three trays laden with mountains of rice and a half a chicken atop each one. Kaplan and I look at each other, and we both know we can't eat anything. We'd barely finished feasting an hour earlier, after all. Sharon, slowly, slowly, cuts and eats, cuts and eats. He looks up at us. "Er, eat something, why don't you? It's really good." "We can't eat, Prime Minister." He finishes his meal and then says, quietly, "Do you think it would be piggish of me if I just tasted a morsel of yours . . . ?" He began tucking in, slowly and methodically, and finished both our portions, too.

"It's a true story," Kaplinsky confirms.

But Arik Sharon's eating was not just a matter of quantities; it was equally a matter of manners. As a little boy, he had to wield his knife and fork with a book tucked under each arm. If he dropped the books, the food would be taken away. To his last day he would eat like this [holding the knife and fork with his arms tightly at his sides], which wasn't easy with his big belly . . . And the pace of his eating was also critical. He would eat very slowly, carefully chewing every mouthful. He would look at every bite before putting it in his mouth. He could eat all day—start in the morning and finish at night. By the same token, he could eat nothing for hours. But if someone said, "Would you like something to eat?" and ordered food, he'd immediately lose his concentration and start asking, "What's happening with the food? When are they bringing the food?" We'd say, "You've ordered falafel from a particular shop. It takes half an hour to get there, half an hour back, a few minutes to pick up the order." But he'd say, "Phone up and find out. Maybe something's happened to the messenger . . ." Once I witnessed him eat nine portions of falafel one after another. How? Slowly . . .

His tastes were catholic, but one particular favorite was a dish that most of his countrymen intensely dislike: Loof. This is a Hebrew corruption of the original British army's meat loaf. The Israeli version came in a can and was a staple in the IDF from the early years right through to the 1980s. For Sharon it remained a staple. "I didn't know it still existed," says Marit Danon. "But it did, and he had to have it. We all joked about it, and he joined in; but he wouldn't give it up. We'd get the staff to fry it up for him in slices, and he would eat it with great gusto, as though it were some gourmet dish, munching away, slowly and deliberately."

Loof, falafel, or cordon bleu—whatever the menu it had to be served on crisp white linen, with white napkins for Sharon and whomever he could get to join him. He hated eating alone and always urged staffers to partake. The staffers, though it wasn't formally part of their jobs, made sure his appetite was catered to. "We didn't want him invading Iraq because he was hungry," Perlman jokes. Conditions at the Israeli prime minister's office, an ugly 1950s office block, are remarkably Spartan.* There is no private dining room for the prime minister, and Sharon would have his white tablecloth and gleaming cutlery laid out on his office desk. To take the edge off the unaesthetic drabness of the place, he would insist on freshly cut flowers in a vase each morning. "I can't stand to see flowers thirsty," he once told Marit when the waterline did not quite reach all the stalks. In the background, a music system quietly played classics or the Hebrew or Russian songs he loved. It had to be on when he walked into the empty room each morning.

Before he walked in, he would pause, without fail, at Marit's desk and say "Good morning, how are you?" to her and other staffers present. "You could see he grew up in a European household," says Marit.

---

* Ehud Olmert, Sharon's successor, planned an office-plus-residence compound near the present office, away from the residential heart of the city. It would have given the incumbent a significantly improved quality of life. But Netanyahu, when he took over in 2009, demonstratively shot down the plan as too lavish and extravagant. As a result, the residents of Rehavia and the adjacent districts are still disturbed at all hours by the sirens and slamming doors of the prime minister's cavalcade. And he himself and his family are still entombed behind the high walls and reinforced windows of the old residence.

"There was something hugely dissonant between his behavior in practice and his 'quintessential sabra' image. He would not go through a door ahead of a woman. At the beginning, we would both stand inside his room with neither of us prepared to go out first. And he would automatically stand—no mean feat for a man of his girth—when a woman entered the room. It took time before he stopped standing for me or before he stopped protesting if I walked next to him carrying a briefcase, instead of him carrying it for me."

Sharon's close aides are still close to each other years later. All of them have nostalgic stories about the interest and concern he showed not only for them but for their families. "I daresay Avigdor has already complimented you on your new hairstyle," the prime minister gushed to the wife of his director general, Avigdor Yitzhaki.[44] "He had to know everything," says Perlman. "He phoned my wife, Roni, in Paris when she was still my fiancée, to see if she'd found a wedding dress. When she said she had, he asked her to describe it to him. She described it and went on to ask, 'Prime Minister, why is this of interest to you?' He said, 'Because I'll want to kiss the bride on her wedding day and I don't want to step on the train.' "[45]

"It was important to him that everyone should get married and have families," another aide recalled.

> The fact that I'd been married for several years and didn't have any children was a matter of constant concern to him. He and Lily would have had six children if they could have. He kept up the pressure, as though he were my father. When I got pregnant, he was really pleased. He insisted that career was no reason not to have children. During his term, lots of people at the office—secretaries, drivers, aides—got married or had children. There was a real abundance in this area. He had us keep a list of all the births. Big families were important to him, perhaps because he'd come from a small one.[46]

"I miss him every day," Marit Danon admitted. "We would talk about books he was reading, books I was reading. Where do you find a CEO in a small company, let alone a prime minister, so caring about the people around him? Once, soon after he took over, he said to me, 'Go after the tea lady and ask her what's wrong. Her eyes look so sad today.' The woman was gobsmacked. She was over her head in personal problems."

His own sadness showed through at night. "Perhaps you'll come upstairs and have a bite to eat?" Perlman recalled the prime minister asking late in the evening at the Jerusalem residence. "We go upstairs and we eat and it's twelve, twelve thirty, one, and I can't go. We're talking on and on. What about? About anything. Just gossiping. I must have left eventually after two, and I remember thinking to myself, he's a powerful man and he's the prime minister, but at the end of the day he's all by himself." Kaplinsky, too, sometimes found himself called into the office at ten or eleven o'clock at night "just to have someone to talk to before going home, alone. What did we talk about? About everything. It always began with the army and spilled over to everything. Everything. Conversations in the night between two people."[47]

There were rumors that he would marry Michal Modai, the widow of his old friend, army comrade, and political colleague Yitzhak Modai, the former finance minister who had died in 1998. A onetime beauty queen, she was still a stately head turner and had made her own public career as the president of World WIZO, a women's Zionist organization. The Sharons and the Modais had been friends for decades.

"Sources?" Modai said.

There were all sorts of sources! My driver at WIZO told me that in his synagogue one Saturday the people were talking about Sharon being alone and needing to get married. Someone said that not every woman can be the wife of the prime minister; you need a representative sort of woman. Someone else said, "What about Michal Modai?" Soon, people started asking my secretary when's the wedding date. A good match, eh? I know the public thought so. But it was complete poppycock. Once we met at an event where he spoke. I went over to him, and of course he kissed me. I said, "Right, we've been photographed together. Now there'll be more rumors." But we'd known each other long enough not to have to stop kissing when we met just because of rumors . . . Did I know he was lonely? I knew from Yitzhak that politics is a tough job and being at the top is that much tougher. But it keeps you busy around the clock, so I really didn't think that loneliness was his problem. Anyway, I wasn't going to drive up to Jerusalem to entertain him.[48]

For Marit Danon, everything in Sharon's character, both the toughness and the introversion, went back to his childhood in Kfar Malal.

He was very talkative; I'd never had a boss who talked so much. Always about Kfar Malal, always about how hard it was. I'm no psychologist, but his pain sounded authentic, no matter how often he retold the same stories: how his mother's hands were worn rough from work; how he himself had to work so hard with his father in the fields; how his family was ostracized; how he never went to other kids' houses and always wondered what they were like inside. He told me that his mother would shut herself away one day each week to write home to her family in Russia from whom she'd been torn away. I found that genuinely moving. I felt the loneliness of this fat little boy coming through. He was always a bit of a fatty, I think. One day, a year or more before he collapsed, we got a letter from the Aharono-witz School in Kfar Malal. They were celebrating their seventieth anniversary, and would the prime minister please write a few words of greeting. The letter sat on his desk for weeks. They kept phoning. He kept asking me, "What should I write?" and I said, "Just write about something nice from third grade or something." He replied, "Marit, don't you understand? There wasn't anything nice there."

CHAPTER 14 · KING OF ISRAEL

On May 22, 2002, Ariel Sharon lumbered into the members' dining room of the Knesset without the sardonic grin that he usually reserved for this seething political bourse, where every grin and grimace is minutely analyzed. He sat down heavily. At a sign from his spokesman, a couple of veteran lobby correspondents joined the table. Younger reporters formed a scrum around them, notebooks poised. They expected to find the prime minister in triumphant mood, firing off quotable one-liners. His government's controversial package of economic austerity measures had just passed comfortably on first reading. It would soon move smoothly into law. Shas's seventeen Knesset members, who had voted against the package two days earlier and caused Sharon an ignominious defeat, all meekly abstained this time around. This was because he had peremptorily and publicly sacked the party's ministers within minutes of the previous vote. He would govern without Shas, he announced to the nation, live on television. The ultra-Orthodox party had thought to strong-arm him; he had swatted it down. Press and public applauded this act of leadership.

Now, beaten and humiliated, Shas was desperately signaling that it wanted to slink back in. By law, Sharon's letters of dismissal would take effect after forty-eight hours. There was still time for him to withdraw them. But Sharon's whole demeanor spoke otherwise. Slinking would not be good enough; he wanted to see Shas crawl. The package would go through two more readings. Abstentions would not do. The bearded, black-suited Shas members, self-appointed tribunes of the poor, would have to raise their hands with the rest of the coalition in favor of the painful cuts to child support and government welfare programs. These were no less painful to the Likud than to Shas, Sharon insisted. The Likud was no less authentic a representative of the poor. The intifada had devastated the economy, and fighting it cost money.

The high-tech sector, powerhouse of Israel's recent prosperity, was still reeling from the global downturn and collapse of the Nasdaq.

Ruby Rivlin, Sharon's faithful follower from the wilderness years, now his minister of communications and political fixer, urged the prime minister to make do with the abstentions. After all, in victory, magnanimity. "Let's talk about something else," Sharon growled. "Something nice." The lobby correspondents complied, regaling him with the latest political gossip. Gradually, he leaned back and relaxed, silently ingesting the little nuggets of useful information.

More than previous prime ministers, Sharon kept coming to the Knesset dining room. He would come to eat hearty schnitzel lunches in his slow and fastidious way, to enjoy an off-the-record laugh with the correspondents, usually at a rival's expense, to radiate confidence at times of crisis. "He would carefully empty two sachets of sweetener into his soup," Yossi Verter of *Haaretz* recalls, "and that was the signal for us to start swapping tidbits of gossip. He would listen avidly but discreetly kept his own counsel, confining himself to a noncommittal 'Really?' or 'What do you say?' to keep jogging us along."

That day late in May, when he banned Shas's vicarious wheedling from his table talk, was a seminal moment in Sharon's prime ministership. For all his determination, frequently stated, to maintain his coalition until the end of the Knesset term in November 2003, he signaled now that he would not be pushed around by any of the partners, even if that meant early elections. Netanyahu had contended that governing would be impossible at the head of such a small ruling party—Likud's paltry nineteen seats—and such a fractured and fractious Knesset. Sharon was out to prove him wrong and then to beat him in the inexorable next round of their unending duel, whenever it took place.

With the intifada and the economic crisis to contend with, that was a tall order at best. Sharon seemed to make things worse for himself by deliberately antagonizing his right-wing allies, including the right wing of his own party. But he was already building a base of public support that would transcend party politics.

The cracks in the Likud ominously widened. Party rules required a meeting of the central committee at least every six months. By early May, Sharon had run out of excuses and postponements. The invitations went out, and he braced himself for a lambasting. It was even worse than he had feared. "You have undermined the nation's security," Netanyahu hurled at him. "Without any democratic process whatever—not in the party, not in the cabinet, not in the Knesset, and above all not in a general election—you have undermined, with your uncalled-for statements, a pillar of our movement's policy and a foundation of our national security. Suddenly the position of the Left supporting a Palestinian state, the position of Sarid and Peres, has become the official policy of the government of Israel." Netanyahu demanded an unequivocal resolution by the central committee rejecting this policy.

The meeting ended in a stinging defeat for Sharon. He left the hall before the result was announced, aware that he was about to be publicly trounced. But despite losing the vote, Sharon had in fact won: Netanyahu had overreached himself. Far from becoming a lame-duck prime minister, spurned by his own party, as Netanyahu's aides were busily spinning the night's events, Sharon had emerged with his stature enhanced, a national leader who put the nation's interest before narrow party advantage. His mandate to continue his policies rested now not on the widely reviled Likud central committee but on the whole electorate.

At the Likud faction meeting in the Knesset the next day "the smell of last night's bad blood hovered in the air," Verter reported. But Sharon, refreshed and relaxed, launched into his statement, looking straight into the television cameras. "I would like to make something clear. The considerations that guide me, that affect my decision making, are solely considerations of state . . . I respect the members of the central committee; but [raising his voice] the responsibility is mine. Two-thirds of the public voted for me, with the intention that I take decisions. And I am taking decisions. In order to achieve security and peace, I must act firmly, sensibly, and patiently. And nothing will sidetrack me from my fixed course, certainly not internal political considerations and personal gambits."[1]

It was in this newly assertive mood that Sharon found himself challenged by Shas over the government's tough economic measures. The malaise was deep. The vast and growing ultra-Orthodox, or *haredi*, sector that Shas represented, where the men studied and the women had babies year after year, was becoming a deadweight that the productive part of the economy could no longer carry. In the Arab sector, too, families were large and unemployment rates high, as women generally did not work. Over the previous decade or so, as the *haredi* sector grew in numbers and with it the power of the *haredi* parties, welfare transfer payments had mushroomed to a whopping 13 percent of GDP.

A shift of emphasis from the settlements to the poor, which Barak had begun to instigate during his short term, sufficed to postpone the day of reckoning so long as the economy hummed along. But the bursting of the Nasdaq bubble in 2000 and the worldwide recession that followed grievously affected the high-tech sector that had become the locomotive pulling Israel toward prosperity. Dozens of Israeli companies registered on the Nasdaq exchange in New York were laid low, and thousands of their high-flying employees in Israel found themselves at the labor exchange.

The intifada compounded Israel's economic woes. While its competitors began climbing out of the crisis, Israel found it hard to attract new investments and harder still to persuade potential investors to come and visit its research laboratories and production lines when buses were blowing up on its streets. More angst for Sharon and his finance minister, Silvan Shalom, came from the governor of the Bank of Israel, a dour economist named David Klein, who insisted on keeping interest rates high throughout 2001 as a bulwark against inflation. In December 2001, he agreed to a 2 percent cut in return for Sharon's and Shalom's solemn promises to tighten the nation's belt.

The government's revenues from taxation, moreover, were shrinking fast as the economy contracted. From September 2001 to April 2002, GDP shrank by 5 percent. Unemployment topped 11 percent. As the deficit grew, a serious collapse of confidence threatened in both domestic and overseas markets. Increasingly, the Finance Ministry found it hard to raise money abroad. Forced to pay more in interest on its bonds, Israel was having to funnel ever more of its resources into servicing its debts. Governor Klein, in a demonstration of his own doubts about the government's capacity to discipline itself, began raising interest rates again, in leaps. In a brief six weeks during April and May he doubled them, from 4.5 percent to 9 percent.

No sooner had the 2002 austerity package been pushed through the Knesset than the Finance Ministry mandarins began planning another round of even deeper cuts, to be incorporated into the state budget for 2003. Government spending would be pruned by another massive nine billion shekels: three billion from defense, despite the intifada; three billion from welfare, despite the political fallout; and another three billion in across-the-board cuts in all the other government departments. The plan was especially aggressive toward unemployment benefits. Criteria for recipients would be severely tightened, and the payments themselves would be reduced.*

---

* The economic recovery finally took hold during Sharon's second term, when Netanyahu served as finance minister, enjoying Sharon's blanket backing. "In his first term, Sharon wanted to be hands-on economic czar," the then finance minister, Shalom, complained. "By the second term, he was focused on [the disengagement from] Gaza. He didn't want Bibi to interfere with that, so he didn't interfere with economic policy." Worse yet, from Shalom's rueful perspective, the tough policies

On October 28, 2002, Sharon was back in the Knesset dining room, doing another of his tough and confident performances. This time the party he was not going to be pushed around by was Labor. The man who would have to eat humble pie was his old army comrade, now his corpulent and pliant defense minister, Binyamin "Fuad" Ben-Eliezer. He insisted that Labor MKs vote in favor of the 2003 budget, which was to have its first reading in the house two days later. At cabinet the day before, he had laid it out with brutal clarity. "Whoever doesn't vote for the budget won't be able to remain in the government."

Henry Kissinger famously once observed that Israel's foreign policy is essentially an extension of its domestic politics. That is similarly the case with its economic policy. Sharon's first government eventually fell over economic policy, but the economic arguments in cabinet were always colored by the ideological divide. "Money for the poor—or money for the settlements?" was Labor's simplistic but compelling slogan.

The stakes could hardly be higher—for both men. Sharon knew, despite his bluster, that if he lost Labor, his government was unlikely to survive. And an election would mean, first, a Likud Party leadership primary against Netanyahu—still a daunting prospect. He was far ahead of his perennial rival in nationwide opinion polls. But the nation didn't vote in the Likud primary; only party members did. And among many of them Bibi was still the preferred leader.

Ben-Eliezer was already in the thick of his own party's primary, fending off a vigorous challenge from the bright new star in Labor's firmament, Haifa's mayor, Amram Mitzna. The pundits had expected

---

that he himself had instituted during the first term began to show results during the second—and Netanyahu got all the credit for them. Netanyahu, moreover, added insult to injury by repeatedly asserting that he had taken over, indeed rescued, an economy on the verge of collapse. This version stuck, and Netanyahu was feted in the political community and in much of the media as an economic wizard.

In fact, he deserved most of the accolades, though Shalom deserved some, too. Shalom's decisions to pare down welfare transfers, especially child allowances, were brave politics. But there was no real alternative given the situation that he and Sharon faced of soaring defense costs and recession throughout the economy. For Netanyahu, who took this emergency policy, expanded it, and institutionalized it, forcing able-bodied people to fend for themselves was a matter of long-held ideological belief, not just of immediate budgetary expediency.

For Sharon, it was a matter of common sense. "They should sweep the streets," he asserted, thumping the table, at a meeting of his economic ministers on unemployment in early July. "Our cities are dirty. They need cleaning. They should work in hospitals or guard in kindergartens. Even if they don't get paid, they should do *something* in return for the unemployment benefits they receive. They shouldn't get these benefits if they don't do anything."

Ben-Eliezer to pick a fight with Sharon toward the year's end, prefer-ably over socioeconomic policy rather than defense, where Sharon was strongest. He had to shore up Labor's distinctive political identity in advance of the general elections the next year.* They all warned that Labor would be crushed if it tried to fight the election from inside Sharon's coalition.

Now, because of the Labor leadership contest, Ben-Eliezer's need to rebel and bolt had become even more pressing. Both Mitzna and the third candidate, Haim Ramon, were demanding that Labor secede at once and accusing Ben-Eliezer of kowtowing to Sharon. At a stormy session of Labor's central committee just hours after Sharon's blunt caution at cabinet, Ben-Eliezer outdid the other two in counterattack-ing the prime minister. "Don't preach to me about responsibility and national unity," he bellowed, apostrophizing Sharon. "What kind of unity is it when the majority of the population keeps having to give more and more and a small minority with political power always man-ages to get more and more?"

The "small minority" were, of course, the settlers. Ben-Eliezer had deftly conflated Labor's limp resistance to the budget's sledgeham-mer blows at the welfare state with the party's comfortably famil-iar (and equally ineffectual) opposition to the settlements, at least the farther-flung ones. He had managed to boil down the dispute to one sound bite: move $145 million from the settlements to the hard-hit "development towns" in the south of the country—and say so. The sum was almost paltry in a budget of $57 billion. Sharon could have moved it easily. The hard part for the prime minister was to do so pub-licly, and thereby acknowledge that the settlements were a drain on the national purse and specifically that they soaked up money that would otherwise have been available to help poor voters get through the hard times. Whatever he himself might already have been contemplating privately for the farther-flung settlements, Sharon had to hang tough over every last one of them, in view of his struggle with Netanyahu and the party hard-liners. He could not give Ben-Eliezer the words he wanted.

Despite Labor's secession, the 2003 budget passed on first reading with a majority of 67, which gave Sharon brief grounds for hope that he might be able to keep going. He tried to woo the hard-line National Union–Yisrael Beiteinu, but that party's leader, Avigdor Lieberman, was withering in debunking his blandishments. "I hear the prime min-ister saying that first thing after the election he will try to re-create

---

* By law, the elections had to be held before November 2003.

the unity government, that he will prefer Shimon Peres and Amram Mitzna to us. What do you think we are, chewing gum to be used and then spat out?"[2]

Lieberman's logic was impeccable. Sharon had been emphasizing, publicly and privately, his firm commitment both to the two-state solution, which President Bush had publicly adopted in his June 24 speech as his "vision," and to the "road map" diplomacy that Washington was evolving with its allies to bring this solution about.* But these policies were precisely what Lieberman and his party opposed.

They were also opposed by Netanyahu, to whom Sharon now offered the Foreign Ministry. This was a brilliant move as Netanyahu would be hard put to reject this call to arms, especially at so fraught a moment in national and international affairs with the Palestinian intifada still raging and the Americans preparing to launch their attack on Iraq soon. If he accepted, that might persuade Lieberman to set aside his own objections and join, too. That would give the government another year in office, with Netanyahu effectively neutralized in the "golden cage" of the Foreign Ministry. If, on the other hand, Netanyahu refused, and thus hastened the government's demise, he would be seen in the party as churlish and in the country at large as extremist. On the face of it, it was a win-win prospect for Sharon.

Netanyahu finally slipped out of Sharon's hammerlock, and applied an awkward one of his own, by announcing that he would accept the proffered Foreign Ministry—but only if the prime minister agreed to hold early elections. The Likud could double its strength, Netanyahu asserted, pointing to the polls.

With Lieberman unbending, Sharon was anyway moving toward the same conclusion. On the evening of November 4, the prime minister assembled his advisers at his Tel Aviv office. Most urged him to go for elections. It would be demeaning, they argued, for him to scratch around for splinter factions or lone MKs to woo in order to rebuild a parliamentary majority. And to try to push the budget through its second and third readings without a majority would be even more distasteful: it would mean endless wheeling and dealing with parties large and small.

What swung him around in the end, according to a participant, were polling figures provided by the in-house pollster, Kalman Gayer. Gayer's figures tracked the inevitable showdown between Sharon and Netanyahu for the leadership of the Likud. Sharon was eight points ahead. "Couldn't be better," Gayer proclaimed. Sharon pondered qui-

---

* See p. 421.

etly. "Gentlemen," he finally declared at 1:30 a.m. "I'm going to the president!" He would ask for elections in ninety days, as the law provided. By the time his various rivals had awoken to what was at hand, the deed would have been done. No time for anyone to try to head him off.

No time, either, for Netanyahu to change his condition. "Since the prime minister has done the right thing," he announced, "and since we are facing weighty challenges, I have informed the prime minister that I am prepared to accept the post of foreign minister."[3] The very next day he was sworn in.

By the end of that week Sharon's sanguine assessment of his prospects was being backed by newspaper polls. *Yedioth Ahronoth* had him defeating Labor in the general election by a larger margin than Netanyahu, though both would win comfortably, regardless of who ran at the head of Labor. *Maariv* showed him opening a significant gap against Netanyahu in the Likud primary: 48 percent to 38. The *Yedioth* poll, moreover, gave Sharon a 67 percent approval rating as prime minister ("good" or "very good") and 65 percent on credibility—more than double Netanyahu's score.

Netanyahu, a veteran and obsessive poll reader, trimmed his rhetoric accordingly. In a speech to the Likud conference on November 12, he predicted a great victory for the party in two and a half months, "and I can promise you now: Arik and I will march together to bring that historic victory for the Likud. We'll march together, Arik and I, I and Arik." In other words, whoever won in the primary, the other would serve under him in the new government.* The party, on course to victory, would preserve its unity. And the subtext: Netanyahu was resigned to losing. Barring bad mistakes, then, or really bad luck, Sharon seemed home and dry.

All the voters understood the extent to which war, peace, and prosperity hinged for Israel on the strength of its alliance with America. "Six times I've made my way from Jerusalem to Washington to meet with the president," Sharon recalled proudly in a speech in July. (By the election, it was seven: he was in the Oval Office again in October.) "Our discussions have stayed secret. These efforts have recently brought about a breakthrough which gives grounds for hope that we

---

* A deal to this effect had been worked out behind the scenes by Uri Shani, on behalf of Sharon, and Yisrael Katz, acting for Netanyahu, who made the initial overture.

can move forward toward a solution . . . George Bush has confronted the Palestinians with a simple choice: terror or peace."[4]

This was a flagrantly upbeat description of a much less simple situation. While the president's June 24 speech, effectively repudiating Arafat, had been enthusiastically welcomed in Jerusalem, the subsequent diplomacy had not produced "agreement . . . over the plan," as Sharon expansively asserted. Rather, the road-map initiative was evolving in Washington, and Sharon was bobbing and weaving to avoid agreeing to it and to avoid being seen as rejecting it.

He was urging his public, though, to look beneath the minutiae of diplomacy to the bedrock of unconcealed sympathy in the Bush White House for Israel, and specifically for Sharon himself. Nowhere was that support more salient than in Washington's responses to the IDF's "targeted assassinations." Time and again, when outrage swept the Muslim world and much of the West, too, over these extrajudicial killings and over the "collateral" deaths and injuries often sustained by innocent bystanders, U.S. spokesmen insisted on Israel's right to act in self-defense against terror. Sometimes, they would add a mild word of advice about the need to think ahead, to a future of peaceful negotiations with the people now suffering the brunt of Israel's fury.

Even when Israel itself was riven by controversy over the justification or the wisdom of such an assassination, the government could count on Washington for support. On the night of July 22, 2002, Israeli jets dropped a one-ton bomb on a house in Gaza where the Hamas military commander, Salah Shehadeh, was known to be staying. Sharon and Ben-Eliezer were assured that only his wife and two aides were with him. They decided that given the significance of Shehadeh in Hamas's military chain of command and the heinousness of the terror attacks that he had personally directed, this extent of "collateral damage" was justifiable.[5]*

Seventeen people were killed in the blast: Shehadeh, his wife and daughter, and an aide, and thirteen innocent civilians, ten of them children, all sleeping in an apartment block next door. The youngest victim was a two-month-old baby. Many Israelis recoiled at these numbers. Condemnations resounded around the world. But in Washington, the furthest the White House would go was to characterize the bombing as "heavy-handed."

Before the attacks on New York and Washington, Israel's targeted

---

* They accepted the air force's contention that a smaller bomb would not do the job. A caution from the deputy head of Shin Bet, Yuval Diskin, that the bomb might cause more widespread carnage in the densely populated district was ignored.

assassinations had sometimes occasioned sharp rebukes from the administration. But after 9/11, U.S. officers were sent to spend time with IDF field units in order to study Israeli techniques and experience in carrying out targeted assassinations.[6]

Sharon himself was an eager advocate of these operations. "I hear the noise of helicopters over the ranch," he would sometimes shout into the phone to a sleepy aide. "Does that mean we can expect good news from Gaza?"[7] Over the first thousand days of the intifada, according to an IDF document, Israel carried out ninety-five targeted assassination operations, more than half of them against Hamas men. In a very high percentage of the attacks the target was killed. In some half a dozen cases he was injured; in another six he escaped unscathed. In one-third of the attacks innocent people were killed.[8]

Over time, and in the face of repeated applications by human rights groups to the High Court of Justice, a rough code of legal and moral conduct evolved to govern the decision making: the targeted assassination must be preventive, not punitive; the target must be "a ticking bomb," poised to commit an imminent terrorist attack; the method chosen must be "proportional" and designed to minimize collateral casualties; and other methods of neutralizing the target, such as arrest, must be either unavailable or too dangerous to the lives of IDF troops. Army lawyers were often involved in the planning. Plainly, though, the term "ticking bomb" was open to interpretation, and there was constant pressure to extend it beyond the man who actually strapped the bomb belt to his body to those who sent him out to kill and die.

Meanwhile, the White House was increasingly committed to making war on Saddam's Iraq,[9] and the road map was seen as a means of enlisting support, both in the Arab world and in the West. Britain's Tony Blair, at the head of a Labour government distinctly less warlike than its leader, was particularly insistent in his pressure on President Bush to demonstrate determination in the Israel-Palestine diplomacy. Bush "hastily blessed the . . . Road Map," writes Martin Indyk, "only as a sop to . . . Tony Blair, who needed the president's endorsement of an Israeli-Palestinian peace initiative to bolster support within his Labor Party for the Iraq War effort."

A less sour interpretation of the diplomacy during the latter half of 2002 gives at least some of the credit to King Abdullah of Jordan and to his prime minister, Marwan Muasher, for nudging President Bush to translate his two-state "vision" into a practical and detailed blueprint for progress. "We assume you're going to take military action [against Saddam] . . . We will do everything we can to support you," the king told the president in the Oval Office on August 1. "But we need more

cover on the Palestinian issue. We need a roadmap on how we're going
to get from where we are now to realizing the vision that you have laid
out." Muasher added bluntly: "Frankly, Mr. President, most Palestinians are skeptical that this vision will be realized . . . We need to define
a roadmap. That starts with security, institutions, the humanitarian
situation, but also outlines the remaining steps till mid-2005, so that
people can know exactly what they are getting."[10]

The various drafts of the road map that now began to circulate
differed from the Mitchell plan and the Tenet plan in their explicit
insistence that the parties perform their various requirements in each
phase in the road map *simultaneously* instead of sequentially. There
could be no more demands by Israel for seven terror-free days on the
Palestinian side before it began to rein in its own forces. "The parties are expected to perform their obligations in parallel."* Thus, in
the first phase, the two sides were to end violence and resume security cooperation; the Palestinians were to "undertake comprehensive
political reform in preparation for statehood . . . including free, fair
and open elections"; Israel was to withdraw to the pre-intifada lines
and freeze settlement building. The international community, which
stood behind the road map, would expect Israel to get on with its
withdrawal and freeze (including the immediate dismantling of the
outposts built since Sharon came to power), while the Palestinians got
on with their program. There was to be no conditionality between the
two sides' performances.

But such conditionality had been the linchpin of Sharon's policy
hitherto. He had accepted the Mitchell plan, which required a settlement freeze, on condition that the Palestinians moved first on security.
He doubted that they would in fact move, and hence never expected
to actually have to implement the freeze. This time, if he accepted the
road map, there would be no such comfortable cushioning. He sent
Weissglas to Washington time and again to try to soften the text and
above all blur this key question of simultaneity versus sequence.

But Sharon and his smooth-talking emissary were given a stern
reminder at this time that even with their sympathizers in the highest
places in Washington they could not have things all their own way.
After a suicide bombing on a bus killed six and injured seventy at an
intersection in the heart of Tel Aviv, Sharon ordered the siege of Arafat

---

* This and other direct quotations are from the text of the "Performance-Based
Roadmap to a Permanent Two-State Solution to the Israeli-Palestinian Conflict,"
which was formally published in April 2003 by the Middle East Quartet, comprising the United States, the EU, Russia, and the UN. See Appendix.

reimposed, tighter than ever this time. IDF tanks and APCs charged back into Ramallah, spraying machine-gun fire. They surrounded the *muqata* again and began demolishing PA administrative buildings with bulldozers and explosives. Arafat's own suite of rooms and offices filled with dust and debris. His aides called the White House on their cell phones, seriously scared this time that Sharon meant to take out the *rais*.[11]

The renewed siege was an exercise in brinkmanship. The Americans, involved in their pre–Iraq War diplomacy at the UN and in the region, were not taking chances. On September 20, Condoleezza Rice called Weissglas to remonstrate. The next day, Ambassador Kurtzer helicoptered to Sharon's ranch to deliver the hands-off-Arafat message. Secretary Powell followed up with a phone call to Sharon. And, with Bush's approval, he instructed the U.S. delegation not to veto a resolution at the UN Security Council condemning the renewed siege.

In Washington, Rice lectured the for-once-silent Weissglas: "Israel has had no better friend than this administration, and you've had no better friend in this administration than me. But I'm telling you, if you do not end this siege in Ramallah, if you don't withdraw your forces from the compound, you are going to have a public rift with the President. This needs to end *now*. If you and I are having this same conversation a week from now, you are going to have a serious problem." Their aides started working on a withdrawal schedule. On September 29 the IDF armor and earthmovers revved up and drove away.

The wrangling over the road map proceeded desultorily until, almost as a relief, the government in Israel imploded and elections loomed. Sharon asked for a time-out: hold off publishing the road map until after the election, scheduled for January 28, 2003. This time, Weissglas was successful, and the administration, despite Blair's chafing and the Jordanians' increasing skepticism, put publication plans in abeyance. And Sharon could justly bask in the comfortable assurances he had received from Bush during his visit to Washington in October that U.S. and allied forces would make every effort to smash Iraqi Scud missile launchers at the outset of the looming war. They would bomb airfields in western Iraq, and they would beef up Israel's ground defenses with more batteries of Patriot missiles. Sharon, who tongue-lashed Shamir during the last Gulf War for his U.S.-dictated passivity, undertook now himself to do nothing to surprise the United States. If Israel were attacked and decided to retaliate, it would inform America first.[12]

That was not the only historical irony of that October visit. President Bush could hardly have been more outspoken in support of the still dangerously teetering Israeli economy. "I understand what terror has done to economy," he told reporters. "Terror has affected our economy; terror has affected the Israeli economy. But we've got great confidence in the Israeli economy. We've got great confidence in the Israeli people. The greatest asset Israel has is the brainpower and ingenuity of her people. And I'm convinced that the economy will be strong."[13]

Bush 41 had denied Likud-led Israel loan guarantees, largely because of Ariel Sharon's provocations, and thereby helped Likud lose an election. Now his son was holding out the promise of such guarantees to the same Sharon, knowing that it would help the Likud under him to win another term in power. Bush and his advisers knew, too, that the president's public backing and the prospect of the guarantees were powerful ammunition for Sharon in his upcoming battle with Netanyahu, who would surely attack him on economic policy.*

Pollsters and pundits all agreed that the interesting fight was the one inside the Likud. Whoever won in there would almost certainly defeat whoever won in Labor. In the countrywide vote by Likud Party members, Sharon romped home by a margin of more than 16 percent. Still, Netanyahu's 40 percent entitled him to the No. 2 spot on the Likud Knesset list, as agreed. The two camps now made ready to fight over the rest of the list. This contest was decided by the three-thousand-odd members of the central committee, gathered in Tel Aviv. The result was a stinging blow to the prime minister. His key lieutenants were all punished by the central committee members, while Netanyahu's top loyalists took the prime spots on the list, followed by an eclectic assortment of newcomers, few of whom owed the prime minister any particular fealty. Omri squeezed in, just. But his vaunted sway over the party activists proved a hollow myth: candidates whom he had sponsored did almost uniformly badly.

The vote was ominous. It showed that Netanyahu, though down, was by no means out. It showed, moreover, that the hard core of the party, despite Shani's and Omri's efforts to bring in new blood, continued to balk at Sharon's relative moderation. He was popular among the general public and among the Likud rank and file, as the leadership primary had shown. But the Likud Party activists were not, in the main, his political supporters and probably never would be.

---

* New loan guarantees from Washington, when they were finally negotiated the following March, covered $9 billion—$1 billion more than Israel had asked for. By then, Netanyahu was serving as Sharon's finance minister, and his tough economic policies were earning broad admiration in the international business community.

In Labor, the leadership primary had produced a revolution. Binyamin Ben-Eliezer's dramatic secession from Sharon's government failed to convince a dispirited membership looking for fresh, untainted politics. Amram Mitzna, the bearded, soft-spoken ex-general and popular mayor of Haifa, took the party by storm. A man with no experience in national politics, who had never served in the Knesset and never held cabinet office, would now lead them against the battle-hardened Sharon.

It was not the first time the two men had crossed swords. Mitzna was the highest-ranking officer to resign in protest at the then defense minister's running of the Lebanon War. His resignation was brief, but it gave him momentary fame. He was back in the public eye in 1987–1989 as CO of Central Command during the first intifada, often sparring with the West Bank settlers. Sharon had objected to his promotion to general. Now, though, their roles were different. "I don't bear a grudge, and I'm not vengeful," Sharon told reporters. "It's not a question of relations between two lovers. It's a matter of policy and politics."

Mitzna, determined not to be sweet-talked into passivity, insisted, "It's the same Sharon, the Sharon who misled the government and the nation in the Lebanon War. He hasn't changed, even if he looks like a dear old granddad."

Sharon proposed to found the policy of his new government after the election—another unity government as broadly based as possible, he promised—on President Bush's blueprint for peace first articulated on June 24 and subsequently elaborated in the yet-unpublished road map. In the traditional prime minister's lecture winding up the annual Herzliya Conference on national security, Sharon provided a somewhat airbrushed picture of the evolving road map. He detailed the many constitutional, administrative, financial, judicial, and above all sweeping security reforms that were required of the Palestinians and skated over the steps that Israel would be required to take. He insisted that the Palestinians would have to make progress on their reforms first, before Israel moved at all.

But he did spell out the two subsequent phases in the road map: a Palestinian state with temporary borders, and then peace negotiations over final status and permanent borders. He made it clear that as long as he was in charge, it wouldn't happen fast. But he also insisted that he was committed to the process. He was at pains to persuade his audience of his sincerity: "My long-standing ideological and political beliefs are well-known to you from the many positions I was privileged to fill during my decades of public service. These [new] decisions are not easy for me . . . However, I have come to the conclusion that in the present regional and international reality Israel must act with courage to accept the political plan which I described. There are risks involved, but also enormous opportunities."[14] A year later, on the same dais, he would shock the world by putting tangible content into those vague but intriguing words.

Mitzna, in his lecture to the same forum, challenged Sharon's vagueness and urged a concrete and specific separation plan. The Gaza Strip should be evacuated unilaterally and urgently, he said. In the West Bank, Israel should seek agreement, but if it proved unattainable, then settlements must be dismantled unilaterally there, too, he said. To this Sharon replied repeatedly during the campaign that his rival was "sowing illusions." Unilateral decisions could not produce a solution, he asserted. "Any unilateral withdrawal or unilateral separation without an agreement means serious disaster for Israel."[15]

Happily for Sharon, many middle-of-the-road voters refused to believe him. "Most of the public back Sharon to carry out Mitzna's policy," *Haaretz* wrote, reporting the findings of an opinion poll. "Without reference to the election results," the pollster's question read, "if it proves impossible to reach a negotiated agreement, would you support or oppose unilateral separation, provided Israel could keep the settlement blocs and a solution were found for Jerusalem?" Fifty-eight percent said they would support it. "And here's the even bigger surprise," the reporter Yossi Verter added: "The same results were registered among Likud voters [as among the public at large]. This is the paradox that Amram Mitzna needs to think about: the majority of the public clearly supports his plan for unilateral separation, but the majority of the public will vote for Sharon, in the hope that he will implement Mitzna's plan."

On New Year's Eve, Sharon's sense of quietly cruising to victory was rudely disturbed. Press reports linked some of the new faces in the Likud's Knesset list to powerful but shady families whose business affairs were close to criminality and whose influence would now extend to the national legislature itself.

The police, prodded by the media, began investigating. When they decided to pounce, though, it was on a relatively harmless piece of political pork, allegedly perpetrated by a veteran and thoroughly respectable MK, Naomi Blumenthal, the deputy minister of national infrastructures. A onetime theater star now married to an eminent eye surgeon, she had invited a group of key central committee activists to Tel Aviv on the night before the central committee vote and put them up in a city hotel at her expense. For this infringement of the election finance rules she was arrested. Blumenthal refused to cooperate with her police interrogators, citing "the right to remain silent."

Ill-advised by his image artists, Sharon now committed an ignoble act of hypocrisy that earned him scant public approbation and would quickly come back to haunt him. He fired Naomi Blumenthal. Not only did she not have the right to remain silent, he wrote to her prissily on December 31. She had "an absolute duty to disclose the circumstances surrounding her election." He could not dump her from the list—she had been duly elected—but he sacked her as a deputy minister. This even though she had not, as yet, been prosecuted. She shot back a lawyer's letter denying his right to interfere in her legal process.

The thinking among Sharon's advisers was to distance him from the sleazy imagery projected by the Likud primary and to portray him as a leader of national stature sternly committed to the rule of law, in defiance of seedy party machinations. This supposedly sophisticated strategy sat uncomfortably with Sharon's long chronicle of close scrapes with the law. It became risibly irrelevant a week later, when *Haaretz* broke the story that quickly became known as "the Cyril Kern affair" and mushroomed into a gray cloud that hung over Sharon for the rest of his life.

The prime minister and his son Gilad, wrote the paper's police reporter, Baruch Kra, were suspected by the state prosecution service of receiving bribes, of fraud, of breach of trust, and of lying to the state comptroller and to the police. Omri Sharon was believed to be involved, too, Kra wrote. The state prosecution had specified all these allegations in an official document sent to the government of South Africa asking permission to interrogate a man named Cyril Kern over his role in the affair. The document was in *Haaretz*'s possession.

The Cyril Kern affair did not drop onto Sharon—or onto the Israeli electorate—out of the clear blue sky. Trouble had been brewing for Sharon for more than a year as investigators, first from the state comptroller's office, then from the police, trawled through the accounts of his September 1999 primary campaign for the leadership of the Likud. He had raised and spent far, far more than the law allowed and done so, moreover, through a shadowy network of front companies created specifically to facilitate, but at the same time to conceal, the flow of funds from Sharon's American supporters to his campaign managers.[16] The Cyril Kern affair was a much uglier mutation of this earlier, multi-tentacled creature that was already being dubbed "the front companies affair."

The saga began back in March 1999. Netanyahu was about to lose the prime ministership to Ehud Barak, and Sharon, while publicly demonstrating support for the sinking Netanyahu as his loyal foreign minister, was at the same time preparing for his own bid for the Likud leadership and perhaps, eventually, for the prime ministership. It was against this backdrop that Sharon's longtime lawyer and adviser Dov Weissglas, on March 3, 1999, set up a company in Tel Aviv named Annex Research. Annex's goals, as described in its articles of association, were "to work for the inculcation and advancement of democratic principles in public, party-political, and rural life in Israel; to initiate educational activities aimed at imbuing young people and adults with democratic values and the culture of good government; to encourage foreign investments in Israel." "There was nothing," as a judge was later pointedly to note, "about Annex handling contributions and expenses for Candidate Ariel Sharon's primary campaign."[17]

In fact, though, that was Annex's sole purpose. Weissglas had set it up on behalf of Yoram Oren, an Israeli living in California who had long been a key fund-raiser in the United States for the Likud and for Sharon. Oren instructed Weissglas to transfer the shares in Annex to four U.S. citizens. In August, a month before the primary, Omri Sharon asked Weissglas to install his schoolroom friend and army buddy Gabriel Manor as CEO of Annex. Annex's official address became Manor's home.

Suddenly, the hitherto dormant company sprang to life. A total of $1.5 million poured into its bank account, mainly from three nonprofit concerns in the United States: the American Israel Research Friendship Foundation, the Center for National Studies and International Relationships, and the College for National Studies. And all of this money, about six million shekels in Israeli currency, poured out again, on Omri's orders and over his friend Manor's signature, in payments for the primary—to political strategists, to a pollster, to a security firm, to public-relations experts, and to a legion of campaign workers who all had a part in Sharon's victory in the primary on September 2. The three American foundations were run by two executives who—"what a coincidence," the same caustic judge was to write years later—were among the four shareholders of Annex. The various service providers were asked by Omri to make out their invoices and receipts to Annex, for services ostensibly rendered to Annex, not to the Sharon campaign, their true client.

Under the Parties Law, the candidates in the Likud leadership primary were limited to raising and spending precisely 826,726.50 shekels.[18] Candidates in primaries were required, moreover, to file detailed returns after their campaign to the party's supervisory board, which in turn would publish them and send them on to the registrar of parties. In November 1999, Sharon's campaign filed meticulous returns showing how it had raised the modest sum of 139,776 shekels and had spent 972,396 shekels, just a little above the legal limit. The documents were prepared by the campaign's accountant, and Sharon himself signed them, as the law required. They were entirely true insofar as they went. Only they failed to mention the other 6 million shekels.

When State Comptroller Eliezer Goldberg, in his routine examination of the 2001 prime ministerial election, alighted on the missing 6 million, they naturally piqued his interest. He determined that of 5.9 million shekels actually paid out by Annex, 1.2 million had been paid for services provided to Sharon *after* the primaries, when he was already chairman of the party. That left 4.7 million that had gone for Sharon's primary campaign—almost six times as much as the law allowed and forty-two times as much as Sharon solemnly attested in his official return to have raised. When questioned about this, Sharon informed the state comptroller, after consulting his lawyers,* that he would repay the whole 4.7 million immediately from his own pocket.

Sharon could have dragged his feet. He could have put up arguments about the sums raised and the sums spent and gotten into a long sparring match with the authorities over the facts and figures. His zeal to pay up was apparently intended to underscore, to Comptroller Goldberg and through him to the entire Israeli public, how dumbfounded and humbly contrite the prime minister was about the whole business. Sharon assured the comptroller that he, the candidate, had taken no part whatever in the running of the money side of his primary campaign. He had left all that to his son Omri, leaving himself free to focus on the politics.

Comptroller Goldberg chose not to comment on the plausibility of this depiction. He wrote that Omri was "clearly in total control of Annex's expenditures; the CEO played merely a formal role and signed the checks." Omri for his part, Goldberg noted, had "refused to answer the state comptroller's questions about Annex and about

---

* Weissglas explained that he could not advise the family in this matter because he, too, was under investigation for having set up Annex. Another lawyer, Dori Klagsbald, was approached. His advice, said Weissglas, was inevitable: repay the money. Every lawyer would have had to say the same, Weissglas explained, given the unequivocal language of the Parties Law (sec. 28). Failure to repay illicit funds could result in a fine, under this section, of up to four times the sum illicitly raised or spent (Weissglas interview, Tel Aviv, July 10, 2008).

the companies which transmitted funds to it, on the grounds that he did not wish to incriminate himself and on additional grounds (not entirely relevant) that 'he did not wish to hurt others.' " Omri's noncooperation with the comptroller in his investigation of the "front companies affair" explains the howl of outrage that went up a year later when Sharon peremptorily fired the popular Blumenthal for doing precisely what Omri had done: she exercised her right to remain silent.

The Cyril Kern affair took up from where the front companies affair left off. The state comptroller's report was published on October 1, 2001. Three days later, on October 4, in keeping with his expansive pledge to repay the errant 4.7 million shekels, Sharon sent a check to Annex for 500,000 shekels from his personal account. His sons, Omri and Gilad, now set about finding the wherewithal to cover the rest of their father's commitment. On October 22, 2001, Gilad took a loan of 4.2 million shekels from the branch of Bank Leumi, a large, nationwide bank, in the sleepy little town of Sderot, near Sycamore Ranch. As collateral, he mortgaged the ranch. The next day, Ariel Sharon sent Annex a check for 4.2 million shekels. A quick and elegant end, it seemed, to a potentially awkward affair.

Only it wasn't. Bank Leumi belatedly realized that Sycamore Ranch couldn't be mortgaged because the Sharons didn't own the freehold: it was state land, farmed on long-term lease. Two weeks later, however, it seemed the Sharons really would be able to draw a final line beneath the whole episode: a sum of $1.49 million was deposited in the brothers' account at a branch in Tel Aviv of the Israel Discount Bank. The money was sent by Cyril Kern, a resident of South Africa, from his account in BAWAG (Bank für Arbeit und Wirtschaft) in Vienna, through J. P. Morgan in New York, and on to Israel Discount Bank in Tel Aviv. On April 30, with this deposit as their surety, the brothers negotiated a loan from Israel Discount Bank of 4.2 million shekels. With this, they paid off the loan they had taken from Bank Leumi in Sderot, which was to have been secured by the mortgage but could not be.

Eight months later, and just three weeks before the election, this whole elaborate edifice came crashing down around the Sharon family with the publication, on January 7, 2003, of the *Haaretz* story. Ariel Sharon appeared to have tripped himself up under questioning. Interrogated by police detectives on April 22 over what was then still the front companies affair, the prime minister had trotted out the version of the loan and the mortgage in Sderot, even though, as the prosecutors explained in their letter to the South African legal authorities, everyone involved knew by then that it was impossible to mortgage the ranch.*

The evolution of the front companies affair into the Cyril Kern affair threatened to add a new and, for Sharon, dangerous aspect to the public's perception of his and his family's conduct. From election finance finagling, the story looked as if it were becoming one of outright bribery, or at least of illicit gift taking by the prime minister and his family. The Israeli political ethos, like that of many democracies, makes a distinction between donations to politicians at election time, even if they exceed or otherwise infringe legal restrictions, and gifts to politicians at other times—which are looked on with greater severity.

The almost comical structure of empty companies with pompous, patriotic names was assumed to have been intended to enable Sharon's longtime patrons and admirers to continue supporting him, especially now that he was bidding for the highest office.† Granted, some of these people had business interests in Israel, which made their support unethical and possibly illegal even beyond the election finance laws infringements. But over the long years, the public had somehow grown inured to Sharon's enduring dalliance with this moneyed circle of American backers. His ranch, which he showed off with such pride, had been paid for by these friends, and his claims that he had paid them back were always taken with a pinch of salt.

Cyril Kern was someone new, at least to the broad public. The media quickly learned that he was indeed a very old friend of Sharon's. The two had met back in 1948 when Kern, a young British Jew, came out to Palestine to fight as a volunteer in the new state's army.

---

* In addition to Ariel Sharon's suspicious answers, the Israeli government lawyers wrote to their South African colleagues, his son Gilad had behaved suspiciously by avoiding for months the standard legal requirement that he specify in writing the source of the $1.49 million that had landed in his and his brother's account. Only after he learned that the police were investigating this transaction did he fill out the requisite standard form, specifying the name of Cyril Kern. The Israelis asked the South Africans to enable Israeli detectives to interrogate Kern, in South Africa, about the money transfer. The Israeli authorities revealed their own inefficiency by admitting to the South Africans that they had no firm evidence that Cyril Kern in fact existed.

† When Sharon was asked by police detectives on April 22, 2002, about the sources of the funds that went through Annex, he reportedly replied: "The sources of their money? I never dealt with these financial matters. I think there's one man who might know, and that's Omri." When the detectives pointed out that Omri was maintaining his right to remain silent, Sharon replied, "Look, Omri's a big boy. He's got to decide himself" ("The Sharon File," www.news1.co.il, October 18, 2005).

He had gone back to England and flourished in the textile business. Later he moved to South Africa. Cyril and Arik, for all their disparities, had been close for more than fifty years. And he was certainly a rich man. But was he rich enough to write a check for $1.49 million to help a friend in trouble? Or was he, like Annex Research, also just a front? His money had been remitted through Austria, from the same bank used by Martin Schlaff. Schlaff had been growing closer to the Sharons in recent years. He'd been a guest at Sycamore Ranch. His assiduous cultivation of Israeli politicians, his involvement in the Jericho casino, his reported plans to build another in Eilat—all these were seen as more sinister, certainly more suspicious, than the activities of Sharon's other, older friends.

The Cyril Kern affair, hugely embarrassing and potentially lethal, accounted for only half of Sharon's woes that first week of January 2003. Another rumbling episode of alleged bribe-taking by the Sharon family came surging to the surface, this one on the pages of the mass-circulation *Yedioth Ahronoth*.

In March 2001, just a month after he took office as prime minister, the paper had published a seven-page exposé concerning an ambitious but disreputable building contractor and Likud activist named David "Dudi" Appel who set out in the late 1990s to buy Patroklos, a scenic and undeveloped island just off the Greek coast thirty miles southeast of Athens.[19] Appel planned to build on the island a vast vacation and recreation complex with many thousands of hotel rooms and holiday apartments, huge shopping malls, golf courses, theme parks, cinemas, an opera house, concert halls, sports stadiums, and fifteen(!) casinos. To buy the island and then to develop it, Appel knew he would need the backing of the Greek authorities. There would have to be legislation to change the designation of the island from a protected archaeological site to a tourist venue. He lobbied vigorously in Athens, with the help of an Israeli-Australian-Greek businessman, Norman Shkolnik, who claimed to have close connections with the powers that be in the Greek capital.

In Israel, Appel lobbied two key figures in his party: Ariel Sharon, the foreign minister; and Ehud Olmert, the mayor of Jerusalem. In January 1999, he persuaded the Israel Labor Party, then in opposition, to invite a delegation from its Greek sister party, Passok, led by the deputy foreign minister, Yiannos Kranidiotis. Appel picked up the tab. He prevailed on Minister of Foreign Affairs Sharon to attend an intimate dinner with the Greek delegation in an apartment he owned in Tel Aviv. Other senior politicians and ex-generals completed the star-studded guest list. Unfortunately, the Greek deputy minister was killed soon after in a freak plane accident. Later in the year, Appel persuaded Olmert to invite the mayor of Athens on an official visit. Again Sharon, now leader of the opposition, graced an intimate dinner with his presence, this time in Appel's home.

All through this period, for reason of various and sundry criminal suspicions against him, the police were tapping Appel's telephone lines and monitoring his copious conversations. They heard him, for instance, promise generous support, both political and logistic, *both* to Sharon *and* to Olmert, who were running against each other in the Likud leadership primary in September 1999. They also heard him discuss with Sharon, albeit in rather general terms, the fact that Sharon's son Gilad was working on the Greek island project and would, as Appel stressed, be earning very well out of it. "He's learned how to lose money till now; now he's going to learn how to make some," Appel assured Sharon. Was the payment to the son in fact a payoff to the father?

Despite *Yedioth*'s efforts to demonstrate a prima facie suspicion of bribery against the prime minister, the "Greek island affair" seemed to fade away after the initial publication in 2001. Neither Sharon nor Gilad was questioned by the police, and no additional evidence was unearthed by the media. Now, though, as the Likud floundered in a wave of corruption stories, the Greek island suddenly surfaced again. On January 2, 2003, *Yedioth* splashed over its front page the contract of employment between Appel and Gilad. He had indeed earned very well for services that remained vague and mysterious. "The $3 Million Deal Between Gilad Sharon and David Appel," the headline read.[20]

Gilad was described in the contract as a consultant. This arrangement had lasted until June 2001, by which time the project had finally run aground and the team working on it was disbanded. Gilad earned some $540,000.

The *Yedioth* reporters were particularly exercised by the bonus clauses in the contract. These provided that if permission was received from the Greek authorities and work was begun, Gilad would receive $1.5 million. Once the project was completed, he would receive another $1.5 million.

This was "hard to fathom," the *Yedioth* team wrote. Gilad's "consultancy work," which *Yedioth* anyway ridiculed (he was thirty at the time, had a degree in agriculture, and had scant experience in business and none in tourism), was ostensibly connected with marketing to tourists, not lobbying governments. "On the face of it, he lacks any qualifications for persuading the government of Greece . . . to provide the requisite licenses. But Ariel Sharon—who lives at Sycamore Ranch, to which all the moneys in the contract were paid—he is very well-known all over the world. Even as leader of the opposition . . ."

The next day, January 4, the Meretz MKs Yossi Sarid and Ran Cohen formally requested the police to investigate the Sharons. "The Sharon family is a pretty good business," the sardonic Sarid observed. "Thousands of firms around the country are folding, but they're turning over millions." *Yedioth* cited unnamed "sources familiar with the case" who said that a police investigation had in fact been conducted and the recommendation was "to indict everyone involved in the affair."

After another day of dwindling poll figures, Sharon himself reacted, trying to reduce the flames and to direct them against his political rivals. "This publication about Gilad is very serious, and it makes me very angry," the prime minister said. "The only reason for publishing the story anew at this time is to hurt me. It's all political. These stories are intended to divert the public's attention from the crucial issues of security that should be at the top of our national agenda."[21] Three days later, Cyril Kern soared out of anonymity to the top of the national agenda.

Sharon and the Likud were in real trouble. The gap with Labor narrowed to just three seats—twenty-seven against twenty-four.[22] The election, from a virtual shoo-in, was suddenly wide open. Labor strategists were striving mightily to lump together all the unsavory characters and stories highlighted by the Likud faction primary with the leader himself in one sinkhole of corruption. Labor's election broadcasts took their inspiration from *The Sopranos*. Sicilian music played in the background as "Sharon and his sons" were shown whispering furtively. It looked as if this might just succeed. Panic began to lap at the Likud campaign.

Sharon, at his best when others panicked, shut himself away in his study at the ranch. He summoned his adman friend Reuven Adler; his Israeli election strategist, Eyal Arad; and his American strategist, Arthur Finkelstein. Together they laid on a "simulation" of the toughest press drubbing imaginable. Sharon parried with vigor. Adler urged him to counterattack from the outset. He was being framed by his political foes. (The state prosecution service was long seen on the right as a last redoubt of the leftist "old elites.") They were out to wrest power by subterfuge. That's what he should say. The others agreed. Sharon sat on alone into the night, preparing the opening statement that he would deliver the following evening, January 9, at the press conference to be broadcast live on prime-time television from his office in Jerusalem.

The statement, as it turned out, was a stunning success, one of the most salient in his career. He did not have himself to thank for that, but, ironically, a justice of the Supreme Court. He began with a searing attack on Labor, which was

> trying to bring down the government by lies. They've gone on a hunting expedition against the Likud. They're trying to make us out as a mafia, as organized crime . . . When they saw that this wasn't helping them, they decided to attack my sons with old stories that have no substance to them.
>
> I withdrew my savings and those of Lily, God bless her memory, and in that way I paid back half a million shekels. Gilad undertook to take care of the rest. He took a loan of four and a half million shekels. I returned the full sum. That was the end of it, from my point of view . . . As far as I knew, the ranch was mortgaged.

Everything was done legally, Sharon insisted, and there were documents to prove it. Gilad earned very well, and he was proud of him, he declared, in reference to the renewed Greek island revelations. As for Cyril Kern, he was a dear friend of fifty years' standing. "He never asked for anything, and he never received anything. He's got no business interests in Israel; he never has had, and he never will have. But he loves us . . . Look what you're doing to him just because he's my friend. So Gilad took a loan from him, which he afterward repaid and paid tax on it. So what? Is that bribery? Is that illicit benefits? What is this? Have you gone completely mad?" Here Sharon brought his fist crashing down onto the desk. "He is a lover of Israel . . . What are you doing to him?!"

By this time Sharon was shouting into dead cameras, though he did not know it. The justice of the Supreme Court Mishael Cheshin, who had been appointed election commissioner for the upcoming general election, ordered the three television channels to pull the plug on the prime minister on the grounds that Sharon was electioneering rather than merely answering the allegations against him. Under Israeli law, electioneering on radio and television during the weeks immediately preceding an election is strictly regulated. The parties are allocated TV and radio time for their official election broadcasts in proportion to their numerical strength in the outgoing Knesset. Other than that, the media must keep candidates off the air—unless they're not talking politics. Sharon was supposed to have been talking forensics; when he digressed, Cheshin silenced him.

Probably, this split-second decision by a judge known for his tempestuous disposition decided the outcome of the election. Sharon railed on for another ten minutes, and then his aides answered questions from journalists. The full proceedings of the press conference were duly reported in the newspapers the next day. A close parsing of them left many questions unanswered. But that didn't seem to matter anymore. What remained etched in the public mind was that Sharon had been shut up when trying to defend himself. His accusations against his political opponents hung in the air. The darkened screen was the most memorable image. Its effect on the voters was immediate. That same night, the Likud began picking up ground again, and Labor receding.

The Cyril Kern leak itself, moreover, began to militate among many voters *for* Sharon instead of against him. A brisk investigation by the police, and incautious telephone discipline by a reporter, quickly uncovered the culprit: a senior prosecutor named Liora Glatt-Berkowitz, one of the attorneys working on the Kern case. She insisted her action had not been political, but it had been ideological. She believed the public needed to know about the suspicions against Sharon before they went into the voting booths. Glatt-Berkowitz's admission played into the hands of Sharon's spinners, who kept pumping out their claims that the allegations against him were part of a plot to unseat him.*

After this roller coaster, the election itself was something of an anticlimax. The Likud won with a substantial (for Israel) thirty-eight seats to Labor's miserable nineteen. Reuven Adler's election slogan, "The people want Sharon," showed penetrating insight into the public psyche. The people wanted him regardless of the criminal allegations welling up around him. Most people presumed that at least some of the suspicions were well-founded, despite his slick "victimhood" spin. Nevertheless, they wanted him. They wanted him to keep fighting the intifada, even though his success there had been, thus far, at best partial. They wanted him to keep running the economy, even though his record there was poor. They wanted him to make his "painful concessions for peace," even though they didn't know what these would be,

---

* Cyril Kern played his part, too, when he was eventually tracked down by journalists in his high-walled home in Cape Town. The loan was a personal gift to help the family's struggling ranch, he told a South African newspaper. "I loaned money to a friend and was very happy to do so." He was not involved in Israeli politics "in any shape or form," and the loan had been repaid with interest.

and he himself probably didn't know yet, either. They wanted him despite the ugly aspects of the party he headed. Even people who voted against him and feared his policies no longer feared him. There was no surge of horror or trepidation on the left after his victory this time, not only because it was expected, but because voters who were horrified last time had since learned that he behaved now with caution and restraint. He had come to be seen, over two frightening and depressing years, as a responsible adult whom, in hard times, people in general felt fairly comfortable to have at the helm, even if they had not voted to put him there.

To the extent, though, that Sharon's election triumph in 2003 was a victory over the coalition of police, prosecution, and press that pursued, leaked, and published his various suspicious-smelling "affairs," it was only a partial victory. They were defeated at the ballot box, but he could not ultimately suppress them. With unflagging persistence, they continued to harry him, and he continued to parry them, to the very end.

Amram Mitzna, the defeated Labor Party leader, had solemnly proclaimed before the election that he would not serve under Sharon in a unity government. He made the same declaration on the night of his defeat. "Sharon hopes that the Labor Party will once again serve as a fig leaf for his failed policies," he told his dispirited cohorts at the party headquarters in south Tel Aviv. "But we do not intend to join him. We intend to replace him." Looking back years later, Mitzna maintained that he was in fact prepared to join a unity government "regardless of what I'd said during the campaign" (and on election night)—if it was based on a policy of separation from the Palestinians, whether by negotiation or unilaterally.

A first postelection meeting with Sharon was barren. Sharon waited a fortnight and invited Mitzna again. Mitzna suggested that the new government prepare a compensation package for settlers who sought voluntarily to relocate back to Israel proper. Sharon reacted negatively as Mitzna must have assumed he would. But they carried on talking. At their third meeting Mitzna said, "You've got to give me something tangible. It can be one settlement." He demanded that understandings between them be drawn up in writing. "But the next day," Mitzna recalled, "Uri Shani phoned to say he was very sorry but the prime minister was not prepared to put anything on paper. He would not commit even to the vague things he had said about 'painful concessions,' about

doing 'great things.' He never spoke explicitly of evacuating settlements. It wasn't I who shut the door on the unity government."[23]

But he shut his ears to what Sharon was saying, says Reuven Adler,
who was present at that third meeting. "Arik said to him, 'Look, we're
not far apart. I'm not drawing you into some kind of honey trap. Join
the government with me.' He was trying to tell him something. But
Mitzna didn't hear it. Either because he wasn't experienced enough in
politics, or because he was one of those people who had such a fixed
opinion of Arik that they could not see, or could not believe, that Arik
was going through a process."[24]*

With Labor out of the running, Sharon quickly sewed up a coalition
with the secularist Shinui Party, the National Religious Party (NRP),
and the National Union–Yisrael Beiteinu. Ehud Olmert did the negotiating with the Shinui leader, Tommy Lapid, his close personal friend,
and Effie Eitam, the NRP's firebrand leader. Olmert persuaded Eitam
that Shinui was not antireligious, just anti-*haredi*. Thanks to Olmert's
resourcefulness, the three disparate factions reached agreement on the
sensitive issues of state and religion.

With this latest service to Sharon, Olmert hoped he would be
rewarded with the prize he had set his heart on, the Ministry of
Finance. It was an open secret that Sharon wanted to shift Silvan Shalom for this key position, which was becoming more crucial as the
state of the economy grew more parlous. Sharon, however, offered
Minister of Foreign Affairs Netanyahu the Finance Ministry. "I see
this as a firing," Netanyahu retorted, plainly startled. Not at all, Sharon assured him. If anything, it was a promotion, but, more important, it was a call to arms. The state of the economy was desperate. He
promised his total support for the tough measures that would have to
be taken. They would work in harmony. Bibi would be, for all intents
and purposes, autonomous in making and executing economic policy.

The pundits argued later over whether Sharon in fact meant
Netanyahu to accept or reject his proposition. Sharon welcomed a
hangdog-looking Silvan Shalom, the current finance minister, into
his office. "I told him, as I'd told him many times before, either the
Finance Ministry or out," Shalom recalled later.[25] "Out," Sharon
replied, smiling, and after a moment of incomprehension and another

---

* The unconsummated flirtation with Sharon, coming on top of the electoral
disappointment, left Mitzna unpopular with virtually everyone in Labor. Three
months later he resigned as leader, replaced—ad interim of course—by the indefatigable Shimon Peres.

of disbelief a smile of gratified serenity spread over Shalom's intense and sad countenance. "Out," or *hutz* in Hebrew, is also the word for "foreign," as in Foreign Ministry, or Misrad Hahutz. Shalom's honor and his political career were saved. "You should have known that I would never hurt you," Sharon told the younger man. "I don't forget the people who stuck with me through the hard times." Shalom might have been forgiven for musing to himself that that was precisely what Sharon had done to David Levy last time around.

Sharon offered Olmert the Ministry of Industry and Trade, his own old stomping ground, but met with an angry rejection. Sharon refused to give up. He began beefing up the meat-and-potatoes offer with succulent side dishes: the Israel Lands Authority, which he had always run himself; the Planning Authority, which had been part of the Prime Minister's Office; ministerial responsibility for state television and radio, a much-sought-after political plum; membership on the cabinet defense committee and the kitchen cabinet; and, finally, the prized title of vice prime minister. This mollified even the wounded Olmert.

An assault on child allowances was the centerpiece of the new government's effort to bring the state budget under control. Welfare and defense were the two areas of runaway spending. Defense was effectively untouchable, for both objective and political reasons. Welfare took the brunt of the cuts. The seemingly remorseless growth of both welfare budgets and welfare constituencies was abruptly reversed. With time, and assisted by an upturn in the global and local economies, the proportion of Israelis in the workforce began to rise. This had been the deepest malaise in the Israeli economy. During Sharon's second term, with Netanyahu at the helm of the economy, this key index of economic health went up from a seriously sick 53 percent to a still-lagging but more respectable 56 percent.

Netanyahu's reforms were a watershed; he deliberately set out to change the structure of the Israeli welfare state. To his critics, he came close to destroying it. Even keen supporters accused him of going too far too fast. The basic reform, so desperately needed, remains in place, though Sharon's successor, Ehud Olmert, took steps to mitigate its harshest effects. It is gradually coaxing *haredi* men and Arab women into the workforce. Birthrates in both communities have begun to fall, more markedly among the Arabs.

In parallel, Netanyahu and his Treasury mandarins declared war on Israel's bloated public sector. Here again, their tough steps to streamline and downsize central government and local authorities were assisted, after mid-2004, by the general economic recovery. More jobs were created in commerce and industry as revenues began to rise again. The private sector grew and flourished. First, exports began to grow, and after mid-2004 the domestic consumer market also began showing signs of recovery.

A sweeping tax reform begun in 2002, when a capital gains tax was first levied on companies, was now extended to include individuals, who were henceforth required to pay tax on most forms of unearned income. At one fell swoop, the tax base was significantly broadened. At the same time, tax rates on earnings were reduced—a central plank in Netanyahu's economic credo.

With Sharon's robust backing, Netanyahu was determined, too, to push through a wholesale reform of the Israeli pension sector. The pension reform became the linchpin of Netanyahu's comprehensive overhaul of the capital market. The old-style "defined benefits" pension system, which was heading inexorably toward bankruptcy, was stopped dead in its tracks. Existing pensions were put under the direct management of the Treasury; new pensions would be run by new funds, based on actuarially sound premises, a pension age raised by law from sixty-five to sixty-seven (for men; women could retire earlier), and the ability to invest in a wide range of financial instruments. In comparison with much larger and more advanced European economies, Israel's decision to grapple with the inherent and ominous weakness of its pensions industry was both bold and timely. As in Western economies, the new pension funds now quickly became major players on the capital market.

Getting the *haredim* out to work was unimpeachably good economics. It was sound sociology, too, and brave politics. "To understand the creation of the coalition in 2003," says Omri Sharon, "you have to understand the showdown with Shas during 2002. My father learned the hard way that Shas's price was too high, that they were so set in their ways you couldn't do anything together with them. They were opposed to any change at all. He was attracted now to doing something without the *haredim*. Doing something really meaningful."[26]

Ilan Cohen, too, who was to become director general of the Prime Minister's Office later in the term, says Sharon deliberately sought a coalition without *haredim* in order to institute the economic reforms that the country so direly needed. But there was a serious downside to this, precisely the downside that Yitzhak Rabin had understood, had feared, and had bent over backward to avoid as he embarked, in 1992–1993, on the repartition of Eretz Yisrael. Rabin, as we have seen, was at pains to ensure that he had Shas in his coalition when he first negotiated with Yasser Arafat. Ehud Barak, too, who saw himself as Rabin's true successor, pointedly ignored his own supporters' pleas to keep Shas out of his government. Intent on a bold, historic attempt at peacemaking, he determinedly sat Shas and Meretz together at his cabinet table.

Sharon, by his own account, was bent on offering "painful concessions" and ending the occupation. With Shas out of government, he would have most of the religious sector arrayed against him and, more important, arrayed against the territorial concessions he intended to make.[27] For many Orthodox Jews, territorial concessions would be depicted as heresy, and Sharon himself would be cast as a heretic—just the scenario that Rabin had so wisely managed to avoid during the crucial first phase of Oslo.

Could Sharon have avoided it, too? The answer, sadly perhaps, is that he was not prepared to try if trying meant kowtowing, as he saw it, to Rabbi Ovadia Yosef, the aged spiritual leader of Shas. He was not prepared, as his son Omri explained, to visit the sage in his home in Jerusalem, because he thought that it was demeaning for a prime minister to do so.[28] There is certainly something to be said for such zealous upholding of prime ministerial dignity. But the plain if lamentable fact was that Rabbi Yosef, then eighty-three, had become accustomed to all the politicians paying him homage at his home and he had come to expect it. The only possible way to swing Shas around, moreover, was a personal conversation with Rabbi Yosef. The rabbi had written magisterial halachic opinions in the past on the need to compromise over the Land of Israel rather than risk more bloodshed. He was, in his heart, a moderate. The Shas politicians, mediocre men who pandered to the increasingly xenophobic sentiment among the party rank and file, tried to repress their leader's principled position and to persuade him to repress it, too. Sharon needed to cut through them and reach the sage himself. But he refused to do so.

CHAPTER 15 · ABOUT-FACE

On March 13, 2003, Sharon's bureau chief, Dov Weissglas, and his national security adviser, Efraim Halevy, found themselves hustled into the Oval Office. They were on a secret one-day mission to Washington to reassure administration officials that Sharon would not muscle in on the impending war with Iraq. But the president wanted to talk to them not about the war but about the push for peace in Palestine that he hoped would follow the overthrow of Saddam Hussein.

Bush confided to the Israelis that the Iraq War was now at hand. He would not wait, he said, for a third UN Security Council resolution. He informed them that he would be making a public statement on the road map. Without mincing words, he demanded that both Sharon and AIPAC, the powerful pro-Israel lobby in Washington, swallow it in silent approbation. The last thing he needed at this delicate juncture was discord with Congress over Israel-Palestine.

The next day, Secretary Powell by his side, Bush informed reporters in the Rose Garden:

We have reached a hopeful moment for progress toward the vision of Middle Eastern peace that I outlined last June. I spoke of a day when two states, Israel and Palestine, will live side by side in peace and security . . . We expect that . . . a Palestinian Prime Minister will be confirmed soon. Immediately upon confirmation, the road map for peace will be given to the Palestinians and the Israelis. The United States has developed this plan over the last several months in close cooperation with Russia, the European Union, and the United Nations. Once this road map is delivered, we will expect and welcome contributions from Israel and the Palestinians to this document that will advance true peace . . . America is committed, and I am personally committed, to implementing our road map toward peace.[1]

Bush took no questions and strode off. The import was clear: the road map would be issued shortly, and any further haggling over it would take place *after* it was made public (and hence would not be of much weight).

The war began the following week. In Israel, which had been a target of Saddam Hussein's Scud missiles during Desert Storm in 1991, there was little public trepidation this time. The government asked people to prepare sealed rooms again, with plastic sheets and masking tape designed to ward off clouds of chemical or biological poison. Very few did. It wasn't that the public or the military questioned the U.S.-U.K. intelligence assessments that Saddam had, or intended to produce, weapons of mass destruction. They just presumed he wouldn't, or couldn't, hurl them at Israel. Perhaps this blithe confidence reflected an element of lingering anticlimax after the national trauma thirteen years earlier, when people spent weeks in their sweaty sealed rooms but the Scuds carried conventional explosives and even they were less than devastating. Perhaps, too, it reflected the more recent and much more scarring trauma of the suicide bombings, with the mood of resilience cum resignation that they engendered.

On April 30, Prime Minister Mahmoud Abbas (Abu Mazen) and his new cabinet were sworn in in Ramallah, and within hours the Quartet (the United States, Russia, the EU, and the UN) published the road map. In practice, though, as Abu Mazen himself ruefully admitted later, Arafat never relinquished his grip on key security organs, which in part at least accounted for Abu Mazen's failure to build the "empowered prime ministership" that the Quartet intended.

The text of the road map was ambitious. It spelled out the three-phase process culminating in "a final and comprehensive settlement of the Israel-Palestinian conflict by 2005." Sharon, in other words, long before the end of his current term, would be signing a peace treaty with the new state of Palestine (and hopefully with Syria and Lebanon, too). Granted, plenty of target dates had been set and unmet in Middle East peacemaking before. But this was an American president at the very pinnacle of his international power and influence, as it seemed then, speaking in the name of a quartet of key players on the world stage.

Phase One of the road map, the phase in which the Palestinians were to end terror and reform their government and Israel was to freeze its settlement building,* also required solemn public declarations of intent from the two sides. The "Israeli leadership" was to issue

---

* See p. 421; for the full text of the road map, see the Appendix.

an "unequivocal statement affirming its commitment to the two-state vision." For Sharon himself, this at least presented no problem. He had made the rhetorical leap to Palestinian statehood during his first term and had not retreated despite the intense criticism in his own party. For his followers turned critics, however, the road map inevitably triggered a renewed wave of questioning and dissent as their prime minister appeared to accelerate his disturbing metamorphosis. In an interview with *Haaretz* in mid-April, he seemed actively to court the looming crisis.

> QUESTION: Isn't the phrase "painful concessions" an empty slogan?
>
> SHARON: Definitely not. It comes from the depths of my soul. Look, we're talking about the cradle of the Jewish people. Our entire history is linked to these places: Bethlehem, Shiloh, Beth-El. And I know that some of these places we're going to have to give up. As a Jew this causes me agony. But my rational determination to reach an understanding overcomes my emotions . . .
>
> QUESTION: Have you genuinely accepted the idea of two states for two nations? Do you seriously intend to carry out the [re]partition of western Palestine?
>
> SHARON: I think this is something that is going to happen. We have to look at it realistically: in the end there will be a Palestinian state. I see things firstly from our own perspective. I don't think we should be ruling over another people and running its life. I don't think we have the strength for that. It is too heavy a burden on our people, and it gives rise to serious moral problems and serious economic problems.

Weissglas later explained Sharon's acceptance of the road map in the context of his deepening determination to bring an end to the conflict. "Nothing would have made him happier than if the Palestinians had fulfilled their part of the road map. But he never really believed they would do so, even after Arafat's ostensible devolution of power, indeed even after the *rais*'s death the following year."* That deep-seated skep-

---

* Weissglas says:

Sharon's brilliant gambit—and I say this with the utmost lack of modesty—is that we agreed [to the road map] knowing that the result would be different. The road map is purely "performance based." Theoretically, if the Palestinians had fully implemented the first stage, we could have been in "permanent

ticism, says Weissglas, was the psychological and conceptual basis of Sharon's subsequent move to unilateralism, from the end of 2003. It was, he says, a radical change of tactic in pursuit of the same strategy: ending the conflict.

Sharon had changed from obdurate confrontationist to determined peacemaker, Weissglas insists, before he, Weissglas, took over as bureau chief, in the spring of 2002. His own contribution, says Weissglas, was "the realization that the tail was wagging the dog in Israeli policy making." The tail in this metaphor was the settlers.

> I saw that people's perceived attitudes to the settlers determined their access to the prime minister. For instance, the new American ambassador, Dan Kurtzer, was held to be hostile to the settlers, so he was kept out in the cold. Javier Solana, the EU's foreign policy chief whom I discovered to be a real friend of Israel, was virtually persona non grata in the Prime Minister's Office specifically because of his opposition to the settlements. Everything was subordinated to the settlements . . . the army, the budget, everything. What changed in Sharon, in a word, was that the spell of the settlements was broken.

Sharon's acceptance of the road map seems to bear this out. He rammed it down his party's throat not merely as an act of tactical expediency but as an avowed ideological break from the cherished illusion that the occupation could go on forever. "The Palestinian state is hardly my life's dream," Sharon declared at cabinet on May 25. "But looking ahead, it is not right for Israel to rule over three and a half million Palestinians. I know every mountain and every hill. I know the ideology. But we have to find a solution for the future generations."

The weekend before the cabinet discussion, Sharon, Weissglas, and Omri had spent hours working the phones. There was no point talking to the National Religious Party and National Union–Yisrael Beiteinu ministers; they were certain to vote against it. They remon-

---

status" negotiations with Arafat before the end of 2003. And the monitoring was not in our hands. We took a huge risk. But we took it so cleverly, God forgive me for praising myself. We insisted that the monitoring must be U.S.-led. Sharon said, "In matters of security, a U.S. general will not lie." We insisted on a soldier, not a politician who might bullshit and say that what the Palestinians had done on security was satisfactory . . . And sure enough—it was unsatisfactory. In fact they did nothing. Don't forget, the road map incorporated into its first phase both the Tenet plan and the Zinni plan, detailed and comprehensive work papers on how the PA was to suppress terrorism, disarm the militias, and so forth.

strated instead with wavering Likud ministers. In the event, the road map was endorsed in cabinet by a majority of 12 to 7, with 4 abstentions. Among the Likud ministers, 7 voted in favor (the other 5 aye voters were the Shinui ministers); 7 others abstained or voted against. Verter of *Haaretz* had no doubt he was reporting on a huge upheaval. "The significance of yesterday's vote was so terrifying for most of the cabinet ministers that they could only attempt to obfuscate it, to roll their eyes, and to explain that anyway nothing would come out of it: the terror would not be eliminated, the incitement would not be stopped, the reforms in the PA would not be passed—and Israel would not be required to carry out its part. 'In practice,' [the Likud education minister] Limor Livnat insisted, 'the cabinet did not accept the map.'" Verter, rightly, harbored no such illusions. "Anyone who has been listening to Ariel Sharon's public pronouncements over these past two years had no need to be surprised."[2]

The split in the party was even more starkly in evidence at the Likud caucus in the Knesset the following day. "Let me tell you in the clearest words I know," a still-angry Sharon told the faction members, many of whom were openly critical of the cabinet decision. "I am going to make every effort to reach a political settlement of the conflict . . . I also happen to think that the idea that we can continue to hold three and a half million Palestinians under occupation—you can bridle at the word, but that's what it is, occupation—that idea is bad for Israel, bad for the Palestinians, bad for our economy. We need to free ourselves from control over three and a half million Palestinians, whose numbers are rising all the time. We have to reach a political settlement."

For Israeli right-wingers the word "occupation" itself was anathema. Its use by another Israeli automatically branded him or her as a leftist, a defeatist, a self-hating Jew. The territories had been "liberated" in 1967 and were "administered," or at most "disputed," not occupied. A number of Likudniks, aghast and outraged, roped in the like-minded attorney general, Elyakim Rubinstein, to try to roll back the waves of heresy emanating from their leader. Perhaps, they hoped against hope, it was all a huge slip of the tongue. Rubinstein urged the prime minister to use the neutered euphemism of Israeli officialdom, "disputed territories."

Sharon brushed him aside. The next day, briefing the Knesset Foreign Affairs and Defense Committee, he pointedly rehearsed the statement he had made at the caucus. "I want to restate my position . . . I will make every effort to reach a political settlement, because that is Israel's vital interest. And I also think that the idea that we can continue to hold three and a half million Palestinians under occupation—you can bridle at the word, but that's what it is . . . ," and so on and so forth, word for word.[3]

President Bush invited Sharon and Abu Mazen to a joint summit the following week with him and Jordan's king, Abdullah, at the Jordanian Red Sea port-resort of Aqaba. Bush himself conferred the day before with other Arab heads of state at Sharm el-Sheikh in Egypt. He hoped to obtain goodwill gestures toward Israel from some of the moderate Arab governments in recognition of the road-map breakthrough. But the Saudis refused, and the Americans had to make do with words of encouragement from the Arab leaders for Abu Mazen, the newly installed Palestinian prime minister who was to deliver the next day at Aqaba the "unequivocal statement reiterating Israel's right to exist in peace and security and ending all acts of violence . . . and incitement" required by the road map of the Palestinians as part of their Phase One obligations.

Abu Mazen, overriding his colleagues and advisers, delivered a conciliatory text that he had worked through with the Americans. "We do not ignore the suffering of the Jews throughout history," he declared. "It is time to bring all this suffering to an end . . . We repeat our renunciation of terror against the Israelis wherever they might be. Such methods are inconsistent with our religious and moral traditions . . . The armed intifada must end . . . And to establish the Palestinian state, we emphasize our determination to implement our pledges: the rule of law, a single political authority, weapons only in the hands of those who are in charge of upholding the law and order, and political diversity within the framework of democracy."

The Palestinians reacted testily to what they felt was Sharon's inadequate response. "He was supposed to call for a complete end to violence from *both* sides. He didn't say that," one PA official complained. Sharon declared that "there can be no compromise with terror, and Israel, together with all free nations, will continue fighting terrorism until its final defeat . . . There can be no peace . . . without the abandonment and elimination of terrorism, violence and incitement."

But what he went on to say, speaking in Hebrew, was bold and forceful in the context of his domestic politics. The Palestinians should have recognized that. "We want to make it clear to our Palestinian colleagues that we understand the importance of territorial contiguity in Judea and Samaria for a viable Palestinian state . . . Israeli policy will reflect that. We accept, too, the principle that no unilateral action by any party should determine the outcome of our negotiations." In plain language, that meant the old Sharon dream of isolated Palestinian cantons was now publicly and finally buried as far as Sharon was concerned, and the age of Israeli landgrabs for building Jewish settlements in the territories was over. Sharon added: "On the matter of the illegal settlement-outposts, I want to repeat that Israel is a country ruled by law. That being the case, we shall start immediately upon removing the illegal outposts."

There was a rebellious mood at the Jerusalem convention center where the Likud central committee convened three days later. Demonstrators milled around outside, howling abuse at Sharon and the ministers who supported him. They were especially hostile toward Omri Sharon, surrounding his car and shouting in unison, "Look where you've led your father." In the hall, hundreds of settler-delegates and their sympathizers set up a raucous cacophony with tin whistles. When Sharon entered, the noise became deafening. When Netanyahu rose to speak, it turned into a friendly chant of "Bibi, Bibi." Netanyahu said a Palestinian state would be "a faculty for Hamas and al-Qaeda." He was implacably opposed to it. He was careful, though, not to speak directly against Sharon. Others were less reticent. "How can the prime minister want to give away our ancient patrimony to others?" Uzi Landau, a lifelong hard-liner, hurled at Sharon. "This is a sad day for the Likud and a terrible day for the country. Terror has triumphed."

Sharon, in his speech, avoided the buzzword "occupation." It probably would have triggered a riot; as it was, there was scuffling in the gallery between his supporters and his opponents. Rather, in cautious, measured sentences, he proceeded on what would become, as his second term unfolded, a gradual, steady process of disengagement from the collective discipline of his own party. He recalled Menachem Begin, who spoke in the Knesset of that "extra little bit of responsibility" that rests on a prime minister. "I bear the responsibility," Sharon declared. "The responsibility lies on my shoulders." He had promised the party at its last convention a great victory in the general election, and he had delivered it. But he had also promised the nation "to bring peace and security and I intend to fulfill that, too. For true peace, I said, I am prepared to make painful concessions. Very painful concessions . . . The people delivered its verdict, and I intend to keep my promise."

He did not even look up at the hecklers, let alone respond to them. He did not raise his voice at them, or ask for quiet, or wait for quiet. He ignored them totally and delivered his prepared text as though they were listening in silent and respectful attention. He pitched his speech not at the rowdy audience in the hall but at the nation as a whole, watching him live on prime-time news.

. . .

The national leader who transcended and faintly despised mere party politics made a point of despising, too, the insistent attempts to impute "hidden agendas" to his dramatic change of policy. But his narrative, still unfolding, of a leader courageous enough to break with his own past, was already being challenged by an alternative narrative, much less heroic. "The prime minister was no longer a free agent," the then chairman of the National Security Council and former Mossad director, Efraim Halevy, asserted years later. "He was not in charge. He was acting under duress . . . Weissglas had a hold over him. I don't know where it came from. From somewhere outside government."

This remarkable indictment could be dismissed as the resentful recrimination of the country's top intelligence official who was later unceremoniously ousted from the inner sanctum of policy making by Sharon and Weissglas—were it not for the fact that Halevy's indictment closely tallies with the indictment of *another* top defense official, the then army chief of staff, Lieutenant General Moshe Ya'alon. "I suspected a sinister, symbiotic relationship between Sharon and Weissglas," Ya'alon recalled, "based on other, concealed interests."

Ya'alon also fought with Weissglas and was also eventually dumped by Sharon. Sharon's aides, from Weissglas down, dismiss both Halevy's and Ya'alon's strictures as the fulminations of the disaffected. They embellish this verdict with anecdotes and reminiscences designed to make the two men appear stupid and petty. This in turn raises troubling questions as to how stupid and petty men could have risen to head the Mossad and the IDF. Ya'alon went on to join the Likud (after Sharon left it) and serves, at this writing, as a deputy prime minister.

For Halevy, the warning lights flashed following his brief trip with Weissglas to Washington in March 2003 and their unexpected audience in the Oval Office, where Bush extolled the benefits of the soon-to-be-published road map. "I knew that the road map was anathema for Sharon," Halevy recalled.

The road map, he explained, undercut the essence of Sharon's long-held policy that Israel must strive for a stable interim agreement with the Palestinians because a permanent agreement was unachievable given the wide differences in the two sides' positions on basic issues. The road map proposed to reconcile those differences within two years and produce precisely the permanent peace that Sharon considered unattainable. Thus, for instance, the road map envisaged shared sovereignty in Jerusalem—it prescribes "a negotiated resolution on the status of Jerusalem that takes into account the *political* and religious concerns of both sides"—which for Sharon, Halevy maintained, was totally unacceptable.

Halevy therefore expected a spirited struggle by Israel to try to change the tenor of the road map. "Weissglas reported that the U.S. would 'accept' Israel's reservations. I'm not sure the Americans even bothered to file them in their archives," Halevy said. "Sharon signed off on the partition of Jerusalem. Why did he change his mind? Why did he accept a document that he himself had said for months was one of the greatest threats to Israel?

"I was reminded in some way of what I had read of President Wilson and [his close aide] Colonel House, who became the de facto president. Sharon was no longer seeing people who had been close to him. He was surrounded. He was closeted. He couldn't reach out to talk to people if he wanted to. Weissglas had a hold over him."[4]

For Ya'alon, "Things started happening that seemed murky and dishonest." With Abu Mazen installed as prime minister, Israel resolved to hand back security control over several West Bank towns to the Palestinian Authority. One such town was Jericho, and Weissglas met with the Palestinian chief negotiator, Saeb Erekat, to organize the transfer. The Defense Ministry's intention, says Ya'alon, was to remove the roadblocks around Jericho and enable Palestinians to enter and leave freely. But Weissglas told Erekat the town would be reopened to Israelis, too, Ya'alon asserted.

He recalled:

I phone [Minister of Defense] Mofaz. He's angry. He speaks to Sharon's office—and Duby [Weissglas] denies it. Then our brigadier meets with the PA brigadier with a view to transferring Jericho, and the meeting explodes. Two weeks pass, Duby's still denying it, but we're told, "Try to be flexible toward the PA." That's what Mofaz instructs me, but it's clear that he's been instructed by the Prime Minister's Office.

Now, this isn't the first time Weissglas isn't telling the truth. I started suspecting that there are other interests at play here . . . the casino in Jericho. I remembered the photo from the 2001 election campaign of Duby with Omri and Muhammad Rashid going off to meet with Martin Schlaff in Vienna.* I know that Duby Weissglas represents the interests of Martin Schlaff in Israel, as his attorney. Two years before, when the IDF shelled the casino, he wrote a letter threatening to sue the officers involved.[5]

---

* Schlaff's company owned the Jericho casino; see p. 365.

In the event, Jericho remained closed to Israelis, and the casino stayed shut. That incontrovertible fact is cited by Sharon's supporters to refute the allegations implied by Ya'alon. By the same token, says Avigdor Yitzhaki, the director general of the Prime Minister's Office (2001–2004), a casino ship belonging to Schlaff—and the subject of much anti-Sharon rumormongering—remained empty and abandoned in the Red Sea resort of Eilat throughout Sharon's term because the owners could not get a government license to operate it. "Hardly proof of Schlaff's reputed omnipotence in Sharon's Israel," Yitzhaki notes sourly.

Neither Halevy nor Ya'alon was speaking out publicly at this time, and their alternative narrative, focusing on Weissglas, remained, for the moment, relatively muted. The related theory that Sharon was moving leftward in order to curry favor with the media, and thereby somehow ease the pressure of the criminal investigations against him and his sons, was in the air already, but with nowhere near the resonance it was to receive later, when the settlers embraced it as their battle cry. Amir Oren, a columnist on *Haaretz* and longtime critic of Sharon, suggested in an article in June 2003 that Sharon "has his back to the wall. Two parties will be asking him tough questions: Bush about the future, and the police about the past."[6]

Sharon's "leftward" turn over the road map was all the more remarkable given the spike in Palestinian suicide-terror attacks during this period. The intifada, though no longer at the level of sustained intensity that preceded Defensive Shield, nevertheless still spread indiscriminate carnage and pain throughout the country. Yet Sharon had cruised to victory in the election in February. His approval rating dropped from May to June, but it still stood at a solid 47 percent and remained at that figure in July.[7]

Part of the reason for the Israeli public's relative optimism despite the continuing terror was a sense, or at least a hope, that things might finally be changing on the other side. Abu Mazen's public opposition to the intifada's resort to lethal violence was a matter of public record and could not but impress Israelis, whatever the depth of their skepticism regarding his true powers and Arafat's true relinquishment of powers.

The sole significant test in Israeli eyes, as Abu Mazen well knew, was whether the incidence of violence declined. In his low-key, businesslike way he immediately arranged to meet with Hamas leaders in Gaza and tried to draw them into a general cease-fire. At the beginning of July 2003, against the odds and despite unanimously downbeat punditry, Abu Mazen got all the Palestinian factions to agree to a *hudna,* or temporary truce. Israel was to respond by stopping its "targeted assassinations" and also by releasing hundreds of Palestinian prisoners. In addition, in accordance with its obligations under the first phase of the road map, Israel began dismantling illegal settlement-outposts in the heart of the West Bank. Television crews duly recorded IDF soldiers exchanging shoves and punches with "hilltop youths," as the young settlement activists were dubbed.

Sharon himself had told a part-incredulous, part-hostile group of settler leaders on June 17 that he intended to fulfill Israel's part of the road map "without winks and nods and without sleights of hand." These, of course, had been the stock-in-trade of his intimate collusion with these same leaders for the past twenty-six years. He intended to remove fifteen of the illegal outposts at once and more later, Sharon said. The settlers felt he was moving toward the dismantlement of established settlements, too. "For all these years you were our compass," Pinhas Wallerstein, a veteran and prominent settler leader, wailed. "And now you're abandoning us." "I love the hills of Samaria no less than you," Sharon replied. "Sometimes it's hard to decide which hill is more beautiful. But a new reality has come into being . . . We have made commitments, and I am determined to honor them. We must try this new path; perhaps it will lead us to security."

The settlers for their part said they would fight him, albeit without violence. Among those present was Ze'ev Hever, whom everyone called Zambish, a Gush Emunim activist who had been close to Sharon for decades and whom, unlike some of the others, Sharon genuinely liked. Unlike those who found it hard to believe that the wink-and-nod days were over, Hever understood that something fundamental had changed in their old champion. Sharon had "lost control" of the road-map process, Hever told his comrades. The prime minister's sole focus of concern now was Washington, and as Washington's appetite grew, so Sharon would feed it more and more settlements—first outposts, then established communities. His conclusion, Hever said, was that they must fight him all the way, from the first tiny outpost. No deals, no compromises.[8]

With the *hudna* in place, Abu Mazen was invited to the White House. He met with Sharon in Jerusalem ahead of his U.S. trip. Their talk was businesslike and without rancor. Their aides kept up frequent contact. For the first time in nearly three years, a breath of optimism wafted through Palestine and Israel. The United States sent a full-time peace envoy to the region, the veteran diplomat John Wolf, charged with monitoring progress in implementation of the road map.

Prodded by the Americans, Sharon gave orders to transfer to the PA responsibility for security in the city of Bethlehem and in the Gaza Strip, apart from the Gaza settlement enclaves and the main north-south highway that runs through the Strip. IDF troops moved out of these areas. July was the least violent month since the intifada began: three deaths on the Israeli side, seven on the Palestinian.[9] Talks began on transferring security in four other West Bank cities. "Tensions were reduced," the U.S. envoy Wolf recorded. "Quality of life in Gaza and metropolitan Israel went up sharply. The Gaza agreement enabled Palestinians to move freely [in the Strip], people could go to the beach . . . Stores which had hardly been open at all were staying open until ten or eleven at night . . . So this was a moment of opportunity. It got people's hopes up."[10]

It was a pitifully brief moment. For Israelis, all the hopes collapsed with a terrible suicide bus bombing in Jerusalem on August 19. The Hamas bomber, a married man and university graduate, was disguised as an Orthodox Jew. He boarded a No. 2 bus on the edge of the old *haredi* district of Mea Shearim and detonated his explosive belt, obliterating himself and taking the lives of sixteen adults and seven children. Hamas in Hebron took the credit for this atrocity. It was intended, it said, to avenge the deaths of two Hebron activists, one Islamic Jihad and the other Hamas, at the hands of IDF troops. Two days later, Israeli helicopters struck in Gaza again. This time, there was no collateral killing. The target was Ismail Abu Shanab, a senior leader of Hamas. He and his two bodyguards died in their car under a hail of rockets.

Hamas and Islamic Jihad announced the obvious: the *hudna* was finished. "Israel has a right to defend herself," the White House spokesman commented coldly. Secretary of State Powell and John Wolf desperately urged Abu Mazen and his lieutenants to crack down on the Islamist militants and avert a new round of terror and reprisals. "I'll do it, I'll do it," Mohammed Dahlan, the Gaza commander, assured the U.S. envoy. "I'll start tonight, I've got my men ready." But Arafat would not let him use his men against the militants. Arafat refused to endorse the agreement with Israel transferring security control in four more West Bank cities. Days later, inevitably, Abu Mazen resigned. In a parting speech before a tense and stormy Palestinian parliament in Ramallah on September 6, with angry demonstrators battling his security men outside, the moderate, well-meaning leader laid the main burden of blame for his failure on Arafat, for refusing to forgo his powers and enable the new prime minister to govern.

Abu Mazen had made a start, however modest, on the huge job of uprooting the corruption and maladministration that had entrenched themselves in Arafat's PA. Several particularly degenerate police officers were removed. Traffic cops returned to city streets. Jails were fixed up; courts resumed functioning with a semblance of due process. No less important, his minister of finance, Salam Fayyad, a former official of the World Bank and later of the International Monetary Fund, began to forge a rational and effective system of budgeting and administration, with civil servants and security men paid into their bank accounts rather than by cash handouts from their bosses. In many ways, as it turned out later, the short-lived Abu Mazen–Salam Fayyad partnership in 2003 was a forerunner of their much longer and much more effective cooperation—the one as president of the PA, the other as prime minister—later in the decade.

In later interviews, Abu Mazen tended to soften his verdict on Arafat and to attach more of the blame for the collapse of the *hudna* and of his prime ministerial experiment to Sharon and the Americans (not, however, to himself). Many Israelis in the peace camp agreed with his criticism of Sharon's behavior during these potentially transformational—but wasted—months. In June, Sharon knew Abu Mazen was negotiating earnestly with Hamas to achieve a *hudna*. Yet he referred to him as "a chick that's not yet grown feathers." Until he grew feathers, Sharon continued insultingly, Israel would take care of terrorism itself. His aides made sure the slighting remark, made at cabinet, was immediately leaked.

In another comment about Abu Mazen around this time, no less inane but more telling, Sharon observed that "Abu Mazen, too, is still an Arab." This provides an unguarded glimpse into the deep reservoir of his distaste and distrust for the neighboring nation. That never changed, even though his policy on an eventual accommodation with the Palestinians changed so radically. It helps to explain—though not to excuse—his shortsighted approach to Abu Mazen's prime ministership in 2003 and his inexplicable, almost perverse failure to coordinate the Gaza withdrawal with President Abu Mazen—Arafat was dead by then—in 2005. Unilateralism, as we shall see, was presented by Sharon and his aides as a policy of last resort in the absence of a credible negotiating partner. In fact, though, in a very profound way, for Sharon it was a policy of first resort, even of first choice.

Sharon's single most frustrating refusal from Abu Mazen's point of view was to release a significant number of prisoners as part of the *hudna* package. Israel held thousands of Palestinians in its jails. To the Palestinians many of them were political prisoners or freedom fighters. To the Israelis they were members of illegal organizations or outright terrorists. Sharon laid down as his basic guideline that "terrorists with blood on their hands" would not be freed. That still left plenty of scope for a generous gesture that, more than anything else, would have shored up Abu Mazen's standing on his own side. In the event, Israel released only four hundred men, most of whom were serving relatively short sentences that were anyway nearing completion.

The ostensible removal of settlement-outposts, many of which were back in business the morning after their forcible "dismantlement" by the army, was another protracted and gratuitous insult to Abu Mazen of which the Palestinians became quickly and acutely aware. A list of outposts purportedly evacuated turned out to comprise lone shacks, uninhabited, which the settlers themselves offered to take down in "deals" with the Defense Ministry. Sharon's lofty rhetoric about the rule of law and his solemn promises to the Americans were honored in the breach.[11]

With the *hudna* dead, the tit for tat of terror and reprisal resumed. On September 6, an IAF warplane dropped a half-ton bomb on a building in Gaza City. Israeli intelligence had hard information that Sheikh Ahmed Yassin and all the top Hamas leadership would be meeting inside. There were long discussions over the appropriate ordnance; no one wanted a repeat of the Shehadeh disaster.* The bomb destroyed the third floor, where the meeting was understood to be taking place. In fact it was held on the ground floor, perhaps because of the difficulty of getting Sheikh Yassin's wheelchair upstairs. Yassin and the fourteen others escaped almost unscathed.

"Israel will pay a high price for this crime," the quadriplegic cleric warned. Three days later two suicide bombers took fifteen lives: in Tel Aviv, a bomber exploded alongside a group of off-duty soldiers waiting for rides; in Jerusalem, a father and daughter were among the dead in a wrecked café. The next day, Israel struck from the air again in Gaza, rocketing the home of the Hamas leader Mahmoud Zahar. His son and a bodyguard were killed and two dozen others injured; Zahar himself escaped. On October 5, a woman suicide bomber from Jenin killed twenty-one customers in a restaurant in Haifa. Fifty more were injured.

Sharon suspended all dealings with the PA government. After Abu Mazen's departure, Arafat installed the much more pliant Abu Ala

---

* See p. 419.
* See p. 419.

(Ahmed Qureia) in the post of "prime minister with executive powers," but it was clear to all that real power continued to reside with the *rais*. Sharon refused to meet with Arafat. He pushed through cabinet a resolution "to remove this obstacle [that is, Arafat] in the manner and time of our choosing." But the Americans had not removed their objection to Arafat's physical elimination. The *rais* remained in the *muqata*. The road map was turning into a dead letter.

On October 15, the United States suffered its own casualties from Gazan terror. A massive roadside bomb ripped through an armored van, killing three security men. They were escorting an American cultural attaché whose assignment was to interview applicants for Fulbright scholarships. The State Department promptly banned all further travel by its personnel to Gaza.

While there had clearly been a disappointing setback on the Palestinian side, Washington was losing patience with both sides. Moreover, as the initial, sweeping success of the Iraq invasion turned to ashes, accusations proliferated that somehow Israel or its sympathizers in America had dragged the administration into the war. Yasser Arafat was one of the earliest to charge that Israel actively "incited" in favor of war against Iraq.[12]

It was a charge echoed at the time both on the right and on the left of American politics. Bill Keller of *The New York Times* ridiculed it. "A less conspiracy-minded observer," he wrote, "might point out that the long-standing Bushite animosity toward Iraq is complex and hardly secret, and the fact that our interests coincide with Israel's does not mean that a Zionist fifth column has hijacked the president's brain . . . What is demonstrably true is that Israelis believe that the war in Iraq is—to use a phrase that is a staple of Jewish satire—good for the Jews."[13] But as the postwar occupation of Iraq went from bad to worse, the innuendo began to hurt. The strategic fallout, moreover, looked less good for the Jews in Israeli eyes. The Mossad feared that terror operatives now streaming to Iraq from all over the Middle East would, in time, filter into Jordan and Lebanon and join the Palestinian intifada against Israel.

The gathering gloom on the diplomatic front was exacerbated by another turn for the worse in Israel's economic woes. Netanyahu's tough medicine earlier in the year was not working yet; another dose was needed. Many families were hurting badly. People who had managed in the past to keep their heads above water, just, now found themselves slipping into real poverty as vital welfare subsidies for children, for old people, for single mothers, for the unemployed, were all slashed. A single mother from the small Negev town of Mitzpe

Ramon, Vikki Knafo, caught the national mood when she struck out, in the blazing heat of July, on a long, lonely march to the capital to protest her inability to provide for her three young children. By the time she arrived, she had become an icon. Some six hundred other single mothers joined her in a tent encampment outside the Finance Ministry. Netanyahu refused to meet her. But his advisers were seriously worried over the image of heartlessness that her protest was tarring him with. Inevitably, it rubbed off on Sharon, too. His poll figures and those of the government began to slide.

"When sorrows come," as Sharon the ardent theatergoer must have heard more than once from King Claudius, "they come not single spies but in battalions." While the wiliness of Arafat, the weakness of Abu Mazen, and the troubles of the economy were all known or predictable challenges, he now ran into a flurry of awkward and unexpected episodes that sapped his public standing. That pattern was not starkly clear at the time as events moved along in their ragged way. It has been reconstructed subsequently, perhaps too obsessively, by commentators seeking the key to Sharon's cataclysmic move at year's end that suddenly changed everything.

The first unpredicted blow came in September 2003, from an unexpected source. A group of twenty-seven pilots in the air force reserves signed a letter declaring, "We, veteran pilots and pilots still on active service . . . object to carrying out illegal and immoral attacks . . . in the territories." They sent it to the commander of the air force, General Dan Halutz, with a copy to *Yedioth Ahronoth*, where it appeared as the cover story of the paper's popular magazine, *Seven Days*, on the eve of Rosh Hashanah, the Jewish New Year. "We, for whom the IDF and specifically the IAF are inseparable parts of our lives, refuse to continue hitting innocent civilians. Such actions . . . are the direct result of long occupation which corrupts all of Israeli society. The continuing occupation mortally damages Israel's security and its moral strength." The pilots claimed there was a great deal of "gray refusal" in the air force. Many reserve pilots, they told reporters, and even some still in full-time uniform, found quiet ways to opt out of bombing or rocketing missions in the territories. They ended their letter with a declaration: "We will continue to serve in the Israel Defense Forces and in the Israel Air Force on any mission for the defense of the State of Israel."

This inspired another embarrassing and worrisome protest from within the nation's elite. Three months later, thirteen reservists from the semisecret Sayeret Matkal commando announced that they, too, would "no longer participate in the regime of oppression in the territories." In a letter addressed directly to Sharon (with a copy to the media), they wrote of their "deep anxiety for the future of the State of Israel as a democratic, Zionist, and Jewish state and for its moral and ethical character." They declared that they were no longer "prepared to serve as a defensive shield" for the policy of expanding the settlements. "We will not take part in depriving millions of people of their human rights. We will not corrupt our own humanity in the service of an army of occupation. We can no longer remain silent." They signed off with their unit's motto, "Who Dares Succeeds," which had thrilled generations of the best Israeli youth striving to win a place in this most exclusive unit, its exploits shrouded in martial mystique.

The Sayeret protest was made public on December 22. But it had been in the making for weeks. And meanwhile, if the reserve pilots and commandos could be dismissed or at least pigeonholed as a bunch of leftists, nothing of that applied to another high-profile group who inveighed against the corroding evil of the occupation and the short-sightedness of the Sharon government. They were four former chiefs of the Shin Bet security service: Avraham Shalom (1980–1986), Ya'akov Peri (1988–1995), Carmi Gillon (1995–1996), and Ami Ayalon (1996–2000). They didn't all especially like each other, as Gillon explained to the *Yedioth Ahronoth* journalists Sima Kadmon and Alex Fishman on November 14. But they had decided to come together to do this unique joint interview, run across the cover and five inside pages of *Yedioth*'s weekend political supplement, because they truly believed the country was endangering its future.[14]

"If we don't give up the goal of 'Greater Israel,' " said Shalom, "and if we don't stop treating the other side in the disgraceful way we do, and if we don't start understanding that he, too, has feelings and that he, too, is suffering—then we're on the way to the abyss." What was "disgraceful"? the two reporters asked. The roadblocks? "Everything. Everything is disgraceful," Shalom replied. "We humiliate the Palestinian all the time, individually and collectively." This from the head of a service that had famously honed humiliation into a supereffective technique of interrogation and intimidation. But there was more. All four ex-chiefs criticized the fundamental paradigm of Sharon's policy: first crush terror, then move to negotiation. It was a mistake, said Gillon. "No, you're wrong," said Shalom. "It's an excuse."

All four agreed that there would have to be a showdown with the settlers. But they maintained that the great majority of settlers, if treated empathetically, if praised for their pioneering spirit and offered reasonable compensation, would leave quietly. "Arik Sharon's the one who can do it," said Peri. "The man who built the settlements is the man who can dismantle them. He keeps talking about painful concessions. This is the painful concession he must make: taking down the settlements." Ayalon added: "The obsession of today's policy making about whether we have a partner on the other side is a huge mistake. In the present terrible situation, with people being killed in restaurants and buses, the only way forward is unilaterally. If Israel, tomorrow morning, got up and got out of the Gaza Strip, and seriously started taking down illegal settlements [on the West Bank], I believe, based on many years of intimate knowledge, that the Palestinians would come to the negotiating table."

The Shin Bet chiefs' presentation was an analysis of rare honesty and arresting cogency from people who knew what they were talking about. It laid out, unvarnished, the rock-bottom fundamentals of Israel's condition. Yet it did not massively succeed in the one immediate and practical call that the four men made. They asked people to sign on to Ayalon's "People's Choice," a grassroots peace initiative that he was promoting together with the Palestinian intellectual and political leader Sari Nusseibeh. This called for two states for the two nations, based on the 1967 borders and with each having its capital in Jerusalem. A quarter of a million Israelis eventually signed on, not enough to force the government's hand.

But any relief in government circles was short-lived. A separate but similar initiative promoted jointly by Yossi Beilin, the architect of Oslo and now the leader of the left-wing Meretz Party, and Yasser Abed Rabbo, a former PA minister, won support and plaudits from all around the world. Their "Geneva Accord," signed under Swiss government auspices on December 1, also envisaged a two-state solution based on the 1967 lines with one-to-one swaps of territory to enable Israel to annex the larger blocs of settlements adjacent to the border. Sharon fumed. "They are trying to do what only a government can do—negotiate and sign agreements," he told reporters. "They're causing only confusion and damage."

Basically, the document filled out the agreements almost reached at Taba in the dying days of Ehud Barak's government. Those in turn had been based on the Clinton Parameters, and indeed Bill Clinton sent warm greetings to the nongovernment Israeli and Palestinian delegations and guests gathered in Geneva for the signing. Another former American president, Jimmy Carter, attended the signing ceremony himself. And—much more troubling from Sharon's standpoint—the current American secretary of state, Colin Powell, received his "old friend" Yossi Beilin at the State Department a few days after the signing.

There was more trouble for Sharon. In December, an emergency session of the UN General Assembly resolved to refer Israel's separation fence to the International Court of Justice at The Hague. This action followed the cabinet's approval, on October 1, of plans for the still-unbuilt sections of the fence that entailed deep incursions into the West Bank in order to encompass Jewish settlements. Tens of thousands of Palestinians would be encompassed, too, under these plans. Many of them would be cut off from their own fields and have to pass through IDF-manned gates as they went about their daily lives.

This was already the case, on a much smaller scale, with the first section of the fence, between Salem and Kassem, which had been completed during the summer and had already proved its effectiveness as a barrier to terrorists. Abu Mazen complained of the fence's nibbling of West Bank lands, and of the much more extensive incursions now being planned, when he visited the White House in July.

In ostensible deference to American objections, the October 1 cabinet decision left gaps in the proposed incursive sections of the fence, as though to indicate that they were not final. But Washington refused to buy so transparent a ploy. "The gaps in and of themselves do not satisfy me," Powell told *The Washington Post*. "The question is what becomes of the gaps in due course."

Sharon faced a two-pronged legal fight over the fence, one at home and the other in The Hague. Regular demonstrations at points along the fence by Israeli, Palestinian, and foreign peace activists began to attract international media attention. A UN Security Council resolution condemning the cabinet's October 1 decision was vetoed by the United States, but the General Assembly could not be blocked in this way. The assembly asked the International Court of Justice "whether Israel is legally obligated as an occupying Power to dismantle the barrier." The answer seemed predictable, and while it would not have binding force, it was nevertheless another looming cloud on Sharon's darkening horizon.

Sharon's response was a bombshell: he announced Israel's unilateral disengagement from all of the Gaza Strip and from a part of the northern West Bank. All the settlements in these areas would be dismantled. All the soldiers stationed there would be withdrawn.

Everyone spoke of it as a bombshell, and yet, strangely, everyone claimed to have seen it coming. And they were right: it was clearly discernible in Sharon's public statements over a period of months. He did not seek to hide it and then suddenly spring it on the public. On the contrary, he deliberately "floated balloons" with the words "unilateral" and "disengagement" emblazoned on them, to gauge, presumably, how people would react. And yet, however much they had, or should have, anticipated or feared or hoped for the unilateral disengagement, depending on their views, when Sharon finally announced it, everyone was stunned. Peaceniks were stunned and ecstatic. Settlers were stunned and distraught. Most important for Sharon, the broad mainstream was stunned and supportive. The polls never wavered on that, from the day the disengagement was announced till the day it was carried out, eighteen months later.

One early balloon was flown by Ehud Olmert, plainly with Sharon's compliance. In the second week of November, the deputy prime minister called in a *Haaretz* journalist to explain what he "personally" felt about the way things were going. "Very soon," he confided, "the government is going to have to address the demographic issue with the utmost seriousness and resolve. This issue above all others will dictate the solution that we must adopt. In the absence of a negotiated agreement—and I do not believe in the realistic prospect of an agreement—we need to implement a unilateral alternative."[15]

On November 23, Sharon was questioned at cabinet and replied cryptically that he was indeed thinking about unilateral steps and when he'd decided he would ask for the cabinet's approval.

What Sharon didn't tell the cabinet was that on an official visit to Italy two days earlier, he and Weissglas had taken time out to meet discreetly with Elliott Abrams, the top Middle East man on the U.S. National Security Council, and to fill him in on Sharon's thinking (in advance of the cabinet's approval).*

Olmert, meanwhile, signaled the new thinking to the Israeli public in still starker terms. "The present situation will lead to the end of Israel as a Jewish state," he told *Yedioth Ahronoth* on December 5.

---

* There is some uncertainty as to what precisely Sharon and Weissglas said, what precisely Abrams understood, and what he reported back to Washington (Kurtzer interview, Herzliya, July 28, 2008). Abrams himself, in a later interview, seems to have been more impressed by the food than the conversation:

It was at dinner . . . we were at Sharon's hotel, the Hilton. And then they bring food. Jeez. And it's big slabs of meat and they absolutely do not look kosher! And Dov [Weissglas] goes ahead and cuts out a big slice, and I'm thinking it's very pink . . . it might be ham, and I said to Sharon, "OK, what kind of meat do you think that is?" And Sharon said, "It is better not to ask." (Bregman, *Elusive Peace*, 280–81)

We are approaching the point at which the Palestinians will become the majority and they will forgo their own independent state and demand instead the right to vote in Israel. The day that happens we shall have lost everything . . . I'm for a state with 80 percent Jews and 20 percent Arabs [roughly the proportions within the pre-1967 lines]. Its borders will not be those of Greater Israel, in which I previously believed. Arik thinks about these things all the time . . . There has never been a prime minister who has made the intellectual and emotional leap that Arik has made from the settlements to the road map.[16]*

At first, the American administration was uncomfortable with whatever it was that Sharon was cooking up. On December 15, Minister of Foreign Affairs Silvan Shalom met with National Security Adviser Condoleezza Rice in Washington and came away seriously rattled. "I woke up Sharon in the middle of the night," Shalom recalled, "and I told him, 'She says that if you come out with your unilateral plan, it will cause a rift between the U.S. and Israel.' Because they saw it as a cop-out from the road map. 'She demands that you say that it's part of the road map, that it will be carried out in close coordination with the U.S., and that settlers from Gaza will not end up in the West Bank.' "

Sharon decided to put those points into the speech he was planning to give three days later.

He spoke on Thursday, December 18, the last evening of the annual Herzliya Conference. The conference organizers were told to schedule him precisely in time for the prime-time TV news. Sharon himself spent the whole previous evening and day alone in his "tower" study at the ranch, looking out on his land and writing. He knew that after this speech, nothing would be the same for him anymore.

Two paragraphs in, he made it clear which way he was headed:

---

* A bout of flu at the beginning of December enabled Sharon to deliver another heavy hint through the mouth of Ehud Olmert, whom he asked to stand in for him at the annual graveside memorial ceremony for Ben-Gurion. "Let us assume that we can conquer the whole of Eretz Yisrael by force of arms," Sharon (through Olmert) quoted the founding father. "I'm sure we can. But what then? We will create a single state. But the state will want to be democratic. There will be general elections—and we will be in the minority . . . When the choice before us was the whole of Eretz Yisrael but no Jewish state, or a Jewish state but not the whole of Eretz Yisrael, we chose a Jewish state." To drive the point home, Sharon (Olmert) added: "In the near future, the leaders of Israel will need to gather all their inner strength, all their Zionist faith, in order to determine our destiny with the same remarkable fusion of vision and realism [as Ben-Gurion's] . . . that requires painful compromise for peace."

I do not intend to wait for [the Palestinians] indefinitely . . . If in a few months the Palestinians still continue to disregard their part in implementing the road map, then Israel will initiate the unilateral security step of disengagement from the Palestinians. The purpose of the Disengagement Plan is to reduce terror as much as possible and grant Israeli citizens the maximum level of security. The unilateral steps that Israel will take in the framework of the Disengagement Plan will be fully coordinated with the United States . . . The Disengagement Plan will provide maximum security and minimize friction between Israelis and Palestinians. We are interested in conducting direct negotiations, but . . . we will not wait for them indefinitely.

The Herzliya speech did not lay to rest all the speculation about what the prime minister intended to do and when he intended to do it. True, he was now publicly, dramatically committing to a unilateral withdrawal, if, as was virtually taken for granted, the Palestinians did not take the security measures that would satisfy him. But withdrawal from where? From Gaza only? From all of Gaza? From some of the West Bank, too? If so, how much? All in one go, or in stages?

Sharon himself said, "I know you would like to hear names [of settlements to be dismantled], but we should leave something for later." Was he being coy? Was he reluctant to end the guessing game to which he was subjecting the whole country, and plainly enjoying? Or was he not yet clear in his own mind about how he wanted his new policy of unilateralism to play out in practice?

The speech itself indicated an ambition larger than withdrawal from Gaza. In his very first mention of the new key word, "disengagement," Sharon spoke of it as "disengagement from the Palestinians." Not merely from the Palestinians of Gaza (from whom, in fact, most Israelis were disengaged, given that a virtually impermeable security fence surrounded the Gaza Strip and that Gazans were no longer allowed to work in Israel), but from "the Palestinians." He continued: "The Disengagement Plan will include the redeployment of IDF forces along new security lines and a change in the deployment of settlements, which will reduce as much as possible the number of Israelis located in the heart of the Palestinian population. We will draw provisional security lines, and the IDF will be deployed along them. Security will be provided by IDF deployment, the security fence, and other physical obstacles. The Disengagement Plan will reduce friction between us and the Palestinians."

Without question, then, he was thinking of withdrawal in the West Bank, too, and not merely from the four isolated settlements at the northern end of the West Bank, which were the only ones eventually included in the disengagement plan.

Sharon added: "The relocation of settlements will be made, first and foremost, in order to draw the most efficient security line possible . . . This security line will not constitute the permanent border of the State of Israel. However, as long as implementation of the road map is not resumed, the IDF will be deployed along that line." But of course the Gaza Strip border *was* undisputedly the "permanent border of the State of Israel," so he must have had in mind some line in the West Bank. He began the next paragraph with "Israel will greatly accelerate the construction of the security fence. Today we can already see it taking shape." Plainly, he was planning or at least considering a very ambitious disengagement that would bring Israel back to the line of the security fence that he was in the process of erecting in the West Bank. The route of the fence approved by the cabinet in October encompassed some 16 percent of the West Bank.[17] This was destined to shrink substantially. But so were the dimensions of the disengagement.

The idea of withdrawing to the fence was in fact one of four proposals originally considered within Sharon's close circle and discussed with the Americans.[18] It was the most ambitious. In the event, Sharon decided on the least ambitious of the proposals under review: withdrawal from the Gaza Strip and from just three (later four) settlements in the northern West Bank. Still, it was a momentous decision, an entirely new departure. He announced it on February 2, through the veteran *Haaretz* columnist Yoel Marcus.

Sharon had invited Marcus to his residence in Jerusalem for a long, leisurely breakfast. He had scheduled a session with the Likud Knesset faction in the afternoon and may have intended to publicize his dramatic announcement there first, with Marcus following up with their interview in the newspaper the next morning. That was how things used to work before the age of the Internet. Marcus, too, may have been planning his next day's article as he drove back to Tel Aviv at midday. He briefed the *Haaretz* editor, Hanoch Marmari, on what he had heard and was sent posthaste to write a story for the paper's Web site. An hour later the country was in uproar.

"Of course there'll be uproar in the country," Sharon had predicted in the interview. "It won't be easy. I'll have trouble in the Likud . . . If there's no choice, I'll change the composition of the government. I take the protests inside the Likud seriously, but I mustn't let them change what I think is the right thing to do in the national interest. People have got to understand that there's a difference between pristine ideology and practical reality. [My plan] will sustain Israel into the future with the maximum possible security."

The wave of outraged reaction flooded from the divided Likud faction across the rightist and religious spectrum. The Judea, Samaria, and Gaza Settlement Council warned ominously that if Sharon presented his plan in Washington the following week, "he will lose his moral right to remain in power." The transport minister, Avigdor Lieberman, leader of the National Union–Yisrael Beiteinu faction, said the plan was "a road accident involving the entire nation." Shaul Yahalom of the National Religious Party, another coalition partner now likely to leave, said Sharon was "undergoing a mutation into a leftist; his moral duty is to resign."

An intensive dialogue now took place between Jerusalem and Washington over the intended dimensions of Sharon's disengagement. The Americans tried to nudge Israel toward a more sweeping withdrawal on the West Bank. But the Americans were arguing among *them*selves, too, about how hard to push Sharon and how much to offer him by way of a U.S. quid pro quo, which Israel was asking for in return for the disengagement. Sharon and Weissglas were angling for a major statement by the administration shifting U.S. policy significantly toward Israel. "Sharon's position," says Dan Kurtzer, "was, I want as much as I can get for the minimum I have to give. The U.S. position was, We're prepared to support this [disengagement], but there's a minimum we need."

The American-Israeli diplomacy culminated in a hugely significant exchange of letters between Bush and Sharon in April 2004.* In his letter, Sharon committed to carry out the disengagement. In his response, President Bush committed to back Israel on two vital issues: the Palestinian refugees would not return en masse to the State of Israel; and—by clear implication—the large settlement blocs on the West Bank, close to the 1967 line, would remain part of Israel in a final status agreement. Sharon regarded the exchange of letters as his most salient achievement as prime minister. He was probably right.

The key word in Bush's text is "realistic." On the refugees he wrote:

The United States is strongly committed to Israel's security and well-being as a Jewish state. It seems clear that an agreed, just, fair and realistic framework for a solution to the Palestinian refugee issue

---

* See Appendix.

as part of any final status agreement will need to be found through the establishment of a Palestinian state, and the settling of Palestinian refugees there, rather than in Israel.

And on the issue of borders the president wrote:

As part of a final peace settlement, Israel must have secure and recognized borders, which should emerge from negotiations between the parties in accordance with UNSC Resolutions 242 and 338. In light of new realities on the ground, including already existing major Israeli populations centers, it is unrealistic to expect that the outcome of final status negotiations will be a full and complete return to the armistice lines of 1949, and all previous efforts to negotiate a two-state solution have reached the same conclusion. It is realistic to expect that any final status agreement will only be achieved on the basis of mutually agreed changes that reflect these realities.

Dov Weissglas explained:

As Sharon saw it, the quid pro quo had to come from the U.S. because the disengagement was to be unilateral. The Palestinians were not a party to anything. We said to the Americans: We are in effect delivering part of the permanent solution, therefore your quid pro quo should also be something that affects the permanent solution. That was the basic rationale beneath our understandings with the administration. And they knew full well that this was the first time since 1967 that something was happening on the ground in Palestine.

"Permanent solution" means refugees, borders, and Jerusalem, the three "permanent status issues" [as defined in the Camp David Accords of 1993]. On Jerusalem, the American position was a categorical Not Now. But they were prepared to talk about the other two, and their position was: boldness for boldness. They made it clear from the outset that for Gaza alone we get nothing. Much approbation and praise, of course, because, after all, they wanted us to get out of the territories. But that's it. They said withdrawal from Gaza alone would not be a sufficiently dramatic move to require the U.S. to prejudge at this stage the permanent solution of the conflict. That's what we were asking for, in essence: a statement from the U.S. that would take positions favorable to Israel on the permanent status issues.

Weissglas uses the word "prejudge" advisedly. Formally, as the Americans were stressing to angry and anxious Arab leaders, the

United States would not prejudge the outcome of the eventual Israeli-Palestinian peace negotiations. The United States was only a third party; the parties to the conflict themselves would ultimately have to make the decisions. Weissglas: "The Americans kept stressing that as a matter of legal logic they couldn't undertake in the name of the Palestinians that the large blocs would be part of Israel or that the refugees would not return to Israel. They said, 'We can only say what our opinion will be if we're asked about these matters.' To which my response was 'Good enough!' We could hardly have dreamed for more."

Basically, though neither Bush nor Sharon would have stated it in these terms, the April 14 exchange of letters was a re-enshrinement in American policy of the Clinton Parameters that Bill Clinton and Ehud Barak had agreed to. The vast difference was that Sharon proposed actually to *do* something, unilaterally, that would begin to turn the policy into a reality. The Clinton Parameters had become (and continue to be) the near-universal recipe for the two-state solution to the Israeli-Palestinian conflict. Arafat's recalcitrance and Israeli right-wing, settler-led rejectionism were together destroying the hope of a two-state solution ever being realized. Sharon's disengagement plan suddenly reversed that tragic process. He single-handedly—unilaterally—restored the prospect of the two-state solution, which is the only hope of peace.

Sharon's gradual, reluctant change of attitude toward the fence, from flat rejection to vigorous endorsement, was an integral part of his steady shift from dogmatism to realism that led to the disengagement from Gaza and a small part of the West Bank and would have led, had he remained healthy, to sweeping withdrawals from the West Bank, too. "We're watching a film in which there was a power outage halfway through," Weissglas says.

This was the firm assessment, too, of Brigadier General (res.) Eival Gilady, deputy head of the IDF's planning branch at the time, who was involved both in the discussions within Israel and in the negotiations with the Americans. Withdrawal to the fence always remained the overall concept behind the disengagement, Gilady says; Sharon embraced it in principle—and presumably would have implemented it in practice, had he not "gone to sleep two years too soon"—as Israel's middle-term strategy pending eventual peace negotiations with the (reformed and security-effective) Palestinian Authority. In those eventual negotiations, Gilady says, the fence "was to become the reference point" for mutually agreed border adjustments.

The fence as it eventually emerged from all the various legal, diplomatic, and political challenges, says Gilady, was to encompass some 7–8 percent of the West Bank. It would take in 76 percent of the Jewish settlers living in the large blocs of settlements close to the old border and 0.7 percent of the Palestinian population. The "concept," he says, was "to encourage as many as possible of the remaining 24 percent of settlers, over a period of two years, to move of their own free will into Israel proper or into the settlement blocs."

Weissglas adds:

The disengagement from Gaza, though a complete step in itself, was intended to dovetail into a further move. This was based on two principles: (a) the road map—in other words, no peace negotiations until the first phase of the road map is implemented; and (b) the understanding that to leave things as they were would mean a dangerous deadlock that eventually would engulf us all.

Therefore, the logic was to continue in the West Bank with a series of similar actions . . . To create a situation of two nations living side by side in quiet—I'm not saying in peace—in coexistence, with economic development, with us helping them to build their economy, so that when we eventually reach the permanent status negotiations, things that now look important would suddenly look less important. We hoped that the fence would help create this reality. That Jews living on the other side of the fence would start coming back to Israel proper. We hoped that the Palestinians' growing economic prosperity would help them to impose law and order, and security, on the West Bank, and we would gradually withdraw our troops from town after town, area after area—without the pomp and fanfare of permanent status negotiations, which would doubtless run aground over Jerusalem.

This was absolutely Sharon's thinking. In October 2005, after the disengagement, we were together for a weekend at a rural resort in the Galilee—he, his sons, Adler, me, and my wife—and we had hours to talk about the future. And that was how he saw it. We set up a high-level team under [the director general of the Foreign Ministry, Aharon] Abramovitz, whose task was to draw up a list of problems—problems, not solutions—that would arise when we began applying this strategy to the West Bank. Security: what forces would need to remain on the other side of the fence. Currency, transport, telecommunications, health, everything . . . How you create a de facto reality of two states without the political label and let life take its course and, in time, eventually negotiate the permanent status accords.

The Bush-Sharon letters of April 2004 were accompanied by a "side letter" from Weissglas to Rice. On settlement building, which Israel was supposed to freeze (it never did) under the road map but had now in effect been legitimized inside the blocs,[19] the letter undertook that "an effort will be made in the next few days to have a better definition of the construction line of settlements in Judea and Samaria [the West Bank]. An Israeli team, in conjunction with Ambassador Kurtzer, will review aerial photos of settlements." And on the illegal outposts, which Sharon had repeatedly pledged to remove, the letter promised "a list of unauthorized outposts with indicative dates of their removal . . . within 30 days."

"I'd go to Duby every week and a half after this," Kurtzer recalled, "and say, 'Do you want to start doing this?' And he would say, 'Yes, yes,' and start shuffling his papers. And he'd say, 'Let's start with one of the easy settlements.' And he'd send me to an official at Defense who would launch a whole exercise of mapping and GPS and all the rest of it. But at the end of the day nothing happened, because they didn't want to do it."*

E ven allowing for an ongoing, genuine change of policy thinking on Sharon's part, most commentators assumed that the prime minister and his advisers had devised the disengagement at this particular time in order to haul him back up from the ominous decline in his fortunes that dogged him during the summer and fall of 2003. Yoel Marcus, analyzing his celebrated interview, wrote that Sharon had "woken up to realize that while he's been sticking to his guns, the world has moved away from him, and the Israeli public, too, has begun to lose its confidence in his credibility and wisdom . . . The turning point was the pilots' letter in September." Ze'ev Schiff, too, wrote of the troubling effect on Sharon of the pilots' letter and the petition of the Sayeret Matkal reservists. Sharon had been especially disturbed by the broad support for the "Geneva Accord" because it meant, to him,

---

* In truth, nor did Kurtzer want to do it. His colleagues at State regarded the Weissglas-Rice side letter as little short of a disaster because it gave official U.S. sanction to settlement activity within the "construction line," wherever that was, of each individual settlement within the blocs. "We would rather have had settlement activity without the sanction than with the sanction," Kurtzer admitted. But that was the U.S. policy as formulated by Rice and her staff in Weissglas's letter, and it prevailed. Weissglas's verdict on Kurtzer: "A nice chap, but a bit strange, and he wasn't really in the loop about the big moves. Ambassadors are a bit passé."

that many Israelis were prepared to agree to a Palestinian state even before the Palestinians had put an end to terrorism. That, to Sharon, was the antithesis of the road map. Hence, according to Schiff, the disengagement.[20]

Such mixing of politics and policy is the entirely legitimate recourse of an elected leader responsive to the shifting moods of his own public and to changing circumstances internationally. Weissglas might dress up Sharon's thinking as wholly strategic, but everyone knows that for a prime minister, especially an Israeli one, strategy and politics are inseparable and often indistinguishable. The kerfuffle over how extensive the disengagement was going to be hardly broadcast prolonged strategic thinking or steely resolve. Rather, it broadcast last-minute scrambling to achieve maximum popular and political gains from a long-contemplated but suddenly urgent change of policy. This was readily perceived—and largely condoned—by a public captivated by the hopefulness and boldness of the prime minister's new initiative.

Between Sharon's narrative as recounted by Weissglas and Gilady and the alternative narrative as constructed by his most implacable critics, there is a wide swath of legitimate middle ground. In October, Weissglas buttonholed two of Sharon's aides and pressed them urgently to prepare material "on demography. 'Everything's demography now . . . I'm talking about withdrawal from the Gaza Strip . . . Write about the settlements on the West Bank, too. Arik's opposed to that, but soon he'll agree.' "[21]

Legitimate, or beyond the line of legitimacy? Weissglas said of himself, "If I have to sum up my role, it was to read Sharon's thoughts even when he hadn't yet articulated them."[22] This begs the obvious question: "Even when he hadn't yet thought them?" Moshe Ya'alon, then the IDF chief of staff, recalled Weissglas trying to persuade him to support the disengagement plan with the argument "Look how he's falling in the polls!" Legitimate? The question of how legitimate it is for considerations of domestic popularity to dictate foreign policy preoccupies all democracies. But that brazen appeal by the prime minister's political aide to the state's No. 1 soldier crossed the legitimacy line. It did not, though, delegitimize the new policy shift.

Ya'alon's criticism, however, is deeper than that. He condemns both the *method* and the *motive* of the decision making. The method, he asserts, was irresponsible and hence led to a flawed decision. The motive, he believes, was corrupt. "There was no proper process of consultation," Ya'alon charges. "Here we are embarking on a major strategic move, and the army and other defense agencies have been kept in the dark. There is no serious, professional analysis of what Israel can gain from the move and what it can't . . . Basic military questions need to be considered, but no one has given them any thought."*

To Ya'alon, the only reasonable motivation cited for the disengagement was the fear that with the eclipse of Abu Mazen and the road map, the vacuum would be filled by other international initiatives inimical to Israel. But he does not believe that was the true rationale. "I felt from up close that the true concern was Sharon's political decline, both as a result of the criminal investigations and as a result of the pilots' letter, the Sayeret's petition, the 'Geneva Accord,' and all those other developments. That was my strong sense at the time. I had no hard evidence. If I'd have had evidence, I would have turned it over to the proper authorities and resigned. I did actually consider resigning. But I decided it would cause greater damage to the army and to Israeli democracy."

QUESTION: How was the disengagement going to help Sharon get out of his criminal investigations?

YA'ALON: He thought, and he turned out to be right, that if he undertook an initiative like the disengagement, he would be *etrogized*!† The media would wrap him and *etrogize* him. They wouldn't play up so prominently the allegations of corruption that were swirling around him. It's a question of headlines, of editorials. The nation reads of a new initiative full of hope for the future, and it sees the media supporting and promoting it. Drugging the public, if you like. Sharon read the map aright. Politically, his move was brilliant.

---

* Ya'alon dismisses the involvement of Brigadier General Eival Gilady—a representative, after all, of the defense establishment—in the early, secret stages of the initiative as "improper . . . This is a case of improper behavior by an improper officer . . . That's why he had to quit the army and was not promoted to commander of the planning branch as he wished . . . In army planning procedures people come up with all sorts of scenarios. To make out that one such scenario was the basis of the disengagement plan, and hence arrogate the disengagement to oneself, was not exactly accurate."

† *Etrogization* was a word invented later by the prominent political commentator Amnon Abramovitz to depict what he said was the media's mollycoddling of Sharon during this period. An *etrog* is a species of citrus used in Jewish ritual on the Festival of Tabernacles, or Sukkot. It has a delicate little crownlike growth at its tip. If that breaks off, the fruit is no longer kosher for the ritual. The *etrog* is traditionally wrapped in layers of wadding to protect it. By analogy, Sharon, though embroiled in criminal inquiries, was wrapped in protective wadding by the Israeli media, which strongly supported his disengagement plan.

QUESTION: But how does that save him from the judicial process?

YA'ALON: Judges and law enforcement officials are people, members of the public, part of the country. They're influenced. Every judicial system, in its court verdicts, in its decisions whether to indict or not, reflects the norms of the society in which it operates. Does this influence a particular attorney general or a particular state prosecutor? I would hope not. But I'm not sure. I'm not sure if people aren't influenced subconsciously. I'm not sure if they don't think to themselves: "If I indict the prime minister now, when he's in the middle of a major withdrawal initiative, *Haaretz* will slaughter me!" [Laughs.][23] Don't underestimate the power of the press.

The alternative narrative seemed to have the timing on its side. Sharon unveiled his disengagement plan precisely the day after a new attorney general took office. No more would the witty, rumpled, stern, but ultimately soft Elyakim Rubinstein hold the key to the prime minister's legal and hence political future. In his seven years as attorney general, the religiously pious and reputedly rightist Rubinstein had ordered police investigations against all three prime ministers whose governments he advised.* But he stopped short of indicting any of them.

The new man, Menachem "Menny" Mazuz, had risen to the position of deputy attorney general over years of quiet toil inside the Ministry of Justice. His political sympathies were unknown. As a member of the secular intelligentsia, he most likely favored peace over "Greater Israel." If so, he might hesitate before bringing down a prime minister actively engaged in withdrawing Israeli forces and settlements from sizable swaths of the occupied territories. That, at any rate, was the buzz that quickly began to circulate on the right.

On Mazuz's desk soon after he settled into his new office was a recommendation from his most senior subordinate, State Attorney Edna Arbel, to indict Sharon for receiving bribes. Her recommendation, moreover, was public knowledge; she or someone else had made sure to leak it. Furthermore, Arbel was angling to become a justice of the Supreme Court. If she succeeded, Mazuz knew, he would meet her again, probably frequently, during his term as attorney general. But the configuration between them would be different then: he would be pleading before her. He would need to be brave, some would say

---

* The attorney general in Israel is both the official legal adviser to the government and the head of the state prosecution service. Efforts to divide up these two discrete roles between two separate officeholders have thus far foundered.

foolhardy, to overrule her now. All this was uncomfortably clear to Sharon, his sons, and the rest of his friends and advisers on the "ranch forum."

To appreciate quite how bad Sharon's situation and his survival prospects were at this crucial moment in his prime ministership, we need to wade back into the two affairs that were threatening to end his career in obloquy. The "Greek island affair," the subject of Arbel's recommendation to indict him, had been looming steadily larger since Sharon had fobbed it off a year before in his famously blacked-out television broadcast. He had boasted to viewers of his son Gilad's business prowess and high earning potential. Gilad hadn't even been questioned by the police, he had added smugly.

Since then, both Gilad and he himself had undergone lengthy police questioning. Gilad, on July 31, 2003, and again on September 3, stolidly exercised his right to remain silent. He also refused to hand over documents and tape-recordings that the police wanted. They couldn't obtain a search warrant to look for them, Gilad's lawyers argued, because Gilad lived in the home of a serving Knesset member, Ariel Sharon, which was protected by his parliamentary immunity.

Sharon père had received the police interrogators at his official residence in Jerusalem on October 30, 2003, and sat with them for six straight hours. He spoke a great deal and even joked with the detectives, a police source disclosed later. But at the end of the day, the source complained, the prime minister didn't provide clear answers to the questions he was asked.[1] He stuck to his guns: he had nothing to do with Gilad's business affairs; he was not the owner of Sycamore Ranch (his sons were); there was no connection between Gilad's contract with the building contractor Appel and Appel's help to him during the 1999 Likud primary. Nor was his own involvement in hosting the Greek delegation in any way connected, or criminal.

In December, there was some (relatively) good news for the Sharons. The Tel Aviv prosecutor's office recommended indicting Appel for giving bribes to various officials, including Sharon, but recommended closing the file on Sharon for accepting bribes—on grounds of lack of sufficient evidence. In Israeli law it is possible, though highly unusual, to indict a bribe giver while exculpating the bribe taker because he did not have the requisite criminal intent. He did not know, in other words, that he was being bribed.

But the relief at Sycamore Ranch was short-lived. Edna Arbel, it soon became clear, was not adopting the recommendation from Tel Aviv; she believed Sharon should be indicted, too. On January 21, 2004, during the "interregnum" between the retirement of Attorney

General Rubinstein and the appointment of Attorney General Mazuz, Arbel, as acting attorney general, quickly filed the indictment against Appel for bribing Sharon. This was widely seen as an attempt to present Mazuz with a fait accompli. He would have to indict Sharon, too, or else resort to that seldom-used distinction between bribe giver and bribe taker. He would have to contend, in effect, that the Sharons were too naive to understand what Appel was about. "Senior officials are to be held to a stricter standard," Arbel asserted in a speech. "In offenses involving governmental corruption we are obliged to indict, unequivocally obliged."

Reluctantly, Sharon and his aides began discussing a retreat to a new line of defense: the law providing that a prime minister, unlike other ministers, is not required to resign if indicted, only if convicted. This would be a hard line to defend in the battlefield of public opinion. But they made ready to try.

Under the strict letter of the law, they had a good case. Whereas the Supreme Court had laid down a strong judge-made line of precedent, starting back in 1993, that a government minister, if indicted, must resign or must be removed by the prime minister, statute law provided explicitly that a prime minister need step down only if he was convicted of a serious crime and his conviction was upheld on appeal. In Sharon's case, the general expectation was that even if he were indicted, the trial and appeal would take many months or even years. No rush to resign, then, the prime minister's advisers contended.

Would public opinion go along with that? Much would depend on lawyers' arguments. The statute protecting the prime minister from summary removal was originally passed as part of the reform of the electoral system in the 1990s. Under that reform, the status of the prime minister became constitutionally different from that of other ministers. He was a semi-president. He was elected personally and directly by the public, in a separate ballot.

Since then, though, the electoral system had been changed back, mainly, as we saw,* at Sharon's own dogged insistence. The prime minister was now, once again, in constitutional terms just a name on his party's list of Knesset candidates, no different from the others, all elected in one single ballot.

But—and here was the rub—while many other provisions in the law had been changed back or abrogated by the Knesset, this one, about his removal from office for committing a crime, had been kept intact. An oversight, argued Sharon's adversaries. Now that the electoral sys-

---

* See p. 367.

tem had been changed back, the law reverted to the Supreme Court precedent. Not so, argued Knesset Speaker Rivlin, who was a member of the law committee in 2001. "We wanted to shore up the special standing of the prime minister even after the election system returned to the one-ballot vote."

Edna Arbel was very clearly of the hard-liners' mind. "The moment a criminal indictment is filed against a public figure, he is duty-bound to suspend himself from office," she declared. She did not refer explicitly to the case of a prime minister, or specifically to Prime Minister Sharon. But behind the scenes she was working furiously to connect the dots.

By March 28, aided by a team of six handpicked government attorneys, Edna Arbel had completed her last major opus as state attorney and submitted it to Mazuz: *The State of Israel v. Ariel Sharon*. It was a complete draft indictment, accusing the prime minister and his son Gilad of taking bribes from David Appel, both in the form of political support from Appel in Sharon's 1999 primary campaign and in the form of cash paid by Appel into the account of Sycamore Ranch as Gilad's ostensible salary. In return, according to the draft indictment, Sharon had helped Appel with his plans to build a vast new residential suburb near the town of Lod and with his even vaster (but unsuccessful) plans to build the holiday paradise on the Greek island.

During the 1990s, the draft indictment recounted, Appel spent some $40 million buying up agricultural land in four villages around Lod. The largest tracts were in the village of Ginaton. His investment strategy depended on the lands eventually being rezoned from agricultural to residential. That was where Sharon came in. As the minister of national infrastructures with control over the powerful Israel Lands Authority (ILA), and later as prime minister, still with direct control over the ILA, Sharon took part in Appel's plot by trying to get the bureaucrats to do the developer's bidding.

As minister of infrastructures, he failed. Two successive directors of the ILA stood firm against Appel's applications and against Sharon's relatively subtle attempts to push them through. As prime minister, Sharon took the gloves off, the draft indictment charged. He announced that he was making the expansion and development of the down-at-heel town of Lod his "personal priority." "Following that, defendant No. 1 [Sharon] took action to transfer lands in the Lod area, including the land of Ginaton, from the ILA to the Municipality of Lod, and to rezone the land for residential purposes. He did so knowing that the Ginaton lands had been acquired by Appel, that the ILA disapproved of residential building on them, and that his action would significantly further the commercial interests of Appel and his company."

Regarding the Greek island, the draft indictment chronicled Sharon's participation during 1999 at the dinners Appel gave for the two high-level Greek delegations whose visits to Israel he had arranged.* During that same year, Appel hired Gilad "for work of indeterminate nature," in the words of the draft indictment, on the Greek island project. He was to receive $10,000 a month, plus a $1.5 million bonus when the Greek authorities licensed the project, plus another $1.5 million bonus once the project was up and running. "Appel and defendant No. 2 [Gilad] reached their employment agreement even though Appel had no idea of defendant No. 2's professional abilities—other than that defendant No. 2 had no knowledge whatever of the field in which he was to be employed. Appel made the agreement with defendant No. 2 . . . in order to obtain the active help of defendant No. 1 both in promoting his real estate project in Lod and in advancing his Greek island project."

Gilad's services to the project, in quantity and quality, were "worth far less than what he was paid . . . For part of the time he did no work at all." Yet Appel remitted to the Sycamore Ranch account a total of 2.6 million shekels over a period of less than two years, as Gilad's salary. Appel also organized political and logistical help for Sharon in the 1999 Likud leadership primary. He promised to field "300 'suicidal' activists" on Sharon's behalf, and "he was active in circles susceptible to his influence in order to bring about the election of defendant No. 1 as leader of the Likud."

Whatever the contentions in the hypothetical dispute between jurists, it is reasonable to assume that Sharon would have been forced out of office by massive political and media pressure had he been indicted as Arbel recommended. The charge was bribery, plain and unequivocal. It was not the nebulous catchall charge of breach of faith that had often been filed against unethical politicians, but less often made to stick.

Arbel's indictment, however, was never filed. On June 15, 2004, Attorney General Mazuz announced that he was overruling her and closing the case against Sharon. The facts and findings, he said, didn't "even come close to a reasonable chance of conviction." He publicly accused Arbel of aiming at Sharon and then drawing the rings around him to turn her shot into a bull's-eye. Arbel, meanwhile, had been appointed to the Supreme Court.

---

* See pp. 431–32.

Mazuz, always low-key and unemotional, first telephoned the prime minister and informed him matter-of-factly of his decision. Sharon, at his most controlled, was similarly matter-of-fact. Mazuz then walked into a pre-convened press conference at the Justice Ministry and informed the nation and the world that he was closing the case. Beyond the personal drama, of course, his closely argued seventy-six-page legal opinion meant one thing: the disengagement plan was still on course.

His firm position, Mazuz explained, was that a public official, even a prime minister, should be judged by the same standards as anyone else. Not more leniently, but not more stringently either. The same burden of proof was needed to justify an indictment of a senior official. This, he insisted, contradicting Arbel, was the clear import of the Supreme Court precedents.

In Sharon's case, that burden of proof had not been discharged. Not with regard to the alleged bribe: political help and cash payments. And not with regard to the alleged quid pro quo: Sharon's attending the dinners and pushing for the rezoning of the Lod lands.

Sharon had known Appel for years, Mazuz wrote. He had known Appel's father. Their families were friendly. Appel had often supported Sharon in the party. But he supported other people, too. In the 1999 primary he did seem to have helped Sharon in various ways, though the evidence was sketchy. At the end of the day, Mazuz wrote, Appel seemed to have helped Olmert more than he helped Sharon. Sharon in his interrogation admitted that he'd asked for Appel's help but said he'd taken Appel's pledges of support with a grain of salt. "These kinds of promises—sometimes they're kept, sometimes they're not. I never saw them as a binding commitment. Nor does anyone. Everyone knows the game . . . People feel important when politicians ask their help." Mazuz tended to agree. "To discharge the burden of proof, you have to take account of the overall relationship between the giver and the receiver [of the alleged bribe], and the overall circumstances of the case. You have to take account of what is considered acceptable, in life in general and in political life in particular."

As for Gilad's salary, the heart of the case, Mazuz conceded it was indeed generous. The whole Greek island project, he wrote, was "grandiose, some would say megalomaniacal." The envisaged investment was $16 billion(!). The actual investment Appel made was substantial, and so were the salaries he paid to a string of professionals he hired. Mazuz refused to regard Gilad's employment as a charade, as Arbel had done. He cited the testimony of the senior company accountant and an outside advertising consultant to the effect that Gilad had headed up the marketing and advertising side of the project, had put in long hours at the office, and had done his job well. There were dozens of businesslike, work-related conversations between him and Appel among the police wiretaps of Appel's phone lines, although there were also political and personal conversations between them.

Regarding the lands around Lod, Mazuz wrote that all the evidence showed that as minister of infrastructures Sharon never pressured his officials to accede to Appel's demands. And as prime minister, Mazuz continued, there was no proof that Sharon exerted undue influence on behalf of the Lod building plans. Granted, he pushed through a cabinet decision to "save Lod" through varied and extensive government-backed projects. These were handled by professional planning committees staffed by civil servants. There was no evidence of improper pressure from above or rubber-stamping by cowed officials. Sharon played a similarly active role in promoting development plans for other towns, where Appel had no commercial interests.

So, despite the suspicions, there was not sufficient proof that the political help and the cash from Appel had been bribes. Even if they were, Mazuz went on to argue, there was not sufficient evidence that Sharon *understood* them to be bribes. He knew that Gilad was receiving a high salary. But there was no evidence to show that he understood it to be linked to his ability to help Appel as foreign minister and later as leader of the opposition. In other words, there was no clear evidence of mens rea, or criminal intent, on the prime minister's part.

The same state-of-mind test applied to Gilad, Mazuz wrote. The police tapes showed that Gilad seriously feared Appel might not pay up as agreed. That would hardly have been the case had he thought the salary was intended as a bribe for his father. There was no hint in Gilad's behavior of any feeling of guilt or need to conceal or disguise the money, nor any hint in the tapes that he was disingenuous in regard to the money.

Finally, Mazuz analyzed a tapped telephone call between Sharon and Appel in September 1999 in which Sharon asked the developer, "Is the island in our hands already?"* Arbel and her team deduced that Sharon was fully familiar with the details of the project, but Mazuz said the taped conversation showed exactly the opposite. Sharon did not know how far offshore the island was ("Only 700–800 meters? So it's not a long boat ride?"). He urged vaguely that they build to withstand earthquakes. But he evinced little real interest and

---

* Sharon was being funny; his reference was to the famous words of General Mordechai Gur, the paratroop commander, during the Six-Day War: "The Temple Mount is in our hands."

kept on trying to steer the conversation back to party politics. "Hasn't Gilad got you excited about the project?" Appel asks wistfully. "Our boy's a very discreet boy, you know," Sharon replied. "He never talks about business." Appel replied by praising Gilad's work and assuring his father that he would be making good money out of it. Hardly what he would have said, wrote Mazuz, if they both knew it was a bribe. Appel invited Sharon and Lily to "our new home in Greece," and Sharon accepted, "but I'll pay my own way," he said.

Sharon's enemies gulped. It was hard to tar the gauche, straitlaced, somewhat owlish Mazuz with the brush of too-intimate contact with Sharon's coterie. Still, some whispered that his labored, casuistic opinion was the payoff for his unanticipated appointment as attorney general, a job, they insisted, several sizes too big for him. But that implied the collusion, at least passive, of Tommy Lapid, the Shinui Party leader and minister of justice, who had recommended the appointment. This was thoroughly improbable, as even the whisperers were forced to agree.

An alternative line of attack was that Mazuz, after a career in the rarefied air of the judicial bureaucracy, was just too naive and unworldly to understand how he had been duped. Repeatedly, he cited the *absence* of any incriminating material in the thousands of hours of taped telephone conversations as proof that there had been no crime. But didn't he realize that all the alleged plotters assumed as a matter of course that Appel's lines were tapped? Sharon himself let the veil slip in a rare unguarded moment in November 1999 when he arranged with Appel to have lunch in Raanana and added, apparently for the benefit of the tappers, "That's not a code word; it's the site of a kosher restaurant."[2]

Yossi Sarid of Meretz, Eitan Cabel of Labor, and the Movement for Quality Government all applied to the High Court of Justice to order the attorney general to reconsider. A bench of seven justices, however, decided by 6–1 not to intervene. The majority opinion coldly dismissed the claim that Mazuz had let Sharon's lofty status influence his forensic decision making. Mazuz's decision not to indict was entirely reasonable—as was, the judges stressed, Arbel's recommendation to indict. "It is quite possible that jurists of equal abilities should reach different assessments," Justice Eliahu Matza wrote in the majority opinion. Chief Justice Aharon Barak concurred, as did all the others—apart from Justice Mishael Cheshin, the judge who shut down Sharon's TV broadcast before the last election. "I am sorry,"

Cheshin wrote in his dissenting judgment, "but I have the greatest difficulty concurring with my learned friends. To my mind, the facts speak for themselves. Gilad Sharon, the son of Ariel Sharon, received huge sums of money from Appel . . . These vast sums were to be paid to a man who had no prior experience in the business for which he was hired to engage in . . . Granted, [Ariel] Sharon didn't know much more than the fact that his son was getting 'a high salary.' But that much he knew."

Sharon had got the better of Cheshin again. But he was by no means out of the woods. The Cyril Kern affair had been growing murkier and more impenetrable as detectives followed the trail of mysterious bank transfers to South Africa, to Austria, to New York, and to the Virgin Islands. Gilad was embroiled in an ugly battle to protect his bank records from the prying eyes of police investigators. Omri faced the possibility of prosecution for the election finance offenses exposed in the original front companies affair.

As the investigations proceeded, Kern increasingly appeared to the police to have been a front himself. In an affidavit to the South African minister of justice in January 2003, Kern indicated that the "money which I arranged be sent to Gilad Sharon to whom I have been known since birth as Uncle Cyril" was not in fact his money:

On or about October 2001, Gilad indicated to me that his business needed about $1.5 million which he intended to borrow as a short-term loan . . . I did not inquire about his motives, needs, or reasons, knowing well that he would not ask if he did not really need and if he was not sure he could repay.

Therefore in January 2002, I arranged for a foreign trust to hand Gilad about $1.5 million without any conditions or qualifying requirements on its utilization or purpose about which I made no inquiry. The loan was extended under the sole condition that it would be repaid as soon as possible in the same currency and would carry an arm-length 3-percent interest rate compounding annually.

The loan to Kern had indeed been repaid, thanks to a *second* transfer of money, *also* from BAWAG (Bank für Arbeit und Wirtschaft) in Vienna, which had landed in Gilad's Tel Aviv account in two installments, in November and December 2002. Who had sent it? Gilad was zealously upholding his right to remain silent. The police claimed that Gilad had solicited the second transfer, after he learned that they were investigating the *first* transfer from Kern. They formally asked the Austrian authorities to be allowed to extend their investigation to

Vienna, to interrogate people there and to scour BAWAG bank records. But they were repeatedly rebuffed. The Austrian Justice Ministry, and then the Austrian courts, stonewalled. Raising political donations was not a crime, Austrian law enforcement officials argued, ignoring the Israelis' suspicion that the moneys were bribes. Anyway, the transfers had gone to Gilad and Omri, not to the Israeli prime minister. Moreover, Austrian banking secrecy protected the transfers. The Israelis concluded that whoever had sent the money from Vienna was not only rich but powerful.

By early 2004, the police had come to believe there had in fact been a *third* transfer to the Sharon brothers, also apparently of $1.5 million—making $4.5 million in all—and this last sum seemed to have remained with the family after they had paid off their bank loan and paid back Cyril Kern. The police suggested that Sharon's old Israeli-American friend Arie Genger, who, it turned out, had lent money to Kern in the past, was involved. So, they believed, was Martin Schlaff, the reclusive Austrian-Jewish businessman and part owner of the casino at Jericho together with the Palestinian Authority, and, as it now turned out, together with BAWAG, too. Were Genger, and perhaps Schlaff, involved in the *original* donations, through the U.S. front companies, for the 1999 election campaign? If so, the whole saga was an elaborate loop. Genger was questioned and asserted his right to remain silent.[3]

With Vienna inhospitable and Genger inscrutable, the police could only try to force the equally uncooperative Gilad to furnish the information they lacked. In June 2003, at police request, a Tel Aviv magistrate had ordered Gilad to produce all the documents in his possession connected with the investigation. He refused. This was an attempt, he argued, to unseat his father undemocratically. In August, another magistrate ruled that he couldn't refuse. He was asserting his right to stay silent on the grounds that he might incriminate someone else (his father). But the law, wrote Magistrate Daniella Shirizli, recognized only the grounds of not incriminating oneself. He must produce the documents forthwith.

Gilad obtained from another magistrate a stay of execution pending his appeal from the first magistrate to a higher court. But the second magistrate ruled that he must deposit the documents in a court safe for the time being. Gilad appealed *this* ruling before yet another court. If he agreed to deposit the documents, he argued, he would be admitting he had them in his possession. But he had made no such admission, insisting on his right to silence. This second appeal was accepted in the Tel Aviv District Court on August 13, 2003. Now the state appealed, and in December 2003 the Supreme Court ruled that Gilad must hand over all the documents to a magistrate, who would decide which of them could be read by the police and which would remain protected by Gilad's right to silence.

Gilad grudgingly turned over some documents, but the prosecutors claimed they were ones that the police had anyway, whereas the ones the police wanted, Gilad had failed to provide. Among these latter were documents and bank statements relating to a company called Charnington Ltd., which Gilad and Cyril Kern had apparently set up in 2002 as a vehicle for doing business together (or, as the police suspected, for transferring illicit moneys).

In February 2004, the Tel Aviv District Court ordered Gilad to instruct BAWAG to send him all the relevant statements regarding the money transfers and regarding Charnington Ltd. and to hand them over to the police. Yet again, he appealed to the Supreme Court. There, finally, on March 29, 2004, five justices held against him and ruled that he must hand over documents and tapes connected to both the Cyril Kern affair and the Greek island affair. His lawyer announced that he would have to contact "various third parties such as the Austrian bank" and ask them for the documents. "But no one says they're going to give them to us."

The police, meanwhile, raided the offices of a lawyer and an accountant in Tel Aviv thought to have set up Charnington Ltd. for Gilad and Kern and impounded documents and computers. In April 2004, the prosecutors were back in Magistrate Daniella Shirizli's court, arguing that lawyer-client privilege should not apply to at least some of this material. For the first time, they referred explicitly to Martin Schlaff, who, they said, was believed to have paid money into Charnington ostensibly for "consultancy work" undertaken by Gilad and Kern. The material they wanted could throw light, they said, on the intimate relationship between Schlaff and the Sharons.

On May 6, 2004, Gilad informed the court that he had no written record regarding consultancy services he had performed in return for $3 million that had been deposited in his account in Austria. The contract had been verbal, he explained. "Three million dollars are deposited in your account," asked the prosecutor, "and you don't remember seeing any document relating to the source of this fee?" Gilad: "There is no such document because all the agreements were made orally, but . . ." "*Don't say 'but,'*" Gilad's lawyer, David Libai, cut in. "Nothing in writing?" the prosecutor persisted. "After all, it is $3 million." "Well, maybe it was mentioned in a fax. I don't remember."

On July 4, Judge Shirizli ruled that Gilad had fulfilled his duty under the court order to hand over the documents in his possession regarding the Cyril Kern affair. The yearlong battle in the courts seemed to have ended, at least for the moment. Gilad had emerged unscathed, or at any rate unprosecuted.

But in the court of public opinion, in the salons and the streets of Israel, and most especially among the settlers and their political hinterland, the suspicions against the Sharons became the shrillest battle cry against the prime minister's disengagement policy. Settler activists who for years, indeed for decades, had celebrated Arik Sharon as their hero and their leader, regularly dismissing all his various brushes with the law as the lies and slanders of the Left, now embraced the latest slew of allegations against him with holy zeal.

Zvi Hendel of the National Union, the only Knesset member who actually lived in a settlement in the Gaza Strip, captured this upsurge of righteous indignation with a sound bite that became an instant slogan: "The depth of the disengagement is as the depth of the investigation."* Sharon, he explained, was "a base and corrupt man." Sharon had only dreamed up the disengagement when it seemed that the family would be prosecuted over the Greek island affair. Hendel laid it on with all the rancor of a jilted lover. "For years he [Sharon] called us the salt of the earth, and now he spits in our faces and kicks us in the head with a great muddy boot."[4]

So prevalent did this alleged nexus between the "affairs" and the disengagement become, especially on the political right, that when the attorney general announced his decision in June 2004 to close the Greek island file, the joke around the Knesset was that Sharon responded: "If I'd have known that, I'd never have started with this disengagement."

The campaign to impugn Sharon's motives was to continue unabated long after Sharon himself had physically collapsed and his government had come to a peremptory end. In the settler community and its hinterland, his corruption and its purportedly causal effect on his policy making became axiomatic, almost articles of religious faith.

The settler leaders' dissemination of the "depth . . . depth" theory was all the more cynical and manipulative because it was they themselves, years earlier, who had been the first to sense—and to

---

* This was an adaptation of a policy slogan from the Rabin years, when Israel tried hesitantly to negotiate with Syria. "The depth of the withdrawal is as the depth of the peace," the government declared, meaning that if Syria were prepared for full peace with trade, tourism, and diplomatic ties, then Israel would be prepared to make a full (or almost full) withdrawal from the Golan Heights.

warn—that Sharon was showing signs of softening on the Palestinian question. Yet that was long before the "affairs" crashed down on him. Moreover, the one man among their leadership who had developed a genuine intimacy with Sharon over the years, Ze'ev "Zambish" Hever, flatly rejected the "depth . . . depth" theory. In a documentary film made after the disengagement in which he was interviewed extensively, Zambish pointedly refused to support or give any credence to this allegation. Sharon, he insisted, had acted in what he believed—wrongly in the view of the settlers, but sincerely—was Israel's national interest.[5]

By contrast, Sharon found himself suddenly basking in the warm approbation of media at home and abroad—the same media that over the years had expended millions of words criticizing and excoriating him. Soon enough, this unwonted media praise was itself adduced by Sharon's opponents on the right to reinforce the "depth . . . depth" theory. The disengagement, they claimed, was a sophisticated ploy designed to play to the largely dovish press gallery in order to soften coverage of and commentary on the "affairs." The *etrogization* argument advanced by the former chief of staff Moshe Ya'alon became a central part of the public debate surrounding the disengagement.

Sharon himself, for all his ostensibly contemptuous indifference to the alternative narrative and its various purveyors, did put on record one blunt rebuttal of it as he set out on this last act of his life's drama. "There is no connection," he told political reporters on February 4, "between the disengagement from Gaza and the police investigations. I am doing the disengagement not because of the investigations, but in spite of them."[6]

DUE PROCESS

The political fight to stop the disengagement began within days of the interview with Yoel Marcus. Yisrael Katz, once Sharon's street-smart political fixer, subsequently a Bibi man, and now the minister of agriculture but trying his best to befriend both rivals, proposed a referendum among the membership of the Likud Party. His reasoning was subtle—subtly insidious, some of Sharon's advisers feared—and could not easily be dismissed. "We have some 300,000 party members across the country," Katz argued. (In fact there were just under 200,000.) "A Likud prime minister must be able to show that his policy has the support of the majority of his own voters."[7]

Sharon, assured by his pollsters of the broad national support his new policy was attracting, would ideally have preferred a nationwide plebiscite. He knew that the narrower the voter base, the more susceptible it would be to a pavement-pounding, door-knocking campaign by young settlers and their urban sympathizers. He feared their efficacy and their contagious zeal. But there was no provision for an ad hoc nationwide plebiscite under existing law, and Attorney General Mazuz ruled that one could not therefore be held using the existing election machinery. Special legislation would have to be drafted and passed in the Knesset—a veritable invitation for endless filibusters and other foot-dragging contrivances. The Likud, on the other hand, as an independent political party, could organize a referendum among its members without any need for legislation.

By March 2004, the right wing of the Likud Knesset faction was in open revolt and threatening to withhold their votes from government legislation in the house. The coalition partners further to the right, the National Union–Yisrael Beiteinu and the National Religious Party, were already bucking the coalition whip almost daily. A policy statement by the prime minister on March 15 was approved by an embarrassing majority of one: 46 votes to 45. Labor and Meretz were still voting as opposition parties. Shimon Peres, the Labor leader, encouraged Sharon to move ahead with his disengagement plan and expand it to the West Bank. He made it clear to Sharon that when it came to the test, Labor would side with him. Yossi Sarid, the head of Meretz, said he didn't believe it would ever actually come to the test. "There's no plan and there never was. There won't be any disengagement in the foreseeable future." But Sarid, too, despite his skepticism, promised (hypothetical) support. "If any practical step is actually submitted to the Knesset, if we see a single settlement moving, we'll vote in favor."[8]

At a session of the Likud Party convention in Tel Aviv on March 30, Sharon, facing Edna Arbel's recommended indictment, was given a rousing ovation. But when he spoke of his disengagement plan, the clapping turned to boos. Clearly he had no majority for it in this forum. He announced, to general approbation, that he would accept Yisrael Katz's proposal for a party-wide referendum in the interests of preserving party unity. The result, he declared, "will obligate every representative of the party, starting with me."

The Yesha (Hebrew acronym for Judea, Samaria, and Gaza) Council, the settlement umbrella body generously funded by the state, swung into action. The Likud voters registry was "divided up" among the settlers of the Gaza Strip. Every settler family, beefed up by youngsters from the West Bank settlements, "adopted" a cluster of five eligible voters. They would phone them, e-mail them, visit their homes, befriend their families, inundate them with material about the idyllic, pastoral life in the Gaza communities that Sharon proposed cruelly to eradicate.

Sharon's strategy of persuasion was three-pronged. First, he argued, the disengagement plan itself was sad but eminently sensible in the long run because there was *no* prospect in *any* conceivable peace arrangement of Israelis remaining in Gaza. "What have we got to look for there?" became the slangy, unofficial slogan of the disengagement. (The official slogan, proposed by Reuven Adler, was "The disengagement—good for Israel.") It was a favorite phrase of Shaul Mofaz, the popular, intifada-fighting chief of staff who now stood alongside Sharon as his defense minister and, significantly, as his outspoken backer in the disengagement venture.

Second, both Sharon and Mofaz made it brutally clear that the army would not be scurrying out of Gaza in disarray, as it had—in their view, at any rate—out of south Lebanon in May 2000. Hamas, unlike Hezbollah in Lebanon, would not be able to claim it had driven Israel out. On March 22, the air force took aim again at Sheikh Yassin, the paraplegic Hamas leader. This time, using rockets, it did not err. The sheikh in his wheelchair and nine others, among them his bodyguards, were killed in a street outside a mosque just after dawn prayers. At the Likud convention on March 30, the first wave of cheering for Sharon broke out when the chairman, Yisrael Katz, thanked him "for the decision to eliminate Sheikh Yassin."

Less than a month later the rocket-firing helicopters struck again, assassinating Yassin's successor, Abdel Aziz Rantissi, as he drove through Gaza City. The United States said it was "deeply troubled" by the sheikh's killing, but its ambassador at the UN, John Negroponte, vetoed a Security Council resolution that sought to condemn Israel for the action but was "silent," as the U.S. envoy explained, "about terrorist atrocities committed by Hamas." Between March and May, in addition to the high-profile assassinations, the army mounted penetration raids and sharpshooter ambushes deep inside the Gaza refugee camps, taking a heavy toll of armed militants.[9]

Sharon's third line of argument was the significance of his exchange of letters with President Bush. "Not since the State of Israel was created has there been such strong and broad political support as there is in the president's letter," Sharon proclaimed in the Knesset on his return from Washington. "The letter is an integral part of the disengagement plan. The president of the United States expresses his overwhelming support for the plan. He sees it as a historic step."

Significantly, Sharon's invocation of the president's commitments was predicated on the Likud voters' assent, albeit unspoken, to Israel's eventual withdrawal from most of the West Bank as well as from all of the Gaza Strip. George Bush's implicit endorsement of the large settlement blocs along the Israel–West Bank border ("new realities on the ground, including already existing major Israeli population centers") was meaningful and positive only in the context of the two-state solution, with the envisaged Palestinian state comprising all the West Bank and Gaza apart from those settlement blocs. Sharon had long been advocating the two-state scenario as the ultimate—albeit far-off, vaguely defined—solution to the Israeli-Palestinian conflict. But he had never won his party's approval for it. The pristine Likud ideology of "Greater Israel" still held the hearts of many Likudniks, even if in their heads they knew it was untenable. For the Israeli public at large, however, the message was clear—and broadly applauded.

When Sharon returned from Washington in mid-April, polling of the party members showed him comfortably ahead. But in the fortnight to the vote his lead evaporated. The euphoria in the prime minister's camp gave way to worry, then to panic. Recriminations began within the team. "We deserved to lose," Uri Shani said, looking back. "We didn't really have a campaign at all. No billboards, no meetings, no media, nothing. While the other side, quite rightly, was working flat out." Shani, the departed bureau chief, had been brought back into the inner coterie to help run the referendum. "We lost because we were perceived as high-handed and condescending, as though it were beneath the dignity of a prime minister to campaign for his policy in his own party. Party voters felt their prime minister didn't give a damn for them."[10]

The weekend before the vote, with the polls now running clearly against him, Sharon's tone grew dire. "The extreme right wing has brought down governments before, and now it's trying to bring me down," he told *Maariv*. The night before the vote, his prerecorded voice appealed directly to party members over their telephones. "This is a fateful moment in the history of our country," he warned. "I don't want to think what will happen if the disengagement plan is rejected. I don't want to think what will happen in defense, in foreign policy, in economics, on Main Street, in the stock exchange . . . The Likud must not disengage from the people."

It was desperate stuff and probably could not have reversed the groundswell now building among the Likud voters against the disengagement plan. In the event, the groundswell became a landslide. A gruesome terror attack in Gaza on polling day, May 2, sealed the prime minister's defeat. An entire family—a mother, Tali Hatuel, and her four daughters—were murdered in broad daylight as they drove out of the Katif settlement bloc in Gaza on their way to Ashkelon, just across the border, where their husband/father, David, worked as a school headmaster. Islamic Jihad and Fatah's al-Aqsa Brigades claimed joint responsibility. They said the attack was an act of revenge for the death of Sheikh Yassin and was unconnected to the referendum. Sharon said it was the Palestinian way of trying to destroy the disengagement plan. "That is why I am fighting for my plan." But even he, the inveterate optimist, knew then that he had lost.

Tali and David Hatuel had intended to spend the afternoon with their kids outside one of the Likud polling stations in Ashkelon, canvassing voters to reject the prime minister's plan. Their bullet-riddled car still bore a sticker, "A Jewish heart does not disengage." At the funeral, attended by thousands in Ashkelon that same evening, the National Religious Party leader, Effie Eitam, called on Likud voters to fulfill Tali's posthumous wish while the polling stations were still open.

More than persuading potential supporters to oppose the plan, the terror attack persuaded many simply to stay at home. The turnout barely topped 50 percent: 99,652 out of 193,190 eligible voters. The margin of Sharon's defeat among those who did vote was close to 20 percent. It was a rout.

That same night, Sharon snapped back. Neither the defeat nor the accompanying embarrassment, nor indeed his solemn promises to abide by the voters' decision, were going to sidetrack him. He convened his close aides in his office in Tel Aviv. Within minutes an official announcement went out to the political reporters: he would not resign. The Likud's attorney, Eitan Haberman, conveniently produced a legal opinion to the effect that the party's constitution gave no binding authority to the referendum. "The chairman wanted to know what the rank and file thinks. Now he knows what they think."

Sharon himself issued a statement expressing his "sadness and disappointment" over the way the vote had gone. He knew that "very many members of the Israeli public support my plan and feel the same disappointment I do." He would consult with his ministers and then decide how to proceed. Unofficially, his aides assured the press that the disengagement would go forward. That was what the country clearly wanted even if the Likud voters didn't.

Before the week was out, Sharon made his intentions clear in the most poignant manner imaginable: he reiterated them to the bereaved David Hatuel and other mourners at the shiva for the slaughtered family. "I've come to be with you in your pain," he said, sitting down heavily. "I've gone through tragedies in my life. I can understand your pain." Relatives and neighbors from Gush Katif soon began taxing him with questions about the disengagement. "The disengagement plan has got to be implemented," Sharon replied, "so that things can be better for all of us in other places."

This immediately set off a chorus of angry exclamations. "What," one of Tali's sisters shouted, "you've come here to make political speeches?!" "I didn't intend to," Sharon replied. "I was asked, so I answered." That was probably disingenuous. He doubtless anticipated that he would be asked and came prepared with his unequivocal message: the disengagement would go ahead, regardless of the Likud vote. Perhaps he was being manipulative: visiting the bereaved family in order to point up to the general public the terrible and inexorable price in blood of holding on to the Gaza settlements. Still, the shiva visit took guts. "Why don't you talk to us?" one settler demanded. "Why don't you listen to us?" "I will come and talk," Sharon replied. "I'm not afraid of anyone."

One haunting remark from Tali's father, Shlomo Malka, evoked the potent pall of religious ecstasy and fatalism that was already creeping over the nine-thousand-odd Gaza settlers, most of whom were Orthodox, and over their extended families. "Two weeks ago I spoke to Tali about all the talk of evacuating the settlements from Gaza," the stricken father told Sharon. "I said it looked hopeless. She said leaders can talk but in the end it is Almighty God alone who decides these things." Fifteen months later, on the eve of the disengagement, with tens of thousands of troops and police massed around the settlements, prominent rabbis were still assuring the settlers that Almighty God would not let it happen.

The fact that it did eventually happen, despite these exhortations cum prophecies, was due above all to the strength of public opinion in general, which never wavered in its support for Sharon's disengagement. Two disasters that now struck the IDF in Gaza on two consecutive days, taking the lives of eleven soldiers, were horrific confirmation for most Israelis that the alternative to withdrawal was endless, pointless bloodletting. On May 11, an armored personnel carrier hit a mine on the outskirts of Gaza City. Six men died. They had been part of a search-and-destroy operation against homemade-rocket workshops. The next day, on the Philadelphi road running along the Gaza-Sinai border, another APC was blown up. Five more soldiers died, and three were wounded. The nation was horrified and mortified at media footage showing other soldiers crawling along Philadelphi literally on their hands and knees, looking for body parts of their dead comrades to collect in plastic bags for burial.

The following Saturday night, a pro-peace demonstration in Rabin Square, Tel Aviv, turned into a huge outpouring of popular support for the disengagement and, however grudgingly, for Sharon. This was the square where the legendary 400,000 howled for his head twenty-two years earlier, after Sabra and Shatila. There were no 400,000 there this time. But there were 150,000 by conservative estimates, and some among them were peaceniks who had attended that earlier, unforgettable gathering. Naturally perhaps, there was still a lingering reluctance—it would dissipate over the months ahead as the attacks against him from the Right intensified—to demonstrate support *for* Sharon. But the Labor Party leader, Shimon Peres, struck the popular note, and was noisily applauded, when he declared, "This is not a demonstration of the Left; this is a demonstration of the majority."

The following week, Sharon gave the army the green light for a major armored sweep through Rafah and the Gaza-Sinai border area nearby, which was honeycombed with tunnels through which arms and explosives were getting into the Strip. Dozens of Palestinian militants were killed during the weeklong operation. But innocents died, too, among them seven Palestinian demonstrators hit by tank fire that the IDF claimed was intended only to warn them away. Many homes close to the border were deliberately demolished by bulldozers or damaged beyond habitation by the tanks and armored personnel carriers. The purpose of this Israeli escalation in southern Gaza, beyond curbing the tunnel traffic, was to hurt Hamas and Islamic Jihad and to pave the way for Palestinian Authority forces under the local strongman Mohammed Dahlan to take control of the Strip when the IDF eventually pulled out.[11]

In general, at this time, the fight against the intifada seemed at last to be delivering results. The incidence of terrorist attacks inside Israel dropped sharply through 2004. In the first six months of the year, nightly arrest operations by the army and the Shin Bet on the West Bank rounded up some two thousand Palestinian militants and suspected militants. Israel was able to forestall planned suicide attacks through its intelligence dominance—itself the result of IDF control of the territory and the information culled from those detained during Defensive Shield and thereafter, plus the fence, which slowed the infiltrations and gave time to combat them.*

---

* The fence was not impermeable, but its efficacy was incontrovertible. From January 2004 to August 2005 there were ten suicide attacks inside Israel. Of these,

Life inside Israel slowly returned to a sort of normalcy. Terror attacks were down to one every month or two. People seemed able to block out the more frequent attacks involving settler victims in the territories. The economy began to pick up. Growth in 2003 was 1.3 percent; in 2004, 4.3 percent. On the West Bank, too, Israel's intelligence dominance enabled less massive deployments of troops and firepower. Military operations were more focused instead of the large-scale lashings out that typified the earlier years of the intifada. Palestinian civilian casualties went down. The network of roadblocks that had virtually paralyzed intercity travel was thinned out. Life for the Palestinians was still restricted and hard, but the atmosphere of permanent, ubiquitous war eased.

Fortified by the army's successes and by the outpouring of popular support for his plan, Sharon made ready to charge back into the political fray. "You know me," he told a gathering of old comrades from the Alexandroni Brigade, assembled at Latrun in May to inaugurate a memorial site to their suffering and resilience in 1948. "You know that when I fight for something that's right, I persevere. That is what I intend to do with the disengagement. It is vital for Israel, and I am going to make it happen."

A week later, on May 30, he presented the cabinet with a "new plan," ostensibly in response to the Likud vote. It was no different from the old plan—the same evacuation of all of Gaza and four settlements in northern Samaria—except that it was "phased." The settlements to be abandoned were divided into four groups. The cabinet was to approve the entire plan now, then approve each phase of the evacuation separately when the time came.

"The prime minister pledged to abide by the results of the referendum," Netanyahu noted tartly at cabinet. "He didn't say he'd abide by them if he won and throw them in the trash can if he lost. What kind of democratic message is that to the public?" "Don't preach to me about loyalty to the Likud," Sharon shot back. "I created the Likud. And I restored it from nineteen seats to thirty-eight. The Likud is no less precious to me than to anyone else."

As each minister had his say, it grew clear that Sharon was poised to lose. The majority was 12 to 11. Eight of the Likud's ministers were threatening to vote with the National Union–Yisrael Beiteinu (two ministers) and the National Religious Party (two ministers). Sharon adjourned the meeting without a decision.

The days and nights that followed were a marathon of speeches,

---

three were in Jerusalem and two in Beersheba—areas where the fence had not yet been completed.

negotiations, and ceaseless media spin, most of it demeaning to Sharon. Tzipi Livni, firmly in Sharon's camp but with ambitions far bigger than her present post of minister of immigrant absorption, came up with a bridging proposal whereby the cabinet would approve the disengagement plan but would explicitly state that this did not, yet, mean it was approving the evacuation of any settlements.

Netanyahu responded by demanding that building and development work, much of it paid for by the state, continue in the Gaza settlements right up to the moment of that second cabinet decision. Sharon balked, ordered Livni to stop negotiating, and ordered his secretaries to send formal letters of dismissal to Benny Elon and Avigdor Lieberman, the ministers of the National Union–Yisrael Beiteinu. With those two out, the balance at cabinet would swing back in his favor.

On the following Sunday morning, as the cabinet met for what Sharon confidently announced would be a historic session, the High Court of Justice considered urgent applications against the two ministers' peremptory dismissal. The cabinet adjourned for three hours. Justice Edmond Levy suggested the vote be postponed for a day. Sharon ordered the state attorneys to resist with all vigor this unwarranted interference by the judiciary in the business of the executive. Justice Levy backed off and dismissed the application, though he added an obiter dictum criticizing the autocratic firings.

Netanyahu, accepting that the cabinet arithmetic was about to tilt against him—and recognizing, too, that public opinion was strongly in favor of the disengagement—softened his demands. Sharon embraced Livni's compromise, and Netanyahu and some others voted for it, too, producing a final result of 14 ministers in favor and 7 against in a now-shrunken cabinet of 21. The official communiqué stated that the cabinet had "approved the amended disengagement plan." It added that "this is not a decision to evacuate settlements . . . The cabinet will meet again to hold a separate discussion and decide whether to evacuate settlements or not, if so which settlements and at what pace to evacuate them in accordance with the circumstances then prevailing."

Within moments of gaveling the meeting closed, Sharon was out in front of the cameras and microphones riding roughshod over these nuances and declaring triumphantly that "the cabinet has accepted my plan; the disengagement has begun." In a speech some hours later he added, "Israel today has taken a fateful step for her future. The cabinet, by approving my disengagement plan, has sent a clear and unequivocal message to the Israeli nation, to our Palestinian neighbors, and to the whole world: Israel is taking its future into its own hands. The majority of the people of Israel understand the tremendous importance of today's cabinet decision."

Tommy Lapid, the Shinui leader, added, "Today may be the start of a real peace process with the Palestinians, even though the move we've decided on is unilateral."

Sharon's cavalier performance after the cabinet was ammunition for the "undemocratic behavior" charges that opponents of the disengagement now fired at him with increasing vehemence. He had betrayed his own policy platform on which he was elected prime minister, the critics accused. He had betrayed the majority vote of his own party, which he had pledged to accept. And he had fired his own ministers to influence cabinet decision making.

The ousted tourism minister, Benny Elon, bewailed "Israel's degeneration to the status of an undemocratic country. An entire coalition faction is fired in order to produce a majority, and the prime minister's not ashamed to say so openly. And if there's still no majority? I suppose he'll fire another three ministers?!"[12] "He is nothing more than a dictator," Uri Ariel of the National Union asserted in the Knesset. "That's not incitement; it's the truth. How do I know he's a dictator? Because he does the things dictators do! He tells the people he won't hold a national plebiscite but will conduct a referendum in the Likud. He says he'll accept the results of the referendum, but when they don't go his way, he bins them! He knows he doesn't have a majority in his own party, so he ignores them."[13]

Uzi Landau, leader of the Likud rebels—Sharon fired him from the cabinet in October—described the prime minister's behavior as "lawful but stinking." In a memorable speech to the Knesset in January 2005, Landau challenged

> my many honorable friends on the left to imagine, just for a moment, that Shimon Peres had won the last elections and that he was prime minister, and that a few months later he were to sigh deeply and invite himself to the Herzliya Conference and tell the people there: "Ladies and Gentlemen, from where I'm sitting now, everything looks different. Begin was right. Shamir was right. Sharon was right. From now on our policy will be: Not one inch. We must strengthen the settlements; we must annex the West Bank." I ask you, my friends, in all honesty, what would you do? What would you say? Wouldn't you rise up against him and shout and take to the streets. Wouldn't you

demand new elections, or at the very least a plebiscite . . . ? What this Sharon government has done is immoral and undemocratic.

A week later, also in the Knesset, another articulate rightist resorted to a Mafia metaphor to excoriate Sharon's assault on Israel's democracy. "He runs his party on Sicilian lines," said Yuri Shtern, now of Yisrael Beiteinu but formerly a Likud man himself. "He's taken the platform of Labor, which lost the election, and of Meretz and the Arab parties, and he says: 'This is now our doctrine, this is now our policy.' "[14] In May, Shtern switched from Sicily to Siberia. "Apart from the disengagement plan itself, which is one of the most destructive and dangerous things that ever happened to this country, and let's still hope it won't be implemented, there is . . . the antidemocratic aspect of it." Law enforcement methods against opponents of the plan were "so Soviet, so totalitarian," the Russian-immigrant MK asserted. The authorities were preparing special jails for detained protesters. "This is a real Israeli gulag . . . The Shin Bet is trying to infiltrate its agents into the ranks of the demonstrators . . . It is employing KGB methods in order to suppress dissent."*

There was a heavy irony in this outpouring of democratic indignation. The Israeli settlements in the occupied territories, and the settlers who lived in them, were—and still are—the embodiment of anti-democracy, in that they are instrumental in denying the Palestinians their political rights. The Palestinians have neither a state of their own nor the right to vote in the state that has occupied them for more than four decades. A move to end the occupation, or part of it at least, was therefore inherently pro-democratic, both for the Palestinians and for Israel, whatever its supposed procedural flaws. The gimmick of invoking purported democratic norms to justify undemocratic ends was just that, a hollow gimmick.

But beyond that fundamental hypocrisy in his critics' argument, there was in fact no violation by Sharon of the norms of parliamentary

---

* Shtern asserted that a Russian-immigrant scientist living on a settlement in Samaria had been rousted from his bed at dawn by plainclothes detectives who broke into his home without a warrant, handcuffed him, impounded his computer, and hauled him to their car "without his shoes, without his glasses, without anything. I know this family for twenty years. The wife's father taught me at university . . . This whole family were Zionist activists back in Russia. The KGB searched their home looking for Hebrew books. But they were less violent than these guys." The settler was still in police detention, Shtern added, even though there was no arrest warrant. "How can a man be detained without an arrest warrant?"

"Maybe he's an Arab," the Arab MK Ahmad Tibi chimed in.

democracy. A prime minister in a parliamentary system is beholden solely to the parliament. Not to his election platform, not to his party, not to his coalition agreement. Party allegiance, and multiparty agreements, are susceptible to change at any moment during the life of a parliament, provided the parliament approves. As long as the prime minister retains the confidence of the majority in parliament, he rules.

That is the legal basis of parliamentary life. It sometimes results in a government and a parliament falling out of step with the majority of public opinion that installed them. So long as a government retains its majority in parliament, the public is powerless to oust it. But that was never the case with Sharon. His consistent majority in the Knesset reflected an even bigger majority of the public who wanted to see the disengagement plan go through. The polls were unanimous on that throughout the period. So in terms not only of legal procedure but of political substance, Sharon was on firm democratic ground.

The following year and a half the remainder of Sharon's public career, as it turned out, was dominated by one thing only: the disengagement. For fourteen months after the cabinet vote in June 2004, public life in Israel centered on the single question, will he go ahead with it, or, in a variant, *can* he go ahead with it? Sharon himself, once recovered from the Likud referendum debacle, never doubted the answer: he would and he could.

His challenge during those fourteen months was how to translate public support into political strength while not risking another trial by ballot. His tactics were fluid as the political tides ebbed and flowed chaotically under the impact of his tectonic shift. The one constant was Shimon Peres's support: he knew he could rely on his old rival and friend, who never wavered in his own recognition of the disengagement as a historic turning point. But Peres's authority over Labor was tenuous and waning.

Sharon proclaimed in July that he was "extremely happy" with the present coalition, but if it proved impossible to carry out the disengagement with this coalition, he would have to create a different one. To his unruly Likud Knesset faction he explained: "This coalition is the best possible one from our point of view, and I'd like it to continue. But there's just one problem: the members of the coalition want to keep it going, but they don't want to vote for it in no-confidence motions in the Knesset."[1]

As long as Sharon had been under the threat of a criminal prosecution for bribery, there was no realistic prospect of Labor agreeing to join the government. But Attorney General Mazuz's decision, on June 15, 2004, to close the case against Sharon gave Peres the boost he needed. "I would not forgive myself," he told the Labor Knesset members on July 12, "if our hesitations led to the disengagement not happening."

Peres won over his own waverers but was blocked by the Likud rebels. They proposed a motion to their party convention in August stating baldly that "this convention objects to Labor joining the government" and won a majority of 843 to 612. Omri Sharon tried to save the day with a less specific counter-motion that merely approved "negotiations with any Zionist party with a view to broadening the coalition." But that, too, was defeated, by 765 to 760. Sharon, nevertheless, discreetly assured Peres that the disengagement plan and the plan to bring Labor into the government were both still firmly on course. He was not about to hand over the country, he said, to the Likud convention.[2]

Sharon was determined to avoid a violent showdown with the settlers if possible. Some supporters of disengagement positively spoiled for a fight between the settlers and the army. They believed that if the settler movement were broken, spiritually and if need be physically, subsequent withdrawal on the West Bank would be easier. Sharon believed the opposite. The smaller the trauma, he thought, the greater his victory over the settlers. In this, the settlers agreed with him. They resolved, therefore, to make the trauma of disengagement powerful, painful, and unforgettable. Their fight was thus dual-purpose: to prevent the disengagement by parliamentary and extra-parliamentary means if possible, and, if that proved impossible, then to make it hugely, indelibly traumatic.

They were to fail on both counts but to succeed on a third, which turned out no less significant: shaping the narrative after the event. From a momentous but largely nonviolent anticlimax, they conjured up a tale of tragedy and despair. To assist them in this (still-ongoing) project, they needed the Gaza Strip settlers to have been shabbily treated by the state. The state played into their hands by submerging a generous relocation and compensation effort under a welter of slow-moving bureaucracy.

The administrative plans for the disengagement got off to an indifferent start partly because the settlers in the Gaza Strip refused to have anything to do with them and partly because the government bureaucracy itself took time to move into high gear.[3] Some basic decisions were taken around the time of the cabinet vote in June 2004. The evacuation was to begin on September 2, 2005,[4] and to take two weeks. The date of the cabinet vote was fixed as the determining deadline: whoever lived in the Gaza and north Samaria settlements on that day would be eligible for compensation from the state.

But what compensation? Would it be just a generous lump sum of money, with which the settlers—there were roughly nine thousand of them—would then be expected to make new homes and lives for themselves? That, in large part, was the compensation policy that the Begin government adopted back in 1982, when Sharon, as defense minister, evacuated six thousand people from eighteen rural and urban settlements in Sinai as part of the peace with Egypt.* It was not a success. The millions in taxpayer money paid out to them made them reviled in press and public as cynical freeloaders who had gone to live in Sinai only a few years before and now were cashing in. Many squandered their new wealth on luxuries or lost it in a crash on the Tel Aviv stock market in 1983. Many needed psychological help for years after, and many others succumbed to chronic illness or complained of the early onset of old age.

The most successful evacuees from Sinai were those who resolved to stick together as communities and, with the state's help, were able to move collectively to new farming villages inside Israel. But they were the minority. Academic studies of this Israeli experience and of comparable episodes elsewhere concluded that money alone is not enough. People whose lives are dislocated in this way need help to recover. They need close support and counsel in their personal lives and their work or business. And they make the transition far better if they can keep together and reconstitute their communities in new locations.

"That was the way we wanted to go," says Yonatan Bassi, who in August 2004 was appointed the head of an ad hoc government authority called Sela[†] whose purpose would be to supervise a compensation and resettlement program. "We knew it would be better for the people and cheaper for the state."

Bassi was a man whom Sharon felt comfortable with. A kibbutznik-farmer from the Beit She'an valley and a colonel in the reserves, he had served in the 1980s as director general of the Ministry of Agriculture (under a Labor Party minister). Efficient, decisive, and discreet, he had had to deal as director general with Sycamore Ranch's various problems with milk and mutton and the like,[‡] and he managed to emerge respected all around. He was, moreover, one of that shrinking breed: a religious Zionist who favored peace and compromise and saw the settlements in the occupied territories as an albatross around Israel's neck.

It was a hard and thankless job right from the start. Bassi was boycotted and excoriated within his own national-religious milieu. Hundreds demonstrated against "Yonatan the hangman" (it rhymes better

---

* See p. 170.
† A Hebrew acronym: Assistance for the Gaza Evacuees.
‡ See p. 269.

in Hebrew). Eventually, he had to move out of his kibbutz, where he had lived for decades, to a smaller but less dictatorial one nearby.

He and his handful of staffers did not really know what the bulk of the settlers wanted, because the bulk of the settlers refused to talk to Sela. There were exceptions. The people in the four north Samaria settlements were more pragmatic. But in Gush Katif and most of the other Gaza Strip settlements the dominant spirit was of rejection, resistance, and denial. "Hayo lo tihye"—"It will not come to pass"—was the watchword, rehearsed by leading nationalist rabbis and fervently believed, in the most literal sense, by many of the settlers. The disengagement was a nightmare or an ordeal sent to try them. God would intervene to stop it somehow.

That was not so far-fetched a prognosis in the summer of 2004 as it seems in hindsight. The political battle was not yet decided, nor was the fight for the hearts and minds of the public. On July 25, in their first major demonstration against the disengagement, the settlers and their supporters deployed 130,000 people (this was the official police figure; the organizers claimed it was higher) in a human chain that extended for fifty-six miles—from Gush Katif to the Western Wall in Jerusalem. Men and women, students, schoolchildren, babies in strollers, all turned out along the highways and the streets of Jerusalem. At 6:45 as the sun went down, they all held hands, from Yitzhak and Shlomit Shamir, settlers in the original Kfar Darom, near Gaza, before 1948, to David Hatuel, the bereaved husband and father, who stood at the Wall and declared, "We have the willpower to continue to pursue our lives in all parts of the Land of Israel."[5]

It was an impressive show of strength and discipline. But beneath the atmosphere of civilized, even good-natured mass protest, there was an undercurrent of talk of eventual violence and even bloodshed if Sharon did not back down. "Why don't you talk to the settlers?" Ruby Rivlin asked Sharon privately a couple weeks later. Instead of replying, the prime minister asked a secretary to bring in a copy of a recent article from *The New York Times*. "I asked [a nineteen-year-old U.S.-born woman settler] if she would use the M-16 only against Arabs," the reporter wrote, "or against Jews who came to tear down her outpost."

> "God forbid," she said. "We wouldn't want to hurt a Jewish soldier."
> What about a Jewish prime minister?
> "Sharon is forfeiting his right to live," she said.
> I asked her if she would like to kill him.
> "It's not for me to do. If the rabbis say it, then someone will do it. He is working against God."[6]

Such talk was taken seriously. That was inevitable, given the guilt-laden memory of Rabin's murder only nine years before. Sharon's security, already tight, was tightened still more.[7]

More troubling, because more feasible, were various forms of violence that the authorities feared would be launched in order to foil the disengagement. They feared a Jewish terror attack on the Haram al-Sharif (Temple Mount) in Jerusalem, intended to trigger a massive military conflagration in Palestine and in the wider region and in that way prevent the disengagement. They feared random Jewish terror attacks on Palestinians, also designed to cause widespread unrest and thus divert troops from the disengagement.

They feared that small groups of diehards would take up arms against the evacuating forces (or against themselves: there were threats of suicide as the deadline approached). They expected mass resistance by thousands of young people, from the West Bank settlements and from Israel proper, whose religious and political leaders proclaimed openly that they intended to "invade" the Gaza Strip ahead of the army and thwart the disengagement. They feared that violent confrontations between the soldiers and these "infiltrators" would protract the evacuation process and heighten the risk of attacks on both soldiers and settlers by Palestinian militants.

In addition, the government feared large-scale mutiny* among the troops—that is, refusal on religious grounds to obey orders connected to the disengagement. Some of the nationalist rabbis unequivocally ordered the soldiers to disobey. Some were equally unequivocal in forbidding and condemning such mutiny. But many, like a good number of politicians on the right, wrapped themselves in convenient obfuscation. Hanging over the various scenarios of violence was a fog of deliberate doublespeak that condoned, legitimized, even encouraged some of the violent scenarios while purporting to disapprove of violence. As they broadcast their own mixed messages, some rightist leaders accused Sharon and the army of deliberately hyping the fear of violence as a Soviet-style provocation against the settlers. The settler leaders insisted, moreover, that their planned acts of passive resistance, even if technically illegal, were within the accepted parameters of extra-parliamentary protest. But, as with their determination that Sharon's behavior was antidemocratic, they determined arbitrarily what the accepted parameters were.

The army was especially anxious about possible widespread mutiny

---

* The Hebrew term used was *sarvanut,* literally, refusal.

in reserve battalions. The plans called for units of the border police and of the regular army to perform the actual evacuation, but fairly large reserve forces would have to be called up to take over the deployments of these regular units along the borders and in the West Bank. "We must keep the army out of this ugly contest," Sharon urged at cabinet in September. "The talk we've been hearing is actually intended to foment civil war. I regard with the utmost gravity the threats that have been made against army officers and security personnel."[8]

Benzy Lieberman, chairman of the Yesha Council and a master of the doublespeak, compiled the "Ten Commandments for the Struggle Against the Disengagement." It contained an ostensibly stern prohibition against "verbal or physical violence against the soldiers who will be sent, God forbid, to illicitly uproot the settlers." But it immediately continued, "Advancement of the plan by trampling the norms of democracy lays the responsibility on the prime minister for the nation being torn asunder, God forbid."[9]

Lieberman hewed to this zigzag line throughout the months ahead. "We shall do everything in order to cast the 'expulsion law' onto the trash heap of history," he declared. "There are still plenty of actions that can be undertaken, and we believe with unshakable confidence that this law will not be implemented." If the "day of disaster" came around nevertheless, "thousands of people opposed to the disengagement will flock to Gush Katif and be there with the inhabitants."

What would those thousands do there? Lieberman left that vague. Plainly, though, throughout this period the settlers and their supporters were not thinking in terms of protesting a policy that would ultimately, inexorably, be implemented; they fully intended to prevent its implementation. Extremists and moderates "are united by one common denominator," the *Haaretz* defense correspondent wrote in October. "They share a profound conviction that they have it in their power still to prevent the prime minister's plan from being fulfilled."

Yoel Marcus, the leading columnist, bared the heart of the problem:

In the torrent of incitement flooding the land like a hurricane, there is nothing more pernicious than the claim that Sharon does not have a mandate to carry out the disengagement from Gaza. For when you say a leader does not have a mandate, you are depicting him as an impostor who seized power by force. In which case anything he does is illegitimate, and anything his opponents do to rebel against him is permissible, including killing him. The settlers, the rabbis, the extreme Right, have together created a situation in which the critical

Knesset debate on the disengagement will be conducted in an atmosphere of putsch, of yearning for the political assassination of a leader who was elected by the majority of the people.

The settlement leaders and the extremists who have raised the banner of rebellion have no mandate for anything at all . . . Nobody empowered rabbis to give orders to politicians or to order soldiers to disobey their commanders, as though we were living under a regime of ayatollahs. But the fear campaign against Sharon won't work. He's not afraid. He's determined to win the Knesset's approval and to carry out the disengagement as planned. He does have a mandate. And how![10]

Marcus's powerful defense was perfectly timed; three days later Sharon was to seek the Knesset's approval for the disengagement plan. The government submitted to the house a package that included the cabinet decision (the "Livni compromise") on phased withdrawal, details of the withdrawal and compensation plans, and—a key point for Sharon—a copy of President Bush's letter of April 14.

The Gaza settlements were divided into four groups, and there would be a separate cabinet decision before withdrawal began from each one of them. The IDF would maintain its deployment, at least initially, along the Philadelphi road, the border zone between Gaza and Egypt. Later, Israel might withdraw from there, too (it did), and might facilitate the building of an airport and a seaport in the Gaza Strip (it did not). Israel would "aspire to" leaving all civilian buildings intact (that was subsequently reversed, and the settlers' homes were all demolished) and leaving intact, too, all water, electricity, and sewerage infrastructure. Military installations would be dismantled and removed.

The government pledged to continue building the separation fence on the West Bank in accordance with "humanitarian considerations" as determined by the high court. The proposed removal of the four settlements in northern Samaria would provide territorial contiguity for the Palestinians in that area, the government statement said, and Israel undertook to ease roadblocks and travel restrictions elsewhere in the West Bank.

As for the Gaza Strip, after the disengagement "there will no longer be any basis to contend that it is occupied territory." Nevertheless, Israel would continue "to supervise and guard" Gaza's land borders; it would exercise exclusive control over Gaza's airspace; and it would "continue to conduct military operations in Gaza's coastal waters. Israel also reserves the right to self-defense and to the use of force against threats emanating from Gaza." These provisos did in fact furnish a basis in the years ahead for contentions, by the Palestinians and by much of the international community, that Gaza remained occupied despite the withdrawal of the army and the settlers from its territory.

It was, in the opening words of Speaker Ruby Rivlin, to a packed house on October 25, "the moment of truth for the nation, and we here in the Knesset carry the responsibility, for better or worse. Each of us must answer to his conscience."

"This decision is unbearably hard for me," Sharon began his speech. "In all my years as a military commander, as a politician, as a minister, and now as prime minister I have never had to take such a hard decision."

"So why are you doing it?!" A barrage of catcalls opened up from the Right. Speaker Rivlin gaveled furiously. Sharon let the storm subside and continued:

> I know full well what this decision means for the thousands of Israelis who have been living in the Gaza region for so many years, who were sent there by previous governments, who built homes there and planted trees there and grew flowers and raised boys and girls who have known no other home. I know full well. I sent them. I was party to this project. Many of these people are my personal friends. I feel their pain, their fury, their despair.
>
> But as deeply as I understand what they are going through, I believe as deeply in the need to take this decision for disengagement, and I am determined as deeply to carry it out. I am convinced in the depths of my soul and with my entire intellect that this disengagement will strengthen Israel's hold on territory vital for its existence, will win the support and appreciation of countries near and far, will reduce enmity, will break down boycott and siege, and will advance us on the path of peace with the Palestinians and our other neighbors.

By this time, the heckling from the Right had become a constant and raucous cacophony. Whenever the row subsided a little, Sharon read on doggedly from his text, which he had spent the whole of the previous day at the ranch writing and meticulously rewriting.

It was going to be a long debate. All 120 Knesset members had registered to speak, plus two ministers, Shaul Mofaz and Natan Sharansky, who were not MKs. Rivlin gave them each five minutes. Like a soccer referee, he stopped the clock whenever the heckling drowned out the speaker. But he warned that any speaker answering a heckler did so on his own time. "I haven't got to the point yet," a Shas minister complained when the five-minute guillotine descended on him. "Sorry," Rivlin replied, "you shouldn't have argued with them." He allocated two whole days for the debate, with the vote set for the night of October 26.

"We do not want to rule forever over millions of Palestinians, whose number doubles every generation," Sharon declared. A new chorus of outrage erupted from his own party rebels and the parties to the right. "Israel aspires to be a model of democracy. It cannot live with this reality indefinitely. The disengagement plan opens the gate to a different reality."

That was the crux of it: bringing an end to the occupation. That was how the disengagement was seen on both sides, by supporters and opponents alike. Sharon's stress on demography was echoed by the two other grand old men of the house, Shimon Peres of Labor and Shinui's Tommy Lapid. "In western Palestine today there are 5.2 million Jews and 4.8 million non-Jews," Peres said.

In another five years there will be 5.8 million Jews and 6.5 million non-Jews. We will lose the majority. We will destroy Herzl's vision of a Jewish state. How can we keep a Jewish state if it doesn't have a Jewish majority? . . . A hundred years of Jewish history can be destroyed because of the hysteria of one section of the people, because of their false messianism . . . Ben-Gurion was so right when he said: Better a model democracy on part of Eretz Yisrael than the whole of Eretz Yisrael without a majority, without democracy, without the moral vocation put into practice.

Lapid said the withdrawal from Gaza was unavoidable. "Nor will it be the last withdrawal. It is unavoidable because none of the self-professed Eretz Yisrael lovers among us has an answer to the unanswerable question: In order to rule over 3.5 million Palestinians we need to forgo the democratic character of the state, or else give them the vote and forgo the Jewish and Zionist character of the state. I myself want a Jewish and Zionist state, and I do not want a state that rules over another nation against its will. What the prime minister is initiating today is the first step in the right direction."

This coalescence of statesmanlike logic at the start of the debate augured well for its outcome. Peres was nominally still leader of the opposition, while Lapid was a key partner in the dwindling coalition. Both were clearly determined not to let Sharon fall. Would their support be enough in the face of a fragmenting Likud?

A fortnight before, things had looked far less sanguine for the prime minister. At the opening of the Knesset's winter term, on October 11, he suffered a stinging defeat in the house. Fifty-three members declined to endorse his statement setting out the government's legislative program for the months ahead. Only 44 voted in favor. Most of the Likud rebels left before the vote because of the reference in his speech to the disengagement plan. Labor, which had promised him a "safety net" for the disengagement, voted solidly against him because of his—that is Netanyahu's and his—economic policy. "Swinish capitalism," Peres called the regime of drastic cuts and savings. "Six thousand millionaires and six million beggars," he said, summing up the results of Netanyahu's exertions.

Sharon seemed caught in a cleft stick. His coalition supported his economic policies but did not support his disengagement plan in sufficient numbers. The opposition enthusiastically supported the disengagement but decried his economic policy. Worse yet, the new national budget was due up before the Knesset soon.

Netanyahu, silver-tongued as ever, suggested to Sharon that they keep the disengagement funding out of the budget bill. That way, he argued, the existing coalition could vote for the budget, while an ad hoc coalition of Labor, Shinui, and half of the Likud, with sundry small parties, would pass the disengagement legislation. Sharon demurred. It would mean, in effect, he said, enshrining the split in the Likud.[11] How did Netanyahu himself propose to act in the upcoming Knesset vote on the disengagement? The finance minister was noncommittal.

Making matters even worse for the prime minister was an idiotic interview given by his chief of staff, Dov Weissglas, to *Haaretz*. The top aide, at his flip and garrulous worst, told the reporter that the disengagement "is really formaldehyde. It supplies the amount of formaldehyde required so that there should not be a negotiating process with the Palestinians."[12] Looking back years later, and attempting to sound sheepish and remorseful, Weissglas disparaged his own ignorance of chemistry. "Elliott Abrams told me I should have said deep freeze," he recalled. He had meant, he said, preserving the U.S. commitment to the road map as a living organism, not as a dead specimen.[13]

The formaldehyde line, which resonated around the world and brought ridicule and obloquy on Sharon, does read more like a trying-to-be-cute misstatement rather than an indiscreet betrayal of his boss's secret determination never to cede another inch of land. Weissglas never believed that was Sharon's intention.

"I've got things to say today to our Arab neighbors," Sharon continued in his Knesset speech. He spoke of all the wars, and the wars between the wars, the terror, and the harsh reprisal actions that Israel took over the years. Many innocent noncombatants died in these wars. And grief met with grief. I want you to know that we never intended to build our lives in this homeland on the ruins of yours . . . We were attacked and we fought for our lives, with our backs to the sea. Many died, and many lost homes and fields and orchards, and became refugees. That is the way of war, but war is not an immutable divine decree. We grieve today the sacrifice of innocent people on your side. We never chose the path of premeditated killing.

Sharon ended the speech, perhaps the most significant of his life, with a pointed quotation from Menachem Begin about the settler leaders:

"I once said in an argument with the Gush Emunim people"—I'm quoting Menachem Begin now—"that I love them today and I will go on loving them tomorrow. I said to them: You are wonderful pioneers, builders of the Land, settlers of barren tracts, in the rain and the cold, in conditions of hardship. But you've got one weakness: You have developed a certain messiah complex. You ought to remember . . . [A new barrage of heckling from the Right drowns Sharon's words.] You ought to remember that before you were born or when you were still small children, there were other days when other men endangered their lives day and night, worked and sacrificed, without an iota of any messiah complex."

This was the ultimate insult. Sharon had adopted not only the policy of the Left but also its ideology, built on a deep aversion to the religious-nationalist ethos. Citing Begin, but really taking him out of the context of his lifelong policy and beliefs, Sharon rounded on the religious nationalists who furnished the flesh and the spirit of the settlement movement that he himself had championed for so many years. It was a poignant moment, and also a deeply significant one. It exposed the brutal rupture with Gush Emunim that lay beneath the decision to disengage unilaterally from Gaza and northern Samaria.

That rupture is key to understanding the full import and lasting promise of the disengagement. Unilateralism was not merely a default option, dictated by the lack—or, more accurately, Sharon's firm perception of the lack—of a credible negotiating partner on the Palestinian side. Unilateralism was first and foremost an internal political act, within Israeli society. It was a momentous step to free Israeli policy making from the stranglehold of the settlers, with their religious and nationalist agenda that Sharon now forthrightly condemned as a "messiah complex." Yuri Shtern, the gifted young immigrant MK,[14] understood the enormity of Sharon's betrayal. "*You* are the false messiah," he shouted out. But Sharon, having delivered his bludgeon blow, read on, unmoved. "I call on the whole nation of Israel to unite at this decisive moment and to build a great dam against the internecine hatred that is driving many to a madly irrational stance."

It was a historic moment, but it is not well remembered, because it was eclipsed by the drama that was enacted in the Knesset chamber the following night, live before the eyes of the entire nation watching transfixed on prime-time television. This was a drama without words, almost like a silent film. Words were being spoken from the podium, by the final speakers in the marathon, two-day debate. But they served merely as background sound. All cameras, and all eyes, were on Sharon's face as he sat impassive, no muscle moving, in his seat at the head of the government table, in the center of the Knesset chamber. For more than an hour he sat there, listening to the debate, waiting for the vote, fobbing off various emissaries and go-betweens with messages from Netanyahu and his friends, who were threatening to vote against the disengagement. "Meet? With them? No way," he was heard to whisper loudly. "If they want to see me, they can come here."

The putsch, as Sharon's aides called it, had been brewing behind the scenes throughout the debate. "The only way to carry out this disengagement," Netanyahu warned the Likud caucus during the first day of the debate, "is to have it endorsed first in a national referendum. Let the people decide. I don't doubt the result will be favorable. But holding the referendum will defuse the land mine; even the people of Gush Katif will accept the verdict of the nation. The alternative," he asserted, "is no government and no coalition."

Later that night, in a Jerusalem hotel, Netanyahu and his ministerial co-conspirators issued an ultimatum for publication in the morning newspapers: either Sharon agreed to hold a referendum, or they would vote in the Knesset against the disengagement plan. In the morning, the National Religious Party published a similar threat: Sharon must pledge to hold a referendum, or their four MKs would secede from the coalition.* To strengthen their own and Netanyahu's hand, the NRP produced a document signed by prominent rabbis of the national-religious camp undertaking to accept the verdict of a referendum, whichever way it went.

---

* Two of the party's original six MKs had already seceded from the coalition.

At four in the afternoon, as the debate droned on in the plenary, Sharon did one of his theatrical performances in the members' dining room. Veritably encased by an extra-thick phalanx of bodyguards, he took just two questions from the throng of reporters. The NRP? He wasn't handcuffing anyone to the cabinet table, he replied. A referendum? "What *are* you talking about?" he replied, his voice heavy with sarcasm.

From the streets and parks around the Knesset precinct, the sound of mournful singing wafted in. Thousands of children from the settlements of the West Bank and Gaza had been bused in, their schools shut for the day, to hold a prayer vigil in the open air as the legislators prepared to vote. "Mercy," they sang plaintively, "have mercy, O Lord our God, on thy people Israel." Dressed in T-shirts bearing the legend "We have love in our hearts, and it will triumph," the children recited Psalms, led by the two retired chief rabbis of the state Mordechai Eliahu and Avraham Shapira. "The holy Torah says, 'To your seed I have given this land,' " Rabbi Eliahu intoned. "Not to Esau and not to Ishmael. We will not disengage from the Land of Israel. God will confound the plan, and it will not happen."

Knesset Speaker Rivlin, tears in his eyes, told the children, "We hope the decision will not be taken forcing you to leave your homes and your schools. There, in the Knesset building, fateful decisions are taken. But if, God forbid, the decree is issued against all of us, then, though wearing sackcloth and ashes, we must acquiesce, we must accept it. We will make every effort to prevent decisions that break our hearts. But if they are taken nevertheless, you children must understand that what the government and the Knesset decide is binding on all of us. On you, too, and on your parents."[15]

Contrary to parliamentary practice, the Likud rebels and the parties of the Right had refused to pair any of their members with a Shinui member sick with cancer and a pro-disengagement Likud man who had recently undergone brain surgery. At seven forty, ratcheting up the tension, the surgery patient, Eli Aflalo, was wheeled into the chamber, wearing a large wool cap on his head. Led by Sharon, members flocked around him to shake his hand and wish him well. Sharon himself now took his place and began his steely-nerved vigil.

Downstairs, Netanyahu and his friends were still fluttering about, counting and recounting the likely vote, desperately trying to cut a deal with the members of the three small Arab opposition parties. Two Arab MKs, members of Ra'am, were determined to vote in favor. The other six, representing Hadash and Balad, had all made speeches against it. But which way would they vote? Ahmad Tibi of Hadash calmly ate his hummus in the members' dining room as Labor and Meretz members clustered around him, warning that he and his colleagues, perhaps unwittingly, were about to become co-conspirators in a rightist parliamentary coup.

In the chamber, Rivlin announced the roll-call vote. "But, Mr. Speaker," a Labor member called out, "you promised you wouldn't start till all members were here. Where's Bibi?!" Rivlin replied that all 119 members were present in the building; only Yehudit Naot, the member ill with cancer, was absent. As the names were called, it became clear that two groups of members were not in the chamber: Netanyahu and his followers, still lingering in the corridor outside, and the six Arab MKs from Hadash and Balad, who sidled in as the vote ended.

The Knesset clerk, following protocol, repeated the names of the absentees. "Mohammad Barakeh."

"Later," the Arab MK replied.

Speaker Rivlin: "There is no 'later.' This is the second round. I'll register you as absent."

Clerk (repeating): "Mohammad Barakeh."

Barakeh: "Abstain."

At that moment, the tension suddenly gave way to stifled shouts of relief and rejoicing on the left—the Left now incongruously but incontrovertibly led by Arik Sharon—and muttered acknowledgments on the right that any hope of an alliance of opposites to topple Sharon had just died. One after another, the Arab members now took their places and replied "Abstain" to the clerk's query. If the Arabs abstained, Sharon was home and dry, regardless of what Netanyahu and his allies did. Sheepishly, the discomfited putschists filed in, too, and, in swallowed undertones, whispered their replies.

CLERK: Yisrael Katz.
KATZ: For.
CLERK: Limor Livnat.
LIVNAT: For.
CLERK: Danny Naveh.
NAVEH: For.
CLERK: Benjamin Netanyahu.
NETANYAHU: For.[16]

Sharon, surrounded by ecstatic members, stood and slowly made his way out. At the exit he stopped and surveyed his young aides, bright-eyed and exultant. "Learn a lesson," he said. "Never, never give way to pressure. You can change your mind. You can be persuaded. But never fold before threats." Back in his Knesset suite he immediately summoned Uzi Landau and Michael Ratzon, the Likud minister and deputy minister who had voted against the disengagement, and handed them their letters of dismissal. Identical letters had been prepared for Netanyahu and his friends. "I'm not rejoicing," he told select journalists over the phone as he rode home to the ranch. "This wasn't a happy decision. It was an important decision, but a sad one."

Netanyahu, meanwhile, compounding his discomfiture in the chamber, held a hasty press conference in the corridor outside where he categorically undertook to resign from the government within two weeks unless Sharon agreed to hold a referendum. This was also carried live on television, and he was shown perspiring freely. The contrast between the sweaty, harassed-looking Bibi and the cool and in-control Arik etched itself on the minds of the viewers.

Despite his huge victory that night, Sharon's government was still threatened and his disengagement policy still uncertain of final political success. To stay in power, he needed to pass the budget. But to stay in power, he clearly needed a more stable coalition—in other words, a coalition with Labor back inside it. The two goals seemed incompatible: Labor was opposed to the budget, and the Likud was opposed to Labor. The architect of the budget, moreover, Bibi Netanyahu, was now openly threatening to quit over the disengagement. If he did, would that not bring the Likud rebels to oppose the budget? Sharon could end up without Labor *and* without a budget. First, though, another moment of gratification: on October 27, the day after the Knesset drama, the government submitted its disengagement compensation bill to the house, and a week later it passed its first reading by a majority of 64 to 44 with 9 abstentions.

"Even those of you who oppose the disengagement shouldn't oppose this bill," Sharon reasoned at cabinet. "It's designed to make things easier for the settlers who will lose their homes and businesses." It provided up to $750,000 compensation for farming families for their homes and farms. Some MKs complained that these sums were overly generous by any realistic standards. But there was little appetite in the house, among supporters or opponents of the disengagement alike, to fight the Gaza settlers head-on over money, and the rates of compensation were not pared down.

The government did not detail the anticipated expenditure in the legislation. But the explanatory notes prepared for the MKs suggested an overall outlay of 2.5–3 billion shekels excluding the costs of the military-police operation—a very large sum, but not debilitating. Pro-disengagement advocates asserted that the sum would soon be made up by a surge in exports as Israel's general international situation picked up as a result of the disengagement.

Netanyahu, meanwhile, was wrestling with his own rash ultimatum. His co-conspirators had quickly detached themselves from the failed putsch. Netanyahu knew that if he walked out, he would walk alone. It was Yasser Arafat's dramatically deteriorating health that provided him with the pretext he needed to climb down. The Palestinian leader, still cooped up in the *muqata,* had been growing weaker since mid-October. At first, he seemed to be suffering from a stomach condition. Later, doctors diagnosed a disease of the blood. Now he lay dying in a hospital outside Paris. With Arafat gone, there might be radical changes in the region, Netanyahu explained to the prime minister on November 9, hours before his two-week deadline expired. He had therefore decided to remain in the cabinet.

Sharon's response to Arafat's terminal illness was restrained, especially given his long loathing of the man. At first, the Israeli intelligence agencies, like the doctors the PA brought in from around the Arab world, failed to understand how grave the *rais*'s condition was.* Sharon was reluctant to let him leave for treatment abroad. "Our people say he's not so ill," Sharon told Weissglas over the phone to Europe. He didn't want Arafat traveling around the world and bad-mouthing the disengagement, he said.

Weissglas, on a train between Brussels and London, went to work quickly. Soon he phoned Sharon back with a firsthand report from one of Arafat's closest advisers: Arafat was sinking. Sharon ordered the army to facilitate Arafat's transfer, by Jordanian government helicopter and then French government airplane, to a hospital in France. After his death, the Palestinians demanded that Arafat be buried on the Haram al-Sharif, the Temple Mount. Sharon refused, fearing the grave would become a rallying site for Palestinian resistance in Jerusalem. But he overrode the Shin Bet's urgings that Arafat be laid to rest in Gaza,[17] and he agreed to a grave site in the grounds of the battered *muqata* in Ramallah.

"Recent events could be a historic turning point," he said in a statement on Arafat's death. "Israel is a peace-seeking nation . . . If after the Arafat era ends a new Palestinian leadership arises, a leadership

---

* Assuming, that is, that they were not responsible for it. In late 2012, French investigators began an inquiry into claims that Arafat died of polonium poisoning.

that carries out the Palestinians' commitments under the road map, then we shall have the opportunity to coordinate various steps with them and also to resume political negotiations." But he made it clear that while this was his vague hope, his immediate and unwavering intention was to carry out the disengagement unilaterally.

But there would be no disengagement if there was no government, and there would be no government, come March 31, if there was no budget. The Likud rebels still stolidly refused to vote for the budget. Now, however, extremism of another kind gave Sharon his lucky break. In his dogged search for Knesset votes, Sharon had been flirting with the *haredim* of United Torah Judaism. He promised them 290 million shekels for their schools and yeshivas if they supported the budget bill. It was a fairly modest allurement, but for Shinui's Tommy Lapid it was a nefarious bribe that he and his party could not countenance. If Sharon went ahead, Lapid warned, Shinui would secede. It would continue backing the disengagement policy, though, from the opposition.

Sharon's response was instant. If the Shinui ministers voted against the budget, he replied, he would sack them at once and open negotiations with Labor and the *haredim* to form a new government. His own party, he reasoned, would support him this time—because not to do so would be to trigger the premature end of the Likud-led government.

That is precisely what happened. On December 1, the government submitted the budget bill to the house. Shinui voted against it, and it was duly defeated. No sooner had the voting ended than Sharon summoned the five Shinui ministers and handed each of them a letter of dismissal. His coalition now comprised just the forty Likud MKs, and almost half of them were in profound political rebellion against him. He now called for an urgent session of the Likud convention. There, as he had done unsuccessfully three months earlier, Sharon asked for the delegates' consent to coalition talks with Labor. To sweeten the pill, he made it clear that he hoped to co-opt the ultra-Orthodox United Torah Judaism, too. This time, he won a comfortable majority: 1,410 votes to 856, or 62 percent.

Still moving swiftly, Sharon sent his aides to negotiate with Labor. Every portfolio in the rejiggered cabinet was available, he announced expansively, "except the prime ministership; that's not vacant." Peres, in equally lofty tones, declared that his party was "not interested in portfolios, only in policies." The reality, of course, was less lofty. Not every portfolio was available. In fact, not one of the top ones was. Sharon, for sound political reasons, did not propose to shunt aside either

Netanyahu at Finance or Mofaz at Defense. As for the Foreign Ministry, Silvan Shalom threatened that if Sharon dumped him to make way for Peres, "there'll be no government at all." He was strong enough in the party to make that come true, or at any rate to cause Sharon serious grief.

Peres grandly waived his claim to the Foreign Ministry. Instead, he proposed, he would just have the title of vice prime minister, with no ministry of his own. Sharon received a list of the areas that his would-be vice prime minister wanted to run. It included relations with the Arab world; relations with the donor states to the Palestinian Authority; responsibility for peace negotiations with the PA; responsibility for all the diplomacy surrounding the disengagement both with the PA and with the wider world; responsibility for the secret intelligence agencies; and responsibility for the national security council. It would have left both Sharon and Shalom largely unemployed. But Sharon made light of it. Peres wasn't going to back out now, he reckoned, because of strife over turf. But Shalom was less philosophical. He insisted that Sharon defend him from the Labor leader's intended depredations. He demanded a paper from the prime minister enshrining his areas of responsibility as foreign minister.

"You don't know how to work!" Yisrael Maimon, the cabinet secretary, remembers Sharon bawling at him and Weissglas. "You just have no idea of how to work! Get a piece of paper and start writing. Write to Silvan as follows, yes. Write to him, eh, that he is responsible, eh, for relations with Togo. And, eh, with Equatorial Guinea, yes. And with all of the Scandinavian countries. Fill up three whole pages, yes, with areas that he's responsible for. Every country. Look on the map. Then he'll have lots of responsibilities. When are you two going to learn how to work?!"[18]

No less hilarious—and the whole country shared this one—was the fact, turned up by government lawyers, that the law did not allow for two vice prime ministers. Ehud Olmert had the title already, and he wasn't about to give it up for Peres. Say something happened to Sharon, God forbid. The prime ministership would fall into the Labor leader's hands for ninety days, until new elections were held. That could be disastrous for the Likud. The law would have to be amended. That would take weeks. Peres was adamant: the seven other Labor ministers would not be sworn in until he, too, could be sworn in as vice prime minister (II).

It took till the second week of January. But the delay was a blessing because it enabled Sharon to bring United Torah Judaism (UTJ) in, too, despite desperate efforts by the settlers and the Likud rebels to persuade the *haredi* party to stay out. UTJ had only five seats, paltry compared with Labor's nineteen. But it was important beyond its number. The *haredi* party's accession to the coalition meant, in effect, a political schism within Orthodoxy. Rabbi Yosef Shalom Eliashiv, the ninety-four-year-old spiritual leader of a key faction in UTJ, explained that Sharon had enough votes to ensure the disengagement anyway. He didn't depend on UTJ's five. He had Labor and Shinui and Meretz and the Arab parties lined up behind the policy, apart from the majority of his own Likud Party.

But that was naive, and there was nothing naive about the aged rabbi. He knew that UTJ's entry eased the way in for Labor, thereby salvaging the budget and giving the government a new lease on life. The national-religious rabbis' cry, moreover, that the disengagement was heresy would ring hollow now that the black-garbed, bearded MKs of the ultra-Orthodox UTJ were part of the disengagement government.

The *haredim* were still deeply resentful of the economic reforms that had drastically cut back child allowances and plunged thousands of their families into penury. They had not forgiven Sharon for keeping them out of his government in 2003 so that Netanyahu could go ahead and make those cuts. These people, moreover, many too poor to own cars, had been savagely hit by the bus bombings in Jerusalem during the years of the intifada. Many ordinary *haredim* sympathized with the Gaza settlers. Left to their own devices, many might have taken to the streets on the settlers' behalf.

But *haredim* are never left to their own devices. *Haredi* politics is tightly run by the rabbis, and the rabbis, in the main, still cleave to the old ideological-theological ambivalence toward the Zionist state. This means two general rules for rabbinical decision makers: that *haredi* parties should not be the ones to determine Israel's defense and foreign policy, but that if they nevertheless find themselves in that role, they should support a moderate, unaggressive policy that does not "stir hatred among the nations." Hence Rabbi Eliashiv's somewhat disingenuous claim that the UTJ would not have the casting votes on the disengagement. Hence, too, his decision, wittingly taken, which in effect enabled the disengagement to happen. The settlers sent delegations of their own rabbis to importune the *haredi* sage. But he had made up his mind. "The waiting period is over," Yossi Verter wrote on January 7, when Rabbi Eliashiv's decision was announced. "Nothing now stands in the way of Sharon carrying out his disengagement plan. Nothing but the madness of the extremists."[19]

• • •

The elderly rabbi's ruling meant that the showdown, when it came, pitted just one of the two wings of Jewish Orthodoxy in Israel against the serried ranks of soldiers and policemen deployed to seal off the Gaza Strip from would-be "reinforcements" for the doomed settlements. This proved significant indeed. The *haredim* had shown over the years that they were capable, when aroused, of bringing out tens of thousands, and on occasion even hundreds of thousands, onto the streets to demonstrate. Their young men could be obstreperous, and on occasion violent, when protesting for a cause sanctioned by their rabbis.

But in the mass protests that took place during the lead-up to the Gaza disengagement, the *haredim* were entirely absent. Rabbi Eliashiv's decision to join the government meant that protesting against the disengagement was not sanctioned. His ruling, moreover, spilled over to the Orthodox Sephardim who saw Shas as their political affiliation and Rabbi Ovadia Yosef as their spiritual authority. They were all absent, too, even though Shas was formally in the opposition.

As a result, the anti-disengagement demonstrations that took place during the summer of 2005 in the south of the country, while large and threatening, were essentially homogeneous in their composition. Overwhelmingly, the protesters were national-religious people. Almost all the men and boys wore the trademark knitted *kippa* skullcaps (as distinct from the *haredi* black ones). And the women, unlike *haredi* women, demonstrated alongside their menfolk.

The anti-disengagement movement's chosen color was orange, in emulation of Ukraine's pro-democracy revolution then gripping the world's attention. Orange lit up the land. Orange bunting fluttered from balconies and trees. At intersections, youngsters in orange T-shirts offered drivers orange ribbons to tie to their cars. Married young women in the national-religious community wore orange in their head scarves. Sharon's admen friends tried to launch a "counter-revolution" in blue. But the patriotic blue ribbons—Israel's flag is blue and white—though universally available, failed to catch on.

Orange's ubiquity was deceiving, though. The polls told a different story. In March 2005, Sharon's approval rating in *Haaretz*'s tracking poll was up in January. It slid slightly in April, but he was still ahead 49 to 19 against Netanyahu. More important, 68.5 percent said they supported the impending disengagement, and only 27.6 percent said they opposed it.

Asked at this time if he would go down south and take command of the troops himself if the disengagement ran into trouble, an ostensibly unworried Sharon replied breezily, "You worry too much."[20] But beneath the confident facade, he was still worried. He decided to dismiss the army chief of staff, Moshe Ya'alon, who had spoken of the forthcoming disengagement as "a tailwind for terror." It was not exactly a dismissal (though Ya'alon took it as such). Formally, the chief of staff is appointed for three years, and Ya'alon's three-year term was up in May. But the tradition was that chiefs of staff got a fourth year unless they had seriously fouled up. Minister of Defense Mofaz, Ya'alon recalled later, informed him almost offhandedly that it had been decided to do away with that tradition—starting immediately.[21]

The man chosen to replace Ya'alon was a former commander of the air force, Dan Halutz, a brilliant, soft-spoken general whom Sharon had reportedly wanted to appoint chief of staff back in 2002 but had been dissuaded. No air force commander had ever gone on to become chief of staff in the IDF's history.

The settler lobby, citing this prior preference, immediately began tarring Halutz as a longtime Sharon crony and favorite of the "ranch forum." The less conspiratorial theory, which Sharon himself seemed quietly to encourage, was that the air force chief was the natural, indeed perfect choice given the looming threat of Iran's nuclear ambitions. The overriding military priority, it was hinted, was preparing an aerial strike on Iran's nuclear facilities if all other means of neutralizing them failed.

For the moment, though, the main challenge facing Halutz and the army was the disengagement. "The State of Israel stands on the eve of a major and significant operation," Halutz declared at his swearing-in ceremony on May 31. "The decision of the government and the Knesset will be carried out with the proper sensitivity and with the requisite determination . . . No refusal to obey orders will be tolerated . . . The IDF has one chain of command, and only one: the military hierarchy, which is subordinate to the political echelon." Sharon and Mofaz looked on in manifest approval.[22]

The crucial standoff—and crucial test of the new chief of staff's mettle—came in mid-July with a huge march toward the Gaza border by anti-disengagement protesters from all over the country. Tens of thousands of West Bank settlers converged on the torrid Negev village of Kfar Maimon, where they were joined by columns of sympathizers from inside Israel proper. Adults took off work; children skipped school. Whole families marched and prepared to encamp at "the gates of Gaza." Thousands of young men and boys intended to break through police and army lines and head for Gush Katif, where they would join the local settlers and—in vast numbers, as they hoped—offer determined resistance to the forces sent to carry out the disengagement.

Sharon, Halutz, and the police commissioner, Moshe Karadi, understood that the challenge for them was to ensure there was no such mass incursion. They deployed phalanxes of soldiers and police to block the road to Gaza. They made it clear to the seething, angry mass of demonstrators that no one would be allowed through and that they would use force if need be to impose the blockade.

As dusk fell, the police herded the streams of marchers into the village itself, where, by agreement between their leaders and the police commanders, they were to spend the night. But in the morning they were surprised to find themselves effectively besieged, with the main gates of the village welded shut and thousands of police and soldiers blocking every other possible exit. There was only one way out: back home northward. Rousing rhetoric kept people's spirits up for two hot and dusty days. "Kfar Maimon is one of the great Zionist actions of our generation," Pinhas Wallerstein, a prominent settlement leader, assured his wilting cohorts. "We want Family Sharon to go to hell. Our march continues." On the third day the buses, which the police copiously supplied, began to fill up one after another and head off north.

It was the settler leaders who blinked first. Sharon and the police chiefs were fulsome in their praise of the "sagacity and responsibility" of these leaders for having prevented a violent confrontation. In fact, though, as both sides knew and neither was interested in trumpeting, the demonstrators had been deterred. Confronted by thick cordons of mounted police backed by thousands of troops, their leaders realized, perhaps for the first time, that Sharon meant business. Until then, various acts of civil disobedience—some clearly criminal, such as scattering nails on main highways and planting fake bombs in public places—had gone unpunished. Mass anti-disengagement demonstrations in Jerusalem in January and in Tel Aviv in March had left the impression that the settler leaders could marshal hundreds of thousands of supporters at will. The atmosphere in the country was of civil disobedience. The standoff at Kfar Maimon started to change that.

There was a rerun two weeks later, this time centering on the Negev townships and Sderot and Ofakim. Once again, the army and the police deployed in force. They could not close off these sprawling townships. Instead, lines of troops, standing shoulder to shoulder, stretched out across the desert, blocking any mass march on Gaza. Jeep patrols chased youngsters trying to strike out in twos and threes across the dunes and reach the Gaza Strip perimeter.

On the main road south from Ofakim, blocked by dense rows of mounted police, thousands of demonstrators sat on the asphalt listening to a rabbi rail against "the Amalekites" who, he said, lived across the border in Gaza. The settler leaders "negotiated" with the police, demanding their democratic right to proceed down the highway. Once again, the negotiations were a charade. Once again, both sides extolled the "responsibility" of the settler leaders. In fact, an army and a police force, determinedly led, had snuffed out an incipient insurrection.

In essence, that is what happened in the disengagement itself, a fortnight later. It is perhaps heartless to apply the term "anticlimax" to the heartrending scenes of eviction and destruction that played out live on television before a transfixed and sympathetic nation. But sympathy was not to be confused with support. On the eve of the disengagement in August a well-researched poll showed 57 percent of Jewish Israelis supporting it. (Virtually all Arab Israelis were presumed to support it, too.)

Some 36 percent of those questioned feared that the evacuation would result in bloodshed. But these fears were very quickly allayed as columns of black-clad police and troops moved into settlement after settlement, gently but firmly escorting the settler families to waiting vehicles and out, through the Kissufim crossing, into Israel. The police and the soldiers, both men and women, had been well trained, and counseled by psychologists to inure them to the insults, threats, and pleas directed at them by the settlers.

The policemen and soldiers went about their unpleasant business with impassive faces, closely monitored by their officers. Whoever broke down—confronted, for instance, by a young child clinging to his bed and wailing bitterly or by the rabbi of a synagogue, wrapped in his prayer shawl, holding a Torah scroll and defiantly imploring heavenly intercession—would quickly be withdrawn and replaced. The supply of replacement troops seemed inexhaustible.

In effect, it was. Some forty thousand soldiers and police were involved, in one form or another, in the disengagement operation. Resistance was simply swamped by this vast force, massed in effective concentrations, moving steadily through the twenty-one Jewish settlements in the Gaza Strip. All the prior talk of passive resistance, and indeed of active resistance, evaporated in the face of this display of the state's physical power.

Again the claim was made, in real time and later, that the Gush Emunim leaders and rabbis voluntarily prevailed on their young followers to exercise restraint, to eschew violence, to confine themselves to verbal assault, passive protest, and symbolic confrontation. In fact, they backed down in the face of vastly superior numbers. The army, deployed in concentric rings, continued to prevent would-be settler reinforcements from reaching the Strip. Had they discerned weakness or irresolution in the political echelon—Sharon and Mofaz—or among the generals, the settler leaders would doubtless have tried to exploit it and would have urged their followers to resist more vigorously.

As it was, the drama soon became melodrama. Once it was clear there would be no real violence, the focus turned to the TV cameras. Having finally given up any thought of serious physical resistance, and with even the most messianic among them despairing at last of divine intervention, the settler leaders and rabbis concentrated on enhancing and exacerbating the trauma of the eviction. The word they used was "expulsion," in Hebrew *girush,* a term redolent of Jewish suffering through the ages.* "A Jew does not expel a Jew" was another of the slogans coined by the leadership—the Yesha Council was long adept at picking bright advertising agencies—chanted at the soldiers and police by young evacuees, arms locked, clinging to the synagogue pews, prolonging the disheartening chore for their evictors.

They played to the nationwide television audience, watching live and re-watching evening roundups of the day's evictions and demolitions. Their purpose was to sear into the national memory the painful scenes of rupture and dislocation, of individual grief and family suffering. This, they hoped, would build broader, more effective resistance to further withdrawals and dismantlement of settlements on the West Bank in the future. They portrayed Gush Katif as a pastoral Garden of Eden that Sharon was brutally uprooting. The television cameras panned one last time across the leafy streets, the red-roofed homes, the long greenhouses full of flowers and vegetables, the synagogues and yeshivas, crowded with praying, weeping men and women. Thousands, probably millions of Israelis wept with them.

In eight days, it was all over. The disengagement took less time even than the military planners had hoped. Between August 15 and 22, all twenty-one settlements in the Gaza Strip were emptied of their inhabitants and given over to the wreckers, whose lumbering mechanical monsters made short shrift of the ranch-style, cinder-block homes. Only the synagogues were left standing, emptied of their Torah arks, pulpits, and pews. The only semi-serious altercation took place at Kfar Darom, where young men barricaded themselves on the roof of the synagogue and threw whitewash and various bric-a-brac onto soldiers clambering up ladders to fetch them down. In the end, helicopters lowered metal cages onto the rooftop, and the youngsters were herded

---

* *Girush Sfarad* is the Hebrew term for the expulsion of the Jews from Spain, in 1492, after centuries of flourishing cultural, civil, and commercial life there.

in and deposited in buses that took them to jail. That fracas, too, attended by much screaming and wailing, was staged with one eye on the cameras. In northern Samaria, two of the four settlements emptied out before the army arrived. The other two, reinforced by some two thousand youngsters, put up a show of resistance that was quickly and quietly defused.

The disengagement did etch a deep and lasting trauma. But it was largely confined to the settler community itself and its ideological-political hinterland—the national-religious camp. Youngsters there who had been swayed by the rabbis' confident imprecations to heaven were shattered now by God's apparent apathy. Some of those same rabbis now spoke of an ideological or theological rupture between religious Zionism and the Zionist state (which in their book was Zionist no more).

But the more striking phenomenon, in the wake of the disengagement, was how manifestly the trauma did *not* permeate the wider Israeli public, outside the national-religious camp. The tears of sympathy quickly dried. The national mood was not of sadness but of relief over how well it had all gone, tinged perhaps with embarrassment over having been rattled by the settlers' threats of civil strife. Those who hadn't been rattled now went around saying, "We told you so"—which added to the general sense of anticlimax. Within days, the story was off the front pages. Israelis who had delayed their vacations now embarked on them with gusto, making the most of the last days of school holidays.

For Sharon, the following weeks were an untrammeled splurge of *gloria mundi*. At the UN General Assembly in New York in September statesmen from dozens of countries literally vied for face time and a photo op with the Israeli leader, who, by universal consensus, had taken the Middle East a giant step forward. Bringing peace to the region would be "my calling and my primary goal for the coming years," Sharon vowed in his speech to the General Assembly. "The successful implementation of the Disengagement Plan opens up a window of opportunity for advancing toward peace, in accordance with the sequence of the Roadmap. The State of Israel is committed to the Roadmap."

The general assessment, at home and abroad, given the success of the disengagement, was that more withdrawal and dismantlement of settlements on the West Bank would follow, whether through negotiation with the Palestinians or in further unilateral steps. The original import of the Herzliya speech would be revived. Sharon himself insisted the disengagement was a one-off event, never to be repeated.

But this unequivocal assertion itself was then subjected to equivocal parsing by his aides and close advisers. They created a deliberate cloud of obfuscation around his intentions, pumping out contradictory statements on the record and off. Sharon's wink-and-nod policy, which for so long had characterized the expansion of Israel's settlement map, was now, it seemed, to be applied to its contraction.

The obfuscation was designed, at first, to preserve the option of running for prime minister again at the head of the Likud. Sharon's coterie was divided over this. Sharon himself had signaled repeatedly over the summer months that the time and effort he was spending pandering to his half-disaffected party were increasingly weighing him down. The disparity between his standing in the public and his standing in his own party grew wider and more incongruous in the wake of the successful disengagement. He was determined that things would be different in the next Knesset. Either the party would change, or else he would change parties. Speculation over a new, centrist "Sharon party" mounted from day to day.

Matters came to a head at a rowdy Likud central committee meeting on September 25–26. The issue on the agenda, ostensibly formal, was whether to bring forward the party's leadership primaries. In practice, as Sharon declared, the move was an attempt by the rebels to unseat him and restore Netanyahu to the party leadership. The Likud primaries would inevitably trigger early general elections. The present Knesset still had more than a year to run. But so determined were Sharon's party rivals to dislodge him that they were prepared to forgo that year in power. They did not feel, at the end of the day, that their party was in power. The party leader had effectively crossed the lines.

On the evening of the twenty-fifth, with Sharon on the rostrum and about to speak, the sound system mysteriously failed. Three times the prime minister climbed up, in the hope that the electricity would come on, and three times he returned to his seat amid mounting pandemonium. Eventually, he got up and, with his phalanx of security men and aides, exited the hall. The smirks on some of the faces around him fed media speculation—encouraged by the Netanyahu camp—that the electricity cut was a deliberate provocation by Sharon's side, designed to portray him as victim and his rivals as thugs.

Provocation or not, that was indeed the prevalent reaction in the public. Feeding the conspiracy theory was the fact that Sharon's aides distributed the text of his speech to journalists before he failed to deliver it. So he had the best of both worlds: the speech was published, and he did not have to read it out over the cacophony of pro-Bibi hecklers.

This unspoken speech was more a parting speech than a staying-and-fighting speech. He took his time writing it, up in his tower above his fields. As things turned out, it was his parting message not just to the Likud but to the nation.

> We need to decide if the Likud is going to position itself at the center of the national consensus or at the extremist margin of our national politics . . . It was I who founded the real Likud, under the leadership of the late Menachem Begin. I served in the coalition he created with the Democratic Movement for Change, with Moshe Dayan . . . when he signed the peace treaty with Egypt, when he took the painful decision to evacuate and dismantle all the Jewish settlements in Sinai. Responsibility and sagacity—that is the real Likud. A large, centrist, national-liberal movement, not flinching from hard decisions and painful concessions, leading responsibly, sagaciously, in the true national interest.

This was something of an ellipsis of the Likud's and his own past history, not to say a tendentious, indeed mendacious, rewrite. But its point was not to re-chronicle the past but to chart the future.

> Today we have an opportunity we've never had before . . . We need to state the truth, which everyone knows: when we reach peace negotiations, not everything will remain in our hands. We have a dream that is good and just. But there is the reality that is harsh and demanding. We cannot have a Jewish and democratic state and continue to rule over the whole of Eretz Yisrael. If we insist on fulfilling the whole dream, we could end up losing everything. Literally everything. That is where the extremist path leads . . . Our future efforts must focus on shoring up our hold on Jerusalem, completing the security fence, strengthening the large settlement blocs, the Jordan valley and security areas, the Negev, the Galilee, the Golan Heights.[23]

There was still obfuscation here. "The Jordan valley" and "security areas" were deliberately vague designations, open to Sharon's old, expansive designs on the Palestinian territory. But no one was minded to read such machinations into his text. Friend and foe alike assumed he intended a further substantial contraction of the settlement deployment during his next term. No one doubted that he would have a next term, whether at the head of the Likud or, as seemed increasingly likely, at the head of a new, centrist party whose platform, essentially, would have one plank: unilateralism. The word coming into vogue to express this future political thinking was *hitkansut,* perhaps best translated as "ingathering." The word conveys a sense of strength, of cohesion, rather than of withdrawal and shrinkage.

The committee of top civil servants set up discreetly by Weissglas after the Gaza disengagement* was instructed explicitly to study options and scenarios for a unilateral withdrawal or series of withdrawals from the West Bank.[24] "Where will Sharon go from here?" Aluf Benn asked in *Haaretz* on November 21, the day Sharon finally announced his decision to leave the Likud and found his own party. "He's sticking to the road map—that's the plan for a Palestinian state, for anyone who's forgotten. He denies there'll be another disengagement. Despite that, though, it's clear that the withdrawal from Gaza will not be the last. Instead of disengagement, Israel will evolve a program of *hitkansut,* rolling up the far-flung settlements on the West Bank and shoring up the big settlement blocs."[25]

That same day, November 21, Sharon made his move, announcing on prime-time television that he was leaving the Likud and founding a new party. An early general election had become inevitable. Labor had elected a new leader, Amir Peretz, and was preparing to secede from the government. "The Likud in its present form cannot lead the country to its national goals," Sharon explained. The new party didn't have a name yet. Sharon called it the Party of National Responsibility. Later it became Kadima, which means in Hebrew "forward."

Ehud Olmert, Tzipi Livni, Meir Sheetrit, Roni Bar-On, and other Likud moderates hailed the move and joined up enthusiastically. So did Shimon Peres, recently ousted from the Labor leadership, and other prominent Labor figures like Haim Ramon and Dalia Itzik. Mayors and other elected officials waited hopefully for a call from Sharon or Omri inviting them to join. The Sharons reached out, too, to prominent nonpoliticians in academe and the arts, seeking to broaden the new party's evolving list of Knesset candidates. Minister of Defense Shaul Mofaz hesitated. At first he announced that he was staying in the Likud and would fight Netanyahu for the leadership. But the polls eventually persuaded him to jump aboard the Kadima bandwagon.

The polls were showing the new party at around forty seats. Sharon's advisers predicted an even better result. Labor looked like winning twenty-odd. The prospect, therefore, was of a large, homogeneous, and compliant governing party with a sizable, like-minded coalition

---

* See p. 467.

partner at its side and scant need for additional, smaller allies with their exhausting quibbles and demands. It must have seemed a luxurious vista to Sharon.

He hardly had time to contemplate it. On January 4, 2006, he was felled by a massive stroke. Olmert took over automatically as acting prime minister. Later in the month, Olmert was elected unopposed as leader of Kadima, the new party. He led it to victory in the general election, which took place on March 28, and was sworn in as prime minister on May 4.

Olmert's embrace of *hitkansut* was unequivocal, both in the election campaign and in his early policy statements as prime minister. He would try to negotiate with the Palestinians under the road map, he declared, but if there was no progress, he would embark on further unilateral withdrawals on the West Bank with a view to establishing an interim borderline pending eventual peace negotiations.

The civil servants committee submitted its preliminary report in May. The committee pointed out numerous difficulties—diplomatic, military, political, economic, and legal—that the government would inevitably encounter, whichever unilateral option it chose. The committee was not tasked with recommending a particular option. But it emphasized the possibility of dismantling settlements in the outlying areas of the West Bank while leaving the army deployed in those areas, or some of them, for an interim period.

Olmert adopted none of the options. In February 2006, while still the acting prime minister, he sent ten thousand troops and police to dismantle the West Bank "illegal outpost" of Amona, near the large settlement of Ofra. A violent melee ensued in which dozens of policemen and some three hundred protesters were injured, among them three rightist Knesset members. Nine buildings that had been ordered demolished by the high court were duly flattened. But Gush Emunim and its supporters touted the battle of Amona as a victory. They had demonstrated that their spirit, thought broken by the Gaza disengagement, was not broken after all. It was being steadily restored, especially among their cadres of young people.

But no further major confrontations between government forces and settlers took place during the Olmert years (2006–2009). Nor were there any further unilateral withdrawals by Israel. In November 2007, the Bush administration launched a new peace initiative at an international conference in Annapolis, Maryland. The phases of the road map were effectively to be telescoped into a comprehensive negotiation. All the core issues were to be on the table. The declared goal was the two-state solution—a Palestinian state in the West Bank and Gaza living alongside the State of Israel. Sustained, discreet talks between Olmert and Mahmoud Abbas, the Palestinian president, during the following year came close to reaching a comprehensive agreement.[26] The talks petered out, though, after Olmert's forced resignation announcement in September 2008, under a welter of financial allegations. Kadima, now led by Tzipi Livni, again emerged the largest party from elections in February 2009. But she failed to form a government. The new rightist-religious government led by the Likud, under Benjamin Netanyahu, refused to pick up the Olmert-Abbas negotiations from where they had left off. Sporadic diplomacy by the United States over the next four years produced no progress.

Would Sharon have done better? Would he have done what he (and Olmert) intended to do, leading Israel out of (most of) the occupied West Bank, by agreement or—more likely—unilaterally? The disappointing election result in 2006 is the first piece in this intriguing, hypothetical puzzle. Kadima under Olmert managed only twenty-nine seats in the election in March.* Two months into the new government, moreover, Israel was at war. In July 2006, Olmert unleashed the air force, and then the army, to attack deep into southern Lebanon in reprisal for the ambush by Hezbollah of a military patrol along the Lebanon border fence. The north of Israel was virtually paralyzed as, day after day, Hezbollah rockets rained down from across the border.

A UN-brokered cease-fire ended this four-week Second Lebanon War without a clear-cut victory for Israel. Sharon loyalists muttered that he would never have ordered war so peremptorily, but once it had been launched, he would never have fought it so hesitantly. Olmert for his part implied privately that Sharon's reluctance to confront Hezbollah had enabled the Shiite movement's massive stockpiling of rockets and other hardware over years. There were unflattering off-the-record references within the new government to Sharon's supposed "Lebanon trauma."

Whether because of the war and its aftermath—Olmert was censured by a commission of inquiry for the way he ran it—or because he lacked the political strength and courage, Olmert failed to implement anything of his vaunted *hitkansut* policy. Amona was effectively the last word between him and the settlers. He allowed the game-changing potential of Sharon's Gaza disengagement to wither. He allowed himself and his government to be cowed by the settlers and their politi-

---

* Labor won 19 and Likud only 12; turnout was a low 63 percent.

cal supporters. He enabled the settlers to recover their confidence and their political clout. The huge domestic victory of the disengagement was frittered away. Three years later, the settlers and their cohorts were effectively back in power, an integral part of Netanyahu's new, rightist-religious government.

Yet to an important extent the dispiriting aftermath of the Gaza disengagement was Sharon's fault as much as his successor's. Sharon left the job half done not only because he was struck down before he could complete it but also because he failed to build strong and lasting foundations that would have made the unilateral disengagement from Gaza the indestructible basis of a two-state solution to the conflict. Sharon's high-handedness toward the Palestinians sowed the flaws in the disengagement that eroded its historic significance for both peoples.

Even though his basic strategic decision was that Israel must act unilaterally, there was room—and need—for close coordination on a tactical level with the Palestinian Authority. Sharon's disdain for "the Arabs" meant that he did not sufficiently apply himself to this aspect of the disengagement. There was enough coordination, mainly in the form of dire threats, to ensure that not a shot was fired by any Palestinian militant group in Gaza throughout the period of the actual disengagement. But Israel could have done much more to help ensure that the PA security forces took firm control of the Gaza Strip in the wake of the IDF's departure. In the event, Hamas and its allies were able to strengthen their deployment, in defiance of the Palestinian Authority. Hamas and Islamic Jihad militants seemed able to resume firing their Qassam rockets and mortar shells over the border almost at will.

Sharon's high-handedness and insensitivity toward the PA caused or at least contributed to Israel's failure to implement an elaborate agreement on access, trade, and communications with Gaza in the immediate follow-up to the disengagement. Condoleezza Rice, the U.S. secretary of state, spent long hours in Israel in mid-November 2005 personally negotiating the clauses. She called the deal "a major step forward" that would allow the Palestinians to "live ordinary lives" and would establish a new "pattern of cooperation" between the two sides. "For the first time since 1967, Palestinians will gain control over entry and exit from their territory," she said.[27]

The agreement provided for the implementation, after years of delay, of the "safe passage" between Gaza and the West Bank that Israel had undertaken to establish under the Oslo Accords. A detailed schedule of bus routes and timetables was worked out under Rice's urging. But it soon fell into disuse as Israel reacted to repeated rocket fire and terror attacks by shutting down or constricting access to Gaza. There was logic in this position, but it bred bitter disillusionment on the other side and played into the hands of the Palestinian opposition, Hamas.

Was it Sharon's shortsighted disdain for the Palestinian Authority that engendered his relative passivity, too, in the face of Hamas's determination to run in Palestinian parliamentary elections scheduled for January 2006? He did protest to the Americans. He demanded that Hamas be required to lay down its weapons and amend its charter calling for the elimination of the Jewish state as the preconditions for its eligibility. The Americans' "passion for democracy is so fervent," he complained, "some of them believe that the simple fact of holding elections is enough to found a democracy."[28]

Had he thrown the full weight of his post-disengagement prestige behind his argument with Washington, the outcome might have been different. As it was, Hamas emerged victorious from the election in January. A year later, after attempts at Fatah-Hamas unity rule, violent clashes broke out in Gaza between the two Palestinian movements. PA-Fatah forces were roundly defeated, and Hamas set up its own Islamic regime in the Strip. Israel in response imposed a partial siege on the Strip, preventing exports and drastically limiting imports in the vain hope of toppling the Hamas government.

Sharon's ineffective response in the face of the resumed rocket fire from Gaza continues to trouble and mystify his close aides and political supporters to the present day. "I am not prepared for this to continue!" he fumed at cabinet on September 24, slamming his fist down on the table. The cabinet had been convened on a Saturday night after a flurry of Qassam rockets rained down on the township of Sderot, close to Sycamore Ranch. "For three years I've been asking you to deploy half a battery and start shooting," he admonished the military commanders.

But the attorney general ruled—as Sharon knew he would—that artillery fire into a built-up area would be illegal under the laws of war. "Do something tonight to put a stop to it!" Sharon demanded of the defense minister. "Er . . . I think it's going to take longer than that," Shaul Mofaz replied quietly. Someone suggested a ground incursion. "We didn't leave Gaza in order to go back in," Sharon growled.[29]

He knew the rocket (and mortar) fire was threatening to discredit the disengagement in the Israeli public mind—the arena of its most telling and most significant success. But he had no simple solution. He could only rail and make vague threats. A friend and former adviser recalls talking to him on the car telephone one evening as he drove home to the ranch. "Have you reached Ashkelon?" the friend asked. "Do you see the lights of Gaza?" "Yes, I do," Sharon replied. "Why do you? Why are the lights still on in Gaza when rockets are falling on Sderot?! It was you who invented the idea of hitting their infrastructure. And it worked in the past!" "It's going to happen," Sharon replied. "You'll see, it is going to happen."[30]

But nothing happened as long as Sharon was in office. The sporadic rocket fire and limited IDF responses continued for years, until eventually the Olmert government launched a massive and controversial armored incursion into the Gaza Strip, Operation Cast Lead, in December 2008.* Persistent spinning by the settlers and by Netanyahu largely persuaded the Israeli public over the years that the disengagement had brought on the rocket fire. The fact that rockets had been fired before the disengagement, both at the Jewish settlements inside the Gaza Strip and at towns and villages in sovereign Israel, was blurred. The fact that much higher casualties, civilian and military, were sustained before the disengagement than after was glossed over. It was undeniably true, though, that larger and more deadly rockets were smuggled into Gaza—and fired from Gaza into Israel—in the years after the disengagement. Steadily, their range increased, from Ashkelon to Ashdod to Beersheba and, by 2012, to the outskirts of Tel Aviv.

The fall of Gaza into Hamas's hands seriously undermined the disengagement in the Israeli public's mind. "We can't make the same mistake in Judea and Samaria" became Netanyahu's watchword. It was catchy and seemed cogent. But it was founded on the tragic rupture of Sharon's new strategy of unilateralism before it could be consummated.

Why didn't Sharon encompass more of the West Bank in his first (and as it turned out, sadly, his only) disengagement? Why did he plump for the least ambitious of the alternative proposals presented to him? Weissglas, making the best case for his client, says the chief consideration was security. The Gaza Strip was effectively sealed off from Israel by a fence. The fence around the West Bank was still unfinished.

Unilateral disengagement from Gaza, therefore, was much more easily done. The army's role in Gaza, moreover, was almost entirely a garrison role: guarding the settlements and protecting their access routes. Unlike in the West Bank, the troops did not enter the Palestin-

---

* Some fourteen hundred Palestinians were killed, among them hundreds of civilians, and the damage to property was extensive. Thirteen Israelis died in the operation.

ian cities and refugee camps in the Gaza Strip to make arrests and generally enforce the occupation. The withdrawal, therefore, Weiss-glas argued, did not significantly weaken Israel's security control of the Palestinians, because the army was not engaged in direct control over the Palestinians of Gaza in the years before the disengagement.

> The IDF presence in Judea and Samaria, on the other hand, does not function solely as a garrison guarding the settlements. It is a constant, active, and important component in Israel's daily security. That's the difference. And that's why the process on the West Bank needed to be slower, more deliberate, maybe more coordinated with the Palestinian Authority. We obviously couldn't just get up and get out like in Gaza. So we began looking for a formula in the West Bank that would not be a replica of the disengagement from Gaza, because of the very different circumstances. We intended to complete the fence in the West Bank as quickly as possible and in that way reduce drastically the suicide-bombing threat.

A good, lawyerlike case. But not good enough. Not good enough to explain why the rockets and mortar bombs from Gaza were allowed to resume. But also, and more important, not good enough to explain Sharon's initial decision to go for a minimalist disengagement. Like Rabin at Oslo, Sharon proposed to leap the chasm between Palestinian occupation and Palestinian statehood in two bounds. Granted, he could not have evacuated all the outlying settlements, those beyond the "settlement blocs," in one sweep. But he could have enunciated a clear and unequivocal plan to do so in stages. That would have dispelled doubts about his own intentions and instilled hope in place of skepticism among the Palestinians and the wider Arab world.

Still, the Gaza disengagement, for all its flaws and limitations, was a monumental change of direction for Israel. After decades of settling in the occupied territories and thus denying the Palestinians the prospect of independence, Israel began physically divesting itself of these territories and thus making space for the Palestinians to have their state, too. Despite subsequent disappointments and disillusionment on both sides, despite well-grounded criticism of how the disengagement was done, one precedent-setting fact stands out as indisputable: settlements *can* be dismantled and settlers removed. It is politically possible for an Israeli government to do it. Indeed, it is not even that difficult to do—provided there is the will, the strength, and the leadership to do it.

Sharon spent long years building the settlements and abetting the settlers in their drive to impose the Jewish state on its Palestinian neighbors. Then, very late, he understood what this hubristic policy endangered: the very survival of Israel as a Jewish and democratic state. Despite the frustrating and heartbreaking regression in peace prospects in the years since the Gaza disengagement, the impact of his last, audacious act may yet prove irreversible. And if it does, Zionism will have been saved.

CHAPTER 18 · TO SLEEP, TOO SOON

How many children do you have?" Sharon asked his cabinet secretary, Yisrael Maimon, and his director general, Ilan Cohen. "Two," Maimon answered quietly. Sharon knew the answer, but he was in a jolly, joshing mood. "Only two?! Go home! You heard what the professor said. Why are you wasting your time in meetings?"

The meeting just ended, on the afternoon of December 18, 2005, had been with Professor Sergio DellaPergola, a prominent Jerusalem sociologist who came with a team from a think tank to discuss Jewish demography. The scholar demonstrated with graphs and charts how dramatically Israel would benefit if ordinary (that is, not *haredi*) families had three or four children instead of an average of just over two. Sharon followed his arguments closely.

DellaPergola was delighted. Earlier in the year he had made an initial presentation to the prime minister and his staff, and Sharon, though friendly and welcoming, seemed to snooze through most of it. Now the prime minister gave the professor a hearty handshake and told his aide Lior Shilat, in a voice loud enough for everyone to hear, "We must meet with these people again."

The last visitor of the day was Shimon Peres, the vice prime minister, back from a trip to Europe. Later, Peres said he thought Sharon looked a little pale. When Peres left, Marit Danon came into the room with papers for the prime minister to sign. "We were talking. I asked him to decide about some event he was invited to, and suddenly I felt his speech was strange. I knew what it was; my late father had had a stroke." She summoned Shilat to stay with Sharon while she went into the next room to phone Gilad and Sharon's doctor, Boleslav Goldman. "Bolek said, straight to hospital. But by the time I went back to his room, a matter of a minute or two, he was over it and behaving like at the end of any normal day. He said his polite good evenings to the girls in the front office and headed out to the ranch. They didn't notice anything."[1]

But as soon as the convoy of cars started driving, Sharon felt dizzy again. Gilad, over the phone, instructed them to drive to Tel Hashomer hospital near Tel Aviv, Dr. Goldman's hospital. But Goldman, also by phone, countermanded that. "He sounds confused," Goldman said. "Take him at once to the nearest hospital." The convoy turned around and sped toward the Hadassah Medical Center, on the western outskirts of Jerusalem.

When he was admitted, Sharon was still groggy. He couldn't count his fingers or read his watch.[2] But he quickly improved. The CT and MRI examinations showed a brief and minor stroke, a transient ischemic attack in medical language. He seemed to have survived unscathed. Still, for an overweight seventy-seven-year-old, with the burden of a country on his shoulders, a stroke, even a minor one, was no joke.

Nevertheless, he and his team of aides did all they could to make light of it. At 11:15 p.m., barely three hours after his admission—and an hour or so before the newspaper deadlines—Sharon made a series of phone calls from his hospital bed to six key political reporters, three from the print press and three from the television channels. With all of them he slipped in the pun line "We're going forward." The word "forward" in Hebrew is *kadima,* the name of his new party. He seemed to sound fine and said he felt fine, and they took him at his word.

On December 19, the day after his admission, Professor Tamir Ben-Hur, the head of neurology at Hadassah, told reporters that the stroke had passed without leaving any permanent damage. The professor denied, moreover, that Sharon had been confused on arrival. "There have been all sorts of speculations. Sharon did not lose consciousness, he was not half conscious, he did not suffer from any distortion or paralysis. And he was not confused," though the stroke had affected his speech. He would be discharged the next day, Ben-Hur announced. Hadassah wanted him to stay in his Jerusalem residence, within easy reach of the hospital, rather than returning to the ranch. "We would like him to rest. That's why we're keeping him in another night, because we know he won't be allowed to rest properly once he's discharged."

The professor's statement was made in close coordination with Sharon's aides, who themselves were working under the tight supervision of Reuven Adler, the advertising and public-relations tycoon and the prime minister's intimate friend. Guided by Adler, the aides announced that Sharon's discharge from the hospital, on the morning of December 21, would be open to coverage by the media. "He looks absolutely fine," one aide said. "We want everyone to see him." Meanwhile, they reported, the prime minister was conducting the nation's business from his hospital bed.

When Sharon appeared the next morning before the cameras, flanked by the hospital director and the doctors who had attended him, his face looked waxen, and his neck seemed suddenly shrunken so that it no longer filled out his shirt collar. But he walked unaided and smiled at everyone, and his voice sounded strong. "I would like to thank the hospital staff for their dedicated care. A hospital is not an enjoyable place, but I spent two good days with you. I was moved to see Israelis' great concern for my health, and I thank them with all my heart. Now I must hurry to get back to work and move forward." The *kadima* pun again. It sounded as worn and faux jovial as he looked.

Adler's strategy was double-pronged: to project, as best he could, a business-as-usual aura around the prime minister and to persuade voters that Kadima was more than a one-man band. This latter was a tall order, given that the new party's campaign until that point had been focused on Sharon, on his past successes and the promise he held out for the future. Ehud Olmert, Meir Sheetrit, and other ministers took to the airwaves to assure the public that while everyone was relieved that Sharon was quickly bouncing back, Kadima had a strong and seasoned batting order backing him up.

Of world leaders, Hosni Mubarak was the first to phone in, the Prime Minister's Bureau reported. Mahmoud Abbas followed soon after, and Elliott Abrams on behalf of Bush and Rice. After Sharon left the hospital, Bush called him at his home. "Watch what you eat, start physical training, and work fewer hours," the president said. "I worry about you, my friend."

Despite Professor Ben-Hur's optimism and the breezy hype of the Prime Minister's Bureau, the press was restless. Other medical experts, not involved in Sharon's case, sounded more cautious than Ben-Hur when asked to spell out possible complications of even a mild stroke for a man of Sharon's age and girth. The chances of a recurrence seemed higher than the Hadassah team appeared to admit. There was a nagging sense of guilt, moreover, among journalists. Why had a prime minister deep into his seventies been allowed to rule for five years, and now run for reelection, without providing the public with any serious accounting of his state of health? In other countries that would be unacceptable. Many had laws requiring full disclosure by senior officeholders. The most Sharon ever offered were bragging brush-offs about his family's longevity genes and sarcastic assurances that his bill of health was sounder than those of his political rivals. But was it?

Now, under the pressure of the sudden, dramatic story, which should have been anticipated but wasn't, the media swung to the other extreme. Whole hours of airtime and pages of print were given over to analyzing the little that was known, or surmised, about Sharon's state of health. His war wounds, his bad eye,* the stones he had had in his urinary tract, and above all his obesity were meticulously picked over by experts, hacks, and quacks. At the same time, the media turned all their guns on the Prime Minister's Bureau and his doctors, insisting on the public's right to know the facts.

Acceding, ostensibly at least, to this demand, Dr. Goldman and his colleague at Tel Hashomer hospital and fellow friend of Sharon's, Dr. Shlomo Segev, together with members of the Hadassah team, called a press conference on December 26 to deliver what was billed as Sharon's "complete medical file" and a "medical summary" of his recent illness. The day before, his first day back at work, Sharon turned in a vintage performance chairing the weekly cabinet meeting. He opened the proceedings by sending Christmas greetings to Israel's Christian citizens and Hanukkah blessings for the upcoming Jewish festival, a key custom of which is the eating of oily, jam-filled doughnuts and even oilier potato pancakes. "I hope you will all eat doughnuts and pancakes," he exhorted the cabinet members and the wider public. "Eating them is absolutely permissible. But I strongly advise you not to overdo it." The ministers roared.[3]

The next day, the doctors informed the country that Sharon had a hole in his heart from birth that had probably caused the stroke or blood clot to the brain. The signs of the stroke, moreover, though minor, had not fully worn off until the day after his admission. It was a "stroke," therefore, or cerebral vascular attack (CVA), rather than a transient ischemic attack, because it was discernible in examinations for more than twenty-four hours before finally vanishing. Still, it did vanish, and the doctors were optimistic that it would not recur. Sharon

---

* Sharon's vision was impaired in one eye after he suffered a detached retina during an airplane trip while serving as leader of the opposition. Omri confirmed this in conversations for this book. He confirmed, too, that the Sharon team was able deftly to head off public discourse around this matter. The public, in fact, was largely unaware of the prime minister's reduced-sight problem, although vision professionals, watching closely how Sharon held his head, did discern his virtual non-use of one eye.

didn't have high blood pressure or high sugar levels in the blood, and he did not smoke—all factors that increase the risk of a recurrence.

Sharon would undergo an angioplasty procedure to close the hole in his heart and thereby further reduce the chance of clots in the future.* Many people had such holes, and the procedure was fairly common, though not so commonly undertaken for elderly patients. It was a short procedure; it would be carried out under sedation rather than general anesthetic. Sharon would undergo it in a couple of weeks, and meanwhile he was receiving the blood-thinning drug Clexane, administered by injection twice a day.† These would be stopped before the angioplasty procedure, and if that went well, they wouldn't be resumed.

Other than that, the doctors said, Sharon took pills for gout, which he had contracted twenty years before in his left big toe, and suffered various aches and pains from his 1948 war wounds. Dr. Segev said he weighed 260 pounds before his recent hospitalization, and Dr. Goldman said he had lost six and a half pounds in the past week. "He is significantly overweight, and I'd be happy if he brought it down," Goldman added. "I've been talking to him about it for the past thirty years, and I'll keep talking to him for the next thirty years."

The doctors insisted, at that time and subsequently, that neither Sharon nor his staff had told them what to say and what not to say to the public. They did not explain, though, why political correspondents had been invited to the press conference rather than medical correspondents, who might have asked them informed and pertinent questions. In the event, a surge of such questions flooded the media as the medical correspondents, aided by outside medical experts, tried to analyze what had been disclosed. *Haaretz*'s veteran medical correspondent, Ran Reznick, cast doubt on the purported disclosure of Sharon's weight offered at the press conference. An unnamed "senior doctor" whom he had consulted noted that first-year medical students were taught to estimate patients' weight by looking at them. In this doctor's estimation Sharon weighed between 285 and 310 pounds.[4]

For Reznick, this was the tip of the iceberg of suspicious secrecy, if not outright deceit. He had felt from the outset that the doctors were cooperating with Sharon's aides and associates to deliberately

---

* The term "angioplasty," which usually refers to catheter procedures for unblocking heart valves and arteries, is also loosely used for this form of procedure, a patent foramen ovale (PFO) closure.

† Manufactured by Sanofi-Aventis; marketed in the United States under the name Lovenox.

play down the seriousness of the medical setback that had befallen him just when a truly historic election victory was within his grasp. (They angrily and bitterly deny this to the present day.) On December 20, Reznick cited unnamed outside doctors who criticized the original, upbeat press briefing at Hadassah as premature. Damage assessment could not seriously begin until seventy-two hours had elapsed after a stroke, one expert said.[5]

Whatever the image the staff tried to project to the outside world, behind the thick glass doors of the "aquarium," as the Prime Minister's Bureau is known, there was a certain atmosphere of understated trepidation. "He wasn't quite the same," Marit Danon recalls. He was working less: following doctors' orders, the staff pruned his schedule, paring down the workload and carving out time for him to rest. But that wasn't it. "He kept saying to me, 'You know, Marit, it happened to me at the wrong time.' I said, 'Prime Minister, we can't pick our times. The main thing is you're back on your feet, back at your job.' But he seemed withdrawn throughout those two weeks, kind of pensive and a little sad, really."

Others, too, found him downcast and irritable during this waiting period. People who had seen him close-up in battle, or in political battles, supremely cool and controlled when all around him floundered were frankly surprised at his apparent nerviness over what was being billed as a relatively common medical procedure. Uri Shani remembers calling Sharon on Wednesday, January 4, the day before the scheduled angioplasty. "He sounded scared. Unlike our usual, brief conversations, this one went on for a long time. I tried to sound cheerful. 'If anything goes wrong, Omri and I will come around to look after you,' I said. But he was really worried."[6]

Part, at least, of Sharon's bad humor that day may have been attributable to a news item broadcast on Channel 10 TV News the night before. The police, according to this report, now suspected that Martin Schlaff, the Austrian millionaire, and his brother, James, had funneled $3 million to the Sharon family in the wake of the original election financing shortfall that gave rise to the Cyril Kern affair. Part of the money, they believed, had been used to pay back the illegal campaign contributions, and the rest had remained in the Sharons' hands.

This latest twist in the still-grinding investigation came on top of the knowledge that Omri, who had taken the rap for the election finance offenses, would in all likelihood serve time. Three weeks earlier, Omri had signed a plea bargain with the state prosecution. The punishment was to be determined by the judge, but the prosecutors were demanding a jail term and would not make do with a suspended sentence or a period of community service. Just a week before, Omri had resigned from the Knesset in preparation for his sentencing.*

"In the afternoon," Marit Danon recalled,

> Arik called in Ehud Olmert, and in the presence of Yisrael Maimon, the cabinet secretary, he formally transferred his authority "for the three hours or so that I'll be under sedation." It was a bit embarrassing for everyone, and I suppose to relieve the embarrassment, Olmert joshed, "Tell me, Prime Minister, during these three hours can I fire all your people?" Sharon replied, "You can fire the lot of them, but not Marit. Don't touch Marit." Later, after it happened, Olmert phoned me at the hospital. "Marit, you remember what he said. As far as I'm concerned, what he said is like a will."

It happened at 8:30 that night, at the ranch. When the second cerebral vascular attack struck, Sharon was twenty-five minutes from the nearest hospital at Beersheba, a full fifty-five minutes by speeding ambulance from Hadassah in Jerusalem. But from the moment he felt ill till the ambulance began its journey, another precious hour and a half elapsed. "If he had been close to the hospital, we could have saved him," Professor Chaim Lotan, the Hadassah head of cardiology, said four years later. "The whole story of him having been at the ranch, and without a doctor alongside him—it's all a very sorry business."[7]

But that merely begs the question: Why didn't the Hadassah doctors insist that their patient stay close to the hospital until his angioplasty? Why didn't they insist on attaching a qualified doctor 24/7 to

---

* Writing in *Haaretz* two days later, Yossi Sarid, chairman of Meretz and leader of the opposition during Sharon's second term, described his monthly meetings, required by law, with the prime minister:

> Now it is permissible to reveal what we really talked about in those regular security briefings. You're going to be surprised: The first ten minutes were devoted to the security briefing; then we went over to enjoyably pulverizing various politicians from various parties—both his and mine—and then we swapped gossip about our families. He talked about his sons and I about my sons and my daughter, and we would cluck and coo together over our beloved grandchildren. He loved talking about them. His face would light up. He was the ultimate family man. I am convinced that the fates of Omri and Gilad in the labyrinth of their various investigations affected his health ("Eulogy for the Prime Minister, Not for Sharon," *Haaretz*, January 6, 2006).

his immediate personal staff? Why didn't they forbid him to go to the ranch, at least on the night before the angioplasty? And his sons? And his aides? And his friend Reuven Adler? Why weren't they proffering the advice that plain common sense dictated?

A former close aide still fumes when he thinks about the days and nights between the two CVAs. "Among all the people around him, wasn't there a single one who could have stood up and shouted, 'What's going on here?! Have you all gone mad?! He mustn't be discharged from the hospital!' Instead, he was discharged after a day and a half. The doctors told him, stay close to Hadassah. But on the Friday [December 30] he told the security detail, 'Yallah! To the ranch!' "[8] Marit Danon is more indulgent. "Look," she says gently, "he's got the security people with him all the time. He's an elderly man. I think myself that in times like that a person needs the embrace of his loved ones."

Professor Lotan of Hadassah explained that the wait was at the prime minister's insistence. "We wanted to do the procedure as quickly as possible," he says. "But Hanukkah was at hand, and in accordance with the prime minister's own decision and desire, the procedure was postponed for two and a half weeks. And for that period it was decided to give him Clexane, the blood thinner. When he left here [Hadassah], we were sure he'd stay in Jerusalem. But he wanted to light Hanukkah candles with his grandchildren."*

After the little handover ceremony at the office in Jerusalem, Sharon had left for the ranch.† At 5:00 p.m., the Shin Bet paramedic administered what was to be the last Clexane injection. Sharon watched television in his room and snoozed a little. After 8:00, he asked to be put through to Weissglas, then to Adler, then to his military aide, General Gadi Shamni. He asked Shamni to put him through to the chief of staff, Dan Halutz. His last call was to Maimon, the cabinet secretary. The duty secretary making the calls thought she sensed something strange in Sharon's voice. "I'm putting you through," she said to Maimon, "but listen to him. He doesn't sound right to me." Maimon felt the same. He called Sharon's daughter-in-law, Inbal. "Yes," she said, "we've seen it."[9]

At around 9:00 she called in the paramedic, who took his blood pressure and found it far too high. His speech seemed slightly slurred, and he said he felt a weakness in his left side. The paramedic, fol-

---

* The eight-day festival started that year on December 26 and ended on January 2.
† Hanukkah had in fact ended by then. Sharon had spent three of the eight nights at the ranch: Friday night, December 30–Sunday night, January 1.

lowing standing orders, wanted to have Sharon taken immediately to the nearest hospital, Soroka Medical Center in Beersheba. He phoned his superior, a Shin Bet doctor. Inbal and Gilad meanwhile phoned Dr. Segev at his home in Tel Aviv, who said he would set out for the ranch immediately. Gilad said he didn't want his father to be taken to Soroka. The Shin Bet doctor instructed the paramedic to do what Dr. Segev said.*

Sharon went to the bathroom and collapsed. The paramedic decided not to wait any longer and asked the Shin Bet security team to evacuate the prime minister as quickly as possible. The bodyguards came running in with a stretcher, while the ambulance† backed up toward the front door. Now, though, incredibly, they discovered that the stretcher was too small to carry Sharon. This delay took another fifteen or twenty minutes. Eventually, they got him into the ambulance. Just as the doors were closing, Segev drove up. He got into the ambulance with Sharon, the paramedic, Gilad, and Inbal, and it drove off to Jerusalem. The time was 9:53 p.m.

Ten minutes into the drive, one of the Shin Bet detail suggested they transfer to a helicopter to cut the time to Hadassah. But Segev said the jogging around might be harmful. He knew now that Sharon was having another, more serious stroke. His left side was paralyzed. But he was still conscious and responsive, and Segev said nothing that would cause him more anxiety. When Maimon phoned to ask whether everything was all right or whether he should effect the transfer of authority from Sharon to Olmert immediately, Segev replied, "Everything's all right. No need to do anything special." Maimon duly informed Attorney General Mazuz and Olmert that the prime minister was functioning.

Ten minutes out of Jerusalem, Sharon began vomiting. By the time they reached the hospital, his eyes were closed, and he had ceased communicating with those around him. Maimon, waiting at the hospital as Sharon was wheeled in behind hastily erected screens, now asked Segev for a fuller account. Within minutes, Maimon phoned back to Olmert and Mazuz and told them Olmert must step in as acting prime minister at once.[10]

Half an hour after Sharon's admission—by this time television teams, local and foreign, were setting up in the hospital precincts while police and security men swarmed around belatedly "sterilizing" the area—Hadassah's director, Shlomo Mor-Yosef, announced

---

* Segev denies that he told the paramedic to wait till he arrived.
† Part of the prime minister's motor convoy.

that the prime minister had suffered "a significant cerebral episode." He was now in a drug-induced coma and on a ventilator. Maimon announced that authority had been transferred to Olmert. Ten minutes later, Professor Mor-Yosef came out again to say that the prime minister had undergone a scan that showed bleeding in the brain and was being taken to the operating room. The deputy director of Hadassah, Dr. Shmuel Shapira, delivered the next update. Sharon was suffering from massive bleeding in the brain, he said, "and everyone knows what that means." This time, it seemed, neither the doctors nor the aides were gilding the lily. The nation's two chief rabbis called on the public to pray and to recite Psalms—the ancient Jewish recourse in times of grave crisis.

Hadassah's two top neurosurgeons, Felix Umansky and José Cohen, both immigrants from Argentina, began an operation on Sharon's head that was to go on through the night and not end till 9:30 on the morning of Thursday, January 5. The purpose was to stop the bleeding and to drain the blood that had gathered and congealed. At 4:45 a.m., a CT scan showed that the main hemorrhage had been stopped but there was still bleeding from other, lesser sources. The operation resumed. In the morning a bulletin described his condition as "serious but stable." At midday Mor-Yosef said Sharon would stay ventilated and deeply sedated for seventy-two hours. Only then, after he was gradually taken off the sedation, would the doctors be able to assess his true condition.

The subtext was painfully clear. In not-for-attribution briefings to the reporters, the doctors spelled it out: The damage to the brain was extensive and very probably irreversible. Sharon's career was over. The only question was whether his life would continue, and if so, at what level of mental and physical capacity.

The next day, Friday, January 6, a CT scan showed new bleeding, and Sharon underwent yet another operation, this one five hours long, by Umansky and Cohen. Mor-Yosef announced that while the right side of the brain was damaged, the left side was intact. Cohen, however, in a Friday night television interview, firmly discounted any unwarranted optimism. "To say that after such a serious trauma there will not be any cognitive problems is just not to recognize reality," he explained.

The following week, the doctors began reducing the drugs that kept Sharon sedated. Day by day the dose dropped, but Sharon did not awaken. Mor-Yosef reported that Sharon had moved his right hand, that he had responded to pain stimulus. Again he seemed to be holding out hope, without real grounds. On January 16, heartbreakingly,

Gilad called the doctors to his father's room to see for themselves that Sharon responded when he heard a recording of his grandchildren's voices and laughter. He had blinked and opened his eyes, Gilad insisted. He had even wept. But by the time the doctors came, Sharon's eyes were shut again. "This was the impression of family members from movements of the patient's eyelids," the hospital explained. "The medical significance of these movements is unclear."

Outside experts were less equivocal. "The fact that Sharon opened his eyes has no clinical significance," said Professor Martin Rabey, head of neurology at Assaf Harofeh Medical Center near Tel Aviv. He and other neurologists explained that patients in vegetative condition were sometimes capable of opening their eyes and even responding to certain stimuli, such as the sound of their own names. Some were even able to laugh or cry. "For some reason," said Rabey sourly, "they are not explaining this, and, unfortunately, they are allowing people to get their hopes up."

Rabey's remark reflected the veritable firestorm of criticism that had been raging against Hadassah within the medical profession since Sharon's second CVA. "VIP syndrome" had run riot, in the view of the critics. On the one hand, Sharon's chances of recovering from the first, minor stroke seemed to have been prejudiced by overtreatment: many experts both in Israel and abroad believed that the angioplasty posed an unnecessary risk. For a non-VIP aged seventy-seven, who had lived his whole life with the heart defect, it would probably not have been prescribed. On the other hand, a non-VIP would not have been allowed to postpone the angioplasty for a fortnight, would not have been allowed to return to work just days after the minor stroke but would have been ordered to rest, and would not have been allowed to spend his nights out of range of the hospital. In Sharon's case—thus the critics—all these wrong decisions served one single and medically illegitimate purpose: to play down, in this preelection period, the gravity of his condition and project him to the electorate as working and functioning normally.

Haaretz stoked the controversy by revealing on January 10 that Sharon had been suffering from cerebral amyloid angiopathy (CAA), a weakness of the blood vessels in his brain that made the danger of a hemorrhage even greater. This significant information had been withheld from the public at the press conference on December 26, the paper wrote. Was that because CAA, fairly common among elderly people, was a condition associated with Alzheimer's disease—the last thing the Sharon camp needed the voters to learn about before the election?

Reznick of *Haaretz* reported that a senior doctor at Hadassah—

unnamed—termed the decision to administer Clexane despite the
CAA "a gross mistake." Other doctors agreed. "If Sharon's doctors
knew he suffered from CAA, they should not have given him blood
thinners," wrote Professor Amos Korchin, head of neurology at Tel
Aviv University. Hadassah itself, increasingly beleaguered, insisted it
would not fight back against its critics while the fight was still ongoing
to save Sharon. Two months later, Hadassah's director, Mor-Yosef,
conceded that the press conference on December 26 "was not
well-advised . . . We said what we believed needed to be said. There
was no manipulation, though, certainly not deliberate."

Sharon's condition took a sudden turn for the worse on February 11. His vital signs began to waver, and doctors noticed a telltale swelling of his abdomen. He was rushed into surgery, and some
twenty inches of gangrenous intestine were removed. Again his life
was in danger, but again he pulled through and resumed his vegetative existence. After three months, he was moved from Hadassah to
a rehabilitation center at Tel Hashomer hospital near Tel Aviv. There,
still protected around the clock by bodyguards, he remained. Every
day, save when Omri was in prison, one or the other or both of his
sons spent time with him.

"Would Sharon want the treatment he's getting?" Professor Korchin
asked in an article in *Haaretz* soon after the second stroke. Another
neurologist, unnamed, asserted unequivocally that the second brain
operation, on January 6, was unhelpful and superfluous. "The first
operation was carried out to stanch a massive hemorrhage. Two of
the top neurosurgeons did everything they could. In my opinion, there
was no point or purpose opening his skull a second time."

Other doctors questioned whether even the first operation had a
realistic chance of saving the brain. Another example, then, of the
"VIP syndrome" that dictated every facet of Sharon's case? The sur-
geons were summoned to await his arrival. He was on the operating table within minutes of his admission. Says one seasoned medical
observer: "If Buzaglo [the Israeli version of Everyman] had arrived
at Hadassah in the condition in which Sharon arrived, he would not
have survived long enough to undergo the first operation. By the time
the hospital had gotten itself ready to perform it, the patient would
have died." Another senior physician at Hadassah proposes "Israel
syndrome" rather than "VIP syndrome" to explain Sharon's treatment
after the second stroke. Buzaglo, too, he insists, would have been operated on at Hadassah if his family, having been made aware of the
risks and likelihood of permanent cognitive damage, had demanded

it. Sharon's identity was not a factor in the medical decision making, this physician asserts.

In most other countries, he says, that would not be the case. Patients in Sharon's condition would not be sent to surgery. Certainly their families' wishes as regards the possibility of surgery would not be canvassed by the hospital staff and would not influence the decision making. Israeli society and Israeli medicine are different in this respect, for better or for worse.

Perhaps Sharon and his family would ultimately have been better off had the stricken prime minister not been treated. That question remained both hypothetical and irrelevant, as did the questions that surfaced periodically over the years in Israel and abroad as to why he was being "kept alive." Israeli law and Jewish ethics provided no alternative once his life had been saved.

"The moment a patient's pulse stops, you focus solely on saving him," Professor Lotan reflected four years after Sharon's CVA.

In 99 percent of such cases, resuscitation efforts fail, and the patient either dies or else survives with such massive brain damage that you say to yourself, why did I do it? People lie unconscious for fifteen years, and meanwhile their families are ruined. The wife can't remarry. The financial burden is overwhelming. The children's lives are destroyed. And you say to yourself: At the end of the day I did more harm than good to the patient and his family. But it's not our task as doctors to take such decisions . . . As a doctor, I am obligated to save lives.

If I could turn the clock back, what would I do? Well, we're all wise men after the event. But if I could, I would schedule the procedure for sooner and keep him in Jerusalem, under twenty-four-hour observation, until then . . . Of course I have failures in my work. But this was the most traumatic episode for me. Especially because Sharon was at the most flourishing moment in his career, a moment of hope for all of us.[11]

ACKNOWLEDGMENTS

Three people have given me their constant, unflagging support during my years of work on this book. Toby Eady, agent and friend, was critically present at the conception, when Sonny Mehta, the chairman and editor in chief of Knopf, contemplated an informed, clear-eyed look at the life of Ariel Sharon. And he has been present throughout the laborious gestation, always concerned, always cheering, always inspiring confidence.

Jackie Landau has been more than a loving, comforting, sustaining wife through this period of our lives. She has been an active collaborator on the project from the outset, a judicious editor, a stern but constructive critic, and throughout a devoted partner.

Shira Philosof was efficient and discerning as my research assistant. She was actively involved in every aspect of the work. As we progressed, slowly and—thanks to her—methodically, she became my counselor, confidante, and friend.

The unfinished product needed two brilliant editors to whip it into shape. Juliette Mitchell lopped it down to reasonable size with a briskness that belied deep and subtle sensitivity. Dan Frank, at Knopf, applied his deservedly famous skill and authority to the prose, to the arguments, and to the structure. With a light, empathetic, but rigorous touch, he elevated my efforts to an altogether higher plane of cogency and readability.

My dear friend Jerrold Kessel read the manuscript in an early and prolix form. He was dying, and he wanted to review ideas that we had often discussed together. His advice, as always, was trenchant and caring. I miss him every day. The book is dedicated to his memory.

I discussed some of the ideas at an early stage, too, with a much-admired colleague who was taken from us tragically: Peter David of *The Economist*. In his understated but incisive way, he offered astute and erudite insights.

I am hugely beholden to my colleague from *Haaretz* Yossi Verter, the foremost political commentator in Israel, as much for his forbearance and his unfailing humor as for his vast fund of knowledge and understanding.

Finally, I readily and gratefully acknowledge my debt to my friends Orith Shochat, Motti Friedman, Chemi Shalev, Charlotte Halle, Peter Hirschberg, and Jonathan Cummings for their patience, their wisdom, and their encouragement throughout this endeavor.

INTERVIEWS

Many people kindly agreed to be interviewed for this book. I have added to their names a brief, noncomprehensive, identifying note. Not everything they said was on the record. Several other people spoke entirely off the record. I am very grateful to all of them for their time and their help.

Aharon Abramowitz, director general, Ministry of Justice, Ministry of Foreign Affairs
Reuven Adler, advertising executive, friend and adviser to Sharon
Ofir Akunis, Knesset member
Gideon Altschuler, IDF colonel
Moshe Arens, ambassador to the United States, defense minister
Uri Avneri, journalist, Knesset member
Danny Ayalon, ambassador to the United States, deputy foreign minister
Clinton Bailey, writer and researcher on the Bedouin
Ehud Barak, IDF chief of staff, prime minister, defense minister
Mitchell Barak, pollster
Yonatan Bassi, kibbutznik, head of Gaza Settlers' Evacuation Authority
Yossi Beilin, justice minister, negotiator
Avi Benayahu, IDF spokesman
Binyamin Ben-Eliezer, defense minister
Meir Ben-Meir, water commissioner
Yehuda Ben-Meir, deputy foreign minister
Eytan Bentsur, director general of the Foreign Ministry
William A. Brown, U.S. diplomat, ambassador to Israel
Odelia Carmon, spokesperson for Sharon, Netanyahu
Ilan Cohen, director general of the Prime Minister's Office
Ran Cohen, industry and trade minister
Marit Danon, secretary to prime ministers
Sergio DellaPergola, professor, demographer
Rachel Dolev, IDF chief censor, aide to Sharon as CO of Southern Command

Dahlia Eliashiv, school classmate of Sharon
Jackie Even, IDF general
Avi Gil, director general of the Foreign Ministry
Eival Gilady, IDF planner
Ra'anan Gissin, spokesman for Sharon
Dore Gold, ambassador to the UN
Eitan Haber, journalist, aide to Yitzhak Rabin
Dudu Halevy, *Time* magazine Israel correspondent
Efraim Halevy, head of Mossad, national security adviser to Sharon
Moshe Kaplinsky, IDF general, military aide to Sharon
Yisrael Katz, transport minister
Yaakov Kedmi, diplomat to U.S.S.R., later to Russia
David Kimche, deputy head of Mossad, director general of the Foreign
    Ministry
Menachem Klein, professor, expert on Jerusalem
Alice Krieger, aide to Sharon as minister of agriculture
Dan Kurtzer, U.S. diplomat, ambassador to Israel
Eli Landau, aide to Sharon, mayor of Herzliya
Asher Levy, Sharon's commander in 1948, IDF general
Meirav Levy, aide to Sharon
Samuel Winfield Lewis, U.S. diplomat, ambassador to Israel
Amnon Lipkin-Shahak, IDF chief of staff, negotiator, tourism minister
Tzipi Livni, foreign minister, leader of Kadima Party
Yisrael Maimon, cabinet secretary
Amram Mitzna, IDF general, Labor Party chairman
Michal Modai, president, Women's International Zionist Organization
Shaul Mofaz, IDF chief of staff, negotiator, defense minister
Mibi Mozer, media and libel lawyer
Yitzhak Navon, aide to Ben-Gurion, education minister, president
Ya'akov Ne'eman, finance minister, justice minister
Benjamin Netanyahu, prime minister
Moshe Nissim, finance minister, justice minister
Nimrod Novik, aide to Shimon Peres, analyst
Amir Oren, journalist
Zevulun Orlev, welfare minister
Tomer Orni, aide to Sharon as minister of infrastructures and foreign
    minister
Shimon Peres, defense minister, prime minister, president
Arnon Perlman, aide and spokesman to Sharon
Alon Pinkas, consul general in New York
Dalia Rabin, deputy minister of defense
Haim Ramon, health minister, justice minister
Amnon Reshef, IDF general
Reuven Rivlin, communications minister, Knesset Speaker

Gideon Sa'ar, cabinet secretary, education minister
Yehoshua Saguy, IDF general, head of Military Intelligence
Yossi Sarid, education minister
Shaya Segal, political adviser to Sharon, Netanyahu
Silvan Shalom, finance minister, foreign minister
Uri Shani, bureau chief for Sharon
Natan Sharansky, interior minister, housing minister
Asi Shariv, spokesman for Sharon, consul general in New York
Omri Sharon, Knesset member
Gilead Sher, negotiator
Lior Shilat, aide to Sharon
Azmi Shuaibi, Palestinian legislator, minister
Uri Simchoni, IDF general
Yuval Steinitz, finance minister
Avraham Tamir, IDF general
Dov Tamari, IDF general
Dov Weissglas, lawyer and bureau chief for Sharon
Moshe Ya'alon, IDF chief of staff
Avigdor Yitzhaki, director general of the Prime Minister's Office
Aharon Zeevi-Farkas, IDF general, head of Military Intelligence
Mordechai Zippori, IDF brigadier general, communications minister

I wish I could include Ariel Sharon in this list of interviewees. I wish I'd had the journalistic good sense to spend more time talking to him during his wilderness years. But like so many Israelis, I wrote him off as yesterday's man. I did have a number of conversations with him during his term as prime minister, in my capacity as a newspaper editor. I told him I'd been commissioned to write a book about him, that I'd set it aside for the duration of his prime ministership and of my editorship, and that I'd get back to it, *Deo volente*. He responded, as always, with courteous interest.

Omri, his son, gave me several lengthy interviews for this book. He was constantly suspicious, usually reticent, but ultimately helpful, and I am grateful.

APPENDIX

I

UN Security Council Resolution 242
November 22, 1967

The Security Council,

Expressing its continuing concern with the grave situation in the Middle East,

Emphasizing the inadmissibility of the acquisition of territory by war and the need to work for a just and lasting peace in which every State in the area can live in security,

Emphasizing further that all Member States in their acceptance of the Charter of the United Nations have undertaken a commitment to act in accordance with Article 2 of the Charter,

1. *Affirms* that the fulfillment of Charter principles requires the establishment of a just and lasting peace in the Middle East which should include the application of both the following principles:
   (i) Withdrawal of Israel armed forces from territories occupied in the recent conflict;
   (ii) Termination of all claims or states of belligerency and respect for and acknowledgement of the sovereignty, territorial integrity and political independence of every State in the area and their right to live in peace within secure and recognized boundaries free from threats or acts of force;
2. *Affirms further* the necessity
   (i) For guaranteeing freedom of navigation through international waterways in the area;
   (ii) For achieving a just settlement of the refugee problem;

(iii) For guaranteeing the territorial inviolability and political independence of every State in the area, through measures including the establishment of demilitarized zones;

3. *Requests* the Secretary-General to designate a Special Representative to proceed to the Middle East to establish and maintain contacts with the States concerned in order to promote agreement and assist efforts to achieve a peaceful and accepted settlement in accordance with the provisions and principles in this resolution;

4. *Requests* the Secretary-General to report to the Security Council on the progress of the efforts of the Special Representative as soon as possible.

II
UN Security Council Resolution 338
October 22, 1973

The Security Council,

1. *Calls upon* all parties to the present fighting to cease all firing and terminate all military activity immediately, no later than 12 hours after the moment of the adoption of this decision, in the positions they now occupy;

2. *Calls upon* all parties concerned to start immediately after the cease-fire the implementation of Security Council Resolution 242 (1967) in all of its parts;

3. *Decides* that, immediately and concurrently with the cease-fire, negotiations start between the parties concerned under appropriate auspices aimed at establishing a just and durable peace in the Middle East.

III
Camp David Accords
September 17, 1978

The Framework for Peace in the Middle East (Excerpts)

Muhammad Anwar al-Sadat, President of the Arab Republic of Egypt, and Menachem Begin, Prime Minister of Israel, met with Jimmy Carter, President of the United States of America, at Camp David from September 5 to September 17, 1978, and have agreed on the following framework for peace in the Middle East. They invite other parties to the Arab-Israel conflict to adhere to it.

Preamble

The search for peace in the Middle East must be guided by the following:

- The agreed basis for a peaceful settlement of the conflict between Israel and its neighbors is United Nations Security Council Resolution 242, in all its parts . . . The historic initiative of President Sadat in visiting Jerusalem and the reception accorded to him by the parliament, government and people of Israel, and the reciprocal visit of Prime Minister Begin to Ismailia, the peace proposals made by both leaders, as well as the warm reception of these missions by the peoples of both countries, have created an unprecedented opportunity for peace which must not be lost if this generation and future generations are to be spared the tragedies of war . . .
- Peace requires respect for the sovereignty, territorial integrity and political independence of every state in the area and their right to live in peace within secure and recognized boundaries free from threats or acts of force . . .
- Security is enhanced by a relationship of peace and by cooperation between nations which enjoy normal relations. In addition, under the terms of peace treaties, the parties can, on the basis of reciprocity, agree to special security arrangements such as demilitarized zones, limited armaments areas, early warning stations, the presence of international forces, liaison, agreed measures for monitoring and other arrangements that they agree are useful.

Framework

Taking these factors into account, the parties are determined to reach a just, comprehensive, and durable settlement of the Middle East conflict through the conclusion of peace treaties based on Security Council resolutions 242 and 338 in all their parts. Their purpose is to achieve peace and good neighborly relations. They recognize that for peace to endure, it must involve all those who have been most deeply affected by the conflict. They therefore agree that this framework, as appropriate, is intended by them to constitute a basis for peace not only between Egypt and Israel, but also between Israel and each of its other neighbors which is prepared to negotiate peace with Israel on this basis. With that objective in mind, they have agreed to proceed as follows:

A. West Bank and Gaza

1. Egypt, Israel, Jordan and the representatives of the Palestinian people should participate in negotiations on the resolution of the Palestinian problem in all its aspects. To achieve that objective, negotiations relating to the West Bank and Gaza should proceed in three stages:

a. Egypt and Israel agree that, in order to ensure a peaceful and orderly transfer of authority, and taking into account the security concerns of all the parties, there should be transitional arrangements for the West Bank and Gaza for a period not exceeding five years. In order to provide full autonomy to the inhabitants, under these arrangements the Israeli military government and its civilian administration will be withdrawn as soon as a self-governing authority has been freely elected by the inhabitants of these areas to replace the existing military government. To negotiate the details of a transitional arrangement, Jordan will be invited to join the negotiations on the basis of this framework. These new arrangements should give due consideration both to the principle of self-government by the inhabitants of these territories and to the legitimate security concerns of the parties involved.

b. Egypt, Israel, and Jordan will agree on the modalities for establishing an elected self-governing authority in the West Bank and Gaza. The delegations of Egypt and Jordan may include Palestinians from the West Bank and Gaza or other Palestinians as mutually agreed. The parties will negotiate an agreement which will define the powers and responsibilities of the self-governing authority to be exercised in the West Bank and Gaza. A withdrawal of Israeli armed forces will take place and there will be a redeployment of the remaining Israeli forces into specified security locations. The agreement will also include arrangements for assuring internal and external security and public order. A strong local police force will be established, which may include Jordanian citizens. In addition, Israeli and Jordanian forces will participate in joint patrols and in the manning of control posts to assure the security of the borders.

c. When the self-governing authority (administrative council) in the West Bank and Gaza is established and inaugurated, the transitional period of five years will begin. As soon as possible, but not later than the third year after the beginning of the transitional period, negotiations will take place to determine the final status of the West Bank and Gaza and its relationship with its neighbors and to conclude a peace treaty between Israel and Jordan by the end of the transitional period. These negotiations will be conducted among Egypt, Israel, Jordan and the elected representatives of the inhabitants of the West Bank and Gaza . . . The negotiations shall be based on all the provisions and principles of UN Security Council Resolution 242. The negotiations will resolve, among other matters, the location of the boundaries and the nature of the security arrangements. The solution from the negotiations must also recognize the legitimate right of the Palestinian peoples and their just requirements . . .

B. Framework for the Conclusion of a Peace Treaty Between Egypt and Israel (Excerpts)

In order to achieve peace between them, Israel and Egypt agree to negotiate in good faith with a goal of concluding within three months of the signing of this framework a peace treaty between them . . . [The] terms of the peace treaty will be implemented between two and three years after the peace treaty is signed.

The following matters are agreed between the parties:

1. the full exercise of Egyptian sovereignty up to the internationally recognized border between Egypt and mandated Palestine;
2. the withdrawal of Israeli armed forces from the Sinai;
3. the use of airfields left by the Israelis . . . for civilian purposes only . . .
4. the right of free passage by ships of Israel through the Gulf of Suez and the Suez Canal on the basis of the Constantinople Convention of 1888 applying to all nations; the Strait of Tiran and Gulf of Aqaba are international waterways to be open to all nations for unimpeded and nonsuspendable freedom of navigation and overflight;
5. the construction of a highway between the Sinai and Jordan near Eilat with guaranteed free and peaceful passage by Egypt and Jordan;
6. the stationing of military forces listed below.

Stationing of Forces

- No more than one division (mechanized or infantry) of Egyptian armed forces will be stationed within an area lying approximately 50 km. (30 miles) east of the Gulf of Suez and the Suez Canal.
- Only United Nations forces and civil police equipped with light weapons to perform normal police functions will be stationed within an area lying west of the international border and the Gulf of Aqaba, varying in width from 20 km. (12 miles) to 40 km. (24 miles).
- In the area within 3 km. (1.8 miles) east of the international border there will be Israeli limited military forces not to exceed four infantry battalions and United Nations observers . . .
- Early warning stations may exist to ensure compliance with the terms of the agreement.
- After a peace treaty is signed, and after the interim withdrawal is complete, normal relations will be established between Egypt and Israel, including full recognition, including diplomatic, economic and cultural relations; termination of economic boycotts and barriers to the free movement of goods and people; and mutual protection of citizens by the due process of law.

Interim Withdrawal

- Between three months and nine months after the signing of the peace treaty, all Israeli forces will withdraw east of a line extending from a point east of El-Arish to Ras Muhammad . . .

For the Government of
the Arab Republic of Egypt:
Muhammed Anwar al-Sadat

For the Government of Israel:
Menachem Begin

Witnessed by:
Jimmy Carter,
President of the United States of America

IV
The Oslo Accords
September 1993

Israel-PLO Recognition:
Exchange of Letters Between PM Rabin and Chairman Arafat

Letter from Yasser Arafat to Prime Minister Rabin

September 9, 1993

Yitzhak Rabin
Prime Minister of Israel

Mr. Prime Minister,
The signing of the Declaration of Principles marks a new era in the history of the Middle East. In firm conviction thereof, I would like to confirm the following PLO commitments:
The PLO recognizes the right of the State of Israel to exist in peace and security.
The PLO accepts United Nations Security Council Resolutions 242 and 338.
The PLO commits itself to the Middle East peace process, and to a peaceful resolution of the conflict between the two sides and declares that all outstanding issues relating to permanent status will be resolved through negotiations.
The PLO considers that the signing of the Declaration of Principles constitutes a historic event, inaugurating a new epoch of peaceful coexistence, free from violence and all other acts which endanger peace and stability. Accordingly, the PLO renounces the use of terrorism and other acts of violence and will assume responsibility over all PLO elements and personnel in order to assure their compliance, prevent violations and discipline violators.
In view of the promise of a new era and the signing of the Declaration of Principles and based on Palestinian acceptance of Security Council Resolutions 242 and 338, the PLO affirms that those articles of the Palestinian Covenant which deny Israel's right to exist, and the provisions of the Covenant which are inconsistent with the commitments of this letter are now inoperative and no longer valid. Consequently, the PLO undertakes to submit to the Palestinian

National Council for formal approval the necessary changes in regard to the Palestinian Covenant.

Sincerely,
Yasser Arafat
Chairman
The Palestine Liberation Organization

Letter from Prime Minister Rabin to Yasser Arafat

September 9, 1993

Yasser Arafat
Chairman
The Palestinian Liberation Organization

Mr. Chairman,

In response to your letter of September 9, 1993, I wish to confirm to you that, in light of the PLO commitments included in your letter, the Government of Israel has decided to recognize the PLO as the representative of the Palestinian people and commence negotiations with the PLO within the Middle East peace process.

Yitzhak Rabin
Prime Minister of Israel

Declaration of Principles on Interim Self-Government Arrangements, September 13, 1993 (Excerpts)

The Government of the State of Israel and the P.L.O. team . . . representing the Palestinian people, agree that it is time to put an end to decades of confrontation and conflict, recognize their mutual legitimate and political rights, and strive to live in peaceful coexistence and mutual dignity and security and achieve a just, lasting and comprehensive peace settlement and historic reconciliation through the agreed political process. Accordingly, the two sides agree to the following principles:

Article I
Aim of the Negotiations

The aim of the Israeli-Palestinian negotiations within the current Middle East peace process is, among other things, to establish a Palestinian Interim

Self-Government Authority, the elected Council (the "Council"), for the Palestinian people in the West Bank and the Gaza Strip, for a transitional period not exceeding five years, leading to a permanent settlement based on Security Council Resolutions 242 and 338.

It is understood that the interim arrangements are an integral part of the whole peace process and that the negotiations on the permanent status will lead to the implementation of Security Council Resolutions 242 and 338.

Article III
Elections

1. In order that the Palestinian people in the West Bank and Gaza Strip may govern themselves according to democratic principles, direct, free and general political elections will be held for the Council under agreed supervision and international observation, while the Palestinian police will ensure public order.
2. An agreement will be concluded on the exact mode and conditions of the elections . . .
3. These elections will constitute a significant interim preparatory step toward the realization of the legitimate rights of the Palestinian people and their just requirements.

Article IV
Jurisdiction

Jurisdiction of the Council will cover West Bank and Gaza Strip territory, except for issues that will be negotiated in the permanent status negotiations. The two sides view the West Bank and the Gaza Strip as a single territorial unit, whose integrity will be preserved during the interim period.

Article V
Transitional Period and Permanent Status Negotiations

1. The five-year transitional period will begin upon the withdrawal from the Gaza Strip and Jericho area.
2. Permanent status negotiations will commence as soon as possible, but not later than the beginning of the third year of the interim period, between the Government of Israel and the Palestinian people representatives.
3. It is understood that these negotiations shall cover remaining issues, including: Jerusalem, refugees, settlements, security arrangements, borders, relations and cooperation with other neighbors, and other issues of common interest.
4. The two parties agree that the outcome of the permanent status

negotiations should not be prejudiced or preempted by agreements reached for the interim period.

Article VI
Preparatory Transfer of Powers and Responsibilities

1. Upon the entry into force of this Declaration of Principles and the withdrawal from the Gaza Strip and the Jericho area, a transfer of authority from the Israeli military government and its Civil Administration to the authorized Palestinians for this task, as detailed herein, will commence. This transfer of authority will be of a preparatory nature until the inauguration of the Council.
2. Immediately after the entry into force of this Declaration of Principles and the withdrawal from the Gaza Strip and Jericho area, with the view to promoting economic development in the West Bank and Gaza Strip, authority will be transferred to the Palestinians on the following spheres: education and culture, health, social welfare, direct taxation, and tourism. The Palestinian side will commence in building the Palestinian police force, as agreed upon. Pending the inauguration of the Council, the two parties may negotiate the transfer of additional powers and responsibilities, as agreed upon.

Article VII
Interim Agreement

1. The Israeli and Palestinian delegations will negotiate an agreement on the interim period (the "Interim Agreement").
2. The Interim Agreement shall specify, among other things, the structure of the Council, the number of its members, and the transfer of powers and responsibilities from the Israeli military government and its Civil Administration to the Council. The Interim Agreement shall also specify the Council's executive authority, legislative authority in accordance with Article IX below, and the independent Palestinian judicial organs . . .
5. After the inauguration of the Council, the Civil Administration will be dissolved, and the Israeli military government will be withdrawn.

Article XIII
Redeployment of Israeli Forces

1. After the entry into force of this Declaration of Principles, and not later than the eve of elections for the Council, a redeployment of Israeli military forces in the West Bank and the Gaza Strip will

take place, in addition to withdrawal of Israeli forces carried out in accordance with Article XIV.

2. In redeploying its military forces, Israel will be guided by the principle that its military forces should be redeployed outside populated areas.

3. Further redeployments to specified locations will be gradually implemented commensurate with the assumption of responsibility for public order and internal security by the Palestinian police force pursuant to Article VIII above.

Article XIV
Israeli Withdrawal from the Gaza Strip and Jericho Area

Israel will withdraw from the Gaza Strip and Jericho area, as detailed in the protocol attached as Annex II.

Done at Washington, D.C., this thirteenth day of September, 1993.

V
The Mitchell Report
April 30, 2001

Summary of Recommendations (Excerpts)

The Government of Israel (GOI) and the Palestinian Authority (PA) must act swiftly and decisively to halt the violence. Their immediate objectives then should be to rebuild confidence and resume negotiations . . .

End the Violence

- The GOI and the PA should reaffirm their commitment to existing agreements and undertakings and should immediately implement an unconditional cessation of violence.
- The GOI and PA should immediately resume security cooperation.

Rebuild Confidence

- The PA and GOI should work together to establish a meaningful "cooling off period" and implement additional confidence building measures . . .
- The PA and GOI should resume their efforts to identify, condemn and discourage incitement in all its forms.
- The PA should make clear through concrete action to Palestinians and Israelis alike that terrorism is reprehensible and unacceptable, and that the PA will make a 100 percent effort to prevent terrorist operations and to punish perpetrators. This effort should include immediate steps to apprehend and incarcerate terrorists operating within the PA's jurisdiction.
- The GOI should freeze all settlement activity, including the "natural growth" of existing settlements.
- The GOI should ensure that the IDF adopt and enforce policies and procedures encouraging non-lethal responses to unarmed demonstrators, with a view to minimizing casualties and friction between the two communities.
- The PA should prevent gunmen from using Palestinian populated areas to fire upon Israeli populated areas and IDF positions. This tactic places civilians on both sides at unnecessary risk.
- The GOI should lift closures, transfer to the PA all tax revenues owed, and permit Palestinians who had been employed in Israel to return to their jobs; and should ensure that security forces and settlers refrain from the destruction of homes and roads, as well as trees and other agricultural property in Palestinian areas . . .

- The PA and GOI should consider a joint undertaking to preserve and protect holy places sacred to the traditions of Jews, Muslims, and Christians.
- The GOI and PA should jointly endorse and support the work of Palestinian and Israeli non-governmental organizations involved in cross-community initiatives linking the two peoples.

Resume Negotiations

- In the spirit of the Sharm el-Sheikh agreements and understandings of 1999 and 2000, we recommend that the parties meet to reaffirm their commitment to signed agreements and mutual understandings, and take corresponding action. This should be the basis for resuming full and meaningful negotiations.

George J. Mitchell, Chairman
Former Member and Majority Leader of the United States Senate

Suleyman Demirel
9th President of the Republic of Turkey

Thorbjoern Jagland
Minister of Foreign Affairs of Norway

Warren B. Rudman
Former Member of the United States Senate

Javier Solana
High European Representative for the Common Foreign and Security Policy, European Union

VI
The Road Map
April 30, 2003 (Excerpts)

The following is a performance-based and goal-driven road map, with clear phases, timelines, target dates, and benchmarks aiming at progress through reciprocal steps by the two parties in the political, security, economic, humanitarian, and institution-building fields, under the auspices of the Quartet [the United States, European Union, United Nations, and Russia]. The destination is a final and comprehensive settlement of the Israel-Palestinian conflict by 2005, as presented in President Bush's speech of 24 June, and welcomed by the EU, Russia and the UN . . .

A two-state solution to the Israeli-Palestinian conflict will only be achieved through an end to violence and terrorism, when the Palestinian people have a leadership acting decisively against terror and willing and able to build a practicing democracy based on tolerance and liberty, and through Israel's readiness to do what is necessary for a democratic Palestinian state to be established, and a clear, unambiguous acceptance by both parties of the goal of a negotiated settlement as described below . . .

Phase I: Ending Terror and Violence, Normalizing Palestinian Life, and Building Palestinian Institutions—Present to May 2003

In Phase I, the Palestinians immediately undertake an unconditional cessation of violence . . . [S]uch action should be accompanied by supportive measures undertaken by Israel. Palestinians and Israelis resume security cooperation based on the Tenet work plan to end violence, terrorism, and incitement through restructured and effective Palestinian security services. Palestinians undertake comprehensive political reform in preparation for statehood, including drafting a Palestinian constitution, and free, fair and open elections upon the basis of those measures. Israel takes all necessary steps to help normalize Palestinian life. Israel withdraws from Palestinian areas occupied from September 28, 2000, and the two sides restore the status quo that existed at that time, as security performance and cooperation progress. Israel also freezes all settlement activity, consistent with the Mitchell report.

At the outset of Phase I:

- Palestinian leadership issues unequivocal statement reiterating Israel's right to exist in peace and security and calling for an immediate and unconditional ceasefire to end armed activity and all acts of violence against Israelis anywhere. All official Palestinian institutions end incitement against Israel.
- Israeli leadership issues unequivocal statement affirming its commit-

ment to the two-state vision of an independent, viable, sovereign Palestinian state living in peace and security alongside Israel, as expressed by President Bush, and calling for an immediate end to violence against Palestinians everywhere. All official Israeli institutions end incitement against Palestinians.

Security

- Palestinians declare an unequivocal end to violence and terrorism and undertake visible efforts on the ground to arrest, disrupt, and restrain individuals and groups conducting and planning violent attacks on Israelis anywhere.
- Rebuilt and refocused Palestinian Authority security apparatus begins sustained, targeted, and effective operations aimed at confronting all those engaged in terror and dismantlement of terrorist capabilities and infrastructure. This includes commencing confiscation of illegal weapons and consolidation of security authority, free of association with terror and corruption.
- GOI takes no actions undermining trust, including deportations, attacks on civilians; confiscation and/or demolition of Palestinian homes and property, as a punitive measure or to facilitate Israeli construction; destruction of Palestinian institutions and infrastructure; and other measures specified in the Tenet work plan . . .
- Implementation, as previously agreed, of U.S. rebuilding, training and resumed security cooperation plan in collaboration with outside oversight board (U.S.-Egypt-Jordan). Quartet support for efforts to achieve a lasting, comprehensive cease-fire.
  - All Palestinian security organizations are consolidated into three services reporting to an empowered Interior Minister.
  - Restructured/retrained Palestinian security forces and IDF counterparts progressively resume security cooperation and other undertakings in implementation of the Tenet work plan, including regular senior-level meetings, with the participation of U.S. security officials.
- Arab states cut off public and private funding and all other forms of support for groups supporting and engaging in violence and terror.
- All donors providing budgetary support for the Palestinians channel these funds through the Palestinian Ministry of Finance's Single Treasury Account.
- As comprehensive security performance moves forward, IDF withdraws progressively from areas occupied since September 28, 2000, and the two sides restore the status quo that existed prior to September 28, 2000. Palestinian security forces redeploy to areas vacated by IDF.

Palestinian Institution-Building

- Immediate action on credible process to produce draft constitution for Palestinian statehood . . .
- Appointment of interim prime minister or cabinet with empowered executive authority/decision-making body.
- GOI fully facilitates travel of Palestinian officials for PLC and Cabinet sessions, internationally supervised security retraining, electoral and other reform activity . . .
- Palestinian performance on judicial, administrative, and economic benchmarks, as established by the International Task Force on Palestinian Reform.
- As early as possible . . . Palestinians hold free, open, and fair elections.
- GOI facilitates Task Force election assistance, registration of voters, movement of candidates and voting officials. Support for NGOs involved in the election process.
- GOI reopens Palestinian Chamber of Commerce and other closed Palestinian institutions in East Jerusalem . . .

Settlements

- GOI immediately dismantles settlement outposts erected since March 2001.
- Consistent with the Mitchell Report, GOI freezes all settlement activity (including natural growth of settlements).

Phase II: Transition—June 2003–December 2003

In the second phase, efforts are focused on the option of creating an independent Palestinian state with provisional borders and attributes of sovereignty, based on the new constitution, as a way station to a permanent status settlement. As has been noted, this goal can be achieved when the Palestinian people have a leadership acting decisively against terror, willing and able to build a practicing democracy based on tolerance and liberty. With such a leadership, reformed civil institutions and security structures, the Palestinians will have the active support of the Quartet and the broader international community in establishing an independent, viable, state.

Progress into Phase II will be based upon the consensus judgment of the Quartet of whether conditions are appropriate to proceed, taking into account performance of both parties . . . Phase II starts after Palestinian elections and ends with possible creation of an independent Palestinian state with provisional borders in 2003 . . .

- International Conference: Convened by the Quartet, in consultation

with the parties, immediately after the successful conclusion of
Palestinian elections, to support Palestinian economic recovery
and launch a process, leading to establishment of an independent
Palestinian state with provisional borders.

- Such a meeting would be inclusive, based on the goal of
  a comprehensive Middle East peace (including between
  Israel and Syria, and Israel and Lebanon), and based on
  the principles described in the preamble to this document.
- Arab states restore pre-intifada links to Israel (trade
  offices, etc.).
- Revival of multilateral engagement on issues including
  regional water resources, environment, economic
  development, refugees, and arms control issues . . .
- Quartet members promote international recognition of Palestinian
  state, including possible UN membership.

Phase III: Permanent Status Agreement and End of the Israeli-Palestinian Conflict—2004–2005

Progress into Phase III, based on consensus judgment of Quartet . . .
Phase III objectives are consolidation of reform and stabilization of Palestinian institutions, sustained, effective Palestinian security performance,
and Israeli-Palestinian negotiations aimed at a permanent status agreement
in 2005.

- Second International Conference: Convened by Quartet, in consultation with the parties, at beginning of 2004 . . . to launch a process
  with the active, sustained, and operational support of the Quartet,
  leading to a final, permanent status resolution in 2005, including on borders, Jerusalem, refugees, settlements; and, to support
  progress toward a comprehensive Middle East settlement between
  Israel and Lebanon and Israel and Syria, to be achieved as soon
  as possible.
- Parties reach final and comprehensive permanent status agreement
  that ends the Israel-Palestinian conflict in 2005 . . . includ[ing] an
  agreed, just, fair, and realistic solution to the refugee issue, and a
  negotiated resolution on the status of Jerusalem that takes into
  account the political and religious concerns of both sides, and protects
  the religious interests of Jews, Christians, and Muslims worldwide,
  and fulfills the vision of two states, Israel and sovereign, independent,
  democratic and viable Palestine, living side-by-side in peace and
  security.
- Arab state acceptance of full normal relations with Israel and security
  for all the states of the region in the context of a comprehensive Arab-
  Israeli peace.

VII
Agreed Documents on Movement and Access from and to Gaza
November 15, 2005 (Excerpts)

Rafah

Rafah will be opened as soon as it is ready to operate at an international standard in accordance with the specifications of this agreement and as soon as the 3rd party [the European Union] is on site, with a target date of November 25.

Crossing Points

The passages will operate continuously. On an urgent basis, Israel will permit the export of all agricultural products from Gaza during this 2005 harvest season. The new and additional scanner will be installed and fully operational by December 31. At that time, the number of export trucks per day to be processed through Karni will reach 150, and 400 by end-2006 . . . Israel will permit export of agricultural produce from Gaza and will facilitate its speedy exit and onward movement so that quality and freshness can be maintained . . .

- The PA will ensure that the passages will be protected on the Palestinian side of the border . . .

Link Between Gaza and the West Bank

Israel will allow the passage of convoys to facilitate the movements of goods and persons. Specifically:

- Establish bus convoys by December 15.
- Establish truck convoys by January 15.
- Work out detailed implementation arrangements in a bilateral committee of the GoI and PA with participation as needed from the Quartet team and the USSC [U.S. Security Coordinator].

It is understood that security is a prime and continuing concern for Israel and that appropriate arrangements to ensure security will be adopted.

Movement Within the West Bank

Consistent with Israel's security needs, to facilitate movement of people and goods within the West Bank and to minimize disruption to Palestinian lives, the ongoing work between Israel and the U.S. to establish an agreed list of obstacles to movement and develop a plan to reduce them to the maximum extent possible will be accelerated so that the work can be completed by December 31.

Gaza Seaport

Construction of a seaport can commence. The GoI will undertake to assure donors that it will not interfere with operation of the port . . .

Airport

The parties agree on the importance of the airport. Discussions will continue on the issues of security arrangements, construction, and operation . . .

Third Party

The 3rd party will have the authority to ensure that the PA complies with all applicable rules and regulations concerning the Rafah crossing point and the terms of this agreement. In case of non-compliance the 3rd party has the authority to order the re-examination and reassessment of any passenger, luggage, vehicle or goods. While the request is being processed, the person, luggage, vehicle or cargo in question will not be allowed to leave the premises of the Rafah crossing point.

The 3rd party will assist the PA to build capacity—training, equipment and technical assistance—on border management and customs.

NOTES

Preface: *Land of Hope*

1. Marit Danon interview, Jerusalem, November 2009.
2. Omri Sharon interview, Tel Aviv, January 2011.

Chapter 1: *Poor Little Fat Boy*

1. Yigal Sarna, "His Childhood," *Hadashot,* September 15, 1985.
2. "Man of the Year," *HaOlam Hazeh,* September 24, 1973.
3. Dahlia Eliashiv interview, Kfar Saba, November 8, 2006.
4. Yuval Steinitz interview, Jerusalem, April 30, 2008.
5. Ariel Sharon, *Warrior,* 35.
6. "Arik Sharon's *Saison,*" *Haaretz,* August 1, 1983.
7. "It's All Talk," Israel Radio, February 8, 1990.
8. "An Etzel Fighter: Sharon Commanded a *Saison* Posse." *Arutz Sheva Israel National News,* June 28, 2005.
9. Ibid.
10. Ariel Sharon, *Warrior,* 37.
11. Mordechai Zippori interview, Karmei Yosef, January 30, 2007.
12. Ariel Sharon, *Warrior,* 38.
13. Bregman, *Israel's Wars,* 19.
14. Ariel Sharon, *Warrior,* 44.
15. Omri Sharon interview, Tel Aviv, December 2010.
16. Hefez and Bloom, *Shepherd,* 28.
17. Ariel Sharon, *Warrior,* 54–58.
18. Hefez and Bloom, *Shepherd,* 32.
19. Ariel Sharon, *Warrior,* 62.
20. Dan, *Ariel Sharon,* 13.
21. Ibid.
22. Asher Levy interviews, Tel Aviv and Latrun, March 12, 13, 2008.

23. Ariel Sharon, *Warrior,* 65.
24. Ibid.
25. Ibid., 72.
26. Northern Command, File C/A/3/7, September 1952, Top Secret, IDF Archives.
27. Ariel Sharon, *Warrior,* 76.
28. Ibid.
29. Morris, *Israel's Border Wars, 1949–1956,* 136, 150.
30. Benziman, *Sharon,* 40.
31. Har-Zion, *Chapters of a Diary,* 161.
32. Moshe Dayan, *Story of My Life* [Hebrew], 114.
33. Gideon Altschuler interview, Karmei Yosef, February 28, 2007.
34. Ariel Sharon, *Warrior,* 89.
35. Morris, *Israel's Border Wars, 1949–1956,* 278.
36. Ibid., 203.
37. Ariel Sharon, *Warrior,* 91.
38. Moshe Dayan, *Story of My Life* [Hebrew], 115.
39. Ariel Sharon to Chief of Operations, January 5, 1954, IDF Archives.
40. Altschuler interview.
41. Hefez and Bloom, *Shepherd,* 28.
42. Gilad Harel, "The Azoun Raid," personal testimony to the Paratroop Brigade book and Web site *The First Ten Years;* Yitzhak Gibli and Aharon Davidi, interviews in *The Sixth Night,* a documentary broadcast by Israel Television Channel 2 in June 1996.
43. Ariel Sharon, "Reprisal Actions: How We Were, and How We Fought" (lecture, Sapir College, March 20, 2003).
44. Moshe Dayan, *Story of My Life* [Hebrew], 132.
45. Ibid., 641.
46. Ariel Sharon, *Warrior,* 100.
47. Bar-On, *Gates of Gaza,* 258.
48. Moshe Dayan, *Story of My Life,* 173; Moshe Dayan, *Story of My Life* [Hebrew], 179.
49. Morris, *Israel's Border Wars, 1949–1956,* 312-13.
50. Ariel Sharon, *Warrior,* 111.
51. Shmuel Tamir, *Son of This Land,* 2:1138–39.
52. Commander of Battalion 890 to Chief of Staff, June 27, 1955, IDF Archives.
53. Morris, *Israel's Border Wars, 1949–1956,* 413.
54. Ibid., 361–62.
55. Bar-On, *Gates of Gaza,* 25.
56. Golani, *There Will Be War Next Summer,* 235.
57. Morris, *Israel's Border Wars, 1949–1956,* 426.
58. Peres, *Battling for Peace,* 113.
59. Peres, *Ben-Gurion,* 169.

60. In *There Will Be War Next Summer,* Golani writes that Meir Amit, the chief of operations on the General Staff, and Uzi Narkiss, his deputy, were out of the loop and that senior officers in Southern Command—and Sharon, too—were unaware of the political purpose of the parachute drop.

61. Defense Ministry protocols, cited by Amir Oren, "38 Soldiers Died in Vain. Who Approved? Who Lied?," *Haaretz,* October 26, 2006.

62. Laskov's report to Dayan, December 4, 1956, cited in Oren, "38 Soldiers Died in Vain."

63. Golani, *There Will Be War Next Summer,* 526–27, citing Ze'evi's testimony to Laskov. Golani writes, too, that in addition to the tanks and the infantry that Sharon mentions, the "reconnaissance patrol" included a 120-millimeter mortar battery, ammunition trucks, and fuel tanker-trucks. He cites the official war record of Southern Command, which refers to "a belligerent reconnaissance force sent out in the direction of the pass."

64. Ariel Sharon, *Warrior,* 147.

65. Ibid., 150.

66. Golani, *There Will Be War Next Summer,* 519.

67. Ibid.

68. Dov Tamari interview, Caesarea, March 10, 2007.

69. Eitan Haber, "Paratroop Brigade 202 Rules the Country," *Yedioth Ahronoth,* March 5, 1982.

70. Nahum Barnea, "Doers, Motta Gur Style," *Koteret Rashit,* October 29, 1986.

71. Yitzhak Navon interview, Jerusalem, June 26, 2007.

72. Moshe Dayan, *Story of My Life,* 243.

73. Shimon Peres interview, Tel Aviv, July 11, 2006.

74. Ariel Sharon, *Warrior,* 156.

Chapter 2: Probationer

1. Yitzhak Navon, personal archives.

2. Ariel Sharon, *Warrior,* 158.

3. Ibid.

4. Peres interview.

5. Hefez and Bloom, *Shepherd,* 146.

6. Benziman, *Sharon,* 82.

7. Strangely, that date is inaccurate: the correct date was May 6.

8. Anonymous interview, Tel Aviv, November 2006.

9. Sarit Yishai-Levy, *Hadashot,* September 11, 1988.

10. Benziman, *Sharon,* 87.

11. Rabin, *Service Notebook,* 1:118.

12. Ibid., 119–20.

13. Ehud Barak interview, Tel Aviv, July 23, 2006.
14. Rabin, *Service Notebook*, 1:118.
15. Ariel Sharon, *Warrior*, 179.
16. Yael Dayan, *Soldier's Diary*, 8.
17. Zippori, *In a Straight Line*, 150.
18. Bregman, *Israel's Wars*, 68.
19. Colonel (res.) Ami Gluska, Hebrew University of Jerusalem doctoral thesis, cited in Amir Oren, "IDF Research Paper: Sharon Spoke with Rabin in 1967 About 'Seizing Power to Take a Decision' to Go to War," *Haaretz*, November 16, 2004; Ami Gluska, *Eshkol, Give the Order* (Tel Aviv: Ministry of Defense, 2004).
20. Peres, *Ben-Gurion*, 193.
21. Ze'ev Schiff, "Surprising Conversations," *Haaretz*, June 1, 2007.
22. Ariel Sharon, *Warrior*, 185.
23. Bregman, *Israel's Wars*, 81; Rabin, *Service Notebook*, 1:182.
24. Benziman, *Sharon*, 95.
25. Rabin, *Service Notebook*, 1:188.
26. Ariel Sharon, *Warrior*, 201.
27. Nir Mann, "History Doesn't Repeat Itself," *Yedioth Ahronoth*, June 1, 2007.
28. Ariel Sharon, *Warrior*, 214.
29. Shmuel Tamir, *Son of This Land*, 1,411.
30. Benziman, *Sharon*, 106.
31. Ibid.
32. Hefez and Bloom, *Shepherd*, 189.
33. Bregman, *Israel's Wars*, 93, citing Abdel Magid Farid, secretary-general of the Egyptian presidency, in his *Nasser: The Final Years* (Reading, U.K.: Ithaca Press, 1994).
34. Adan, *On the Banks of the Suez*, 43.
35. Herzog, *War of Atonement*, 5–12.
36. Hefez and Bloom, *Shepherd*, 202.
37. Ariel Sharon, *Warrior*, 238.
38. Ibid., 231.
39. Ze'ev Schiff, "Argument in Gaza," *Haaretz*, March 2, 1972.
40. Benziman, *Sharon*, 117.
41. "Not a Single Minister Proposed Bringing Back the Bedouin," *Maariv*, May 5, 1972.
42. Nadel, *Between the Two Wars*, 133.
43. Adan, *On the Banks of the Suez*, 247.
44. Herzog, *War of Atonement*, 22.
45. Ariel Sharon, *Warrior*, 264.
46. Hefez and Bloom, *Shepherd*, 222.
47. Ariel Sharon, *Warrior*, 271.
48. Ran Kislev, "He Offered Himself as a Minister," *Haaretz*, July 13, 1973.

49. Dan, *Ariel Sharon,* 57.
50. "Sharon Calls for an Alternative Alignment Against the Ruling Alignment of Labor-Mapam," *Maariv,* July 18, 1973.
51. Ariel Sharon, *Warrior,* 266.

Chapter 3: Desert Storm

1. Herzog, *War of Atonement,* 151.
2. Ariel Sharon, *Warrior,* 269–70.
3. Ibid., 288.
4. Argaman, *Pale Was the Night,* 285. The book is a biography of Dr. Pinhas Sussman, who served as commander of Sharon's war room during the Yom Kippur War and, two decades later, as director general of the Ministry of Defense when Sharon was prime minister.
5. Ibid.
6. Ariel Sharon, *Warrior,* 294–95.
7. "Sharon to the Commission: I Tried to Rescue the Strongpoints," *Haaretz,* January 1, 1995.
8. Bergman and Meltzer, *Yom Kippur War,* 79.
9. Protocol: Consultation with the Prime Minister, July 10, 1973, 2:50 p.m.
10. Bartov, *Dado,* 2:74; Herzog, *War of Atonement,* 84, 2:73–74.
11. Bartov, *Dado,* 2:74.
12. Ariel Sharon, *Warrior,* 299.
13. Bartov, *Dado,* 2:86.
14. Ariel Sharon, *Warrior,* 301–2.
15. Adan, *On the Banks of the Suez,* 130.
16. Protocol: Consultation with the Prime Minister, August 10, 1973, 7:50 p.m. Lieutenant General (res.) Haim Bar-Lev and Minister Yigal Allon report on their tour of the fronts.
17. Ze'ev Schiff, "The Rashomon Effect on October 8," *Haaretz,* December 7, 1975.
18. Yehoshua Saguy interview, Rishon Lezion, August 30, 2007.
19. Avraham Tamir interviews, Tel Aviv, August 20, 24, 2006.
20. Asher Levy interview, Tel Aviv, March 12, 2008.
21. Protocol: Consultation with the Prime Minister, August 10, 1973, 7:50 p.m.
22. Protocol: Consultation with the Prime Minister, September 10, 1973, 7:30 a.m.
23. Ariel Sharon, *Warrior,* 305.
24. Bergman and Meltzer, *Yom Kippur War,* 157.
25. Argaman, *Pale Was the Night,* 302.
26. Excerpts from radio recordings; Bergman and Meltzer, *Yom Kippur War,* 140–50.
27. Amnon Reshef interviews, Tel Aviv, October 17, 31, 2006.
28. Herzog, *War of Atonement,* 194–95.

29. Bartov, *Dado,* 2:132.
30. Benziman, *Sharon,* 145–47.
31. Altschuler interview, August 20, 2006.
32. Tamir interview.
33. Herzog, *War of Atonement,* 199.
34. Gai, *Bar-Lev,* 258.
35. Adan, *On the Banks of the Suez,* 163–65.
36. Herzog, *War of Atonement,* 203–6.
37. Ibid.
38. "Sharon: A Bit Complicated, but Doable," tape recordings, *Ynet,* May 9, 2011.
39. Herzog, *Arab-Israeli Wars,* 212.
40. Reshef interview, October 17, 31, 2006.
41. Ariel Sharon, *Warrior,* 315–19.
42. Reshef interview, October 17, 31, 2006.
43. Bartov, *Dado,* 2:242–47.
44. Ariel Sharon, *Warrior,* 325–26.
45. Jackie Even interviews, Holon, September 21, 25, 2006.
46. Ariel Sharon, *Warrior,* 328.
47. Ibid., 330.
48. Herzog, *War of Atonement,* 242.
49. Schiff, *October Earthquake,* 226.
50. Tamir interview, August 20, 2006.
51. Asher Levy interview, March 12, 2008.

Chapter 4: Advise and Dissent

1. Ehud Barak interview, Tel Aviv, July 2006.
2. Bar-Lev had demobilized by then and returned to his ministry desk, and so his interview, the army explained, unlike Sharon's, was not an infringement of the rules. The author, then a young writer on *The Jerusalem Post,* derided this distinction in an article headlined "Why Criticize Sharon and Not Bar-Lev?"
3. "Arik Sharon: Agreement with Egypt Cannot Be Based on Trusting Sadat," *Maariv,* January 21, 1974.
4. Meir, *My Life,* 378.
5. Uri Avneri, "Arik, King of Israel: Man of the Year, 1980–81," *HaOlam Hazeh,* September 27, 1981.
6. Yoel Marcus, "Sharon and Dayan: Gods Again," *Haaretz,* February 21, 1975.
7. Ariel Sharon, *Warrior,* 331.
8. "Evidence Before the Agranat Commission," *Yedioth Ahronoth,* October 8, 2008.

9. Benziman, *Sharon*, 180.
10. Avraham Tamir, *Soldier in Search of Peace*, 10.
11. Rabin, *Service Notebook*, 2:550.
12. Ibid.
13. *Knesset Record*, July 31, 1974.
14. Yaacov Erez and Yosef Walter, " 'A Good Deal,' the Negotiators Rejoiced," *Maariv*, December 9, 1975.
15. Eldar and Zertal, *Lords of the Land*, 73.
16. Yair Kotler, "Let's Talk Like a Couple of Horse Thieves," *Haaretz*, November 26, 1976.
17. " 'Sharon Is a Danger to Democracy,' Ehrlich Wrote in '77," *Yedioth Ahronoth*, July 1, 1983.
18. Amnon Barzilai, "Sharon: A Supreme Effort to Save Israel," *Haaretz*, November 17, 1976.
19. Moshe Nissim interview, Tel Aviv, January 9, 2008.
20. Naor, *Begin in Power*, 31–32.

Chapter 5: His Will Be Done

1. Hefez and Bloom, *Shepherd*, 318.
2. Moshe Dayan, *Shall the Sword Devour Forever?*, 17–18.
3. Naor, *Begin in Power*, 165–66.
4. Ariel Sharon, *Warrior*, 369–70.
5. Boaz Gaon, "What Happened to Arik?," *NRG*, June 5, 2003.
6. Ariel Sharon, *Warrior*, 354.
7. Ibid.
8. Aluf Benn, "The Settlers Have No Property Rights over Their Homes," *Haaretz*, April 5, 2004.
9. Avraham Tamir, *Soldier in Search of Peace*, 41; Ezer Weizman, *The Battle for Peace*, 342.
10. Chief Justice Barak referred to Begin's response in a speech in 2007: "Without Judges There Will Be No Democracy," *Haaretz*, November 7, 2007.
11. Motion for the Agenda, Yossi Sarid (Labor): To Evacuate Elon Moreh, *Knesset Record*, December 12, 1979.
12. Naor, *Begin in Power*, 214; Shilon, *Begin, 1913–1992*, 338.
13. Ariel Sharon, *Warrior*, 386.
14. Shilon, *Begin, 1913–1992*, 329.
15. Moshe Arens interview, Tel Aviv, May 30, 2006.
16. Naor, *Begin in Power*, 259–62.
17. Uri Avneri, "Arik, King of Israel," *HaOlam Hazeh*, September 27, 1981.
18. Ariel Sharon, *Warrior*, 366.
19. "The Battle for the Mountain," *Haaretz*, December 28, 2001.

20. Hagar Lahav, "MK el-Sana: Arabs Become Unwilling Building Offenders Because of Government Policy," *Haaretz,* October 31, 1996.
21. "War of Notes," *Haaretz,* April 13, 2007.
22. Arye Naor, in the documentary film *Tammuz,* dir. Nir Toib, 2006.
23. Naor, *Begin in Power,* 262.
24. Ariel Sharon, *Warrior,* 430.
25. Naor, *Begin in Power,* 262–65.
26. Teddy Preuss, "Sharon Could Use the IDF for Internal Purposes and Embroil Us Abroad," *Davar,* July 17, 1981.
27. Arye Naor testimony, December 26, 2000, and January 8, 2001, Begin Heritage Center Archives.
28. Sima Kadmon, "Arik Sharon: Interview," *Maariv,* July 8, 1994.
29. Ben Caspit, "At Oslo They Were Amateurs," *Maariv,* December 7, 1997.
30. Yosef Waxman, "Begin Will Decide When Yamit Is to Be Evacuated," *Maariv,* January 4, 1982.
31. Ariel Sharon, *Warrior,* 402.
32. Ambassador Samuel W. Lewis, interview with Peter Jessup, August 9, 1998, Association for Diplomatic Studies and Training, Foreign Affairs Oral History Project.
33. Ariel Sharon, *Warrior,* 414.
34. Yossi Melman, "Captain America," *Haaretz,* September 26, 2008.
35. Sam Lewis interview, Jerusalem, 2010.
36. Shiffer, *Snowball,* 53.
37. Naor, *Begin in Power,* 268.
38. Shiffer, *Snowball,* 66.
39. Ibid.
40. Ariel Sharon, *Warrior,* 439.
41. Avi Bettleheim and Avraham Tirosh, "Begin Proposed War in Lebanon in December 1981 After the Golan Law," special report, *Maariv,* June 3, 1983.
42. Schiff and Ya'ari, *False War,* 117.
43. Yeshayahu Ben Porat, "Conversations with Arik Sharon," *Yedioth Ahronoth,* June 10, 1983.
44. Minister of Energy Yitzhak Berman, interviewed by Israel TV in *A Second Look—the Road to Lebanon,* broadcast June 6, 1989, Israel Broadcasting Authority archive, 4249–4256/01.

Chapter 6: Through the Mire

1. Bregman, *Israel's Wars,* 158.
2. Naor, *Begin in Power,* 280.
3. Benziman, *Sharon,* 242.

4. Bregman, *Israel's Wars,* 159.
5. Yitzhak Berman interview, December 4, 2000, Begin Heritage Center Archives.
6. Nissim interview.
7. Herzog, *Arab-Israeli Wars,* 336. This book, updated after Herzog's death by Major General (res.) Shlomo Gazit, served as an important source for these accounts of the military moves in the Lebanon War, as did Bregman's *Israel's Wars.*
8. Bettleheim and Tirosh, "Begin Proposed War in Lebanon."
9. *A Second Look—the Road to Lebanon,* June 6, 1989, Israel Broadcasting Authority archive 4249–4256/01.
10. Eitan, *Soldier's Story,* 236–37.
11. Naor, *Begin in Power,* 301.
12. Bregman, *Israel's Wars,* 172.
13. Naor, *Begin in Power,* 301; Herzog, *Arab-Israeli Wars,* 338.
14. Herzog, *Arab-Israeli Wars,* [page tk].
15. Schiff and Ya'ari, *False War,* 224.
16. Naor, *Begin in Power,* 291.
17. Lewis, interview with Jessup.
18. Herzog, *Arab-Israeli Wars,* 340.
19. Statement by the Government on the Political and Military Situation, *Knesset Record,* June 29, 1982.
20. Bettleheim and Tirosh, "Begin Proposed War in Lebanon"; Naor, *Begin in Power,* 324.
21. Shultz, *Turmoil and Triumph,* 54–55.
22. Ibid., 58–59.
23. Schiff and Ya'ari, *False War,* 275.
24. Yehuda Litani, "Begin Levels Implied Criticism at Sharon," *Haaretz,* August 9, 1982; Schiff and Ya'ari, *False War,* 277.
25. Bettleheim and Tirosh, "Begin Proposed War in Lebanon."
26. "Demands in Labor for Commission of Inquiry," *Haaretz,* August 16, 1982.
27. Ariel Sharon, *Warrior,* 493.
28. Ibid., 496.
29. Schiff and Ya'ari, *False War,* 286.
30. Shiffer, *Snowball,* 116.
31. Yitzhak Shamir, oral testimony, February 6, 1995, State Archives; cited in Shilon, *Begin, 1913–1992,* 400.
32. David Kimche, *Last Option,* 157.
33. Herzog, *Arab-Israeli Wars,* 353.
34. Shilon, *Begin, 1913–1992,* 401.
35. Schiff and Ya'ari, *False War,* 354.
36. Ibid.

37. Eitan, *Soldier's Story*, 340.
38. The Commission of Inquiry into the Events at the Refugee Camps in Beirut, 1983. Final Report. [The Kahan Report], 16.
39. Schiff and Ya'ari, *False War*, 325–27.
40. Shultz, *Turmoil and Triumph*, 101.
41. Ariel Sharon, *Warrior*, 504.
42. Kahan Report, 27.
43. Ariel Sharon, *Warrior*, 505.
44. Kahan Report, 21.
45. Ibid., 15.
46. Ibid., 27.
47. Eitan, *Soldier's Story*, 343–44.
48. Israel Television, Interview of the Week, September 26, 1982, ITV Archive 1343/01.
49. Nissim interview.
50. Naor, *Begin in Power*, 332.
51. Yitzhak Zamir interview, July 24, 2001, Begin Heritage Center Archives.
52. Ariel Sharon, *Warrior*, 521.
53. Shultz, *Turmoil and Triumph*, 196ff.; Schiff and Ya'ari, *False War*, 372ff.
54. Yoel Marcus, "Look Who's Talking," *Haaretz*, February 15, 1985.

Chapter 7: On the Farm

1. Yeshayahu Ben Porat, "A Leadership That Abandons Responsibility Is Itself Abandoned by the People," *Yedioth Ahronoth*, June 10, 1983.
2. Bruria Avidan-Barir, "Twice I Didn't Tell the Truth to Ben-Gurion," *La'isha*, September 9, 1985.
3. Amnon Barzilai, "When I Left the Defense Ministry Our Situation Was Better Than Now," *Haaretz*, February 15, 1985.
4. Orly Azulai Katz, "Sharon's Waiting for Shamir," *Yedioth Ahronoth*, February 14, 1986.
5. Avidan-Barir, "Twice I Didn't Tell the Truth to Ben-Gurion."
6. Dan, *Ariel Sharon*, 121–22; David K. Shipler, "Sharon Is Offered Chance to Remain in Begin's Cabinet," *New York Times*, February 12, 1983.
7. William E. Smith, "The Verdict Is Guilty," *Time*, February 21, 1983.
8. Shilon, *Begin, 1913–1992*, 419–21.
9. Naor, *Begin in Power*, 345.
10. Yisrael Katz interview, Tel Aviv, August 4, 2008.
11. Amnon Barzilai, "Arik, Party Man," *Haaretz*, November 9, 1984.
12. Peres interview.
13. Reuven Adler interviews, Tel Aviv, October, December 2007; Yisrael Katz interview, Tel Aviv, August 4, 2008.

Chapter 8: Wars Old and New

1. Yosef Harif, "Only One or Two of My Would-Be Successors Are Satisfactory," *Maariv*, June 26, 1992.
2. See, for instance, Baker, *Politics of Diplomacy*, 556.
3. Interview of the Week: Sharon on Sabra and Shatila (interviewer, Yoram Ronen), September 26, 1982, Israel Television archives 1343/01.
4. Yossi Beilin interview, Tel Aviv, July 2008.
5. Ariel Sharon, "Lebanon and Israel's Security"; "Peace for Galilee in the Perspective of Past Wars"; "Peace for Galilee: Aims, Achievements—and Obstructions," *Yedioth Ahronoth*, May 24, May 31, June 7, 1985.
6. Ilan Shechori, "Begin to *Haaretz:* The Time Has Not Yet Come for Me to Speak," *Haaretz*, August 13, 1987.
7. Ze'ev Schiff, "The Forty-Kilometer Mystery," *Haaretz*, August 28, 1987.
8. Btselem, http://www.btselem.org/Hebrew/Statistics/First_Intifada_Tables .asp; "Balance-Sheet of Occupation," *Haaretz*, July 15, 1993.
9. Katz interview.
10. "Sharon: If I Were Defense Minister There Wouldn't Be an Intifada," *Yedioth Ahronoth*, June 22, 1988.
11. "Sharon: One Man, Peres, Prevented Proper Handling of the Riots," *Yedioth Ahronoth*, March 16, 1988.

Chapter 9: Jordan Is Palestine?

1. Ariel Sharon, "The Palestinian Problem—the Lie and the Danger," *Yedioth Ahronoth*, July 26, 1985.
2. Peres, *Battling for Peace*, 264.
3. "Sharon: Presenting the International Conference as a Mere Opening Event Is a Fraud," *Maariv*, May 11, 1987.
4. "Shamir: 'We'll examine it in depth and then we'll decide,'" *Haaretz*, May 5, 1987.
5. *Maariv*, March 12, 1988.
6. Baker, *Politics of Diplomacy*, 115ff.
7. Author's conversation with Shamir, 1990.
8. Milo's brother, Matti, is married to Begin's daughter Hassia.
9. Israel Television archives, 2292/90.
10. Yeshayahu Ben Porat, "I Prevented Shamir's Ouster by His Own Loyalists," *Yedioth Ahronoth*, June 15, 1990.
11. Joel Greenberg, "Rabbi Eliezer Schach, 103; Leader of Orthodox in Israel," *New York Times*, November 3, 2001.
12. Baker, *Politics of Diplomacy*, 132.
13. Ibid., 387.
14. IAF Web site, www.iaf.org.il; *Haaretz; Ynet*. Arens, *Broken Covenant* (201), attributes thirteen fatalities to the Scuds.

15. Arens, *Broken Covenant,* 180.
16. *Knesset Record,* December 25, 1985.
17. TV interview with Eli Yatzpan, February 23, 2005.
18. Avi Ganor, "A License to Make Money," *Haaretz,* March 29, 1991.
19. Anonymous interview, Tel Aviv, June 2008.
20. State Comptroller's Annual Report No. 42, 192–93.

Chapter 10: Backwoodsman

1. Interview with a senior political adviser to Sharon, subsequently a senior political adviser to Benjamin Netanyahu, who requested anonymity, Tel Aviv, June 2008.
2. *Knesset Record,* July 27, 1992.
3. Moshe Vardi telephone interview, February 12, 2009.
4. "Democracy and the Jewish State," *Yedioth Ahronoth,* May 28, 1993.
5. Ilan Shchori and Yerach Tal, "Labor Intends to Sign a Coalition Agreement with Meretz, Shas, and Tsomet," *Haaretz,* June 25, 1992; Akiva Eldar, "A Government of Elderly Doves," *Haaretz,* July 13, 1992.
6. "In Place of Autonomy," *Yedioth Ahronoth,* August 7, 1992.
7. These freedoms were severely curtailed by Sharon as prime minister during the second intifada (from October 2000). The IDF, citing its war against Palestinian suicide terror, imposed a system of military roadblocks throughout the territories.
8. Sima Kadmon, "Arik Sharon: An Interview," *Maariv,* July 8, 1994.
9. For the texts of Resolutions 242 and 338, and the Oslo Accords, see Appendix.
10. "Disengagement, the Palestinian Economy, and the Settlements," World Bank, working paper, June 23, 2004.
11. Eitan Haber interview, Ramat Gan, February 17, 2009.
12. Author's conversations with Yossi Beilin, 1993–2008.
13. Kadmon, "Arik Sharon."
14. Nadav Shragai, "Tens of Thousands Demonstrate in Jlm Against the Agreement; Damage PM's Car," *Haaretz,* October 6, 1995; Daniel Ben-Simon, "Chronicle of a Murder Foretold," *Haaretz,* November 4, 2005.
15. *Haaretz, Yedioth Ahronoth, Maariv,* October 6, 1995.
16. Itim News Agency, "MK Sharon Calls for Passive Resistance to Hebron Eviction," *Haaretz,* March 30, 1994.
17. David Landau and Aviva Lori, "Worried About the Jewish People in 3,000 Years' Time," *Haaretz,* August 10, 1995.
18. Dalia Rabin interview, Tel Aviv, March 29, 2009.
19. Benjamin Netanyahu interview, Tel Aviv, May 5, 2006.
20. Ibid.
21. Zvi Zerahia and Nadav Shragai, "Sharon Sworn in as Minister of

National Infrastructures; Thanked Levy for Showing True Friendship," *Haaretz,* July 9, 1996.

22. David Makovsky, "The U.S. Fears: Sharon's Promotion Will Further Complicate the Peace Process," *Haaretz,* June 6, 1997; Yossi Verter, "Beilin: European Figures Warn Against Sharon's Appointment as Minister of Finance," *Haaretz,* June 6, 1997.

23. Ross, *Missing Peace,* 339.

24. "Sharon: We Worked Hard to Get This Prime Minister; Stop Complaining," *Haaretz,* June 20, 1997.

25. This episode earned him an *Economist* cover, with the memorable caption "Serial Bungler."

26. Danny Yatom, telephone interview, April 6, 2009.

27. Amira Hass, "At a Mass Rally in Gaza Yassin Thanks Hussein, Arafat, and the Arab MKs," *Haaretz,* October 7, 1997.

28. Meir Ben-Meir interview, Yokneam, April 13, 2009.

29. Israel-Jordan Peace Treaty, Annex II: Water and Related Matters.

Chapter 11: Last Man Standing

1. Motions for the Agenda: The Meeting Between Minister Sharon and Mr. Abu Mazen, *Knesset Record,* July 2, 1997.

2. *Yedioth Ahronoth,* June 26, 1997; Shiffer was no stranger to the ranch himself. He had been much in favor with the Sharons before the Lebanon War. But writing a book critical of the campaign changed his designation from friend to foe, especially on Lily's list. Now, a decade and a half later, there was rumored to be a thaw. His article was read with care.

3. Yerach Tal, "Senior U.S. Officials Reject Sharon's Cantons Scheme," *Haaretz,* November 24, 1997; Shimon Shiffer, "Sharon: A Palestinian State Is a Fait Accompli," *Yedioth Ahronoth,* November 25, 1997.

4. Yossi Verter, "Netanyahu-Sharon Ties Improving," *Haaretz,* August 13, 1997.

5. Amira Segev, "Sharon: I Told the PM, I Don't Know Whether to Help Your Right Hand or Your Left Hand," *Haaretz,* November 12, 1997.

6. Ross, *Missing Peace,* 493.

7. Danny Rubinstein, "Sharon Sent Greetings 'to Arafat and His Family,' " *Haaretz,* December 31, 2000. Rubinstein, a veteran Arab affairs commentator, wrote a biography of the Palestinian leader: *The Mystery of Arafat* (South Royalton, Vt.: Steerforth Press, 1995).

8. Dr. Azmi Shuaibi interview, Oslo, December 9, 2009.

9. Ze'ev Schiff, "Sharon Asked the Palestinians Not to Condemn His Appointment," *Haaretz,* October 15, 1998.

10. Cf. Dan, *Ariel Sharon,* 145–46: "Sharon was against it, since Clinton could no longer honor his word, but he was in the minority."

11. Eldar and Zertal, *Lords of the Land,* 170.

12. Tomer Orni interviews, London, December 6–7, 2009.
13. Yoram Bronowski, "Tragic Heroes," *Haaretz,* October 30, 1998.
14. Eytan Bentsur interview, Tel Aviv, March 24, 2009.
15. Ibid.
16. Ze'ev Schiff, "Sharon Offers Syria Withdrawal from Lebanon Before the Election," *Haaretz,* April 13, 1999.
17. Ze'ev Schiff, "Netanyahu Was Close to an Agreement to Withdraw from the Golan," *Haaretz,* May 28, 1999.
18. "Sharon: This Is How I Blocked the Negotiations with Syria," *Maariv,* June 2, 1999.
19. Daniel Pipes, "The Road to Damascus: What Netanyahu Almost Gave Away," *New Republic,* July 5, 1999.
20. Netanyahu interview.
21. Arens interview, May 30, 2006; telephone interview, March 19, 2009.

Chapter 12: Summit

1. "Sharon: I'm Running," *Maariv,* June 2, 1999. Later that summer, as the primaries campaign heated up, Sharon observed that he was "loath to flaunt my medical records: they might make other people ill." *Yedioth Ahronoth,* August 27, 1999.
2. Nahum Barnea, "Plan for February," *Yedioth Ahronoth,* August 20, 1999.
3. Bregman, *Elusive Peace,* 3. This important book, based mainly on interviews, was written to accompany the BBC television series *Israel and the Arabs* by Brook Lapping Productions.
4. Ibid., 11, citing General (res.) Danny Yatom, Barak's senior aide and the former Mossad chief.
5. Ofir Akunis interview, Tel Aviv, June 7, 2009.
6. Anonymous interviews, Jerusalem, 2008–2009.
7. Ross, *Missing Peace,* 539.
8. Nonconfidence Resolution in the Prime Minister Submitted by the Likud Faction: His Policy Regarding Palestinian Activity in Jerusalem, *Knesset Record,* February 21, 2000.
9. Ross, *Missing Peace,* 585.
10. Akunis interview.
11. Anonymous interview.
12. Ross, *Missing Peace,* 599.
13. Ben-Ami, in Bregman, *Elusive Peace,* 68.
14. Bregman, *Elusive Peace,* 77.
15. Ibid.
16. Ben-Ami, *Front Without a Rearguard,* 224. See also Ben-Ami, *Scars of War, Wounds of Peace.*
17. Indyk, *Innocent Abroad,* 313, 330, 335.

18. No-Confidence Motion by the National Union Faction: Israel's Sovereignty over Jerusalem, *Knesset Record,* July 24, 2000.
19. No-Confidence Motion by the Likud Faction: The Prime Minister's Method of Negotiating at Camp David, *Knesset Record,* July 31, 2000.
20. Motion by the Likud Faction: The Prime Minister's Trips Abroad to Negotiate with the Palestinians, Contravening Cabinet Decisions, *Knesset Record,* August 15, 2000.
21. They have since divorced and each remarried.
22. Sher, *Just Beyond Reach,* 282.
23. Harel and Isacharoff, *Seventh War,* 15. A similar account of the Arafat-Barak conversation appears in Bregman, *Elusive Peace,* 123.
24. Ben-Ami, *Front Without a Rearguard,* 287. Rajoub denied this version in his testimony before the Mitchell Commission and in his interview with Bregman, *Elusive Peace.*
25. Yossi Verter, "Sharon Will Climb Down—and Get the Second Spot," *Haaretz,* September 28, 2000.
26. Amira Hass and Baruch Kra, "Visit by Sharon and the Likud on the Temple Mount Provokes a Storm," *Haaretz,* September 29, 2000.
27. Uri Dan, whom the others kept out of this forum but who still tried to maintain his close relationship with Sharon, was enthusiastically in favor. In his book, he recalls accompanying Sharon, then minister of commerce, one freezing dawn in the mid-1980s on a demonstrative visit to the Wall after Palestinians had thrown stones at Jewish worshippers. "For Sharon, it was not a provocation but a confirmation of Israeli sovereignty over the site." Dan, *Ariel Sharon,* 159.
28. Omri Sharon interviews, Yavne, 2008–2009.
29. "Senior Likudniks Stayed Away," *Yedioth Ahronoth,* September 29, 2000.
30. Harel and Isacharoff, *Seventh War,* 18ff.
31. A report in *Maariv,* undenied, said the IDF's Central Command fired 850,000 rounds of light-arms ammunition during the first month of the intifada. Ibid., 36.
32. Indyk, *Innocent Abroad,* 352.
33. Dan, *Ariel Sharon,* 176.
34. Ben-Ami, *Front Without a Rearguard,* 297ff.
35. Bregman, *Elusive Peace,* 129.
36. Yoel Marcus, "Rock of Our Existence—Part II," *Haaretz,* October 3, 2000.
37. Ron Ben-Yishai, "Just Not Arafat," *Yedioth Ahronoth,* October 2, 2000.
38. Ze'ev Schiff, "Some Lessons from the Riots," *Haaretz,* October 27, 2000.
39. Special Session in Memory of Prime Minister and Defense Minister Yitzhak Rabin, Blessed Be His Memory, *Knesset Record,* November 9, 2000.
40. Indyk, *Innocent Abroad,* 359.

41. Ben-Ami, *Front Without a Rearguard,* 382.
42. Indyk, *Innocent Abroad,* 373–74.
43. Arieli and Sfard, *Wall of Folly,* 40.
44. Ibid., 41.
45. Yossi Verter, "Meridor: If the Clinton Parameters Become an Agreement, I'm Voting Sharon," *Haaretz,* December 28, 2000.
46. Adler interviews, Tel Aviv, October–December 2007.

Chapter 13: Power Failure

1. Danny Ayalon interview, Jerusalem, December 24, 2007.
2. Harel and Isacharoff, *Seventh War,* 109.
3. Danon interview, Jerusalem, November 4, 2009.
4. Bregman, *Elusive Peace,* 151ff.; Harel and Isacharoff, *Seventh War,* 110.
5. Shaul Mofaz interview, Tel Aviv, March 3, 2008.
6. See Sean Yom and Basel Saleh, "Palestinian Suicide Bombers: A Statistical Analysis."
7. Lior Shilat interview, Jerusalem, October 26, 2009.
8. Uri Shani interviews, Tel Aviv, September 2009.
9. Arnon Perlman interviews, Tel Aviv, June 2007.
10. Moshe Kaplinsky interview, Tel Aviv, July 6, 2007.
11. "The Cease-Fire: A Roadside Bomb in Samaria; Mortars in Gaza," *Ynet,* June 4, 2001.
12. Shani interview.
13. Ibid.
14. Anonymous interview, Tel Aviv, June 30, 2008.
15. Omri Sharon interview, Yavne, August 11, 2009; phone conversation, August 23, 2009.
16. Avi Gil interview, Jerusalem, December 2009.
17. Binyamin Ben-Eliezer interview, Tel Aviv, March 20, 2008.
18. Danon interview.
19. Shani interview.
20. Miller, *Much Too Promised Land,* 333.
21. Dan Kurtzer interview, Herzliya, July 2009.
22. "The White House: Sharon's Statement About Appeasement of the Arab World Is Unacceptable," *Ynet,* October 5, 2001.
23. Miller, *Much Too Promised Land,* 336.
24. *New York Times,* September 12, 2001.
25. Harel and Isacharoff, *Seventh War,* 169.
26. "Sharon: There Are Some Things I Have to Do Which I Don't Like," *Haaretz,* January 1, 2001.
27. Bregman, *Elusive Peace,* 168–69.
28. Clancy, *Battle Ready,* 394.
29. Ibid., 395.

30. Mofaz interview.
31. Harel and Isacharoff, *Seventh War,* 181–88.
32. "The Netanyahu Effect Takes Its Toll," *Haaretz,* December 5, 2001.
33. Yossi Verter, "Sharon Against the Central Committee," *Haaretz,* July 23, 2001.
34. Bregman, *Elusive Peace,* 178.
35. Miller, *Much Too Promised Land,* 341.
36. Clancy, *Battle Ready,* 402.
37. Bregman, *Elusive Peace,* 186.
38. The account that follows of Operation Defensive Shield relies heavily on Harel and Isacharoff, *Seventh War.*
39. Clancy, *Battle Ready,* 404.
40. Powell, in Bregman, *Elusive Peace,* 196.
41. Ibid., 200.
42. Bregman, *Elusive Peace,* 212.
43. Ibid., 215.
44. Avigdor Yitzhaki interview, Tel Aviv, March 26, 2008.
45. Perlman interview.
46. Anonymous interview, Tel Aviv, December 6, 2006.
47. Kaplinsky interview.
48. Michal Modai interview, Tel Aviv, November 22, 2006.

Chapter 14: King of Israel

1. Yossi Verter, "Sharon Reassures: My Policy Will Take No Account of 'Political Considerations,' " *Haaretz,* May 14, 2002.
2. Appointment of Defense Minister, *Knesset Record,* November 4, 2002.
3. "Netanyahu to Be Sworn in Today," *Haaretz,* November 6, 2002.
4. Speech to Tenth Annual Caesarea Economic Forum, July 9, 2002.
5. Harel and Isacharoff, *Seventh War,* 196–97. The authors cite an unnamed senior officer who told them the Israeli policy makers were ready to countenance ten innocent fatalities in order to kill Shehadeh. "It was a choice between the lives of ten Palestinians and the lives of tens of Israelis."
6. Ibid., 172.
7. Ibid., 195.
8. Ibid., 199, 202. Bregman's figures in *Elusive Peace* are similar: thirty-three Palestinians assassinated in 2001 and thirty-seven in 2002.
9. When Richard Haass, director of policy planning at State, sought to raise his concerns about a war with Rice in early July, the national security adviser "cut him off. 'Save your breath,' she told him, in Haass's recollection. 'The president has made up his mind.' " Bumiller, *Condoleezza Rice,* 185.
10. Bregman, *Elusive Peace,* 231–33.

11. Ibid., 235–42.

12. Hefez and Bloom, *Shepherd*, 629–31.

13. http://georgewbush-whitehouse.archives.gov/news/releases/2002/10/20021016–13.html.

14. Keynote Address to the Herzliya Conference, 2002.

15. "Sharon: Mitzna's Plan Is an Illusion," *Haaretz*, December 23, 2002.

16. The State Comptroller's Report on the Parties' Accounts for the Prime Ministerial Election, February 6, 2001, and on the Parties' Current Accounts for the Period 1.6.1999–28.2.2001, October 1, 2001.

17. Tel Aviv chief magistrate Edna Beckenstein, sentencing Omri Sharon and Gabriel Manor, February 14, 2006.

18. Ibid. The ceiling was a factor of how long a particular campaign lasted; the longest campaign period covered by the law was nine months.

19. Mordechai Gilat, Michal Grayevsky, and Mali Kempner, "The Greek Island Affair," *Shiva Yamim/Yedioth Ahronoth*, March 16, 2001. The following paragraphs also draw on the Draft Indictment Against Ariel Sharon and Gilad Sharon, March 2004; and on the Decision of the Attorney General in the Matter of Ariel Sharon and Gilad Sharon in the Greek Island Affair and Appel's Lands, June 15, 2004.

20. The story carried a triple byline: By Mordechai Gilat, Gidi Weitz, and Michal Grayevsky.

21. "Sharon Fuming: 'UK Interfering in Election,' " *Yedioth Ahronoth*, January 5, 2003.

22. Hefez and Bloom, *Shepherd*, 652.

23. Amram Mitzna interview, Yeruham, December 25, 2007.

24. Adler interview, Tel Aviv, October 25, 2007.

25. Silvan Shalom interview, Tel Aviv, December 21, 2006.

26. Omri Sharon interview, Tel Aviv, March 24, 2010.

27. United Torah Judaism, as we shall see, joined Sharon's government in 2005, before the disengagement.

28. Omri Sharon interview, Tel Aviv, January 5, 2011.

Chapter 15: About-Face

1. U.S. Department of State Web site.

2. Yossi Verter, "The Hawks Succumbed to Sharon's Power," *Haaretz*, May 26, 2003.

3. Hefez and Bloom, *Shepherd*, 696.

4. Efraim Halevy interview, Tel Aviv, May 20, 2008.

5. Moshe Ya'alon interview, Jerusalem, June 12, 2008.

6. Amir Oren, "The Thousand-Day War," *Haaretz*, June 3, 2003.

7. *Maariv*–Hagal Hahadash poll.

8. Uzi Benziman, "The *Hudna* Came Too Soon," *Haaretz*, June 20, 2003.

9. Drucker and Shelah, *Boomerang*, 324.

10. Bregman, *Elusive Peace*, 268.
11. Harel and Isacharoff, *Seventh War*, 305, 315.
12. "Israel Inciting U.S. to Iraq War, Says Arafat," *Daily Times* (Lahore), March 3, 2003.
13. Bill Keller, "Is It Good for the Jews?," *New York Times*, March 8, 2003.
14. The main headline of *Yedioth* that day was "Four Shin Bet Chiefs Warn: Israel Is in Serious Danger."
15. David Landau, "Unilateral, Though Not Unequivocal," *Haaretz*, November 14, 2003.
16. Nahum Barnea, "Olmert Withdraws from the Territories," *Yedioth Ahronoth*, December 5, 2003.
17. Dov Weissglas interviews, Tel Aviv, July 10, 27, August 24, 2008, September 15, 2010; Eival Gilady interviews, Tel Aviv, February and May 2008. Arieli and Sfard put the encompassed areas at closer to 20 percent. *Wall of Folly*, 97.
18. Gilady interviews, February 26, 2008; May 8, 2008.
19. Kurtzer interview.
20. "Sharon: Corrections," *Haaretz*, December 3, 2003.
21. Drucker and Shelah, *Boomerang*, 258–59.
22. Weissglas interview, Tel Aviv, July 10, 2008.
23. The author was editor in chief of *Haaretz* at the time of the disengagement.

Chapter 16: Island in the Sun

1. "Dispute Among Police over Sharon's Involvement," *Haaretz*, October 31, 2003.
2. Amir Oren, "Wise Men and Presidents," *Haaretz*, October 3, 2006.
3. Baruch Kra, "Gilad Sharon Repaid Kern with Another Mysterious Transfer from the Austrian Bank," *Haaretz*, August 27, 2003.
4. "Hendel: Sharon Is Base and Corrupt," *Haaretz*, October 25, 2004.
5. *Sharon*, dir. Dror Moreh, 2007.
6. Hefez and Bloom, *Shepherd*, 731.
7. Tsur, *Disengaging from the Strip*, 172.
8. The Prime Minister's Disengagement Plan and Policy in the Territories, *Knesset Record*, March 15, 2004.
9. Harel and Isacharoff, *Seventh War*, 208ff., 321ff.
10. Shani interview.
11. Harel and Isacharoff, *Seventh War*, 324.
12. Tsur, *Disengaging from the Strip*, 194.
13. Debate on the Implementation of the Disengagement Law, *Knesset Record*, November 2, 2004.
14. Motion for the Agenda by National Union–Yisrael Beiteinu: The Gov-

ernment's Reliance on the Extreme Left, *Knesset Record,* January 17, 2005.

Chapter 17: *"You Worry Too Much"*

1. Tsur, *Disengaging from the Strip,* 199.
2. Hefez and Bloom, *Shepherd,* 753.
3. The following section draws heavily on the Final Report of the Judicial Commission of Inquiry into the State Authorities' Handling of the People Evacuated from Gush Katif and Northern Samaria. This commission, under the Supreme Court justice Yehoshua Matza, was created by the State Control Committee of the Knesset in February 2009, following a series of critical reports submitted by the state comptroller. As provided by the Commissions of Inquiry Law, the three members of the commission were appointed by the chief justice of the Supreme Court. The commission published an interim report in September 2009 and its final report in June 2010.
4. The date was later brought forward to July 20, to ensure completion well before the Jewish High Holidays, which fell in early October. The date was then changed again to August 15, so as not to coincide with the annual mourning period for the destruction of the Temple. This ends with the fast of Tisha B'Av, which fell that year on August 14. Subsequently, nevertheless, national-religious circles have incorporated mourning for Gush Katif into the Tisha B'Av rites.
5. "Land of Israel Supporters Buoyed by Human Chain," *Arutz Sheva Israel National News,* July 26, 2004.
6. Jeffrey Goldberg, "Protect Sharon from the Right," *New York Times,* August 5, 2004; Yossi Verter, "Sharon and the Right," *Haaretz,* August 13, 2004.
7. Hefez and Bloom, *Shepherd,* 754.
8. Arik Bender, Ben Caspit, and Yifat Zohar, "The Calls on the Right Are Intended to Foment Civil War," *Maariv-NRG,* September 12, 2004.
9. "The People Is Against Withdrawal—and the People Is Us," *Maariv-NRG,* September 12, 2004.
10. Yoel Marcus, "He's Got a Mandate. And How!," *Haaretz,* October 22, 2004.
11. Yossi Verter, "Obsessively," *Haaretz,* October 22, 2004.
12. "Top PM Aide: Gaza Plan Aims to Freeze the Peace Process," *Haaretz,* October 6, 2004.
13. Weissglas interview, Tel Aviv, June 18, 2008.
14. He died in 2007, at the age of fifty-seven.
15. Nadav Shragai, "The Settlers Invoke Heaven," *Haaretz,* October 27, 2004.

16. Government Statement on the Amended Disengagement Plan, *Knesset Record*, October 26, 2004.
17. Hefez and Bloom, *Shepherd*, 762.
18. Yisrael Maimon interview, Tel Aviv, June 2008.
19. Yossi Verter, "Rabbi Eliashiv Rules," *Haaretz*, January 7, 2005.
20. Conversation with author, March 22, 2005.
21. Ya'alon interview.
22. "IDF Bids Farewell to Ya'alon and Welcomes the Disengagement CoS, Dan Halutz," *Haaretz*, June 1, 2005.
23. "It Is Impossible to Have a Jewish and Democratic State and to Rule over the Whole Land," *Haaretz*, September 26, 2005.
24. Aharon Abramowitz (committee chairman) interview, Mevasseret Zion, December 2010.
25. Aluf Benn, "He's Leaving the Likud for an 'Ingathering Plan,' " *Haaretz*, November 21, 2005.
26. "Abbas: Olmert Negotiations Would Have Succeeded," JPost.com, October 14, 2012; conversations with Olmert.
27. Robin Wright, "Rice Cites 'Progress' in Talks to Open Gaza Border Crossing," *Washington Post*, November 15, 2005.
28. Dan, *Ariel Sharon*, 250.
29. Yossi Verter, "Men in a Trap," *Haaretz*, March 7, 2008.
30. Anonymous interview, August 2008.

Chapter 18: To Sleep, Too Soon

1. Danon interview.
2. "Sharon Was Unable to Count His Fingers," *Maariv*, December 19, 2005.
3. "Sharon: Don't Overdo the Doughnuts," *Haaretz*, December 26, 2005.
4. Ran Reznick, "How Much Does Sharon Really Weigh?," *Haaretz*, December 27, 2005.
5. "The Doctors: Sharon's Not in Danger but He Must Rest," *Haaretz*, December 20, 2005.
6. Shani interview, September 30, 2009.
7. Neri Livneh, "Decade in Review: The Day the Prime Minister Was Felled by a Stroke," *Haaretz*, December 25, 2009.
8. Anonymous interview.
9. Aluf Benn, Tamara Traubman, and Ran Reznick, "Sharon to Have Another CT This Morning," *Haaretz*, January 6, 2006.
10. Ibid.
11. Livneh, "Decade in Review."

BIBLIOGRAPHY

Adan, Avraham. *On the Banks of the Suez*. Novato, Calif.: Presidio Press, 1980.

Arens, Moshe. *Broken Covenant: American Foreign Policy and the Crisis Between the U.S. and Israel*. New York: Simon & Schuster, 1995.

Argaman, Josef. *Pale Was the Night*. Tel Aviv: Miskal–Yedioth Ahronoth Books and Chemed Books, 2002.

Arieli, Shaul, and Michael Sfard. *The Wall of Folly*. Tel Aviv: Books in the Attic and Yedioth Ahronoth, 2008.

Baker, James A., III. *The Politics of Diplomacy*. With Thomas M. DeFrank. New York: G. P. Putman's Sons, 1995.

Bar-On, Mordechai. *The Gates of Gaza: Israel's Defense and Foreign Policy, 1955–1957* [in Hebrew]. Tel Aviv: Am Oved, 1992.

Bartov, Hanoch. *Dado: 48 Years and Another 20 Days* [in Hebrew]. 2 vols. Tel Aviv: Maariv Book Guild, 1978.

Bar-Zohar, Michael. *Ben-Gurion: A Political Biography* [in Hebrew]. Tel Aviv: Am Oved, 1975.

———. *Phoenix: Shimon Peres: A Political Biography* [in Hebrew]. Tel Aviv: Miskal–Yedioth Ahronoth Books and Chemed Books, 2006.

Ben-Ami, Shlomo. *A Front Without a Rearguard: A Voyage to the Boundaries of the Peace Process* [in Hebrew]. Tel Aviv: Miskal–Yedioth Ahronoth Books and Chemed Books, 2004.

———. *Scars of War, Wounds of Peace: The Israel-Arab Tragedy*. New York: Oxford University Press, 2006.

Benziman, Uzi. *Nothing but the Truth* [in Hebrew]. Jerusalem: Keter, 2002.

———. *Sharon: An Israeli Caesar* [in Hebrew]. Tel Aviv: Adam, 1985.

Bergman, Ronen, and Gil Meltzer. *The Yom Kippur War: Moment of Truth* [in Hebrew]. Tel Aviv: Miskal–Yedioth Ahronoth Books and Chemed Books, 2003.

Bregman, Ahron. *Elusive Peace: How the Holy Land Defeated America*. London: Penguin Books, 2005.

————. *Israel's Wars*. New York: Routledge, 2002.

Bumiller, Elisabeth. *Condoleezza Rice: An American Life*. New York: Random House, 2007.

Carver, Field Marshal Lord. *The Apostles of Mobility: The Theory and Practice of Armoured Warfare*. New York: Holmes & Meier, 1979.

Clancy, Tom. *Battle Ready*. With Tony Zinni and Tony Koltz. New York: G. P. Putnam's Sons, 2004.

Clinton, Bill. *My Life*. New York: Alfred A. Knopf, 2004.

Dan, Uri. *Ariel Sharon: An Intimate Portrait*. New York: Palgrave Macmillan, 2006.

Dayan, Moshe. *Shall the Sword Devour Forever?* [in Hebrew]. Jerusalem: Edanim–Yedioth Ahronoth, 1981.

————. *Story of My Life*. New York: William Morrow, 1976.

————. *Story of My Life* [in Hebrew]. Tel Aviv: Edanim, 1976.

Dayan, Yael. *A Soldier's Diary: Sinai, 1967*. London: Weidenfeld & Nicolson, 1967.

De Young, Karen. *Soldier: The Life of Colin Powell*. New York: Vintage Books, 2007.

Drucker, Raviv. *Harakiri* [in Hebrew]. Tel Aviv: Miskal–Yedioth Ahronoth Books and Chemed Books, 2002.

Drucker, Raviv, and Ofer Shelah. *Boomerang* [in Hebrew]. Jerusalem: Keter, 2005.

Eban, Abba. *An Autobiography*. New York: Random House, 1977.

Edelist, Ran. *Ehud Barak, Fighting the Demons* [in Hebrew]. Tel Aviv: Kinneret, Zmora-Bitan, and Miskal-Yedioth, 2003.

Eitan, Raful. *A Soldier's Story*. New York: SPI Books/Shapolsky, 1992.

Eldar, Akiva, and Idith Zertal. *Lords of the Land* [in Hebrew]. Tel Aviv: Kinneret, Zmora-Bitan, 2004.

Gai, Carmit. *Bar-Lev* [in Hebrew]. Tel Aviv: Am Oved, Sifriat Hapoalim, 1998.

Golani, Motti. *There Will Be War Next Summer . . . : The Road to the Sinai War, 1955–1956* [in Hebrew]. Tel Aviv: Ministry of Defense Publishing House, 1997.

Gorenberg, Gershom. *The Accidental Empire: Israel and the Birth of the Settlements, 1967–1977*. New York: Times Books, 2006.

Haig, Alexander M., Jr. *Caveat: Realism, Reagan, and Foreign Policy*. New York: Macmillan, 1984.

Halevy, Efraim. *Man in the Shadows*. New York: St. Martin's Press, 2006.

Harel, Amos, and Avi Isacharoff. *The Seventh War* [in Hebrew]. Tel Aviv: Miskal–Yedioth Ahronoth Books and Chemed Books, 2004.

Har-Zion, Meir. *Chapters of a Diary* [in Hebrew]. Tel Aviv: Lewin-Epstein, 1969.

Hefez, Nir, and Gadi Bloom. *The Shepherd* [in Hebrew]. Tel Aviv: Miskal–Yedioth Ahronoth Books, 2005.

Herzog, Chaim. *The Arab-Israeli Wars* [in Hebrew]. Tel Aviv: Yedioth Ahronoth–Chemed Books, 2005.

———. *The War of Atonement*. London: Greenhill Books, 1998.

Huberman, Haggai. *Against All the Odds: Forty Years of Settlement* [in Hebrew]. Tel Aviv: Netzarim Books, 2008.

Indyk, Martin. *Innocent Abroad: An Intimate Account of American Peace Diplomacy in the Middle East*. New York: Simon & Schuster, 2009.

Isaacson, Walter. *Kissinger: A Biography*. London: Faber & Faber, 1992.

Kershner, Isabel. *Barrier: The Seam of the Israeli-Palestinian Conflict*. New York: Palgrave Macmillan, 2005.

Kfir, Ilan. *The Suez Canal Heroes: The Southern Front, October 1973* [in Hebrew]. Tel Aviv: Miskal–Yedioth Ahronoth Books and Chemed Books, 2003.

Kimche, David. *The Last Option*. London: Weidenfeld & Nicolson, 1991.

Kimmerling, Baruch. *Politicide: Ariel Sharon's War Against the Palestinians*. London: Verso, 2003.

Kurtzer, Daniel C., and Scott B. Lasensky. *Negotiating Arab-Israeli Peace: American Leadership in the Middle East*. Washington, D.C.: United States Institute of Peace Press, 2008.

La Guardia, Anton. *Holy Land, Unholy War*. London: Penguin Books, 2007.

Landau, David. *Piety & Power: The World of Jewish Fundamentalism*. London: Secker & Warburg, 1993.

Lustick, Ian S. *For the Land and the Lord: Jewish Fundamentalism in Israel*. New York: Council on Foreign Relations, 1988.

Meir, Golda. *My Life*. London: Weidenfeld & Nicolson, 1975.

Meir, Yedidya, and Sivan Rahav-Meir. *Days of Disengagement: Conversations About the Israeli Evacuation from the Gaza Strip* [in Hebrew]. Tel Aviv: Miskal–Yedioth Ahronoth Books and Chemed Books, 2006.

Miller, Aaron David. *The Much Too Promised Land: America's Elusive Search for Arab-Israeli Peace*. New York: Bantam Books, 2008.

Morris, Benny. *Israel's Border Wars, 1949–1956: Arab Infiltration, Israeli Retaliation, and the Countdown to the Suez War* [in Hebrew]. Tel Aviv: Am Oved, 1996.

———. *Righteous Victims: A History of the Zionist-Arab Conflict, 1881–2001* [in Hebrew]. Tel Aviv: Am Oved, 2003.

Nadel, Chaim. *Between the Two Wars* [in Hebrew]. Tel Aviv: Ministry of Defense Publishing House, 2006.

Nakdimon, Shlomo. *Tammuz in Flames: The Bombing of the Iraqi Reactor* [in Hebrew]. Tel Aviv: Edanim–Yedioth Ahronoth, 1986.

Naor, Arye. *Begin in Power: A Personal Testimony* [in Hebrew]. Tel Aviv: Yedioth Ahronoth Books, 1993.

———. *Cabinet at War: The Functioning of the Israeli Cabinet During the Lebanon War* [in Hebrew]. Tel Aviv: Lahav, 1986.

Oren, Michael B. *Six Days of War: June 1967 and the Making of the Modern Middle East*. New York: Oxford University Press, 2002.

Peres, Shimon. *Battling for Peace*. Edited by David Landau. New York: Random House, 1995.

———. *Ben-Gurion: A Political Life: Shimon Peres in Conversation with David Landau*. New York: Schocken/Nextbooks, 2011.

Perlmutter, Amos, Michael Handel, and Uri Bar-Joseph. *Two Minutes over Baghdad*. London: Corgi Books, 1982.

Pundak, Yitzhak. *Five Missions* [in Hebrew]. Tel Aviv: Yaron Golan, 2000.

Rabin, Yitzhak. *Service Notebook*. With Dov Goldstein [in Hebrew]. 2 vols. Tel Aviv: Maariv Book Guild, 1979.

Reeves, Richard. *President Reagan: The Triumph of Imagination*. New York: Simon & Schuster, 1981.

Rosenthal, Yemima, ed. *David Ben-Gurion, the first Prime Minister, Selected Papers (1947–1963)* [in Hebrew]. Jerusalem: Israel State Archives, 1997.

Ross, Dennis. *The Missing Peace: The Inside Story of the Fight for Middle East Peace*. New York: Farrar, Straus & Giroux, 2004.

Schiff, Ze'ev. *October Earthquake* [in Hebrew]. Tel Aviv: Zmora, Bitan, Modan, 1974.

Schiff, Ze'ev, and Ehud Ya'ari. *False War* [in Hebrew]. Tel Aviv: Schocken, 1984.

Shamir, Yitzhak. *Summing Up: An Autobiography*. London: Weidenfeld & Nicolson, 1994.

Sharon, Ariel. *Warrior: An Autobiography*. With David Chanoff. New York: Simon & Schuster, 1989.

Sharon, Gilad. *Sharon: The Life of a Leader*. New York: HarperCollins, 2011.

Shavit, Ari. *Partition: Disengagement and Beyond*. Jerusalem: Keter, 2005.

Sher, Gilead. *Just Beyond Reach: The Israel-Palestine Peace Negotiations, 1999–2001* [in Hebrew]. Tel Aviv: Miskal–Yedioth Ahronoth Books and Chemed Books, 2001.

Shiffer, Shimon. *Snowball: The Story Behind the Lebanon War* [in Hebrew]. Tel Aviv: Edanim, 1984.

Shilon, Avi. *Begin, 1913–1992* [in Hebrew]. Tel Aviv: Am Oved, 2007.

Shultz, George P. *Turmoil and Triumph: My Years as Secretary of State*. New York: Charles Scribner's Sons, 1993.

Tamir, Avraham. *A Soldier in Search of Peace*. London: Weidenfeld & Nicolson, 1988.

Tamir, Shmuel. *Son of This Land* [in Hebrew]. 2 vols. Tel Aviv: Zmora Bitan, 2002.

Taub, Gadi. *The Settlers: And the Struggle over the Meaning of Zionism* [in Hebrew]. Tel Aviv: Miskal–Yedioth Ahronoth Books and Chemed Books, 2007.

Tsur, Nadir. *Disengaging from the Strip: Ariel Sharon and Israel's Withdrawal from the Gaza Strip* [in Hebrew]. Jerusalem: Tzivonim, 2006.

Unger, Craig. *The Fall of the House of Bush.* New York: Scribner, 2007.

Weissglas, Dov. *Ariel Sharon: A Prime Minister* [in Hebrew]. Tel Aviv: Miskal–Yedioth Ahronoth Books and Chemed Books, 2012.

Weizman, Ezer. *The Battle for Peace.* Jerusalem: Edanim Publishers, 1981.

Ya'alon, Moshe. *The Longer Shorter Way* [in Hebrew]. Tel Aviv: Miskal–Yedioth Ahronoth Books and Chemed Books, 2008.

Yenuka, Moshe. *From Kibbiya to the Mitle* [in Hebrew]. Tel Aviv: Bitan, 1967.

Zippori, Mordechai. *In a Straight Line* [in Hebrew]. Tel Aviv: Chemed Books, 1997.

Official Report

The Commission of Inquiry into the Events at the Refugee Camps in Beirut, 1983. Final Report.

Newspapers and Periodicals

*Al HaMishmar**
Bamahane
*Davar**
Globes
Haaretz
*Hadashot**
Ha'Ir
Hamodia
HaOlam Hazeh
*Hatzofe**
*Koteret Rashit**
Nekuda
Yated Neeman
Yedioth Ahronoth

*Now defunct.

Archives

My research assistant, Shira Philosof, and I relied heavily on a number of archives during our work. I am grateful to their staffs for the kindness they showed us:

Menachem Begin Heritage Center Archives
Beit Ariela Library: newspapers and periodicals department
Ben-Gurion Research Institute for the Study of Israel and Zionism archive
Haaretz daily newspaper archive
Israel Broadcasting Authority archive
Israel Defense Forces and Defense Establishment Archives
Israel State Archives
Jabotinsky Institute archive
Maariv daily newspaper archive
Yitzhak Rabin Center archive

INDEX

ILLUSTRATION CREDITS

Mordechai Scheinerman: courtesy of Natana Levine
Arik and Dita: courtesy of Natana Levine
Farmyard: courtesy of Natana Levine
Family portrait: courtesy of Natana Levine
Avigail: courtesy of Natana Levine
No annexation: courtesy of Natana Levine
At the beach: courtesy of Natana Levine
Seder night: courtesy of Natana Levine
Miriam and Dita: courtesy of Natana Levine
Young Sharon: courtesy of Natana Levine
Neck-deep in fighting": January 1948. Israel Defense Forces and Defense
    Establishment Archives (IDF Archives)
Meir Har-Zion : IDF Archives, Assaf Kutin.
"Hostile takeover": IDF Archives, Avraham Vered
Moshe Dayan : Israel Government Press Office (IGPO)
"Ate from the same mess-tin": IDF Archives, Avraham Vered
Rehavam Ze'evi and Arik: IDF Archives, Avraham Vered
David Ben-Gurion: IDF Archives, Avraham Vered
Gur, Arik, Lily and Vera: IDF Archives, Avraham Vered. Courtesy of
    Gilad Sharon
May 1967: IDF Archives
Yael Dayan: IDF Archives, Amos Zucker
Generals Tal, Sharon, Gavish, Yoffe: IDF Archives
Arik and Ze'evi: IDF Archives
Arik and Omri: IPPA photo archive
Haim Bar-Lev and Dayan: IDF Archives, Giora Gera
General Yoffe: IGPO
Not up to the job: IPPA photo archive
Colonel Amnon Reshef: IDF Archives, Eli Chen
October 8: IDF Archives, Shlomo Arad
Tanks: IDF Archives

Amphibious bridging tugs: Shlomo Arad
Bar-Lev: IGPO, Yossi Greenberg
M-113 armored personnel carrier: IDF Archives
Rolling bridge: IDF Archives, IDF Spokesman
Dayan and Abrasha Tamir: IDF Archives
Yaffa Yarkoni: Isaac Shokal
"King of Israel": IGPO, Moshe Milner
Rabin: Uzi Keren, Haaretz Newspaper Archives ©
Ministerial repast: Israel Sun, Israel Simyonski
Anwar Sadat: Israel Sun
Begin, Burg, and Katzover: IGPO, Chanania Herman
Hebron Hills: IDF Archives
Near the Canal: IDF Archives
With his defense minister: IGPO, Nati Harnik
Sa'ad Hadad: IDF Archives
Begin and Hadad: IDF Archives, IDF Spokesman
Beaufort: IDF Archives, Ministry of Defense
Lebanon, June 1982: Shlomo Arad
Yitzhak Shamir and Mordechai Zipori: IDF Archives, IDF Spokesman
Rabin, Eitan, Tamir; IDF Archives, Uri Dan
Bashir Gemayel: IDF and Defense Establishment Archives, Uri Dan
Arik and Raful: IDF Archives
Arik and Raful: IDF Archives
Honor guard: Uzi Keren, Haaretz Newspaper Archives ©
Protesters: Uzi Keren, Haaretz Newspaper Archives ©
With unfurled maps: Israel Sun
Yisrael Katz: Moshe Shai
Lily: IGPO, Nati Harnik
Druze feast: Leon Minster, Haaretz Newspaper Archives ©
Arik, Modai, and Levy: Moshe Shai
"Night of the Microphones": Moshe Shai
Minister of Housing: Israel Sun, Ilan Ossendryver
From Russia: Israel Sun, Ilan Ossendryver
Sycamore Ranch soiree: Micky Kratzman, Haaretz Newspaper Archives ©
Election night, 1992: Micky Kratzman, Haaretz Newspaper Archives ©
King Hussein: IGPO, Amos Ben Gershom
Netanyahu: IGPO, Ya'acov Sa'ar
Yonatan: Moshe Shai
Ehud Barak: IGPO, Avi Ohayon
Temple Mount: AFP/Getty images
Reuven Adler: Nir Kedar, Haaretz Newspaper Archives ©
Uri Dan, Cyril Kern, Arie Genger: David Rubinger
Coalition: IGPO, Amos Ben Gershom
Marit Danon: IGPO, Moshe Milner

Mayor Giuliani: IGPO, Amos Ben Gershom
Shaul Mofaz and Binyamin Ben-Eliezer: IGPO, Moshe Milner
"Teaching you where the fish pees from": Amos Biderman, Haaretz
  Newspaper Archives ©
Bus-bombing: IGPO, Avi Ohayon
Dov Weissglas: Lior Mizrachi, Baubau Agency, Haaretz Newspaper
  Archives ©
"Arik and I, I and Arik.": Israel Sun
Michal Modai: IGPO, Avi Ohayon
Comfortable, confident, enjoying the job: Baubau Agency, Haaretz News-
  paper Archives ©
Oval Office: IGPO, Moshe Milner
Aqaba, June 2003: Israel Sun, Ariel Jerozolimski
"The president liked Sharon": Alon Ron, Haaretz Newspaper Archives ©
Mahmoud Abbas: IGPO, Avi Ohayon
Peace diplomacy cartoon: Eran Wolkowski, Haaretz Newspaper Archives ©
Rotem: IGPO, Avi Ohayon
Yitzchak David Grossman: IGPO, Amos Ben Gershom
Naomi Blumenthal: Pavel Wohlberg, Haaretz Newspaper Archives ©
Dan Halutz and Moshe Ya'alon: Reuters
Omri: Lior Mizrachi, Baubau Agency, Haaretz Newspaper Archives ©
Tommy Lapid: Lior Mizrachi, Baubau Agency, Haaretz Newspaper
  Archives ©
Festival of Tabernacles: IGPO, Avi Ohayon
Atzmona: IGPO, Amos Ben Gershom
Crawford, Texas: IGPO, Avi Ohayon
Disengagement: IGPO, Mark Neyman
Kfar Darom: IGPO, Yossi Zamir
Hannuka: Lior Mizrachi, Baubau Agency, Haaretz Newspaper Archives ©
Omri goes to jail: Israel Sun, Kfir Sivan

David Landau immigrated to Israel from the United Kingdom as a young man. His career in journalism began in 1970 at *The Jerusalem Post,* and he joined *Haaretz* in 1993 as news editor. He was the founder and editor in chief of the *Haaretz*'s English edition from 1997 to 2004 and is currently the Israel correspondent for *The Economist.* Landau collaborated with Israel's president Shimon Peres on Peres's memoir, *Battling for Peace.* He published, with President Peres, *Ben-Gurion: A Political Life.* He is also the author of *Piety and Power,* an account of the increasingly significant role the ultra-Orthodox (*haredi*) play in Israel, the United States, and Europe. Landau graduated in law from University College London and studied in leading yeshivas in Israel. He is married with children and grandchildren and currently lives in Jerusalem.

A NOTE ON THE TYPE

The text of this book was set in Sabon, a typeface designed by Jan Tschichold (1902–1974), the well-known German typographer. Based loosely on the original designs by Claude Garamond (c. 1480–1561), Sabon is unique in that it was explicitly designed for hotmetal composition on both the Monotype and Linotype machines as well as for filmsetting. Designed in 1966 in Frankfurt, Sabon was named for the famous Lyons punch cutter Jacques Sabon, who is thought to have brought some of Garamond's matrices to Frankfurt.

COMPOSED BY *North Market Street Graphics, Lancaster, Pennsylvania*

PRINTED AND BOUND BY *Berryville Graphics, Berryville Virginia*

DESIGNED BY *Iris Weinstein*